PENGUIN BOOKS

THE NEW PENGUIN RUSSIAN COURSE

Nicholas J. Brown was born in Cambridge in 1948 and first took an interest in things Russian at the age of three, when he met a pictorial version of the folk tale 'The Fox and the Rolling-Pin' (see Lesson 25). He took up Russian properly at George Heriot's School, Edinburgh, continued his studies at the universities of Birmingham, Moscow and Edinburgh, and, for good measure, married a Russian in New York. He first taught Russian at the New University of Ulster in the early 1970s and is now Senior Lecturer in Russian at the School of Slavonic and East European Studies (SSEES), part of University College London. He is the author of two other Russian textbooks and a Russian learners' dictionary.

NICHOLAS J. BROWN

Senior Lecturer in Russian
School of Slavonic and East European Studies
University College London

THE NEW PENGUIN
RUSSIAN COURSE

PENGUIN BOOKS

PENGUIN BOOKS

Published by the Penguin Group
Penguin Books Ltd, 80 Strand, London WC2R 0RL, England
Penguin Putnam Inc., 375 Hudson Street, New York, New York 10014, USA
Penguin Books Australia Ltd, 250 Camberwell Road, Camberwell, Victoria 3124, Australia
Penguin Books Canada Ltd, 10 Alcorn Avenue, Toronto, Ontario, Canada M4V 3B2
Penguin Books India (P) Ltd, 11 Community Centre, Panchsheel Park, New Delhi – 110 017, India
Penguin Books (NZ) Ltd, Cnr Rosedale and Airborne Roads, Albany, Auckland, New Zealand
Penguin Books (South Africa) (Pty) Ltd, 24 Sturdee Avenue, Rosebank 2196, South Africa

Penguin Books Ltd, Registered Offices: 80 Strand, London WC2R 0RL, England

www.penguin.com

First published 1996
035

Copyright © Nicholas J. Brown, 1996
All rights reserved

The moral right of the author has been asserted

Typeset by Transet Ltd, Coventry
Printed in England by Clays Ltd, St Ives plc

ISBN-13: 978–0–140–12041–7

www.greenpenguin.co.uk

For
Margaret and Arthur Brown,
who introduced me to
'The Fox and the Rolling-Pin'

CONTENTS

Notes on Russian Prices. Since the fall of Communism, Russia has been afflicted by serious inflation. Rouble prices have risen a thousandfold in the last few years and continue to rise at an alarming rate. In the sections of this book which deal with money and shopping (Lessons 9 and 10), we have decided to leave the stable pre-inflation prices. These provide better practice for beginners, since they do not involve large numbers in the hundreds and thousands; they are also very much part of Russian folk memory (for example, the price of the standard loaf of bread did not change for thirty years). Some of the dialogues give prices in US dollars, which Russians have used since Communist times as a parallel 'hard' currency for trade, the tourist industry, and 'black market' deals, and as a sensible way to store savings 'under the mattress' (or, as Russians say, **в чулке** 'in a stocking'). If/when Russia returns to financial stability, the author hopes that Russia's central bank will remove several zeros from its hopelessly inflated currency, restore the old rouble–dollar exchange rate which was (officially) about one to one, and enable a grateful population to return to the days of three-rouble notes and two-kopeck coins.

INTRODUCTION

Like its Penguin predecessor, the *New Penguin Russian Course* is a grammar of Russian for adults which aims to take the reader to the equivalent of A-level standard. It is designed primarily as a self-tutor for all those who intend to study this important language without a teacher. This means that there is plenty of explanation, a concern for completeness, a key to all exercises and English translations of all the Russian texts. It can thus also serve as a reference work for students and others who are following a more communicatively based classroom course but want to know the grammar in detail. It includes all the basic structures of the language, a fairly large vocabulary of over 1,500 words, a variety of exercises, and a good number of texts (including conversations) intended both to illustrate the use of the language and also to give information about life in Russia.

Unlike its predecessor, the *NPRC* emphasizes functional and communicative aspects of language learning, in tune with current developments in language teaching. Exercises involving translation from English into Russian include only things the learner might actually need to say (or write) in Russian. Furthermore, the lessons try to distinguish material which is essential for basic competence in Russian from less important points (marked EXTRA), which can safely be ignored by those in a hurry.

The grammar is presented in an order which, in the author's experience, works well with university students. The overall intention is that all the basic grammar of Russian should be covered, but the main concern is usefulness for the foreign learner. The examples and exercises concentrate on the kind and level of Russian which can reasonably be attained by serious students who wish to make themselves understood and to speak correctly but who are not necessarily aiming to become master spies or pass themselves off as Russians. The Russian in the texts, which has all been written and/or carefully checked by native speakers, is in some cases more complicated than the Russian which learners will be able to produce themselves, but one's ability to understand a foreign language is always greater than one's ability to speak or write it.

Each lesson begins with examples of expressions which the learner is likely to need in dealing with Russians and which contain grammar points to be dealt with in the lesson. If you, the student, begin each study period by trying to memorize these expressions, you will have a good functional basis with which you can begin to communicate. The explanations then give you a basic understanding of how the grammar works, with further examples and reading texts.

The theoretical basis of the book as a teaching aid is the notion that traditional structure-based grammar (e.g. 'present tense', 'genitive singular of nouns') and communicative grammar (e.g. 'how to address Russians', 'how to complain about something') should as far as possible be combined. Thus the functional usefulness of each structure is made the main reason for learning it, and the examples which the student is asked to memorize are clearly relevant to the needs of a foreigner.

Exercises. Each lesson contains one or two grammar exercises to let you check that you have understood the main points; some sentences for translation into Russian concentrating on things you might need or want to say or write in Russian – so the sentences are functional and short; and a comprehension exercise which asks you to find particular information in a text. For those who find Russian–English translation a useful exercise, all the Russian texts in the lessons are translated in the key at the end of the book. There are revision exercises at five-lesson intervals.

Vocabulary. Russian grammar is interesting and fairly easy to follow. Your most demanding task will be the vocabulary. At first, you will feel you are forgetting words as fast as you learn them – but persevere, and the task gets easier. The number of new words is lower in the early lessons (350 in the first ten) and then increases to give you a good working vocabulary of around 1,500 by the end of Lesson 30.

A Note on Modern Russian. Despite all the changes which have taken place in Russia this century, the essentials of the language have been almost unaffected. The spelling reform of 1917–18, whose main effect was the abolition of a number of redundant letters (notably the replacement of ѣ by e), is probably the only major example of government interference – and it is worth noting that the plans for the spelling reform were put forward *before* the 1917 socialist revolution. Under the Communists, many new vocabulary items were introduced, particularly political and industrial terms, but there was no attempt to alter the grammar of the language. The standard remained that of the educated Moscow classes, *not* the workers or the peasants. Indeed, in contrast to their economic and socio-political failures, it can be argued that Russia's Communist rulers had considerable linguistic success. They managed to maintain linguistic continuity with the past while spreading literacy throughout the population, turning Russian into a world language and making it a lingua franca for a sixth of the land surface of the globe. This important language is in all essentials the one used so richly by Tolstoi and Chekhov a hundred years ago; it remains, and will remain, the key to a rich culture, a world-class literature and communication with 150 million native speakers. In the new post-Cold War Europe, we must recognize that Russian is both an important part of the European cultural heritage and also the first language of more Europeans than any other.

SSEES, London, 1996   NJB

ACKNOWLEDGEMENTS

I wish to thank the School of Slavonic and East European Studies of the University of London which granted me a year's leave from teaching and other duties in order to complete this book. I am particularly grateful to Dr Lyudmila Ivanovna Matthews, who read and discussed two separate drafts and made many valuable suggestions. Thanks are also due to Aleksei Il'ich Prokhnevskii and Tat'iana Aleksandrovna Golova, who checked all the Russian, and to Shirley Adams, Joan Fernald, John Garrett and Sarah Hurst, who commented on the manuscript from the learner's point of view.

1

РУ́ССКАЯ А́ЗБУКА

LEARNING TO READ RUSSIAN

Before you finish this lesson you'll be able to pronounce the Russian heading above, which means 'the Russian alphabet'.

1.1 The Russian Cyrillic Alphabet

Russian Cyrillic is based on an alphabet invented around AD 863 by a Macedonian monk, who spoke a South Slavonic language closely related to Russian and also knew Greek; the inventor was later canonized as Saint Cyril, hence the name Cyrillic. This original Slavonic alphabet was based on the Greek one, so some of the letters will be familiar, e.g. п, the Russian p, which you may recognize as the Greek *pi*, used in mathematics.

The alphabet is the first hurdle when you tackle Russian, but it is not a daunting one. Once you know the sounds of the thirty-three letters, you can read Russian words comprehensibly; unlike English, it is generally true to say that Russian words are pronounced as they are written. In this lesson, you will learn the essentials for reading and pronouncing Russian. In Lesson 2, you will find details of the regular minor differences between Russian spelling and pronunciation.

1.2 Learning the Russian Alphabet

To make thirty-three letters easier to learn, we'll divide them into four groups.

(a) The first group contains five letters which are easy to learn:

Capital	Small	Pronunciation
A	a·	[a] as in father
K	к	[k] as in kangaroo
M	м	[m] as in man
O	o	[o] as in bottle – but note that in unstressed" syllables' (i.e. with no stress mark ´) standard Moscow pronunciation of o is closer to [a]. For 'stress', see 2.2.
T	т	[t] as in tan

So now you can read Russian words such as:

тóт	[tot]	'that'
кóт	[kot]	'cat'
так	[tak]	'so'
там	[tam]	'there'
ктó-то	[któ-ta]	'someone' (second o pronounced [a] because it is unstressed). This word has the same rhythm as English 'totter', which is stressed on the o.

(b) The second group contains seven letters which look like English ones but have different sounds:

Capital	Small	Pronunciation
B	в	[v] as in vet
E	e	[ye] as in yes
H	н	[n] as in never
P	p	[r] as in error (rolled as in Scottish English)

---

1 Words marked ' are technical terms which are explained in the lessons and/or in the glossary on page 503. The ' is inserted when a term is first used and occasionally thereafter as a reminder that the term is defined in the glossary. Syllables' (a syllable is a vowel plus preceding consonants) are separated by hyphens (-) in the [bracketed] English transcriptions.

С	с	[s] as in **s**it
У	у	[oo] as in b**oo**t
Х	х	[h] pronounced like the **ch** in Scots lo**ch** or German Ba**ch**

Words for practice:

нет	[nyet]	'no'
Москва́	[mask-vá]	'Moscow'
метро́	[mye-tró]	'metro', 'underground railway'
о́н	[on]	'he'
она́	[a-ná]	'she'
сестра́	[sye-strá]	'sister'
рестора́н	[rye-sta-rán]	'restaurant'

Now try these ones, covering the pronunciation on the right with a piece of paper:

	Translation	**Pronunciation**
са́хар	'sugar'	**[sá-har]**
вам	'to you'	**[vam]**
Ве́ра	'Vera'	**[vyé-ra]**
у́тро	'morning'	**[oʹo-tra]**
Нева́	'Neva'	**[nye-vá]** (river in St Petersburg)
ка́сса	'cash desk'	**[ká-ssa]**
ка́рта	'map'	**[kár-ta]**
ма́рка	'postage stamp'	**[már-ka]**

It is worth going through these lists twice, since you will meet all these useful words again.

(c) The third group contains thirteen letters which look unfamiliar but have familiar sounds:

Capital	**Small**	**Pronunciation**
Б	б	[b] as in **b**et
Г	г	[g] as in **g**et
Д	д	[d] as in **d**ebt
Ё	ё	[yo] as in **yo**nder. (Note: Russians normally omit the two dots, so in books, newspapers etc. this letter *looks* the same as **е** [ye]; however, the dots are printed in dictionaries and books for foreigners)

3

З	**з**	[z] as in **z**oo
И	**и**	[ee] as in **ee**l
Й	**й**	[y] as in bo**y**; **й** forms diphthongs, so **ой** sounds like [oy] in b**oy**, **ай** sounds like the igh in s**igh**, **уй** [ooi] sounds like oui in the name Lo**ui**s
Л	**л**	[l] as in peop**l**e
П	**п**	[p] as in **p**et
Ф	**ф**	[f] as in **f**at
Э	**э**	[e] as in f**e**d
Ю	**ю**	[yoo] as in **u**niverse
Я	**я**	[ya] as in **ya**k

Examples:

мир	**[meer]**	'peace', 'world'
да	**[da]**	'yes'
футбóл	**[foot-ból]**	'football'
спасúбо	**[spa-se´e-ba]**	'thank you'
до свидáния	**[da svee-dá-nee-ya]**	'goodbye' (**до** has no stress, so is pronounced [da])
Югослáвия	**[yoo-ga-slá-vee-ya]**	'Yugoslavia'
Алексáндр	**[a-lye-ksándr]**	'Alexander'
спýтник	**[spo´ot-neek]**	'sputnik', 'travelling companion'
Владивостóк	**[vla-dee-va-stók]**	'Vladivostok'
Россúя	**[ra-sse´e-ya]**	'Russia'
Толстóй	**[tal-stóy]**	'Tolstoi' (author of *War and Peace*)
зимá	**[zee-má]**	'winter'
Белфáст	**[byel-fást]**	'Belfast'
я знáю	**[ya zná-yoo]**	'I know'
Аэрофлóт	**[a-e-ra-flót]**	'Aeroflot' (the Russian airline)
ликёр	**[lee-kyór]**	'liqueur' (**ё** always carries the stress, so there is no need to print the ´ mark on **ё**)
самолёт	**[sa-ma-lyót]**	'aeroplane'
бойкóт	**[bay-kót]**	'boycott'
парк	**[park]**	'park'

кио́ск	[kee-ósk]	'kiosk'
Байка́л	[bay-kál]	'Baikal' (lake in Siberia)
телефо́н	[tye-lye-fón]	'telephone'
Пра́вда	[práv-da]	'*Pravda*' (= truth)

(d) The last group contains eight letters which take longer to learn:

Capital	Small	Pronunciation
Ж	ж	[zh] pronounced like the [s] in plea**s**ure
Ц	ц	[ts] as in i**ts**
Ч	ч	[ch] as in **ch**urch
Ш	ш	[sh] as in **sh**ut
Щ	щ	[shsh] as in Wel**sh sh**eep
Ъ	ъ	'hard sign' – this letter has no sound of its own but represents a very short pause
Ы	ы	[i] as in b**i**t, but with the tongue tip further back
Ь	ь	'soft sign' – [y] as in **y**et, but pronounced simultaneously with the letter before it – so **нь** sounds like the [ny] in can**y**on. Try not to separate the [y] from the preceding letter, particularly at the ends of words; to remind you of this, we shall show the **ь** as a small raised ʸ in our transcriptions, e.g. **со́ль** 'salt' [solʸ]

Examples:

журна́л	[zhoor-nál]	'magazine'
царе́вич	[tsa-ryé-veech]	'son of the tsar'
гости́ница	[ga-ste´e-nee-tsa]	'hotel'
чай	[chay]	'tea'
дру́жба	[dro´ozh-ba]	'friendship'
щи	[shshee]	'cabbage soup'
бо́рщ	[borshsh]	'beetroot soup'

шампа́нское	[sham-pán-ska-ye]	'champagne', 'sparkling wine'
Шотла́ндия	[shat-lán-dee-ya]	'Scotland'
Шостако́вич	[sha-sta-kó-veech]	'Shostakovich'
объе́кт	[ab-yékt]	'object' (the 'hard sign' simply separates the [b] from the [y])
сын	[sin]	'son'
рестора́ны	[rye-sta-rá-ni]	'restaurants'
Крым	[krim]	'Crimea'
ко́фе	[kó-fye]	'coffee'
большо́й	[balʸ-shóy]	'big' (lʸ is l+y pronounced simultaneously, like ly in the name Lyuba)
Кремль	[kryemlʸ]	'the Kremlin'
царь	[tsarʸ]	'tsar' (рь = r+y pronounced together, one of the most difficult of Russian sounds)

If you learn the values of the thirty-three letters given above, you will be understood when you read any Russian word. Read them by the syllables†, as in the transcriptions above: **[Vla-dee-va-stók]**. A syllable† is a vowel plus any preceding consonants; consonants at the end of a word go with the last vowel; if a word contains a large or awkward group of consonants, split the consonants so that some go with the preceding vowel and some with the following one, e.g. **Москва́** 'Moscow' can be read **[Mask-vá]**. While you are learning to read Cyrillic, use that slow pronunciation, syllable by syllable.

Now try this practice exercise. Cover the transcription (and the translation) on the right.

	Pronunciation	**Translation**
Влади́мир	[Vla-deʹe-meer]	'Vladimir'
туале́т	[too-a-lyét]	'toilet'
метро́	[mye-tró]	'metro', 'underground'
тролле́йбус	[tra-llyéy-boos]	'trolleybus'
календа́рь	[ka-lyen-dárʸ]	'calendar'
перестро́йка	[pye-rye-stróy-ka]	'perestroika', 'reorganization'
гла́сность	[glás-nastʸ]	'openness'
Украи́на	[oo-kra-eʹe-na]	'Ukraine'

Сиби́рь	[see-be´er⁷]	'Siberia'
Во́лга	[vól-ga]	'the Volga river'
Ма́нчестер	[mán-chye-styer]	'Manchester'
Би́рмингем	[be´er-meen-gyem]	'Birmingham'
Ливерпу́ль	[lee-vyer-po´ol⁷]	'Liverpool'
Аберди́н	[a-byer-de´en]	'Aberdeen'
По́ртсмут	[pórt-smoot]	'Portsmouth'
Филаде́льфия	[fee-la-dyél⁷-fee-ya]	'Philadelphia'
Майа́ми	[ma-yá-mee]	'Miami'
Го́луэй	[gó-loo-ey]	'Galway'
Ду́блин	[do´ob-leen̄]	'Dublin'
Ме́льбурн	[myél⁷-boorn]	'Melbourne'
Перт	[pyert]	'Perth'
да́ча	[dá-cha]	'country cottage'
хорошо́	[ha-ra-shó]	'good', 'well', 'OK'
до́брое у́тро	[dó-bra-ye o´o-tra]	'good morning'

1.3 The Russian Alphabet in Dictionary Order

Here is the Russian (Cyrillic) alphabet in its normal dictionary order. Cover the transcription on the right and check your pronunciation of the thirty-three letters again. To help you learn the order of the letters, notice that it is similar to the Latin alphabet as far as letter no. 21 (**у**), so you should concentrate on the letters from **ф**.

1	**А а**	[a]	12	**К к**	[k]	23	**Х х**	[h] as in lo**ch**	
2	**Б б**	[b]	13	**Л л**	[l]	24	**Ц ц**	[ts]	
3	**В в**	[v]	14	**М м**	[m]	25	**Ч ч**	[ch] as in **church**	
4	**Г г**	[g]	15	**Н н**	[n]	26	**Ш ш**	[sh]	
5	**Д д**	[d]	16	**О о**	[o]	27	**Щ щ**	[shsh]	
6	**Е е**	[ye]	17	**П п**	[p]	28	**Ъ ъ**	hard sign – brief pause	
7	**Ё ё**	[yo]	18	**Р р**	[r]	29	**Ы ы**	[i]	
8	**Ж ж**	[zh]	19	**С с**	[s]	30	**Ь ь**	[y] as in can**y**on	
9	**З з**	[z]	20	**Т т**	[t]	31	**Э э**	[e]	
10	**И и**	[ee]	21	**У у**	[oo]	32	**Ю ю**	[yoo]	
11	**Й й**	[y]	22	**Ф ф**	[f]	33	**Я я**	[ya]	

1.4 Russian Italics

NOTE: In Russian italic printing, **г** is *г*, **д** is *д*, **и** is *и*, **й** is *й*, **л** is *л*, **п** is *п*, **т** is *m*. You will see in Lesson 2 that most of these resemble the handwritten forms.

EXERCISE 1/1

Read the following words. Can you translate them? The pronunciation and translations are in the key at the end of the book.

1 **Бори́с** ....
2 **да** ....
3 **нет** ....
4 **большо́й** ....
5 **спаси́бо** ....
6 **ру́сская а́збука** (the heading of the lesson) ....
7 **бо́рщ** ....
8 **чай** ....
9 **са́хар** ....
10 **журна́л** ....

EXERCISE 1/2

Here are some common signs. Check your pronunciation in the key at the back of the book.

1 **АЭРОПО́РТ**   AIRPORT
2 **БУФЕ́Т**   SNACKBAR
3 **ГОСТИ́НИЦА**   HOTEL
4 **ДИРЕ́КТОР**   MANAGER, DIRECTOR
5 **ЗАКРЫ́ТО**   CLOSED
6 **ЗАПРЕЩЕНО́**   FORBIDDEN
7 **ИНТУРИ́СТ**   INTOURIST
8 **КА́ССА**   CASH DESK/TICKET OFFICE
9 **К СЕБЕ́**   PULL

10	**НЕ КУРИ́ТЬ**	NO SMOKING
11	**ОТ СЕБЯ́**	PUSH
12	**ПАРИКМА́ХЕРСКАЯ**	HAIRDRESSER/BARBER
13	**ПО́ЧТА**	POST OFFICE
14	**РЕМО́НТ**	CLOSED FOR REPAIRS
15	**РЕСТОРА́Н**	RESTAURANT
16	**ТУАЛЕ́Т**	TOILET

EXERCISE 1/3

What do these say?

1 **БАР**	2 **ПРАВДА**	3 **ТАКСИ**
4 **СТОП**	5 **МОСКВА**	6 **ЛОС АНДЖЕЛЕС**
7 **ПИЦЦА ХАТ**	8 **ВЛАДИМИР ЛЕНИН**	9 **ИЗВЕСТИЯ**
10 **НЬЮ-ЙОРК**	11 **ГЛАСНОСТЬ**	12 **РОЛЛС-РОЙС**
13 **БИТЛЗ**	14 **ШЕКСПИР**	15 **ХЕЛЬСИНКИ**

ПРАВДА

Пицца Хат

In addition to the main material of the lesson, this book will also give you extra information which is not essential to a basic competence in Russian. If you choose to skip these parts, marked EXTRA, or to return to them later, your progress through the lessons will not be hindered.

1.5 EXTRA

(1) The names of the Russian letters

Above we gave only the *pronunciation* of the letters. You need the *names* of the letters only when you read abbreviations (see Lesson 30), just as in English the letters pronounced **[i]**, **[b]**, **[m]** are read **[ay-bee-em]** in the abbreviation IBM.

а [a], **б** [be], **в** [ve], **г** [ge], **д** [de], **е** [ye], **ё** [yo], **ж** [zhe], **з** [ze], **и** [ee], **й** [ee krát-ka-ye ('short ee')], **к** [ka], **л** [el], **м** [em], **н** [en], **о** [o], **п** [pe], **р** [er], **с** [es], **т** [te], **у** [oo], **ф** [ef], **х** [ha], **ц** [tse], **ч** [che], **ш** [sha], **щ** [shsha], **ъ** [tvyór-di znak ('hard sign')], **ы** [yerí], **ь** [myáh-kee znak ('soft sign')], **э** [e], **ю** [yoo], **я** [ya]

So CCCP, the name of the country, is pronounced [es-es-es-ér]. **КГБ** (= the KGB) is pronounced [ka-ge-be].

(2) Transliteration of Russian in English letters

Transliteration is the representation of Russian *letters* by English ones, for example when spelling the names of Russian people and places in English

10

newspapers. *Transcription* (or 'phonetic transcription') is the representation of Russian *sounds*, for example to help foreigners learn to pronounce correctly. Since there are a number of differences between Russian spelling and Russian pronunciation (see Lesson 2), transliteration and transcription can never be the same thing. There are various standard ways of transliterating Russian into English letters. The American Library of Congress system is now generally preferred by those professionals, e.g. compilers of library catalogues, who need to worry about such things as how to spell Russian names consistently in English. Most of the equivalents in the list below are obvious from the pronunciation; those which are not, or which are transliterated differently in other systems, are marked with an asterisk (*):

а = a, **б** = b, **в** = v, **г** = g, **д** = d, *****е** = e, *****ё** = ё, *****ж** = zh, **з** = z, *****и** = i, *****й** = i, **к** = k, **л** = l, **м** = m, **н** = n, **о** = o, **п** = p, **р** = r, **с** = s, **т** = t, *****у** = u, **ф** = f, *****х** = kh, **ц** = ts, **ч** = ch, **ш** = sh, *****щ** = shch, *****ъ** = ", *****ы** = y, *****ь** = ', **э** = e, *****ю** = iu, *****я** = ia.

Example of transliteration[1] (a woman's name):
Наталья Евгеньева Хрущёва = Natal'ia Evgen'eva Khrushchëva

This system is used in this book for proper names (i.e. 'Vania' rather than 'Vanya' for **Ваня**), except where traditional spellings are likely to be much more familiar, e.g. 'Yalta' (rather than 'Ialta') for the town of **Ялта** in the Crimea.

---

[1] For comparison, in the phonetic *transcription* used in this book, this name would be **[na-tá-l'ya yev-gyé-n'ye-va hroo-shshyó-va]**.

11

2

УРÓК НÓМЕР ДВА

RUSSIAN HANDWRITING;
MORE ON PRONUNCIATION

(If your aim is not to speak or write Russian but only to be able to read Russian books and periodicals, you can skip the whole of Lesson 2 – or skim through it now and come back to it later.)

2.1 **Russian Handwriting**

(Even if you decide not to copy out the examples written here, this section will give you some useful alphabet revision and reading practice.)

Russians all learn the same rather florid handwriting style at school. You should form the letters as indicated here, though you will not be misunderstood if you choose not to join the letters or if you make fewer loops.

Here are the handwritten forms of the letters in alphabetical order:

A а [a] *A   a*

Б б [b] *Б   б*

    Баба   **Бáба [bá-ba]** 'Peasant woman'

В в [v] *В   в*

Г г [g] *Г   г*

Д д [d] *Д   д*

    да   **да [da]** 'yes'

12

There is also an old-fashioned form of small **д**: *∂*

Е е [ye] *Ɛ* *е*

где **где [gdye]** 'where'

Ё ё [yo] *Ɛ̈* *ё*

Ж ж [zh] *Ж* *ж*

даже **да́же [dá-zhe]** 'even'

З з [z] *З* *з*

И и [ee] *И* *и*

Иди! **Иди́! [ee-de´e]** 'Go!'

Й й [y] *Й* *й*

Дай! **Дай! [day]** 'Give!'

К к [k] *К* *к*

Л л [l] *Л* *л* The initial short downstroke is an integral part of this letter and must be present, whatever the preceding letter. Look at these examples: *зал* **зал [zal]** 'hall', 'large room' *или* **йли [e´e-lee]** 'or'

М м [m] *М* *м* As in the case of **л**, the initial short downstroke must be present; *Адам* **Ада́м** 'Adam' *Клим* **Клим** 'Clement' (if the downstrokes on **л** and **м** are omitted, the letters become indistinguishable: *Клии*)

Н н [n] *Н* *н*

О о [o] *О* *о*

Он 'Не' If the following letter is **л** or **м**, do not try to join them: *дом* **дом** 'house' *молоко* **молоко́** 'milk'

П п [p] *П* *п*

Р р [r] *Р* *р*

13

С с [s] *С с*

    Спасибо **Спаси́бо [spa-se´e-ba]** 'Thank you'

Т т [t] *Т т*   Note the difference between the printed and handwritten forms.

    Тот **То́т** 'That' *кто-то* **кто́-то [któ-ta]** 'someone'

    нет **нет [nyet]** 'no'

Some Russians 'cross their t's' by putting a bar over the letter, like this: *т̄о̄т̄* **то́т**, but they are in a minority. Another minority writes **т** as *Т т*

У у [oo] *У у*

Ф ф [f] *Ф ф*   Notice that, like all Russian capital letters except **щ** and **ц** with their small 'tails', capital **Ф** does not go below the line. You don't need to spend long practising capital *Ф* , since initial **ф** is rare in Russian.

    Белфаст **Бе́лфаст** 'Belfast' *Футбол* **футбо́л [foot-ból]** 'football'

Х х [h] *Х х*

    Бах **Бах** 'Bach'

Ц ц [ts] *Ц ц*   Keep the loop small, much smaller than the loop of **у**

    у **[oo]** *гостиница* **гости́ница [ga-ste´e-nee-tsa]** 'hotel'

    Царица **Цари́ца [tsa-re´e-tsa]** 'Empress'

Ч ч [ch] *Ч ч*   Note that the bottom stroke of the capital form turns the opposite way from **У** *у* **[oo]**. Make sure that your small form looks different from **г** *г* **[g]**.

    Чай **Чай** 'Tea' *дача* **да́ча [dá-cha]** 'country cottage'

    человек **челове́к [chye-la-vyék]** 'person'

Ш ш [sh] *Ш ш*   Unlike an English w, the last stroke ends at the foot of

14

the letter: *Хорошо* **Хорошо́** 'Good' **[ha-ra-shó]**. Some

Russians put a bar under **ш** *ш* to make it clearly distinct from **и** *и* :

машина **маши́на** 'car'

Щ щ [shsh] *Щ щ* As in the case of **ц** *ц* , keep the loop small:

Щи **Щи [shshee]** 'Cabbage soup' *борщ* **бо́рщ [borshsh]**

'beetroot soup'

Ъ ъ [-] *ъ* There is no need to practise a capital form, since this letter

never starts a word.

объект **объе́кт [ab-yékt]** 'object'

Ы ы [i] *ы* No capital form, since it never starts a word.

сын **сын [sin]** 'son'

Ь ь [y] *ь* No capital form required. Make sure your **ь** *ь* is half the

height of **в** *в* : *царь* **царь [tsar']** 'tsar'

Прокофьев **Проко́фьев** 'Prokofiev'

Э э [e] *Э э* *Этот* **Э́тот [é-tat]** 'This' *Аэрофлот* **Аэрофло́т** 'Aeroflot'

Ю ю [yoo] *Ю ю*

Югославия **Югосла́вия** 'Yugoslavia' *меню* **меню́** 'menu'

Я я [ya] *Я я* Like **л** *л* and **м** *м* , this letter must always have a

distinct initial short downstroke. To help you remember those three

letters, here is a word with all three of them together:

земля **земля́ [zye-mlyá]** 'earth'

Read and copy:

До свида́ния. *До свидания.* **[da svee-dá-nee-ya]** (Goodbye)

Приве́т. *Привет.* **[pree-vyét]** (Greetings/Hi)

Спаси́бо за всё. *Спасибо за всё.* **[spa-se'e-ba za vsyo]**

(Thank you for everything)

Где же письмо? *Где же письмо?* [gdye zhe pees^y-mó] (Where
  is the letter?)

Это мой сын Чáрли. *Это мой сын Чарли.*

  [é-ta moy sin chár-lee] (This is my son Charlie)

Дорогáя Клáра! *Дорогая Клара!* [da-ra-gá-ya klá-ra] (Dear Klara)

Щи да кáша – пи́ща нáша. *Щи да каша – пища наша.*

  [shshee da ká-sha – pe´e-shsha ná-sha] (Cabbage soup and

  kasha are our food)

Я люблю́ футбóл. *Я люблю футбол.* [ya lyoo-blyo´o

  foot-ból] (I love football)

Это хорóшая гости́ница. *Это хорошая гостиница.*

  [é-ta ha-ró-sha-ya ga-ste´e-nee-tsa] (This is a good hotel)

Почему́? *Почему?* [pa-chye-mo´o] (Why?)

Объявлéние. *Объявление.* [ab-ya-vlyé-nee-ye] (Announcement)

2.2 More on Russian Pronunciation: Stress'

As in English, some syllables' are pronounced more prominently than
others. Compare the English word 'phótograph', where the first syllable is
stressed, with 'photógraphy', where the stress is on the second syllable.
Although normal Russian spelling, like English, does not show the place
of the stress, it is important to learn the stress when you learn the word. Be
careful with those Russian words (particularly names) which are sometimes used in English, since the traditional English pronunciation often
does not match the Russian. A good example is the name **Влади́мир**
'Vladimir'. In English we often say Vládimir, but in Russian the stress is
always on the second syllable [Vla-de´e-meer]. Other examples:

The writer Pasternak is **Пастернáк** (not Pásternak)

Nabokov is **Набóков** (not Nábokov)

Oblomov, the man in the dressing-gown in Goncharóv's famous novel, is
  Облóмов (not Óblomov).

16

Russian stress is heavier than in English and it is also much harder to predict which syllable is the stressed one. You will find that different forms of the same word may have different stresses. For example, the Russian for 'hand' is **рука́**, stressed on the end **[roo-ká]**, but 'hands' is **ру́ки**, stressed on the first syllable **[ro´o-kee]**.

If you have to read a word whose stress you do not know, the safest thing is to read it with no stress at all, syllable by syllable.

2.3 **EXTRA: One-Syllable Words and Stress**

Dictionaries and most grammar books do not put a stress mark on one-syllable words, since there is obviously only one place for the stress to fall. We shall follow that practice *except* in the case of one-syllable words containing the letter **o**. There are some short Russian words, particularly prepositions (words like **за** 'for', **от** 'from', **до** 'until'), which are normally pronounced with no stress, as if they were joined to the following word. As you learnt in Lesson 1, **o** sounds very different (like **[a]**) if it is not stressed, so **до** 'until' is pronounced **[da]**. Practise:

до свида́ния [da-svee-dá-nee-ya] 'goodbye', literally 'until meeting'.

The preposition **до** 'until' is unstressed and pronounced as if joined to the word **свида́ния**.

So to help you pronounce correctly, when **o** is pronounced **[o]**, we give it a stress mark (e.g. **бо́рщ**). Pronounce unstressed **o** as **[a]**.

The pronunciation of the vowel letter **o** as **[o]** only when it is stressed (marked **ó** in this book) and elsewhere as **[a]** (like the first letter of the alphabet) is a notable feature of Moscow pronunciation.[1]

---

[1] To be more precise, **o** and **a** in the syllable before the stress both sound like the vowel in 'cup', phonetically **[ʌ]**; in most other unstressed positions they both sound like the a in 'about', phonetically **[ə]**. But for practical purposes think of both vowel letters as being equivalent to unstressed **[a]**.

2.4 **EXTRA: Other Non-Essential Pronunciation Features**

If you simply want to be understood, you can ignore the following details. If you read Russian words as they are spelt, you will not cause misunderstandings. But if you are interested in the details of the small differences between the way Moscow Russian is written and the way it is pronounced, study these six points.

2.5 **Softness'**

Probably the most important feature of a 'good' Russian accent is the correct pronunciation of soft' consonants. 'Soft' means that the consonant is pronounced with a *simultaneous* **y** sound. A consonant is soft if it is followed by **е ё и ю я** or the soft sign **ь**. So the two consonants in **день** [**dyen'**] 'day' are soft. The main thing is to pronounce the **y** simultaneously with the consonant; English speakers tend to pronounce them separately. The word **совéт** 'council' is pronounced [**s-a-v'-é-t**] – five sounds. The **v'** (soft **в**) is one sound. In English we known this word as 'soviet' – six sounds **s-o-v-i-e-t**.

2.6 **Hard' Consonants versus Soft' Consonants**

'Hard' means pronounced like most English consonants, with no [**y**] sound. In the alphabet you learnt in Lesson 1, there are twenty consonant letters. All of these, *except* **ч** and **щ**, represent hard sounds. **ч** and **щ** are always soft (i.e. they always contain a [**y**] sound). Of the other eighteen consonants, fifteen regularly have soft equivalents. If a consonant is to be pronounced soft, it will have **е ё и ю я** or **ь** written after it. So **л** is hard' [**l**], while **ль** is soft' [**l'**]. To a Russian, [**l**] and [**l'**] are completely different sounds, while to an English speaker they may simply sound like variant pronunciations of the same letter 'l'. If you compare your pronunciation of the l in 'people' and the l in 'leaf', you are likely to find (depending on your dialect) that the 'people' l is like **л** while the 'leaf' l is like **ль**. If you

18

have a tape or a teacher, listen for the difference between these two Russian words:

ми́ло [me´e-la] 'nice' – hard[t] **л**
ми́ля [me´e-lya] 'mile' – soft[t] **ль**

Then try:

лук [look] 'onion' – hard[t] l
люк [lyook] 'hatch' – [ly] is soft[t] l

More examples of contrasting hard and soft consonants:

мат [mat] 'bad language', 'abuse' – hard[t] **т**
мать [mat⁷] 'mother' – soft[t] **ть**

мать [mat⁷] 'mother' – hard[t] m
мять [myat⁷] 'to crumple' – soft[t] **[my]**

Before **и** the **[y]** element is less audible but the consonant is none the less soft[t].

бить [beet⁷] 'to beat' – soft[t] b

If the **б** was hard, the vowel would be not **и** but **ы**, as in:

быть [bit⁷] 'to be' – hard[t] b

A possibly helpful note on hard[t] versus soft[t]

The difference between the English pronunciations of 'booty' and 'beauty' is close to the difference between **б** and soft **бь** in Russian. 'Do' and 'dew' give you a good comparison with **ду** and **дю** in Russian. Compare 'fool' and 'fuel' with **дул** and **фюл**, 'poor' and 'pure' with **пур** and **пюр**. The correspondence between 'pure' and **пюр** is not exact, because the **р** and **у** sounds are not simultaneous in 'pure' while the **п** and the **[y]** element from the **ю** are pronounced simultaneously in **пюр**, but for practical purposes the correspondence is close enough.

2.7 The Consonants ж ц ш are Always Hard[t]

Although the letters **е ё и ю я ь** make the preceding consonant soft[t], there are three exceptional consonants: **ж ц ш**. These three letters are always

19

pronounced hard' (i.e. with *no* [y] sound), whatever the following letter. So **женá** 'wife' is pronounced **[zhe-ná]** – the [y] of the letter **e** [ye] simply disappears. **Жёны** 'wives' is pronounced as if written **жóны** [zhó-ni]. **Ты знáешь** 'you know' is pronounced as if written **ты знáеш** [zná-yesh] – the soft sign has no effect and is only there for historical reasons.

You should also be able to hear that after **ж ц** and **ш** the vowel **и** [ee] is pronounced as if it were **ы** [i]:

жить [zhit'] 'to live'
цирк [tsirk] 'circus'

2.8 Voiced' Consonants Can Become Unvoiced'

The first six consonants of the alphabet **б в г д ж з** are all voiced', that is, pronounced with vibration of the vocal cords. At the ends of words these six turn into their unvoiced' equivalents (i.e. pronounced with little or no vibration of the vocal cords):

Voiced		Unvoiced
б [b]	is pronounced	п [p]
в [v]	"	ф [f]
г [g]	"	к [k]
д [d]	"	т [t]
ж [zh]	"	ш [sh]
з [z]	"	с [s]

So **Петербýрг** is pronounced **[pye-tyer-bo´ork]** – **г** [g] becomes [k] at the end of the word.
Горбачёв is **[gar-ba-chyof]** – **в** [v] becomes [f]

Within words, the six voiced consonants above become unvoiced if they stand immediately before an unvoiced consonant (**к п с т ф х ц ч ш щ**). Look at the following examples:

вóдка is pronounced **[vóṭka]** – **д** becomes [t] before **к**
зáвтра 'tomorrow' is **[záftra]** – **в** becomes [f] before **т**
вхóд 'entrance' is **[fhot]** – **в** is [f] before **х**

2.9 Unvoiced' Consonants Can Become Voiced

Similarly, *unvoiced* consonants become *voiced* before the voiced consonants **б г д ж з** (but not **в**). So:

вокзáл 'station' is pronounced **[vag-zál]** – **к** is **[g]** before **з** **[z]**

But the consonants in **Москвá** 'Moscow' are pronounced as written: **[mask-vá]** – **в** does *not* affect preceding unvoiced consonants.

2.10 The Vowels о, е, я in Unstressed Syllables

As you learnt above (2.2), syllables' marked ´ have a heavy stress, heavier than in English. So unstressed' vowels sound much less distinct than stressed' ones. You already know that **о** and **а** sound the same in unstressed syllables. You may also be able to hear that unstressed **е** is almost indistinguishable from unstressed **и**, so that, particularly in the pronunciation of younger speakers, **Петербýрг** (St Petersburg) sounds as if it were written **Питирбýрк [pee-teer-bo´ork]**. The vowel **я**, *in the syllable before the stress*, also sounds like **и**, so that **язы́к** 'language' at normal speed sounds like **[ee-zík]**, rather than **[ya-zík]**.

Remember: IF YOU CHOOSE NOT TO BOTHER WITH THE DETAILS ABOVE, OR IF YOU DECIDE TO LEAVE THEM UNTIL LATER, YOU WILL NOT CAUSE MISUNDERSTANDINGS. As we said in Lesson 1, to get by it is sufficient to know the values of the thirty-three letters of the alphabet and to read words as they are written. There is nothing wrong with a foreign accent, as long as you are comprehensible.

2.11 Pronunciation Practice

	Slow	Normal Speed
Ленингрáд	[lye-neen-grad]	**[lye-neen-grát]** ('Leningrad') – soft **ль**, soft **нь**, **д** becomes **т** at the end of the word
Москвá	[mosk-va]	**[mask-vá]** ('Moscow') – [o] becomes [a] when unstressed

21

Ки́ев	[kee-ev]	[ke´e-ef] ('Kiev') – [v] becomes [f] at the end of the word
Достое́вский	[do-sto-yev-skeey]	[da-sta-yéf-skee] ('Dostoevskii') – [v] becomes [f] before s; [y] is inaudible after [ee]
Пастерна́к	[pa-styer-nak]	[pa-styer-nák] ('Pasternak') – [ty] is one sound, soft ть
во́дка	[vod-ka]	[vót-ka] ('vodka') – д devoiced' before к
пиццери́я	[pee-tse-ree-ya]	[pee-tse-re´e-ya] ('pizzeria') – no [y] sound after ц
Бре́жнев	[bryezh-nyev]	[bryézh-nyef] ('Brezhnev') – в devoiced at end of word
Горбачёв	[gor-ba-chyov]	[gar-ba-chyóf] ('Gorbachev')
Проко́фьев	[pro-ko-fʸ-yev]	[pra-kó-fʸyef] ('Prokofiev' or 'Prokof'ev')
Набо́ков	[na-bo-kov]	[na-bó-kaf] ('Nabokov')
Бе́рнард Шо́у	[byer-nard sho-oo]	[byér-nart shó-oo] ('Bernard Shaw')
Ли́дз	[leedz]	[leets] ('Leeds')

2.12 Exceptional Pronunciation Features

In addition to the above list of regular divergences between spelling and Moscow pronunciation, there are a few less predictable irregularities. Here are some common examples – these are all words which you will meet again:

что́ 'what' pronounced [**sh**to], not [chto]

пожа́луйста 'please' usually pronounced [pa-zhál-sta], without the **уй**

здра́вствуйте 'hello' pronounced [zdrá-stvooy-tye] without the first **в**

его́ 'his' pronounced [ye**v**ó], not [ye**g**ó]

сего́дня 'today' pronounced [sve-**v**ód-nya] not [sye-**g**ód-nya]

ра́дио 'radio' pronounced [rá-dee-o] not [rá-dee-a], because of its
foreign origin

In many recently borrowed words, educated Russians pronounce **e** as **э**, e.g.

те́ннис 'tennis' [té-nees] (not [tyé-nees])

компью́тер 'computer' [kam-pʸo´o-ter] (not [-tyer])

HANDWRITING EXERCISE 2/1

Write out the Russian words in 2.11.

PRONUNCIATION EXERCISE 2/2

Read the following words, fairly new to Russian. Then check your pronunciation (and the translations) in the key.

1 ви́ски. 2 инфля́ция. 3 ма́ркетинг. 4 мю́зикл. 5 но́у-ха́у.
6 персона́льный компью́тер. 7 приватиза́ция. 8 ро́к-му́зыка.
9 стрипти́з. 10 эксклюзи́вное интервью́.

FUN SECTION: PRONUNCIATION EXERCISE 2/3

Here are some reading practice words which English learners sometimes find amusing for one reason or another. Check your pronunciation with the key:

1 щит 'shield'. 2 шит 'sewn'. 3 брат 'brother'. 4 золотоволо́сое
'golden-haired'. 5 защища́ющий 'defending'. 6 нокаути́ровать 'to knock out'. 7 эксперименти́ровать 'to experiment'.
8 достопримеча́тельности 'sights'. 9 человеконенави́стничество
'misanthropy'.

3

УРОК НОМЕР ТРИ

EVERYDAY PHRASES; BASIC GRAMMAR

3.1 Some Everyday Words and Phrases

Here are some useful words and phrases to read and learn. If you've studied the handwriting in Lesson 2, you can also write them out and check your version with the key (exercise 3/1).

Да	[da]	Yes
Нет	[nyet]	No
Это	[é-ta]	This/That/It
Спасибо	[spa-se′e-ba]	Thank you
Доброе утро	[dó-bra-ye o′o-tra]	Good morning
Добрый день	[dó-bri dyen′]	Good day
До свидания	[da svee-dá-nee-ya]	Goodbye
Простите	[pra-ste′e-tye]	Excuse me/I'm sorry

With special pronunciation features:

Пожалуйста	Please/Don't mention it/You're welcome usually pronounced without the **уй** as [pa-zhál-sta]
Здравствуйте	Hello (the commonest greeting) pronounced without the first **в** as [zdrá-stvooy-tye]
Что	What pronounced [shto]
Где	Where [gdye], if pronounced carefully, but if you simply say [dye] without the **г** [g], no one will notice

24

And the numbers up to five:

1 **оди́н** [a-de´en]
2 **два** [dva]
3 **три** [tree]
4 **четы́ре** [chye-tí-rye]
5 **пять** [pyatʸ]

3.2 Some Simple Questions and Answers

A: **Что́** [shto] **э́то?** What's this/What's that?
B: **Э́то чай.** That/This/It is tea.

A: **Спаси́бо.** Thank you.
B: **Пожа́луйста.** Don't mention it.

A: **Что́ э́то?** What's this?
B: **Э́то рубль.** It's a rouble.

A: **Где Влади́мир?** Where is Vladimir?
B: **Во́т о́н.** There he is.

A: **Где чай?** Where is the tea?
B: **Во́т о́н.** Here it is/There it is.

A: **Где во́дка?** Where is the vodka?
B: **Во́т она́.** Here it is/There it is.

A: **Где меню́?** Where is the menu?
B: **Во́т оно́.** Here it is.

A: **Спаси́бо.** Thank you.
B: **Пожа́луйста.** Don't mention it.

A: **Прости́те, э́то вино́?** Excuse me, is this wine?
B: **Нет, э́то во́дка.** No, it's vodka.

3.3 Some Culture: Пожа́луйста in Reply to Спаси́бо 'Thank you'

If someone says **спаси́бо** 'thank you' you should always reply **пожа́луйста [pa-zhál-sta]** 'you're welcome'/'don't mention it'.

3.4 **More on Пожа́луйста 'Please'**

Пожа́луйста is a versatile word. It also means 'please', and 'here you are' when you give something to somebody.

Customer:	**Два, пожа́луйста.**	Two please.
Assistant :	**Пожа́луйста.**	Here you are.
Customer:	**Спаси́бо.**	Thank you.
Assistant :	**Пожа́луйста.**	You're welcome.

3.5 **Some Grammar: No 'is', 'am', 'are'**

You will see from the examples above that Russian manages without any equivalent of the present tense of 'to be' ('am', 'is', 'are')

Э́то чай. This (is) tea.

Note: If both parts of the sentence contain nouns ('Mary is an Englishwoman'), the missing verb can be represented by a dash (**Мэ́ри** [noun] – **англича́нка** [noun]).

3.6 **And No Equivalent of the Articles 'a' and 'the'**

Во́т меню́. Here (is) (a or the) menu.

3.7 **'This'/'That': Э́то**

Э́то is a useful word corresponding to both 'this' and 'that'. It also translates 'it' when 'it' can replace 'this' or 'that' in English, for example in naming things:

A: **Что́ э́то?** What is this/that/it?
B: **Э́то во́дка.** That/This/It is vodka.

EXAMPLES

A: **Что́ э́то?** What's this?/What is it?
B: **Э́то борщ.** It's beetroot soup.

A: **А что́ э́то?** And what's this?
B: **Э́то смета́на.** It's sour cream.
  [é-ta smye-tá-na]

(Russian soup is nearly always served with a spoonful of sour cream floating on the top.)

3.8 Here he/she/it is: Вот он/она́/оно́. Gender

All Russian nouns[1] (i.e. words like 'Ivan', 'vodka', 'taxi', 'beauty') belong to one of three different categories, depending on what the last letter is. These three categories are *masculine* (m), *feminine* (f) and *neuter* (n). Most male beings, like **Влади́мир**, are masculine, but so are days, towns and languages; all these are referred to as 'he' **он**. Most females, like **ма́ма** 'mother', are feminine, but so are vodka (**во́дка**), truth (**пра́вда**) and Moscow (**Москва́**), which are all called 'she' **она́**. The neuter category is the smallest one and includes such things as morning (**у́тро**), wine (**вино́**) and taxi (**такси́**); they are all called 'it' **оно́**. If you know about gender from studying French and German, you will be glad to know that the gender of Russian nouns is much easier to learn since you can nearly always tell the gender from the ending. Here are the details:

(a) Masculine nouns normally end with a consonant or **й**:

борщ 'beetroot soup'
Ива́н 'Ivan'
чай 'tea'

(b) Feminine nouns normally end **-а** or **-я**:

смета́на 'sour cream'
Ната́лья 'Natalia' **[na-tá-lʲya]**
Москва́ 'Moscow'

27

(c) Neuter nouns end **-o** or **-e**:

окно́ 'window'

вино́ 'wine'

упражне́ние 'exercise' **[oo-prazh-nyé-nee-ye]**

So you can normally tell the gender of a noun just by looking at it.

However, there are awkward cases:

(d) Most nouns ending **-ь** (soft sign) are feminine, but there are many masculine ones too, so you have to learn the gender of soft-sign nouns.

Feminine examples:

Сиби́рь 'Siberia' **[see-beʹerʹ]**

мать 'mother' **[matʹ]**

дверь 'door' **[dvyerʹ]**

Masculine examples:

рубль 'rouble' **[rooblʹ]**

И́горь 'Igor' **[eʹe-garʹ]**

день 'day' **[dyenʹ]**

(e) Nouns ending **-a** or **-я** which denote males are masculine:

па́па 'father', 'dad'

Воло́дя 'Volodia' (a familiar form of Vladimir)

дя́дя 'uncle'

(f) If a noun ends **-и** or **-у** or **-ю**, it is likely to be a foreign borrowing and to be *neuter*:

такси́ 'taxi'

меню́ 'menu'

(g) Foreign words denoting females are feminine, whatever their endings:

ле́ди (f) 'lady'

Мэ́ри (f) 'Mary'

Ма́ргарет (f) 'Margaret'

28

But if they do not end **-a**, **-я** or **-ь**, they are indeclinable' (see 5.10).

3.9 It

When you're talking about something which has already been named, 'it' will be **óн/онá/онó**, depending on the gender' of the noun to which 'it' refers.

A: **Где чай?**   Where is the tea?
B: **Вóт óн.**   There it ('he') is.
A: **Где винó?**   Where is the wine?
B: **Вóт онó.**   There it is.

3.10 Vocabulary

Here is the essential vocabulary for this lesson. These are words which you should try to learn:

NOUNS

англичáнка	**[an-glee-chán-ka]**	Englishwoman
бóрщ	**[borshsh]**	beetroot soup
брат	**[brat]**	brother
Вáня (m)	**[va-nya]**	Vania (familiar form of Ivan)
винó	**[vee-nó]**	wine
вóдка	**[vót-ka]**	vodka
Волóдя	**[va-ló-dya]**	Volodia (familiar form of Vladimir)
газéта	**[ga-zyé-ta]**	newspaper
дверь (f)	**[dvyerʸ]**	door
день (m)	**[dyenʸ]**	day
дóм	**[dom]**	house
дя́дя (m)	**[dya-dya]**	uncle
мать (f)	**[matʸ]**	mother
меню́ (n)	**[mye-nyoˊo]**	menu
Москвá	**[mask-vá]**	Moscow

окно́	[ak-nó]	window
па́па (m)	[pá-pa]	father, dad
рубль (m)	[roobl']	rouble
Сиби́рь (f)	[see-be´er']	Siberia
смета́на	[smye-tá-na]	sour cream
такси́ (n)	[tak-se´e]	taxi
упражне́ние	[oo-prazh-nyé-nee-ye]	exercise
у́тро	[o´o-tra]	morning
чай	[chay]	tea
шокола́д	[sha-ka-lat]	chocolate

QUESTION WORDS

| где | [gdye] | where |
| что | [shto] | what |

PRONOUNS

о́н	[on]	he
она́	[a-ná]	she
оно́	[a-nó]	it (referring to neuter nouns)
э́то	[é-ta]	this/that/it

OTHER WORDS

а	[a]	and/but (indicating a slight contrast)
во́т	[vot]	here/there (when pointing)
да	[da]	yes
до́брый день	[dó-bri dyen']	good day
до свида́ния	[da svee-dá-nee-ya]	goodbye
здра́вствуйте	[zdrást-vooy-tye]	hello
нет	[nyet]	no
пожа́луйста	[pa-zhál-sta]	please/don't mention it/ here you are

| простите | [pra-ste´e-tye] | excuse me/I'm sorry |
| спасибо | [spa-se´e-ba] | thank you |

The main problem in learning Russian is making all these unfamiliar words stick in your memory. Unlike French or Spanish, the basic vocabulary of Russian looks quite different from that of English. **Утро** does not look or sound like 'morning', and **здравствуйте** looks like nothing on earth. For many of the words, as well as listening to them being spoken, repeating them, writing them down, you will have to make up deliberate links. Some links are easy: a word like **дом** 'house' can easily be connected to its English equivalent by a link word such as '*dom*estic'; **газета [ga-zyé-ta]** can be linked to its meaning 'newspaper' by the word 'gazette'. But a word like **спасибо** [spa-se´e-ba] 'thank you' takes a little longer, because a link has to be invented. For example, think of *thanking S*arah for *pass*ing the *bu*tter.

3.11 **Dialogues.** (Cover the translation on the right and test yourself.)

| A: **Простите. Что это?** | Excuse me. What is this? |
| B: **Это вино.** | It's/That's wine. |

| A: **А это?** | And this? |
| B: **Это водка.** | That's vodka. |

| A: **А это?** | And what about this? |
| B: **Пепси-Кола.** | Pepsi-Cola. |

| A: **Спасибо.** | Thank you. |
| B: **Пожалуйста.** | Don't mention it. |

| A: **Простите, пожалуйста, что это?** | Excuse me, please, what's this? |
| B: **Это шоколад.** | It's chocolate. |

| A: **Три, пожалуйста.** | Three, please. |
| B: **Пожалуйста.** | Here you are. |

| A: **Спасибо.** | Thank you. |
| B: **Пожалуйста.** | Don't mention it. |

| A: **Где такси?** | Where's the taxi? |
| B: **Вот оно.** | There it (neuter) is. |

31

A: **Где Мэ́ри?**   Where's Mary?

B: **Вот она́.**   There she is.

A: **Где дя́дя Ва́ня?**   Where's Uncle Vanya?

B: **Вот он.**   There he is.

A: **Где Сиби́рь?**   Where's Siberia?

B: **Вот она́.**   There it (feminine) is.

3.12 **EXTRA: Different Equivalents of** 'It'

In identifying sentences (e.g. 'What is this/it?' 'It's a rouble'), 'it' is translated as **э́то**. In such English sentences 'it' can be replaced by 'this' or
'that' ('It/This/That is a rouble'); 'this' and 'that' are also **э́то** in Russian.
So if the predicate[†] (the verb and the part after the verb, e.g. 'is a rouble')
contains a noun, 'it' is always **э́то**.

If you're saying something about a noun which has already been identi-
fied, then you refer to it as **он**, **она́** or **оно́**, depending on the gender:

A: **Где вино́?**   Where is the wine?

B: **Вот оно́.**   There it is.

Remember always to translate 'it' as **э́то** in identifying sentences in which
the predicate[†] is a noun (e.g. 'It's wine'):

A: **Что э́то?**   What's this?

B: **Э́то во́дка. Э́то** (not **она́**) **Ста́рка.**   It's vodka. It's Starka (a type of vodka).

A: **Где во́дка** (feminine)**?**   Where's the vodka?

B: **Вот она́.**   There/Here it ('she') is.

EXERCISE 3/2

Answer the questions, using **Вот**: 'Here/There he/she/it is'

1 **Где А́нна?**   4 **Где дя́дя Ва́ня?**

2 **Где брат?**   5 **Где во́дка?**

3 **Где такси́?**   6 **Где вино́?**

EXERCISE 3/3

Answer the questions in Russian, using the words in brackets:

1 **Что́ э́то?** (It's tea.)
2 **Что́ э́то?** (It's a rouble.)
3 **Э́то во́дка?** (No, it's wine.)
4 **Где такси́?** (There it is.)

EXERCISE 3/4

Say in Russian:

1 Hello.
2 Excuse me, what's that?
3 It's wine.
4 Thank you.
5 Don't mention it.

6 No, this is beetroot soup.
7 Where is the sour cream?
8 Excuse me, please, where is Vanya?
9 There he is.
10 Thank you. Goodbye.

EXERCISE 3/5

Read the names of these towns on the Trans-Siberian Railway and say which are **о́н** ('he'), which **она́** ('she') and which **оно́** ('it'):

1 **Владивосто́к**. 2 **Сковородино́**. 3 **Облу́чье**. 4 **Чита́**. 5 **Слюдя́нка**.
6 **Байка́льск**. 7 **Москва́**.

EXERCISE 3/6

Which of the following are male names and which female?
1 **Христиа́н** [hree-stee-án]. 2 **Юлиа́н** [yoo-lee-án]. 3 **Арка́дий** [ar-ká-dee].
4 **Ма́йя** [má-ya].

Can you guess (or do you know) which of these names in **-ь** are masculine and which feminine?

5 **И́горь** [e´e-gar ͬ]. 6 **Юди́фь** [yoo-de´ef ͬ]. 7 **Любо́вь** [lyoo-bóf ͬ]. 8 **Нине́ль** [nee-nyél ͬ].

ФИНЛЯ́НДИЯ
(FINLAND)

Санкт-
Петербу́рг

Архáнгельск

Москва́

Яросла́вль

Вя́тка

Об

УКРАЙНА
(UKRAINE)

Ни́жний
Но́вгород

Пермь

Екатеринбу́рг   Тюме́нь

Во́лга

Челя́бинск

Омск   Томск

Новосиби́рск

КАЗАХСТА́Н
(KAZAKHSTAN)

0   500 Km

0   500 Miles

РОССИ́Я (РОССИ́ЙСКАЯ ФЕДЕРА́ЦИЯ) (RUSSIA)

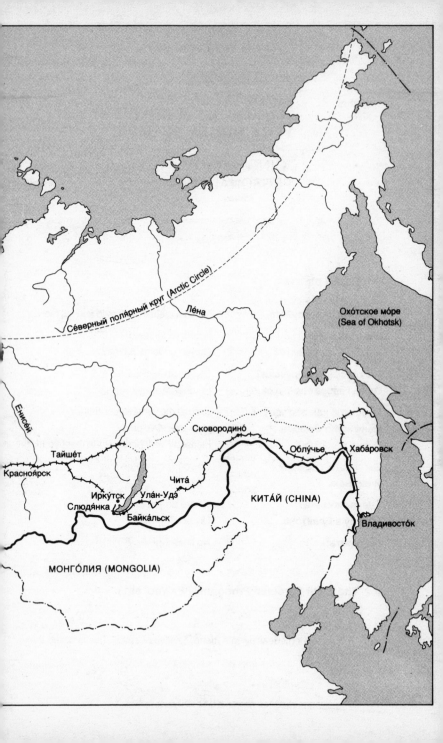

4

DOING THINGS – VERBS;
PERSONAL PRONOUNS

4.1 **Useful phrases**

Скажи́те, пожа́луйста . . .	Tell me, please . . . Could you tell me . . .
Я не понима́ю.	I don't understand.
Вы меня́ понима́ете?	Do you understand me?
Вы говори́те по-ру́сски?	Do you speak Russian?
Он не говори́т по-ру́сски.	He doesn't speak Russian.
Прости́те, как вас зову́т?	Excuse me, what's your name?
Меня́ зову́т Воло́дя.	My name is Volodia.
О́чень прия́тно.	Pleased ('Very pleasant') to meet you.
Вы зна́ете, где Е́ва?	Do you know where Eva is?
Я не зна́ю.	I don't know.
Где вы живёте?	Where do you live?
Я живу́ в Бра́йтоне.	I live in Brighton.
Не кури́ть!	No smoking!

4.2 **The Eight Personal Pronouns' ('I', 'you' etc.)**

я I

ты you (when speaking to a friend, relative or child). This is called the 'familiar' (fam) you.

óн	he ⎤	you met
онá	she ⎬	those in
онó	it ⎦	Lesson 3
мы	we	
вы	you (when speaking to someone you do not know well or to more than one person). This pronoun is the polite or plural (pol/pl) you.	
они́	they	

4.3 **Verbs**

To do things, you need verbs. A verb[t] is a word expressing an action or state, the kind of word which would fit in the gap in the sentence 'She ———— in New York', e.g. works, worked, was, lives, drives. In Russian dictionaries, verbs are listed in their infinitive[t] form (this corresponds to 'to drive', 'to be' etc. in English). Russian infinitive forms normally end **-ть** (e.g. **кури́ть** 'to smoke', **знать** 'to know').

4.4 **Conjugation[t] of Verbs in the Present Tense. Type 1: знать 'to know'**

The present tense[t] describes actions taking place at the moment of speech ('I *work* in Moscow', 'She *is walking* to school'). In Russian there is only one present tense, corresponding to both 'I do' and 'I am doing' in English.

The list of verb forms which go with the eight personal pronouns is known as the *conjugation*[t] of the verb. The form to which the personal endings are attached is called the *stem*[t] of the verb. Most (not all) **знать**-type verbs have a stem which is simply the infinitive form minus the **-ть**. So **знáть** has the stem **знá-**. The endings are underlined.

я знá<u>ю</u>	[zná-yoo]	I know	
ты знá<u>ешь</u>	[zná-yesh]	you (familiar) know	
óн знá<u>ет</u>	[zná-yet]	he knows ⎤	these three forms
онá знá<u>ет</u>	[zná-yet]	she knows ⎬	are always the same
онó знá<u>ет</u>	[zná-yet]	it knows ⎦	in the present tense
			of <u>all</u> verbs
мы знá<u>ем</u>	[zná-yem]	we know	
вы знá<u>ете</u>	[zná-ye-tye]	you (polite/plural) know	

они зна́**ют**	[zná-yoot]	they know

Note: In colloquial (informal) Russian, the pronoun can be omitted, so that 'I know' can be simply **Зна́ю**. But remember that this is informal usage and rare in stylistically neutral[1] Russian.

EXAMPLES

Мы зна́ем, где Ва́ня.	We know where Vanya is.
Вы зна́ете меня́?	Do you know me?

The majority of Russian verbs have this type of conjugation, and we shall call it the **знать** type or Type 1.

4.5 Type 2: говори́ть 'to speak'

The standard example of the second type of present-tense conjugation is **говори́ть** 'to speak'. The stem[1] is **говор-**:

я говорю́	I speak/am speaking
ты говори́шь	you (familiar) speak
о́н говори́т	he speaks
она́ говори́т	she speaks
оно́ говори́т	it speaks
мы говори́м	we speak
вы говори́те	you (polite/familiar) speak
они́ говоря́т	they speak

Note the ending **-ят** of the **они́**-form.

EXAMPLES

Я говорю́ по-ру́сски.	I speak Russian.
Они́ говоря́т по-францу́зски.	They speak French.
Вы говори́те по-англи́йски?	Do you speak English?

4.6 Type 1B: éхать 'to go (by transport)', жить 'to live'

The third (and last) type is a variant of the **знать** type. These verbs have much the same endings as the **знать** type, but the problem is to predict the stem' from the infinitive'. Our first example is the verb **éхать** 'to go (by transport), to ride'. The stem happens to be **éд-** (you just have to learn that, you couldn't guess it) and the conjugation' is:

я **éду**	I go/am going	оно́ **éдет**	it goes
ты **éдешь**	You (familiar) go	мы **éдем**	we go
он **éдет**	he goes	вы **éдете**	you (polite/plural) go
она́ **éдет**	she goes	они́ **éдут**	they go

You can see that the **я** and **они** forms have **-у** where the **знать** type has **-ю** but otherwise the endings are the same.

Here is another example, the verb **жить** 'to live' (despite its **-ить** ending, it is a **éхать**-type verb). The unguessable stem is **жив-** [zhịv] (2.7) and the conjugation is:

я **живу́**	I live/am living	оно́ **живёт**	it lives
ты **живёшь**	you (familiar) live	мы **живём**	we live
он **живёт**	he lives	вы **живёте**	you (polite/plural) live
она́ **живёт**	she lives	они́ **живу́т**	they live

EXAMPLES

Он éдет домо́й.	He's going home.
Я живу́ в Ло́ндоне.	I live in London.

The endings are the same as the endings of **éхать** except for the change of **e** to **ё**. This change is conditioned by the place of the stress: if the letter **e** in a verb ending is stressed, it always turns into **ё** (though remember that Russians don't normally write the dots – see 1.2c).

Another useful example of the **éхать** type is the verb **зва́ть** 'to call', whose stem is **зов-**. The first two forms are a **я зову́, ты зовёшь**, but the one to remember is **(они) зову́т** '(they) call', which turns up in the idiomatic question:

Как вас зову́т? 'How you (they) call?' (= What's your name?).

Вас is the accusative' case' of **вы** 'you'; the details of the accusative are in Lesson 6.

These three sets of similar endings in 4.4–4.6 give the present tense of nearly all Russian verbs. These endings don't take long to learn; the main problem is remembering the stem (and the stress pattern) of verbs like **éхать**, **жить** and **звать**. Although most verbs are like **знать** or **говорить**, there are many irregular infinitives like **жить**. In the vocabularies, we give the **я** and the **ты** form of each verb (since you can work out the other forms from these two).

4.7 Verb Summary Table

Infinitive	**знать** (1)	**говорить** (2)	**жить** (1B)	**éхать** (1B)
Stem	**зна-**	**говор-**	**жив-**	**éд-**
я	-ю	-ю	-ý	-у
ты	-ешь	-ишь	-ёшь	-ешь
óн/онá/онó	-ет	-ит	-ёт	-ет
мы	-ем	-им	-ём	-ем
вы	-ете	-ите	-ёте	-ете
они	-ют	-ят	-ýт	-ут

Stress notes. (1) A few **знать**-type verbs are stressed on the end, so each **е** turns into **ё**. An example is **давáть** 'to give' (12.4), which has the stem **да-**. The stressed endings are: **даю**, **даёшь**, **даёт**, **даём**, **даёте**, **дают**. (2) Many **говорить**-type verbs are stressed on the stem (see 4.9). but the spelling is not affected.

4.8 Negation ('not')

To make a verb negative ('I don't know') simply put **не** 'not' in front of the verb:

Я не знáю.	I don't know.
Óн не понимáет.	He doesn't understand.

4.9 **EXTRA: Stress Patterns**

As you have probably noticed by now, stress is a very tricky subject in Russian, because of the difficulty of predicting where to put it in any word – and to make things even more awkward (or interesting, depending on your point of view) Russians often disagree about the correct place of the stress. As a comparison, English speakers argue about 'cóntroversy' versus 'contróversy', but there are hundreds of such debatable cases in Russian.

Even at this early stage, a few general rules may help:

(a) if the word contains **ё**, the stress always falls on the **ё**, e.g. **живёт** 'lives', so we don't need to put a stress mark on words with **ё**;

(b) if the infinitive of a verb is stressed on any syllable except the last one, e.g. **éхать** 'to travel', the stress is *fixed* (i.e. always in the same place in all of the forms of the conjugation – **éду, éдешь** etc.);

(c) if the infinitive is stressed on the last syllable, e.g. **говорúть** 'to speak', **курúть** 'to smoke', the **я** form is stressed on the ending (**я говорю́, я курю́**); the other five forms will either *all* have the stress on the ending (**ты говорúшь, óн говорúт** etc.) *or* all have the stress on the stem (**ты ку́ришь, óн ку́рит** etc.).

4.10 **A Brief Survey of Russian Grammar: Nouns and Cases**[i]

Russian is an inflected language, which means that the endings of words change according to the grammar of the sentence. For example, the name **Ивáн** (nominative[i] form) becomes **Ивáна** if you mean '*of* Ivan'; it becomes **Ивáну** if you mean '*to* Ivan'; **Ивáн** becomes **Ивáна** in a sentence such as 'I (**Я**) know (**знáю**) Ivan (**Ивáна**)'. Nouns and adjectives each have six different endings, called cases[i] (nominative[i], accusative[i], genitive[i], dative[i], instrumental[i], prepositional[i]). English has a genitive case ending 's, used with people, e.g. 'Ivan's house' (= 'the house of Ivan') and pronouns have accusative forms (he/him, she/her, they/them), but there are very few such changes in comparison with Russian. Like English, Russian also distinguishes singular and plural (as in 'book'/'books'). Verbs (words like 'to do', [she] 'wants', [they] 'know') have different endings depending

41

on who is doing, wanting, knowing etc. and on the tense. All this means
that to a speaker of English, Russian seems to have a 'lot of grammar'.
However, although learning all the endings is a burden at first, the system
is not difficult to understand; you will find that learning vocabulary is a
much bigger task.

To make the sets of endings more digestible, we shall take them in
small doses. However, if you want to tackle the whole system in one go,
you will find grammar tables on pages 378–86.

4.11 **Prepositional' Case'**

As an example of the way nouns change their form, look at these sentences:

Я живу́ в Бра́йтоне.	I live in Brighton.
Óн живёт в Москве́.	He lives in Moscow.
Я е́ду на авто́бусе.	I'm going on a bus (by bus).

After the prepositions **в** 'in' and **на** 'on', most masculine nouns *add* **-e** and
most feminine nouns *change* their last **-a** or **-я** to **-e**.

Москва́ 'Moscow'	**в Москве́** 'in Moscow'
Бра́йтон 'Brighton'	**в Бра́йтоне** 'in Brighton'
авто́бус 'bus'	**на авто́бусе** 'on a bus'

There are more details of these case endings in Lesson 5.

4.12 **Vocabulary (in alphabetical order)**

авто́бус [af-tó-boos] bus
в in
вас you (accusative' – explained in
  Lesson 6)
вы you (polite or plural 4.2)
говори́ть [ga-va-re´et´] to speak
  я говорю́, ты говори́шь
гости́ница hotel
домо́й home, to one's home
е́хать [yé-hat´] to go (by transport)
  я е́ду, ты е́дешь

жить [zhit´] to live
  я живу́, ты живёшь
звать to call
  я зову́, ты зовёшь
здесь [zdyes´] here
здра́вствуй [zdrá-stvooy] hello
  (to someone you call **ты** see 4.13,
  note)
знать to know
  я зна́ю, ты зна́ешь
и and

42

изуча́ть to study
  я изуча́ю, ты изуча́ешь
как how
куда́ (to) where (whither)
кури́ть to smoke
  я курю́, ты ку́ришь
Ло́ндон London
меня́ me (accusative' – explained
  in Lesson 6)
метро́ (n indeclinable 5.10) metro,
  underground
мы we (4.2)
на on
но but
не not
они́ they
о́чень very
по-англи́йски in English
  [pa-an-gle´e-skee]'
подру́га (female) friend
понима́ть to understand
  я понима́ю, ты понима́ешь
по-ру́сски in Russian
по-францу́зски in French
  [pa-fran-tso´o-<u>skee</u>]

почему́ [pa-chye-mo´o] why
прия́тно pleasant
проспе́кт avenue, prospekt
  (wide street)
  проспе́кт Ми́ра Peace Avenue
  (Avenue of Peace)
рабо́тать to work
  я рабо́таю, ты рабо́таешь
Росси́я Russia
ру́сский язы́к Russian language
  [ro´o-skee ee-zík]'
скажи́те [ska-zhí-tye] tell/say
  (imperative' form)
тепе́рь now
то́же [tó-zhe]' too
тролле́йбус trolleybus
ты you (familiar 4.2)
у́лица street
  у́лица Во́лгина Volgin Street
  (Street of Volgin)
хорошо́ [ha-ra-shó] well
я I (4.2)
язы́к [ee-zík]' language

4.13 **Диало́ги Dialogues.** (See Key for Translations.)

(1) **Вот Влади́мир Смирно́в и Мэ́ри Ро́бинсон. Они́ в Москве́, в
гости́нице «Росси́я». Они́ говоря́т по-ру́сски.**
    BC: **Здра́вствуйте, меня́ зову́т Воло́дя. А как вас зову́т?**

---

1. Pronunciation notes: in **-ий** and **-ый** the **й** is inaudible; **я [ya]** before the stress
sounds like **[ee]** (2.10); for **шь, же** and **жи** see 2.7.

MP: Мэ́ри. Я англича́нка.

BC: Вы хорошо́ говори́те по-ру́сски.

MP: Я изуча́ю ру́сский язы́к здесь в Москве́. А вы говори́те по-англи́йски?

BC: Я понима́ю, но́ не говорю́. Где вы живёте, Мэ́ри?

MP: На у́лице Во́лгина. А вы?

BC: На проспе́кте Ми́ра.

(2) В: Здра́вствуй¹, Ната́ша. Ты е́дешь домо́й на авто́бусе?

Н: Здра́вствуй, Ва́ня. Нет, я е́ду на тролле́йбусе.

(3) А: Почему́ Мэ́ри е́дет на тролле́йбусе, а не на метро́?

Б: Я не зна́ю.

(4) В: Как вас зову́т?

Е: Меня́ зову́т Е́ва. А как вас зову́т?

В: Вади́м.

(5) Е: Э́то Ната́ша.

В: О́чень прия́тно. Меня́ зову́т Вади́м.

Н: О́чень прия́тно.

EXERCISE 4/1

Put on the correct endings and translate:

1 Я не зна́( ). 2 О́н не говор́( ) по-ру́сски. 3 Вы хорошо́ говор( ) по-англи́йски. 4 Где вы жив( ) ? 5 Я жив( ) в Ло́ндон( ). 6 Мы изуча́( ) ру́сский язы́к. 7 Мэ́ри жив( ) в Москв( ). 8 Ива́н е́д( ) на авто́бус( ), а Мэ́ри е́д( ) на тролле́йбус( ). 9 Они́ е́д( ) домо́й.

---

1. **Здра́вствуй** 'Hello', to someone you call **ты**. **Здра́вствуйте** is for people you call **вы**. **Здра́вствуйте** is literally an imperative (a command) meaning 'Be healthy'. All imperative forms, such as **Прости́те** 'Excuse me', drop the **-те** (**Прости́**) when you're speaking to someone you call **ты** (Lesson 15).

EXERCISE 4/2

Say in Russian:

1 Excuse me.   2 I don't know.   3 I don't understand.   4 Do you speak English?   5 Where do you live?   6 What is your name?

COMPREHENSION EXERCISE 4/3

(Translation in key)

See if you can find the answers to the following three questions in the text below. The text contains some points you won't meet until Lessons 5–7, but these should not prevent you finding the information you need.

1 What are the names of **A**, **Б** and **В**?
2 Where do **A** and **Б** live and where does **В** study?
3 What are we told about **В**'s knowledge of languages?

Разгово́р в метро́ (Conversation in the metro)

A bumps into his fellow student **Б**, who has a companion **В**.

А: **Здра́вствуй, Ва́ня. Куда́ ты е́дешь?**

Б: **Домо́й, на у́лицу Во́лгина. А ты е́дешь в университе́т?**

А: **Нет, я то́же е́ду домо́й. я тепе́рь живу́ на у́лице Вави́лова.**

Б: **Познако́мьтесь‡. Э́то моя́‡ подру́га Мари́, она́ англича́нка.**
       Она́ изуча́ет ру́сский язы́к здесь в Москве́. Мари́, э́то Ми́ша.

В: **Здра́вствуйте, Ми́ша.**

А: **Прости́те, вас зову́т Мэ́ри?**

В: **Нет, Мари́. Э́то францу́зское‡ и́мя. Но́ я не говорю́ по-**
       францу́зски.

‡ **Extra vocabulary for Exercise 4/3**

Познако́мьтесь Let me introduce you ('Become acquainted').
моя́ my
францу́зское и́мя French name

5

УРÓК НÓМЕР ПЯТЬ

ASKING QUESTIONS;
THE PREPOSITIONAL CASE

5.1 **Phrases**

Где вокзáл?	Where's the station?
Когдá рабóтает музéй?	When is the museum open (When works the museum)?
Почемý ресторáн не рабóтает?	Why is the restaurant closed?
Ктó э́то?	Who is that?
Э́то вóдка?	Is this vodka?
Пря́мо и напрáво.	Straight on and turn right.
Они́ в Сиби́ри.	They're in Siberia.
На такси́.	By taxi.

5.2 **Asking Wh-Questions**

Wh-questions are questions with question words such as 'what', 'who', 'when', 'why', 'how'. You already know **где** 'where', **чтó** 'what', **почемý** 'why'.

Когдá is 'when'.

Когдá рабóтает ресторáн?	When is the restaurant open?

Ктó is 'who'.

Ктó знáет?	Who knows?

Often the emphatic particle **же** is added after the question word:

Где же она?   Where is she?

Же emphasizes the previous word, so the effect is like pronouncing 'Where is she?' with extra emphasis on 'is' (or on 'where').

5.3 **Yes–No Questions**[1]

These are questions which expect the answer 'yes' or 'no'. In Russian they look the same as statements, apart from the question mark:

Это во́дка?   Is this vodka?
Это во́дка.   This is vodka.

In the spoken language, it is intonation which distinguishes **Это во́дка?** (yes–no question[1]) from **Это во́дка** (statement). **Это во́дка?** is pronounced with a sharp rise–fall on **во́** – like saying in English 'Oh, this is *vod*ka, is it?', with a sharp rise and fall on the *vod*. This intonation pattern sounds surprised or indignant in English, but in Russian it is the normal way of asking such questions. Practise the intonation, making sure that your voice goes up and down on the stressed syllable of the word you are asking about:

Вы зна́ете?   Do you know?
Это ко́фе?   Is this coffee?
Он англича́нин?   Is he English?
Она́ англича́нка?   Is she English?
Она́ англича́нка?   Is **she** English?

Notice the voice does *not* go up at the end of the question, *unless* the key stressed syllable happens to be the last thing in the sentence:

Это чай?   Is this tea?

In this case the Russian and English sentences sound very similar in their intonation.

5.4 **Prepositional Case**[1]

In Lesson 4 we met the question 'Where do you live' **Где** (Where) **вы**

47

(you) **живёте** (live)? **[Gdye vi zhi-vyó-tye?]**. And we met answers such as **в Брáйтоне** 'in Brighton', **в Москвé** 'in Moscow', **в гостúнице «Россúя»** 'in the Hotel Russia'. The Russian for 'in' is **в** (the same as the third letter of the alphabet), but after **в** meaning 'in', following nouns have an ending (usually **-e**) called *the prepositional case*. This case ending does not mean anything; it is simply a grammatical ending which must be added after certain prepositions if you want to speak correctly. These prepositions are:

в	in
на	on
о	about, concerning
при (fairly rare)	attached to; in the presence of

So **Петербýрг** 'St Petersburg' with **в** becomes **в Петербýрге [fpye-tyer-bo´or-gye]**[1] 'in St Petersburg'.

В plus **Москвá** becomes **в Москвé [vmask-vyé]**[1] (**а** changes into **e**).

'In Bristol' is **в Брúстоле**.

'On a trolleybus' is **на троллéйбусе**.

DETAILS OF THE PREPOSITIONAL (PREP.)

Nouns which end with a consonant add **-e**; nouns which end **-й**, **-а** or **-о** change the vowel to **-e**.

Лóндон London	**в Лóндоне** in London
музéй museum	**в музéе [vmoo-zyé-ye]** in the museum
Москвá Moscow	**в Москвé** in Moscow
письмó letter	**в письмé** in a/the letter

The awkward category is nouns which end **-ь**; if the noun is masculine the **ь** changes to **-e**, but if it's feminine the **ь** changes to **-и**.

Брúстоль (m) Bristol	**в Брúстоле** in Bristol
Сибúрь (f) Siberia	**в Сибúри** in Siberia
царь (m) tsar	**о царé [a-tsa-ryé]** about the tsar

---

1 Pronunciation note. Russian prepositions are read as if they are joined to the following word. So **в [v]** sounds like **[f]** before unvoiced consonants. See 2.3 and 2.8.

Nouns which end **-я** or **-e** also have the prepositional ending **-e** unless the letter before the **-я** or **-e** is **-и**, in which case the ending is a second **-и**:

мо́ре sea	**в мо́ре** in the sea
Ва́ня Vania	**при Ва́не** in Vania's presence
А́нглия England	**в А́нглии** in England
упражне́ние exercise	**в упражне́нии** in the exercise

5.5 **EXTRA**

Those few nouns, mainly male names, which end **-ий** in the nominative have the prepositional ending **-и**, e.g. **Ю́рий: о Ю́рии** 'about Iurii';

Васи́лий: на Васи́лии 'on Vasilii'

5.6 **Exceptions (Russian Grammar Has Many)**

A few masculine nouns, usually short ones, have **-у́** (always stressed) instead of **-e** in the prepositional case after **в** 'in' and **на** 'on'.

Крым Crimea	**в Крыму́ [fkri-mo´o]** in the Crimea
сад garden, orchard	**в саду́ [fsa-do´o]** in the garden
лес wood, forest	**в лесу́ [vlye-so´o]** in the forest
До́н the Don River	**Росто́в-на-Дону́** Rostov-on-Don
Клин Klin (town NW of Moscow)	**в Клину́** in Klin

But after **о** 'about', these nouns have the normal **-e** ending:

Мы говори́м о са́де.	We're talking about the garden.

The two nouns **мать** 'mother' and **до́чь** 'daughter' always add **-ер-** before any ending. So their prep. case forms are **ма́тери** and **до́чери**.

5.7 **Prepositional Case of Personal Pronouns**

The eight pronouns we met in 4.2 have the following prepositional forms:

nom	prep	example	
я	мне	обо мне [a-ba-mnyé]	about me (**обо** is a variant of **о** used with **мне**)
ты	тебе́	о тебе́	about you (fam)
он	нём	о нём [a-nyóm]	about him
она́	ней	на ней	on her
оно́	нём	в нём [vnyom]	in it
мы	нас	о нас	about us
вы	вас	о вас	about you (pol/pl.)
они́	них	на них	on them

5.8 **В and на: 'in', 'on', 'at'**

'In' is **в**, 'on' is **на**, 'at' will be **в** with enclosed spaces or buildings ('at school' **в шко́ле**) and **на** with open spaces and activities/events ('at work' **на рабо́те**, 'at a concert' **на конце́рте**). Note that English 'in' sometimes corresponds to Russian **на** when the place (e.g. a street) is an open space or was originally an open space (e.g. **вокза́л** 'station').

in the street	**на у́лице**
in the square	**на пло́щади**
in/at the station	**на вокза́ле**

Unpredictable uses of **на** for 'in'/'at', e.g. **на Украи́не** 'in the Ukraine', are shown in the vocabularies.

5.9 **Что́ as a Conjunction¹ = 'that'**

As well as 'what', **что́** is also a conjunction¹ which joins clauses¹:

Она́ говори́т, что́ Ва́ня в Сиби́ри. She says that Vania is in Siberia.

Note that the **что** cannot normally be missed out in Russian, though you can say 'She says Vania is in Siberia' in English. Note also that the comma in front of **что** is compulsory – Russian schoolchildren get bad marks in their exams if they miss out the commas.

5.10 Indeclinable Nouns

Some nouns borrowed into Russian from other languages are indeclinable, that is, they do not obey Russian grammatical rules and never change their endings regardless of the grammar of the sentence. The principal categories are these:

(a) words ending **-и, -у, -ю** e.g. **такси** 'taxi', **меню** 'menu' – these words are neuter;

(b) female names ending with a consonant (or anything other than **-а, -я, -ь**), e.g. **Анн** 'Anne', **Джейн Óстин** 'Jane Austen', **Мэ́ри** 'Mary' – these words are of course feminine. So, while names like 'John Smith' **Джо́н Смит** are treated as normal masculine nouns and decline (**Мы говори́м о Джо́не Сми́те**), 'Jane Smith' **Джейн Смит** is indeclinable (**Мы говори́м о Джейн Смит**).

(c) many (but not all) foreign words ending **-о**, e.g. **пальто́** 'overcoat' (from an old French word *paletot*), **кино́** 'cinema', **метро́** 'metro', 'underground railway', **ра́дио** 'radio' (in this word the last letter is pronounced [o] not [a]). These words are neuter; **в кино́** 'in the cinema'.

(d) Note the unusual case of **ко́фе** 'coffee'. This indeclinable word is *masculine* in formal, educated Russian: **Где ко́фе? Вот он.** Although in informal colloquial Russian it is sometimes neuter, foreigners are advised to keep to formal norms.

In other cases, foreign words are treated like native ones. **Ло́ндон** 'London' and **компью́тер** 'computer' are normal masculine nouns (**на компью́тере** 'on the computer'); **Де́бора** 'Deborah' and **Пе́пси-Ко́ла** 'Pepsi-Cola' decline as feminine nouns.

5.11 Vocabulary

англича́нин Englishman

А́нглия England (also, loosely, 'Britain')

вокза́л [vag-zál] station, terminus
  на вокза́ле at the station

во́н там over there (pointing)

же (emphasizes previous word)

институ́т institute (university-level institution specializing in one area, e.g. physics or foreign languages)

когда́ when

ко́фе (m indeclinable) coffee

Крым prep. case **в Крыму́** Crimea (Black Sea peninsula)

кто́ prep. case **ко́м** who

лес prep. case **в лесу́** wood, forest

мо́ре sea

музе́й museum

нале́во to the left

напра́во to the right

но́мер number

о + prep. case about, concerning

об А́нглии about England
  (**о** becomes **об** before **а и о у э**)

письмо́ [pees′-mó] letter

пло́щадь (f) **[pló-shshat′]** square
  на пло́щади [na-pló-shsha-dee] in/on a square

по́чта post office
  на по́чте at the post office

при + prep. case attached to; at the time of

пря́мо straight on

рестора́н restaurant

сад prep. case **в саду́** garden, orchard

там there (opposite of **здесь** 'here')

туале́т toilet

Украи́на Ukraine
  на Украи́не in the Ukraine

университе́т university

царь (m) tsar (emperor)

центр centre

5.12 Dialogues (Translation in Key)

1 А: Где Москва́?
   Б: В Росси́и.

2 А: Где Ло́ндон?
   Б: В А́нглии.

3 А: Где Ки́ев?
   Б: На Украи́не.

4 А: Где Я́лта?
   Б: В Крыму́.

5 А: Где рабо́тает дя́дя Ва́ня?
  Б: В Петербу́рге.

6 А: О чём[1] вы говори́те?
  Б: О Росси́и.

7 А: Вы говори́те о Мэ́ри?
  Б: Нет, мы говори́м не о ней, а о тебе́.

8 А: Где вы живёте?
  Б: В гости́нице «Росси́я».[2]
  А: А где живу́т Джон и Ма́ргарет?
  Б: То́же в «Росси́и».[2]

9 А: Где Ирку́тск?
  Б: В Сиби́ри.

10 А: Где живёт Мэ́ри Ро́бинсон?
  Б: В Москве́, на у́лице Во́лгина. А в А́нглии она́ живёт в Бри́столе.

11 А: Скажи́те, пожа́луйста, где у́лица Во́лгина?
  Б: Пря́мо и напра́во.

12 А: Скажи́те, пожа́луйста, где здесь туале́т?
  Б: Нале́во.
  А: Спаси́бо.
  Б: Пожа́луйста.

13 А: Где вы живёте, Ива́н Петро́вич?
  Б: Я живу́ в Воро́неже, в це́нтре.

14 А: Мэ́ри изуча́ет ру́сский язы́к в университе́те?
  Б: Нет, она́ изуча́ет ру́сский язы́к в институ́те.

15 А: Прости́те, пожа́луйста, вы не зна́ете, где здесь по́чта?
  Б: Дом но́мер два.
  А: А где э́то?
  Б: Вон там, напра́во.
  А: Спаси́бо.
  Б: Пожа́луйста.

---

1 **Чём** is the prepositional case of **что́**.

2 A name in quotation marks is not declined if its generic noun (hotel, newspaper, novel etc.) precedes it (**в газе́те «Пра́вда»** 'in the newspaper *Pravda*'). It *is* declined if the generic noun is omitted (**в «Пра́вде»** 'in *Pravda*').

EXERCISE 5/1

Answer the question **Где она?** 'Where is she?', putting the correct ending on the word in brackets:

1 В (Ло́ндон). 2 В (Росси́я). 3 В (гости́ница). 4 В (Нью-Йо́рк).
5 В (Австра́лия). 6 В (Аме́рика). 7 В (го́род). 8 В (Сиби́рь).
9 В (Крым). 10 В (до́м). 11 На (у́лица). 12 На (пло́щадь).

EXERCISE 5/2

О ко́м вы говори́те? About whom are you speaking?

1 О (Ва́ня). 2 О (Мари́я). 3 Об (Ива́н). 4 Об (Анн Бра́ун). 5 О (она́).
6 О (он).

EXERCISE 5/3

Say in Russian:

1 Where is the toilet? 2 Is this beetroot soup? 3 Do you live in the centre?
4 I live in England, in Oxford. 5 We're talking about you.

COMPREHENSION EXERCISE 5/4

Work out what the names are in the following and write them out in English and Russian (nominative[1] form):

1 **Я живу́ в Ду́блине.** 2 **Она́ живёт в Га́мбурге, в Герма́нии.**
3 **Мы говори́м об Анто́не Па́вловиче Че́хове.** 4 **Они́ сейча́с в Росто́ве-на-Дону́.**

EXERCISE 5/5
REVISION OF LESSONS 1–5

(Refer to the numbered sections if you need to check something.)

Pronounce:

1 **Москва́** (1.2). 2 **Здра́вствуйте!** (3.1). 3 **Что́ э́то** (3.1). 4 **Пожа́луйста** (3.1). 5 **Э́то ко́фе?** (5.3).

Say in Russian:

6 Thank you (3.1). 7 Please (3.1). 8 Goodbye (3.1). 9 Excuse me (3.1).

Ask:

10 What's this? (3.2). 11 Is this tea? (5.3). 12 Excuse me, what's your name? (4.1). 13 Do you know where the metro is? (4.1). 14 Do you speak English? (4.5).

Answer:

15 I live in England/Manchester/Dublin (4.6, 5.4). 16 I don't know (4.7). 17 I speak Russian (4.5).

Put on the required endings:

18 **Я е́д_____ на авто́бус_____**. (4.4, 5.4). 19 **Они́ е́д_____ домо́й** (4.6). 20 **Он жив_____ в Москв_____** (4.6, 5.4). 21 **Они́ жив_____ в Сиби́р_____** (5.4). 22 **На пло́щад_____** (5.4.) 23 **Она́ изуча́_____ ру́сский язы́к в Росси́_____** (4.12, 5.4).

6

УРÓК НÓМЕР ШЕСТЬ

POSSESSION; GOING PLACES;
THE ACCUSATIVE CASE

6.1 Phrases

Э́то мóй сын.	This is my son.
Где моя́ гости́ница?	Where is my hotel?
Вы зна́ете Ната́шу?	Do you know Natasha?
Вы лю́бите му́зыку?	Do you like music?
Подожди́те мину́ту.	Wait a minute.
Позови́те, пожа́луйста, Га́лю.	Please call Galia = May I speak to Galia? (when telephoning)
Позови́те Ива́на Петрóвича.	Call Ivan Petrovich.
Спаси́бо за письмó.	Thank you for the letter.
Я е́ду в Москву́.	I'm going to Moscow.
Как ва́ше и́мя и óтчество?	What are your name and patronymic?

6.2 Possessives

m	f	n	
мóй	моя́	моё	my
твóй	твоя́	твоё	your (fam)
наш	на́ша	на́ше	our
ваш	ва́ша	ва́ше	your (pol/pl.)

56

These words agree[1] with the gender of the noun:

мо́й сын my son   **моя́ до́чь** my daughter   **моё письмо́** my letter

наш сын our son   **на́ша до́чь** our daughter   **на́ше письмо́** our letter

m/f/n

его́ [ye-<u>v</u>ó]	his (NB: **г** pronounced [**v**] in this word)
её [ye-yó]	her
его́ [ye-<u>v</u>ó]	its
их	their

These words are indeclinable[1], so they do not vary, whatever the following noun or the grammar of the sentence.

его́ сын/до́чь/письмо́	his son/daughter/letter
их сын/до́чь/письмо́	their son/daughter/letter

6.3 The Accusative Case

The accusative case is a set of endings which do not have any precise meaning but which are required in the kinds of grammatical situations where we use 'her' instead of 'she' in English. For example, the object of a verb is typically in the accusative. We say 'I know *her*', not 'I know she'. 'Her' is the accusative of 'she', used after verbs like 'know', 'like', 'hit'. But unlike English, it is not only Russian pronouns (**я** 'I', **ты** 'you', **мы** 'we' etc.) which have special forms for the accusative, but also many nouns, particularly nouns ending **-a** and **-я**.

Nouns ending **-a** or **-я**, *whether masculine or feminine*, change **-a** to **-y** and **-я** to **-ю** in the accusative. So **Москва́** becomes **Москву́** in a sentence like:

Я люблю́ Москву́.	I love Moscow (like 'I love her').
Она́ лю́бит дя́дю Ва́ню.	She loves Uncle Vanya.

Feminine nouns ending in a soft sign (**ь**) do not change:

Он лю́бит до́чь.	He loves (his) daughter.

Masculine nouns ending in a consonant, soft sign (**ь**) or **й** do not change (unless they denote people or animals – see 6.4). Neuter nouns (including **и́мя** 'name') do not change.

Я зна́ю Петербу́рг.	I know St Petersburg.
Я люблю́ вино́.	I love wine.
Е́ва лю́бит чай.	Eva loves tea.

6.4 Animate' Masculine Nouns

Nouns denoting people and animals (but not plants are called *animate'* in Russian. Animate nouns have certain special grammatical features. One of these features is a special accusative ending for masculine animate nouns:

-a added to nouns ending with a consonant

-я for nouns with the soft' endings **-ь** or **-й**, which are replaced by the **я**; notice the **-ь** or **-й** are not needed because the [y] sound they represent is contained in the **я** [ya]

Ива́н:

Вы зна́ете Ива́на?	Do you know Ivan?

И́горь:

Вы зна́ете И́горя?	Do you know Igor'?

Андре́й:

Вы зна́ете Андре́я?	Do you know Andrei?

6.5 Feminine Animate Nouns

Notice that *feminine* animate nouns behave just like inanimate ones (**а→у я→ю ь→ь**):

Вы зна́ете Москву́? (inanimate)

Вы зна́ете Ма́шу? (animate)

6.6 EXTRA on Animate Nouns

Although it is usually obvious whether a noun is animate or not, there are non-obvious cases. For example, singular nouns denoting groups of people, e.g. **наро́д** 'a people, nation', **а́рмия** 'army', are *in*animate. Also inanimate are nouns denoting parts of animate beings: **лицо́** 'face' is inanimate (but **лицо́** meaning 'person' is animate). There are doubtful cases: **микро́бы** 'microbes' are inanimate for most people, but sometimes animate for biologists; dolls and other anthropomorphic toys, e.g. **матрёшки**, the wooden dolls which fit inside each other, are usually animate, as are the court-cards (**туз** 'ace', **коро́ль** 'king', **да́ма** 'queen', **вале́т** 'jack') in card-games.

6.7 Accusative Case of Pronouns

Just as 'me' is the accusative of 'I', so **меня́** is the accusative of **я**. Here is the full list of personal accusative pronouns:

Nominative		Accusative	
я	I	**меня́**	me
ты	you	**тебя́**	you
о́н	he	**его́ [ye-vó]**	him
она́	she	**её**	her
оно́	it	**его́ [ye-vó]**	it
мы	we	**нас**	us
вы	you	**вас**	you
они́	they	**их**	them

6.8 Uses of the Accusative

(1) After verbs, where you would use 'him' not 'he' in English ('I know him' not 'I know he'):

Я зна́ю Ива́на.	I know Ivan.
Вы зна́ете его́ [ye-vó]?	Do you know him?

(2) In time expressions of duration and frequency:

Подожди́те мину́ту.	Wait *a minute*.
Я здесь уже́ неде́лю.	I've been here *for a week*. (literally 'I am here already a week' – **неде́ля** 'week')

59

раз в го́д   once a year (**раз** 'once', 'one time')

(3) With **в** 'into' and **на** 'on to' to express motion to somewhere:

Мы е́дем в Москву́.   We are travelling to Moscow.

(4) With the prepositions **че́рез** 'through', 'across', **за** 'for' (in return for)

че́рез лес   through the forest
че́рез у́лицу   across the street
Спаси́бо за письмо́.   Thank you for the letter.

че́рез 'through' is also used with time words to mean 'after the named period of time has elapsed':

Че́рез неде́лю мы е́дем в   In a week's time we're going to
  Сиби́рь.   Siberia.

6.9 'To Go on Foot': Идти́

You already know **е́хать** 'to go by transport' (a Type-1B verb – see Lesson 4). 'To go on foot' is the verb **идти́**, an unusual verb as you can see from its ending **-ти**. The stem is **ид-**, and the endings are the same as those of **жить** 'to live':

я иду́	**мы идём**
ты идёшь	**вы идёте**
о́н/она́ идёт	**они́ иду́т**

As mentioned in 6.8 (3) above, to describe motion *to* some destination, you use the same two prepositions **в** and **на** which you met in Lesson 4, but in this meaning of motion from place to place, you use them with the *accusative* instead of the prepositional. So **в Москву́** (acc.) means 'to Moscow', while **в Москве́** (prep.) means 'in Moscow'.

Я иду́ в центр.   I am going (on foot) to the centre.
Мэ́ри идёт в гости́ницу.   Mary is going to the hotel.
Вы идёте на рабо́ту?   Are you going to work?

EXERCISE 6/1

Put the possessives in the correct form:

1 (My) _____ **сын.** 2 (Our) _____ **до́чь.** 3 (His) _____ **мать.** 4 (Your) _____ **гости́ница.** 5 (Her) _____ **муж.**

EXERCISE 6/2

Where necessary, change the endings of the nouns:

1 **Я люблю́ (му́зыка) _____.**
2 **Она́ лю́бит (муж) _____?**
3 **Позови́те, пожа́луйста, (Любо́вь) _____ (Влади́мировна) _____.**
4 **Подожди́те (мину́та) _____.**
5 **Спаси́бо за (чай) _____.**
6 **Спаси́бо за (во́дка) _____.**

6.10 Russian Names and How to be Polite (or Familiar)

FIRST NAMES FIRST

The first Russians you meet socially are likely to give you their names as **Ната́ша** 'Natasha', **Воло́дя** 'Volodia', **Та́ня** 'Tania' and so on, all ending in the sound [**a**]. These are short or 'intimate' forms of their 'official' first names. On her birth certificate **Ната́ша** is **Ната́лья** (f), **Воло́дя** is **Влади́мир** (m), **Та́ня** is **Татья́на** (f). Here are some of the commonest Russian first names:

	'Official'	'Intimate'
Females	Еле́на	Ле́на
	Ната́лья (or -ия)	Ната́ша
	Татья́на	Та́ня
	О́льга	О́ля
	Мари́я	Ма́ша
	Ири́на	И́ра
	Светла́на	Све́та
	Гали́на	Га́ля

61

Males		
	Алекса́ндр	**Са́ша**
	Бори́с	**Бо́ря**
	Влади́мир	**Воло́дя**
	Ива́н	**Ва́ня**
	Михаи́л	**Ми́ша**
	Никола́й	**Ко́ля**
	Па́вел	**Па́ша**
	Серге́й	**Серёжа**

Strictly speaking, these 'intimate' forms are only to be used when you are on **ты** terms with your new acquaintance, but Russians (for example tour guides or street traders) will often introduce themselves to you with their intimate names because these forms are easier for foreigners.

6.11 **Patronymics**

However, in more formal circumstances a new Russian acquaintance will be introduced with his or her full first name *and middle name*, which is formed from the father's official first name and is called a 'patronymic' (in Russian **о́тчество** from the word **оте́ц** 'father'). Male patronymics end **-ович** or **-евич** (meaning 'son of'), female ones end **-овна** or **-евна** ('daughter of'). The ending **-ович/-овна** follows hard consonants (**Ива́н** – **Ива́нович/Ива́новна**); **-евич/-евна** is the corresponding 'soft' ending, replacing the **й** or **ь** of names such as **И́горь** (**И́горевич/И́горевна**) or **Андре́й** (**Андре́евич/Андре́евна**). Note that if the name ends **-ий** (**Васи́лий**), the **и** is replaced by a soft sign (**Васи́льевич/Васи́льевна**).

So you may hear:

– **Познако́мьтесь, пожа́луйста, э́то Влади́мир Бори́сович.** 'Let me introduce you (become acquainted), please, this is Vladimir Borisovich ('son of Boris').'

Ива́н Ива́нович Ivan Ivanovich (son of Ivan)

Бори́с Серге́евич Boris son of Sergei (**-евич** for names ending **ь** or **й**)

Все́волод Влади́мирович Vsevolod son of Vladimir

Ната́лья Ива́новна Natalia daughter of Ivan

Мари́я Серге́евна Maria daughter of Sergei (**-евна** for names ending **ь** or **й**)

These long double names are in such common use between people who call each other **вы** that patronymics are usually shortened in speech, dropping the **-ов-** or **-ев-** (unless stressed). So **Сергéевич** is normally pronounced **Сергéич**, **Ивáновна** is pronounced **Ивáнна**. However, a patronymic such as **Петрóвич**, stressed on the **-óв-**, cannot be shortened in that way.

Russians do not expect you as a foreigner to have a patronymic, though there is nothing to stop you creating one – (**Рéджинальдович/Джóновна/ Дáрэнович/Джóрджевна** or whatever). If you do not want to leave a blank against **óтчество** on Russian forms, you can put in your middle name(s), if you have any.

6.12 EXTRA: Exceptional Patronymics

A small number of male official first names (i.e. not intimate forms) end **-a** e.g. **Никúта**. Such names are rare. They form patronymics as follows:

Ильá (Elias): **Ильúч/Ильúнична**
Кузьмá: Кузьмúч/Кузьмúнична
Лукá (Luke): **Лукúч/Лукúнична**
Никúта: Никúтич/Никúтична
Фомá (Thomas): **Фомúч/Фомúнична**

6.13 EXTRA On Choice of Names

Russians are conservative when naming children, keeping to a relatively small number of old, safe names such as **Елéна**, **Николáй**, **Владúмир**, **Натáлья**. You will probably find that all the Russian men you meet share about a dozen names, while the women have about two dozen. There was a fashion in the thirties for more 'international' names such as **Рóберт**, **Эдуáрд**, and immediately after the revolution for new, revolutionary names, but now people prefer to play safe. In the case of boys, parents always bear in mind that an 'unfortunate' choice of name (**Спýтник** 'Sputnik', **Трáктор** 'Tractor'), which seemed all right at the time, will be inflicted on the grandchildren too through the patronymic. Some relics of the revolutionary names survive: **Вило́ра** (from the initial letters of **Влади́мир Ильи́ч Ле́нин организа́тор револю́ции** – 'V.I.L. Organizer of the Revolution'; **Рикс** (**Рабо́чих и крестья́н сою́з** 'Union of the Workers and Peasants'), **Рем** or **Рема** (**Револю́ция мирова́я** 'World Revolution') **Марле́н** ('Marx and Lenin'), **Владле́н** ('Vladimir Lenin'), **Нине́ль** ([nee-nyélʲ] a female name – **Ле́нин** backwards).

6.14 Surnames

Every Russian has a surname or family name (**фами́лия**), typically ending -ов, -ев, -ёв, -ин or -ын for men (**Бре́жнев, Горбачёв, Каре́нин, Солжени́цын**), and -ова, -ева, -ина, -ына for women (**Бре́жнева, Горбачёва, Каре́нина**). The commonest Russian surnames are **Ивано́в/Ивано́ва, Попо́в/Попо́ва, Смирно́в/Смирно́ва** (though in Russian jokes the equivalent of 'Smith, Jones and Brown' is **Ивано́в, Петро́в и Си́доров**). Some surnames, for example **Достое́вский**, are adjectives, so the feminine form ends -ая (**Достое́вская** – see 7.3).

Surnames with other endings, e.g. **Пастерна́к, Го́голь** (the writer Gogol'), **Шмидт** (Schmidt), **Бра́ун** (Brown), **По́уп** (Pope) do not have feminine forms. As you might expect (5.10), they decline for males, but as *female* names are indeclinable: **Вы зна́ете Ри́чарда По́упа?** 'Do you know Richard Pope (acc.)?'; **Вы зна́ете Ба́рбару По́уп?** 'Do you know Barbara Pope?'

6.15 Etiquette

Acquaintances who call each other **вы** will normally use the first name and patronymic. So if **Ива́н Ива́нович Смирно́в** meets his acquaintance **Ири́на Петро́вна Попо́ва**, the conversation may begin:

И.И.: Здра́вствуйте, Ири́на Петро́вна.
И.П.: Здра́вствуйте, Ива́н Ива́нович.

Children use **вы** to adults and call their teachers by their **и́мя-о́тчество**. Adults reply with **ты**, and use the intimate form of the first name. So if little Tat'iana meets her friend's mother Klara Aleksandrovna, the conversation may start:

Т.: Здра́вствуйте, Кла́ра Алекса́ндровна.
К.А.: Здра́вствуй, Та́ня.

Although you, as a foreigner, may not be expected to handle the long double names, your politeness will be appreciated if you make the effort. When you meet someone you are likely to have to deal with again, ask **Прости́те, как ва́ше и́мя и о́тчество?** 'Excuse me, what ('how') are your name and patronymic?' If you address **Ива́н Ива́нович Смирно́в** as **Ива́н Ива́нович**, that is the equivalent of calling him Mr Smirnov in English. Although every Russian has a surname, there are no generally used equivalents of Mr/Mrs/Miss/Ms.

When talking to or about foreigners, Russians usually use Russified versions of foreign titles: **ми́стер Смит, ми́ссис/мисс Уо́лкер** for 'Mr Smith' and 'Mrs/Miss Walker', **мосье́** for 'monsieur', **фра́у** for German 'Frau', and so on.

6.16 Vocabulary (in Alphabetical Order)

ваш your (pol/pl. 6.2)
год [got] year
   prep. **в году́ [vga-doó]** in a year
де́душка (m) grandfather
дочь (f) prep. **до́чери** (5.6) daughter
его́ [ye-vó] his; its (6.2)
её [ye-yó] her (6.2)
жена́ wife
за + acc. for (in return for)
   спаси́бо за + acc. thank you
   for (sth)
за́втра [záf-tra] tomorrow
идти́ [eet-te´e] to go (on foot)
   я иду́, ты идёшь

и́мя (neuter!) forename, first name
их their (6.2)
люби́ть to love, be fond of
   я люблю́,[1] ты лю́бишь
магази́н shop
мину́та minute
мой (6.2) my
муж [moosh] husband
му́зыка music
наш (6.2) our
неде́ля week
непло́хо not bad, not badly
оте́ц (acc **отца́**) father
о́тчество [ó-chye-stva] patronymic

---

1. Every **говори́ть**-type (type 2) verb whose stem ends **б в м п** or **ф** (all labial [lip] consonants) has this extra **-л-** in the 'I' (**я**) form.

подожди́те (**подожди́** with **ты**)
  wait (imper¹)
пожива́ть to live, get along
  Как пожива́ет . . . ? How is . . . ?
поздравля́ю! congratulations!
  (= I congratulate)
познако́мьтесь meet (become
  acquainted) (imper¹)
  [pa-zna-kóm'-tyes']
позови́те (**позови́** with **ты**) call
  (imperative form)

рабо́та work
  на рабо́те at work
  на рабо́ту to work
сейча́с now, at the moment
сын son
так so
тво́й your (fam 6.2)
уже́ [oo-zhé] already
фами́лия surname
час hour
че́рез + acc. through; across; after
  (a period of time)

6.17 **Dialogues** (Translation in Key)

Вади́м: Вы лю́бите му́зыку?
Ёва: О́чень. Я люблю́ Гли́нку и Бородина́.
Вади́м: А Проко́фьева?
Ёва: Не о́чень.

КМ: Здра́вствуйте, Михаи́л Петро́вич, как вы живёте?
МП: Непло́хо, Константи́н Миха́йлович. А вы?
КМ: То́же непло́хо.
МП: Куда́ вы идёте?
КМ: На рабо́ту. А вы?
МП: Я иду́ в магази́н. А как пожива́ет ва́ша жена́, Ната́лья
  Бори́совна?
КМ: Хорошо́. За́втра она́ е́дет в Москву́. На́ша до́чь Ни́на
  живёт там уже́ го́д. Вы зна́ете её му́жа Андре́я?
МП: Да, я его́ зна́ю.
КМ: А их сы́на зову́т Ми́ша.
МП: Сы́на?! Так вы уже́ де́душка, Константи́н Миха́йлович.
  Поздравля́ю вас!

EXERCISE 6/3

Using **позовите** 'call' and the accusative form of the name, call the following to the telephone:

1 Call **Ива́н**, please (= May I speak to Ivan, please?).
2 Call **И́горь Петро́вич**.
3 Please call **Ната́ша**.
4 Please call **Ната́лья Алекса́ндровна**.

EXERCISE 6/4

Say in Russian:

1 Good morning, Ivan Petrovich.
2 Where is our hotel?
3 Thank you for the wine.
4 Please wait a minute.
5 Is that your (pol) wife?

EXERCISE 6/5

What are the nominative forms of the names of the five people mentioned in these two dialogues?

А: **Позови́те, пожа́луйста, Михаи́ла Серге́евича и Людми́лу Андре́евну.**
Б: **Сейча́с.**

А: **Вы лю́бите Ма́рка Тве́на?**
Б: **Нет. Я люблю́ Сэ́линджера и А́гату Кри́сти.**

7

УРÓК НÓМЕР СЕМЬ

DESCRIBING THINGS: ADJECTIVES

7.1 Phrases with Adjectives

Большóй теáтр	Bolshoi (Big) Theatre
рýсский язы́к	Russian language
Дóбрый день	Good day
Тверскáя ýлица	Tver' Street (Moscow's main street)
Дóброе ýтро	Good morning
в Большóм теáтре	in the Bolshoi Theatre
на Крáсной плóщади	in (on) Red Square

Pronunciation note: the **й** in the endings **-ый** and **-ий** is inaudible, so there's no need to make an effort to pronounce it.

7.2 Adjectives

An adjective is a word such as 'good', 'interesting', 'Soviet' which can describe a noun, that is, any word which fits in the gap in a sentence such as 'It's a _____ thing'. In Russian, adjectives have endings which must agree with the noun, that is, if the noun is neuter (**ýтро** 'morning'), then the adjective must have a neuter ending too (the ending **-ое** on **дóброе** in **Дóброе ýтро** 'Good morning').

If you look in a dictionary, you will find adjectives in their masculine nominative[1] form. There are three possible masculine endings: **-ый** (the commonest), **-ий** and **-óй**. These endings are all related: **-ый** is the

68

commonest one, **-ий** is the ending if the last consonant of the adjective is soft (7.5) or one of the spelling rule consonants (8.3), and **-ой** replaces **-ый** and **-ий** if the adjective is stressed on the ending.

Three standard examples are:

но́вый	new
ру́сский	Russian
второ́й	second

Russian adjectives are much simpler than nouns. First, once you know the basic endings, you find that there are really no exceptions. Second, once you have learnt the stress on the masculine form, the stress is on the same syllable in all other forms of the adjective.

7.3 Feminine Adjective Ending: -ая

Here are the feminine forms of our three typical adjectives:

но́вая	**но́вая у́лица**	new street
ру́сская	**ру́сская газе́та**	Russian newspaper
втора́я	**втора́я дверь**	the second door

7.4 Neuter Adjectives: -ое

но́вое	**но́вое и́мя**	new name
ру́сское	**ру́сское и́мя**	Russian name
второ́е	**второ́е упражне́ние**	second exercise

EXERCISE 7/1

Put on the required endings:

1 **За́падн(ый)____ Сиби́рь** (f) Western Siberia. 2 **Ру́сск(ий)____ чай** Russian tea. 3 **Но́в(ый)____ гости́ница** new hotel. 4 **Кра́сн(ый)____ пло́щадь** Red Square. 5 **Больш(о́й)____ кварти́ра** large flat.

6 **Ма́леньк(ий)**____ **окно́** small window. 7 **Пу́шкинск(ий)**____ **пло́щадь**
Pushkin Square. 8 **Брита́нск(ий)**____ **посо́льство** The British Embassy.

7.5 Soft Adjectives (-ний)

There are a few 'soft' adjectives ending -**ний**. These have -**ий** where
но́вый has -**ый**, -**яя** where **но́вый** has -**ая**, -**ее** where **но́вый** has -**ое**.
Most 'soft' adjectives have a time meaning, e.g. the parts of the day and
the seasons. Here is a list of the commonest:

m		f	n
после́дний	last	после́дняя	после́днее
у́тренний	morning	у́тренняя	у́треннее
вече́рний	evening	вече́рняя	вече́рнее
весе́нний	spring	весе́нняя	весе́ннее
зи́мний	winter	зи́мняя	зи́мнее
ле́тний	summer	ле́тняя	ле́тнее
осе́нний	autumn	осе́нняя	осе́ннее

вече́рняя газе́та	evening newspaper
весе́нний день	spring day
зи́мнее пальто́	winter overcoat
ле́тняя ночь	summer night
осе́нняя пого́да	autumn weather

For **хоро́ший** 'good' see 8.10.

7.6 An Exception: the Тре́тий ('Third') Type

The only important exception is **тре́тий** 'third', whose endings do not fit
in any of our categories above. This adjective has the ending -**ья** in the
feminine and -**ье** in the neuter:

тре́тий день	third day
тре́т**ья** ночь	third night
тре́т**ье** у́тро	third morning

7.7 EXTRA: More Examples of the трéтий Type

The other (rare) adjectives of the **трéтий** type are nearly all derived from the names of living things, particularly animals, e.g. **собáчий** 'dog's (**собáчья жизнь** 'dog's life'), **кошáчий** 'cat's' (**кошáчья шерсть** 'cat fur'). One to note is **бóжий** from **бог** 'god' (**бóжья мúлость** 'God's mercy').

EXERCISE 7/2

Put on the required endings:

1 **Послéдн____ минýта** The last minute. 2 **Зúмн____ ýтро** Winter morning.
3 **Трéт____ урóк** The third lesson. 4 **Трéт____ ýлица** The third street.

7.8 Какóй 'What (kind of) . . .'?

If you want to ask what something is like, use the adjective **какóй** (same endings as **вторóй**):

Какáя э́то машúна?	What kind of car is it?
Какáя погóда в Москвé?	What's the weather like in Moscow?
Какóе э́то винó?	What wine is this?

7.9 'This' and 'That': Э́тот and Тóт

When used in noun phrases ('this house', 'that woman'), 'this' and 'that' are translated by **э́тот**, which agrees with its noun like this:

m	f	n
э́тот дóм	**э́та кнúга**	**э́то письмó**
this house	this book	this letter

Э́тот дóм стáрый.	This house is old.
Э́та кнúга моя́.	This book is mine.

71

If you wish to contrast 'this' (i.e. near me) with 'that' (i.e. not near me), you can translate 'that' with the word **тот**, which has the same endings as **этот**:

тот дом	**та книга**	**то письмо**
that house	that book	that letter

Эта книга моя, а та книга ваша. This book is mine and that one is yours.

7.10 EXTRA: Эта книга моя versus Это книга

Note the difference between **этот/эта** in sentences such as 'This book is mine' **Эта книга моя** and indeclinable **это** in sentences such as 'This is my book' **Это моя книга** (Lesson 3). In **Эта книга моя**, 'this' and 'book' are part of the same noun phrase and therefore agree. In **Это моя книга** 'This is my book', **это** and **книга** belong to different parts of the sentence. Note also that because **это**, the neuter form of **этот**, looks and sounds the same as indeclinable **это**, **Это письмо** has two meanings: it means both 'This letter' and 'This is a letter'.

7.11 Prepositional Case of Adjectives

If the noun is in the prepositional case, the adjective must agree[1], i.e. be in the same case as the noun. The endings are:

m and n (always the same): **-ом** for the **новый/русский/другой** types
-ем for soft adjectives (with **-ний**) and
adjectives like **хороший** 'good' (see 8.10)

в новом городе/кафе	in a new town/café
в русском городе/кафе	in a Russian town/café
в другом городе/кафе	in another town/café
в зимнем городе/пальто	in a wintry town/winter overcoat

третий 'third' has **-ьем**
| **в третьем доме/письме** | in the third house/letter |

The f equivalent of **-ом** is **-ой**; the f equivalent of **-ем** is **-ей**:

в но́в**ой** кни́ге	in a new book
в ру́сск**ой** кни́ге	in a Russian book
в друг**о́й** кни́ге	in another book
в зи́мн**ей** ша́пке	in a winter hat
в тре́ть**ей** кни́ге	in the third book

7.12 Accusative of Adjectives

Masculine (m) and neuter (n)

If the noun doesn't change, the adjective doesn't change:

Ру́сский язы́к (m nom.) **краси́вый.**	Russian is beautiful.
Я зна́ю ру́сский язы́к (m acc.).	I know Russian.
Э́то на́ше но́вое метро́ (n nom.).	This is our new metro.
Я люблю́ на́ше но́вое метро́ (n acc.).	I love our new metro.

With *masculine* animate¹ nouns (people and animals), adjectives of the **но́вый/ру́сский/второ́й** types end **-ого** (note that **г** in this ending is pronounced [v]):

Вы зна́ете но́вого ру́сского сосе́да?	Do you know the new Russian neighbour?
Она́ лю́бит второ́го му́жа?	Does she love her second husband?

Adjectives of the **после́дний** and **тре́тий** types have **-его** (**г** again pronounced [v]):

Мы зна́ем после́днего царя́.	We know the last tsar.
Вы зна́ете её тре́тьего му́жа?	Do you know her third husband?

This alternation of **о** and **е** in the endings **-ого** and **-его** is part of a pattern in adjective endings. Compare the endings **-ом** and **-ем** of the prepositions in 7.11 above.

Feminine (f)

-ая becomes **-ую**
-яя becomes **-юю**
тре́тья becomes **тре́тью**

nom.: **холо́дная зи́мняя пого́да** cold winter weather
    Вы лю́бите холо́дную зи́мнюю пого́ду? Do you like cold winter weather?

7.13 Accusative of мо́й, тво́й, наш, ваш, э́тот, то́т

m inanimate and n: same as nominative
Вы зна́ете мо́й/наш/то́т го́род? Do you know my/our/that town?
О́н лю́бит на́ше/э́то вино́. He loves our/this wine.

m animate
Вы зна́ете моего́/на́шего дру́га? Do you know my/our friend?
Она́ лю́бит э́того/ She loves this/that Englishman.
    того́ англича́нина.

f
Вы зна́ете мою́/на́шу до́чь? Do you know my/our daughter?
Я зна́ю э́ту/ту же́нщину. I know this/that woman.

7.14 Prepositional of Possessives (мо́й etc.), э́тот and то́т

m and n
в моём/твоём до́ме/письме́ in my/your house/letter
    (note the dots)
в на́шем/ва́шем до́ме/письме́ in our/your house/letter
в э́том/то́м до́ме/письме́ in this/that house/letter

f
в мое́й/тво́ей кни́ге in my/your book
в на́шей/ва́шей кни́ге in our/your book
в э́той/то́й кни́ге in this/that book

7.15 Example Phrases

Э́та кни́га на ру́сском языке́. This book is in Russian (Russians say
                            'on' a language, not 'in').

на Кра́сной пло́щади	on Red Square
в Большо́м теа́тре	at the Bolshoi Theatre
в тре́тьей кварти́ре	in flat number three (the third flat)
в вече́рней газе́те	in the evening paper
в ле́тнем кафе́	in the summer café (street café)

7.16 Adverbs

Adverbs' are words which can fill the gap in a sentence such as 'She speaks Russian _____', e.g. quickly, well, often, impressively. English adverbs are often formed from adjectives by adding -ly (nicely, cleverly, coldly etc.). The commonest adverb ending in Russian is **-о**, replacing the **-ый/-ий/-о́й** adjective ending. Adverbs are always indeclinable'. Examples:

краси́вый beautiful	краси́во beautifully
интере́сный interesting	интере́сно interestingly
холо́дный cold	хо́лодно coldly (NB stress)
хоро́ший good (see Lesson 8.10)	хорошо́ well (NB stress)
Она́ говори́т хорошо́.	She speaks well.

7.17 Vocabulary (with Pronunciation Check)

америка́нский American (adj)
[a-mye-ree-ка́n-skee]
большо́й [balʸ-shóy] large
брита́нский [bree-tа́n-skee] British
ва́нная (f adj) [vа́-nna-ya] bathroom
вече́рний [vye-chyе́r-nee]
evening (adj)
второ́й [fta-róy] second
гла́вный [glа́v-ni] main
го́род [gó-rat] town, city
до́брый [dó-bri] good, kind
до́ма [dó-ma] at home
есть [yestʸ] is/are (8.9)
за́падный [zа́-pad-ni] western

зи́мний [ze´em-nee] winter
знамени́тый [zna-mye-ne´e-ti]
famous
интере́сный [een-tye-ryе́-sni]
interesting
како́й [ka-kóy] what kind of
кварти́ра [kvar-te´e-ra] flat,
apartment
кни́га [kne´e-ga] book
краси́вый [kra-se´e-vi] beautiful,
attractive
кра́сный [krа́-sni] red
Кремль (m) [kryemlʸ] the Kremlin
(fortress)

75

ку́хня [ko´oh-nya] kitchen
 в or **на ку́хне** in the kitchen
ле́тний [lyét-nee] summer
ма́ленький [má-lyen^y-kee] small
мост [most] bridge
 prep. **на мосту́ [na-ma-sto´o]**
 on a bridge
но́вый [nó-vi] new
пальто́ (n indeclinable) **[pal^y-tó]**
 overcoat
пе́рвый [pyér-vi] first
план [plan] plan, street map
пого́да [pa-gó-da] weather
пока́зывать (+acc.) **[pa-ká-zi-vat^y]**
 to show (something)
 я пока́зываю, ты
 пока́зываешь
после́дний [pa-slyéd-nee] last
посо́льство [pa-sól^y-stva] embassy
река́ acc. **ре́ку [rye-ká ryé-koo]**
 river

ру́сский [ro´o-skee] Russian
ря́дом [ryá-dam] nearby, alongside
сего́дня [NB: **sye-vód-nya]** today
спа́льня [spál^y-nya] bedroom
ста́нция [stán-tsi-ya] station
 (on metro or in country)
 на ста́нции [na-stán-tsi-ee] at
 a station
ста́рый [stá-ri] old
та́кже [tág-zhe] also, in addition
теа́тр [tye-átr] theatre
тёплый [tyó-pli] warm
тот [tot] that (7.9)
тре́тий [tryé-tee] third (7.6)
холо́дный [ha-lód-ni] cold
шко́ла [shkó-la] school
эта́ж [e-tásh] floor, storey
 на этаже́ [na-e-ta-zhé] on
 a floor
э́тот [é-tat] this (7.9)

7.18 **Те́ксты Texts** (Translations in Key)

А: Москва́ – большо́й го́род. В Москве́ краси́вая река́,
 знамени́тый университе́т. Вы уже́ зна́ете Кра́сную пло́щадь,
 Большо́й теа́тр, Тверску́ю у́лицу.
Б: Зна́ю. Тверска́я у́лица – э́то гла́вная у́лица.
А: (Пока́зывает на пла́не) Вот Тверска́я, вот Но́вый Арба́т, а вот
 ста́рый Арба́т, о́чень ста́рая у́лица. Э́то гости́ница «Росси́я»,
 о́чень больша́я гости́ница. Здесь Кремль, ря́дом Большо́й
 Ка́менный‡ мост, а э́то брита́нское посо́льство, на
 на́бережной‡. Вот америка́нское посо́льство, а во́т
 кана́дское‡.

*

А: Доброе утро.
Б: Добрый день.
А: Почему вы в зимнем пальто? Погода сегодня тёплая.
Б: Это не зимнее пальто, а летнее.

*

Мы живём в Москве. Мы – это я, Павел Павлович Петров, моя жена Светлана Александровна и наша дочь Елена. В школе её зовут Лена, а дома мы её зовём Ленуша. Моя мать, Зинаида Егоровна, тоже живёт в Москве. Она живёт в старом доме в центре, а мы живём в новой квартире в новом доме на юго-западе‡. Наш дом на проспекте Вернадского. Вы знаете станцию «Юго-западная»‡? Мы живём на третьем этаже. В нашей квартире есть прихожая‡, большая комната, спальня. Есть также маленькая кухня, ванная и туалет.

‡ **Extra Vocabulary for Texts**

каменный [ká-mye-ni] stone (adj)

канадский [ka-nát-skee] Canadian

набережная (f adj) embankment
  [ná-bye-ryezh-na-ya]

прихожая (f adj) [pree-hó-zha-ya]
  entrance hall

юго-запад [yo´o-ga-zá-pat] the south-west

  на юго-западе in the south-west

«Юго-западная» (f adj) 'South Western' (metro station)
  [yo´o-ga-zá-pad-na-ya]

EXERCISE 7/3

Put on the required endings and translate:

1 Он живёт в Западн____ Сибир____. 2 Вы знаете нов____ гостиниц____? 3 Они ид____ на Красн____ площадь. 4 Она в зимн____ пальто. 5 Вы знаете мо____ втор____ жен____? 6 В эт____ магазин____ работает мо____ дочь. 7 Она показывает нов____ зимн____ пальто. 8 – Как____ сегодня погода? – Тёпл____.

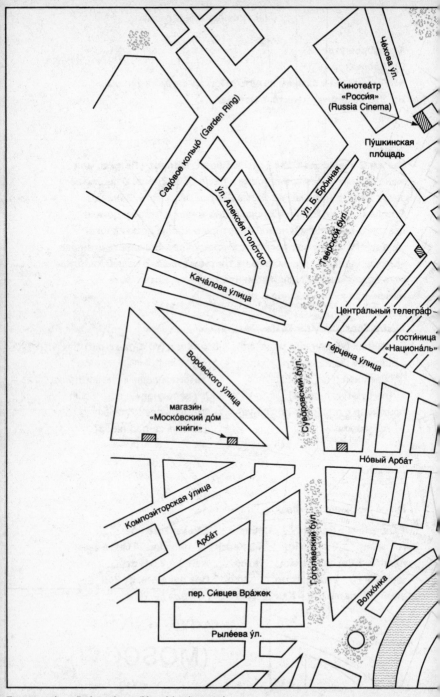

План центра́льной ча́сти го́рода (Map of the city centre)

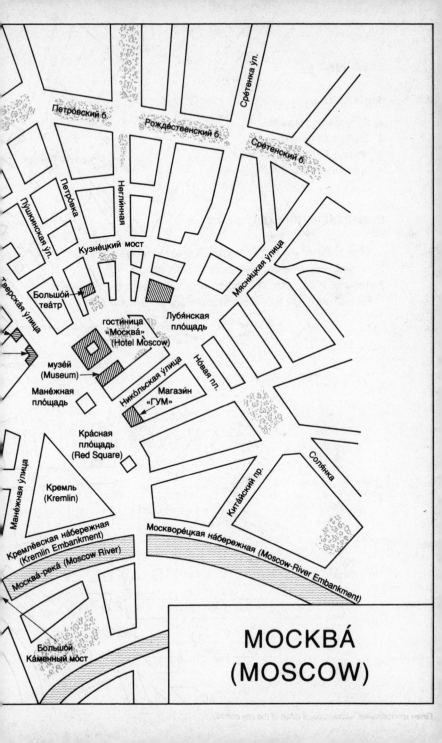

EXERCISE 7/4

Say in Russian:

1 Where is Red Square?
2 She is in (on) Red Square.
3 We're going to Red Square.
4 Is this book yours?

COMPREHENSION EXERCISE 7/5

1 What is the most direct route from GUM to Miasnitskaia Street?
2 On which square does the Natsional' Hotel stand?
3 Tell an English visitor who knows enough Russian to read the street names how to get from Great Stone Bridge to Pushkin Square.

8

УРО́К НО́МЕР ВО́СЕМЬ

PLURALS; SPELLING RULES;
BUYING THINGS

8.1 **Key Phrases**

Где на́ши места́?	Where are our seats (places)?
Да́йте, пожа́луйста, апельси́ны.	Give (me) (some) oranges, please.
Где мои́ друзья́?	Where are my friends?
Есть америка́нские газе́ты?	Are there (any) American newspapers?
Пирожки́, пожа́луйста.	(Some) pies, please.
Есть блины́?	Are there pancakes?
Во́т де́ньги.	Here is the money.

8.2 **Nominative Plural of Masculine and Feminine Nouns**

All the phrases in 8.1 contain nouns in the form of the nominative plural ('seats', 'oranges', 'friends' etc.). To make nouns plural, the basic ending for both masculine and feminine nouns is **-ы**. Masculine nouns add **-ы**, feminine nouns replace their **-a** with **-ы**. So:

блин 'pancake' becomes **блины́** 'pancakes'
газе́та 'newspaper' becomes **газе́ты** 'newspapers'

The ending **-ы** has the variant **-и**, depending on the last consonant of the noun. If the masculine noun ends with a soft sign (**ь**) or **й**, then the plural ending replaces the soft sign or **й** with **-и**. If the feminine noun ends **ь** or **я**, then the ending replacing the **ь** or **я** is also **и**:

дверь door	**две́ри** doors
неде́ля week	**неде́ли** weeks

8.3 Spelling Rule 1

In addition, you have to know the so-called 'spelling rules', which affect the spelling of endings right through the grammar. The first spelling rule, which we need to form plurals correctly, is as follows:

After the following seven letters, where you would expect **-ы**, for example in the plural, you always find **-и** instead.

г	⎫	these three letters are all
к	⎬	pronounced in the same
х	⎭	place, at the back of the mouth
ж	⎫	these are two of the three consonants
ш	⎭	which are always hard (see 2.7)
ч	⎫	these are the two consonants
щ	⎭	which are always soft (2.6).

This rule has no particular logic to it. It is simply a result of sound and spelling changes in the history of Russian. But it is worth learning, since you will need it frequently.

Because of this rule, the plural of **язы́к** 'language' is **языки́** (not **языкы́**), the plural of **кни́га** 'book' is **кни́ги** 'books' (not **кни́гы**). (This rule also explains why the ending of the adjectives **ру́сский** 'Russian' and **хоро́ший** 'good' is **-ий** and not **-ый** as in **но́вый** 'new' – see 7.2.)

8.4 Nominative Plural of Neuter Nouns

Replace the ending **-o** with **-a** and (usually) change the place of the stress. Nouns ending **-e** replace the ending **-e** with **-я**.

ме́сто 'place'	**места́** 'places'
окно́ 'window'	**о́кна** 'windows'
вино́ 'wine'	**ви́на** 'wines'
упражне́ние 'exercise'	**упражне́ния** 'exercises'

8.5 Plural Exceptions (Nouns We've Met So Far)

англича́нин	Englishman	**англича́не**	Englishmen
до́м	house	**дома́**	houses
брат	brother	**бра́тья**	brothers
го́род	town	**города́**	towns
до́чь	daughter	**до́чери**	daughters (that extra **-ер-**)
друг	friend	**друзья́**	friends
и́мя	name	**имена́**	names
мать	mother	**ма́тери**	mothers (extra **-ер-**)
муж	husband	**мужья́**	husbands
сын	son	**сыновья́**	sons
я́блоко	apple	**я́блоки**	apples

These are unpredictable. The biggest category of exceptions is short masculine nouns ending in a consonant and stressed on the stem in the singular, many of which end in **-á** in the plural. **До́м** 'house' **дома́** 'houses' is a good example. Many names of professions and jobs also end **-á**, for example **профе́ссор** 'professor' **профессора́** 'professors', **дире́ктор** 'director' **директора́** 'directors'; in this type of case, which is getting more widespread, the stress of the singular is not a factor. You will meet variants. **Инжене́р** 'engineer' in dictionaries has the plural **инжене́ры**, but many engineers call themselves **инженера́**. Irregular plural forms will be shown in the vocabularies.

8.6 Mobile' or 'Fill' Vowels: от(é)ц pl. отцы́

Some masculine nouns which end consonant + **е** (or **о**) + consonant, e.g. **оте́ц** 'father', drop the **е** or **о** whenever an ending is added. So the plural of **оте́ц** is not **отецы** but **отцы́**. These disappearing vowels are called 'mobile' or 'fill' vowels and they are shown in parentheses in the vocabularies like this: **от(é)ц**

Other examples:

америка́н(е)ц	American	pl. **америка́нцы**
продав(é)ц	sales assistant	pl. **продавцы́**
пирож(ó)к	pie	pl. **пирожки́**

д(е)нь (m)	day	pl. **дни**
ры́н(о)к	market	**на ры́нке** (prep.) at the market

The ending **-ец**, common with names of nationalities, nearly always has a mobile **е**, e.g. **япо́н(е)ц** 'Japanese' pl. **япо́нцы**.

The endings **-е́ец** [yé-yets], **-а́ец**, **-о́ец**, e.g. in **европе́(е)ц** 'a European', also have a mobile **е**, but when the **е** drops out it leaves the consonantal **[y]** sound in the form of the letter **й**. So the plural of **европе́(е)ц** 'European' is **европе́йцы**.

Other examples:

кита́(е)ц Chinese pl. **кита́йцы**
валли́(е)ц Welshman pl. **валли́йцы**

8.7 Nominative Plural of Adjectives

All adjectives in the nom. plural end **-ые** (or **-ие** for soft adjectives and those whose stem ends with one of the seven 'spelling rule' letters **г, к, х, ж, ч, ш, щ** – see 8.3 above).

но́вые кни́ги	new books
ста́рые друзья́	old friends
больши́е де́ньги	big money (a lot of money)
после́дние дни	last days
ру́сские блины́	Russian pancakes

8.8 Nominative Plurals of Possessives and Demonstratives

мой/моя́/моё	**мои́ [ma-e´e]**	my
твой/твоя́/твоё	**твои́ [tva-e´e]**	your (fam)
наш/на́ша/на́ше	**на́ши [ná-shi]**	our
ваш/ва́ша/ва́ше	**ва́ши [vá-shi]**	your (pol/pl.)
э́тот/э́та/э́то	**э́ти [é-tee]**	these
тот/та/то́	**те [tye]**	those

Его́, **её** and **их** are indeclinable, so do not change in the plural.

Examples:

мои друзья	my friends
наши деньги	our money
эти яблоки	these apples
его слова	his/its words

EXERCISE 8/1

Make the nouns plural and translate:

Regular examples: 1 улица. 2 троллейбус. 3 университет.
4 школа. 5 музей. 6 продав(е)ц. 7 письмо. 8 площадь. 9 минута.
10 неделя. 11 фамилия. Spelling-rule examples: 12 книга. 13 язык.
14 пирож(о)к. Irregular examples: 15 дочь. 16 дом. 17 англичанин.
18 лес. 19 такси. 20 сын. 21 имя. 22 яблоко. 23 друг.

EXERCISE 8/2

Make the adjectives and possessives nominative plural and translate:

1 русская книга. 2 этот язык. 3 летний день. 4 наш сын. 5 старый
город. 6 мой друг. 7 большой магазин. 8 тот год. 9 ваше место.
10 это упражнение.

The nominative plural forms you met above are also the endings of the
accusative plural *except* for all phrases involving *animate* nouns.

| Дайте эти яблоки, пожалуйста. | Please give (me) these apples. |
| Я люблю русские блины. | I love Russian pancakes. |

Animate accusatives, e.g. 'I love Russian girls', are in Lesson 10.

8.9 Есть 'is', 'are'

If you want to ask if something is available, use **есть**, with the rise–fall
intonation you met in 5.3:

Чай есть? or **Есть чай?**	Is there tea?
Блины́ есть? or **Есть блины́?**	Are there pancakes?
Ко́фе есть?	Is there coffee?
Есть.	There is.
Пирожки́ есть?	Are there pies?
Пирожки́ есть.	There are pies. (Pies are available.)

Although Russian does not normally require an equivalent of 'am', 'is', 'are' (**Он ру́сский** 'He (is) Russian'), **есть** is used for all forms of the present tense of 'to be' when 'to be' means 'to exist' or 'to be present'.

Бог есть.	God is. (God exists.)
Чай есть.	There is tea.

8.10 Spelling Rule 2

Spelling Rule 1 (8.3) concerns the occurrence of **и** where you would other-wise expect **ы**. So the normal nominative adjective ending is **-ый** (**но́вый** 'new'), but 'Russian' is **ру́сский** and 'good' is **хоро́ший**. Rule 2 accounts for the occurrence of **е** where you would expect **о**. It affects **хоро́ший** and all adjectives ending **-жий**, **-ший**, **-чий**, **-щий**, e.g. **све́жий** 'fresh', **горя́чий** 'hot', **сле́дующий** 'next'.

After **ж, ч, ш, щ** and **ц** (the last four of the letters in Rule 1 plus **ц**), you find **е** where adjectives like **но́вый** have **о**. So the nominative neuter end-ing of **хоро́ший** is **хоро́шее** (not **-ое**), and the prepositional endings are **-ем** and **-ей** (7.11), not **-ом** and **-ой**.

хоро́шее ру́сское вино́	good Russian wine
све́жее яйцо́	a fresh egg
в горя́чей воде́	in hot water
в хоро́шем ру́сском рестора́не	in a good Russian restaurant

This rule also explains why **наш** 'our' and **ваш** 'your' never have **о** after the **ш**:

в на́шем но́вом до́ме	in our new house

Rule 2 also applies to **ц**, as we shall see when we meet the rule again in grammatical endings involving nouns (16.2). There are almost no adjectives ending **-цый**, but should you ever meet **ку́цый** 'tailless' or **краснолицый** 'red-faced', the neuter forms will be **ку́цее** and **краснолицее**.

Note. Rule 2 does *not* apply to stressed ó, so **большо́й** 'big' has **о**, not **е**, after **ш**. However, **большо́й** is unique. There are no other adjectives ending **-шо́й**, and none ending **-жо́й**, **-чо́й**, **-що́й** or **-цо́й**.

8.11 Vocabulary

апельси́н orange

бе́лый white

блин pancake
   pl. **блины́**

бутербро́д [boo-tyer-brót] open sandwich

вку́сный [fko´o-sni] tasty

вода́ acc. **во́ду** water

всегда́ [fsyeg-dá] always

горя́чий hot

да́йте give (imperative¹)

де́лать to do; to make
   я де́лаю, ты де́лаешь

де́ньги (pl.) **[dyén'-gee]** money

дорого́й dear, expensive

друг [drook] friend
   pl. **друзья́**

е́сли if

есть [yest'] (there) is, (there) are

карто́фель (m) (no plural) potatoes

кефи́р fermented milk drink

кило́ (n indeclinable) kilo(gram)

килогра́мм kilogram

колбаса́ salami

ма́сло butter, oil

ме́сто pl. **места́** place, seat

молоко́ milk

моло́чный milk, dairy (adj)

мя́со meat

отде́л [ad-dyél] section (of a shop)

пирож(ó)к [pee-ra-zhók] pie

плохо́й bad

покупа́ть to buy
   я покупа́ю, ты покупа́ешь

продава́ть to sell (**знать** -type, stem **прода-**, stressed on the end – 4.7)
   я продаю́, ты продаёшь

продав(е́)ц sales assistant

проду́кты (m pl.) groceries, food

ры́н(о)к market
   на ры́нке in/at the market

са́хар sugar

све́жий (8.10) **[svyé-zhi]** fresh

сле́дующий (8.10) following, next

сло́во word

сыр cheese

то́лько only

фрукт a piece of fruit

хлеб bread

хоро́ший (8.10) **[ha-ró-shi]** good

чёрный black

87

я́блоко apple   **яйцо́ [yee-tsó]** egg
  pl. **я́блоки**   pl. **я́йца [yáy-tsa]**

8.12 Dialogues (Translation in Key)

1 Проду́кты

Мэ́ри:	Каки́е проду́кты ру́сские покупа́ют в магази́не?
Воло́дя:	В магази́не мы покупа́ем колбасу́, сыр, молоко́, я́йца, ма́сло, карто́фель, са́хар. И хлеб, коне́чно, чёрный и бе́лый. Ру́сский хлеб о́чень вку́сный, всегда́ све́жий. Мы о́чень лю́бим де́лать бутербро́ды.
Мэ́ри:	А фру́кты?
Воло́дя:	Фру́кты мы покупа́ем на ры́нке. Они́ дороги́е, но све́жие. Мы покупа́ем я́блоки и апельси́ны, е́сли есть.
Мэ́ри:	Где вы покупа́ете мя́со?
Воло́дя:	В магази́не мя́со плохо́е. Хоро́шее, све́жее мя́со есть то́лько на ры́нке.

2 Фру́кты

А́нна:	Где продаю́т‡ апельси́ны?
Бори́с:	То́лько на ры́нке.
А́нна:	А я́блоки?
Бори́с:	Я́блоки есть в магази́не, но они́ плохи́е.

‡ Where do they sell oranges?/Where does one sell oranges?/Where are oranges sold? If you use the third person plural (the 'they' form) of the verb without **они́**, the meaning becomes impersonal. **Говоря́т, что ру́сский хлеб всегда́ све́жий** 'It is said that Russian bread is always fresh'.

3 На ры́нке

А:	Э́ти пирожки́ ва́ши?
Б:	Мои́.
А:	Они́ све́жие?

Б: Свéжие, óчень хорóшие.

А: Дáйте, пожáлуйста, килогрáмм.

4 В магазúне

Мэ́ри: Скажúте, пожáлуйста, в какóм отдéле продаю́т
             кефúр?

Продавéц: В молóчном.

Мэ́ри: А я́йца?

Продавéц: Тóже в молóчном.

Мэ́ри: Спасúбо.

EXERCISE 8/3

Say in Russian:

1 Is there (any) coffee? 2 Are there (any) fresh sandwiches? 3 Where are
your friends? 4 I love Russian pancakes. 5 Black bread, please. 6 Give
(me) these oranges, please.

COMPREHENSION EXERCISE 8/4

Here is a list of fifteen of the peoples of Europe. Guess who is who and
see if you can work out the masculine singular form of each nationality,
bearing in mind the example **америкáн(е)ц/америкáнцы** in the section
on mobile vowels (8.6 above). The capital city of each nationality is given
in brackets.

**В Еврóпе живу́т белору́сы (Минск), валлúйцы (Кáрдифф), вéнгры
(Будапéшт), ирлáндцы (Дýблин), испáнцы (Мадрúд), латыши́
(Рúга), литóвцы (Вúльнюс), нéмцы (Берлúн), поля́ки (Варшáва),
францу́зы (Парúж), рýсские (Москвá), украúнцы (Кúев), швéды
(Стокгóльм), шотлáндцы (Эдинбýрг), эстóнцы (Тáллинн).**

1 Гренла́ндия (Greenland)
2 Исла́ндия (Iceland)
3 Ирла́ндия (Ireland)
4 Великобрита́ния (Great Britain)
5 Фра́нция (France)
6 Португа́лия (Portugal)
7 Испа́ния (Spain)
8 Бе́льгия (Belgium)
9 Нидерла́нды (Netherlands)
10 Герма́ния (Germany)
11 Да́ния (Denmark)
12 Норве́гия (Norway)
13 Шве́ция (Sweden)
14 Финля́ндия (Finland)
15 Росси́я (Росси́йская Федера́ция)
   (Russia or Russian Federation)
16 Эсто́ния (Estonia)
17 Ла́твия (Latvia)
18 Литва́ (Lithuania)
19 Москва́ (Moscow)
20 Белору́ссия (Belarus)
21 По́льша (Poland)
22 Че́хия (Czech Republic)
23 Склова́кия (Slovakia)
24 Украи́на (Ukraine)
25 Молда́вия (Moldova)
26 Гру́зия (Georgia)
27 Азербайджа́н (Azerbaijan)
28 Арме́ния (Armenia)
29 Румы́ния (Romania)
30 Болга́рия (Bulgaria)
31 Гре́ция (Greece)
32 Алба́ния (Albania)
33 Македо́ния (Macedonia)
34 Се́рбия (Serbia)
35 Черного́рия (Montenegro)
36 Бо́сния (Bosnia)
37 Хорва́тия (Croatia)
38 Ве́нгрия (Hungary)
39 А́встрия (Austria)
40 Швейца́рия (Switzerland)
41 Ита́лия (Italy)
42 Ту́рция (Turkey)
43 Люксембу́рг (Luxembourg)
44 Слове́ния (Slovenia)

0   600 Km

0   300 Miles

ЕВРО́ПА (EUROPE)

9

УРÓК НÓМЕР ДÉВЯТЬ

NUMBERS; THE GENITIVE CASE

9.1 **Key Expressions**

Скóлько э́то стóит?	How much does this cost?
оди́н рубль	one rouble
два рубля́	two roubles
четы́ре рубля́	four roubles
пять рублéй	five roubles
С вас дéсять дóлларов.	You owe ten dollars.
однá копéйка	one kopeck
две копéйки	two kopecks
пять копéек	five kopecks
пять часóв	five hours
часóв пять	about five hours
нéсколько часóв	several hours
кварти́ра Натáши	Natasha's flat
до свидáния	goodbye (= until meeting)
нет винá	there is no wine

9.2 **Numbers**

1 **оди́н** (m)/**однá** (f) **однó** (n)
2 **два** (m and n)/**две** (f)
3 **три**

4	четы́ре
5	пять
6	шесть
7	семь
8	во́семь
9	де́вять
10	де́сять
11	оди́ннадцать [a-de´e-na-tsatʸ]
12	двена́дцать [dvye-ná-tsatʸ]
13	трина́дцать [tree-ná-tsatʸ]
14	четы́рнадцать [chye-tír-na-tsatʸ]
15	пятна́дцать [peet-ná-tsatʸ]
16	шестна́дцать [shes-ná-tsatʸ]
17	семна́дцать [syem-ná-tsatʸ]
18	восемна́дцать [va-syem-ná-tsatʸ]
19	девятна́дцать [dye-veet-ná-tsatʸ]
20	два́дцать [dvá-tsatʸ]
21	два́дцать оди́н (m)/два́дцать одна́ (f)/два́дцать одно́ (n)
22	два́дцать два (m and n)/два́дцать две (f)
23	два́дцать три
30	три́дцать [tre´e-tsatʸ]
40	со́рок
50	пятьдеся́т [pee-dye-syát]
60	шестьдеся́т [shez-dye-syát]
70	се́мьдесят
80	во́семьдесят
90	девяно́сто
100	сто́
101	сто́ оди́н (m)/сто́ одна́ (f)/сто́ одно́ (n)
125	сто́ два́дцать пять
200	две́сти
300	три́ста
400	четы́реста
500	пятьсо́т [peet-sót]
600	шестьсо́т [shes-sót]
700	семьсо́т
800	восемьсо́т
900	девятьсо́т [dye-veet-sót]

1000	тысяча [tí-sya-cha] or (faster) [tí-shsha]
1357	тысяча триста пятьдесят семь
2000	две тысячи
5000	пять тысяч

To help you spell: Notice that no Russian one-word number has more than one soft sign (e.g. 50 **пятьдесят** – no soft sign at the end). In numbers below 40, the soft sign is at the end (e.g. 10 **десять**. In words above 40, the soft sign is in the middle.

9.3 'Five (of) roubles': Numbers are Used with the Genitive Case

The genitive case, whose basic meaning is 'of' as in 'the name *of* the girl', is in Russian used with numbers and other quantity words. That is, Russians say 'five of books', 'ten of roubles', 'much of money'. In English we use similar constructions such as 'a lot *of* money', 'a great deal *of* work', 'hundreds *of* books'.

9.4 Formation of the Genitive Singular (abbreviated 'gen.sg.')

These forms are straightforward:

Masculine (m) and neuter (n) nouns have -a or -я

-a is added to masculine nouns ending in a consonant and replaces the **-o** of neuter nouns:

друг 'friend'	друга 'of a friend'
письмо 'letter'	письма 'of a letter'

-я replaces the **ь** (soft sign) or **й** of masculine nouns and the **-e** of neuter nouns:

рубль 'rouble'	рубля 'of a rouble' (note stress)
Игорь 'Igor'	Игоря 'of Igor'
музей 'museum'	музея 'of a museum'
море 'sea'	моря 'of the sea'
свидание 'meeting'	свидания 'of a meeting'

Note: The ten neuter nouns ending **-мя** have genitive **-ени**:

вре́мя 'time'	**вре́мени** 'of time'
и́мя 'name'	**и́мени** 'of a name'

Feminine nouns (and masculine nouns with feminine endings) all have -ы or -и

Replace nominative **-а** with **-ы**:

Москва́ 'Moscow'	**Москвы́** 'of Moscow'
па́па 'dad'	**па́пы** 'dad's'

Replace **-я** or **-ь** with **-и**:

неде́ля 'week'	**неде́ли** 'of a week'
дверь 'door'	**две́ри** 'of a door'
Ва́ня 'Vania'	**Ва́ни** 'of Vania/Vania's'

Remember that Spelling Rule 1 (8.3) will apply to nouns ending **-ка, -га, -ха, -жа, -ча, -ша, -ща**. They all have genitive **-и** instead of **-ы**.

копе́йка 'kopeck'	**копе́йки** 'of a kopeck'
кни́га 'book'	**кни́ги** 'of a book'
Са́ша 'Sasha'	**Са́ши** 'of Sasha/Sasha's'

Note. **до́чь** 'daughter' and **мать** 'mother' always add **-ер-** before any case ending, so their genitive forms are **до́чери** 'of daughter' and **ма́тери** 'of mother' (same as the prep. case).

9.5 Uses of the Genitive

The genitive, the commonest case after the nominative and accusative, has five main uses:

(a) With numbers and quantity words:

три рубля́ 'three roubles' (lit. 'three of rouble')
мно́го вре́мени 'a lot of time'

If you invert the number and the noun, the meaning is 'about', 'approximately'

рубля́ три 'about three roubles'

After the numbers **два/две** 'two', **три** 'three', **четы́ре** 'four' and any number ending **два/две, три, четы́ре** (e.g. **два́дцать три** 'twenty-three'), the noun is genitive singular:

два рубля́   two roubles = two of rouble

Numbers from **пять** 'five' upwards are followed by the genitive plural – see 9.9 below.

(b) Possession, corresponding to 's' in 'Ivan's house', and related meanings, corresponding to *of*, e.g. in 'map *of* the town':

до́м Ива́на	Ivan's house
план го́рода	map of the town
и́мя до́чери	daughter's name

(c) After a large number of prepositions – see lesson 10.6:

до свида́ния   goodbye ('until meeting')

(d) With **нет** meaning 'there isn't' (see 10.5 for more examples). **Нет** 'there isn't' is the opposite of **есть** 'there is' (8.9). It is a different word from **нет** 'no' (the opposite of **да**):

Есть is used with the nominative: **Есть ча́й** 'There is tea'
Нет is used with the genitive: **Нет ча́я** 'There is no tea'
Нет вре́мени 'There is no time' ('There is not of time')

(e) The genitive is also used after negated transitive' verbs. This topic is dealt with in Lesson 24.

Она́ не зна́ет языка́.   She doesn't know the language.

EXERCISE 9/1

Put the bracketed nouns in the genitive:

1 **Два (рубль)**. 2 **Три (письмо́)**. 3 **И́мя (сын)**. 4 **Три (же́нщина)**. 5 **У́лицы (Москва́)** 'The streets of Moscow'. 6 **Две (кни́га)**. 7 **Две (до́чь)**.

8 **Стака́н (молоко́)** 'a glass of milk'. 9 **До (свида́ние)**. 10 **Нет (ко́фе)** 'There's no coffee'.

EXERCISE 9/2

Say in Russian:

1 Two kopecks. 2 There's no sugar. 3 Three words. 4 Two sons. 5 Two weeks. 6 Volgin Street (= street of Volgin). 7 Masha's husband. 8 A bottle (**буты́лка**) of wine. 9 The number of the house. 10 There is no tea.

9.6 Genitive Plural (abbreviated 'gen.pl.')

This is the most complex ending in Russian. The five main rules are given here. Other, less important, rules are given in the 'EXTRA' section. The genitive plural form of awkward nouns (e.g. **копе́йка** – **копе́ек** 'of kopecks') is given in the vocabularies.

(a) All nouns ending **-ь**, *whether m or f*, replace the soft sign with **-ей** (which is often stressed, i.e. **-е́й**, particularly if the noun is short, but the stress is hard to predict).

рубль (m) 'rouble'	**рубле́й** 'of roubles'
д(е)нь (m) 'day'	**дне́й** 'of days'
пло́щадь (f) 'square'	**площаде́й** 'of squares'
жи́тель (m) 'inhabitant'	**жи́телей** 'of inhabitants'

Remember that **мать** and **до́чь** always have **-ер-** before endings:

мать 'mother'	**матере́й** 'of mothers'
до́чь 'daughter'	**дочере́й** 'of daughters'

(b) Nouns ending **-ж, -ч, -ш, -щ** add **-ей** (as in (a), often stressed **-е́й**):

эта́ж 'floor'	**этаже́й** 'of floors'
врач 'doctor'	**враче́й** 'of doctors'
това́рищ 'comrade'	**това́рищей** 'of comrades'

97

(c) Most other masculine nouns ending with a consonant add **-ов** (so the common ending **-ов**, by coincidence, means 'of')

язы́к 'language'	**языко́в** 'of languages'
авто́бус 'bus'	**авто́бусов** 'of buses'

Spelling Rule 2 (8.10) applies to nouns ending **-ц**, i.e. their gen.pl. is **-цо́в** when stressed, otherwise **-цев** (the gen.pl. has the same stress as the nom.pl.).

от(е́)ц 'father'	**отцо́в** 'of fathers'
америка́н(е)ц 'American'	**америка́нцев** 'of Americans'
ме́сяц 'month'	**ме́сяцев** 'of months'

(d) Feminine nouns with **-а** in the nominative *and* neuter nouns with **-о** simply lose their **-а** or **-о** (so they have a 'zero ending'):

у́лица 'street'	**у́лиц_** 'of streets'
ты́сяча 'thousand'	**ты́сяч_** 'of thousands'
сло́во 'word'	**сло́в_** 'of words'

(e) All nouns ending **-ия** and **-ие** replace the **-я** or **-е** with **-й** (and the stress never shifts):

фами́лия 'surname'	**фами́лий** 'of surnames'
упражне́ние 'exercise'	**упражне́ний** 'of exercises'

9.7 Genitive Plural of Other Nouns

Apart from these five main rules, covering most nouns, there are minor rules, given in EXTRA section 9.8. However, if a noun does not obey one of the rules above, its genitive plural (gen.pl.) is always given in the vocabulary list, and you will probably find it easier to learn such forms as exceptions. Here are the exceptional nouns we have met so far:

	gen.pl.		gen.pl.
англича́нин 'Englishman'	**англича́н_**	**сын** 'son'	**сынове́й**
англича́нка 'Englishwoman'	**англича́нок**	**друг** 'friend'	**друзе́й**
де́душка 'grandfather'	**де́душек**	**дя́дя** 'uncle'	**дя́дей**
письмо́ 'letter'	**пи́сем**	**мо́ре** 'sea'	**море́й**
окно́ 'window'	**о́кон**	**брат** 'brother'	**бра́тьев**
спа́льня 'bedroom'	**спа́лен**	**музе́й** 'museum'	**музе́ев**

яйцо́ 'egg'	я́иц	и́мя 'name'	имён
де́ньги 'money'	де́нег	го́д 'year'	лет (lit.
копе́йка 'kopeck'	копе́ек		'of
неде́ля 'week'	неде́ль		summers')
ку́хня 'kitchen'	ку́хонь		

9.8 EXTRA: Further Details of the Genitive Plural

If you do wish to know what the minor rules behind many of the exceptions are, here is a list. But, as stated above, it is probably simpler to learn the gen.pl. of awkward nouns as you meet them.

(f) Nouns with irregular nominative plurals ending *un*stressed **-ья** (e.g. **брат** – **бра́тья** 'brothers') repeat the irregular stem (**бра́ть-**) in all forms of the plural.

брат 'brother' nom.pl. **бра́тья**	**бра́тьев** 'of brothers'
де́рево 'tree' nom.pl. **дере́вья**	**дере́вьев** 'of trees'

(g) Nouns with nom.pl. forms ending *stressed* **-ья́** have gen.pl. **-е́й** (with no soft sign – note that the gen.pl. ending **-ей** *never* has a soft sign before it):

сын 'son' nom.pl. **сыновья́**	**сынове́й** 'of sons'
муж 'husband' nom.pl. **мужья́**	**муже́й** 'of husbands'

(h) Nouns ending **-й** have **-ев**:

музе́й 'museum' nom.pl. **музе́и**	**музе́ев** 'of museums'

(i) Nouns ending **-жка, -чка, -шка** have **-жек, -чек, -шек** in the gen.pl. Nouns ending **-цка, -ька** (rare) become **-цек, -ек**. That is, rule (d) applies (i.e. delete final **-а**), and the final consonant group is split with a 'mobile' **e**:

ло́жка 'spoon'	**ло́жек** 'of spoons'
де́вушка 'girl'	**де́вушек** 'of girls'
до́чка 'little daughter'	**до́чек** 'of little daughters'
по́лька 'Polish woman'	**по́лек** 'of Polish women'

(j) Other consonants + **ка** become consonant + **ок**:

англича́нка 'Englishwoman'	**англича́нок** 'of Englishwomen'
ма́рка 'postage stamp'	**ма́рок** 'of postage stamps'

(k) Other **-a** and **-o** nouns with 'awkward' consonant groups also split the final consonants with **o** or **e**.

окно́ 'window'	**о́кон** (same stress as nom.pl. **о́кна**)
письмо́ 'letter'	**пи́сем** (**e** replaces the soft sign)

Note: The consonant groups **-тв, -гр, -рт** are *not* split. So the gen.pl. of **посо́льство** 'embassy' is **посо́льств** (by rule (d)).

(l) Nouns ending **-йка** have **-ек**:

копе́йка 'kopeck'	**копе́ек**

(m) Nouns ending consonant + **я** generally replace the **я** with **ь**, but if the ending is consonant + **ня**, the ending of the gen.pl. is consonant + **ен**:

неде́ля 'week'	**неде́ль**
кастрю́ля 'saucepan'	**кастрю́ль**
пе́сня 'song'	**пе́сен**
спа́льня 'bedroom'	**спа́лен**

(n) Nouns ending **-анин** or **янин**, and six other animate nouns ending **-ин** lose the final **-ин**:

англича́нин 'Englishman'	**англича́н**
граждани́н 'citizen'	**гра́ждан**
боя́рин 'boyar'	**боя́р**

There are plenty of unpredictable cases. Even native Russian speakers are sometimes unsure of the genitive plural of rare words – and, like foreigners, have to check in a dictionary.

9.9 Genitive Plural after Numbers 5, 6 etc.

While **два, три, четы́ре** and numbers ending 2, 3 and 4 are followed by the genitive singular (**два рубля́** 'two of rouble' 9.5), **пять** and upwards are followed by the genitive *plural*, e.g. **пять рубле́й** 'five of roubles'.

де́сять до́лларов	ten dollars ('of dollars')
сто́ два́дцать сло́в	a hundred and twenty words

EXERCISE 9/3

Translate and put the required endings on the bracketed words:

1 **Пять (рубль).** 2 **Де́сять (до́м).** 3 **Шесть (но́чь).** 4 **Три́ста (жи́тель).** 5 **Семь (эта́ж).** 6 **Сто́ два́дцать шесть (кни́га).** 7 **Двена́дцать (упражне́ние).** 8 **Девятна́дцать (врач).** 9 **Пять (бутербро́д).** 10 **Два́дцать (ме́сто).** 11 **Со́рок (газе́та).** 12 **Де́вять (апельси́н).** 13 **Две́сти (америка́н(е)ц).** 14 **Пять (ты́сяча).** 15 **Килогра́мм (я́блоко).** 16 **Шесть (друг).** 17 **Нет (де́ньги).** 18 **Со́рок (копе́йка).** 19 **Оди́ннадцать (письмо́).** 20 **Се́мьдесят (англича́нин).** 21 **Оди́ннадцать (неде́ля).** 22 **Четы́реста пятьдеся́т (го́д).** 23 **Семь (мо́ре).** 24 **Во́семь (и́мя).** 25 **Девяно́сто (англича́нка).**

EXERCISE 9/4

Read, adding the genitive plural endings:

(1) **10 рубл___ 30 копе́___.** (2) **5 час___.** (3) **15 мину́т___.** (4) **5 неде́л___.** (5) **80 апельси́н___.** (6) **50 до́ллар___.** (7) **20 (день) _____.** (8) **5 ме́сяц___.** (9) **100 сло́в___.** (10) **260 кварти́р___.**

9.10 One: оди́н etc. (Table 7)

Note that one (**оди́н, одна́, одно́** etc.) is not a numeral (i.e. it is not a quantity word followed by the genitive case). It behaves like an adjective, agreeing[†] with the following noun, and has the same endings as **э́тот, э́та, э́то** 'this'. The **и** of **од(и́)н** is a mobile[†] vowel (8.6).

Я зна́ю одну́ де́вушку.	I know one girl (acc.).
Я зна́ю одного́ америка́нца.	I know one American (animate acc.).

All numbers which end with a form of **оди́н**, e.g. 21, 151, behave in the same way and any accompanying noun is *singular*:

Я зна́ю сто́ два́дцать одну́ де́вушку. I know 121 girls ('121 girl').

9.11 Last Number Determines Agreement

It is a general rule that the last number determines the form of the noun:

два́дцать оди́н до́ллар_	twenty-one dollars
два́дцать четы́ре до́ллара	twenty-four dollars
два́дцать семь до́лларов	twenty-seven dollars
четы́ре-пять до́лларов	four or five dollars

EXERCISE 9/5

Put the required endings on the words in brackets and translate:

1 **Три (мину́та)**. 2 **Пять (мину́та)**. 3 **Два́дцать одна́ (мину́та)**. 4 **Два (год)**. 5 **Де́сять (год)**. 6 **Сто́ два́дцать три (день)**. 7 **Ты́сяча две́сти шестьдеся́т оди́н (до́ллар)**. 8 **Четы́ре (дочь)**. 9 **Со́рок (оди́н) (копе́йка)**. 10 **Я зна́ю два́дцать (оди́н студе́нт)**.

9.12 Other Quantity Words

Other quantity words also take the genitive – singular or plural, according to meaning:

мно́го	much, many, a lot
мно́го друзе́й (gen.pl.)	many friends
мно́го са́хара (gen.sg.)	a lot of sugar
ма́ло	few, little
ма́ло са́хара	not much sugar
не́сколько	some, a few
не́сколько мину́т (gen.pl.)	a few minutes
ско́лько?	how much? how many?
Ско́лько вре́мени? (gen.sg)	How much time? What time is it?

102

Ско́лько часо́в? (gen.pl.)	How many hours?
сто́лько	so many, so much
сто́лько рабо́ты (gen.sg.)	so much work
бо́льше	more
бо́льше де́нег	more money
ме́ньше	less, fewer
ме́ньше слов	fewer words

9.13 **Vocabulary**

бо́льше + gen. more

буты́лка gen.pl. **буты́лок** bottle

валю́тный currency, foreign currency (adj)

вегетариа́нка gen.pl. **вегетариа́нок** (female) vegetarian

ведь you know/isn't it/aren't you, etc. (indicating that the speaker expects agreement)

вре́мя gen.sg. **вре́мени** time

грамм gen.pl. **гра́ммов** or **грамм** gram(me)

де́вушка gen.pl. **де́вушек** girl

до + gen. as far as; until

до́ллар dollar

ещё что́-нибудь? anything else? (lit. 'more anything')

жи́тель (m) inhabitant

и́ли or

иногда́ sometimes

ка́ждый each, every

копе́йка gen.pl. **копе́ек** kopeck (1/100th of a rouble)

ма́ло + gen. little, not much

ме́ньше + gen. less

ме́сяц gen.pl. **ме́сяцев** month

миллио́н million

мно́го + gen. much, many

мо́жет быть perhaps

ночь (f) gen.pl. **ноче́й** (NB stress) night

о́вощи gen.pl. **овоще́й** vegetables

от + gen. from

полкило́ (indecl) half a kilo

получа́ть + acc. to receive, get

  я получа́ю, ты получа́ешь

поэ́тому so, consequently

раз gen.pl. **раз** a time

ра́зный various

роди́тели (sg. **роди́тель** m) parents

рубль (m) rouble

ру́сский (m) (adj) a Russian (man)

с вас you owe (idiom lit. 'from you')

сда́ча change (money returned)

ско́лько + gen. how much, how many

сто́ить + acc . to cost

  Ско́лько э́то сто́ит?

  How much does this cost?

  Ско́лько они́ сто́ят?

  How much do they cost?

то́чно exactly

туда́ there (motion 'thither')

фу́нт pound (weight and currency)

ходи́ть to go (there and back, on foot)

я хожу́, ты хо́дишь

что́-нибудь anything

9.14 Dialogues (Translation in Key)

Buying things

(1)

А: Да́йте, пожа́луйста, три ко́фе, три ча́я, пять бутербро́дов и пять пирожко́в.

Б: С вас четы́ре рубля́ два́дцать во́семь копе́ек.

А: Пожа́луйста.

Б: Вот сда́ча - пять рубле́й се́мьдесят две копе́йки.

А: Спаси́бо.

Б: Пожа́луйста.

(2)

А: Да́йте, пожа́луйста, две́сти гра́ммов сы́ра и по́лкило́ колбасы́.

Б: Семь рубле́й два́дцать шесть копе́ек.

(3)

А: Ско́лько э́то сто́ит?

Б: Двена́дцать рубле́й килогра́мм.

А: Четы́реста гра́ммов, пожа́луйста.

Б: Пожа́луйста. Четы́ре рубля́ во́семьдесят копе́ек.

(4)

А: Пожа́луйста, да́йте кило́ я́блок.

Б: Ещё что́-нибудь?

А: Ско́лько сто́ят апельси́ны?

Б: Четы́рнадцать рубле́й.

А: По́лкило́, пожа́луйста.

Б: С вас шестна́дцать рубле́й.

Population figures

А: Ско́лько жи́телей в Москве́? Два-три миллио́на?

Б: Нет, бо́льше. Во́семь миллио́нов. А в Петербу́рге жи́телей ме́ньше – четы́ре миллио́на.

А: А ско́лько в Росси́и?

Б: Я не зна́ю то́чно. Мо́жет быть, сто́ пятьдеся́т миллио́нов.

EXERCISE 9/6

Read the following 1990 prices in Russian:

часы́ (watch)	**21 рубль**
видеомагнитофо́н (video recorder)	**1 200 рубле́й**
мотоци́кл «Ура́л» ('Ural' motorbike)	**1 873 рубля́**
автомоби́ль «Жигули́» ВАЗ 21063 (Zhiguli/Lada car)	**9 000 рубле́й**
цветно́й телеви́зор (colour tv)	**755 рубле́й**
электри́ческнй самова́р (electric samovar)	**52 рубля́**
микрокалькуля́тор (pocket calculator)	**50 рубле́й**
электроми́ксер (electric mixer)	**35 рубле́й**
радиоприёмник (radio)	**36 рубле́й 60 копе́ек**

COMPREHENSION EXERCISE 9/7

1 How long has Mary been in Moscow?

2 How often does she go to the market?

3 Why doesn't she buy more vegetarian food in the foreign currency food shop?

Воло́дя: Ско́лько ме́сяцев вы уже́ в Москве́, Мэ́ри?

Мэ́ри: Уже́ три ме́сяца, и́ли, е́сли то́чно, оди́ннадцать неде́ль и четы́ре дня.

Воло́дя: Как вы живёте? Ведь вы вегетариа́нка, а ру́сские о́чень лю́бят мя́со.

Мэ́ри: Я покупа́ю мно́го проду́ктов на ры́нке. Я хожу́ туда́ два – три ра́за в неде́лю[†]. Иногда́ я хожу́ в валю́тный магази́н «Садко́». Там есть ра́зные моло́чные проду́кты,

мно́го овоще́й и фру́ктов, но́ всё сто́ит до́рого[‡].
Килогра́мм сы́ра сто́ит пять фу́нтов, де́сять яи́ц сто́ят
два фу́нта. Я получа́ю от роди́телей то́лько сто́
два́дцать фу́нтов в ме́сяц, поэ́тому я покупа́ю там о́чень
ма́ло.

[‡]**два–три ра́за в неде́лю**	two or three times a week (lit. 'in week' – accusative, 6.8 (2))
[‡]**всё сто́ит до́рого**	everything costs a lot

10

УРÓК НÓМЕР ДÉСЯТЬ

'TO HAVE'; MORE ON THE GENITIVE

10.1 **Key Phrases**

У вас есть кóфе?	Have you any coffee?
У вас есть дéти?	Have you any children?
Чáя нет.	There's no tea.
У меня́ нет дóлларов.	I have no dollars.
Свобóдных мест нет.	There are no seats left.

10.2 **To Have**

In Russian there is no commonly used verb corresponding to 'to have'. When you want to say 'Have you any children?', you use a construction which literally translates as 'By you is children?' **У вас есть дéти? У** means 'by', **вас** is the genitive form of the word **вы** 'you', **есть** means 'is' in the sense of 'exists', and **дéти** is 'children'.

У вас есть кóфе?	Do you have coffee?
У вас есть вóдка?	Do you have vodka?

The answer could be simply:

Есть.

This is literally 'Is' or 'Exists', but here it corresponds to 'There is' or 'We do.'

У вас есть сын?	Do you have a son?
Есть.	I do.

Or the answer could be **Нет** 'No, I don't'.

If you want to say 'My brother has a car', the structure is the same: **у** + genitive of the possessor + **есть** + thing possessed in the nominative:

У бра́та есть маши́на.	(My) brother has a car. ('By brother is car.')

10.3 **Genitive Pronouns**

The genitive forms of **я, ты** etc. are the same as the accusative forms we met in 6.7: **меня́, тебя́, его́** [ye-vó], **её, его́, нас, вас, их**.

Remember that after a preposition, **его́, её** and **их** have an initial **н**: **него́, неё, них**. Here are examples of the 'have' construction with all the personal pronouns:

У меня́ есть сын.	I have a son.
У тебя́ есть до́ллар?	Do you have a dollar?
У него́ есть жена́?	Does he have a wife?
У неё есть муж?	Does she have a husband?
У нас есть вре́мя.	We have time.
У вас есть де́ньги?	Have you any money?
У них есть де́ти?	Have they any children?

You will also meet the **У вас** construction without the **есть**. For example, **У вас большо́й дом?** 'Is your house large?' In this case you are not being asked whether you have a house, but whether your house is a big one or not. That is, the question with **есть** asks about existence ('Do you or do you not have a house?'); without the **есть**, the question asks about some feature of the thing possessed.

У вас есть сын?	'Do you have a son?' (Does a son exist?')

If you reply, **Да, есть**, the next question might be: **У вас сын большо́й и́ли ма́ленький?** 'Is your son big or small?'

Exercise 10/1

Translate:

1 **У Вади́ма есть жена́?** 2 **У него́ есть ру́сская подру́га.** 3 **У Е́вы есть брат?** 4 **Бра́та у неё нет.** 5 Do you have (any) white wine? 6 They have a daughter and two sons. 7 Does she have (any) money?

10.4 EXTRA: име́ть 'to have'

There is also a verb **име́ть** (**знать**-type): **я име́ю, ты име́ешь** 'to have'. This verb is not used in the everyday sense of possession ('I have a car' is **У меня́ есть маши́на**, *not* **Я име́ю маши́ну**). Instead, it is used with abstract nouns in a number of fixed expressions:

име́ть пра́во 'to have the right'
име́ть ме́сто 'to take place'
име́ть возмо́жность 'to have the opportunity'
име́ть в виду́ 'to have/bear in mind'
име́ть значе́ние 'to matter'

Вы име́ете пра́во. You have the right.
Э́то не име́ет значе́ния (gen.). It doesn't matter.

10.5 There isn't: нет + genitive

The opposite of **есть** 'there is/there exists' is **нет** 'there isn't'. This word looks and sounds the same as the word **нет** meaning 'no', but it is actually a shortened form of the phrase **не есть** 'not there is'.

Whatever there isn't is put in the *genitive* case:

A: **Чай есть?** Is there tea?
B: **Ча́я нет.** There is no tea.

A: **У вас есть са́хар?** Have you any sugar?
B: **Са́хара нет.** There's no sugar/No, we haven't.

Note the idiomatic use of **нет** + person to mean 'not here'.

Вади́ма (gen.) **нет.**	Vadim isn't here/Vadim isn't in.
Её (gen.) **нет до́ма.**	She's not at home.

You may guess that 'I don't have . . .'/'I haven't got . . .' is **У меня́ нет** + genitive:

У меня́ нет дете́й.	I have no children.
У бра́та нет маши́ны.	My brother has no car.

10.6 Prepositions Used with the Genitive

без	without
ко́фе без молока́	coffee without milk, black coffee
для	for
письмо́ для Вади́ма	a letter for Vadim
до	until
до свида́ния	until (our) meeting, goodbye
из	from (out of) – opposite of **в** + acc. ('into')
из Москвы́	from Moscow
оди́н из её друзе́й	one of ('out of') her friends
кро́ме	except
все кро́ме Е́вы	everybody except Eva
ми́мо	past
Мы е́дем ми́мо Лубя́нки.	We're passing the Lubianka (KGB HQ).
о́коло	near/approximately
о́коло до́ма	near the house
от	from (people)
пи́сьма от друзе́й	letters from friends
по́сле	after
по́сле уро́ка	after the lesson
про́тив	opposite, against
про́тив магази́на	opposite the shop
ра́ди	for the sake of
ра́ди дете́й	for the sake of the children
с	from – opposite of **на** + acc. ('on to')

с вокза́л<u>а</u>	from the station
у	by, near; at (someone's place), *chez*
у окн<u>а́</u>	by the window
у нас	in our house/ in our country/ at our place

10.7 **EXTRA: Another Fourteen Prepositions with the Genitive**

близ 'near', **вблизи́** 'near', **вдоль** 'along', **вме́сто** 'instead of', **вне** 'outside', **внутри́** 'inside', **во́зле** 'near', **вокру́г** 'around', **из-за** 'because of', **из-под** 'from under', **накану́не** 'on the eve of', **поми́мо** 'apart from'/'besides', **посреди́** 'in the middle of', **среди́** 'among'/'in the middle of'.

из-за пого́ды	because of the weather
вдоль рек<u>и́</u>	along the river
среди́ друз<u>е́й</u>	among one's friends

10.8 **EXTRA: Partitive¹ ('Some') Genitive**

A minor use of the genitive case is to express the meaning 'some' with food and drink nouns:

Да́йте вод<u>ы́</u>/вин<u>а́</u>/хле́б<u>а</u>. Give me some water/some wine/some bread. (**Да́йте хлеб** corresponds to 'Give me bread' or 'Give me the bread'.)

A small number of nouns have a special **у/ю** ending for the partitive. You may hear the question:

Вы хоти́те ча́ю? Would you like some tea?

Ча́ю, with a special genitive ending **-ю** (an alternative to **-я**), is the partitive¹ genitive of **чай** 'tea'. Other nouns which *may* have this **-у** ending are **са́хар** 'sugar', **мёд** 'honey', **сыр** 'cheese':

ло́жка са́хар<u>у</u> (or **са́хар<u>а</u>**)	a spoonful of sugar

10.9 Genitive of Adjectives

The genitive singular for all adjectives with masculine or neuter nouns is **-ого** or **-его**. The **г** is pronounced [v]. This is the same adjective ending you used with accusative masculine animate nouns in 7.12. With feminine nouns the adjective ending is **-ой** or **-ей**, the same endings as in the prepositional (7.11). Here are the four types of adjective we met in Lesson 7:

но́вый 'new' (all adjectives ending **-ый** or **-о́й**)

письмо́ от но́в<u>ого</u> [nó-va-<u>va</u>] дру́га	a letter from a new friend
и́мя но́в<u>ой</u> подру́ги	the name of the new female friend

ру́сский 'Russian' (all adjectives ending **-гий, -кий, -хий**):

кни́ги из ру́сск<u>ого</u> магази́на	books from a Russian shop
письмо́ от ру́сск<u>ой</u> подру́ги	a letter from a female Russian friend

хоро́ший 'good' (**е** not **о** after Spelling Rule letters **ж, ч, ш, щ, ц**):

Нет хоро́ш<u>его</u> вина́.	There isn't any good wine.
от хоро́ш<u>ей</u> подру́ги	from a good (female) friend

после́дний 'last' (soft adjective – in the nominative they all end **-ний**):

у́тро после́дн<u>его</u> дня	the morning of the last day
до после́дн<u>ей</u> мину́ты	until the last minute

Remember the extra **ь** in **тре́тий** 'third' (7.6)

у́тро тре́т<u>ьего</u> дня	the morning of the third day
из тре́т<u>ьей</u> кварти́ры	from the third flat (flat three)

EXERCISE 10/2

Put the required endings on the words in brackets and translate:

1 Мэ́ри получа́ет пи́сьма от (ру́сский друг). 2 О́коло (Большо́й теа́тр) есть ста́нция метро́. 3 (Воло́дя) нет до́ма. 4 Для (друзья́) мы покупа́ем буты́лку (хоро́шее вино́). 5 Сего́дня по́сле (рабо́та) все, кро́ме (Са́ша), иду́т в теа́тр. 6 Пожа́луйста, да́йте два (килогра́мм) (све́жая колбаса́).

10.10 Genitive Plural of Adjectives

Unlike nouns, the adjective endings are as usual simple and regular and the same for all genders: **-ых** for the **но́вый/друго́й** types and **-их** for all the others:

У нас нет но́в<u>ых</u> книг.	We have no new books.
от ру́сск<u>их</u> друзе́й	from Russian friends
цена́ хоро́ш<u>их</u> я́блок	the price of good apples
ми́мо после́дн<u>их</u> домо́в	past the last houses
Свобо́дн<u>ых</u> мест нет.	There are no free places. (There are no seats left.)

10.11 Genitive of Possessives and Demonstratives

Мо́й/тво́й/наш/ваш have adjective endings which are the same as those of **хоро́ший**: **-его/-ей** in the singular and **-их** in the plural:

У мо<u>его́</u> (NB stress) бра́та нет де́нег.	My brother has no money.
без тво<u>е́й</u> жены́	without your wife
кварти́ра на́<u>шего</u> дру́га	our friend's flat
письмо́ от мо<u>и́х</u> ру́сских друзе́й	a letter from my Russian friends
имена́ ва́<u>ших</u> дете́й	the names of your children

Э́тот and **тот** have the adjective endings of **но́вый** in the singular (**э́<u>того</u>/э́<u>той</u>, <u>того́</u>** (NB stress)/**<u>той</u>**), but in the genitive plural **э́тот** has **э́т<u>их</u>** and **тот** has **т<u>ех</u>** i.e. the n.pl. endings (8.8) plus **x**.

ми́мо э́<u>того</u> но́в<u>ого</u> до́ма	past this new house
до <u>того́</u> дня	until that day
от э́<u>той</u>/<u>той</u> де́вушки	from this/that girl
цена́ э́т<u>их</u> я́блок	the price of these apples
от т<u>ех</u> де́вушек	from those girls

EXERCISE 10/3

Translate:

1 У ва́ших ру́сских друзе́й есть де́ти? 2 Почему́ у вас нет све́жих фру́ктов? 3 Óколо на́шего до́ма есть институ́т иностра́нных языко́в. 4 Их нет до́ма. 5 Here is a letter from my Russian (female) friend. 6 A kilo of these large apples, please. 7 We have a few (9.12) books for your friends. 8 Two bottles of red wine and one bottle of Russian vodka. 9 He has a lot of interesting books. 10 We have no Russian money.

10.12 Accusative Plural of Animates = Genitive Plural

In 8/2 it was mentioned that all *animate* nouns (people and animals) of whatever gender have special endings in the accusative plural. These endings, and the endings of any accompanying adjectives, possessives and demonstratives, are the *same as the endings of the genitive plural*.

Я люблю́ ру́сских де́вушек.   I love Russian girls.

  ру́сских де́вушек also means 'of Russian girls'

Мы зна́ем э́тих америка́нцев.   We know these Americans.

  э́тих америка́нцев also means 'of these Americans'

Éва лю́бит англи́йских соба́к_.   Eva loves English dogs.

10.13 Adjectives with Numerals

There are no surprises with **оди́н** or numerals which are followed by the genitive plural:

Я зна́ю шестьдеся́т одно́ ру́сское (nom.sg.) **сло́во** (nom.sg.) I know 61
  Russian words

пять но́вых (gen.pl.) **слов** (gen.pl.) five new words

But after **два, три, четы́ре,** nouns are in the *genitive singular* (9.5) and any adjectives are in the *genitive plural* with masculine and neuter nouns and in the *nominative plural* with feminine ones:

два иностра́нных (gen.pl.) **языка́** (gen.sg.) two foreign languages

три но́вых (gen.pl.) **сло́ва** (gen.sg.) three new words
две краси́вые (nom.pl.) **де́вушки** (gen.sg.) two pretty girls
четы́ре но́вые (nom.pl.) **кни́ги** (gen.sg.) four new books

The grammar of Russian numerals has other intriguing complications. For details see Lesson 22.

EXERCISE 10/4

Put the required endings on the words in brackets:

1 Она́ зна́ет (мои́ америка́нские друзья́). 2 Три́дцать пять (америка́нский до́ллар). 3 Она́ покупа́ет пять (больша́я буты́лка) со́ка и (одна́ ма́ленькая буты́лка) вина́. 4 Мэ́ри зна́ет три (иностра́нный язы́к).

10.14 **EXTRA 2, 3, 4 with Feminine Adjectives**

Note: It is permissible to use the genitive plural with feminine nouns too, which makes things a little simpler: **две молоды́х де́вушки**. However, Russians prefer to use the *nominative* plural of adjectives with all those feminine nouns whose genitive singular is identical to the nominative plural – **де́вушки** (gen.sg. 'of a girl') = **де́вушки** (nom.pl. 'girls'). Those feminine nouns which have different stresses in the genitive singular and nominative plural (e.g. **реки́** 'of a river' – **ре́ки** 'rivers') are more likely to have genitive adjectives: **две ру́сских** (gen.pl.) **реки́** (gen.sg.) 'two Russian rivers'.

10.15 **Question Word ли 'whether'**

Yes/no questions (5.3) can also be asked with **ли** (a particle¹ you will meet again with the meaning 'whether'). No question intonation is required, so you may prefer it if you have difficulty getting used to the rise–fall intonation pattern described in 5.3. The question particle **ли** is always the *second* item in the question. A typical example is:

Нет ли у вас . . .	Don't you have . . . ?
Нет ли у вас до́лларов?	You wouldn't have dollars, would you?

This question is an alternative way of asking:

У вас нет до́лларов? with rise–fall on **нет**.

Other examples:

Бы́ли ли вы в Москве́?	Have you been to Moscow?
(Cf. **Вы бы́ли в Москве́?** with rise–fall on **бы́ли**)	
Éсть ли у вас «Пра́вда»?	Do you have *Pravda*?
(Cf. **У вас есть «Пра́вда»?** with rise–fall on **есть**)	
Говори́те ли вы по-ру́сски?	Do you speak Russian?
Нет ли у них све́жих фру́ктов?	Don't they have any fresh fruit?

Note the colloquial phrase **что ли**) 'is it?'/'am I?'/'are you?' etc., (expressing surprise or hesitation), always placed at the end.

Сто́ до́лларов, что ли?	A hundred dollars, is it?
Óн ру́сский, что ли?	He's a Russian, is he?

10.16 Vocabulary

авиаконве́рт airmail envelope
англи́йский English
бана́н banana
без + gen. without
биле́т ticket
брать + acc. to take
  я беру́, ты берёшь
всё (from **весь** 'all') everything
буфе́т snackbar
вещь (f) gen.pl. **веще́й** thing
всего́ in all/only
вчера́ yesterday
де́ти, (sing. **ребён(о)к**) children
  gen.pl. **дете́й**

для + gen. for
зна́чит so (that means)
из + gen. out of, from
иностра́нный foreign
к сожале́нию unfortunately
ка́рта map
конве́рт envelope
коне́чно [ka-nyésh-na] of course
кро́ме + gen. apart from, except
ли (question word); whether
  что ли? am I? is it? etc. – see
  10.15
ма́рка gen.pl. **ма́рок** stamp
маши́на car; machine

116

ми́мо + gen. past

напро́тив opposite (place adverb)

нет + gen. there isn't/there aren't

неудо́бно it's awkward

о́коло + gen. near; approximately

пиро́г (**из** + gen.) (large) pie (made of) (**пирожо́к** small pie)

по́сле + gen. after

посмотри́те look (imperative)

почто́вый postage (adj)

прия́тный pleasant

про́сто simply

про́тив + gen. opposite

путеводи́тель (m) guidebook

ра́ди + gen. for the sake of

разгово́р conversation

разме́р size, dimension

ры́ба fish

ры́бный fish (adj)

с + gen. off, from

свобо́дный free

сего́дня у́тром [sye-<u>v</u>ód-nya] this morning

сли́шком too (excessively)

слова́рь (m) gen.sg. **словаря́** dictionary

соба́ка dog

совсе́м completely

совсе́м нет + gen. none at all

со́к juice

специа́льно specially

сре́дний average; middle

сто́лько + gen. so much, so many

сюрпри́з surprise

так как since (because)

тако́й such

у + gen. near; by

цена́ pl. **це́ны** price

You have now met about 350 Russian words. If you feel you've forgotten most of them, that's normal. Just go back and learn them again. Once you've made the first few hundred stick, it then gets easier and easier to learn new ones.

10.17 **Разгово́ры в буфе́те и в магази́не** Snackbar and Shop Conversations

(1)

А: **У вас есть чай?**

Б: **Нет, но́ есть со́к.**

А: **А ко́фе есть?**

Б: **Есть.**

(2)

А: **Есть ли у вас бана́ны?**

Б: **Нет. Бана́нов нет.**

А: А что́ же у вас есть?

Б: Есть я́блоки. Други́х фру́ктов нет.

(3)

А: А что́ у вас есть вы́пить[‡]?

Б: Вино́. Бе́лое, кра́сное. Во́дки нет.

А: Пожа́луйста, да́йте буты́лку бе́лого вина́.

Б: Пожа́луйста.

[‡]Что́ у вас есть вы́пить? What have you got to drink (alcohol)?

На по́чте At the Post Office

А: Скажи́те, пожа́луйста, нет ли у вас авиаконве́ртов?

Б: Есть.

А: А ско́лько сто́ит тако́й конве́рт?

Б: Авиаконве́рт сто́ит пятьдеся́т четы́ре копе́йки.

А: Пожа́луйста, два конве́рта.

Б: Оди́н рубль во́семь копе́ек.

А: Хорошо́.

In the Map Section

А: Скажи́те, пожа́луйста, у вас есть план го́рода?

Б: К сожале́нию, сейча́с нет, но́ есть путеводи́тель.

А: А ка́рты Росси́и есть?

Б: Ка́рты есть. Посмотри́те во́т э́ту.

А: Нет, э́та ка́рта сли́шком ма́ленькая. У вас нет большо́й ка́рты?

Б: Больши́х нет. Но́ есть во́т така́я, сре́дних разме́ров.

А: Хорошо́. Я беру́ э́ту. Ско́лько она́ сто́ит?

Б: Четы́рнадцать копе́ек.

А: Всего́ четы́рнадцать копе́ек! Так ма́ло! Како́й прия́тный сюрпри́з!

В ры́бном магази́не In the Fish Shop (a Typical Shortage Joke)

Покупа́тель[‡]:   Скажи́те, пожа́луйста, у вас нет мя́са?

Продаве́ц: Нет, э́то ры́бный магази́н. У нас нет ры́бы. Мя́са нет в магази́не напро́тив.

[‡]Customer ('buyer').

10.18 **Signs (Everyday Genitives)**

Свобо́дных мест нет.	There are no free seats (restaurant).
ме́сто 'place', 'seat'	
Биле́тов нет.	There are no tickets left.
биле́т 'ticket'	
Отде́л зака́зов	Orders Section (Section of Orders) –
зака́з 'order'	part of a shop where certain categories of people (e.g. war veterans, mothers of large families) may order scarce goods
Ме́сто для куре́ния	Place for Smoking (Smoking Permitted
куре́ние 'smoking'	here)
Ко́мната ма́тери и ребёнка	Mother and Child Room in stations and
мать 'mother'	airports (for changing nappies etc.)
ребён(о)к 'child'	
у́лица Чайко́вского [a-va]	Chaikovskii Street (Street of Chaikovskii)
Ка́мера хране́ния	Left luggage room (room of keeping)
хране́ние 'keeping'	

COMPREHENSION EXERCISE 10/5 (Translation in Key)

1 What has Vadim borrowed from Eva's parents in the last two days?
2 Does Eva have any brothers?
3 Does Eva's mother like Vadim?

Вади́м: Нет ли у тебя́ почто́вых ма́рок? У меня́ три письма́ для
англи́йских друзе́й, но совсе́м нет ма́рок.

Е́ва: У меня́ то́лько две шестикопе́ечные‡ ма́рки. Спроси́‡ у
мои́х роди́телей.

Вади́м: Неудо́бно. Я беру́ у‡ них сто́лько ра́зных веще́й – вчера́
не́сколько англи́йских газе́т, сего́дня у́тром два
англи́йских словаря́ . . .

Е́ва: Так как у них нет сы́на, ты для них – как сын. Ты
име́ешь‡ пра́во брать всё, что ты хо́чешь‡.

Вади́м: А для тебя́ я кто – тво́й брат, что́ ли?

Éва: Нет, коне́чно. Ты про́сто оди́н из мои́х друзе́й.

Вади́м: Спаси́бо. Зна́чит, я про́сто оди́н из твои́х друзе́й. Но́ меня́ лю́бят твои́ роди́тели.

Éва: Да, сего́дня ма́ма де́лает пиро́г из све́жих я́блок, специа́льно для тебя́.

‡**Extra Vocabulary**

‡**шестикопе́ечный** six-kopeck (adj)

‡**Спроси́ у мои́х роди́телей.** Ask my parents ('Ask at my parents').

‡**Я беру́ у них.** I borrow from them ('I take at them').

‡**ты име́ешь пра́во** you have the right (10.4)

‡**всё, что ты хо́чешь** everything that you want

EXERCISE 10/6
REVISION OF LESSONS 6–10

You should be able to say the following in Russian:

1 I don't understand.
2 Do you speak English?
3 Do you live in Moscow?
4 Do you know where the post office is?
5 He doesn't speak Russian.
6 Thank you for the letter.
7 What are her name and patronymic?
8 I'm going to Red Square.
9 I'm not very fond of Borodin.
10 I think that McDonald's (**Макдо́налдс**) is in Pushkin Square.
11 My friends live in this street.
12 Twenty-five dollars.
13 There is the house of my friend Ivan.
14 There is no milk today.
15 Have you any English books?
16 Excuse me, do you have any coffee?

17 I have many Russian friends.
18 Natasha has two small sons.
19 Give me a bottle of good white wine, please.
20 Do you know these girls?

11

УРÓК НÓМЕР ОДИ́ННАДЦАТЬ

THE PAST; REFLEXIVE VERBS

11.1 Key Phrases

Вы бы́ли в Лóндоне?	Have you been in London?
Я не знал.	I didn't know (man speaking).
Я не зна́ла.	I didn't know (woman speaking).
Как э́то называ́ется?	What ('How') is this called?

11.2 Talking about the Past

Ива́н был здесь вчера́.	Ivan was here yesterday.
Ната́ша была́ в Пари́же.	Natasha was in Paris.

When you want to talk about the past in English, you use forms like 'I *was*', 'She *knew*', 'We *were talking*', 'I *have been*' to Moscow'. These verb forms are all forms of the past tense. The past tense of verbs is very easy in Russian, much easier than the present tense. To make the past tense of most verbs, there are two simple steps. First, you take off the **-ть** of the dictionary form (the infinitive, corresponding to 'to know') and replace it with **-л**. Second, you make the ending match (agree with) the gender (m, f or n) and number (singular or plural) of the subject, according to the following table:

m sing	f sing	n sing	m/f/n plural
-л	**-ла**	**-ло**	**-ли**

So the past tense of **знать** 'to know' is:

óн знал	**онá знáла**	**онó знáло**	**они́ знáли**
he knew	she knew	it knew	they knew

óн не знал
he didn't know

Other examples

рабóта/ть 'to work' **я рабóтал, я рабóтала, мы рабóтали** 'worked'
продавá/ть 'to sell' **я продавáл, я продавáла, вы продавáли** 'sold'
жи/ть 'to live' **я жил, я жилá, óн жил, онá жилá** 'lived'

быть 'to be', which does not have a normal present tense, forms its past tense like any other verb:

óн был	**онá былá**	**онó бы́ло**	**они́ бы́ли**
he was	she was	it was	they were
	(NB stress)		

Remember that the gender of the subject must be shown if the subject is singular. So if you are a man, your past tense forms end **-л**, but if you are a woman, the past tense forms of all your verbs end **-ла**. So if you want to say 'I was in Moscow', the Russian will be

either **Я был в Москвé** (man speaking)
  or **Я былá в Москвé** (woman speaking)

And if you're using **ты**, the verb ending will also depend on the sex of the person you're talking to:

Ты был в Лóндоне? Were you (man) in London?
Ты былá в Лóндоне? Were you (woman) in London?

However, **вы** always takes a plural past tense ending, even if you are talking to one person:

Иван Петрóвич, вы бы́ли в Сиби́ри? Ivan Petrovich, have you been
  in Siberia?

Here is the complete list with **быть**:

я был (m), **я былá** (f) I was
ты был (m), **ты былá** (f) you were (fam)

óн был	he was
онá былá	she was
онó бы́ло	it was
мы бы́ли	we were
вы бы́ли	you were (pol./pl.)

Remember **вы** always takes plural past tense endings, even if you are talking to one person.

| они́ бы́ли | they were |

Note that the negative forms of **быть** have an unusual stress pattern. The stress moves to the **не** *except* in the feminine:

я <u>не</u> был	I wasn't (m)
я не былá	I wasn't (f)
онó <u>не</u> было	it wasn't
мы <u>не</u> были	we weren't

11.3 Past of есть and нет 'there isn't'

Since **есть** 'there is/are' is the present tense of **быть**, the past-tense forms of **есть** are those of **быть**:

| У нас есть дóллары. | We have dollars (10.2). |
| У нас бы́ли дóллары. | We had dollars ('By us were dollars'). |

The past of **нет** + genitive is **не́ было** (note stress) + genitive

Нет чáя.	There's no tea (10.5).
Не́ было чáя.	There was no tea.
У нас совсéм не́ было дóлларов.	We had no dollars at all.

11.4 **EXTRA: Stress of the Past Tense**

As a general rule, if the infinitive has only one syllable (**жить, брать**), the feminine form will be stressed on the **-á** (**онá жилá**, 'she lived'; **онá бралá** 'she took'), while the other forms will be stressed on the stem (**они́** жи́ли, они́ бра́ли). **Знать** is an exception: **она́ зна́ла** 'she knew'. Where the stress moves, this will be shown in the vocabularies.

Longer verbs (**продава́ть** 'to sell') are likely to have fixed stress (**она́ продава́ла** 'she sold'). But verbs with prefixes (Lesson 19) normally have the same stress pattern as the root verb; so **избра́ть** 'to pick out', 'to elect' has the past tense **она́ избрала́** 'she elected' because it is derived from the verb **брать** 'to take', which has the past tense **она́ брала́** 'she took'.

The shift of the stress to **не́** with **быть** (see examples above) is found with a small number of one-syllable verbs, e.g. **жить** 'to live' (**он не́ жил, мы не́ жили**) and **дать** 'to give' (12.7), but the only important one is **быть**, because its negative forms are so common.

11.5 Exceptional Verbs

If the infinitive ends in something other than **-ть** (e.g. **идти́** 'to go' 6.9, **мочь** 'to be able' 11.8), then the masculine singular past tense stem cannot easily be predicted (the m past of **мочь** is **мо́г** 'was able'). However, once you know the masculine form, the other forms always end **-ла, -ло, -ли**:

мочь 'to be able' **я мо́г, я могла́, оно́ могло́, они́ могли́** (was able, could)

Note the odd past tense of **идти́** 'to go on foot', which has both an unexpected stem **ш(ё)** and a fleeting vowel.

он шёл, она́ шла́, оно́ шло́, они́ шли 'he/she/it/they was/were going'

No other Russian verb has such a difference of stem between the infinitive and the past tense.

EXERCISE 11/1

Make the verbs in brackets past tense and translate:

1 Ива́н (быть) в Москве́.
2 Ма́ша то́же (быть) в Москве́.
3 Я (быть) в Ки́еве два дня.

4 Они́ (рабо́тать) весь день.

5 Я (рабо́тать) вчера́.

6 Вы (знать), что она́ (быть) в Берли́не?

7 Вы (ви́деть 'to see') моего́ му́жа?

8 Она́ не (мочь) рабо́тать.

9 Мы (идти́) ме́дленно.

10 Когда́ я (ви́деть) его́, он (идти́) в магази́н.

11 У вас (есть) друзья́ в Москве́?

12 У неё (есть) ру́сский друг.

13 В буфе́те (нет) молока́.

14 У нас (нет) ру́сских де́нег.

11.6 Reflexive¹ Verbs

Many Russian verbs have a suffix **-ся**, which is short for **себя́**, meaning 'self' (21.4). Our example is **одева́ться** [a-dye-vá-tsa] 'to dress oneself'. Note that **-ться** is always pronounced [tsa]. These verbs are called reflexive¹. The suffix **-ся** (pronounced [sa] after **т**), which becomes **сь** [s'] after a vowel, is simply added to the endings you already know (present tense – Lesson 4; past tense above).

Одева́ть 'to dress (someone)' has the **знать**-type endings **одева́ю**, **одева́ешь**, so the endings of **одева́ться** 'to dress oneself' are:

я одева́юсь I dress myself   **мы одева́емся** we dress ourselves
[a-dye-vá-yoos']   [a-dye-vá-yem-sya]

ты одева́ешься you dress yourself   **вы одева́етесь** you dress yourself
[a-dye-vá-yesh-sya]   [a-dye-vá-ye-tyes']

он одева́ется he dresses himself   **они́ одева́ются** they dress themselves
[a-dye-vá-ye-<u>tsa</u>]   [a-dye-vá-yoo-<u>tsa</u>]

Она́ одева́ет ма́льчика. She dresses the boy.
Она́ одева́ется краси́во. She dresses (herself) well.

The past tense works in the same way (**ся** added after consonants, **сь** after vowels):

я одева́лся I dressed myself (man speaking)
я одева́лась I dressed myself (woman speaking)
мы одева́лись we dressed ourselves

In English we often omit the 'self' ('I dressed') but in Russian the **-ся** is not optional. Apart from **одева́ться, мы́ться** 'to wash oneself' (**я мо́юсь, ты мо́ешься**), **бри́ться** 'to shave (oneself)' (**я бре́юсь, ты бре́ешься**), there are a large number of verbs which have a reflexive suffix **-ся** for no obvious reason:

улыба́ться	to smile
улыба́юсь, улыба́ешься	
смея́ться	to laugh
смею́сь, смеёшься	
серди́ться	to be angry
сержу́сь, се́рдишься	
руга́ться	to swear
руга́юсь, руга́ешься	

You simply have to learn that these verbs have **-ся** suffixes, even though there is no meaning of 'self'.

Another common use of **-ся** is with verbs like **открыва́ть** 'to open', **закрыва́ть** 'to close', **начина́ть** 'to begin', when they are used 'intransitively', that is, the thing which opens, closes, or begins is made the subject of the sentence and there is no object in the accusative case. Compare transitive¹ (a) with intransitive¹ (b):

(a) **Ива́н начина́ет конце́рт.** Ivan begins the concert.
(b) **Конце́рт начина́ется.** The concert begins ('itself').

Конце́рт начина́ет . . . is an incomplete construction to a Russian, who expects to hear an object in the accusative case or a following verb, e.g. **Конце́рт начина́ет надоеда́ть** 'The concert begins to bore' or **Конце́рт начина́ет но́вую се́рию** 'The concert begins a new series'; if there is no following noun or infinitive, then the reflexive ending is added 'The concert begins itself' (**Конце́рт начина́ется**). This structure is common with verbs (e.g. **открыва́ть** 'to open') which are normally followed by an accusative noun ('He opens the door') or an infinitive verb ('He continues to talk') but which can also be used with an inanimate noun as subject ('The door opens'):

Я открыва́ю дверь.	I open the door.
Дверь открыва́ется.	The door opens.
Мы продолжа́ем уро́к.	We continue the lesson.

Уро́к продолжа́ет<u>ся</u>.	The lesson continues.
Мы продолжа́ем рабо́тать.	We continue to work.
Рабо́та продолжа́ет<u>ся</u>.	The work continues.

11.7 Common Phrases with Reflexive Verbs

Когда́ открыва́ется магази́н?	When does the shop open?
ка́жется . . .	it seems (often corresponding to
(from **каза́ться** 'to seem')	'I think')
Ка́жется, о́н до́ма.	I think he's at home.
Каза́лось . . .	It seemed . . .
О́н, каза́лось, серди́лся.	He seemed to be angry.
	('He, it seemed, was angry.')
Сади́тесь.	Take a seat. (Sit yourself down.)
(**сади́ться** 'to sit down')	
Как э́то называ́ется?	What is this called? (What does this
(**называ́ться** 'to be called' of	call itself?)
things, not people)	
Раздева́йтесь.	Take your coat off. (Undress
(**раздева́ться** 'to undress')	yourself.)
Наде́юсь.	I hope (so).
(**надея́ться** 'to hope')	
Не толка́йтесь.	Don't push.
(**толка́ться** 'to push', ' to shove')	

EXERCISE 11/2

Translate the verbs:

1 **Почему́ О́ля не** (smiles)? 2 **Мы** (got dressed). 3 **Дверь** (opens).
4 **Две́ри** (opened). 5 **Когда́** (begins) **фильм?**

128

11.8 **Vocabulary**

Балти́йское мо́ре Baltic Sea
боле́знь (f) disease
быть (only present form **есть**) to be
вели́кий great
весь gen. pl. **всех** (Table 4) all
ви́деть: ви́жу, ви́дишь to see
всё равно́ nevertheless, all the
same
все (pl. of **весь**) everybody
до́ждь (m) gen.sg. **дождя́** rain
до́лго for a long time
заходи́те come in (to guest)
из-за (+ gen.) because of
извини́те за (+ acc.) excuse me
for
иска́ть (+ acc. or gen.): **ищу́,
и́щешь** to look for, to seek
ка́жется [ká-zhe-tsa] it seems,
I think
кино́ (n indecl) cinema
конце́рт concert
на конце́рте at a concert
красота́ beauty
крестья́нин nom.pl. **крестья́не**
peasant
gen. pl. **крестья́н**
ма́ма mother, mum(my)
мо́чь: могу́, мо́жешь, мо́гут to
be able
(past **мо́г, могла́, могло́,
могли́**)
называ́ть (+ acc.) (like **знать**) to
name (sth)
называ́ться [na-zi-vá-tsa] to be
called (of thing, not person)

начина́ть(ся) (11.6) (like **знать**)
to begin
**наде́яться: наде́юсь,
наде́ешься** to hope
Нева́ Neva River
неда́вно recently
ничего́! [nee-chye-vó] it doesn't
matter/that's all right
ничего́ [nee-chye-vó] не + verb
nothing
ну́жно it's necessary
одева́ть(ся) (like **знать**) (11.6) to
dress (oneself)
ожида́ть (+ gen.) (like **знать**) to
expect (something/someone)
опозда́ние lateness
открыва́ть(ся) (like **знать**) (11.6)
to open
по́рт prep. **в порту́** port
пра́вда truth
Пра́вда? Is that so?
продолжа́ть(ся) (like **знать**)
(11.6) to continue
проходи́те go through (imper)
про́шлый previous, last
в про́шлом году́ last year
раздева́йтесь take your coat off
серди́ться: сержу́сь, се́рдишься
to be angry
слы́шать: слы́шу, слы́шишь to
hear
смея́ться: смею́сь, смеёшься to
laugh
смотре́ть (+ acc.) to watch; to
look at (the content of)

смотрю́, смо́тришь
смотре́ть на (+ acc.) to look at
(the surface of)
сосе́д pl. сосе́ди gen.pl. сосе́дей
neighbour
стоя́ть: стою́, стои́шь to stand
стро́ить: стро́ю, стро́ишь to
build
стро́иться to be built ('build itself')
та́почки gen.pl. та́почек slippers
тума́н mist, fog

уже́ нет (+ gen.) there is/are
no more
улыба́ться [oo-li-bá-tsa] to smile
улыба́юсь, улыба́ешься
фильм film
хо́лод cold
час hour
в семь часо́в at seven o'clock
шу́тка gen.pl. шу́ток joke
Эрмита́ж the Hermitage
(St Petersburg museum)

11.9 Диало́ги

(1)

ВП: Вы бы́ли в Петербу́рге?

Е́ва: Да. В про́шлом году́. Я была́ там четы́ре дня.

ВП: Что́ вы там ви́дели?

Е́ва: Я ви́дела Не́вский проспе́кт, Неву́, Петропа́вловскую
кре́пость, была́ в Эрмита́же, коне́чно. Я не зна́ла, что́
Петербу́рг тако́й краси́вый го́род. Я мно́го слы́шала об
э́том го́роде, но всё равно́ я не ожида́ла тако́й красоты́.

(2)

Е́ва: Когда́ начина́ется конце́рт?

Вади́м: Ка́жется, в семь часо́в. Почему́ ты улыба́ешься?

Е́ва: Я зна́ю, что́ биле́тов уже́ нет. Но в кино́ идёт хоро́ший
америка́нский фильм. Ма́ма вчера́ смотре́ла. Она́
говори́т, что́ все смея́лись.

(3)

КМ: Ми́лости про́сим[‡]! Заходи́те! Раздева́йтесь. Во́т та́почки.

АБ: Кла́ра Миха́йловна, извини́те за опозда́ние. Наде́юсь, вы
не се́рдитесь. Я о́чень до́лго иска́ла такси́.

КМ: Ничего́, ничего́. Проходи́те, пожа́луйста.

АБ: Свобо́дных маши́н не́ было совсе́м. Я не зна́ла, что́ де́лать.

КМ:	Познако́мьтесь, э́то наш сосе́д, Влади́мир Петро́вич. О́н неда́вно был в Ло́ндоне.
АБ:	О́чень прия́тно. Меня́ зову́т А́нна Бори́совна. А что́ вы там ви́дели?
ВП:	К сожале́нию, из-за тума́на я ничего́ не ви́дел.
АБ:	Пра́вда? Почему́ вы смеётесь?
ВП:	Э́то шу́тка, коне́чно. Тума́нов не́ было. Но́ постоя́нно шёл до́ждь.

‡ми́лости про́сим! welcome! (to guests)

COMPREHENSION EXERCISE 11/3

(Translation in key)

Основа́ние Петербу́рга The Founding of St Petersburg (1703)

1 Was St Petersburg founded on a completely empty site?
2 What hardships did the peasant labour force endure?

Ру́сский царь Пётр Вели́кий счита́л, что́ ну́жно стро́ить но́вый по́рт на Балти́йском мо́ре. Э́то го́род Санкт-Петербу́рг, и́ли Петербу́рг, как его́ обы́чно называ́ют. Э́то но́вое «окно́ в Евро́пу»‡ стро́или на реке́ Неве́, где на о́строве‡ уже́ стоя́ла Петропа́вловская‡ кре́пость.

Петербу́рг стро́ился бы́стро. Для постро́йки‡ го́рода со всех концо́в‡ Росси́и ка́ждый го́д посыла́ли ты́сячи крестья́н. Они́ рабо́тали в хо́лоде, постоя́нно шёл до́ждь и дул ве́тер. Они́ стоя́ли по коле́ни‡ в воде́ и грязи́. Ка́ждый го́д ты́сячи люде́й погиба́ли‡ от боле́зней, го́лода и непоси́льного‡ труда́.

‡Extra vocabulary (less common words and phrases, not worth learning at this stage). In alphabetical order:

вет(е)р wind	**дуть** to blow
го́лод hunger	**со всех концо́в (кон(е́)ц** end)
грязь (f) mud	from all corners ('ends')
в грязи́ in mud	

непоси́льный excessive, over-demanding

«онко́ в Евро́пу» window on ('into') Europe

о́стров pl. **острова́** island

Петропа́вловская кре́пость Peter and Paul Fortress

по коле́ни up to (their) knees

погиба́ть to perish

постро́йка construction

посыла́ть to send

счита́ть [shshee-tátʲ] to consider

труд labour, work

12

УРÓК НÓМЕР ДВЕНÁДЦАТЬ

THE FUTURE; ASPECT;
THE DATIVE CASE

12.1 Useful Phrases

Я позвонЮ́ зáвтра.	I'll phone tomorrow.
Я приéду в срéду.	I'll come on Wednesday.
Вы нам скáжете?	Will you tell us?
Я хочÚ пойтú в Кремль.	I want to go to the Kremlin.
Москвá мне нрáвится.	I like Moscow.

12.2 Aspect: Imperfective (ⁱ) and Perfective (ᵖ) Verbs

If you look up any verb, e.g. 'to write', in an English–Russian dictionary, you will usually find *two* Russian verbs. 'To telephone' is both **звонúть** and **позвонúть**. **Звонúть** is called the *imperfective aspect* form of this verb, and **позвонúть** is called the *perfective aspect* form. The imperfective and perfective forms are usually, but not always, fairly similar to look at.

All the verbs you have met so far in this book (apart from some imperative[t] forms) have been imperfective. From now on imperfectives will be marked ⁱ, and perfectives ᵖ.

The present tense is always formed from imperfective verbs. The future is most often formed from perfective verbs, as in this lesson. The meaning of the two aspects, their use in the past tense, and the imperfective future are dealt with in Lessons 13 and 14.

12.3 Future Tense

A major use of perfective verbs is the formation of the future tense. If you
add to perfective verbs the same verb endings which you met with imperfective verbs in Lesson 4, the meaning is future.

звони́ть¹ to telephone	позвони́ть^p to telephone
present tense	future tense
я звоню́ I phone/am phoning	я позвоню́ I'll phone
ты звони́шь you phone	ты позвони́шь you'll phone
о́н звони́т he phones	о́н позвони́т he'll phone
мы звони́м we phone	мы позвони́м we'll phone
вы звони́те you phone	вы позвони́те you'll phone
они́ звоня́т they phone	они́ позвоня́т they'll phone

Another example

The perfective of **отдыха́ть**¹ 'to rest' is **отдохну́ть**^p. **Отдохну́ть**^p is a
жить- type verb with the stem **отдохн-**. So:

я отдыха́ю is 'I rest' and **я отдохну́** is 'I shall rest'/'I'll take a rest'
ты отдыха́ешь 'you rest' **ты отдохнёшь** 'you'll rest'

12.4 More Pairs of Imperfective and Perfective Verbs

Notice that a perfective (e.g. **пое́хать**^p) formed from an imperfective
(**е́хать**¹) by the addition of a prefix (**по-** in this case) always has the same
conjugation (endings) as the imperfective:

де́лать¹ to do	сде́лать^p
я де́лаю, ты де́лаешь I do etc.	я сде́лаю, ты сде́лаешь I'll do etc.
идти́¹ to go on foot	пойти́^p
я иду́, ты идёшь I go etc.	я пойду́, ты пойдёшь I'll go etc.
е́хать¹ to go by transport	пое́хать^p
я е́ду, ты е́дешь I go etc.	я пое́ду, ты пое́дешь I'll go etc.
пока́зывать¹ to show	показа́ть^p
я пока́зываю, ты пока́зываешь	я покажу́, ты пока́жешь I'll show etc.

покупа́ть¹ to buy	купи́ть ᵖ
я покупа́ю, ты покупа́ешь	я куплю́, ты ку́пишь I'll buy
ви́деть¹ to see	уви́деть ᵖ
я ви́жу, ты ви́дишь	я уви́жу, ты уви́дишь I'll see
помога́ть¹ to help	помо́чь ᵖ
я помога́ю, ты помога́ешь	я помогу́, ты помо́жешь, они́ помо́гут I'll help
дава́ть¹ to give (stem да-)	дать ᵖ (irregular verb)
я даю́, ты даёшь	я дам, ты дашь, он даст, мы дади́м, вы дади́те, они́ даду́т

Мы идём¹ на Кра́сную пло́щадь.	We're going to Red Square.
Мы пойдём ᵖ на Кра́сную пло́щадь.	We'll go to Red Square.
Я ви́жу¹ её ка́ждый день.	I see her every day.
Я уви́жу ᵖ её за́втра.	I'll see her tomorrow.
Они́ не помога́ют.¹	They're not helping.
Они́ не помо́гут.ᵖ	They won't help.

Very occasionally, the i and p partners look very different:

говори́ть¹ to say	сказа́ть ᵖ
я говорю́, ты говори́шь	я скажу́, ты ска́жешь I'll say
брать¹ to take	взять ᵖ
я беру́, ты берёшь	я возьму́, ты возьмёшь I'll take

Она́ говори́т¹ «спаси́бо».	She says 'thank you'.
Она́ ска́жет ᵖ «спаси́бо».	She'll say 'thank you'.
Мы берём¹ шампа́нское.	We're taking champagne.
Мы возьмём ᵖ шампа́нское.	We'll take champagne.

EXERCISE 12/1

Translate into Russian:

1 I'll help. 2 Will you help? 3 We'll see her tomorrow. 4 We'll go to Red Square. 5 They won't go (by transport). 6 I'll buy this book. 7 We shall rest. 8 He won't come. 9 I'm taking this book. 10 I'll say two words.

12.5 Хоте́ть[i] 'to want'

There are very few irregular (unpredictable) verb conjugations in Russian (though there are plenty of awkward infinitives). One unpredictable verb is **хоте́ть**, which has **е́хать**-type endings in the singular and **говори́ть**- type in the plural:

я хочу́	I want	**мы хоти́м**	we want
ты хо́чешь	you (fam) want	**вы хоти́те**	you (pol./pl.) want
он хо́чет	he wants	**они́ хотя́т**	they want

Most commonly this verb is used with an infinitive ('I want to go to the circus'). If what you want to do is a single event, use the *perfective* infinitive:

Я хочу́ пойти́[p] **в Эрмита́ж.**	I want to go to the Hermitage.
Я хочу́ пое́хать[p] **в Ки́ев.**	I want to go to Kiev.

If what you want to do is to be repeated or has no specified duration, use the imperfective:

Мы хоти́м говори́ть[i] **по-ру́сски.**	We want to speak Russian.

Compare:

Я хочу́ прочита́ть[p] **э́ту кни́гу.**	I want to read (and finish) this book.
Я хочу́ чита́ть[i] **ру́сские кни́ги.**	I want to read Russian books (in general, no specified number)

Note also:

Я хочу́ пить[i] **.**	I'm thirsty.
Я хочу́ вы́пить[p] **.**	I want a drink (a strongly alcoholic one, not beer).

Хоте́ть can be used with a noun in either the accusative case (with specific objects) or the genitive (with abstract objects, or in the partitive meaning – see 10.8), but constructions with an infinitive are much commoner:

Что́ вы хоти́те?	What do you want? (The questioner supposes you want something definite.)
Я хочу́ бутербро́д.	I want a sandwich (a specific thing).
Мы хоти́м ми́ра.	We want peace (abstract noun).
Хоти́те ча́ю?	Like some tea? (partitive 10.8)

Хотéть[1] is a good example of a verb whose meaning (a state, not an action) is naturally associated with the imperfective aspect. However, there is a perfective **захотéть**[p], which means 'to start to want', 'to conceive a desire', and is used quite frequently to form the future:

Мóжет быть, зáвтра онú захотя́т[p] **пойтú в теáтр.**

Tomorrow they may decide that they want (lit. 'perhaps they will begin to want') to go to the theatre.

EXERCISE 12/2

Translate into Russian:

1 What do you want? 2 I want to go (p) to Siberia. 3 We don't want (to). 4 They want to buy vodka. 5 Do you (fam) want to have a drink (p)?

12.6 **Dative Case: Pronouns**

The basic meaning of the dative case endings is 'to' as in 'She gave it *to me*'. The dative forms of the personal pronouns are:

я	мне	to me	
ты	тебé	to you (fam.)	
óн	емý	to him	**немý** after prepositions[1]
онá	ей	to her	**ней** after prepositions
онó	емý	to it	**немý** after prepositions
мы	нам	to us	
вы	вам	to you (pol/pl.)	
онú	им	to them	**ним** after prepositions

Онá даст[p] **мне пять рублéй.**	She'll give (to) me five roubles.
к немý	towards him
Вы дадúте[p] **емý дéсять рублéй?**	Will you give him ten roubles?

12.7 **Дать 'To Give': Another Irregular Verb**

Like **хотéть**[1] in 12.5 above, **дать**[p] is an awkward verb:

я дам	I'll give	мы дади́м	we'll give
ты да́шь	you'll give	вы дади́те	you'll give
о́н да́ст	he'll give	они́ даду́т	they'll give

The only other verb of this type is **есть**' 'to eat' – see 12.18.

12.8 Нра́виться 'To Please'

Note the use of the dative in the Russian structure corresponding to 'Do you like . . .?' using the verb **нра́виться** (third person **нра́вится/нра́вятся**) 'to please':

Вам нра́вится Москва́? Do you like Moscow? (lit. 'To you pleases Moscow?')

Москва́ мне не нра́вится. I don't like Moscow ('Moscow to me does not please').

Мне ва́ши де́ти о́чень нра́вятся. I like your children very much. ('To me your children very please').

A common question is:

Как вам нра́вится . . .? What do you think of . . .?

Как вам нра́вится э́тот фильм? What do you think of this film?

Люби́ть 'to like/love' (with the accusative) can be used when the feeling is stronger:

Я люблю́ Москву́. I love/am very fond of Moscow.

12.9 Formation of the Dative Singular of Nouns

The dative is an easy case to form:

Masculine nouns ending in a consonant add **-у**:

дру́г friend **дру́гу** to a friend

Masculine nouns ending **-ь** or **-й** replace the **ь** or **й** with **-ю**:

И́горь Igor **И́горю** to Igor

Васи́лий Vasilii **Васи́лию** to Vasilii

Neuter nouns replace **-o** with **-y** and **-e** with **-ю**:

окно́ window	**окну́** to the window
сожале́ние regret	**к сожале́нию** unfortunately ('to regret')
сча́стье happiness, luck	**к сча́стью** fortunately ('to happiness')

И́мя 'name' has dative **и́мени** (same as the genitive form)

Feminine nouns (and masculine nouns ending **-а/-я**) have the same endings as in the prepositional case (see 5.4):

Ната́ша	**Ната́ше** to Natasha
А́ня	**А́не** to Ania
Сиби́рь	**Сиби́ри** to Siberia
мать	**ма́тери** to mother
Росси́я	**Росси́и** to Russia
Ва́ня	**Ва́не** to Vanya
Я позвоню́ Ива́ну.	I'll phone (to) Ivan.
Я дам Ма́ше пять до́лларов.	I'll give (to) Masha five dollars.
Она́ помога́ет му́жу.	She helps (to) her husband.
Он не помога́ет жене́.	He doesn't help (to) his wife.

(**помога́ть/помо́чь**ᵖ 'to help' is followed by the dative case)

EXERCISE 12/3

Put dative endings on the words in brackets and translate:

1 **Я дам (вы) пять до́лларов.** 2 **Вы (я) помо́жете?** 3 **Я покажу́ письмо́ (жена́).** 4 **Я позвоню́ (Е́ва и Вади́м).** 5 **К (сча́стье), ру́сские хотя́т ми́ра.**

12.10 Formation of the Dative Plural

All nouns, regardless of gender, add either **-ам** or **-ям** to the stem of the nominative plural (Lesson 8). That means:

(a) If the nominative plural (see Lesson 8) ends **-ы** or **-а**, replace the **-ы** or **-а** with **-ам**:

дома́ houses	**дома́м** (**до́м** 'house')
де́вушки girls	**де́вушкам** (**де́вушка** 'girl')
пи́сьма letters	**пи́сьмам** (**письмо́** 'letter')
имена́ names	**имена́м** (**и́мя** 'name')

(b) If the nom. plural ends **-и** or **-я**, replace the **и** or **я** with **ям**:

друзья́ friends	**друзья́м** 'to friends' (**друг** 'friend')
ма́тери mothers	**матеря́м** 'to mothers' (**мать** 'mother')
неде́ли weeks	**неде́лям** 'to weeks' (**неде́ля** 'week')

12.11 The Last Two Spelling Rules (3 and 4)

Rule 3. After **г, к, х, ч, ж, ш, щ, ц** (all the eight letters involved in Rules 1 and 2), you always find **а** not **я**. So the dative plural of **кни́га** 'book' (pl. **кни́ги**) is **кни́гам** (not **ки́йгям**). 'They are learning Russian' from the **говори́ть**-type verb **учи́ть** 'to learn' is **они́ у́чат** (*not* **у́чят**) **ру́сский язы́к**.

Rule 4. After those same eight letters, you always find **у**, not **ю**. So 'I am learning Russian' is **я учу́** (not **учю́**) **ру́сский язы́к**.

12.12 The Main Uses of the Dative

(1) To translate *to* a person in sentences such as 'I wrote *to my friend*' (**Я писа́л дру́гу** – **у** is the dative ending), 'I shall give ten dollars to the waiter' (**Я дам де́сять до́лларов официа́нту**). The dative is the opposite of **от** + genitive 'from'.

(2) In impersonal constructions with words like **на́до** 'it is necessary', **мо́жно** 'it's possible', the person affected is in the dative, e.g. **Ему́ мо́жно** 'He's allowed to' (lit. 'To him it is possible'). See Lesson 14 for the details.

(3) After certain verbs, including most verbs of speaking and communicating and many which have a sense of giving something:

говори́ть/сказа́тьᵖ 'to say', 'to tell' (*to* someone)
расска́зывать/рассказа́тьᵖ 'to tell (a story)' (*to* someone)
дава́ть/датьᵖ 'to give' (*to* someone)
приноси́ть/принести́ᵖ 'to bring' (*to* someone)

помога́ть/помо́чьᵖ 'to help'
разреша́ть/разреши́тьᵖ 'to permit'

Я <u>ему́</u> скажу́.	I'll tell him.
О́н расска́зывал <u>нам</u> о Сиби́ри.	He told us about Siberia.
Она́ помога́ет роди́телям.	She helps her parents.

(4) After the prepositions **к** 'towards'/'to (a person)' and **по** 'along', 'according to' and various other meanings depending on context (**по** is the vaguest of Russian prepositions).

Я ходи́л к друзья́м.	I went to (see) my friends.
по го́роду	around the town (**го́род** 'town')
по у́лицам	along the streets (**у́лица** 'street')
по пла́ну	according to plan (**план** 'plan')
по по́чте	by post (**по́чта** 'post', 'post office')
по и́мени	by name (**и́мя** 'name')

The dative is the least common case of nouns.

12.13 Dative of Adjectives, Possessives, Demonstratives (э́тот and то́т)

Check that you know the prepositional endings of adjectives, possessives and demonstratives (7.11, 7.14). The masculine and neuter endings of the dative simply require the addition of **у** to the **-ом** or **-ем** of the prepositional, i.e. the dative endings are always **-ому** or **-ему**. The feminine dative is the same as the feminine prepositional, i.e. always **-ой** or **-ей**.

на́шему хоро́шему дру́гу	to our good friend (cf. prepositional **о на́шем хоро́шем дру́ге**)
специали́ст по ру́сскому теа́тру	a specialist on the Russian theatre
тому́ официа́нту	to that waiter
мое́й ру́сской подру́ге	to my Russian friend (same endings as prep.)

141

по зи́мн<u>ему</u> го́роду	across the wintry town (**зи́мн<u>ий</u>** 'winter', 'wintry' has soft endings)
Я помога́ю э́т<u>ой</u> де́вушке.	I'm helping this girl.

Note: all forms of **мой** and **твой** are stressed on the last syllable, so the m and n dative forms are **моему́** and **твоему́** (prepositional: **моём/твоём**; remember that **ё** only occurs in stressed syllables – 1.2 (c), 4.9 (a)):

моему́ дру́гу	to my friend

12.14 Dative Plural of Adjectives, Possessives, Demonstratives

Adjectives ending **-ый** or **-ой** have **-ым**
Adjectives ending **-ий** have **-им**

но́в<u>ым</u> друзья́<u>м</u>	to new friends
ру́сск<u>им</u> друзья́<u>м</u>	to Russian friends

The possessives and demonstratives (**этот/тот**) simply add **-м** to the ending of the nominative plural (8.8):

мои́м друзья́м	to my friends (**мои́ друзья́** 'my friends')
э́тим де́тям	to these children (**э́ти де́ти** 'these children')
т<u>ем</u> де́вушкам	to those girls (**те де́вушки** 'those girls')

For the forms of **тре́тий** 'third', see Table 5.

12.15 Common Phrases with the Dative

К вокза́лу	To the station
К поезда́м	To the trains
Това́ры по сни́женн<u>ым</u> це́н<u>ам</u>	Goods at reduced prices
Вход посторо́нн<u>им</u> воспрещён	Private (entry *to strangers* forbidden)

12.16 EXTRA: Minor Uses of the Dative

With four rarer prepositions: **благодаря** 'thanks to', **согла́сно** 'according to', **вопреки́** 'in spite of', **навстре́чу** 'towards':

благодаря́ хоро́шей пого́де	thanks to the good weather
согла́сно пла́ну	according to the plan
Навстре́чу нам шёл де́душка.	Grandfather was coming towards us (to meet us).

In infinitive phrases (**Что́ де́лать?** 'What is to be done?') you can add a subject in the dative:

Что нам де́лать? What are we to do? ('What to us to do?')

EXERCISE 12/4

Put in the dative singular:

1 **моя́ жена́**. 2 **ваш ру́сский друг Воло́дя**. 3 **э́тот интере́сный англича́нин**.

EXERCISE 12/5

Put dative plural endings on the words in brackets:

1 **к (на́ши роди́тели)**. 2 **по (э́ти у́лицы)**. 3 **Он помога́ет (те америка́нцы)**. 4 **Я позвоню́ (мои́ друзья́)**. 5 **Она́ специали́ст по (Соединённые Шта́ты)**.

12.17 Prepositional Plural

It is convenient to deal with the plural of the prepositional case (Lesson 5) after the dative plural, since for both adjectives and nouns the prepositional endings can always be derived from the dative endings by replacing the final **-м** with **-х**.

Dative plural:	**мои́м друзья́м**	to my friends
	тем де́вушкам	to those girls
	но́вым города́м	to new towns
Prepositional plural:	**о мои́х друзья́х**	about my friends
	о тех де́вушках	about those girls
	в но́вых города́х	in new towns

So the prep plural endings for nouns are always **-ах** or **-ях**. The prep.pl. endings for adjectives are always **-ых** or **-их**. Since the dat.pl. of **тот** 'that' and **весь** 'all' are **тем** and **всем**, the prep.pl. are **тех** and **всех**.

EXERCISE 12/6

Put the words in brackets in the dat. or prep. case and translate:

1 Я расска́зывала (ру́сские друзья́) о (на́ши де́ти). 2 Во (все ру́сские дома́) ча́сто говоря́т о (Соединённые Шта́ты). 3 Проду́кты в (э́ти магази́ны) (мы) не нра́вятся.

12.18 Vocabulary

бифште́кс [beef-shtéks] meat rissole, hamburger

блю́до pl. **блю́да** dish, course of a meal

бу́дьте добры́ be so good (polite phrase before a request)

вегетариа́н(е)ц (male) vegetarian

вегетариа́нский vegetarian (adj)

взятьᵖ **(брать**ᶦ**) возьму́, возьмёшь** to take

вы́питьᵖ (see **пить**ᶦ) (+ acc.) to have a drink

вы́пью, вы́пьешь

гость (m) gen.pl. **госте́й** guest

идти́ᶦ **(пойти́**ᵖ**) в го́сти к** (+ dat.) to go visiting someone

быть в гостя́х у (+ gen.) to be visiting someone

гриб pl **грибы́** mushroom

дава́тьᶦ**/дать**ᵖ (see 12.7) to give

далеко́ (от + gen.) far (from)

естьᶦ **(съесть**ᵖ**)** (+ acc.) (past **ел, е́ла**) to eat

ем, ешь, ест, еди́м, еди́те, едя́т

звони́тьᶦ **(по-**ᵖ**)** (+ dat.) to telephone (someone)

звоню́, звони́шь

капу́ста (no pl.) cabbage

144

котле́ты по-ки́евски Chicken Kiev (with butter and garlic)

кро́ме того́ also, in addition ('besides that')

кры́мский Crimean

ли́ния line

минера́льный mineral (adj)

мир peace; world

нра́виться (**по–**[р]) (see 12.8) to please

  мне нра́вится I like

обе́д dinner; meal

обе́дать (**по–**[р]) (like **знать**) to dine, have a meal

отдыха́ть/отдохну́ть[р] (12.3) to rest

официа́нт waiter

официа́нтка gen.pl. **официа́нток** waitress

пить (**вы–**[р]) **пью, пьёшь** (+ acc.) to drink

пое́хать[р] (**е́хать**) to go (by transport)

  пое́ду, пое́дешь

пойдём в го́сти let's go visiting

помидо́р tomato

пообе́дать[р] (see **обе́дать**) to dine, have a meal

посети́тель (m) customer

пото́м then, next

потому́ что because

предупрежда́ть (**знать** – type) to warn

прийти́[р] (**приходи́ть**) to arrive, come

  приду́, придёшь

принеси́те bring (imperative)

принести́[р] (+ acc. + dat.) to bring (something to someone)

  принесу́, принесёшь

  (**приноси́ть, приношу́, прино́сишь**)

прямо́й direct, straight

рассказа́ть[р] (**расска́зывать**) to tell, talk about (to somebody)

  расскажу́, расска́жешь (+dat.)

сала́т salad

сказа́ть[р] (**говори́ть**) (+ acc. + dat.) to say (something to someone)

  скажу́, ска́жешь

семья́, gen.pl. **семе́й** family

слу́шать (**по**[р]) (+ acc.) to listen to

  слу́шаю, слу́шаешь

Соединённые Шта́ты Аме́рики United States of America

страна́ pl. **стра́ны** country

то́ then (in that case)

тогда́ at that time, in that case

уйти́[р] (**уходи́ть**) to leave

  я уйду́, ты уйдёшь

хоте́ть (**за–**[р]) (see 12.5) to want

ча́сто often

чита́ть (**про–**[р]) (like **знать**) (+ acc.) to read

шампа́нское n adj champagne, sparkling wine

12.19 Диало́ги Dialogues

В рестора́не In the Restaurant

Официа́нтка:	До́брый день.
Посети́тель:	Здра́вствуйте.
Официа́нтка:	Что́ вы хоти́те?
Посети́тель:	Мы хоти́м пообе́дать.
Официа́нтка:	Пожа́луйста.
Посети́тель:	А что́ у вас есть?
Официа́нтка:	У нас есть грибы́ в смета́не, ры́бный сала́т, бифште́кс [beef-shtéks], бефстро́ганов‡, котле́ты по-ки́евски. Что́ вы хоти́те?
Посети́тель:	Моя́ жена́ возьмёт грибы́ и котле́ты, а я возьму́ грибы́ и бефстро́ганов. Минера́льная вода́ есть?
Официа́нтка:	Да.
Посети́тель:	А что́ у вас есть вы́пить?
Официа́нтка:	У нас есть шампа́нское и вино́.
Посети́тель:	Пожа́луйста, принеси́те мое́й жене́ буты́лку минера́льной воды́, а мне кра́сное вино́.
Официа́нтка:	Хорошо́. Я принесу́ вам на́ше кры́мское кра́сное.

‡**бефстро́ганов** Beef Stroganov (chopped beef in a cream sauce)

Посети́тель:	Официа́нт, бу́дьте добры́.
Официа́нт:	Я вас слу́шаю‡.
Посети́тель:	Я вегетариа́нец. У вас есть вегетариа́нские блю́да?
Официа́нт:	Да. Вы хоти́те ры́бу?
Посети́тель:	Нет, я ем то́лько о́вощи.
Официа́нт:	Хорошо́, я принесу́ вам карто́фель, капу́сту и помидо́ры.
Посети́тель:	Спаси́бо.

‡**Я вас слу́шаю** What would you like? ('I'm listening to you')

Пойдём в го́сти Let's Go Visiting

Е́ва:	Куда́ мы пойдём?
Вади́м:	Дава́й пойдём к твои́м друзья́м.

Éва:	К кому́ мы пойдём?
Вади́м:	К Ве́ре и Оле́гу.

В гостя́х Visiting Friends

Ве́ра:	Хоти́те вы́пить?
Éва:	Нет, спаси́бо. Я хочу́ бутербро́д - и Пе́пси, е́сли есть.
Вади́м:	А я вы́пью.
Éва:	Предупрежда́ю: е́сли ты вы́пьешь мно́го, то́ я уйду́ без тебя́.

COMPREHENSION EXERCISE 12/7

1 What are Vadim's three objections to going to visit Natal'ia Petrovna and Boris Karlovich?

2 How does Eva win the argument?

Éва:	Дава́й пое́дем к мои́м друзья́м.
Вади́м:	К Ве́ре и Оле́гу?
Éва:	Нет, к Ната́лье Петро́вне и её семье́.
Вади́м:	Я не хочу́ е́хать к ним. Ведь[‡] они́ живу́т в Соко́льниках[‡]. Это о́чень далеко́.
Éва:	Туда́ идёт пряма́я ли́ния метро́.
Вади́м:	Кро́ме того́, Ната́лья Петро́вна постоя́нно говори́т о ма́леньких де́тях. Мне э́то неинтере́сно[‡].
Éва:	Её муж расска́жет тебе́ о стра́нах За́падной Евро́пы. Бори́с Ка́рлович - специали́ст[‡] по Европе́йскому[‡] Сою́зу, о́н ча́сто путеше́ствует[‡] по э́тим стра́нам.
Вади́м:	Я не хочу́ слу́шать ле́кцию[‡] по эконо́мике[‡]. Пое́дем к Ве́ре.
Éва:	Мне ка́жется, ты не хо́чешь е́хать к Ната́лье и Бори́су то́лько потому́, что они́ не пьют. А Ве́ра даст[‡] тебе́ вы́пить.
Вади́м:	Как тебе́ не сты́дно[‡] ! Ты же зна́ешь, что мне нра́вится тре́звый[‡] о́браз[‡] жи́зни Ната́льи Петро́вны и её му́жа.

147

Éва: **Тогда́ пое́дем к мои́м тре́звенникам‡. Сейча́с я им позвоню́, а пото́м мы позвони́м ма́ме и ска́жем, что́ мы к обе́ду не придём.**

‡ Extra Vocabulary

ведь you know

даст тебе́ вы́пить will let you have a drink ('will give to you to drink')

Европе́йский Сою́з European Union

За́падная Евро́па Western Europe

ле́кция lecture

неинтере́сно uninteresting, boring

о́браз kind, type

   о́браз жи́зни way of life

путеше́ствовать' (по + dat.) to travel (around)

   путеше́ствую, путеше́ствуешь

Соко́льники Sokol'niki (Moscow district north-east of the centre)

специали́ст (по + dat.) specialist in

сты́дно shameful

   как тебе́ не сты́дно you ought to be ashamed

тре́звенник abstainer

тре́звый sober

эконо́мика economics

13

УРÓК НÓМЕР ТРИНÁДЦАТЬ

ASPECT IN THE PAST; USE OF TENSES

13.1 Key Examples of Aspect in the Past Tense

(a) идти́ⁱ/пойти́ᵖ to go (on foot)

Мы шли́ по у́лице.	We were walking along the street.
Вади́м пошёлᵖ домóй.	Vadim went home.

(b) забыва́ть ⁱ/забы́тьᵖ to forget

Онá чáсто забывáлаⁱ егó и́мя.	She often forgot his name.
Сегóдня онá забы́лаᵖ позвони́ть.	Today she forgot to phone.

(c) быть ⁱ to be

Онá былá дóма.	She was at home.

(d) писáть ⁱ/написáтьᵖ to write

Я писáлⁱ весь день.	I wrote all day.
Я написáлᵖ два письмá.	I wrote two letters.

(e) звони́ть ⁱ/позвони́тьᵖ to telephone

Éва не звони́лаⁱ.	Eva didn't phone.
Éва не позвони́лаᵖ.	Eva failed to phone.

(f) звони́ть/позвони́тьᵖ to telephone

Я звони́ла', но вас не́ бы́ло.   I phoned but you weren't in.

Я позвони́ла ͬ и сказа́ла ͬ, что   I phoned and said I'd come.
приду́.

13.2 Use of Aspect in the Past

Both perfective and imperfective verbs have past tense forms. The rules
for making the past tense of perfective verbs are exactly the same as for
imperfective verbs (see 11.2). The past tense of imperfective verbs, as you
know from Lesson 11, corresponds to English 'I did' or 'I was doing'. The
past tense of *perfective* verbs, on the other hand, has an extra element of
meaning. Basically, the perfective past indicates that the action was a completed whole. So, while the imperfective **она́ чита́ла'** means 'she read' or
'she was reading', the perfective **она́ прочита́ла** means 'she read (and
finished what she was reading or read a specific amount)'; because of its
meaning, the perfective **прочита́ть** will nearly always have an object noun
(e.g. **письмо́** 'letter', **две кни́ги** 'two books') specifying how much was read.

The six sets of sentences above are typical examples of the use of the
aspects in the past tense. Here are some general rules for the use of the
imperfective and the perfective, using the examples above.

Imperfective[i]

(a) Actions in process (unfinished actions) are always imperfective.

If you use the English continuous past (I *was* do*ing* something; We *were*
read*ing*), the Russian equivalent will always be imperfective. 'We were
walking' indicates an action in process (i.e. unfinished), so it cannot be
perfective (it cannot be a completed whole). **Мы шли'** – 'We were walking'. **Мы пошли́ ͬ**, on the other hand, means 'We went (somewhere)' or
'We set off'.

(b) Actions repeated habitually or an unspecified number of times are
imperfective.

Она́ ча́сто забыва́ла' 'She often forgot'. **Мы звони́ли' ка́ждый день**
'We telephoned every day'. But **Сего́дня она́ забы́ла ͬ** ('Today she
forgot') indicates that we are talking about one single occasion.

(c) Verbs denoting states rather than actions are normally imperfective.

Óн был' дóма 'He was at home', **Онú жúли' в Москвé** 'They lived in Moscow'.

(d) Expressions of duration ('all day', 'for three hours') require the imperfective.

Я писáл' весь день 'I wrote/was writing all day'. This sentence does not indicate how much I wrote or whether I finished what I was writing, so it has to be imperfective. You will find that duration phrases such as 'for a long time' (**дóлго**), 'for three hours' (**три часá**), 'all night' (**всю нóчь**) always go with imperfective verbs.[1]

(e) If there was no action, use the imperfective.

Онá не звонúла'.   She didn't phone.

(f) Actions attempted but without result are imperfective.

Я вам звонúла'.   I telephoned you (but you weren't in).

Perfective[p]

(i) Use the perfective for completed single events.

Мы пошлú[p] домóй.   We went home.

(ii) Sequences of actions, except when they are repeated actions (see (b) above) are perfective, since each action must be finished before the next one can take place.

Я позвонúла[p] и сказáла[p],   I phoned and said I'd come.
  чтó придý.

(iii) With negation (**не**) the perfective indicates failure to do something.

Онá не позвонúла[p].   She failed to phone (though she was
                                expected to).

---

1. Except for perfective verbs with the prefix **про-** meaning 'to spend a specified amount of time doing something' e.g. **Мы прóжили[p] там три гóда** 'We lived there for three years.'

13.3 EXTRA: Minor Uses of the Imperfective

(a) The imperfective is also used in the past in cases where the fact of completion is irrelevant. **Вы чита́ли¹ «Войну́ и мир»?** 'Have you read *War and Peace*?' I'm not concerned with whether you finished the book or not, only with whether you have some knowledge of it. The question **Вы прочита́ли ᵖ «Войну́ и мир»?** would correspond to 'Have you finished *War and Peace*?'

(b) The past imperfective is also used for actions which, though completed, were reversed or undone or cancelled. This situation is common with verbs of motion:

Мой друг приезжа́л¹ ко мне.   My friend came to (visit) me (and left again).

Мой друг прие́хал ᵖ ко мне.   My friend has come to (visit) me (and is here now).

In **Мой друг приезжа́л¹ ко мне** my friend 'undid' his arrival by leaving again.

Я открыва́л¹ окно́.   I opened the window (and later closed it)/I had the window open.

13.4 Aspect of the Infinitive

In sentences such as 'I want to work', you have to make the same choice between the aspects of the infinitive (**Я хочу́ рабо́тать¹/я хочу́ порабо́тать ᵖ**). If you mean 'work in general (e.g. to have a job)' or aren't specifying how much work you're going to do, use the imperfective. If you mean to do a fixed amount of work and then stop, use the more specific perfective **порабо́тать ᵖ** 'to do a bit of work'.

Я реши́л чита́ть¹ э́ту кни́гу.   I have decided to read this book (not necessarily all of it).

Я реши́л прочита́ть ᵖ э́ту кни́гу.   I have decided to read this book (and finish it).

In many situations the choice of aspect in the infinitive will seem difficult, but, fortunately, you are unlikely to cause any serious misunderstandings if you choose the wrong one.

One handy rule to note is this: after the verbs **начина́ть/нача́ть**ᵖ 'to begin', **продолжа́ть** 'to continue' and **конча́ть/ко́нчить**ᵖ 'to finish', any infinitive is *always* imperfective:

Я начина́ю понима́тьⁱ.	I am beginning to understand.
Она́ продолжа́лаⁱ **чита́ть**ⁱ.	She continued to read.
Когда́ вы ко́нчитеᵖ **писа́ть**ⁱ**?**	When will you finish writing?

EXERCISE 13/1

Say why the verbs are ⁱ or ᵖ in the following story:

Е́ва и Вади́м шлиⁱ **по Тверско́й у́лице и говори́ли**ⁱ **о её друзья́х. Вдруг Е́ва вспо́мнила**ᵖ**, что она́ забы́ла**ᵖ **позвони́ть**ᵖ **Ве́ре. Обы́чно она́ ей звони́ла**ⁱ **ка́ждое у́тро, но сего́дня она́ ей не позвони́ла**ᵖ**.**

– Я хочу́ⁱ **позвони́ть**ᵖ**, – сказа́ла**ᵖ **она́ Вади́му. – На́до найти́**ᵖ **автома́т.**

Они́ иска́лиⁱ **его́ де́сять мину́т и наконе́ц нашли́**ᵖ **о́коло гости́ницы «Интури́ст».**

Eva and Vadim were walking along Tverskaia Street, talking about her friends. Suddenly Eva remembered (**вспомина́ть/вспо́мнить**ᵖ 'to recall') that she had forgotten to ring Vera. Usually she rang her every morning, but today she hadn't rung her.

– I want to make a phone call, – she said to Vadim. – We need to find (**находи́ть/найти́**ᵖ 'to find') a call-box.

They searched (**иска́ть**ⁱ 'to search for', 'to seek') ('for it') for ten minutes and finally found (**нашли́** – past of **найти́**ᵖ) one near the Hotel 'Intourist'.

13.5 Use of Tenses: Reported Speech

He said he spoke (past) Russian.

Он сказа́л, что он говори́т (pres.) **по-ру́сски.**

In Russian, when someone's words are reported, the tense (past, present or future) of the original words stays unchanged. So if Mary says **Я говорю** (pres.) **по-ру́сски**, then any report of her words ('Mary said that she spoke Russian') will keep the present tense (**Мэ́ри сказа́ла, что она́ говори́т по-ру́сски**). English grammar is more complicated here. Notice how in English a future tense statement (e.g. Vadim: I shall phone Vera) acquires a 'would' form if it is reported: ('Vadim said that he *would* phone Vera'). In Russian the future tense remains.

Вади́м: Я позвоню́ Ве́ре.

Reported speech: **Вади́м сказа́л, что он позвони́т** (fut.) **Ве́ре.**

Other examples:

Vera: I was (past) in London.

Report: Vera said that she had been (pluperfect) in London.

Ве́ра: Я была́ (past) **в Ло́ндоне.**

Report: **Ве́ра сказа́ла, что она́ была́** (past) **в Ло́ндоне.**

This preference for keeping the tense of the original words is extended to cover seeing, hearing and other forms of perception in addition to verbs of speaking:

I heard you were now living (i.e. are living) in Siberia.

Я слы́шал, что вы сейча́с живёте в Сиби́ри.

I knew he was Russian.

Я знал, что он ру́сский ('I knew that he *is* Russian').

We thought he was in Berlin.

Мы ду́мали, что он в Берли́не (pres.).

Vera realized that he was annoyed (i.e. that he is annoyed).

Ве́ра поняла́, что он се́рдится (pres.).

13.6 **Whether: ли**

The same retention of the original tense is found in reported yes–no questions. In English, if John asked 'Does Anna speak Russian?', the question will be reported as 'John asked if Anna spoke (past tense) Russian.' Whenever English 'if' can be replaced by 'whether', 'if' *must* be translated as **ли** (*not* **éсли**). This is the same **ли** as in the structure for yes–no questions in 10.15; **ли** is placed second in the clause¹, and the verb tense is the same as in the original question.

Джóн спроси́л: «Áнна говори́т (Говори́т ли Áнна) по-ру́сски?»
John asked: 'Does Anna speak Russian?'

Report of John's question:

Джóн спроси́л, говори́т (pres.) **ли Áнна по-ру́сски.**
John asked if Anna *spoke* (past) Russian.

More examples:

I asked if (=whether) Boris was at home. (Actual question: 'Is Boris at home?')

Я спроси́ла, дóма ли Бори́с (present tense).

The reported question **Я спроси́ла, был ли Бори́с дóма** would correspond to 'I asked if Boris *had been* at home.'

This same construction with **ли** is used in all structures involving 'whether' or 'if' in the meaning 'whether'.

I didn't know if (=whether) she would come. (Actual thoughts: 'I didn't know if she *will* come.')

Я не знал, придёт (future) **ли онá.**

EXERCISE 13/2

Translate:

1 **Мы спроси́ли, знáет ли онá Бори́са Петрóвича.** 2 **Éва не знáла, уви́дит ли онá Вади́ма.** 3 I don't know if he speaks Russian. 4 I don't know if she'll telephone tomorrow. 5 We didn't know if she spoke English. 6 She asked whether I was an American. 7 I'll ask her if she wants to go to the theatre.

13.7 Learning

One of the first topics on which you are likely to become fluent is the question of how you started to learn Russian and what other languages you know:

to study: **изуча́ть**¹ +acc. – **я изуча́ю, ты изуча́ешь**

or

to learn **учи́ть**¹ +acc. – **я учу́, ты у́чишь, они́ у́чат** (note **у** (not **ю**) and **а** (not **я**) after **ч** – Spelling Rules 3 and 4 (12.11)

Я изуча́ю ру́сский язы́к уже́ пять ме́сяцев.
I have been studying Russian for five months (lit. 'I am studying Russian language already five months').

Я учу́ ру́сский язы́к уже́ шесть лет.
I have been learning Russian for six years.

Both **изуча́ть**¹ and **учи́ть**¹ mean 'to study', but **учи́ть**, like 'to learn', has connotations of memorizing. Both verbs can be used of learning a language. But 'I'm learning these words' (i.e. committing them to memory) is **Я учу́ э́ти слова́**, while 'She's studying mathematics' (not 'She's learning mathematics') should be **Она́ изуча́ет матема́тику**.

The perfective of **изуча́ть**¹ is **изучи́ть**ᵖ (**изучу́, изу́чишь**) and the perfective of **учи́ть**¹ is **вы́учить**ᵖ (**вы́учу, вы́учишь**). Since perfective verbs always describe a successful, completed act, **изучи́ть**ᵖ and **вы́учить**ᵖ correspond to 'to master', 'to learn successfully':

Мэ́ри вы́училаᵖ **ру́сский язы́к.** Mary mastered Russian.
Бори́с Ка́рлович изучи́лᵖ **эконо́мику А́нглии.** Boris Karlovich has made a thorough study of the British economy.

Note: If you want to say that you're studying without saying *what* you're studying, use the reflexive verb **учи́ться** 'to study' (somewhere):

Я учу́сь в Ло́ндоне. I'm studying in London.

13.8 **Vocabulary**

Аме́рика America
бы́стро quickly
ва́жный important
вдруг suddenly
возмо́жность (f) possibility,

opportunity
войти́ᵖ **войду́, войдёшь** past
вошёл, вошла́ – like **идти́**
(входи́ть¹ like **ходи́ть)** to
enter

вообще́ altogether, totally

во́т почему́ that is why

вспомина́ть (like **знать**) (**вспо́мнить**ᵖ **вспо́мню, вспо́мнишь**) (+ acc.) to remember, recall

вы́учитьᵖ (see **учи́ть**) (+ acc.) to master (13.7)

давно́ long ago, since long ago

де́ло в то́м, что́ . . . the thing is that . . .

журнали́ст journalist

забыва́ть (like **знать**) (+ acc.) (**забы́ть**ᵖ **забу́ду, забу́дешь**) to forget

засмея́тьсяᵖ (**смея́ться**) **засмею́сь, засмеёшься** to start laughing

изуча́ть (like **знать**) to study (13.7)

изучи́тьᵖ **изучу́, изу́чишь** to master (13.7)

ку́рсы (pl. of **курс**) classes, a course of study

литерату́ра literature

ма́льчик boy

мно́гие (pl. adj.) many (people)

молодо́й young

нача́тьᵖ (**начина́ть** like **знать**) **начну́, начнёшь** past **на́чал, начала́, на́чали** + 'inf to begin

наза́д ago; back

наро́д people, nation

находи́ть **нахожу́, нахо́дишь** (**найти́**ᵖ **найду́, найдёшь** past **нашёл, нашла́**) to find

немно́го (+ gen.) a little

обы́чно usually

око́нчитьᵖ (+ acc.) **око́нчу, око́нчишь** (**ока́нчивать** like **знать**) to finish, graduate from

оригина́л original

останови́тьᵖ (+ acc.) **остановлю́, остано́вишь** (**остана́вливать** like **знать**) to stop (something)

отве́титьᵖ (+ dat.) **отве́чу, отве́тишь** (**отвеча́ть** like **знать**) to answer (someone)

относи́ться **к** (+ dat.) to relate to, regard, treat

переводи́ть **перевожу́, перево́дишь** (**перевести́**ᵖ) to translate

перее́хатьᵖ **перее́ду, перее́дешь** (**переезжа́ть** like **знать**) to move (house); to drive across

писа́ть (**на-**ᵖ) **пишу́, пи́шешь** to write

повезло́ (+ dat. of person) (someone) was lucky

мне повезло́ I was lucky (idiom)

по-мо́ему in my opinion

по-неме́цки (in) German

поня́тьᵖ **пойму́, поймёшь** past **по́нял, поняла́, по́няли** (**понима́ть** like **знать**) to understand, realize

популя́рный popular

посмотре́тьᵖ **(на + acc.)**
  (смотре́тьⁱ **смотрю́,**
  смо́тришь) to have a look (at)
поступи́тьᵖ **(в + acc.) поступлю́,**
  посту́пишь (поступа́тьⁱ like
  знать) to enter
  (university etc.)
почти́ almost
преподава́тель (m) teacher, lecturer
преподава́тьⁱ **(+ acc.) преподаю́,**
  преподаёшь to teach
прие́хатьᵖ **прие́ду, прие́дешь**
  (приезжа́тьⁱ like **знать)** to
  arrive (by transport)
приказа́тьᵖ **(+ dat. + inf)**
  прикажу́, прика́жешь
  (прика́зыватьⁱ like **знать)** to
  order someone to do sth
прожи́тьᵖ **проживу́, проживёшь**
  (житьⁱ**)** to live (for a specified
  period)
равноду́шно indifferently, with
  indifference
ра́дость (f) joy
  от ра́дости from joy
реши́тьᵖ **решу́, реши́шь (+ acc.)**
  (реша́тьⁱⁱ like **знать)** to decide;
  to solve

роди́тьсяᵖ to be born
  past **роди́лся, родила́сь**
рома́н novel; love affair
сам (m)/**сама́** (f)/**са́ми** (pl.) oneself
  (see Table 4)
смо́чьᵖ **смогу́, смо́жешь, смо́гут**
  to be able (to), manage (to)
  (мо́чьⁱ**)** (+ inf) past **смо́г,**
  смогла́, смогло́, смогли́
совреме́нный modern,
  contemporary
спра́шиватьⁱ (like **знать)**
  (спроси́тьᵖ **спрошу́,**
  спро́сишь) to ask
  (a question)
счита́тьⁱ (like **знать)** to consider,
  count
телеви́зор television
тру́дный difficult
уме́тьⁱ **уме́ю, уме́ешь** (+ inf.) to
  know how to
учи́тьⁱ **учу́, у́чишь (вы́-**ᵖ**)** to study
  (see 13.7)
учи́тьсяⁱ **учу́сь, у́чишься** to study
  (somewhere – see 13.7)
шофёр driver

13.9 Два те́кста

НН:	Когда́ вы на́чали изуча́ть ру́сский язы́к?
Мэ́ри:	Четы́ре го́да наза́д.
НН:	Вам ру́сский язы́к нра́вится?
Мэ́ри:	О́чень. Но́ о́н о́чень тру́дный.

НН: Какие языки вы знаете, кроме русского?

Мэри: Я говорю немного по-французски. В наших школах почти все дети учат французский. И я умею читать по-немецки, но не говорю.

НН: А русский язык у вас‡ популярный?

Мэри: Многие хотят его изучать, потому что все знают, что это очень важный язык в современном мире. Но возможностей изучать его у нас‡ в школах мало. Я сама ходила на вечерние курсы. Мне повезло: в моём городе есть институт, где уже давно преподают русский язык. Вообще англичане относятся к иностранным языкам равнодушно. Обычно они считают, что весь мир говорит по-английски.

НН: А почему вы решили изучать русский?

Мэри: Дело в том, что несколько лет назад я начала читать романы Достоевского – по-английски, конечно. Потом я захотела читать русскую литературу в оригинале. Вот почему я решила записаться на‡ курсы. Я не знаю, смогу ли я выучить язык, но я уже прочитала три романа Достоевского по-русски.

НН: По-моему, вы его уже выучили.

‡**у вас** in your country (10.6)

‡**записаться**ᵖ **на** + acc to enrol for

Старый анекдот An Old Joke

Журналист проводил‡ **опрос на улицах Москвы:**

– Простите, где вы родились ᵖ?

– В Санкт-Петербурге.

– А где вы окончили ᵖ школу?

– В Петрограде.

– А где вы живёте теперь?

– В Ленинграде.

– А где вы хотите жить ᶦ?

– В Санкт-Петербурге.

‡**проводить**ᶦ **опрос** to conduct a survey

159

Note: Peter's city on the Neva, founded 1703, was officially **Санкт-Петербу́рг** until the First World War, though the name was often shortened to **Петербу́рг. Санкт** 'saint', **Петер** 'Peter' and **бург** 'town' are all German borrowings; the Russian equivalents would be **свято́й, Пётр** and **го́род** or **град**. During the War, in 1914, the German-sounding name was Russified into **Петрогра́д**. In 1924, after Lenin's death, the city acquired its Communist-era name **Ленингра́д**.

EXERCISE 13/3

Translate, noting the aspects:

Ве́ра родила́сь^р в Москве́. Она́ прожила́^р там три го́да, пото́м семья́ перее́хала^р в Ирку́тск. Там она́ око́нчила^р шко́лу и поступи́ла^р в институ́т. Когда́ она́ учи́ласьⁱ в институ́те, она́ влюби́лась^р в молодо́го преподава́теля. Так как он преподава́лⁱ англи́йский язы́к и переводи́лⁱ англи́йский рома́н, она́ реши́ла^р, что то́же хо́чет изуча́тьⁱ англи́йский. Поэ́тому она́ начала́^р ходи́тьⁱ на вече́рние ку́рсы.

влюби́ться^р в + acc. to fall in love with

EXERCISE 13/4

Say in Russian:

1 I have been studying Russian (for) three months.
2 We want to master Russian.
3 Mary moved to Moscow and quickly mastered Russian.
4 I don't know if Vadim speaks English.
5 If he speaks English, I'll give him this novel.

COMPREHENSION EXERCISE 13/5

A Brezhnev Joke (Translation in key)

1 Why did Brezhnev order his chauffeur to stop?

2 What was his first question to the small boy?

3 Why did the boy think Brezhnev was his American uncle?

Бре́жнев е́халⁱ на маши́не по одному́ из моско́вских проспе́ктов. Он реши́л^p посмотре́ть^p, как живёт сове́тский[‡] наро́д. Он приказа́л^p шофёру останови́ть^p маши́ну у многоэта́жного[‡] до́ма. Он вошёл^{p‡} в до́м и позвони́л^p в пе́рвую кварти́ру. Дверь откры́л^p ма́ленький ма́льчик. Бре́жнев спроси́л^p ма́льчика, есть ли у него́ в до́ме телеви́зор.

   — Есть, — отве́тил ма́льчик.

   — А холоди́льник[‡]?

   — Есть.

   — А магнитофо́н[‡]?

   — Есть.

   — Так во́т[‡], всё э́то дал^p тебе́ я!

Ма́льчик засмея́лся^p от ра́дости:

   — Ма́ма, па́па, дя́дя Ми́ша из Аме́рики прие́хал^p!

‡Extra vocabulary

вошёл^p entered (past of **войти́**^p 'to enter')

магнитофо́н tape recorder

многоэта́жный many-floored

сове́тский Soviet (adj)

так во́т well then (idiom)

холоди́льник refrigerator

Note: Leonid Il'ich Brezhnev was the General Secretary of the Soviet Communist Party from 1964 to 1982.

14

УРÓК НÓМЕР ЧЕТЫ́РНАДЦАТЬ

ASPECT IN THE FUTURE; IMPERSONAL CONSTRUCTIONS

14.1 Key Expressions

Я бу́ду до́ма.	I shall be at home.
За́втра мы бу́дем отдыха́ть.	Tomorrow we shall rest.
Я бу́ду писа́ть ча́сто.	I shall write often.
Вы бу́дете смея́ться, нó . . .	You're going to think this funny, but . . .
	('You will laugh, but . . .')
Éсли бу́дет вре́мя . . .	If there is time . . .
Мóжно?	May I?
Мне хо́лодно.	I'm cold.

14.2 The Future of быть

я бу́ду	I shall (I'll) be
ты бу́дешь	you (fam) will (you'll) be
óн/она́/онó бу́дет	he/she/it will ('ll) be
мы бу́дем	we'll be
вы бу́дете	you (pol/pl.)'ll be
они́ бу́дут	they'll be
Я бу́ду в Москве́.	I shall be in Moscow.
Вы бу́дете здесь за́втра?	Will you be here tomorrow?

14.3 **Imperfective Future**

As in the past tense, Russian has a choice of aspects in the future too. The imperfective future is easy. Simply use the future forms of **быть** (14.2) plus the *imperfective infinitive* of the required verb.

Я бу́ду говори́ть по-ру́сски.	I'll speak/be speaking Russian (literally, 'I shall be to speak . . .').
Где ты бу́дешь жить?	Where will you live?
Она́ бу́дет говори́ть по-ру́сски?	Will she speak Russian?
Мы бу́дем отдыха́ть в Крыму́.	We're going to take a holiday ('rest') in the Crimea.
В Москве́ вы бу́дете жить у нас.	In Moscow you will stay (live) with us.
Они́ бу́дут писа́ть ча́сто.	They will write often.

(Note that the future of **быть** is simply **я бу́ду** etc., as in 14.2, *never* **Я бу́ду быть**. 'I shall be in Moscow': **Я бу́ду в Москве́**)

The choice of aspect in the future follows the same basic principles as the choice in the past (i.e. the imperfective simply names the action, while the perfective specifies that the action is seen as a completed whole). But in practice the choice in the future will seem much simpler. *Rule of thumb*: In most cases (90 per cent) use the *perfective*, as in Lesson 12. Use the *imperfective* only if the action will be unfinished or repeated.

EXERCISE 14/1

Translate, using the imperfective future:

1 I shall be in Moscow. 2 Will she be at home tomorrow? 3 We shall study Russian. 4 Tomorrow I shall be working. 5 In Moscow I shall speak only Russian. 6 They will telephone every day.

14.4 **Use of Tenses: Future for English Present**

In Russian, after the conjunctions **когда́** 'when', **е́сли** 'if' (never 'whether'), **пока́ . . . не** 'until', the future tense (i or p) must be used *if the meaning is future* (English often uses the present):

Когда́ я бу́ду¹ в Москве́, я позвоню́ᵖ его́ сестре́.
When I am (will be) in Moscow, I'll phone his sister.

Éсли вы бу́дете¹ изуча́ть¹ ру́сский язы́к, вы полу́чите ᵖ хоро́шую рабо́ту.
If you study (will study) Russian, you will get a good job.

Éсли вы изу́чите ᵖ ру́сский язы́к, вы полу́чите ᵖ хоро́шую рабо́ту.
If you master (will master) Russian, you will get a good job.

Я скажу́ᵖ сёстрам, когда́ их уви́жуᵖ (future).
I'll tell (my) sisters when I see (pres.) them (i.e. when I will see them).

Éсли бу́дет¹ вре́мя, мы пойдём ᵖ в Ру́сский музе́й.
If there is (will be) time, we'll go to the Russian Museum.

Вади́м не уйдёт ᵖ, пока́ Éва не позвони́т ᵖ.
Vadim won't leave until Eva phones (will phone).

Be careful to note the aspect when translating such **когда́** and **éсли** clauses:

Когда́ я бу́ду отдыха́ть¹, я начну́ чита́ть «Войну́ и мир».
When I'm on holiday ('shall be resting' – action in process), I'll start reading *War and Peace*.

Когда́ я отдохну́ᵖ, я начну́ чита́ть «Войну́ и мир».
When I've had a holiday ('when I finish resting' – completed action), I'll start reading *War and Peace*.

EXERCISE 14/2

Translate:

1 **Когда́ мы бу́дем в Москве́, мы бу́дем жить в гости́нице «Росси́я».** 2 **Éсли вы напи́шете ей письмо́, она́ отве́тит.** 3 **Éсли Вади́м вы́пьет мно́го, Éва уйдёт без него́.** 4 **Мы вам ска́жем, когда́ вы прие́дете.** 5 **Когда́ мы пообе́даем ᵖ, мы посмо́трим телеви́зор.** 6 When I'm (14.4) in Moscow, I shall speak only Russian. 7 When Eva arrives ᵖ, Vadim will phone us. 8 If you (pol. pl.) give ᵖ him ten dollars, he'll give you the tickets. 9 I don't know if (14.4) she will be at home.

14.5 **EXTRA: Planned Future**

Do not confuse the 'hidden' future of 'If you write (= will write) she'll answer' (14.4) with the planned future of 'I'm working tomorrow', where the present ('We're working') is used with a future time word ('tomorrow') to show that some future event is regarded as an accepted fact. In the case of the planned future, Russian and English have the same usage. **Завтра я работаю** (pres.) 'Tomorrow I'm working' (pres.). **Через месяц мы едем** (pres.) **в Сибирь** 'In a month's time we're going (pres.) to Siberia.'

14.6 **Dative in Impersonal Constructions**

Many English constructions such as 'It is cold today', 'I have to go', 'He needs to study' have Russian equivalents in which 'is cold', 'have to', 'needs' are translated not by verbs but by indeclinable adverb-type words usually ending **-o** (e.g. **холодно** 'is cold', **нужно** 'is necessary'). Words like **нужно** are often called 'category of state' words (**категория состояния**), because they describe states, not actions. If you want to indicate the person who is affected by the state of affairs (e.g. 'I am cold'), in Russian the person is in the *dative* (12.6) case (**Мне холодно** literally 'To me is cold'). Look at these useful examples:

Сегодня холодно.	It's cold today. (Today is cold.)
Ему холодно.	He's cold. (To him is cold.)
В театре жарко.	The theatre is hot. (It's hot in the theatre.)
Ей тепло.	She's warm. (To her is warm.)
Надо/Нужно идти.	It's necessary to go.
Мне надо идти.	I have to go.
Здесь скучно. [sko´osh-na]	It's boring here.
Нам здесь скучно.	We're bored here. (To us here is boring.)
Можно открыть окно?	Is it possible to (May I) open the window?
Можно мне войти?	May I come in? (Is it possible to me to come in?)

165

Now read through this list and then try to find idiomatic translations for the examples which follow, covering up the answers below with a piece of paper:

необходи́мо	(it) is essential
интере́сно	(it) is interesting
светло́	(it) is light
ну́жно (like **на́до**)	(it) is necessary

1 **Вам необходи́мо купи́ть ша́пку.**
2 **Вам интере́сно смотре́ть футбо́л?**
3 **В э́той ко́мнате о́чень светло́.**
4 **Нам ну́жно купи́ть две буты́лки минера́льной воды́.**

1 You must buy a hat. (To you is essential to buy a hat.)
2 Do you like watching football?/Do you find watching football interesting? (To you is interesting to watch football?)
3 This room is very light. (In this room is very light.)
4 We need to/have to buy two bottles of mineral water. (To us is necessary to buy . . .)

Note that it is not common in Russian for a place (e.g. 'Siberia') to be the subject¹ when the sentence describes something that happens *in* the place:

В Сиби́ри хо́лодно.	Siberia is cold. ('In Siberia is cold.')
В ко́мнате светло́.	The room is light. ('In the room is light.')
На у́лице шу́мно.	The street is noisy.

Note also **нельзя́** 'it is not possible', 'it is not permitted', which behaves in the same way though it does not end **-о**.

Кури́ть нельзя́.	Smoking is not permitted.
Вам нельзя́ здесь кури́ть.	You may not smoke here.

These indeclinable words can be made past tense by placing **бы́ло** 'was' after the 'state' word. (**Бы́ло** can also be placed before the 'state' word, particularly those like **хо́лодно** or **интере́сно** which are also used as adjectives i.e. **хо́лодный** 'cold', **интере́сный** 'interesting'.)

Нам на́до бы́ло позвони́ть^p.	We had to make a phone call.
	('To us was necessary to phone.')
Нам бы́ло хо́лодно.	We were cold.
Нельзя́ бы́ло найти́^p такси́.	It was impossible to find a taxi.

Similarly, to make these 'state' words future, put **бу́дет** after (or before) them:

Вам на́до бу́дет позвони́тьᵖ.	You will have to phone.
Мо́жно бу́дет верну́тьсяᵖ **на такси́.**	It will be possible to come back by taxi.
Там бу́дет хо́лодно.	It will be cold there.

Note some special features of negation with these words:

The opposite of **мо́жно** is *not* **не мо́жно**. Use either **нельзя́** ('it's impossible'/'it's not permitted') or **невозмо́жно** ('it's impossible')

Нельзя́ открыва́тьⁱ **окно́.**	It is not permitted to open the window.
Нельзя́/Невозмо́жно бы́ло откры́тьᵖ **окно́.**	It was impossible to open the window.

(Note the use of the i infinitive in the meaning of 'not permitted' and the use of the p infinitive in the meaning 'it's impossible' – see 15.11.)

Не на́до and **не ну́жно** both have the meaning 'one shouldn't'/'don't' (as well as 'it is not necessary'):

Не на́до говори́тьⁱ **об э́том.**	Don't talk about that.
Не на́до так мно́го рабо́татьⁱ.	You shouldn't/it's not necessary to work so much.
А: Е́сли хоти́те, я вам расскажу́ об эконо́мике Сиби́ри.	If you like, I'll tell you about the economy of Siberia.
В: Не на́до.	I'd rather you didn't.

Other 'state' words:

Жаль (or **жа́лко).**	It's a pity.
Жаль, что́ вас там не́ было.	It's a pity you weren't there.
Мне жа́лко тебя́ (gen.).	I'm sorry for you.
пора́ . . .	it's time . . .
Нам пора́ идти́.	It's time for us to go.
неохо́та (coll)	one doesn't feel like + verb
Мне неохо́та об э́том говори́тьⁱ.	I don't want to talk about it.
Сты́дно.	It's shameful.
Как вам не сты́дно?!	You should be ashamed of yourself!
Е́сли вы напьётесьᵖ**, вам пото́м бу́дет сты́дно**	If you get drunk, you'll feel ashamed afterwards.

EXERCISE 14/3

Translate:

1 – **Вам не хо́лодно? – Нет, мне да́же тепло́.** 2 **В Москве́ в а́вгусте нам бы́ло жа́рко.** 3 – **Мо́жно откры́ть окно́? – Пожа́луйста, но́ бу́дет шу́мно.** 4 **За́втра ну́жно бу́дет купи́ть ша́пку.** 5 Is it possible to buy^p vodka here? 6 This room is very cold. 7 You will not be bored. 8 Vadim is not allowed to drink.

14.7 **Vocabulary**

а́вгуст August

беспоко́иться¹ **беспоко́юсь, беспоко́ишься** to worry
  не беспоко́йся don't worry

верну́тьсяᵖ **верну́сь, вернёшься** to return, come back
  (возвраща́ться¹ like **знать)**

возража́ть¹ (like **знать)**
  (возрази́тьᵖ **возражу́, возрази́шь)** to object

война́ war

вре́дно harmful, it's harmful (14.6)

годовщи́на anniversary

го́лос pl. **голоса́** voice

гро́мкий loud

да́же even

жаль (жа́лко) it's a pity (14.6)

жа́рко hot (of weather), it's hot (14.6)

же́нщина woman

интере́сно (it's) interesting (14.6)

ко́мната room

компа́ния company

краси́во it's attractive

ле́том in summer

мо́жно it's possible, one may (14.6)

мужско́й male

на́до (= ну́жно) it's necessary, one must (14.6)

напи́тьсяᵖ **напью́сь, напьёшься (напива́ться**¹ like **знать)** to get drunk

настрое́ние mood
  для настрое́ния for a (good) mood (= to relax)

невозмо́жно (+ ᵖinf) it's impossible (to do sth) (14.6)

недалеко́ not far

нельзя́ it's not allowed; it's impossible (14.6)

немно́жко a little (diminutive¹ of **немно́го)**

необходи́мо it's essential (14.6)

о́сенью in autumn

оста́тьсяᵖ **оста́нусь, оста́нешься (остава́ться**¹ **остаю́сь, остаёшься)** to remain, stay

откры́тьᵖ **откро́ю, откро́ешь (открыва́ть**¹ like **знать)** to open

отмеча́ть¹ (like знать) (отме́тить°
   отме́чу, отме́тишь) to mark,
   celebrate
пока́ . . . не until (14.4)
поня́тно comprehensible (= I see)
пора́ (+ inf) it's time (to do sth)
   (14.6)
пья́ный drunk
разво́д divorce
сестра́ pl. сёстры, g.pl. сестёр,
   dat.pl. сёстрам sister
сиде́ть¹ (по-°) сижу́, сиди́шь to
   sit, be sitting
ску́чно [sko´o-shna] boring, it's
   boring (14.6)

сты́дно shameful (14.6)
суббо́та Saturday
   в суббо́ту on Saturday
тепло́ it's warm (14.6)
ти́хо quiet, it's quiet (14.6)
тру́дно difficult, it's difficult (14.6)
уе́хать° уе́ду, уе́дешь to leave
   (by transport)
   (уезжа́ть¹ like знать)
хо́лодно it's cold (14.6)
ша́пка g.pl. ша́пок hat (no brim)
шу́мно noisy, it's noisy (14.6)
юг south
   на ю́ге in the south

14.8 Dialogues (Translation in Key)

Вади́м: Ты не бу́дешь возража́ть, е́сли в суббо́ту я пойду́ к
Алёше? Мы бу́дем отмеча́ть годовщи́ну его́ разво́да. В
мужско́й компа́нии, коне́чно, без же́нщин.

Е́ва: Поня́тно. Зна́чит, ты бу́дешь пить во́дку весь ве́чер. А
тебе́ пить вре́дно.

Вади́м: Я вы́пью немно́жко, то́лько для настрое́ния. Я зна́ю, что
на́до пить в ме́ру.‡

Е́ва: Е́сли ты напьёшься, тебе́ пото́м бу́дет сты́дно.

Вади́м: Не беспоко́йся.

‡**в ме́ру** in moderation (**ме́ра** measure)

COMPREHENSION EXERCISE 14/4

(Translation in key)

1 What three reasons does VP give for choosing to spend the summer in
his Moscow flat rather than in the Crimea?

2 What is AM's reaction to his summer plans?

3 What will VP do in the autumn?

ВП:	Где вы бу́дете отдыха́ть ле́том?
АМ:	На ю́ге, в Крыму́, недалеко́ от Я́лты. Там о́чень краси́во.
ВП:	Мне ле́том в Крыму́ не нра́вится. О́чень жа́рко. И тру́дно найти́ ко́мнату.
АМ:	А мо́жно вас спроси́ть, что́ вы бу́дете де́лать в а́вгусте?
ВП:	Вы бу́дете смея́ться, но мы реши́ли оста́ться в Москве́. Мы бу́дем сиде́ть до́ма и смотре́ть телеви́зор.
АМ:	Но́ ведь бу́дет ску́чно [sko´o-shna].
ВП:	Зато́‡ бу́дет ти́хо. Все сосе́ди уе́дут, не бу́дет слы́шно‡ ни‡ пья́ных голосо́в, ни ру́гани‡, ни гро́мкой ро́к-му́зыки‡.
АМ:	А в на́шем до́ме звукоизоля́ция‡ хоро́шая.
ВП:	У нас о́чень шу́мно. Пото́м о́сенью, когда́ все верну́тся в Москву́, мы бу́дем отдыха́ть в Со́чи, у мое́й сестры́.

‡Extra Vocabulary

зато́ on the other hand
(in compensation)
звукоизоля́ция sound-proofing
ни . . . ни neither . . . nor
ро́к-му́зыка rock music

ру́гань (f) swearing
слы́шно audible
не бу́дет слы́шно + gen. we
won't hear ('won't be audible')

15

УРО́К НО́МЕР ПЯТНА́ДЦАТЬ

REQUESTS AND THE IMPERATIVE

15.1 **Key Examples**

Скажи́те, пожа́луйста	Tell (me), please/Could you tell me?
Покажи́те, пожа́луйста	Show (me), please/Would you show me?
Прости́те, пожа́луйста.	Excuse (me), please.
Уходи́те.	Go away.
Приходи́те к нам.	Come and see us.
Сади́тесь.	Take a seat.
Да́йте, пожа́луйста.	Give (me), please/Could you give me?
Помоги́те нам.	Help us.
Говори́те ме́дленно.	Speak slowly.
Не забу́дьте.	Don't forget.

15.2 **Asking People to Do Things: Imperative Form**

When we ask people to do things in English, we tend to use such polite constructions as 'Would you pass me the bread?', 'Could you open the window, please?' Russians make such requests with a form of the verb called the imperative[t] (the form for giving commands), which ends **-йте**, **-ите** or **-ьте**, depending on the verb. The imperative in English is the same as the infinitive (without 'to'), as in 'Pass the bread', 'Give me that book, please'. 'Give me that book please' sounds abrupt in English, but its literal equivalent **Да́йте[p] мне э́ту кни́гу, пожа́луйста** is normal usage in Russian.

171

We have already met examples of the imperative. If you have learnt these, then you already know all the possible types.

Да́йтеᵖ, **пожа́луйста** . . . (8)	Please give (me) . . .
Раздева́йтесь (11).	Take your coat off.
Скажи́теᵖ, **пожа́луйста** . . . (4.11)	Please tell (me) . . .
Прости́теᵖ (3).	Excuse (me).
Познако́мьтесьᵖ (11) . . .	Meet (Become acquainted) . . .

The three possible endings are **-йте**, **-ите**, **-ьте**, if you are speaking to someone you call **вы**. If you are speaking to someone you call **ты**, leave off the **-те**. Reflexive verbs add **ся** after **й** or **ь** and **сь** after **и** or **те**.

(a) **-й(те)** is the ending if the stem of the verb ends with a vowel (for 'stem' see 4.4), e.g.

чита́тьⁱ 'to read' stem **чита́-** imper **чита́й(те)**
Ва́ня, чита́йⁱ, **пожа́луйста.** Vanya, read, please.
датьᵖ 'to give' stem **да-** imper **да́й(те)**
Да́йтеᵖ, **пожа́луйста, два стака́на.** Please give (me) two glasses.
беспоко́итьсяⁱ 'to worry', stem **беспоко́-**
Не беспоко́йсяⁱ/**Не беспоко́йтесь**ⁱ. Don't worry.

All **знать**-type verbs have this ending.

EXERCISE 15/1

Make the verbs imperative:

1 (**Дать**ᵖ) **мне ваш телефо́н** 'Give me your telephone number.'
2 (**Послу́шать**ᵖ) **меня́, пожа́луйста!** 'Please listen to me.'
3 (**Одева́ться**ⁱ), **пожа́луйста, уже́ пора́ е́хать** 'Please get dressed, it's time we were leaving.'

(b) **й(те)** is the ending if the stem of the **ты**- form ends in a consonant and the **я**-form of the present (i-verbs) or future (p-verbs) is stressed on the end. This is the ending for most **говори́ть**- and **жить**- type verbs.

приходи́тьⁱ 'to come' stem **приход-** (as in **ты прихо́дишь**), stress of **я прихожу́** on ending, so imper **приходи́(те)**

172

Приходи́ к нам за́втра. Come (fam) and see us tomorrow.

говори́ть 'to say, speak' **я говорю́, ты говори́шь** stem **говор-**, stress on end, so the imperative is **говори́(те)**

Говори́те, пожа́луйста, ме́дленно. Speak slowly, please.

сказа́тьᵖ 'to say' **я скажу́, ты ска́жешь** stem **скаж-**, stress on end, so the imperative is **скажи́(те)**

Скажи́теᵖ**, пожа́луйста, где здесь кино́?** Could you tell me where the cinema is, please?

сади́ться 'to sit down' **я сажу́сь, ты сади́шься** stem **сад-**, stress on ending, so the imperative is **сади́сь/сади́тесь** 'take a seat'

EXERCISE 15/2

Make the verbs imperative:

1 **(Принести́**ᵖ**) нам шампа́нское, пожа́луйста** 'Bring us champagne, please.' 2 **Не (уходи́ть)** 'Don't go away!' 3 **(Купи́ть**ᵖ**) два биле́та** 'Buy two tickets.' 4 **(Посмотре́ть**ᵖ**) на неё!** 'Look at her!'

(c) **-ь(те)** is the ending for verbs whose stem ends in a consonant with the stress on the stem. So the difference from type (b) is determined by the place of the stress on the **я**-form of the present/future.

забы́тьᵖ 'to forget' **я забу́ду, ты забу́дешь**, stem **забу́д-**, stress on the stem in all forms, so imper **забу́дь(те)**:

Не забу́дьтеᵖ **сказа́ть ей об э́том.** Don't forget to tell her about it.

познако́митьсяᵖ 'to become acquainted' **я познако́млюсь, ты познако́мишься**, stem **познако́м-** (from the **ты**-form), stress on the stem in the **я**-form, so imper **познако́мьтесь (познако́мься)**

Познако́мьтесь. Мэ́ри, э́то Воло́дя. Mary, meet Volodia.

Быть 'to be' forms its imperative from the stem **бу́д-** of the future tense:

Бу́дьте здоро́вы! Be healthy! (Set phrase)

Бу́дьте добры́.   Be so good. (Set phrase introducing a
                          request)

This ending **-ь(те)** is by far the least common of the three.

EXERCISE 15/3

Make the infinitives imperative:

1 (**Оста́ться**ᴾ 14.7) **здесь** 'Stay here.' 2 **Пожа́луйста, (отве́тить**ᴾ**) на
два вопро́са** 'Please answer two questions.' 3 **Ва́ня, не (забы́ть**ᴾ**)
позвони́ть Е́ве** 'Vania, don't forget to ring Eva.'

15.3 **Choice of Aspect**

Rule 1: Use the *perfective* for commands and requests involving single
events:

Скажи́теᴾ**, пожа́луйста . . .**   Could you tell me . . .
Позови́теᴾ**, пожа́луйста, Е́ву.**   Please call Eva.

Rule 2: Use the *imperfective* for commands to do something repeatedly or
without time limitation, as you would expect from the general rules of
aspect usage:

Пиши́теⁱ **мне ча́сто.**   Write to me often. (Compare **Напиши́те**ᴾ
                                  ей письмо́ 'Write her a letter'.)

Говори́теⁱ **по-ру́сски,**   Speak Russian please. (Compare
  пожа́луйста.   **Скажи́те**ᴾ **э́то по-ру́сски,**
                                  пожа́луйста 'Say that in Russian,
                                  please.')

Rule 3: Use the *imperfective* for negative commands (Don't . . .) with **не**:

Не уходи́теⁱ**.**   Don't go away.
Не спра́шивайтеⁱ**.**   Don't ask.

174

Rule 4: Use the *imperfective* for invitations.

Приходи́теⁱ **к нам.**	Do come and see us.
Бери́теⁱ **ещё**	Take some more (food).
Сади́тесьⁱ**.**	Take a seat.

EXERCISE 15/4

Translate and account for the choice of aspect:

1 **Приходи́те**ⁱ **к нам в го́сти в суббо́ту.** 2 **Откро́йте**ᵖ **окно́, пожа́луйста.** 3 – **Мо́жно закури́ть**ᵖ ('to light a cigarette')? – **Пожа́луйста, кури́те**ⁱ**.** 4 **Отве́тьте**ᵖ **на два вопро́са.** 5 **Да́йте**ᵖ **мне ваш телефо́н.** 6 **Бери́те**ⁱ **пирожо́к.** 7 **Не уходи́те**ⁱ **.**

EXERCISE 15/5

Translate, using the imperative forms:

1 Phoneᵖ me tomorrow. 2 Could you tellᵖ me where the station is? 3 Don't forgetᵖ to bringᵖ the juice. 4 Writeⁱ to us often. 5 Do have a seatⁱ. 6 Would you giveᵖ me two tickets, please? 6 Don't openⁱ the window. This room is cold.

15.4 **Imperative Exceptions**

There aren't many exceptions. Of the verbs we have met so far, only the following need to be noted:

питьⁱ 'to drink' has **пей(те)** 'drink'

All prefixed forms of **пить** (e.g. **вы́пить**ᵖ 'to have a drink') have the same ending:

Вы́пейтеᵖ**.**	Have a drink.

The imperative of both **е́хать**ⁱ (**е́ду, е́дешь**) and **пое́хать**ᵖ 'to go by trans-port' is **поезжа́й(те)**ⁱ/ᵖ.

Помо́чьᴾ (**помогу́, помо́жешь**) 'to help' has **помоги́(те)** (*not* **поможи́(те)**))

In this lesson you meet **вы́йти**ᴾ (**вы́йду, вы́йдешь**) 'to go out', which has the imperative **вы́йди(те)** (not **вы́йдь(те)**), probably because all the other **-ити** ('go') verbs have **-й(те)** in the imperative (**вы́йти** is the only one stressed on the stem).

Any other exceptions are shown in the vocabularies.

15.5 **EXTRA: An Unexpected Idiomatic Use of the Imperative**

The **ты-** imperative is occasionally used idiomatically with the meaning 'If . . .'

Будь я на твоём ме́сте, я бы ушла́ от него́. 'If I were you (in your place), I would leave him.'

Знай они́, что . . . 'If they had known that . . ./If they knew that . . .'

15.6 **EXTRA: Two More Imperative Aspect Rules**

Rule 5. Negative commands which are warnings rather than prohibitions ('Mind you don't . . .') can be perfective. There aren't many of these. Just learn the following:

Не забу́дь(те)ᴾ.	Mind you don't forget.
Не упади́(те)ᴾ.	Don't fall/Watch your step.
Не простуди́тесьᴾ.	Mind you don't catch a cold.

Rule 6. Insistent or peremptory commands may be *imperfective*, particularly when you are telling people to get on with something they know they ought to do. The customs officer asking you to open your case will say **Откро́йте**ᴾ, **пожа́луйста** 'Open it, please', using the perfective as in Rule 1. If you hesitate, he may repeat the command as **Открыва́йте**ᴵ! 'Go on, open it (as you know you're supposed to)'.

15.7 First Person Imperative

The equivalent of 'Let's' in 'Let's go to Red Square' is **Давáй(те)** plus either the first person plural (the **мы** form) of the *future perfective or* the *imperfective infinitive*, depending on whether the proposal is for a single action (p) or a repeated one (i).

Давáйте пойдёмᵖ **на Крáсную плóщадь.**	Let's go to Red Square. (**Давáйте** to someone you call **вы**)
Давáй позвонúмᵖ **Кáте.**	Let's ring Katia. (**Давáй** to someone you call **ты**)
Давáйте прочитáемᵖ **её письмó.**	Let's read her letter. (Completed act of reading with amount specified)
Давáйте читáтьⁱ.	Let's read. (No amount specified)
Давáйте поговорúмᵖ.	Let's have a talk. (**Поговорúть**ᵖ means 'to do a little talking'.)
Давáйте говорúтьⁱ **по-рýсски.**	Let's talk Russian. (No amount or time limit specified)

The imperfective infinitive is a shortened version of the imperfective future, i.e. **Давáйте (бýдем) говорúть** (14.3). If the imperative is negative ('Let's not . . .'), the **бýдем** must be included. 'Let's not talk about that' **Давáйте не бýдем говорúть**ⁱ **об этом.**

15.8 Third-person Imperative ('Let')

If you want some third person to do something, i.e. if you want to say the equivalent of 'Tell her/them to (Let her/them) come back tomorrow', you can use **пусть** (lit. 'let', 'allow') with the third person of the verb:

Пусть (онá) придёт зáвтра.	Let her come tomorrow.
Пусть говорят.	Let them talk.

EXERCISE 15/6

Translate:

1 **Давáйте вы́пьем.** 2 **Давáйте поéдем к Éве и Вадúму.**

3 Не серди́тесь. Пусть е́дут, е́сли хотя́т. 4 Е́сли Воло́дя позвони́т, скажи́те ему, что́ я ушла́. Пусть позвони́т за́втра. 5 Let's speak Russian. 6 Let's phone Eva. 7 Let's not think about work. 8 Let him study French if he wants (to).

15.9 Official Imperative

In official style (e.g. on notices), commands, particularly negative ones ('Don't . . .'), are often in the infinitive. This construction often corresponds to the English 'No' + noun structure.

Не кури́ть! (4.1)	No smoking
Молча́ть!	Be quiet!
Не разгова́ривать!	No talking!
По газо́нам не ходи́ть!	Do not walk on the grass
Не сори́ть!	No litter

15.10 More Everyday Phrases with Imperatives

Разреши́те^р пройти́.	Excuse me (Let me pass).
Переста́ньте^р!	Stop it!
Обрати́те^р внима́ние.	Note/Take note.
Бу́дьтеⁱ осторо́жны.	Be careful (set phrase).
Покажи́те^р э́то, пожа́луйста.	Show me that, please (asking a shop assistant to show you something).
Не кла́ди́теⁱ тру́бку.	Don't hang up (on telephone).
Приходи́теⁱ к нам.	Come and see us (invitation to visit).

15.11 Revision and Summary of Aspect Use: Fourteen Key Examples

The imperfective is used:

(1) for present-tense actions

Я чита́юⁱ.	I read/I am reading.

(2) for uncompleted actions, so that English continuous forms ('I was doing', 'She will be working') always correspond to the imperfective:

Мы шли домо́й.	We were walking home.
Я бу́ду чита́ть весь ве́чер.	I shall be reading all evening.

(3) for states and processes:

Он жил в Москве́.	He lived in Moscow.
Мэ́ри изуча́ла ру́сский язы́к.	Mary studied Russian.
Мы бу́дем жить у друзе́й.	We'll stay with friends.

(4) for negated actions (particularly in the past), to indicate absence of action:

Она́ не приходи́ла.	She didn't come.

(5) with infinitives and the negated imperative (15.3, rule 3) to indicate undesirability of an action:

Не на́до покупа́ть э́ту кни́гу.	You shouldn't buy that book.
Не покупа́йте э́ту кни́гу.	Don't buy that book.
Я сове́тую вам не покупа́ть её.	I advise you not to buy it.

(6) for actions repeated an unspecified number of times:

Я всегда́ звони́ла в семь часо́в.	I always rang at seven.
Я бу́ду писа́ть ча́сто.	I shall write often.
Пиши́те ча́сто.	Write often.

(7) in the past tense, to indicate that the result of an action was cancelled or annulled – particularly with verbs of motion (13.3):

Вчера́ приходи́л мой ру́сский друг.	My Russian friend came yesterday (and left again).
Я открыва́л окно́.	I had the window open (it's closed now).

(8) when the fact of completion is irrelevant:

Вы чита́ли «Войну́ и мир»?	Have you read *War and Peace*? (I'm not concerned with whether you finished it)

179

Кто́ стро́ил¹ Большо́й теа́тр?   Who built the Bolshoi Theatre?
(I want to know the name of the
architect, not to stress the fact that the
theatre was finished)

The perfective is used:

(9) to describe an action as a completed whole, with a beginning and an end:

В суббо́ту я купи́л^p «Пра́вду».   I bought *Pravda* on Saturday.
Я э́то сде́лаю^p за́втра.   I'll do it tomorrow.
Да́йте^p два биле́та, пожа́луйста.   Would you give me two tickets?
Я хочу́ купи́ть^p слова́рь.   I want to buy a dictionary.

(10) to indicate the relevance of the result:

Вы купи́ли^p «Пра́вду» сего́дня?   Have you bought *Pravda* today?
(I.e. perhaps I want to borrow it)

(11) to indicate completion, particularly in sequences of actions, where each action must be finished before the next one can begin:

Вади́м пришёл^p домо́й, вы́пил^p   Vadim came home, drank some water
воды́ и сел^p у окна́.   and sat down by the window.

(12) with infinitives, to show that something is impossible or can't be done:

Откры́ть^p окно́ невозмо́жно.   It's impossible to open the window.
Она́ не могла́ найти́^p такси́.   She couldn't find a taxi.

(13) with negation (**не**) in the past tense, to indicate failure to do something:

Ива́н хоте́л откры́ть окно́,   Ivan wanted to open the window
но не смог^p.   but failed.
Она́ сказа́ла, что придёт,   She said she'd come but (in fact)
но (так и) не пришла́^p.   she didn't.

(14) perfective infinitives and imperatives are used after negation (**не**)
(15.6) to indicate that something might happen by chance:

Я не хочу́ вас оби́деть[p].	I don't want to offend you (by chance).
Не забу́дь[p]**!**	Don't forget.
Смотри́ не упади́[p]**!**	Mind you don't fall.

These example sentences illustrate typical imperfective and perfective situations. Learn these and then try to relate other situations to this list. For example, if 'Have you read *War and Peace*? is **Вы чита́ли**[i] **«Войну́ и мир»?**, then 'Have you seen this film?' is the same type of imperfective situation: **Вы смотре́ли**[i] **э́тот фильм?**

Short Summary: General Rules of Thumb

(a) In the *present*, verbs are imperfective.

(b) In the *future*, use the *perfective*, *unless* the action will be repeated or unfinished.

(c) In the *past* (where about 50 per cent of verbs are perfective and 50 per cent are imperfective), remember that the perfective always carries the meaning 'action seen as a completed whole', while the imperfective simply names the action without saying anything about completion.

(d) In the *imperative*, use the *perfective* (plus **пожа́луйста**) for polite commands and requests (**Скажи́те**[p], **пожа́луйста** . . . 'Could you tell me . . .' Use the imperfective for invitations, repeated or unfinished actions, and for negated commands and requests (**Не де́лайте**[i] **э́того** 'Don't do that').

(e) For the *infinitive* choose the *perfective* for actions with an intended result (particularly after all verbs meaning 'want', 'to be able or unable', 'try', 'forget' (**Я могу́/не могу́ прийти́**[p] **за́втра** 'I can/can't come tomorrow'). Use the *imperfective* after all verbs meaning 'begin', 'continue' and 'finish' (**Он на́чал писа́ть**[i] 'He started writing'), and for repeated, unfinished and undesirable actions, particularly with all phrases meaning 'one shouldn't', 'it's not allowed', 'it's not necessary' (**Не на́до её приглаша́ть**[i] 'You shouldn't invite her').

15.12 **EXTRA: Linguistic Note on Aspect**

Aspect is about *how* actions take place in time; tense is about *when*. We have aspect in English too: the difference between 'He was reading

'War and Peace' and 'He read War and Peace' is a difference of aspect, not of tense (they're both past tense). 'He was reading' tells us that the reading was in process, not finished; 'he read' simply tells us what kind of activity it was – perhaps he finished the book (as in 'He read War and Peace in sixty-five minutes'), perhaps he didn't (as in 'He read War and Peace for a couple of hours and realized he would never finish it').

EXERCISE 15/7

Translate, noting the aspects:

Юра: Вы чита́лиⁱ рома́н «А́нна Каре́нина»?

Ши́рли: Пока́ нет. Я купи́ла^p его́ в про́шлом году́. Хоте́лаⁱ прочита́ть^p, но я мно́го рабо́талаⁱ, о́чень устава́лаⁱ и ничего́ не успева́лаⁱ. Во́т бу́ду в а́вгусте отдыха́тьⁱ, тогда́ обяза́тельно прочита́ю^p.

Юра: Когда́ прочита́ете^p, мы поговори́м^p, о то́м, понима́лⁱ ли Толсто́й же́нское се́рдце.

15.13 Vocabulary

боя́тьсяⁱ бою́сь, бои́шься
  (+ gen.) to be afraid (of)
ве́чером in the evening
вниз down
вы́йти^p вы́йду, вы́йдешь past
  вы́шел, вы́шла, вы́шли
  imper **вы́йди(те)^p**
  (выходи́тьⁱ выхожу́,
  выхо́дишь) to go out
вы́ход exit
дово́льно fairly, quite
дойти́^p дойду́, дойдёшь
  (**до** + gen.) past **дошёл,**
  дошла́, дошли́ (доходи́тьⁱ)

to reach (on foot)
ещё раз again
жда́ть (подо-^p) жду, ждёшь
  (+ acc.) to wait for (someone)
же́нский female
запи́ска g.pl. **запи́сок** note
зда́ние building
клие́нт client
любо́й any (any one you like)
мо́чьⁱ (с-^p) могу́, мо́жешь, мо́гут
  past **мо́г, могла́, могло́, могли́**
  to be able
надое́ло that's enough, I'm tired
  (of it)

182

наказа́ть[p] **накажу́, нака́жешь,** (**нака́зывать**' like **знать**) to punish

напо́мнить[p] **напо́мню, напо́мнишь** (**напомина́ть**' like **знать**) (+ dat.) to remind (someone)

находи́ться' **нахожу́сь, нахо́дишься** to be situated **где нахо́дится . . .?** where is . . .?

обяза́тельно definitely, without fail

освободи́ться[p] **освобожу́сь, освободи́шься** (**освобожда́ться**' like **знать**) to become free

оста́вить[p] **оста́влю, оста́вишь** (**оставля́ть** like **знать**) (+ acc.) to leave (sth)

переда́ть[p] (like **дать** 12.7) to pass, transmit, give a message (**передава́ть**' like **дава́ть**') (+ dat.) (to someone)

пересе́сть[p] **переся́ду, переся́дешь** (**переса́живаться**') (**на** + acc.) to change (from one form of transport to another)

переста́ть (+ ' inf) **переста́ну, переста́нешь** (**перестава́ть**') to stop (doing sth)

перехо́д street crossing

пла́кать' **пла́чу, пла́чешь** to cry (**за-**[p] 'to start crying')

поверну́ть[p] **поверну́, повернёшь** (**повора́чивать**' like **знать**) to turn (change direction)

поговори́ть[p] (of **говори́ть**') to talk

for a while (cf. **сказа́ть**[p] 'to say')

подзе́мный underground

пока́ нет not yet (while not)

прое́хать[p] **прое́ду, прое́дешь** (**проезжа́ть**' like **знать**) (**в/на** + acc.) to travel to

проси́ть' (**по-**[p]) + acc. + inf. **прошу́, про́сишь** to ask someone to do something

пусть let (15.8)

разреша́ть' (like **знать**) (+ dat.) (**разреши́ть**[p] **разрешу́, разреши́шь**) to allow (someone)

сади́ться' **сажу́сь, сади́шься** (see **сесть**[p]) to sit down; (**на** + acc.) to take (transport)

секрета́рь (m) gen.sg. **секретаря́** secretary (male or female)

се́рдце gen.pl. **серде́ц** heart

сесть[p] **ся́ду, ся́дешь** past **сел, се́ла** (see **сади́ться**') to sit down; (**на** + acc.) to take (transport)

сле́ва on the left

собо́р Васи́лия Блаже́нного St Basil's on Red Square ('the Cathedral of Vasilii the Blessed')

спусти́ться[p] **спущу́сь, спу́стишься** (**спуска́ться**' like **знать**) to go down

сторона́ acc. **сто́рону,** pl. **сто́роны** gen.pl. **сторо́н** side, direction **в сто́рону** (+ gen.) in the direction of

телефо́н telephone

то́лько что́ (+ past) just (= very recently)

трамва́й gen.pl. **трамва́ев** tram

тури́ст tourist

успева́ть' (like **знать**) (**успе́ть**ᵖ

успе́ю, успе́ешь) to have time (to do something)

устава́ть' устаю́, устаёшь (**уста́ть**ᵖ уста́ну, уста́нешь) to get tired

четвёртый fourth

15.14 Диало́ги

Two Lost Tourists

Тури́ст: Скажи́те, пожа́луйста, как прое́хать на вокза́л?

Вади́м: Сади́тесь на четвёртый тролле́йбус, вы́йдите на пло́щади, а там переся́дьте на любо́й трамва́й.

*

Тури́ст: Пожа́луйста, скажи́те, как дойти́ до гости́ницы «Росси́я».

Е́ва: Дава́йте посмо́трим план го́рода. Вот гости́ница, недалеко́ от Кремля́. Мы нахо́димся здесь, о́коло рестора́на «Макдо́налдс» на Пу́шкинской пло́щади. Поверни́те напра́во и иди́те пря́мо по Тверско́й. У гости́ницы «Национа́ль» вы уви́дите подзе́мный перехо́д. Спусти́тесь вниз, иди́те пря́мо, найди́те вы́ход на Кра́сную пло́щадь. Иди́те в сто́рону собо́ра Васи́лия Блаже́нного. Сле́ва от собо́ра вы уви́дите большо́е совреме́нное зда́ние. Это и есть‡ «Росси́я».

‡**э́то и есть** that is ('that indeed is')

Разгово́р по телефо́ну A Telephone Conversation

Е́ва: Извини́те, попроси́те‡ Вади́ма к телефо́ну.

НН: Он то́лько что вы́шел. Это Е́ва говори́т?

Е́ва: Да.

НН: Он звони́л вам де́сять мину́т наза́д, но вас‡ не́ было до́ма.

Е́ва: Скажи́те ему́, что я бу́ду до́ма ве́чером. Пусть позвони́т ещё раз.

НН: Обяза́тельно.

‡**Попроси́те** (imper of **попроси́ть** 'to ask') **Вади́ма к телефо́ну.** Ask Vadim (to come) to the phone.

‡**Вас не́ было до́ма.** You weren't at home ('of you wasn't' 10.5).

Людми́ла Петро́вна и ма́ленькая Та́ня

ЛП:	Та́ня! Что́ ты де́лаешь?! Переста́нь!
Та́ня:	Но́ я хочу́.
ЛП:	Не разреша́ю! Нельзя́!
Та́ня:	Почему́ нельзя́?
ЛП:	Та́ня, надое́ло!
Та́ня:	Я тебя́ не бою́сь.
ЛП:	Я тебя́ накажу́.
Та́ня:	Е́сли ты меня́ нака́жешь, я бу́ду пла́кать.

COMPREHENSION EXERCISE 15/8

(Translation in key)

Borisov seeks Ravvinov

1 What four things did Borisov ask the secretary to do during the first call?
2 Did she carry out the four instructions?
3 What did Borisov ask her to do during the third call?
4 How did she propose to carry out his instruction?

Пе́рвый звоно́к First Call

Бори́сов:	Позови́те Равви́нова, пожа́луйста.
Секрета́рь:	К сожале́нию, о́н за́нят‡. Позвони́те че́рез час.
Бори́сов:	Не клади́те тру́бку, пожа́луйста. Переда́йте ему́, что звони́л Бори́сов.
Секрета́рь:	Хорошо́, переда́м.
Бори́сов:	Попроси́те его́ позвони́ть мне по телефо́ну 125-36-47.
Секрета́рь:	Не беспоко́йтесь, я переда́м.

‡**о́н за́нят** he's busy

Второй звонок Second Call

Борисов:	Вас беспокоит‡ Евгений Матвеевич Борисов. Попросите Раввинова к телефону, пожалуйста.
Секретарь:	Он уже ушёл.
Борисов:	Как ушёл?‡ Почему он не позвонил?
Секретарь:	Не знаю. Я ему сказала, что вы звонили.
Борисов:	Пожалуйста, напомните ему ещё раз завтра.
Секретарь:	Обязательно.

‡**Вас беспокоит ... Борисов** 'You is troubling ... Borisov'. Polite formula corresponding to: 'My name is Borisov. Excuse me for troubling you.'
‡**Как ушёл?** 'How can he have left?'

Третий звонок Third Call

Борисов:	Здравствуйте, говорит Борисов. Раввинов на месте‡?
Секретарь:	На месте, но он ждёт клиента.
Борисов:	Когда он освободится, напомните ему, пожалуйста, что я просил его позвонить мне.
Секретарь:	Хорошо, я ему оставлю записку.

‡**Раввинов на месте?** Is Ravvinov in ('on (his) place')?

EXERCISE 15/9
REVISION OF LESSONS 11–15
(Tense, Aspect, Dative)

Say in Russian:

1 I want to buy a hat. 2 We stayed ('lived') in the Hotel 'Intourist'. 3 – Have you read the novel *Anna Karenina*? – No, I haven't. 4 We often telephoned Vadim and Eva. 5 – Will you come tomorrow? – I'll come if I can ('shall be able'). 6 If we have time tomorrow, we'll phone (our) friends. 7 We'll be waiting for you. 8 I'll have a rest, then I'll go (on foot) to Red Square. 9 It's impossible to open this door. 10 Please bring me a bottle of mineral water. 11 Please don't open the window. We're cold. 12 Write (fam) to me often. I shall write to you every week. 13 Don't forget that tomorrow we are going to

(see) Natal'ia Petrovna. 14 Take a seat (pol). I'll come in **(че́рез)** a few minutes. I have to telephone[D] the children. 15 Let's not talk about children.

16

УРО́К НО́МЕР ШЕСТНА́ДЦАТЬ

THE INSTRUMENTAL CASE

16.1 **Useful Phrases**

ве́чером	in the evening
С Но́вым го́дом!	Happy New Year! (lit. 'With New Year')
С удово́льствием!	With pleasure!
ме́жду на́ми	between us
Познако́мьтесь с мои́м дру́гом.	Meet my friend.
Рука́ми не тро́гать	Don't touch (with your hands) (sign in museums)
Я интересу́юсь ру́сской литерату́рой.	I am interested in Russian literature.

16.2 **Instrumental' case**

Here we meet the last of the six cases. For many learners it is the one which is most distinctively Russian. Its primary meaning is 'with' (in the sense *by means of*) as in the sentence 'He wrote with (= by means of) a pencil' – **Он писа́л карандашо́м**. The ending **-ом** on a masculine noun is the instrumental case. It has a number of other uses (see 16.5), particularly with six prepositions including **с** 'with' in the meaning 'accompanied by' or 'together with'.

16.3 Formation of the Instrumental Singular

For m nouns ending in a consonant and neuter nouns ending **o**, the instrumental is **-ом**:

каранда́ш 'pencil'	**карандашо́м**	with (by means of) a pencil
ве́чер 'evening'	**ве́чером**	in the evening
у́тро 'morning'	**у́тром**	in the morning

If the m noun ends with a soft sign **ь** or **й**, replace the **ь** or **й** with **-ем** (**-ём** if stressed); if the neuter noun ends **-е** or **-ё**, add **-м**:

И́горь 'Igor'	**И́горем**	by Igor
д(е)нь 'day'	**днём**	in the daytime/in the afternoon
мо́ре 'sea'	**мо́рем**	by sea

For m and f nouns ending **-a** the instrumental is **-ой**:

весна́ 'spring'	**весно́й**	in the spring
па́па 'dad'	**с па́пой**	with dad

If the noun ends **-я**, replace the **я** with **-ей**. Stressed **я** becomes **ёй**:

Ва́ля 'Valia'	**Ва́лей**	by Valia
семья́ 'family'	**с семьёй**	with the family

Feminine nouns with **-ь** *add* **ю**:

но́чь 'night'	**но́чью**	at night
о́сень 'autumn'	**о́сенью**	in autumn
до́чь 'daughter'	**с до́черью**	with a daughter (remember the extra **-ер-** 5.6)

Remember that Spelling Rule 2 (8.10) will apply to nouns (with <u>un</u>stressed endings) whose last consonant is **ж, ч, ш, щ** or **ц**. After these consonants you find **e** instead of unstressed **o**:

Ма́ша 'Masha'	**с Ма́шей** (not **Ма́шой**)	with Masha
това́рищ 'comrade'	**с това́рищем** (not **-щом**)	with a comrade
америка́нец 'American'	**с америка́нцем**	with an American

(but 'with father' is **с отцо́м** because the ending is stressed)

There are no exceptions to these rules.

189

EXERCISE 16/1

Put the nouns in brackets in the instrumental:

1 **Чай с (варе́нье)** Tea with (together with) jam. 2 **Варе́нье едя́т (ло́жка)** One eats the jam with (by means of) a spoon. 3 **Он придёт (у́тро)** He'll come in the morning. 4 **Я приду́ с (жена́ и дочь)** I'll come with (my) wife and daughter. 5 **С (Са́ша)** With Sasha. 6 **С (царь Никола́й)** With Tsar Nicholas (**царь** is stressed on the ending).

16.4 **Instrumental Plural**

To form the instrumental plural, you need to know the nominative plural (see Lesson 8). If the nominative plural ends **-ы** or **-а**, replace the **ы** or **а** with **-ами**; if the ending of the nom. pl. is **-и** or **-я**, replace the **и** or **я** with **-ями**. The gender of the noun does not matter.

	nom.pl.	inst.pl.
магази́н 'shop'	**магази́ны**	**магази́нами**
до́м 'house'	**дома́**	**дома́ми**
брат 'brother'	**бра́тья**	**бра́тьями**
неде́ля 'week'	**неде́ли**	**неде́лями**
сын 'son'	**сыновья́**	**сыновья́ми**

Don't forget Spelling Rule 3 (**-а** not **-я** 12.11):

кни́га 'book'	**кни́ги**	**кни́гами** (not **-ями**)
това́рищ 'comrade'	**това́рищи**	**това́рищами**

There are four exceptions (apart from some cases with unpredictable stress). These have the ending **-ьми́**:

детьми́ (from **де́ти** 'children')
дочерьми́ (from **до́чери** 'daughters')
лошадьми́ (from **ло́шади** 'horses')
людьми́ (from **лю́ди** 'people')

A few nouns have alternative forms in **-я́ми** (neutral style) and **-ьми́** (bookish style) **дверя́ми – дверьми́** 'doors'.

EXERCISE 16/2

Put on the required endings:

1 **С (сёстры)** 'With sisters.' 2 **С (бутылки)** 'With bottles.' 3 **С (дети)** 'With the children.' 4 **С (американцы)** 'With Americans.'

16.5 Uses of the Instrumental (in Russian творительный падеж 'creative case')

(1) To indicate the instrument used to carry out an action:

Он писал карандашо́м. He wrote with (= by means of) a pencil.
Это мо́жно есть ло́жкой. You can eat this with a spoon.

(2) After six prepositions:

за	behind, beyond	**за две́рью** behind the door	
ме́жду	between	**ме́жду ле́сом и реко́й** between the wood and the river	
над	above	**над го́родом** above the city	
пе́ред	in front of	**пе́ред до́мом** in front of the house	
под	under	**под землёй** under the ground	
с	with	**с удово́льствием** with pleasure	

(3) The instrumental is used with parts of the day and the seasons of the year answering the question 'when?':

у́тро	**у́тром**	in the morning
день	**днём**	in the afternoon
ве́чер	**ве́чером**	in the evening
ночь (f)	**но́чью**	at night
весна́	**весно́й**	in spring
ле́то	**ле́том**	in summer
о́сень (f)	**о́сенью**	in autumn
зима́	**зимо́й**	in winter

(4) The instrumental is used after certain verbs, e.g. **быть** 'to be', **занима́ться** 'to occupy oneself with/to study', **каза́ться** 'to seem',

называ́ться[1] 'to be called', **станови́ться/стать**[2] 'to become', **явля́ться**[1] lit. 'to appear' (frequently used in formal style with the meaning 'to be'):

Она́ ста́ла инжене́р<u>ом</u>.	She became an engineer.
Мы занима́емся исто́ри<u>ей</u> Росси́и.	We are studying the history of Russia.
Он явля́лся дире́ктор<u>ом</u>.	He was the director.

The most important of these is **быть** 'to be'. As you will remember from Lesson 3, the verb **быть** is normally omitted in the present tense (**Я англича́нин** 'I am English') but it has normal past and future forms (**был, была́** etc.; **бу́ду, бу́дешь** etc.). The past and future forms, and also the infinitive, are normally followed by the instrumental:

Его́ оте́ц был врач<u>о́м</u>.	His father was a doctor.
Наш сын бу́дет учи́тел<u>ем</u>.	Our son will be a teacher.
Его́ спу́тник<u>ом</u> был ру́сский бизнесме́н.	His travelling companion was a Russian businessman (see 16.8(b)).

(5) Note the idiomatic use of **с** + inst. to join two human subjects where English uses 'and':

Пришли́ Ива́н <u>с жено́й</u>.	Ivan and his wife came.

English 'X and I' is in Russian **мы с X** ('we with X'):

мы с му́жем	my husband and I
Мы с Е́вой реши́ли пое́хать в Сиби́рь.	Eva and I have decided to go to Siberia.

16.6 Instrumental of Adjectives, Possessives and Demonstratives

Singular. If the nominative adjective ends **-ый** or **-о́й**, the masculine and neuter instrumental ending is **-ым**. Adjectives with nominative **-ий** have instrumental **-им**. Feminine adjectives have **-ой** or **-ей**, exactly the same endings as in the feminine singular of the genitive, dative and prepositional.

с но́в<u>ым</u> ру́сск<u>им</u> дру́гом	with a new Russian friend
с но́в<u>ой</u> ру́сск<u>ой</u> подру́гой	with a new Russian girlfriend

Plural. All genders have **-ыми** (**-ый** and **-ой** adjectives) or **-ими** (**-ий** adjectives):

с но́выми ру́сскими друзья́ми   with new Russian friends

мо́й, тво́й etc. all have **-им** (m and n sg.), **-ей** (f sg.), **-ими** (pl.)

с твои́ми детьми́   with your children
Они́ бы́ли на́шими спу́тниками.   They were our travelling companions.

Two tricky words: **э́тот** and **то́т** (see Table 4).

э́тот 'this' has m/n **э́тим**, f **э́той**, plural **э́тими**
то́т 'that' has m/n **тем**, f **то́й**, plural **те́ми**

с те́ми людьми́   with those people

16.7 Instrumental of Pronouns

я	**мно́й**
ты	**тобо́й**
о́н	**им** (**ним** after prepositions)
она́	**ей** (**ней** after prepositions)
оно́	**им** (**ним** after prepositions)
мы	**на́ми**
вы	**ва́ми**
они́	**и́ми** (**ни́ми** after prepositions)

Я за ва́ми.   I'm behind you (phrase used to book a place in a queue).

Что́ с ним?   What's the matter with him?

Note also: **кто́** 'who' has inst. **кем**; **что́** 'what' has **чем** (Table 4):

Чем вы занима́етесь?   What are you doing? ('With what are you occupying yourself?')

Кем был Дзержи́нский?   Who was Dzerzhinskii?

EXERCISE 16/3

Put the words in brackets in the instrumental and translate:

1 Я давно́ занима́юсь (ру́сская му́зыка.). 2 Мы с (брат) отдыха́ли в Крыму́. 3 Вади́м пьёт ко́фе с (молоко́), а Мэ́ри пьёт во́дку с (апельси́новый 'orange' со́к). 4 Я хочу́ познако́мить вас с (мои́ ру́сские друзья́). 5 Что́ с (она́)? Почему́ она́ не хо́чет разгова́ривать с (мы)?

16.8 EXTRA: Instrumental with быть: Two Problems

(a) With **быть** the nominative *may* be used instead of the instrumental (**Мо́й оте́ц был врач** instead of **врачо́м** 'My father was a doctor'). The nominative is common if the complement (the phrase after **быть**) denotes a permanent characteristic of the subject, i.e. if your father was a doctor all his life. **Че́рчилль был англича́нин** 'Churchill was English' (all his life). The nominative is also very common if the complement is an adjective rather than a noun, e.g. **Пого́да была́ хоро́шая** (nominative) rather than **хоро́шей** (instrumental).

(b) The second problem arises with sentences such as 'The main problem was the grammar'. Which noun, **пробле́ма** 'problem' or **грамма́тика** 'grammar', is in the nominative and which in the instrumental? Generally, the more specific word will be nominative, the more general one instrumental. A good test is to replace the verb 'to be' with the verb 'constitute' and see which order sounds more natural: 'The problem constituted the grammar' or 'Grammar constituted the problem'? The latter, you should agree, so 'grammar' is the subject[t]: **Гла́вной пробле́мой** (inst.) **была́ грамма́тика** (nom.). The word order in neutral Russian requires the new information to come at the end (see 26.8), so if you are stressing 'the grammar', it comes after the verb. If you want to stress 'main problem', you turn the sentence round: **Грамма́тика была́ гла́вной пробле́мой**.

In the example **Мои́м спу́тником был ру́сский бизнесме́н** 'My travelling companion was a Russian businessman' you are saying 'A Russian businessman constituted my travelling companion' and you are indicating that the new information is 'Russian businessman'.

16.9 Declension of Surnames

Russian male surnames normally end **-ын**, **-ин**, **-ов**, **-ёв** or **-ев**. These were originally possessive adjectives (**Ивано́в** meant 'belonging to Ivan'). They have normal noun endings *except* in the instrumental, where the ending is the adjectival **-ым** (not **-ом**). So **Я люблю́ Че́хова** 'I love Chekhov' but **Я занима́юсь Че́ховым** 'I am studying Chekhov'. Female surnames (**-ына**, **-ина**, **-ова**, **-ёва**, **-ева**) are more adjectival. Apart from the accusative (ending **-у**, like a feminine noun), all the other cases have **-ой**, like adjectives. In the plural ('the Ivanovs'), all endings except the nominative are adjectival.

	Mr Ivanov	Mrs/Miss/Ms Ivanov	the Ivanovs
N	**Ивано́в**	**Ивано́ва**	**Ивано́вы**
A	**Ивано́ва**	**Ивано́ву**	**Ивано́вых**
G	**Ивано́ва**	**Ивано́вой** (not **ы**)	**Ивано́вых**
D	**Ивано́ву**	**Ивано́вой** (not **е**)	**Ивано́вым**
I	**Ивано́вым** (not **ом**)	**Ивано́вой**	**Ивано́выми**
P	**Ивано́ве**	**Ивано́вой** (not **е**)	**Ивано́вых**

16.10 Vocabulary

бы́вший former

варе́нье jam, preserves

вме́сте (с + inst.) together (with)

вме́сто (+ gen.) instead of

врач gen.sg. **врача́**[‡] doctor

встава́ть[i] **встаю́, встаёшь** (**встать**[p] **вста́ну, вста́нешь**) to get up

гид guide (person)

гита́ра guitar

гото́вить[i] (**при-**[p]) **гото́влю, гото́вишь** (+ acc.) to prepare; to cook

да́льше further

до́чка gen.pl. **до́чек** (little) daughter

за (+ inst.) (16.5) behind; for ('to fetch')

заво́д factory

на заво́де at a factory

за́втрак breakfast **за за́втраком** at ('behind') breakfast

за́втракать[i] (**по-**[p]) (like **знать**) to breakfast

занима́ться[i] (+ inst.) (like **знать**) to study (something)

знако́мить[i] (**по-**[p]) (+ acc.; **с** + inst.) **знако́млю, знако́мишь** to acquaint someone with

someone, to introduce someone
to someone

знако́миться (по-ᵖ) (**с** + inst.)
to beome acquainted with, to get
to know, to meet

игра́ть (**сыгра́ть**ᵖ) (like **знать**)
to play

инжене́р engineer

иностра́н(е)ц foreigner

интере́с interest

интересова́ться (за-ᵖ) (+ inst.)
интересу́юсь,
интересу́ешься to be
interested (in)

исто́рия history

каранда́ш gen.sg. **карандаша́**‡
pencil

ка́ша kasha, Russian porridge

лимо́н lemon

люби́мый favourite

лю́ди gen.pl. **люде́й** dat.pl.
лю́дям, inst.pl. **людьми́,**
prep.pl. **лю́дях** people (pl. of
челове́к 'person')

ме́жду (+ inst.) between (16.5)

молча́ть (за-ᵖ) **молчу́, молчи́шь**
to keep silent, say nothing

музыка́нт musician

назва́ние name

называ́ться (like **знать**) (+ inst.)
to be called

настоя́щий real, genuine

никогда́ (**не**) never

организа́ция organization

па́л(е)ц g.sg. **па́льца,** pl. **па́льцы**
finger

пе́ред + inst. before, in front of
(16.5)

петь (**с-**ᵖ) **пою́, поёшь** (+ acc.)
to sing (sth)

поёт see **петь** (he) sings

по́здно late

познако́мить(-ся) – see
знако́мить(ся)

председа́тель (m) chairman

привы́чка gen.pl. **привы́чек** habit

профессиона́л professional
(noun)

разгова́ривать (like **знать**)
(**с** + inst.) to converse with, talk to

ра́но early

ра́ньше before; earlier

революционе́р revolutionary

револю́ция revolution

ря́дом (**с** + inst.) beside

случи́тьсяᵖ (**с** + inst.) to happen (to)
Что́ случи́лось? What happened?

снача́ла first, at first

спать (по-ᵖ) **сплю, спишь**
to sleep

спу́тник travelling companion

станови́ться **становлю́сь,**
стано́вишься (**стать**ᵖ) (+ inst.)
to become

статьᵖ **ста́ну, ста́нешь** (+ inst.)
to become

стена́ acc. **сте́ну,** pl. **сте́ны** wall

сто́л gen.sg. **стола́**‡ table

те́ма theme, topic

увлека́ться (like **знать**) (+ inst.)
to be keen on, enthusiastic (about)

удово́льствие pleasure,
satisfaction

у́жин supper

у́жинать (по-ᵖ) (like **знать**)
to have supper

уро́к lesson

уходи́ть[†] **ухожу́, ухо́дишь (уйти́**[р]**)**
to leave

учи́тель (m) pl. **учителя́** teacher,
schoolteacher

хотя́ although

явля́ться[†] **явля́юсь, явля́ешься**
(+ inst.) to be (something)
(used in formal style, not in
conversation)

яи́чница [ye´esh-nee-tsa]
fried eggs

[†]*Stress Note.* If the genitive singular of a masculine noun is shown as stressed on the end (**стола́**), that means all forms of the word are stressed on the end (pl. **столы́**, dat. **столу́** etc.)

16.11 **Текст** (Translation in Key)

У́тром мы с бра́тьями Серге́ем и Алекса́ндром встаём ра́но, одева́емся и идём на ку́хню. Мы за́втракаем обы́чно вме́сте с отцо́м. О́н сиди́т за столо́м[†], пьёт ко́фе с молоко́м и с интере́сом чита́ет газе́ту. С на́ми он почти́ никогда́ не разгова́ривает за за́втраком. Ра́ньше он был учи́телем и за за́втраком всегда́ гото́вил уро́ки. Во́т почему́ у него́ така́я привы́чка – чита́ть и молча́ть за столо́м. Но когда́ мы сади́мся за сто́л[†], он говори́т:

– Здра́вствуйте, ма́льчики! Здра́вствуй, до́чка! Как спа́ли?

– Хорошо́, па́па, – отвеча́ем мы[†].

Пото́м мы начина́ем есть. Мои́ бра́тья обы́чно едя́т ка́шу. Серёжа ест ло́жкой, а Са́ша – па́льцами, так как о́н зна́ет, что́ оте́ц на него́ не смо́трит. Я ем бутербро́ды с сы́ром. Мы пьём чай с лимо́ном и́ли с варе́ньем. Иногда́ ма́ма де́лает мне яи́чницу с колбасо́й, но обы́чно она́ встаёт по́здно.

На́ша ма́ма не лю́бит за́втракать. Она́ встаёт по́сле нас и е́дет на за́вод, где рабо́тает гла́вным инжене́ром[†]. Ве́чером она́ возвраща́ется домо́й, па́па гото́вит у́жин, и мы все у́жинаем вме́сте.

По́сле у́жина мы сиди́м пе́ред телеви́зором, но обы́чно мы не смо́трим. Ма́ма сиди́т ме́жду мно́й и бра́тьями, и мы разгова́риваем. Э́то о́чень прия́тно. К сожале́нию, иногда́ вме́сто разгово́ра Серёжа игра́ет на гита́ре и Са́ша поёт. Хотя́ я

интересу́юсь му́зыкой, я не могу́ их слу́шать, когда́ они́ даю́т
тако́й конце́рт. Они́ говоря́т, что́ хотя́т стать профессиона́лами, но́
по-мо́ему они́ никогда́ не бу́дут настоя́щими музыка́нтами. Когда́
они́ начина́ют, я говорю́, что́ мне на́до занима́ться, и я ухожу́ из
ко́мнаты. Но́ па́па о́чень увлека́ется э́тими конце́ртами и слу́шает
сынове́й с удово́льствием.

‡**сиде́ть за столо́м** (inst.) to sit at ('behind') the table (place)
‡**сади́ться/сесть° за сто́л** (acc.) to sit down at the table (motion)
‡**отвеча́ем мы** 'answer we'. *After* direct speech the verb and the subject
are nearly always in that order in Russian.
‡**рабо́тать** + inst. to work as something

COMPREHENSION EXERCISE 16/4

Volodia and the KGB

1 Which three places mentioned by Volodia have new names?
2 What organization did Dzerzhinskii head?
3 Why does Mary ask if Dzerzhinskii was a foreigner?
4 Of the 'old Bolsheviks' listed by Volodia, which two were women?
5 What two opposing views of the Chekists does Volodia mention?

Воло́дя: Куда́ вы хоти́те пойти́ сего́дня?

Мэ́ри: Я хочу́ познако́миться с достопримеча́тельностями‡
Москвы́. Вы бу́дете мои́м ги́дом?

Воло́дя: С удово́льствием. Дава́йте пое́дем в це́нтр. Сейча́с я
возьму́ план го́рода. Во́т. Пое́дем снача́ла на Охо́тный‡
ряд. Э́то бы́вший проспе́кт Ма́ркса. По нему́ мы дойдём
до Театра́льной‡ пло́щади – она́ ра́ньше называ́лась
пло́щадью Свердло́ва. А во́т и‡ знамени́тый Большо́й
теа́тр. Ря́дом с ним – Ма́лый‡ теа́тр. Пото́м мы пойдём
да́льше, на Лубя́нскую пло́щадь. По́сле револю́ции
Лубя́нка до́лгое‡ вре́мя называ́лась пло́щадью
Дзержи́нского.

Мэ́ри: Ке́м был Дзержи́нский? По-мо́ему, о́н просла́вился‡
че́м-то‡ не о́чень прия́тным.

Воло́дя: Фе́ликс Эдму́ндович Дзержи́нский был одни́м‡ из пе́рвых чеки́стов‡. Точне́е‡, он был председа́телем – Всеросси́йской‡ чрезвыча́йной коми́ссии по борьбе́‡ с контрреволю́цией‡ и сабота́жем – ВЧК‡ [ve-chye-ká].

Мэ́ри: Фе́ликс Эдму́ндович? Он был иностра́нец'?

Воло́дя: По происхожде́нию‡ он был поля́к‡¹.

Мэ́ри: А что случи́лось с его́ Чрезвыча́йной Комми́ссией?

Воло́дя: Эта организа́ция не́сколько раз меня́ла‡ назва́ние: тепе́рь э́то КГБ [ka-ge-bé] – Комите́т‡ Госуда́рственной‡ Безопа́сности‡. Éсли хоти́те, я вам расскажу́ биогра́фию‡ Дзержи́нского.

Мэ́ри: Спаси́бо, я бессо́нницей‡ не страда́ю‡.

Воло́дя: Извини́те, не по́нял.

Мэ́ри: Это была́ шу́тка². А почему́ вы так увлека́етесь э́той те́мой?

Воло́дя: Мои́м люби́мым предме́том‡ в шко́ле была́ исто́рия. Я о́чень интересова́лся ста́рыми большевика́ми‡ – Ле́ниным, Кру́пской, Тро́цким, Буха́риным, Ка́меневым, Зино́вьевым, Коллонта́й, Дзержи́нским и други́ми. В ча́стности‡, я уже́ давно́ занима́юсь Дзержи́нским и его́ помо́щниками‡. Хотя́ тепе́рь мно́гие счита́ют‡ чеки́стов‡ престу́пниками‡, да́же уби́йцами‡, я счита́ю, что они́ бы́ли настоя́щими революционе́рами, пре́данными‡ иде́ям‡ Ле́нина.

Мэ́ри: Мо́жет быть, ве́чером вернёмся к э́той те́ме. А как‡ с на́шим маршру́том‡ по Москве́?

Воло́дя: Хорошо́. Пото́м мы пойдём по Нико́льской у́лице. Пе́ред ва́ми откро́ется‡ вид‡ на Кра́сную пло́щадь, мавзоле́й‡ Ле́нина и, за мавзоле́ем, кремлёвскую‡ сте́ну с ба́шнями‡.

---

1 After **быть** the nominative can be used for permanent features of the subject (see 16.8).

2 In 'It was/will be something' sentences, it is normal to make **быть** agree with the noun. **Это бы́ло шу́ткой** (inst.) is possible but less common.

‡**EXTRA Vocabulary for Comprehension Exercise (in Alphabetical Order)**

ба́шня tower

безопа́сность (f) security, safety

бессо́нница insomnia ('without sleepness')

биогра́фия biography

большеви́к gen. **большевика́** Bolshevik

борьба́ (с + inst.) struggle with/against

вид на + acc. view of

Всеросси́йская чрезвыча́йная коми́ссия All-Russia Special Commission

ВЧК the Cheka (Lenin's secret police 1917–22)

госуда́рственный state (adj)

до́лгое вре́мя for a long time

достопримеча́тельности (f. pl.) sights

и and; even; (used for emphasis) **а во́т и** and here is

иде́я idea

как (с + inst.) what about . . . ?

комите́т committee

контрреволю́ция counter-revolution

кремлёвский Kremlin (adj)

мавзоле́й mausoleum

ма́лый small (rarer form of **ма́ленький**)

маршру́т route

меня́тьⁱ to change

называ́тьсяⁱ (+ inst.) to be called something

одни́м (inst. of **оди́н**) (Table 7) one (same endings as **э́тот**)

откры́тьсяᵖ to open (intrans)

Охо́тный ряд 'Hunting Row'

поля́к Pole

помо́щник assistant

пре́данный (+ dat.) devoted to

предме́т subject (of study); object (thing)

престу́пник criminal

происхожде́ние origin

просла́витьсяᵖ **просла́влюсь, просла́вишься** (+ inst.) **(прославля́ться**ⁱ like **знать**) to become famous (for)

сабота́ж sabotage

страда́тьⁱ (like **знать**) (+ inst.) to suffer (from)

счита́тьⁱ (+ acc.) (+ inst.) to consider sth to be sth

театра́льный theatre (adj), theatrical

точне́е more precisely

уби́йца (m and f) murderer

в ча́стности in particular

чеки́ст Chekist (member of secret police)

чём-то (inst. of **что́-то**) by something

17

УРО́К НО́МЕР СЕМНА́ДЦАТЬ

TIME, DATE, AGE; ORDINAL NUMBERS

17.1 **Phrases: Time, Date, Age**

Мне два́дцать лет.	I am twenty.
в про́шлом году́	last year
в сле́дующем (бу́дущем) году́	next year
Приходи́те в пя́тницу.	Come on Friday.
Мы прие́дем пя́того ма́я.	We'll arrive on the fifth of May.
в ты́сяча девятьсо́т девяно́стом году́	in 1990
в апре́ле девяно́сто пе́рвого го́да	in April (19)91
Кото́рый час?	What time is it?
Ско́лько вре́мени?	What time is it?/How long?
Час.	(It is) one o'clock.
Два ча́са.	(It is) two o'clock/Two hours.
пять мину́т второ́го	(at) five past one
Без пяти́ де́вять.	(It is/At) five to nine.

17.2 **Days of the Week**

Monday	**понеде́льник**	'after Sunday day' from the old word for Sunday **неде́ля** which now means 'week'
Tuesday	**вто́рник [ftó-]**	'second day' – **второ́й** 'second'

201

Wednesday	**среда́**	'middle day' – **сре́дний** 'middle'
Thursday	**четве́рг** [-rk]	'fourth day' – **четвёртый** 'fourth'
Friday	**пя́тница**	'fifth day' – **пя́тый** 'fifth'
Saturday	**суббо́та**	'Sabbath'
Sunday	**воскресе́нье**	'resurrection' (g.pl. **воскресе́ний**)

On a particular day is **в** + the accusative:

в пя́тницу	on Friday
во вто́рник	on Tuesday (**в→во** before a word beginning with **в** + consonant)
в сре́ду	on Wednesday (note stress)

17.3 **Time of day**

Кото́рый час? or **Ско́лько вре́мени?** What time is it?

If the answer is a full hour, say:

Час.	(It is) one o'clock.
Два часа́.	(It is) two o'clock.
Сейча́с пять часо́в.	It is now five o'clock.

See Lesson 9 for the forms of nouns after different numerals.

17.4 **From the Full Hour to Half Past**

If the answer is between the full hour and half-past, Russian says 'It is so many minutes of the xth hour'. The hour from twelve to one is called **пе́рвый час** ('the first hour'); from one to two is 'the second hour' **второ́й час**, and so on. For the list of the Russian equivalents of 'first', 'second' etc., see 17.5 below. 'Ten past one' is 'ten minutes of the second', using the genitive case of **второ́й**, i.e. **второ́го**:

де́сять мину́т второ́го [-ova]	ten past one
два́дцать мину́т пя́того	twenty past four ('twenty minutes of the fifth')
шесть мину́т тре́тьего	six minutes past two

'Half' is **полови́на**, and 'half past six' is 'half of the seventh' **полови́на седьмо́го**.

17.5 Ordinal Numerals (Number Adjectives)

пе́рвый first	**шестна́дцатый** sixteenth
второ́й second	**семна́дцатый** seventeenth
тре́тий (see Table 5) third	**восемна́дцатый** eighteenth
четвёртый fourth	**девятна́дцатый** nineteenth
пя́тый fifth	**двадца́тый** twentieth
шесто́й sixth	**два́дцать пе́рвый** twenty-first
седьмо́й seventh	**тридца́тый** thirtieth
восьмо́й eighth	**сороково́й** fortieth
девя́тый ninth	**пятидеся́тый** fiftieth
деся́тый tenth	**шестидеся́тый** sixtieth
оди́ннадцатый [-a-tsa-ti] eleventh	**семидеся́тый** seventieth
двена́дцатый [-á-tsa-ti] twelfth	**восьмидеся́тый** eightieth
трина́дцатый thirteenth	**девяно́стый** ninetieth
четы́рнадцатый fourteenth	**со́тый** hundredth
пятна́дцатый fifteenth	**сто́ пе́рвый** hundred and first

17.6 Half-past to the Full Hour

From half-past to the full hour, Russian says 'without so many minutes x hours', so 'ten to eight' is 'without ten eight' **без десяти́ во́семь**. After **без** 'without', numbers, like nouns (see 10.6), must stand in the genitive case. The genitive of the numbers up to twenty-five is:

	nominative	genitive
1	**оди́н/одна́/одно́**	**одного́** (m/n)/**одно́й** (f)
2	**два/две**	**двух**
3	**три**	**трёх**
4	**четы́ре**	**четырёх**
5	**пять**	**пяти́**
6	**шесть**	**шести́**

7 семь	семи́
8 во́семь	восьми́
9 де́вять	девяти́
10 де́сять	десяти́
11 оди́ннадцать	оди́ннадцати
12 двена́дцать	двена́дцати
13 трина́дцать	трина́дцати
14 четы́рнадцать	четы́рнадцати
15 пятна́дцать	пятна́дцати
16 шестна́дцать	шестна́дцати
17 семна́дцать	семна́дцати
18 восемна́дцать	восемна́дцати
19 девятна́дцать	девятна́дцати
20 два́дцать	двадцати́
21 два́дцать оди́н/одна́/одно́	двадцати́ одного́/одно́й/одного́
22 два́дцать два/две	двадцати́ двух
23 два́дцать три	двадцати́ трёх
24 два́дцать четы́ре	двадцати́ четырёх
25 два́дцать пять	двадцати́ пяти́

без двадцати́ де́вять	twenty to nine
Сейча́с без двадцати́ пяти́ пять.	It is now twenty-five to five.

As in English, if the number does not divide by five, it is normal to add the word for 'minutes' (**мину́та: мину́ты** (gen.sg.) /**мину́т** (gen.pl.)).

It is nineteen minutes to one.	**Без девятна́дцати мину́т час.**
It is now one minute to four.	**Сейча́с без одно́й мину́ты четы́ре.**

EXERCISE 17/1

Translate:

1 **В воскресе́нье.** 2 **Сейча́с шесть часо́в.** 3 **Сейча́с два́дцать пять мину́т тре́тьего.** 4 On Wednesday. 5 It's ten past four. 6 It's twenty to twelve.

17.7 **At a Time**

To say *at* an hour, simply put **в** in front of the time:

в час	at one o'clock
в де́сять часо́в	at ten o'clock

At half-past **в полови́не** (prepositional case):

в полови́не пя́того	at half past four

For '*at* any other time', use the same form as for 'It is such and such a time':

Он пришёл де́сять мину́т седьмо́го.	He came at ten past six.
(**Сейча́с де́сять мину́т седьмо́го.** It is now ten past six.)	
Я приду́ без пяти́ оди́ннадцать.	I'll come at five to eleven.
(**Сейча́с без пяти́ оди́ннадцать.** It is now five to eleven.)	

17.8 **a.m./p.m.**

Either use the twenty-four hour clock (**в два́дцать оди́н час** 'at 9 p.m.' – 21 hours) or the following divisions of the day and night:

4 a.m. – midday: **утра́** ('of the morning' from **у́тро** 'morning')
midday – 6 p.m.: **дня** ('of the day' from **д(е)нь** 'day')
6 p.m. – midnight: **ве́чера** ('of the evening' from **ве́чер** 'evening')
midnight – 4 a.m.: **но́чи** ('of the night' from **ночь** 'night')

10 p.m.	**де́сять часо́в ве́чера**
He came back at 3 a.m. (three in the morning).	**О́н верну́лся в три часа́ но́чи** ('at three of the night').

EXERCISE 17/2

Translate:

1 **Она́ придёт без пяти́ во́семь.** 2 **Дава́й пойдём туда́ в суббо́ту в полови́не тре́тьего.** 3 **Фильм начина́ется де́сять мину́т восьмо́го.** 4 **Мы прие́дем в де́сять часо́в ве́чера.** 5 I'll come on Wednesday at six. 6 The film starts at ten to seven. 7 He'll telephone at half past four. 8 In London it is 11 p.m.

17.9 **EXTRA: Some Alternatives**

'Midday' can be **двенáдцать часóв** or **пóлдень**; 'midnight' can be **двенáдцать часóв** or **пóлночь**; 'a quarter' can be **пятнáдцать минýт** or **чéтверть** (f).

Óн пришёл в двенáдцать   He came at midnight.
часóв/в пóлночь.

Я позвоню́ без пятнáдцати/без I'll call at a quarter to seven.
чéтверти семь.

There is also an official style for giving times, used in station announcements and on the radio. This uses the twenty-four-hour clock and gives the hours and minutes as follows:

14.53 **Четы́рнадцать часóв пятьдеся́т три минýты**
10.02 **Дéсять часóв две минýты**
23.00 **Двáдцать три нóль-нóль**

Москóвское врéмя – восемнáдцать часóв пятнáдцать минýт.
Moscow Time is 6.15 p.m.

17.10 **Months**

The months, all masculine, are:

	Nominative	Genitive	Prepositional
January	**янвáрь**	**января́**	**в январé**
February	**феврáль**	**февраля́**	**в февралé**
March	**март**	**мáрта**	**в мáрте**
April	**апрéль**	**апрéля**	**в апрéле**
May	**май**	**мáя**	**в мáе**
June	**ию́нь**	**ию́ня**	**в ию́не**
July	**ию́ль**	**ию́ля**	**в ию́ле**
August	**áвгуст**	**áвгуста**	**в áвгусте**

September	**сентя́брь**	**сентября́**	**в сентябре́**
October	**октя́брь**	**октября́**	**в октябре́**
November	**ноя́брь**	**ноября́**	**в ноябре́**
December	**дека́брь**	**декабря́**	**в декабре́**

Note that the first two months and the last four have the stress on the end in the genitive, while the six in the middle have fixed stress on the stem.

'In a month' is **в** + prepositional. Since all the months are masculine, all end **-e** in the prepositional case:

in March **в ма́рте**

in December **в декабре́**

What is the date today? is **Како́е сего́дня число́? Число́** means 'number'. A day in the month is the adjective form of the numeral (see 17.5 above) in its *neuter* form (agreeing with the word **число́** 'number', 'date', which is usually omitted). So 'the first' is **пе́рвое**. The month is then in the genitive ('of April').

| **Сего́дня второ́е января́.** | Today is the second of January. |
| **два́дцать тре́тье ма́я** | the twenty-third of May |

On a date is expressed by the *genitive* ending of the adjective:

| **Я прие́ду восьмо́го ма́я.** | I'll come on the eighth of May. |

17.11 Years

The year is an adjective too, so once again we need the ordinal numerals from 17.5. The year 1991 is 'the thousand nine hundred ninety-first year' **ты́сяча девятьсо́т девяно́сто пе́рвый год**.

| **ты́сяча девятьсо́т со́рок пя́тый год** | 1945 |
| **ты́сяча пятьсо́т пятьдеся́т второ́й год** | 1552 |

Note: It is perfectly acceptable to omit the century if it is obvious:

| **Я роди́лся в со́рок восьмо́м году́.** | I was born in 1948 ('in forty-eighth year'). |

'In a year' is **в** + prepositional case. (Note prep. of **год** is **в году́**.)

В ты́сяча девятьсо́т девяно́сто In 1992
второ́м году́

If the month is included, say 'In May *of* the year (gen.)'

Я родила́сь в ию́не со́рок   I was born in June 1948 ('in June
восьмо́го го́да.   of 48').

EXERCISE 17/3

Translate:

1 **Гла́вные пра́здники в СССР бы́ли пе́рвое января́, пе́рвое ма́я, девя́тое ма́я, седьмо́е ноября́.** 2 **Ле́нин роди́лся два́дцать второ́го апре́ля ты́сяча восемьсо́т семидеся́того го́да.** 3 **Они́ прие́хали в шесть часо́в ве́чера в понеде́льник три́дцать пе́рвого декабря́ ты́сяча девятьсо́т девяно́стого го́да.** 4 On the sixth of April 1991. 5 At 9 a.m. on Friday the eleventh of January. 6 At 5.45 on the tenth of October 1977.

17.12 From (c + gen.), Until (до + gen.), After (по́сле + gen.)

These three prepositions are used with all the time words in the preceding sections.

с шести́ (gen.) **часо́в**   from/since six o'clock
до пя́того октября́   until fifth October
до вто́рника   until Tuesday
с шестьдеся́т седьмо́го го́да   since (19)67

с шести́ часо́в до оди́ннадцати   from six o'clock until eleven
от (+ gen.) . . . **до** can also be used

With dates, **по** + acc. (meaning 'up to and including') is the equivalent of 'inclusive' (American 'thru'):

с деся́того ма́я <u>по</u> пятна́дцатое   from the tenth to the fifteenth of May
inclusive

17.13 Age

To give your age in Russian, you say 'To me (dat.) is twenty-five years'.
Remember that the genitive plural of **год** is **лет** (from **лéто** 'summer'):

Мне (dat.) **двáдцать пять лет.**	I am twenty-five.
Скóлько вам лет?	How old are you? ('How many to you of years?')
Емý трúдцать три гóда.	He is thirty-three.
Ей бы́ло (n.sg. – see 22.12) **двáдцать лет.**	She was twenty.

For other expressions of time and duration, see Lesson 23.

EXERCISE 17/4

Translate:

(1)

A: Скóлько вам лет?

Б: Мне трúдцать четы́ре гóда.

A: Когдá ваш день рождéния?

Б: Двáдцать трéтьего мáрта.

A: Скóлько лет вáшим дéтям?

Б: Сы́ну дéсять лет, а дóчери вóсемь.

A: Вы давнó в Москвé?

Б: С прóшлой пя́тницы.

(2)

A: Вáня, в какóм годý ты стал учúтелем?

Б: В шестьдеся́т трéтьем.

A: Скóлько тебé бы́ло лет тогдá?

Б: Двáдцать три.

(3)

A: Скажúте, пожáлуйста, когдá рабóтает э́тот магазúн?

Б: С девятú утрá до десятú вéчера.

(4)

A: Сейчáс пятнáдцать минýт пя́того.

Б: Как?! На мои́х часа́х‡ ещё нет четырёх.

‡часы́ watch

(5)

Тури́ст: Скажи́те, пожа́луйста, когда́ рабо́тает Ру́сский музе́й?
Ева: Ка́ждый день, кро́ме вто́рника, с девяти́ до шести́.
Тури́ст: Спаси́бо.
Ева: Пожа́луйста.

(6)

А: Скажи́те, пожа́луйста, когда́ открыва́ется э́тот магази́н?
Б: В оди́ннадцать часо́в.
А: А когда́ переры́в на обе́д?
Б: С двух до трёх.

(7)

А: Когда́ в ГУ́Ме переры́в на обе́д?
Б: ГУМ рабо́тает без переры́ва.

(8)

А: Когда́ в гастроно́мах выходно́й день?
Б: Гастроно́мы рабо́тают без выходны́х дней.

17.14 Vocabulary

(See also Days 17.2, Months 17.10, Ordinal Numerals 17.5)

большинство́ majority
бу́дущий future (adj)
бюро́ (n indecl) office
во вре́мя (+ gen.) during (23.3 (h))
выходно́й день day off
гастроно́м food shop
гуля́тьᶦ **(по-**ᵖ**) гуля́ю, гуля́ешь**
    to take a walk
де́тство childhood
закрыва́ть(ся)ᶦ (like **знать**)
    закры́ть(ся)ᵖ **закро́ю,**

закро́ешь to close
замеча́тельный remarkable
зарубе́жный foreign
зате́м then, next (= **пото́м**)
кто ... кто some ... some
москви́ч gen. **москвича́** (stress)
    Muscovite
моско́вский Moscow (adj)
не́который some, certain (adj)
па́мять (f) memory
переры́в break

петербу́ргский Petersburg (adj)

писа́тель (m) writer

по́езд (pl.) поезда́ train

полови́на half

пра́здник [práz-neek] national holiday; festival

приро́да nature (scenery)

проводи́ть' (провести́ᵖ) вре́мя провожу́, прово́дишь to spend ('conduct') time

прогу́лка gen.pl. прогу́лок walk

продово́льственный food (adj), grocery

про́мтова́рный магази́н non-food goods shop (про́м is from промы́шленный 'industrial' and това́р means 'goods' or 'wares')

ро́вно precisely; evenly

рожде́ние birth

день рожде́ния birthday

сме́рть (f) death

сно́ва again

создава́ть' создаю́, создаёшь (созда́тьᵖ like дать 12.7) to create

с(о́)н sleep; dream

пе́ред сно́м before bed ('before sleeping')

среди́ (+ gen.) among

сте́пень (f) degree, extent

до тако́й сте́пени to such a degree

сюда́ here, hither (motion equivalent of здесь)

тишина́ silence, quiet

Ура́л the Urals

на Ура́ле in the Urals

часы́ (pl. of час) watch; clock

чуде́сный wonderful

экску́рсия excursion

17.15 Texts

Moscow Working Hours

Мэ́ри: Когда́ москвичи́ обе́дают днём?

Воло́дя: Кто́ в двена́дцать часо́в, кто́ в час, кто́ в два, кто́ и‡ в три. Не́которые магази́ны закрыва́ются с трёх часо́в до четырёх, иногда́ да́же с четырёх до пяти́. Мно́гие магази́ны рабо́тают без переры́ва.

Мэ́ри: А когда́ они́ открыва́ются у́тром?

Воло́дя: Продово́льственные магази́ны с восьми́, а про́мтова́рные с десяти́.

Мэ́ри: Когда́ они́ закрыва́ются?

Воло́дя: По́здно [pó-zna]. Большинство́ рабо́тает до восьми́,

211

не́которые до десяти́. Но́ бюро́ закрыва́ются ра́ньше, о́коло пяти́.

| Мэ́ри: | А в суббо́ту и воскресе́нье? |
| Воло́дя: | Гастроно́мы рабо́тают ка́ждый день. Бюро́ в э́ти дни не рабо́тают. |

‡**и** even (particle' – see Lesson 30).

In the Hotel Service Bureau

Гость:	Когда́ отхо́дит‡ по́езд в Воро́неж?
Де́вушка:	В оди́ннадцать часо́в ве́чера.
Гость:	А когда́ я смогу́ получи́ть биле́т?
Де́вушка:	За́втра у́тром.
Гость:	Хорошо́. Я приду́ в во́семь часо́в.
Де́вушка:	Это ра́но. Бюро́ открыва́ется в де́вять.
Гость:	Но́ за́втра я не смогу́ прийти́ в де́вять. На́ша экску́рсия по го́роду начнётся в во́семь три́дцать.
Де́вушка:	Тогда́ мы бу́дем ждать вас по́сле экску́рсии. Мы рабо́таем до восьми́ часо́в ве́чера.

‡**отходи́ть** to depart (of a train).

EXERCISE 17/5

Translate:

1 How old is she? 2 I am thirty-six. 3 In 1988 he was forty. 4 I'll come on Tuesday at a quarter to three in the afternoon. 5 Please phone me on the tenth after six. 6 We'll be in Siberia from the ninth of May to the sixteenth of June. 7 I have lived (= am living) in London since 1973.

READING AND COMPREHENSION EXERCISE 17/6

1 Read in Russian (or write out in full) the three dates in the first paragraph: 'in 1840', 'from 1885', 'in May 1892'.
2 Write out Chaikovskii's twelve-part daily timetable in Klin.
3 Which two dates are mentioned in the last paragraph?

4 Why are these two dates significant?

Пётр Ильи́ч Чайко́вский роди́лся на Ура́ле в 1840 году́. Му́зыку он
на́чал сочиня́ть‡ уже́ в де́тстве. Музыка́льное образова́ние‡ он
получи́л в Петербу́ргской консервато́рии‡. С 1885 го́да
Чайко́вский жил в окре́стностях‡ го́рода Кли́на, недалеко́ от
Москвы́. А в до́ме, где тепе́рь до́м-музе́й Чайко́вского, Пётр Ильи́ч
посели́лся‡ в ма́е 1892 го́да. Здесь бы́ло всё, к чему́ Чайко́вский
давно́ стреми́лся‡: замеча́тельная приро́да, тишина́, возмо́жность
писа́ть му́зыку. Он встава́л в восьмо́м‡ часу́ утра́, до девяти́
занима́лся англи́йским языко́м и чита́л. В полови́не деся́того
приступа́л‡ к рабо́те. Рабо́тал Пётр Ильи́ч до ча́су‡ дня. Час
обе́дал, а зате́м ро́вно два часа́ гуля́л. Гуля́л обяза́тельно оди́н‡,
так как во вре́мя прогу́лок почти́ всегда́ сочиня́л му́зыку. С пяти́
до семи́ Пётр Ильи́ч сно́ва рабо́тал. По́сле рабо́ты гуля́л и́ли
игра́л на фортепья́но‡. В во́семь часо́в подава́лся‡ у́жин. По́сле
у́жина Чайко́вский проводи́л вре́мя с гостя́ми, а е́сли госте́й не́
было, чита́л. В оди́ннадцать шёл в свою́‡ ко́мнату, писа́л пи́сьма и
пе́ред сном сно́ва чита́л. В э́том до́ме Чайко́вский создава́л свои́
после́дние произведе́ния‡, среди́ них гениа́льную‡ Шесту́ю
симфо́нию‡.

Тепе́рь Клин – го́род Чайко́вского. До́м П.И. Чайко́вского в
Клину́ стал музе́ем. Два́ ра́за в го́д, седьмо́го ма́я, в день
рожде́ния Петра́ Ильича́, и шесто́го ноября́, в день его́ сме́рти,
сюда́ приезжа́ют оте́чественные‡ и иностра́нные музыка́нты.
И здесь сно́ва звучи́т‡ чуде́сная му́зыка Петра́ Ильича́
Чайко́вского. Тогда́ мно́гие слу́шатели вспомина́ют слова́
вели́кого ру́сского писа́теля Анто́на Па́вловича Че́хова: «Я гото́в‡
день и ночь стоя́ть в почётном‡ карау́ле у крыльца́‡ того́ до́ма, где
живёт Пётр Ильи́ч.»

‡Extra Vocabulary

в восьмо́м часу́ between 7 and 8
  ('in the eighth hour' – see 17.4)
гениа́льный brilliant
гото́в (m) **гото́ва** (f) **гото́вы** (pl.)
  ready (short adj – 29.7)
звуча́ть' **звучи́т** to sound

консервато́рия conservatoire
крыльцо́ porch; front steps
музыка́льный musical
образова́ние education
оди́н/одна́/одно́/одни́ alone
окре́стности (pl.) environs

213

отéчественный home ('of the fatherland', from **отéчество** 'fatherland', 'Russian')

подавáться¹ to be served

поселúтьсяᵖ to take up residence

почётный караýл guard of honour

приступáть¹ **к** (+ dat.) to get down (to), start (on)

произведéние a work (of art)

в свою кóмнату to his own room

симфóния symphony

сочинять¹ (**сочинúть**ᵖ) to compose

стремúться¹ **к** (+ dat.) to strive for, aspire to

фортепьяно piano (modern equivalents are **рояль** (m) ('grand piano') and **пианúно** (indecl) ('upright'))

час hour; one o'clock (17.3)

до чáсу until one o'clock (**чáсу** is a variant of the genitive **чáса**)

18

УРÓК НÓМЕР ВОСЕМНÁДЦАТЬ

THE COMPARATIVE; SUPERLATIVES; RELATIVE CLAUSES WITH **КОТÓРЫЙ**

18.1 Phrases with Comparatives

Э́то бу́дет лу́чше.	That will be better.
Какóе винó дешéвле?	Which wine is cheaper?
Тóт фильм интерéснее.	That film is more interesting.
Быстрéе!	Faster!
Побыстрéе!	A bit faster!
Говори́те мéдленнее!	Speak more slowly!
Дáйте кóфе покрéпче.	Give me stronger coffee.

18.2 Comparative of Adjectives and Adverbs: Examples to Learn

better	**лу́чше**	from	**хорóший** good
cheaper	**дешéвле**	from	**дешёвый** cheap
easier	**лéгче**	from	**лёгкий** easy
larger	**бóльше**	from	**большóй** large
less	**мéньше**	from	**мáленький** small
longer	**длиннéе**	from	**дли́нный** long
more	**бóльше**	from	**большóй** large
more beautiful	**краси́вее**	from	**краси́вый** beautiful
more difficult	**труднéе**	from	**трýдный** difficult
more expensive	**дорóже**	from	**дорогóй** expensive
more interesting	**интерéснее**	from	**интерéсный** interesting

more often	**ча́ще**	from	**ча́сто** often
nicer	**прия́тнее**	from	**прия́тный** pleasant, nice
quicker	**быстре́е**	from	**бы́стрый** quick
shorter	**коро́че**	from	**коро́ткий** short
simpler	**про́ще**	from	**просто́й** simple
slower	**ме́дленнее**	from	**ме́дленный** slow
smaller	**ме́ньше**	from	**ма́ленький** small
stronger	**кре́пче**	from	**кре́пкий** strong
worse	**ху́же**	from	**плохо́й** bad

Use these as adverbs ('Write faster') or as predicative¹ adjectives, i.e. with no following noun, in sentences such as 'This hotel was/will be better' **Э́та гости́ница была́/бу́дет лу́чше**.

In informal Russian, **по-** 'a little' is often added to the comparative:

побыстре́е 'a bit faster', **поме́ньше** 'a little less'

'Than' is **чем**:

Ва́ша ко́мната лу́чше, чем на́ша.	Your room is better than ours.
Петербу́рг краси́вее, чем Москва́.	Petersburg is more beautiful than Moscow.
В Петербу́рге интере́снее, чем в Москве́.	It's more interesting in Petersburg than in Moscow.
Вы говори́те быстре́е, чем я.	You speak faster than me/than I do.
Я зна́ю Е́ву лу́чше, чем Ве́ра (nom.).	I know Eva better than Vera does.
Я зна́ю Е́ву лу́чше, чем Ве́ру (acc.).	I know Eva better than I know Vera.

But in colloquial Russian, instead of **чем** + the *nominative* case, the genitive (with no **чем**) is preferred:

Ва́ша ко́мната лу́чше на́шей (gen.).	Your room is better than ours.
Петербу́рг краси́вее Москвы́ (gen.).	Petersburg is more beautiful than Moscow.
Вы говори́те быстре́е меня́ (gen.).	You speak faster than me/than I do.
Я зна́ю Е́ву лу́чше Ве́ры (gen.).	I know Eva better than Vera does.

18.3 **Formation and Use of Comparatives**

If the last consonant of the adjective or adverb is **н, л, р** or a labial (lip consonant – **п, б, м, в**) simply add the indeclinable ending **-ee**. If the adjective has only two syllables, the stress is generally on the **-ée**.

краси́вый	beautiful	**краси́вее**	more beautiful(ly)
у́мный	clever	**умне́е**	cleverer/more cleverly

Note the stress of:

весёлый	cheerful	**веселе́е**	more cheerful(ly)
холо́дный	cold	**холодне́е**	colder/more coldly

If the adjective or adverb has some other ending, such as **-кий** or **-тый**, the stem changes and the ending is a single indeclinable **-e**. See the list in 18.2. Stress is always on the stem.

бли́зкий	near	**бли́же**
бога́тый	rich	**бога́че**
высо́кий	tall	**вы́ше**
глубо́кий	deep	**глу́бже**
далёкий	far	**да́льше**
молодо́й	young	**моло́же**
ни́зкий	low	**ни́же**
ти́хий	quiet	**ти́ше**
широ́кий	wide	**ши́ре**

Two common adjectives have totally unpredictable comparatives, as in English:

хоро́ший	good	**лу́чше**	better
плохо́й	bad	**ху́же**	worse

Since it is sometimes difficult to work out, or guess, the **-e** comparative of an adjective, it is reassuring to know that there is a simple alternative: just place the word **бо́лее** 'more' (not **бо́льше** in this construction) in front of the adjective, which then has its normal case, gender and number endings. So **бо́лее дешёвый** (m), **бо́лее дешёвая** (f) or **бо́лее дешёвое** (n) is another way of saying **деше́вле** 'cheaper'.

Э́та кни́га бо́лее дешёвая. This book is cheaper.

However, Russians much prefer to use the indeclinable form: **Эта кни́га деше́вле**.

But note that if you put a comparative *before* a noun ('a cheaper book'), you *must* use the **бо́лее** construction:

Я куплю́ бо́лее дешёвую (not **деше́вле**) **кни́гу**. I'll buy a cheaper book.
Она́ была́ в бо́лее дли́нном пла́тье. She was wearing ('in') a longer dress.

With the **бо́лее** comparative, 'than' is always **чем**, never the genitive:

Ве́ра бо́лее интере́сная же́нщина, чем Е́ва.
   Vera is a more interesting woman than Eva.

Russians tend to avoid using the **бо́лее** construction, except with long adjectives (four syllables or more, e.g. **удиви́тельный** 'surprising', **есте́ственный** 'natural' **Это бо́лее есте́ственно** 'That's more natural'). So in equivalents of sentences such as 'I want a lighter room', Russians normally say 'I want a room (which is) lighter'.

Я хочу́ ко́мнату посветле́е[1] (though you can also say **Я хочу́ бо́лее све́тлую ко́мнату**).

'Much' with comparatives is **намно́го** (formal usage) or **гора́здо** (colloquial):

Чай намно́го/гора́здо деше́вле вина́. Tea is much cheaper than wine.

EXERCISE 18/1

Translate:

1 **Како́е вино́ лу́чше?** 2 **Э́ти апельси́ны доро́же.** 3 **Приходи́те к нам поча́ще.** 4 **Побыстре́е, пожа́луйста, уже́ полови́на восьмо́го.** 5 **Е́ва моло́же Ве́ры.** 5 **В Москве́ пого́да была́ лу́чше, чем в Петербу́рге.** 7 **Ру́сский язы́к намно́го трудне́е францу́зского.** 8 **«Война́ и мир» бо́лее дли́нный рома́н, чем «А́нна Каре́нина».** 9 **Ве́ра была́ в бо́лее**

---

1 In this construction, **по-** ('a little') is always added to the comparative.

дорого́м пла́тье, чем Е́ва. 10 Мэ́ри гора́здо интере́снее Е́вы. 11 Мэ́ри интересу́ется Дзержи́нским ме́ньше Воло́ди. 12 Пожа́луйста, да́йте мне рабо́ту поле́гче.

EXERCISE 18/2

Translate the words in brackets:

1 **В Ло́ндоне жизнь** (is better). 2 **Вади́м говори́т** (more slowly than you). 3 **Во́дка сто́ит** (much more expensive) **в рестора́не,** (than in the shop). 4 **Ве́ра зна́ет** (more than Eva). 5 **Достое́вский и Че́хов** (are more interesting) **писа́тели,** (than Tolstoi). 6 **Я покупа́ю вино́** (more often), **чем** (vodka).

18.4 Special Comparatives

When used before a noun, four common adjectives have *declinable* comparative forms which must be used instead of the **бо́лее** construction above. They have the same endings as **хоро́ший**.

хоро́ший	good	лу́чший	better
плохо́й	bad	ху́дший	worse
большо́й	big	бо́льший	bigger (note stress)
ма́ленький	small	ме́ньший	smaller

Е́ва живёт в лу́чш<u>ей</u> кварти́ре, чем Ве́ра. Eva lives in a better flat than Vera (*not* **в бо́лее хоро́шей**).
Е́ва живёт в бо́льш<u>ей</u> кварти́ре. Eva lives in a bigger flat (*not* **в бо́лее большо́й**).

Note 1: If there is no **чем** 'than', **лу́чший** also means 'best', **ху́дший** means 'worst', **ме́ньший** means 'least' (see 18.7):

Вади́м – мой лу́чший друг.   Vadim is my best friend.

Note 2: Two more common adjectives sometimes behave like the four above: **молодо́й** 'young' has the comparative **мла́дший** in the meaning 'junior', and **ста́рый** 'old' has **ста́рший** in the meaning 'senior'. They are also used for 'younger' and 'elder' in family relationships.

Э́то моя́ мла́дшая сестра́.	This is my younger sister.
бо́лее ста́рый дом	an older house
but	
ста́рший офице́р	a senior officer

Note 3: If there is *no* following noun, the comparatives **лу́чший**, **ху́дший**, **бо́льший**, **ме́ньший** *must* be replaced by the indeclinables **лу́чше**, **ху́же**, **бо́льше**, **ме́ньше** (the forms in 18.2):

Э́то ко́мната лу́чше (not **лу́чшая**). This room is better.

(**Э́та ко́мната лу́чшая** (= **Э́то лу́чшая ко́мната**) means 'This room is the *best*/This is the best room' – Note 1)

18.5 Less

Ме́нее 'less' (an alternative form of **ме́ньше**) is used like **бо́лее**.

Неме́цкий язы́к ме́нее тру́дный, чем ру́сский.
German is less difficult than Russian.

More colloquially, you can use **не тако́й . . . как** ('not such . . . as') with adjectives and **не так . . . как** ('not so . . . as') with adverbs:

Францу́зский язы́к не тако́й тру́дный, как ру́сский.	French is not as difficult as Russian.
не так ча́сто, как ра́ньше	not as often as before

18.6 Superlatives

If you want to say 'the cheapest wine', 'the most interesting girl', simply place **са́мый** ('the very') in front of the adjective. **Са́мый** is itself an adjective (same endings as **но́вый**), so it has the same gender, number and case as the adjective which comes after it:

дешёвое вино́	cheap wine
са́мое дешёвое вино́	the cheapest wine
Я говори́л с интере́сной де́вушкой.	I talked to an interesting girl.
Я говори́л с са́мой интере́сной де́вушкой.	I talked to the most interesting girl.

18.7 Superlative Adjectives (see 18.4 Note 2 above)

Although 'best' can be **самый хороший** (as in 18.6), 'worst' can be **самый плохой** and 'smallest'/'least' can be **самый маленький**, it is common to use **лучший** and (less commonly) **худший** and **меньший** (18.4) as superlatives, with or without **самый**:

Вадим – мой (самый)	Vadim is my (very) best friend.
лучший друг.	
в худшем случае	in the worst case

In bookish style, these three superlatives can have the prefix **наи-** ('most'), instead of the word **самый**:

| **наилучший** the very best | **наилучшие годы** the best years |
| **наименьший** the least | **с наименьшим трудом** with the least effort |

наибольший 'biggest' also exists as the superlative of **большой**.

EXERCISE 18/3

Translate:

1 **Мы купим самые дорогие билеты.** 2 **Мы живём в лучшей гостинице.** 3 **Байкал – самое большое озеро в мире.** 4 He bought (ᴾ) the cheapest vodka. 5 This is the easiest exercise.

18.8 EXTRA: Another Type of Superlative: величайший

This type of adjective has the ending **-ейший** or, for certain adjectives (see below), **-айший**. It is rarer than the **самый** type of superlative and differs from it in meaning by being more emotive. It can indicate a high degree of the quality expressed by the adjective ('a very great writer') without necessarily implying that no other case is greater ('*the* greatest writer'):

Пушкин – самый великий русский поэт. Pushkin is *the greatest* Russian poet.

Пу́шкин – велича́йший ру́сский поэ́т. Pushkin is *a very great* Russian poet.

Examples:

чи́стый clean/pure   **чисте́йший** purest/very pure
интере́сный interesting   **интере́снейший** most interesting

Adjectives whose stem ends **к**, **г**, **х** change the **к**, **г**, **х** to **ч**, **ж**, **ш** respectively and add the ending **-а́йший**:

вели́кий great   **велича́йший** greatest
широ́кий wide   **широча́йший** widest
ти́хий quiet   **тиша́йший** quietest
дорого́й dear   **дража́йший** dearest (from **драго́й**,
                                a rarer form of **дорого́й**)

Three **-зкий** adjectives have exceptional forms: **бли́зкий** 'near' **ближа́йший** 'nearest'; **ни́зкий** 'low' **нижа́йший** 'lowest'; **ме́рзкий** 'foul', 'disgusting' **мерзе́йший** 'foulest'.

It is unnecessary to learn this method of forming superlatives. But note these phrases:

Нет ни мале́йшего сомне́ния. There isn't the slightest doubt (from
    ма́лый 'small').
чисте́йший вздо́р utter rubbish ('purest rubbish')
дража́йшая полови́на better half (wife or husband, literally 'dearest half')
с велича́йшим удово́льствием with the greatest of pleasure
в кратча́йший сро́к in the shortest possible time (from **кра́ткий** 'short')
Где ближа́йшая остано́вка авто́буса? Where's the nearest bus-stop?
нижа́йший покло́н kindest greetings ('lowest bow')
мерзе́йшее настрое́ние foulest mood

18.9 Relative Clauses¹ with кото́рый ('Who'/'Which')

If you want to say 'That's the girl *whom* /the film *which* I saw yesterday', the Russian word you need is **кото́рый**. This is an adjective with the same endings as **но́вый**.

Где буты́лки, кото́рые   Where are the bottles which
 стоя́ли здесь?   were standing here?
Во́т де́вушка, кото́рая была́   There's the girl who was in
 в рестора́не.   the restaurant.

It is curious that English makes a distinction here between animate (the girl *who* . . .) and inanimate (the glass *which* . . .) while Russian doesn't.

Кото́рый agrees in number and gender with the noun to which it relates: **Де́вушка, кото́рая** (f sg.) **была́** . . . The girl who was . . .; **Де́вушки, кото́рые** (pl.) **бы́ли** . . . The girls who were . . .

Кото́рый also has case endings, but these depend *not* on the preceding noun but on the role of **кото́рый** in its own clause†. So in the sentence 'This is the girl who(m) you saw yesterday' **Во́т де́вушка** (nom.), **кото́рую** (acc.) **вы ви́дели вчера́** the relative **кото́рую** has an accusative ending because it is the object of **ви́дели**. If in English you say 'who*m* you saw', then you are obeying the same grammatical rule, since 'whom' is the accusative of 'who'.

Во́т официа́нт (m sg. nom.)**, кото́рого** (m sg., acc.) **вы иска́ли.**
There's the waiter (whom) you were looking for.
Где официа́нт, с кото́рым (m sg., inst.) **я говори́л?**
Where's the waiter I was talking to (with whom I was talking)?
Вы зна́ете де́вушек (pl., acc.)**, с кото́рыми** (pl., inst.) **я познако́мился в ба́ре?**
Do you know the girls I met in the bar (with whom I became acquainted)?

EXERCISE 18/4

Put the required ending on **кото́рый**:

1 **Же́нщина, кото́р____ сиди́т в углу́, америка́нка.**
 The woman who is sitting in the corner is American.

2 **Же́нщина, с кото́р____ вы говори́ли, то́же америка́нка.**
 The woman you were talking to is also American.

3 **Пожа́луйста, покажи́те кни́ги, кото́р____ вы купи́ли.**
 Please show me the books which you bought.

4 **Мы живём в гости́нице, кото́р____ постро́или фи́нны.**

We are staying in a hotel which was built by (which built) the Finns.

5 **Мы живём в но́мере** (m), **в котор___ нет телеви́зора.**

We have a room without a television (in which there is no television).

6 **Э́то писа́тель, котор___ я о́чень люблю́.**

He's a writer I like very much.

In English 'which'/'who'/'whom' can be omitted 'There's the waiter (who) you were looking for', but in standard Russian **кото́рый** must always be present in such sentences.

18.10 Use кто/что, not кото́рый, after the pronouns тот 'that', весь 'all'

After the pronouns **тот** 'that' (pl. **те** 'those'), **все** 'everybody' and **всё** 'everything', **кото́рый** is *usually* replaced by **кто** (for animates) or **что** (for inanimates). The verb in the **кто/что** clause[†] is singular if **кто** or **что** is the subject, since **кто** is grammatically a masculine singular word and **что** is grammatically neuter singular. However, some Russians make the verb plural after **кто** if the verb in the main clause is plural.

Те, кто (not **кото́рые**) **был** (possible: **бы́ли**) **на ве́чере, верну́лись в три часа́ но́чи.**

Those who were at the party came back at three in the morning.

Всё, о чём (not **о кото́ром**) **он говори́л, мы уже́ зна́ли.**

Everything which he talked about we already knew.

Тот, о ком вы спра́шивали, уе́хал вчера́.

The one you asked about left yesterday.

Спаси́бо за всё, что вы сде́лали для нас.

Thank you for everything (which) you've done for us.

18.11 Vocabulary (See also comparative lists 18.2, 18.3)

А́зия Asia

америка́нка gen.pl. **америка́нок** American (woman)

анекдо́т joke, anecdote

ах oh

Байка́л Lake Baikal

бар bar

бе́рег prep. **на берегу́** pl. **берега́** bank, shore

бо́лее more

бо́льший (18.4) bigger

води́ть' вожу́, во́дишь (20.2) to take, lead (there and back)

восто́к east

на восто́ке in the east

восто́чный eastern

высо́кий tall

вы́ше taller

глубо́кий deep

гора́ acc. **го́ру,** pl. **го́ры** hill; mountain

грани́ца border

достава́ть' достаю́, достаёшь (доста́ть° доста́ну, доста́нешь) to get hold of, obtain; to reach

дре́вний ancient

занима́ть' занима́ю, занима́ешь, (заня́ть° займу́, займёшь) + acc. to occupy (something)

за́пад (на за́паде) west (in the west)

запа́с stock, reserve

зверь (m) gen.pl. **звере́й** (wild) animal

зо́лото gold

Кита́й China

кон(е́)ц end

кото́рый who/which (18.9)

ле́кция lecture

лу́чше (18.3) **[lo´o-tshe]** better

лу́чший (18.4, 18.7) **[lo´o-tshi]** better, best

Монго́лия Mongolia

мужчи́на (m) **[moo-shshe´e-na]** man

наприме́р for example

нача́ло beginning

огро́мный enormous

о́зеро pl. **озёра** lake

о́стров pl. **острова́** island

отде́льный separate

побли́же a bit closer (18.3)

позавчера́ the day before yesterday

по́мнить' по́мню, по́мнишь to remember

пригласи́ть° приглашу́, пригласи́шь (приглаша́ть' like знать) (+ acc.) to invite (someone)

пти́ца bird

ре́дкий rare

са́мый very, most (18.6)

се́вер (на се́вере) north (in the north)

се́верный northern

специали́ст (по + dat.) specialist (in)

террито́рия territory

худо́й thin; bad

часть (f) gen.pl. **часте́й** part

челове́к pl. **лю́ди** (16.10) person

молодо́й челове́к young man

чем than

чи́стый pure, clean

ю́жный southern

18.12 Текст Viktor Wants to Meet Mary

Воло́дя: Вы по́мните Ви́ктора?

Мэ́ри: Э́то то́т молодо́й челове́к, с кото́рым вы говори́ли вчера́ в ба́ре?

Воло́дя: Нет. Это то́т, кто́ доста́л нам‡ биле́ты в теа́тр на Тага́нке‡.

Мэ́ри: Это не то́т худо́й мужчи́на, с кото́рым мы разгова́ривали у Ве́ры?

Воло́дя: Что́ вы!‡ Это друго́й Ви́ктор. Я говорю́ о то́м Ви́кторе, с кото́рым вы хоте́ли познако́миться побли́же. Высо́кий тако́й‡, вы́ше меня́, с прия́тным го́лосом.

Мэ́ри: Ах да, по́мню. Кото́рый лу́чше всех расска́зывает анекдо́ты.

Воло́дя: То́т са́мый‡. Так во́т‡, он по́мнит вас и хо́чет пригласи́ть на ле́кцию, кото́рую он чита́ет в сре́ду.

Мэ́ри: На каку́ю те́му? Наде́юсь, его́ ле́кция бу́дет интере́снее, чем ле́кция о чеки́стах, на кото́рую вы меня́ води́ли позавчера́.

Воло́дя: Не беспоко́йтесь. Ви́ктор – наш лу́чший специали́ст по ру́сскому теа́тру.

‡**доста́л нам биле́ты** got us ('to us') tickets
‡**теа́тр на Тага́нке** the Taganka Theatre (on Taganka Square in Moscow)
‡**Что́ вы!** Come now! (mild reproach)
‡**высо́кий тако́й** a tall fellow (**тако́й** 'such' used colloquially for emphasis)
‡**то́т са́мый** that's the one ('that very')
‡**так во́т** well then

COMPREHENSION EXERCISE 18/5

Siberian Superlatives and Comparatives:

1 What are the boundaries of Siberia?
2 A geographical feature of Siberia is number one in the world for three things. Find the details.
3 Something else in Siberia is described as number one in the world. What is it?
4 What does **Да́льний Восто́к** ('Far East') mean to a Russian geographer?

Сиби́рь занима́ет бо́льшую часть Се́верной А́зии от ура́льсих‡ го́р на за́паде до Ти́хого‡ океа́на на восто́ке и от берего́в

226

Северного‡ Ледовитого океана на севере до южных степей‡ и границы с Монголией и Китаем.

Сибирские реки Обь, Енисей и Лена входят в десятку‡ самых больших рек мира. Кроме рек, в Сибири есть красивейшие‡ маленькие и большие озёра с чистейшей‡ водой, одно из которых, Байкал – самое древнее, самое глубокое, самое большое в мире пресноводное‡ озеро.

В Сибири находится больше половины природных ресурсов‡ России: уголь‡, нефть‡, газ‡, золото, алмазы‡, редкие металлы‡. А по запасам гидроэнергии‡ она занимает первое место в мире.

Сибирь – это самые разные звери, птицы, ценнейшие‡ рыбы – например, осётр‡, лосось‡.

Географы‡ чаще всего‡ делят‡ Сибирь на Западную Сибирь, Восточную Сибирь и Дальний‡ Восток, который они считают отдельным регионом‡. Дальний Восток – это огромная территория, которая включает Камчатку, Якутию и остров Сахалин. Самыми важными городами являются‡ Хабаровск и Владивосток.

‡Extra Vocabulary for Siberian Text

алмаз diamond

включать' to include

газ gas

географ geographer

гидроэнергия hydroelectric power

дальний far

делить' to divide

десятка a group of ten

красивейший very beautiful (18.8)

лосось (m) salmon

металл metal

нефть (f) oil, petroleum

осётр sturgeon (source of caviare)

пресноводный freshwater

природный natural (**природа** 'nature')

регион region

ресурсы (m pl.) resources

Северный Ледовитый океан the Arctic Ocean

степь (f) steppe (flat, dry grassland)

Тихий океан Pacific Ocean (**тихий** 'quiet')

уг(о)ль (m) coal

уральский Ural (adj)

ценнейший highly valuable (18.8) (**ценный** 'valuable')

чаще всего most often (= 'more often than all' – comparative of **часто** 'often' + gen. of **всё** 'all')

чистейшей very pure (18.8) (**чистый** 'pure')

являются (+ inst.) are – see 16.5 (4)

УРÁЛЬСКИЕ ГÓРЫ
(URAL MOUNTAINS)

ЗÁПАДНАЯ СИБИ́РЬ
(WESTERN SIBERIA)

Среднесиби́рское плоскогóрье
(Central Siberian Plateau)

Обь

Енисéй

Екатеринбу́рг

Челя́бинск

Омск

Новосиби́рск

Красноя́рск

КАЗАХСТÁН
(KAZAKHSTAN)

0   500 Km

0   500 Miles

СИБИ́РЬ (SIBERIA)

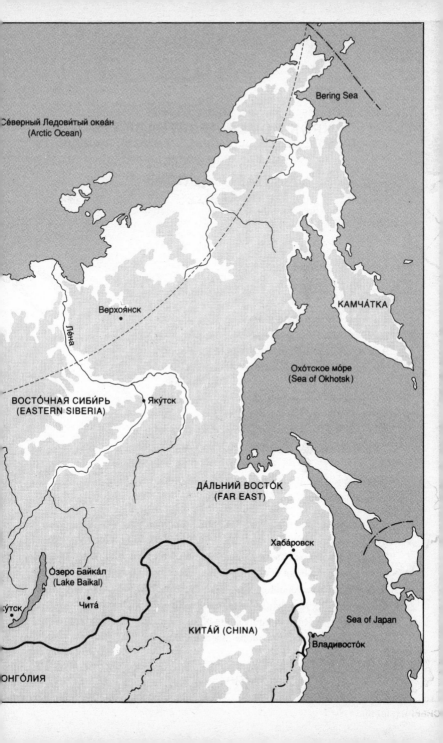

19

УРÓК НÓМЕР ДЕВЯТНÁДЦАТЬ

THE CONDITIONAL;
OBLIGATION (**ДÓЛЖЕН**);
PREFIXES

19.1 **Key Phrases**

Éсли бы я знал, я ушёл бы.	If I'd known, I would have left.
Я бы хотéл(а) вас пригласи́ть.	I would like to invite you.
Я дóлжен/должнá извини́ться.	I must apologize.
Мы должны́ бы́ли отказáться.	We had to refuse.
Проходи́те.	Go through.
Вхóд/вы́ход/перехóд/ухóд	Entrance/exit/crossing/departure

19.2 **Conditional Mood**

Éсли <u>бы</u> я жил(á) в Росси́и, я <u>бы</u> говори́л(а) по-рýсски.

If I lived in Russia, I would speak Russian.

The equivalent of 'would' in Russian is a particle¹ **бы**, which suggests a hypothesis or something contrary to fact or something which you would like to happen. **Бы** has no meaning of its own and is never used without other words; it cannot occur first in the sentence or clause. It adds a meaning of hypothesis, doubt or wish to the verb with which it is used. So **он был** means 'he was' while **он был бы** means 'he would be' or 'he would have been'. In Russian equivalents of such conditional sentences as 'If I knew Russian, I would go alone', there are three points to note:

230

(a) there is a **бы** in *each* clause;

(b) the verbs are always <u>past tense</u>;

(c) it is normal to put one **бы** after **éсли** ('if') and one **бы** before or after the verb in the other clause.

To convert the sentence 'If I am (=shall be) in Moscow, I'll telephone him' into 'If I had been in Moscow, I would have telephoned him', add two **бы**s and make the verbs past tense:

Éсли я бýду в Москвé, я емý позвоню́.	If I'm in Moscow, I'll phone him.
Éсли бы я был в Москвé, я бы емý позвони́л.	If I'd been in Moscow, I would have phoned him.

Since Russian has only one past tense, this sentence could also be translated 'If I was in Moscow, I would phone him.'

The **бы** can also stand after the verb: **я позвони́л бы емý.**

As in English, the conditional can be used for polite requests. 'I would like' is **Я хотéл(а) бы** ('I would want'):

Я хотéла бы поéхать в Сýздаль.   I would like to go to Suzdal'.

EXERCISE 19/1

Translate:

1 Éсли бы онá говори́ла мéдленнее, я бы понялá. 2 Éсли бы мы знáли, чтó вы бýдете в Москвé, мы бы позвони́ли. 3 Вади́м написáл бы Éве письмó, éсли бы у негó бы́ло врéмя. 4 Вéра хотéла бы поговори́ть с вáми.

EXERCISE 19/2

Translate:

1 If he was in Moscow, he would phone[p] us. 2 They would have come[p] if you (pol) had invited[p] them. 3 If Eva knew that Vadim was (= is) drinking wine with us, she would get angry (**рассерди́ться**[p]). 4 I would like to invite[p] you (pol.).

19.3 EXTRA: Он бы

Russian has a very restricted set of verb endings, so those of you who have struggled with subjunctives in German or the Romance languages (Latin, French etc.) will be glad to know that the various contrary-to-present-reality meanings associated with the subjunctive do not involve the learning of any new endings in Russian. The **бы** + past tense construction which you learnt for the conditional above also serves in 'subjunctive'-type situations such as:

I don't know anyone who could help.

Я не зна́ю никого́, кто́ мо́г бы помо́чь (i.e. as far as I know, there is no such person).

I want you to clean up your room (i.e. at present it's a mess).

Я хочу́, что́бы ты убра́л свою́ ко́мнату. (These **что́бы** (=**что́** + **бы**) structures are dealt with in 21.8.)

Бы sometimes occurs without a past-tense verb:

Побо́льше бы таки́х люде́й!	We need more people like that.
На́до бы спроси́ть.	We ought to ask.

19.4 Obligation: до́лжен + infinitive

The closest equivalent of 'I must' is **я до́лжен** (man), **я должна́** (woman). 'Ivan must go' is **Ива́н до́лжен идти́**. 'Must' is a verb in English, but **до́лжен** is an adjective which literally means 'obliged'. It is a special kind of adjective (called a short form – see 29.7) which has only one case, the nominative, and four endings, **до́лжен** (m), **должна́** (f), **должно́** (n), and **должны́** (pl.):

Ива́н до́лжен идти́.	Ivan must go.
А́нна должна́ рабо́тать.	Anna must/has to work.
Вы должны́ извини́ться.	You must apologize.

До́лжен can also express probability or expectation ('should'):

Она́ должна́ ско́ро верну́ться.	She should be back soon.
Э́то лека́рство должно́ помо́чь.	This medicine should help.

Note the phrase **должно быть** 'probably', 'very likely' (lit. 'must be'):

Óн, должно быть, уже вернулся. He has probably already returned.

In the meaning 'have to', the construction **надо/нужно** + dative (Lesson 14.6) and the construction with the adjective **должен** are, with humans, nearly synonymous, though **должен** can carry the meaning of moral obligation (duty) as well as necessity. However, notice (a) that only **должен** has the probability meaning of 'must' ('If she hasn't arrived yet, the train must be late'), and (b) only **должен** is used with inanimate nouns: **Самолёт должен вылететь через два часа** 'The plane should/is due to leave in two hours' (not **Самолёту надо . . .**).

19.5 Past/Future of должен

Since **должен** is an adjective, the past and future are formed with **быть**, but note that the forms of **быть** are placed *after* **должен**:

Óн должен был продать машину.	He had to sell the car.
Мы должны будем извиниться.	We shall have to apologize.

(**Должен** also means 'owing'. In this meaning, **быть** is placed *before* **должен**: **Вы мне должны пять рублей** 'You owe me five roubles'; **Она была мне должна два доллара** 'She owed me two dollars').

EXERCISE 19/3

Put **должен** in the correct form:

1 **Она** (must) **вернуться завтра.** 2 **Óн** (had to) **извиниться.** 3 **Мы** (will have to) **сесть на метро.**

19.6 Prefixes

Russian uses a lot of prefixes[1]. Prefixes (such as, in English, un-, re-, over-) are attached to the beginning of words to add an extra element of meaning to the root[t]. For example, these prefixes can be added to the verb root 'do' to make 'undo', 'redo' and 'overdo'. You know that the prefix **по-** has the basic meaning 'a little' and is particularly common with comparatives (**побо́льше** 'a little more') and as a way of making verbs perfective (**посиде́ть**[p] 'to sit for a while'). It is indeed the commonest prefix in Russian: if you come across a set of the seventeen-volume Soviet Academy of Sciences *Dictionary of Russian* in a library, you will see that one whole volume consists of words beginning with **по-**. But there are another twenty-five or so common prefixes with more or less easily learnt meanings, and they are well worth memorizing as a way of increasing your vocabulary.

You will notice that some of these prefixes, e.g. **без-/бес-** 'without' are similar or identical to prepositions you have met (**без** + gen. 'without').

без-/бес-[‡]	without	
	безалкого́льный	non-alcoholic
	безлю́дный	uninhabited (**лю́ди** 'people')
	беспоко́иться	to be uneasy (**поко́й** peace)
в-/во-	in	
	входи́ть[i]/**войти́**[p]	to go in
	вход	entrance (**хо́д** going)
вз-/вс-[‡]/	up	
воз-/вос-[‡]		
	возвести́[p]	to elevate ('uplead')
	взбить[p]	to beat up **взбить сли́вки** to whip cream
	вздуть[p]	to inflate ('upblow' – **дуть** to blow)
	всплыть[p]	to rise to the surface ('upswim')
	восхо́д	rising ('upgoing') – **восхо́д со́лнца** sunrise
вы-	out	
	вы́йти[p]	to go out
	вы́ход	exit
до-	up to/as far as	
	доходи́ть[i]	to go as far as/to reach,
за-	(1) behind/calling in on the way	
	заходи́ть[i]/**зайти́**[p]	to call in **захо́д со́лнца** sunset ('going behind of the sun')

234

	(2) starting:	
	зазвони́тьᴾ	to start ringing
между-	between	
	междунаро́дный	international (**наро́д** nation)
на-	(1) on	
	находи́ть/найти́	to come upon, to find
	(2) a quantity of	
	наде́латьᴾ (+ acc. or gen)	to make a quantity of something
не-	not	
	неинтере́сно	uninteresting
от-/ото-‡‡	away/back	
	отпуска́ть/отпусти́тьᴾ	to let go (**пуска́ть** to let)
	о́тпуск	leave/holiday (from a job)
пере-	(1) across (trans-)	
	переходи́ть/перейти́ᴾ	to cross
	(2) again (re-)	
	перечи́тывать/	
	перечита́тьᴾ	to reread
	перестро́йка	reconstruction/reorganization (**стро́йка** construction)
по-	a little	
	побо́льше	a little more
	поговори́ть	to talk a bit
под-/	(1) under	
подо-‡‡	**подборо́д(о)к**	chin (**борода́** beard)
	подпи́сывать/подписа́тьᴾ	to sign ('under-write')
	подбира́ть/подобра́тьᴾ	to pick up ('take hold of underneath')
	(2) approaching	
	подходи́ть/подойти́ᴾ	to go up to, approach
пред-	pre-	
	предложе́ние	offer, suggestion (**лож-** means 'put' or 'pose')
	предло́г	preposition
	предвое́нный	pre-war (**война́** war)
при-	(1) arrival	
	приходи́ть/прийти́ᴾ	to arrive

	(2) proximity	
	примо́рский	coastal (**мо́ре** sea)
про-	(1) through/past	
	проходи́ть/пройти́ᴾ	to go through/to pass
	(2) pro-	
	проамерика́нский	pro-American
раз-/	dis-/breaking up/different directions	
рас-‡	**развод́**	divorce ('apart-taking')
	разгово́р	conversation (several people talking)
	раздева́ться	to undress ('dis-dress')
	рассе́янный	scattered (**се́ять** to sow)
с-/со-	(1) off/down	
	сходи́ть/сойти́ᴾ	to go down
	(2) with	
	спу́тник	companion (with-journey-person' from **путь** journey)
у-	away	
	уходи́ть/уйти́ᴾ	to go away/to leave

‡spelt **бес/вос/вс/рас** before the ten unvoiced consonants **к, п, с, т,ф, х, ц, ч, ш, щ**.

‡‡**ото/подо** before some groups of two consonants.

In Lesson 20, there is a special section on prefixes with verbs of motion.

EXERCISE 19/4

Guess the meaning of the following. The words underlined are items from previous lessons combined with prefixes from the list in 19.6 above.

1 <u>отда́ть</u> де́ньги. 2 <u>переда́ть</u> письмо́. 3 <u>разлюби́ть</u> му́жа. 4 друзья́ и <u>не́други</u>. 5 <u>осмотре́ть</u> го́род. 6 <u>при́город</u> Москвы́. 7 <u>ухо́д</u> с рабо́ты. 8 <u>перестро́ить</u> до́м. 9 <u>дое́хать</u> до вокза́ла. 10 <u>бездо́мная</u> соба́ка. 11 <u>предпосле́дний</u> день. 12 <u>предви́деть</u> результа́т.

19.7 EXTRA: Rarer Prefixes

анти- 'anti-' **антивое́нный** 'antiwar'; **вне** 'outside' **внебра́чный** 'extra-marital' (**брак** 'marriage'); **внутри́** 'inside', 'intra' **внутриве́нный** 'intra-venous'; **еже** 'each' **ежедне́вный** 'everyday', 'daily'; **из-/ис-** 'out' **исписа́ть**ᵖ 'to use up (paper, pencil) by writing'; **над-** 'above' **надстро́йка** 'superstructure'; **недо-** 'not as far as'/'insufficient' **недостро́енный** 'un-finished' (of building); **низ-/нис-** 'down' **низложи́ть**ᵖ 'to depose'; **о-/об-** 'about', 'round' **обду́мать**ᵖ 'to consider, think about'; **около-** 'around'; **пол(у)-** 'half', 'semi-' **полуо́стров** 'peninsula' ('semi-island'); **пра-** 'pre-', 'proto-' **пра́дед** 'great grandfather'; **пре-** 'extremely'; **противо-** 'counter-'; **сверх-** 'super-' **сверхчелове́к** 'superman'; **транс-** 'across', 'trans-' **транс-сиби́рский** 'trans-Siberian'; **чрез-/через-/черес-** 'across' **чрезме́рный** 'excessive' ('across measure'); **экстра-** 'extra-' **экстрасе́нс** 'psychic'.

19.8 Vocabulary

ба́бушка gen.pl. **ба́бушек** grandmother

воспи́тыватьⁱ (like **знать**) (+ acc.) to bring up (someone)

всё-таки all the same, nevertheless

встре́титьсяᵖ (**с** + inst.) **встре́чусь, встре́тишься** (**встреча́ться**ⁱ like **знать**) to meet (someone)

вхо́д (**в** + acc.) entrance (to)

дека́н dean (university or institute)

де́ло pl. **дела́** matter

дере́вня gen.pl. **дереве́нь** vil-lage; country (opposite of town)

договори́тьсяᵖ (**с** + inst.) (**догова́риваться**ⁱ like **знать**) to come to an agreement, make

an arrangement (with someone)

до́лжен (19.4) must, obliged

должно́ быть probably ('must be')

доста́точно (+ gen.) enough (of something)

ду́мать (по-) (like **знать**) to think **Как вы ду́маете?** What ('how') do you think?

жизнь (f) life

Забайка́лье region beyond (**за**) Lake Baikal

заверну́тьᵖ (**за** + acc.) **заверну́, завернёшь** (**завора́чивать**ⁱ like **знать**) to turn (round something)

зави́сетьⁱ (**от** + gen.) to depend (on)

Всё зави́сит от пого́ды It all
depends on the weather

записа́тьᵖ **запишу́, запи́шешь
(запи́сывать**ⁱ like **знать)** to
note down

извини́тьсяᵖ **извиню́сь,
извини́шься (извиня́ться**ⁱ)
(like **знать) (за** + acc.) to
apologize (for)

командиро́вка business or study
trip, assignment

перейти́ᵖ **перейду́, перейдёшь**
past **перешёл, перешла́
(переходи́ть**ⁱ) **(че́рез** + acc.)
to cross ('overgo')

пода́р(о)к present, gift

подними́тесь see **подня́ться**

подня́тьсяᵖ **поднalgому́сь,
подни́мешься (поднима́ться**ⁱ
like **знать)** to climb up; to rise

подъе́зд entrance, doorway
('towards drive')

по́мощь (f) help

пройти́ᵖ **пройду́, пройдёшь
(проходи́ть**ⁱ) to go
through/past

профе́ссор pl. **профессора́**
professor

развести́сьᵖ **разведу́сь,
разведёшься** past **развёлся,
развела́сь (разводи́ться**ⁱ
развожу́сь, разво́дишься)
(с + inst.) to get divorced (from
someone)

рассе́янный absent-minded

светофо́р traffic light

серьёзно seriously

сро́чный urgent

тёща mother-in-law (wife's mother)

у́г(о)л prep. **в/на углу́** corner
за́ угол (note stress) round the
corner

19.9 Диало́г Mary Seeks an Absent-Minded Professor

Мэ́ри: Прости́те, вы не зна́ете, где профе́ссор Мирча́нов?
Он до́лжен был встре́титься со мной здесь в два
часа́. Как вы ду́маете, я должна́ подожда́ть?

Секрета́рь: Да, да, я по́мню, что вы договори́лись с Ильёй
Его́ровичем встре́титься сего́дня. Должно́ быть, он
забы́л. По-мо́ему, он уже́ ушёл домо́й. Я бы ему́
напо́мнила, но, к сожале́нию, я была́ всё у́тро у
дека́на.

Мэ́ри: Е́сли бы я зна́ла, что он тако́й рассе́янный, я бы
позвони́ла у́тром. А как мне найти́ его́? Де́ло

238

сро́чное. Я за́втра уезжа́ю в командиро́вку в Забайка́лье.

Секрета́рь: Вы должны́ вы́йти из институ́та, пойти́ пря́мо, пото́м заверну́ть за́ угол у магази́на «Пода́рки». Там перейди́те у́лицу, дойди́те до светофо́ра, пройди́те ми́мо вхо́да в метро́, найди́те до́м но́мер шесть, войди́те в тре́тий подъе́зд, подними́тесь на четвёртый эта́ж и позвони́те в со́рок втору́ю кварти́ру.

Мэ́ри: Спаси́бо, я всё записа́ла.

COMPREHENSION EXERCISE 19/5

1 What does Elena Sidorova want and why?
2 What is her husband's view of her proposal?
3 Does Elena accuse her husband of doing no housework?

У Еле́ны и Па́вла Си́доровых год наза́д родила́сь до́чка Та́ня. Ле́на ду́мает, что жизнь была́ бы ле́гче, е́сли бы ря́дом была́ ба́бушка.

– Я бы не возража́ла, е́сли бы с на́ми жила́ моя́ ма́ма, – говори́т Ле́на. – Она́ помога́ла бы мне гото́вить и воспи́тывать Та́нечку.

– По-мо́ему, я тебе́ помога́ю доста́точно, – возража́ет Па́вел, кото́рый счита́ет, что тёща должна́ оста́ться в дере́вне.

– Е́сли бы ты мне не помога́л, я бы с тобо́й развела́сь! – серьёзно отвеча́ет Ле́на. – Но всё-таки бы́ло бы лу́чше, е́сли бы я не зави́села то́лько от твое́й по́мощи.

20

УРÓК НÓМЕР ДВÁДЦАТЬ

VERBS OF MOTION:
GOING, RUNNING, BRINGING

20.1 Key Examples

В прóшлом годý я éздил(а) в Москвý.	Last year I went to Moscow.
Я чáсто хожý в кинó.	I often go to the cinema.
Вчерá мы никудá не ходи́ли.	We didn't go anywhere yesterday.
Кудá вы идёте?	Where are you going?
Я идý в гости́ницу.	I'm going to the hotel.
Пойдём.	Let's go.
Идёт дóждь.	It's raining.
Кáждый день идёт снег.	It snows every day.
Каки́е сейчáс идýт фи́льмы?	What films are on ('going')?
Как пройти́ на Крáсную плóщадь?	How do I get to Red Square?
Как доéхать до университéта?	How do I reach the university?
Когдá вылетáет самолёт?	When does the plane leave?

20.2 Basic (Unprefixed) Verbs of Motion: ходи́ть', идти́' etc.

'To go on foot' is either **ходи́ть'** or **идти́'** (see 20.3 for perfective forms).
Ходи́ть' means 'to walk in more than one direction' (e.g. there and back),
or 'to walk around'. **Идти́'** means 'to walk in one direction'. So 'I go to the

cinema often' is **Я часто <u>хожу</u> в кино** because each trip to the cinema involves coming back. But 'I'm going to the cinema' (now, or this evening) is **Я иду в кино**, and this means that you're only talking about the trip there.

There are fourteen pairs of verbs which express this distinction between one direction and more than one direction. The eight common ones are:

more than one direction' (multidirectional 'm')	one direction' (unidirectional 'u')	

ходить
  хожу, ходишь
	идти
	  иду, идёшь
	  past **шёл, шла**
		to go (on foot)

ездить
  езжу, ездишь
	ехать
	  еду, едешь
	  imper **поезжайте**
		to go (by transport)

бегать
  бегаю, бегаешь
	бежать
	  бегу, бежишь, они бегут
	  imper **бегите**
		to run

летать
  летаю, летаешь
	лететь
	  лечу, летишь
		to fly

носить
  ношу, носишь
	нести
	  несу, несёшь
	  past **нёс, несла, несло**
		to carry

водить
  вожу, водишь
	вести
	  веду, ведёшь
	  past **вёл, вела, вело**
		to lead (take on foot)

возить
  вожу, возишь
	везти
	  везу, везёшь
	  past **вёз, везла, везло**
		to transport

плавать
  плаваю, плаваешь
	плыть
	  плыву, плывёшь
	  past **плыл, плыла, плыло**
		to swim/to sail

The other six are:

лазить
  лажу, лазишь
	лезть
	  лезут, лезешь
	  past **лез, лезла**
		to climb

241

по́лзать	ползти́	to crawl
по́лзаю, по́лзаешь	ползу́, ползёшь	
	past полз, ползла́, ползло́	
таска́ть	тащи́ть	to drag
таска́ю, таска́ешь	тащу́, та́щишь	
ката́ть	кати́ть	to roll
ката́ю, ката́ешь	качу́, ка́тишь	
гоня́ть	гнать	to chase, drive
гоня́ю, гоня́ешь	гоню́, го́нишь	
	past гнал, гнала́, гна́ло	
броди́ть	брести́	(броди́ть) to wander
брожу́, бро́дишь	бреду́, бредёшь	(брести́) to plod along
	past брёл, брела́, брело́	

All these verbs are *imperfective* forms.

Note that the multidirectional (m) verbs are generally easier to learn than the more irregular unidirectional (u) ones.

Three basic rules determine the choice between the **ходи́ть**-type (m column) and the **идти́**-type (u column):

(1) If the motion involves more than one direction, use the **ходи́ть** (m) type. If the motion is in one direction, use the **идти́** (u) type.

Я хожу́ (m) **в институ́т ка́ждый день.**	I attend the institute every day.
Мы ча́сто е́здим (m) **в Бе́рлин.**	We often go to Berlin (there and back).
Вчера́ мы е́здили‡ (m) **в Заго́рск.**	Yesterday we went to Zagorsk (there and back)‡.
Мы ходи́ли (m) **по го́роду.**	We walked around the town.
Де́ти бе́гали (m) **во дворе́.**	The children were running around in the yard.
Куда́ вы идёте (u)?	Where are you going?
Я бегу́ (u) **в магази́н.**	I'm running to the shop.
За́втра мы лети́м (u) **в Москву́.**	Tomorrow we're flying to Moscow.
Ка́ждый день идёт (u) **дождь.**	It rains every day (rain goes in only one direction, i.e. down).

‡Note that **ходи́ть**-type (m) verbs can be used for a *single* round trip only in the *past* tense.

242

(2) If there is no motion, the multidirectional verbs are used:

Не ходи́те на э́тот фильм.	Don't go to that film.
Вчера́ мы никуда́ не ходи́ли.	Yesterday we didn't go anywhere.
Он никогда́ не лета́ет.	He never flies.

(3) If the number of directions is irrelevant, use the multidirectional verb:

Вы лета́ли когда́-нибудь на самолёте?	Have you ever flown in a plane?
Я люблю́ пла́вать.	I like swimming.

EXERCISE 20/1

Mark the verbs as multidirectional (m) or unidirectional (u) and translate:

1 **В про́шлом году́ мы е́здили в Нью-Йо́рк.**
2 **Ка́ждый день жена́ во́зит дете́й в шко́лу на маши́не.**
3 **Вчера́ она́ води́ла ма́ленького сы́на в парк.**
4 **Куда́ вы та́щите э́ти огро́мные словари́?**
5 **Обы́чно я встаю́ в во́семь часо́в, за́втракаю и в де́вять иду́ на рабо́ту.**
6 **Вре́мя лети́т!**
7 **Беги́те! Фильм начина́ется че́рез пять мину́т.**
8 **Ка́ждый год мы с му́жем е́здим на мо́ре.**
9 **Вы лета́ли когда́-нибудь (ever) на ру́сском самолёте?**
10 **Я не уме́ю пла́вать.**
11 **Не ходи́ на э́тот фильм. Тебе́ бу́дет ску́чно.**
12 **Не иди́ так бы́стро, у нас ещё есть вре́мя.**
13 **Мы не лю́бим бе́гать пе́ред за́втраком.**

You will see from these examples that the unidirectional verbs always have the specific meaning of one direction, while the multidirectional verbs are vaguer – so the m verbs are used when there is no motion or the number of directions doesn't matter (rules 2 and 3 above). So as a 'rule of thumb', use the m verbs in contexts involving repeated motion, e.g. **иногда́** 'sometimes', **ча́сто** 'often', **обы́чно** 'usually', **ка́ждый день** 'every day' (**Я ча́сто хожу́ в теа́тр** 'I often go to the theatre'). With

иногда etc. only use the unidirectional verbs if the motion is clearly in one direction, for example:

Часто идёт (u) **снег.** It often snows.

Обычно я иду (u) **на работу пешком, а домой возвращаюсь на автобусе.** Usually I go to work on foot and return home by bus.

Каждый день я встаю в восемь часов, завтракаю и иду на работу. Every day I get up at eight, breakfast and leave for work. (In this last case you are concerned only with the journey *to* work, *not* with the journey back.)

EXERCISE 20/2

Choose the correct verb (in each pair, the multidirectional one is first):

1 **Куда вы (ходили/шли) в субботу?**
  Where did you go on Saturday?
2 **Мы с женой часто (летаем/летим) в Одéссу.**
  My wife and I often fly to Odessa.
3 **Куда (ходит/идёт) пятый автобус?**
  Where does the number 5 bus go? (What's its destination?)
4 **Как медленно (ползает/ползёт) время!**
  How slowly time crawls! ('How time drags!')
5 **Мы (бродили/брели) по городу весь день.**
  We wandered round the town all day.
6 **Официант (носит/несёт) нам бутылку шампанского.**
  The waiter is bringing us a bottle of champagne.

20.3 Aspect Usage with Multidirectional/Unidirectional Verbs

All twenty-eight verbs can be made perfective by adding **по-**. Note that **по** + **идти** is spelt **пойти**.

По- gives multidirectional verbs the meaning 'a little', 'a limited amount'. So **походить**ᵖ means 'to walk about for a while', **побегать**ᵖ means 'to run about for a while'.

Сейчас будет антракт. Давай походимᵖ **по театру.**
It's the interval. Let's go for a little walk around the theatre.

По- gives unidirectional verbs the meaning 'to make a complete trip in one direction' or, in the right context, 'to start'/'to set off'.

Пойдём!	Let's go/Let's set off.
Где сестра?	Where's your sister?
Она пошла в театр.	She's gone to the theatre.
Пошёл дождь. Все побежали.	It started to rain. Everybody began to run.

To express the meaning 'to make one round trip', multidirectional verbs (except **бродить**) have a different prefix **с-**, e.g. **сбегать**ᵖ 'to run somewhere and come back'. This is a different prefix from **с-** 'off' (19.6).

Я сбегаюᵖ (m) **в магазин за**	I'll run to the shop for some bread
хлебом.	(and come straight back).

Note that for single trips in the *future* the unidirectional verbs are much commoner than the multidirectional ones. Even if you expect to come back, it is normal to say **Завтра я пойду́ в . . .** 'Tomorrow I shall go to . . .'

Летом мы пое́демᵖ (u) **на мо́ре.**	In the summer we'll go to the seaside.

The perfective round-trip verbs (**сходить**ᵖ (m) etc.) are used when you want to emphasize that you're coming back or that you won't be away for long:

Я схожу́ᵖ **к Вади́му.**	I'll pay a call on Vadim (and come back).

Imperfective future forms of the verbs of motion are rare. As you might expect, the imperfective future of multidirectional (**ходить**-type) verbs is used for unfinished multidirectional motion and repeated round trips, while the imperfective future of **идти**-type verbs (very rare) denotes uncompleted motion in one direction:

Я бу́ду ходи́ть на ле́кции профе́ссора Мирча́нова.
I shall attend Professor Mirchanov's lectures (repeated round trips).

Они́ бу́дут ходи́ть по го́роду.
They will be walking round the town.

За́втра в во́семь часо́в я бу́ду идти́ по ва́шей у́лице.
Tomorrow at eight I shall be walking along your street.

EXERCISE 20/3

Translate:

1 Мы походи́ли^p (m) по магази́нам, пото́м пошли́^p (u) в кино́.

2 Мы съе́здили^p (m) в Пари́ж на (for) три дня.

3 Де́ти побе́гали^p (m) в па́рке, уста́ли и пошли́^p (u) домо́й.

4 Сего́дня у́тром мы своди́ли^p (m) Та́ню к врачу́.

5 Мы бу́дем пла́ватьⁱ (m) в бассе́йне (pool) ка́ждое у́тро.

6 Сбе́гай^p (m), пожа́луйста, в магази́н за (for) хле́бом.

20.4 Verbs of Motion with Other Prefixes, e.g. вылета́тьⁱ 'to fly out'

If you put a prefix such as **вы-** 'out' or **про-** 'through' on any of the unprefixed verbs (20.2), you form a new verb which combines the type of motion (flying, running etc.) with the direction specified by the prefix. So **вы + лета́ть**ⁱ means 'out' + 'fly', i.e. 'to fly out', 'to take off' (of an aeroplane). The equivalent perfective is **вы́лететь**^p.

The eleven prefixes (see 19.6) commonly used with verbs of motion are:

в-	in
вы-	out
до-	as far as
за-	calling in (on the way somewhere else)
от-	away (to or from a specified place)
пере-	across
под-	approach
при-	arrival
про-	through/past
с-	off (a different prefix from **с-** 'there and back')
у-	away

Here is the general rule for forming prefixed verbs of motion: if you add a prefix to one of the *multi*directional verbs of motion (e.g. **лета́ть**) you get a new *im*perfective verb (e.g. **вылета́ть**ⁱ). The equivalent perfective verb is formed from the *uni*directional verb (e.g. **вы́лететь**^p).

(Note that **по-** 'a little' and **с-** 'there and back' behave differently and are dealt with separately in 20.3.)

Examples (same conjugation details as in 20.2):

влета́тьⁱ	**влете́ть**ᵖ	to fly in
вылета́тьⁱ	**вы́лететь**ᵖ	to fly out
долета́тьⁱ	**долете́ть**ᵖ	to reach by flying
прилета́тьⁱ	**прилете́ть**ᵖ	to arrive (by plane)
пролета́тьⁱ	**пролете́ть**ᵖ	to fly past or through
относи́тьⁱ	**отнести́**ᵖ	to take away somewhere (by carrying)
переводи́тьⁱ	**перевести́**ᵖ	to lead across/transfer (*also* to translate)
отвози́тьⁱ	**отвезти́**ᵖ	to take somewhere (by transport)

Самолёт вылета́етⁱ **в семь.**	The plane takes off at seven.
Две неде́ли пролете́лиᵖ **как оди́н день.**	The fortnight flew past like a single day.
Па́па вас отвезётᵖ **на вокза́л.**	Dad will drive you to the station.
Éва отнесётᵖ **гря́зные таре́лки на ку́хню.**	Eva will take the dirty plates to the kitchen.
Éва отвела́ᵖ **ру́ку Вади́ма от буты́лки.**	Eva led Vadim's hand away from the bottle.

However, the common verbs **идти́** and **е́здить** change slightly when they are prefixed in this way: **идти́** becomes **-йти́** after a prefix, and prefixes ending with a consonant add **-о-**; **е́здить** becomes **-езжа́ть**. **Ходи́ть** and **е́хать** do not change. Examples:

входи́тьⁱ	**войти́**ᵖ (NB extra **о**)	to enter (on foot)
приходи́тьⁱ	**прийти́**ᵖ	to arrive (on foot)
приезжа́тьⁱ	**прие́хать**ᵖ	to arrive (by transport)
проходи́тьⁱ	**пройти́**ᵖ	to walk through or past

Óн всегда́ приходи́лⁱ **ра́но.**	He always arrived early.
Проходи́теⁱ **в большу́ю ко́мнату.**	Go through into the big room (the living-room in a Russian flat).
По́езд отошёлᵖ **от платфо́рмы.**	The train left the platform.

Заходи́те к нам.　　　　　　　　Call and see us (when
　　　　　　　　　　　　　　　　　　you're passing).

Бе́гать, the multidirectional verb 'to run', changes its stress to **-бега́ть**
when it forms prefixed imperfective verbs:

убега́ть　　　**убежа́ть**ᴾ　　　　　to run away

20.5 Bring

Notice the different equivalents of 'to bring':

приноси́ть/принести́ᴾ	to bring (by carrying)
Принеси́теᴾ**, пожа́луйста, два стака́на.**	Please bring two glasses.
приводи́ть/привести́ᴾ	to bring (by leading)
Приведи́теᴾ **дру́га.**	Bring your friend.
привози́ть/привезти́ᴾ	to bring (by transport)
Я привёзᴾ **вам пода́рок из А́нглии.**	I've brought you a present from England.

Similarly, 'to take away' can be **уноси́ть/унести́**ᴾ (by carrying),
уводи́ть/увести́ᴾ (by leading), **увози́ть/увезти́**ᴾ (by transport).

20.6 Everyday Examples (Prefixed Verbs of Motion together with Prepositions That Normally Accompany Them)

Приходи́те к нам.
Come and see us.
По доро́ге в институ́т мы зайдём в магази́н.
On the way to the institute we'll call at the shop.
Заходи́те к нам.
Do call and see us (when you're passing).
До метро́ довезётᴾ**?**
Will it (this bus/tram etc.) take me to (as far as) the metro station?
Пожа́луйста, отнеси́те таре́лки на ку́хню.
Please take these plates to the kitchen.

Я к вам подойду́ в два часа́.

I'll come up to you (I'll meet you) at two.

Мы прошли́ ми́мо по́чты.

We walked past the post office.

Проходи́те, пожа́луйста. Go in, please. (Go on through.)

О́н с ума́ сошёл?

Has he gone mad? ('Has he gone off his mind?')

Она́ ушла́ с рабо́ты/из университе́та/от му́жа.

She has left her job/the university/her husband.

О́н вы́шел⁰ на де́сять мину́т. Подожди́те, пожа́луйста.

He's gone out for ten minutes. Please wait.

EXERCISE 20/4

Translate:

1 О́н ско́ро прие́дет в Ло́ндон. 2 Она́ вошла́ в ко́мнату. 3 О́н вы́шел из магази́на. 4 Когда́ вы дойдёте до угла́, поверни́те напра́во. 5 Пожа́луйста, отойди́те от окна́. 6 Дава́йте перейдём (че́рез) доро́гу у светофо́ра. 7 О́н подошёл к ней. 8 Уходи́те.

20.7 **EXTRA: Ходи́ть/идти́ with Vehicles**

As a general rule, vehicles, particularly large ones such as trains, boats, buses and trams, go 'on foot' (**ходи́ть/идти́**). In particular, **ходи́ть/идти́** is normal when you are talking about the route of a vehicle or its timetable, as in the first three examples below.

Куда́ идёт э́тот авто́бус? Where does this bus go?

Когда́ отхо́дит по́езд? When does the train leave?

Такси́ идёт в парк. The taxi is going to the depot (it's the end of the driver's shift).

По́езд выхо́дит из тунне́ля. The train is coming out of the tunnel.

Во́т идёт трамва́й. There's a tram coming.

Теплохо́д вы́шел из га́вани. The steamer left the harbour.

But smaller vehicles, particularly **маши́на** 'car', 'lorry', are often used with **е́здить/е́хать** ('to ride').

Маши́на прое́хала че́рез лес и вы́ехала на шоссе́.
The car drove through the wood and came out on to the main road.

Во дво́р въезжа́ет «Во́лга». A 'Volga' (make of car) drives into the yard.

And any land vehicle can be used with **е́здить/е́хать** if you are stressing its movement rather than where it's going:

По́езд е́дет о́чень бы́стро. The train is going very fast.

In many situations with vehicles, **ходи́ть/идти́** ('go on foot') verbs and **е́здить/е́хать** ('ride') verbs are interchangeable: you can also say **По́езд идёт о́чень бы́стро.**

20.8 Aspect with Prefixed Verbs of Motion

The general rules (15.11) apply, of course, but note that it is common to use the *imperfective* to denote *a single round trip in the past*.

Когда́ тебя́ не́ было, заходи́ли¹ Е́ва и Вади́м.
While you were out, Eva and Vadim called (and left again).

Ле́том приезжа́ли¹ мои́ ру́сские друзья́.
My Russian friends came in the summer (and have now gone home).

This is the 'cancellation of result' use of the imperfective, mentioned in Extra 13.3. That is, the result of reaching one's destination is 'cancelled' by returning. Compare:

Вчера́ прие́хала^р моя́ тёща.   My mother-in-law came yesterday (and is staying with me now).

Вчера́ приезжа́ла¹ моя́ тёща.   My mother-in-law came yesterday (and went home).

EXERCISE 20/5

Translate the motion verbs in brackets:

1 **Мы** (are going on foot) **в кино.** 2 **За́втра мы** (are flying) **в Москву́.** 3 **Почему́ они́** (are running)**?** 4 **Вы ча́сто** (go on foot) **в теа́тр?** 5 **В про́шлом году́ мы** (went and came back) **в Пари́ж.** 6 **За́втра мы** (shall go by transport) **в го́род.** 7 **Она́** (is taking by transport) **сы́на к ба́бушке.** 8 **Не** (go on foot) **в э́тот бар. Пи́во** ('beer') **там плохо́е.** 9 **Он всегда́** (arrives on foot) **в семь часо́в.** 10 **Моя́ тёща** (will arrive by transport) **за́втра.** 11 **Та́ня** (ran away). 12 **Официа́нт** (will bring) **чи́стый стака́н** ('glass'). 13 **Пожа́луйста,** (bring by transport) **две буты́лки вина́.** 14 **Мы** (got out) **из авто́буса на Но́вом Арба́те.** 15 **В сентябре́** (came and left again) **мои́ друзья́ из Ми́нска.**

20.9 EXTRA: Other Changes to Verbs of Motion when Prefixed:

пла́вать 'to swim or sail' becomes **-плыва́ть**
   приплыва́ть **приплы́ть**ᵖ 'to arrive' (ship)
ла́зить 'to climb' becomes **-леза́ть**
   влеза́ть **влезть**ᵖ 'to climb in'
по́лзать 'to crawl' becomes **-полза́ть**
   вполза́ть **вползти́**ᵖ 'to crawl in'
таска́ть 'to drag' becomes **-та́скивать**
   выта́скивать **вы́тащить**ᵖ 'to drag out'
ката́ть 'to roll' becomes **-ка́тывать**
   выка́тывать **вы́катить**ᵖ 'to roll out'
броди́ть 'to wander' becomes **-бреда́ть**
   забреда́ть **забрести́**ᵖ 'to wander in'

All the imperfective forms of these verbs are conjugated like **знать**.

Note that the only one of the *uni*directional verbs which changes after a prefix is **идти́** – and its change to **-йти́** is a very minor one.

To drive in is **въезжа́ть** **въе́хать**ᵖ. Note the hard signs. If a verb begins with a [y] sound (e.g. **е́хать [yé-hatʸ]** 'to travel', **яви́ть [yee-ve´etʸ]** 'to show'), any prefix ending with a consonant (**в-** 'in',

об- 'around', 'totality', **под-** 'under', 'approaching') is separated from the
[y] sound by a hard sign: **объезжа́ть/объе́хать**ᵖ 'to drive round',
объявля́ть/объяви́тьᵖ 'to announce', **подъезжа́ть/подъе́хать**ᵖ 'to
drive under/towards'.

20.10 **Vocabulary (See also Verb list 20.2)**

ваго́н carriage

вперёд forward

вы́бежать (выбега́ть') to run out
(20.4)

Герма́ния Germany

гря́зный dirty

доезжа́ть/дое́хатьᵖ **до** (+ gen.)
to reach, go as far as (20.4)

забега́ть/забежа́тьᵖ to call in
(running) (20.4)

закрича́тьᵖ **закричу́, закричи́шь
(крича́ть')** to shout, start shouting

заходи́ть/зайти́ᵖ to call in (20.4)

как раз exactly, just

кинотеа́тр or **кино́** (n indecl) cinema

«Кита́й-город» 'China Town'

Кита́йский проспе́кт 'Chinese
Prospect'

ле́стница staircase

оказа́лосьᵖ it turned out

оказа́тьсяᵖ to turn out; to find
oneself

остано́вка gen.pl. **остано́вок** stop

парк park

пешко́м on foot

побежа́тьᵖ **(бежа́ть')** to run (20.2)

полчаса́ half an hour

прибежа́тьᵖ **(прибега́ть')** to arrive

(running) (20.4)

привезти́ᵖ **(привози́ть')** to bring
by transport (20.5)

привести́ᵖ **(приводи́ть')** to bring
(by leading) (20.5)

прилете́тьᵖ **(прилета́ть')** to arrive
(by air) (20.4)

противополо́жный opposite (adj)

путь (m) (unique noun)
gen./dat./prep. **пути́,** inst.
путём way

самолёт aeroplane

свора́чивать' (like **знать)
(сверну́ть**ᵖ **сверну́,
свернёшь)** to turn off

ско́ро soon

снег prep. **в снегу́,** pl. **снега́** snow

сойти́ᵖ **(сходи́ть')** **с** (+ gen.) to
get off (20.4)

сосе́дний neighbouring, next

стадио́н stadium
на стадио́не at a stadium

стра́нно strange; it's strange

таре́лка g.pl. **таре́лок** plate

убежа́тьᵖ **(убега́ть')** to run away (20.4)

услы́шатьᵖ **услы́шу, услы́шишь
(слы́шать')** to hear

центра́льный central

20.11 Тексты (Translations in Key)

Tania in Motion

– Таня, отнеси, пожалуйста, эту грязную тарелку на кухню и принеси чистую.

Таня убежала.

Через десять минут я пошёл её искать: заходил на кухню, там её не было, тогда я зашёл в спальню к бабушке.

– Таня сюда не забегала?

– Нет. Мне кажется, что я слышала её голос в соседней квартире.

– Странно, – сказал я. – Абрамовы уехали в Германию месяц назад.

Я побежал к соседям. Оказалось, что Абрамовы только что прилетели из Франкфурта. Таня услышала, как они приехали, и выбежала на лестницу.

– Да, Таня у нас, – засмеялись соседи. – Она прибежала минут пятнадцать назад. Скоро мы приведём её домой.

– Папа, посмотри, какие красивые вещи они привезли! – закричала Таня. – Я хочу переехать жить в Германию!

Finding the Way

А: Как проехать на Центральный стадион?

Б: Лучше всего доехать на метро до станции «Спортивная».

А: А сколько туда ехать?

Б: Думаю, полчаса.

*

А: Вы не скажете, как проехать в гостиницу «Россия»?

Б: Вы должны будете сесть на автобус и проехать три остановки.

А: Спасибо.

Б: Пожалуйста.

*

А: Скажите, пожалуйста, как доехать до гостиницы «Россия»?

Б: На метро до станции «Китай-город».

253

А: А мо́жно туда́ дое́хать на авто́бусе?

Б: Мо́жно. Сади́тесь на два́дцать четвёртый авто́бус. Óн идёт по Кита́йскому проспе́кту. Нó лу́чше на метро́.

COMPREHENSION EXERCISE 20/6

1 What are Ivan Petrovich's instructions for getting to his house by metro?
2 How can Eva get there by number 57 bus?
3 Why is the number 10 less suitable?

ИП: Запи́сывайте, как к нам е́хать. На́до сесть на метро́ и дое́хать до ста́нции «Профсою́зная». Иди́те в сто́рону после́днего ваго́на и вы́йдите на у́лицу. Поверни́те нале́во . . .

Éва: Мину́точку. Я запи́сываю: вы́йти на у́лицу и поверну́ть куда́?

ИП: Поверни́те нале́во, дойди́те до угла́ и перейди́те на противополо́жную сто́рону. Поверни́те ещё раз нале́во, иди́те по проспе́кту до на́шей у́лицы.

Éва: Ива́н Петро́вич, нельзя́ ли найти́ бо́лее просто́й путь?

ИП: Éсли вы бу́дете у Вади́ма, вам лу́чше пое́хать на авто́бусе. Пятьдеся́т седьмо́й авто́бус идёт по его́ у́лице. На́до прое́хать четы́ре остано́вки и сойти́ на пя́той, у кинотеа́тра. Ми́мо не прое́дете, кинотеа́тр большо́й, как раз напро́тив остано́вки. Пройди́те по проспе́кту немно́го вперёд, до на́шего до́ма. Мо́жно е́хать и на деся́том авто́бусе, нó óн свора́чивает нале́во, на у́лицу Наро́дного ополче́ния, и до кинотеа́тра не доезжа́ет.

EXERCISE 20/7

Say in Russian:

1 Where are you (fam) going (on foot)? 2 I'm going to Red Square.
3 They've gone to the Kremlin. 4 I go to the cinema often. 5 I went to Novgorod on Wednesday. 6 We go to Russia almost every year. 7 I like to run before breakfast. 8 I shall fly to Tallinn in three days' time. 9 We want to

go to the market. 10 The waiter is bringing (carrying) beetroot soup.
11 Where are you taking (leading) us? 12 Does it rain often?

EXERCISE 20/8
REVISION OF LESSONS 1–20

Translate the following and put the correct endings on the words in brackets.
(You have now done all the verb, noun, pronoun and adjective endings.)

1 Я не (знать). Я не (говорить) по-францу́зски. Я (жить) в
   А́нглии. (pres. 4)
2 Я (дать) пять до́лларов. (fut. 12)
3 Извини́те, что́ мы (прийти́) так по́здно. Мы не (мо́чь) найти́
   такси́. (past 11)
4 (Показа́ть) э́то, пожа́луйста. (Дать) два, пожа́луйста. (imper 15)
5 Е́сли бы я (знать), я (позвони́ть) бы. (cond. 19)
6 Позови́те, пожа́луйста, (Мари́я Фёдоровна) и́ли (Ива́н
   Петро́вич). (acc. 6)
7 Я не могу́ откры́ть (э́та дверь). (acc. 6)
8 Принеси́те, пожа́луйста, пять (буты́лка) (минера́льная вода́),
   три (чай) и пять (пирожо́к). (gen. 9, 10)
9 У (я) нет (ру́сские де́ньги). (gen. 10)
10 Ви́ктор – специали́ст по (ру́сский теа́тр). (dat. 12)
11 Помоги́те (они́), пожа́луйста. Помоги́те (э́ти тури́сты). (dat. 12)
12 Познако́мьтесь с (мо́й но́вый друг). (inst. 16)
13 Я хочу́ познако́миться с (ва́ши друзья́). (inst. 16)
14 У вас есть кни́ги на (англи́йский язы́к)? (prep. 5, 7)
15 Мы говори́ли о (он). (prep. 5)

Say in Russian:

16 Come in, please (i). Take a seat (i).
17 I would like to go (p) to the Bolshoi Theatre.
18 Could you tell me how to get (p) to the institute by metro?
19 Please give (p) me two tickets. Does the film begin at half past seven?
20 I'm sorry I'm late ('for lateness' 11.8). It was very difficult to find (p)
   your house.

21 I spoke (i) to (with) Vladimir Smirnov yesterday. He said (p) that I should telephone (p) you.

22 It is cold in my room. It's also very noisy. The window doesn't close.

23 There is no toilet paper (**туалéтная бумáга**). Please do not say that I should buy *Pravda*.

24 I have reread (p) the letter. I cannot understand (p) it.

25 Cross (p) the road, walk past (p) the shop and turn (p) right.

21

УРÓК НÓМЕР ДВÁДЦАТЬ ОДИ́Н

POSSESSION (**СВÓЙ**);
PURPOSE (**ЧТÓБЫ**)

21.1 **Phrases**

Я люблю́ свóй гóрод.	I love my (own) town.
Онá говори́т о свои́х дéтях.	She talks about her (own) children.
Онá пошлá к себé.	She went to her (own) room.
Чтóбы вы́учить рýсский язы́к, нáдо читáть Чéхова.	To learn Russian, you have to read Chekhov.
Я хочý, чтóбы óн ушёл.	I want him to leave.

21.2 **Свóй: 'Own'**

Свóй means 'own', belonging to the subject of the verb. It has the same declension as **мóй**. It is always used instead of **егó**, **её**, **их** (4.2) and sometimes **мóй**, **твóй**, **наш**, **ваш**, when the subject owns whatever is mentioned in the predicate[t] of the clause[t].

Óн говори́т о <u>своéй</u> рабóте.	He's talking about his job.
Они́ не мóгут найти́ <u>свои́</u> билéты.	They can't find their tickets.
В 11 часóв Чайкóвский шёл в <u>свою́</u> кóмнату.	At 11 o'clock Chaikovskii went to his room.

If the subject is **я**, **мы**, **вы**[‡] the use of **свой**, instead of **мóй**, **наш**, **ваш**, is optional, since it doesn't make any difference in meaning.

257

Я взял <u>свой</u> (or **<u>мой</u>**) **биле́т.**   I took my (my own) ticket.

Возьми́те <u>ва́ше</u> (or **<u>своё</u>**) **пальто́.** (You) Take your coat.‡‡

‡ *Note 1.* When the subject is **ты, свой** is much preferred to **твой**. Say **Ты возьмёшь своё** (not **твоё**) **пальто́?** 'Will you take your coat?'

‡‡ *Note 2.* You can save effort by remembering that *Russians often do not use an equivalent of 'my','his' etc. if the possessor is obvious*. For example, 'I love my wife' would normally be **Я люблю́ жену́** (rather than **свою́ жену́** or **мою́ жену́**) because the hearer can assume that you mean your own wife. 'Take your coat' would be **Возьми́те пальто́** ('Take coat'), with no translation of 'your' if it is clear from the context who owns the coat.

If the subject is third person (he, she, it, they or equivalents), you *must* use **свой** if the thing belongs to the subject. As you see in the next two examples, the meaning changes depending on whether you use **свой** or **его**.

Серге́й не знал, что Ива́н взял   Sergei didn't know that Ivan had
    свой биле́т.   taken his (Ivan's) ticket.

Серге́й не знал, что Ива́н взял   Sergei didn't know that Ivan had
    его́ биле́т.   taken his (i.e. Sergei's) ticket.

Они́ не зна́ют, где их биле́ты.   They don't know where their tickets are.

Be careful not to misuse **свой**. Remember that it refers to the subject of the same clause¹ (see 'Glossary of Grammatical Terms' for 'clause'). So 'They do not know where their tickets are' is **Они́ не зна́ют, где их** (NOT **свои**) **биле́ты** because **где их биле́ты** is a different clause from the one with **они** in it. One simple rule for avoiding mistakes is: DO NOT USE **СВОЙ** IN THE NOMINATIVE CASE.

EXERCISE 21/1

Choose the correct possessive and translate:

Почему́ Ива́н не зна́ет, где (его́, свой) биле́т? Почему́ он не мо́жет найти́ (его́, свой) биле́т? Он не зна́ет, где биле́т потому́, что (его́, своя́) жена́ дала́ (его́, свой) биле́т (её, свое́й) подру́ге.

EXERCISE 21/2

Translate the possessives:

1 **Они́ пошли́ в** (their) **ко́мнату.** 2 **Возьми́** (your) **пальто́. На у́лице хо́лодно.** 3 **Познако́мьтесь. Э́то Ива́н Петро́вич.** (His) **жена́ –** (my) **секрета́рь.** 4 **Ве́ра взяла́** (her) **пальто́, а Е́ва оста́вила** (hers) **до́ма.**

21.3 **EXTRA: On свой**

Occasionally **свой** *is* used in the nominative (meaning 'one's own', 'not somebody else's'), particularly in the 'have' construction (10.2). Examples:

У ка́ждого своё мне́ние.	Each has his or her own opinion.
У ка́ждого свой дом.	Each has his or her own house.
У него́ своя́ маши́на.	He has a car of his own.

Notice also the proverb:

Своя́ руба́шка бли́же к те́лу.	One's own shirt is closer to the body (= charity begins at home).

And the special meaning 'home-made':

Хлеб свой, не из магази́на.	The bread is our own, not from the shop (i.e. we made it ourselves).

You may also meet cases where **свой** refers to a non-nominative subject, e.g.

<u>Мне</u> на́до найти́ <u>свой</u> биле́т.	I must find my ticket.

21.4 **Себя́: Self**

The grammar of **себя́** 'self' is similar to the grammar of **свой**. If the person affected by the action is also the subject of the clause, then **себя́** is used instead of **меня́/тебя́/нас** etc., just as in English we say 'I talk to myself' not 'I talk to me', 'She loves only herself' not 'She loves only her' (i.e. the person loved is the same person as the person who is doing the loving). But unlike **свой**, whose use is compulsory only with third person subjects, **себя** *must* be used if the person affected is the same as the subject.

<u>Вы</u> лю́бите то́лько <u>себя́</u>.	You love only yourself.
Посмотри́ на <u>себя́</u>.	(You) look at yourself.

Since 'self' cannot be the subject of a sentence, **себя** (which is the accusative/genitive form) has no nominative case. The other case forms match those of **тебя́**, namely:

N	—
A/G	себя́
D	себе́
I	собо́й
P	себе́

Ива́н взял бока́л для неё.	Ivan took a glass for her.
Ива́н взял бока́л для себя́.	Ivan took a glass for himself.
Она́ говори́ла о ней.	She talked about her (somebody else).
Она́ говори́ла о себе́.	She talked about herself.

Because the forms of **себя** *must* be used if the subject and the person affected are the same, Russian and English uses of 'self' do not always match:

Мы взя́ли дете́й с собо́й.	We took our children with us ('with ourselves').
Закро́йте дверь за собо́й.	Close the door behind you ('yourself').

EXERCISE 21/3

Say in Russian:

1 Take her with you. 2 Tell us about yourself. 3 She considers (**счита́ет**) herself very interesting (inst.).

21.5 Idioms with себя

Она́ пошла́ к себе́.	She went to her (own) room/home ('to herself').
О́н у себя́.	He's at home/at his own place/ in his own room.
прийти́ в себя́	to come to one's senses/to recover ('to come back into oneself')
У меня́ нет при себе́ де́нег.	I haven't any money on me ('attached to myself').
О́н назва́л себя́.	He gave his name ('named himself').
ОТ СЕБЯ́	PUSH (notice on doors, i.e. 'away from self')
К СЕБЕ́	PULL (i.e. 'towards self')

21.6 **EXTRA**: себя́ versus -ся

Себя́ always means 'self', while the reflexive verb ending **-ся** may express the meaning 'self' less emphatically and sometimes not at all (e.g. in **улыба́ться** 'to smile'). As you know from 11.6, most 'self' verbs (e.g. 'wash oneself' **мы́ться**ⁱ, 'dress oneself' **одева́ться**ⁱ) have **-ся**, but note the following contrasting pair, where the more emphatic 'self' meaning of **себя́** is clear:

счита́тьсяⁱ 'to be considered' (by other people)
счита́тьⁱ **себя́** 'to consider oneself'

О́н счита́ется специали́стом.	He is considered a specialist.
О́н счита́ет себя́ специали́стом.	He considers himself a specialist.

21.7 **Что́бы** [shtó-bi]: in order to

When 'to' has the meaning of purpose ('in order to'), use **что́бы** in Russian:

We live (in order) to work. **Мы живём, что́бы рабо́тать.**

(In order) to master Russian, you have to study three hours every day.

Что́бы вы́учить ру́сский язы́к, на́до занима́ться три часа́ ка́ждый день.

After verbs of motion (but not non-motion verbs), **что́бы** can be omitted:

О́н уе́хал в Герма́нию (что́бы) преподава́ть ру́сский язы́к.
He's gone to Germany to teach Russian.

О́н рабо́тает семь дней в неде́лю, что́бы помога́ть роди́телям жены́.
He works seven days a week to help his wife's parents.

21.8 **Что́бы** in 'Someone Wants Someone To Do Something' constructions

Что́бы, which comes from **что́** + the particle **бы** (see lesson 19) is also used when somebody wants somebody else to do something. The two clauses are linked by **что́бы** and the verb after **что́бы** is *in the past tense* (just as **бы** is followed by the past tense – see 19.2).

Я хочу́, что́бы она́ пришла́   I want her to come on Wednesday.
  в сре́ду.

Мы хоти́м, что́бы вы отдохну́ли.   We want you to have a rest.

Most other verbs which indicate that somebody wants somebody to do (or not to do) something are also followed by the same **что́бы** construction, for example verbs meaning 'to order', 'to wish', 'to insist', 'to demand':

веле́ть[i/p] **(велю́, ты вели́шь)** (+ dative) 'to order

говори́ть[i]/**сказа́ть**[p] 'to tell'

прика́зывать[i]/**приказа́ть**[p] (13) (+ dative) 'to order'

наста́ивать[i] (like **знать**)/**настоя́ть**[p] **(настою́, настои́шь)** 'to insist'

жела́ть/по-[p] (like **знать**) 'to wish'

тре́бовать[i] **(тре́бую, тре́буешь)/по-**[p] 'to demand'

О́н вели́т, что́бы вы   He orders you to come tomorrow.
  пришли́ за́втра.

Мэ́ри сказа́ла, что́бы   Mary told him to wait.
  о́н подожда́л.

Она́ наста́ивает, что́бы   She insists that he apologize.
  о́н извини́лся.

Мы жела́ем, что́бы всё　　　　　We want (wish) everything to go well.
　бы́ло хорошо́.

Тури́сты потре́бовали, что́бы их пересели́ли в другу́ю гости́ницу.
The tourists demanded to be moved to another hotel.

Some verbs can be used either with **что́бы** or with an infinitive. The main ones are **проси́ть/по-**ᵖ (15) 'to request' and **прика́зывать/приказа́ть**ᵖ 'to order':

Я проси́л, что́бы она́ пришла́.　　I asked her to come.
or **Я проси́л её** (acc.) **прийти́.**

Она́ приказа́ла, что́бы он пришёл. She ordered him to come.
or **Она́ приказа́ла ему́** (dat.) **прийти́.**

EXERCISE 21/4

Say in Russian, using **что́бы**:

1 We're going to Russia to study (i) Russian. 2 I want them to come (p) tomorrow. 3 He wants you to ring (p) in the evening. 4 Give me two kopecks to make a phone call (p). 5 We told her to take (p) her coat.

21.9 **Vocabulary**

а́втор author
администра́тор administrator;
　hotel manager
бока́л wineglass
бума́га paper
　туале́тная бума́га toilet paper
ве́ритьᶦ **ве́рю, ве́ришь (по-**ᵖ**)** to
　believe (+ dat. = someone)
　(в + acc. in someone or
　something)
взгляд view
включа́тьᶦ **(like знать)**

(включи́тьᵖ **включу́,**
　включи́шь) to plug in, switch on
вме́сто того́ что́бы (+inf) instead
　of (doing something)
вряд ли hardly, unlikely
вы́зватьᵖ **вы́зову, вы́зовешь**
　(вызыва́тьᶦ **like знать)** to
　summon
выраже́ние expression
выходи́ть/вы́йтиᵖ **из себя́** to
　lose one's temper ('go out of
　oneself')

геро́й gen.pl. **геро́ев** hero

гне́вный angry

го́рничная (f adj) maid

европе́йский European

жа́ловаться (**по-ᴾ**) (**на** + асс.)
жа́луюсь, жа́луешься to
complain (about)

заяви́тьᴾ **заявлю́, зая́вишь** (+
асс.) (**заявля́ть** like **знать**) to
announce (sth)

име́ть в виду́ to bear in mind

каса́ться (like **знать**) (+ gen.)
(**косну́ться**ᴾ **косну́сь,
коснёшься**) to touch (sth); to
concern

что́ каса́ется (+ gen.) as for
('what concerns')

кипят(о́)к boiling water

крова́ть (f) bed

культу́ра culture

лежа́ть лежу́, лежи́шь (**по-ᴾ**) to
lie, be in a lying position

лицо́ pl. **ли́ца** face; person

ма́стер pl. **мастера́** skilled workman

мили́ция police

монтёр electrician

наве́рное probably

наро́чно deliberately

но́мер pl. **номера́** hotel room;
number

обо́и (m pl.) gen.pl. **обо́ев** wallpaper

одина́ковый identical

отноше́ние attitude

перево́дчик translator

перенести́ᴾ (like **нести́**) + асс.

(переноси́ть like **носи́ть)** to
transfer

пересели́тьᴾ (+асс.) **пересели́,
пересели́шь (переселя́ть** like
знать) to move, resettle
(s.o.)

по́вод cause

пое́здка gen.pl. **пое́здок** journey

по́льзоваться (**вос-ᴾ**) (+ inst.)
по́льзуюсь, по́льзуешься to
use (sth)

потре́боватьᴾ (**тре́бовать**)
потре́бую, потре́буешь to
demand

причи́на reason, cause

пробле́ма problem

прове́ритьᴾ **прове́рю,
прове́ришь (проверя́ть** like
знать) (+ асс.) to check

прожива́ющий (m adj) resident

про́сьба request

путеше́ствовать **путеше́ствую,
путеше́ствуешь** to travel

разви́тие development

разделя́ть (like **знать**) + асс.
(**раздели́ть**ᴾ **разделю́,
разде́лишь**) to share

ремо́нт repair(s), maintenance

ро́дина homeland
на ро́дине in one's homeland

розе́тка gen.pl. **розе́ток**
electricity socket, power point

самова́р samovar, urn

свой own (21.2)

себя́ self (21.4)

сеть (f) network; circuit

со́бственный own, personal

спря́татьᴾ спря́чу, спря́чешь
(+ acc.) (**пря́тать**ⁱ) to hide

сра́зу же immediately

сро́чно urgently

стиль (m) style

терпе́тьⁱ (**по-**ᴾ) терплю́, те́рпишь
to endure; to be patient

терпе́ть не могу́ (+ acc.) I can't
stand (s.o. or sth)

тре́боватьⁱ see **по-** to demand
(21.8)

тургру́ппа tourist group

ту́фли (f pl.) gen.pl. **ту́фель**
shoes, house shoes

уважа́тьⁱ (like **знать**) to respect

устра́иватьⁱ (like **знать**) (+ acc.)
(**устро́ить**ᴾ устро́ю, устро́ишь)
to organize (sth); to suit (s.o.)

хотя́ although

цвет pl. **цвета́** colour

ча́йник kettle; teapot

ча́стый frequent

ча́шка gen.pl. **ча́шек** cup

чтóбы [shtó-bi] (in order) to

чу́вствоватьⁱ (**по-**ᴾ) (+ acc.) to
feel (something)

чу́вствую, чу́вствуешь

чу́вствовать себя́ хорошо́
to feel well

электробри́тва electric razor

21.10 В гости́нице In the Hotel

А = Администра́тор
П = Перево́дчик тургру́ппы

П: Здра́вствуйте. У меня́ к вам про́сьба. Ми́стер То́рнтуэйт хо́чет,
чтóбы вы ему́ да́ли друго́й но́мер. Óн говори́т, чтó в егó
но́мере нет розе́тки, а óн хо́чет сде́лать себе́ ча́шку ко́фе.

А: Розе́тка есть обяза́тельно, за крова́тью. Нó вообще́ мы не
лю́бим, чтóбы прожива́ющие включа́ли в сеть нагрева́тельные
прибо́ры.‡ Скажи́те ему́, чтó го́рничная даст ему́ кипято́к из
своего́ самова́ра.

П: Хорошо́, я переда́м.

Че́рез де́сять мину́т . . .

П: Ми́стера То́рнтуэйта э́то не устра́ивает. Óн говори́т, чтó óн не
хо́чет по́льзоваться самова́ром го́рничной. Óн говори́т, чтó,
наве́рное, самова́р у го́рничной гря́зный, а у негó свóй ча́йник,
и óн бу́дет по́льзоваться тóлько свои́м со́бственным
ча́йником.

А: А розе́тку óн нашёл?

П: Нашёл, но он говорит, что она не работает. Кроме того, он жалуется, что он не может включить свою электробритву, что нет туалетной бумаги и что цвет обоев ему не нравится.

А: Хорошо. Я вызову монтёра, чтобы он проверил розетку, и я скажу горничной, чтобы она принесла туалетную бумагу. А что касается обоев, я ничего не могу сделать. Во всех номерах обои одинаковые.

П: От себя скажу‡, что я терпеть не могу этого мистера Торнтуэйта. Он думает только о себе, он всё время сердится, выходит из себя по любому поводу. Когда мы были в московской гостинице и он не мог найти свои туфли, он потребовал, чтобы я срочно вызвал милицию. Пришла милиция, и оказалось, что туфли лежат под его кроватью. Вместо того, чтобы извиниться, он заявил, что горничная нарочно спрятала его туфли, чтобы потом продать их на чёрном рынке.

Подходит англичанин с гневным выражением лица.

П: Мистер Торнтуэйт требует, чтобы его сразу же переселили в другой номер.

А: Хорошо. Есть свободные номера на девятом этаже, хотя там идёт ремонт и вряд ли ему там будет лучше. Я могу попросить, чтобы его переселили туда.

П: Большое спасибо.

А: Пусть мистер Тиран . . . как его . . . Пусть английский гость идёт к себе в номер. Я скажу горничной, чтобы она помогла ему перенести вещи.

‡**нагревательный прибор** heating appliance.

‡**от себя скажу** speaking for myself ('from myself I'll say').

COMPREHENSION EXERCISE 21/5

Ivan Sergeevich Turgenev

1 When was Turgenev born?
2 What was the name of his birthplace? (You may need a map to find the nominative form.)

3 Translate the first sentence of the second paragraph paying special attention to **свою** рóдину, **свой** нарóд, <u>**егó**</u> культýру, <u>**егó**</u> язы́к.
4 He spent a lot of time in Western Europe. What two reasons are mentioned?
5 Did Turgenev want to overthrow the Tsar or did he consider Russia to be paradise on earth?

Извéстный рýсский писáтель Ивáн Сергéевич Тургéнев, áвтор ромáна «Отцы́ и дéти», роди́лся двáдцать восьмóго октября́ (девя́того ноября́ по нóвому сти́лю‡) ты́сяча восемьсóт восемнáдцатого гóда в гóроде Орлé, к ю́гу от Москвы́.

Хотя́ Тургéнев óчень люби́л свою́ рóдину, свой нарóд, егó культýру, егó язы́к, óн проводи́л мнóго врéмени за грани́цей. Óн учи́лся в Берли́не, дóлго жил в Пари́же, путешéствовал по стрáнам Зáпадной Еврóпы, был в Áнглии, где в ты́сяча восемьсóт шестидеся́том годý óн провёл три недéли на Уáйте‡, а в ты́сяча восемьсóт сéмьдесят девя́том годý получи́л почётную‡ стéпень‡ Óксфордского университéта.

Считáется, чтó глáвной причи́ной егó чáстых поéздок за грани́цу былá егó привя́занность‡ к францýзской певи́це‡ П. Виардó, с котóрой óн познакóмился в 1843 годý. Нó мнóгие считáют, чтó óн чýвствовал себя́ лýчше в Зáпадной Еврóпе, чем в Росси́и. Хотя́ óн писáл о проблéмах своéй рóдины, óн был европéйским писáтелем.

Свой лýчший ромáн «Отцы́ и дéти» óн опубликовáл‡ в ты́сяча восемьсóт шестьдеся́т пéрвом годý. На Зáпаде мнóгие знáют э́тот ромáн и егó герóя, «нигили́ста»‡-революционéра Базáрова. Тургéнев уважáл своегó мýжественного‡ герóя, но не разделя́л егó взгля́дов. Чтóбы поня́ть егó двóйственное‡ отношéние к Базáрову, нáдо имéть в видý, чтó Тургéнев хорошó знал все проблéмы своéй отстáлой‡ рóдины, но считáл себя́ либерáлом‡, а не революционéром. Óн не вéрил в необходи́мость‡ револю́ции в Росси́и. Óн был «зáпадником»‡, тó есть óн считáл зáпадно-европéйский, капиталисти́ческий‡ путь разви́тия приéмлемым‡ для Росси́и.

‡**Extra Vocabulary for Turgenev Exercise (in Alphabetical Order):**

двóйственный dual

зáпадник westernizer, i.e. one who believed that Russia could learn from the West; their opponents, the Slavophiles (**славянофи́лы**) believed in a non-western, Slavonic, path

капиталисти́ческий capitalist

либерáл liberal

мýжественный manly, courageous

необходи́мость (f) necessity

нигили́ст nihilist (an 1860s revolutionary who believed that all the existing social institutions should be swept away)

опубликовáтьᵖ to publish

отстáлый backward

певи́ца (female) singer

почётная стéпень honorary degree

привя́занность (f) attachment, affection

приéмлемый acceptable

по нóвому сти́лю new style (by the western calendar adopted after the 1917 revolution)

Уáйт Isle of Wight

22

УРО́К НО́МЕР ДВА́ДЦАТЬ ДВА

FUN WITH NUMBERS

22.1 **Key Phrases**

ме́жду пятью́ и семью́ часа́ми	between five and seven o'clock
бо́льше (бо́лее) пятисо́т рубле́й	more than five hundred roubles
Она́ говори́т на трёх языка́х.	She speaks three languages.
с обе́их сторо́н	from both sides
обе́ими рука́ми	with both hands
на обо́их стола́х	on both tables
со мно́гими ру́сскими	with many Russians
в не́скольких города́х	in several towns

22.2 **The Declension of Numbers and Quantity Words**

The material in this lesson is concerned with the complexities of Russian number usage. If you find the difficulties of doing arithmetic in Russian intriguing, then enjoy yourself. If the grammar of numbers turns you off, then skip through the lesson to see the kinds of situations to avoid, and move on quickly to Lesson 23. The essential material on numbers is in Lessons 9 and 17.

Have you revised 9.5 and 9.9 on 'two dollars' **два до́ллара**, 'five dollars' **пять до́лларов** etc? The two main grammar points to note in this lesson are:

(a) that numbers and quantity words (**пять, сто́, мно́го**) have declensions just as nouns do (**после Ле́нина** 'after Lenin'; **по́сле пяти́** 'after five' – genitive case);

(b) the agreement rules for nouns and numbers in 9.9 (and adjectives 10.13) *do not apply* if the number is in the *gen., dat., inst. or prep.* case ('of three', 'with fifty' etc.). *Note this new rule:* When the number is in one of these four cases, for example the instrumental, any accompanying adjectives and nouns are in the *plural of the same case as the number*. Examples:

(nom./acc. number) **два до́ллара**	two dollars ('of dollar' 9.5)
(inst. number) **с двумя́ до́лларами**	with two dollars ('dollars' in inst. plural)
две молоды́е де́вушки	two young girls (see 10.13)
двум молоды́м де́вушкам	to two young girls (dat. pl.)
два часа́	two o'clock
по́сле двух часо́в	after two o'clock (gen. pl.)
три иностра́нных студе́нта	three foreign students (10.13)
с тремя́ иностра́нными студе́нтами	with three foreign students (inst. pl.)
не́сколько языко́в	several languages
на не́скольких языка́х	in several languages (prep. pl.)

In practice, Russians avoid using numbers, particularly big ones, in cases other than the nom./acc./gen., and you can do the same. For example, a sentence such as 'I arrived with 540 dollars' (instrumental **с пятьюста́ми сорока́ до́лларами**) can be rephrased as 'I had 540 dollars when I arrived' (**Когда́ я прие́хал, у меня́ бы́ло пятьсо́т со́рок до́лларов**).

22.3 Declension Details

Numbers which end with a soft sign in the nominative (e.g. 5–20) behave like soft-sign feminine singular nouns, so the genitive of **пять** is **пяти́** (cf. **Сиби́рь–Сиби́ри**). But many numbers are idiosyncratic. **Два, три** and **четы́ре** have unique declensions, and other numbers have special features too. See the tables on pp. 378–86.

270

As mentioned in Lesson 17 on times and dates, the only number case forms you *have* to know are the genitive forms of the low numbers, up to twenty-five or so (17.6). But for reference purposes it is useful to know how the phrases at the beginning of this lesson are formed.

Оди́н, as you may remember, has the same grammar and endings as **э́тот** ('this'):

Я зна́ю одного́ (note stress) **писа́теля.**	I know one (= a certain) writer.
Я познако́милась с одни́м молоды́м челове́ком.	I got to know a certain ('one') young man.
письмо́ от одно́й де́вушки	a letter from one (a certain) girl

Оди́н also has plural forms (for use with nouns which have no singular):

одни́ часы́	one watch

Оди́н also means 'alone':

Она́ одна́.	She is alone.
Мы одни́.	We are alone.
в одни́х брю́ках (брю́ки 'trousers')	wearing only trousers (in trousers alone)

Два/две, три and **четы́ре** have the following forms:

N	**два**	**три**	**четы́ре**
A	**два/двух**[‡]	**три/трёх**[‡]	**четы́ре/четырёх**[‡]
G	**двух**	**трёх**	**четырёх**
D	**двум**	**трём**	**четырём**
I	**двумя́**	**тремя́**	**четырьмя́**
P	**двух**	**трёх**	**четырёх**

[‡]**Двух, трёх** and **четырёх** are used with animate nouns – see 22.9 below.

пять, шесть, во́с(е)мь etc. look like feminine singular nouns.

N	**пять**	**во́семь**	**пятна́дцать**	**два́дцать**
A	**пять**	**во́семь**	**пятна́дцать**	**два́дцать**
G	**пяти́**	**восьми́**	**пятна́дцати**	**двадцати́**
D	**пяти́**	**восьми́**	**пятна́дцати**	**двадцати́**
I	**пятью́**	**восемью́**	**пятна́дцатью**	**двадцатью́**
P	**пяти́**	**восьми́**	**пятна́дцати**	**двадцати́**

The stress is on the end of 5, 6, 7, 8, 9, 10, 20 and 30. It is fixed on the stem of 11–19.

Со́рок, девяно́сто and **сто́** have strange (but easy) declensions:

N	со́рок	девяно́сто	сто́
A	со́рок	девяно́сто	сто́
G	сорока́	девяно́ста	ста́
D	сорока́	девяно́ста	ста́
I	сорока́	девяно́ста	ста́
P	сорока́	девяно́ста	ста́

The numbers 50, 60, 70, 80, and the hundreds – 200 etc. – are two-part words and both parts decline:

N	пятьдеся́т	во́семьдесят	две́сти	пятьсо́т
A	пятьдеся́т	во́семьдесят	две́сти	пятьсо́т
G	пяти́десяти	восьми́десяти	двухсо́т	пятисо́т
D	пяти́десяти	восьми́десяти	двумста́м	пятиста́м
I	пятью́десятью	восьмью́десятью	двумяста́ми	пятьюста́ми
P	пяти́десяти	восьми́десяти	двухста́х	пятиста́х

The numbers 60 and 70 are like 50; 300 and all the other hundreds are like 200 and 500. Grammar Table 7 (see page 383) gives more examples.

For 'thousand' (**ты́сяча**) and million, see 22.6 below.

EXERCISE 22/1

Translate:

1 **Он придёт ме́жду тремя́ и пятью́ часа́ми.** 2 **Она́ зараба́тывает** (earns) **бо́льше четырёх ты́сяч трёхсо́т до́лларов в ме́сяц.** 3 **В на́шем магази́не продаю́тся кни́ги на восьми́десяти двух языка́х.**

EXERCISE 22/2

Read (or write out) the numbers in Russian:

1 **Пожа́луйста, позвони́те мне до 11 часо́в** Please ring me before eleven. 2 **Я хочу́ вас познако́мить с 2 интере́сными де́вушками** 'I

want to introduce you to two interesting girls. 3 **Мистер Поуп говорит на 8 языках** Mr Pope speaks eight languages. 4 **Администратор получил письмо от 31 американца** The manager has received a letter from thirty-one Americans.

22.4 Both: оба/обе

These words behave like **два/две** 'two', so **оба** is used with m and n nouns, while **обе** goes with f ones. After **оба/обе** in the nom. or acc., the noun is genitive singular:

оба друга	both friends
обе подруги	both female friends

The declensions of **оба** and **обе** are:

M	**оба**	**обе**
A	**оба** (inanim)/**обоих** (anim)	**обе** (inanim)/**обеих** (anim)
G	**обоих**	**обеих**
D	**обоим**	**обеим**
I	**обоими**	**обеими**
P	**обоих**	**обеих**

Here are some phrases you might need:

обеими руками	with both hands
Я знаю их обоих.	I know **them both**.
в обоих случаях	in both cases

Note that 'both' linking two words is **и . . . и**:

Я знаю и Еву, и Вадима.	I know both Eva and Vadim.

22.5 Полтора: One and a Half

One and a half is always translated as **полтора** (**полторы** with feminine nouns), never as **один с половиной**. After **полтора** (which is short for **половина второго** 'half of the second'), use the genitive singular:

Мы ждáли полторá часá (gen. sg.).	We waited for an hour and a half.
полторá килогрáмма	one and a half kilograms

The feminine form is officially **полторы́**:

полторы́ недéли	one and a half weeks

But in informal, colloquial speech **полторá** is used with all nouns.

22.6 **EXTRA: Declension of полторá**

Like all numerals, **полторá/полторы́** decline. The G/D/I/P of both **полторá** and **полторы́** is **полýтора**.

бóльше полýтора ты́сяч (gen. pl.)	more than one and a half thousand

---

22.7 Thousand, Million, Billion

Note that **ты́сяча** (1,000), **миллиóн** (million), **миллиáрд** (US billion = thousand million), and **биллиóн** (million million) are grammatically nouns, not numerals, which means that (a) they have normal noun endings, and (b) they behave like **килогрáмм**, not like **пять**, i.e. following nouns and adjectives are always in the genitive:

с двумя́ килогрáммами апельси́нов	with two kilos of oranges
с двумя́ миллиóнами рублéй (not **рубля́ми**)	with two million roubles
трём ты́сячам америкáнцев (not **америкáнцам**)	to three thousand Americans

But remember (9.11) that in Russian it is always the *last number* which determines agreement:

трём ты́сячам трёмстáм америкáнцам	to 3,300 Americans

Я прочита́л две ты́сячи ру́сс<u>**ких**</u> **книг.**   I have read 2,000 Russian books.

Я прочита́л ты́сячу две́сти одну́ ру́сск<u>**ую**</u> **кни́гу.**   I have read 1,201
   Russian books.

четы́ре-пять ме́сяц<u>**ев**</u> (gen.pl.)   four or five months

22.8 Quantity Words: Declension of мно́го etc.

Мно́го 'many', **не́сколько** 'a few', 'several', and **ско́лько** 'how many'
have the following type of declension:

N   **мно́го**

A   **мно́го** (inanim)/**мно́гих** (anim)

G   **мно́гих**

D   **мно́гим**

I   **мно́гими**

P   **мно́гих**

во мно́гих отноше́ниях	in many respects
Я говори́л со мно́гими тури́стами.	I spoke to many tourists.
в не́скольких места́х	in several places

EXERCISE 22/3

Put the numbers/quantity words in the correct form and translate:

1 **Мы бы́ли в 32 стра́нах.** 2 **Мы е́хали 1,5 часа́.** 3 **Магази́н рабо́тает с
9 утра́ до 5 ве́чера.** 4 **Я познако́мился с (о́бе) де́вушками.** 5 **Мы
побыва́ли во (мно́го) ру́сских города́х.** 6 **Мы разгова́ривали с
(не́сколько) ру́сскими инжене́рами.**

EXERCISE 22/4

Read the following sentences aloud and translate, noting that each second
sentence is a simpler version of the preceding one, avoiding awkward
declined numerals:

1 **Мы прошли пешко́м о́коло 250** (gen.) **киломе́тров.** 2 **Мы прошли пешко́м приме́рно** (= approximately (adverb)) **250** (acc.) **киломе́тров.** 3 **Óн прие́хал с 540** (inst.) **до́лларами.** 4 **Когда́ о́н прие́хал, у него́ бы́ло 540** (nom.) **до́лларов.** 5 **Я приду́ ме́жду 10 и 11 часа́ми.** 6 **Я приду́ в 11-ом** (adj) **часу́** (17.4). 7 **В Москве́ живёт бо́лее 6.500.000** (gen.) **челове́к.** 8 **Населе́ние** (population) **Москвы́ превыша́ет** (exceeds) **6.500.000** (acc.) **челове́к.**

22.9 The Accusative of Numbers with Animate Nouns

General rules. Only the numbers 1, 2, 3 and 4 have animate accusative forms (i.e. **одного́, двух, трёх, четырёх**). Numbers ending 1 decline the 1, but numbers which end 2, 3 and 4, e.g. 22, 32, 5,134, do not have animate accusative forms.

Note these three model sentences:

Я зна́ю её дву́х (anim acc.) **бра́тьев.** I know her two brothers.

Мы хоти́м заказа́ть сто́л на два́дцать два (inanim form) **челове́ка.** We want to book a table for twenty-two people.

Мы хоти́м заказа́ть сто́л на два́дцать одного́ (anim) **челове́ка.** We want to book a table for twenty-one people.

22.10 Collective Numerals

There is another set of number words which you will meet occasionally, particularly when Russians give the number of children in a family. Instead of **два ребёнка** 'two children' ('two of child'), they normally say **дво́е дете́й**, 'a twosome of children'. There are nine of these collective numerals, from two to ten, but only the first three are common:

дво́е 'two', 'a twosome'
тро́е 'three', 'a threesome'
че́тверо 'four', 'a foursome'

The others are **пя́теро, ше́стеро, се́меро, во́сьмеро, де́вятеро, де́сятеро.** You need these collective numerals:

(a) when counting children (**дéти**) and men (**мужчи́ны**):

У неё двóе детéй. 'She has two children' (more idiomatic than **два ребёнка**).

двóе мужчи́н 'two men' (not **два мужчи́ны**)

(b) when counting words which have no singular forms (since **два, три, четы́ре** require the gen. sg.), e.g. **су́тки** 'twenty-four hours', **часы́** 'watch', **брю́ки** 'trousers', **я́сли** 'crèche':

В пóезде мы éхали трóе су́ток. We spent three days and nights on the train.

У меня́ двóе часóв. I have two watches.

На э́том завóде двóе я́слей. This factory has two crèches.

(c) in phrases such as 'There are four of us'. **Нас чéтверо.**

Нас бы́ло трóе. There were three of us.

22.11 **EXTRA: More on Collective Numerals**

Optionally, collective numerals can be used for groups of males (not females or mixed groups), e.g. **двóе солдáт** 'two soldiers' (or **два солдáта**), **трóе учителéй** 'three teachers' (or **три учи́теля**). This usage is rather colloquial. **Трóе мини́стров** ('a threesome of male government ministers') would sound disrespectful; **три мини́стра** is more polite.

The other collective numerals up to ten are, as we saw above: **пя́теро** 'five', **шéстеро** 'six', **сéмеро** 'seven', **вóсьмеро** 'eight', **дéвятеро** 'nine', **дéсятеро** 'ten', but the higher the number, the rarer it is. Instead of **Нас бы́ло пя́теро** 'There were five of us' you can say **Нас бы́ло пять человéк**. Since the numbers **пять, шесть** etc. take the genitive plural, you do not need to use **пя́теро, шéстеро** etc. with words which have no singular. So 'five days and nights' is simply **пять су́ток** (no need to say **пя́теро су́ток**), 'five children' is **пять детéй**.

Like all numerals, **двóе, трóе** etc. decline, but Russians generally avoid structures in which declined forms would be necessary. Here are the declensions of **двóе** ('two') and **чéтверо** ('four'):

N **двóе**   **чéтверо**

A	двóе (inanim) двойх (anim)	чéтверо (inanim)/четверы́х (anim)
G	двойх	четверы́х
D	двойм	четверы́м
I	двойми	четверы́ми
P	двойх	четверы́х

Трóе declines like **двóе**, the others like **чéтверо**.

In a hotel: **нóмер на двойх** 'a room for two (people)', 'a double'
рабóтать за тройх 'to work for three' (do as much as three people).

There are no collective numerals beyond **дéсятеро** 'ten', so there are
problems if you should ever want to say 'twenty-three watches' (**часы́**
m pl. 'watch') or 'eighty-two crèches' (**я́сли** pl. 'crèche'), since numbers
ending 2, 3, 4 require the genitive singular. In such cases, the construction
has to be rewritten to separate the number from the noun, e.g. **Мы
откры́ли я́сли в колйчестве восьмйдесяти двух** 'We have opened
crèches in the quantity (to the total) of eighty-two.'

22.12 Verb Agreement with Numbers

The general rule is: when the subject is a numeral, make the verb neuter
singular:

У меня́ бы́ло пятьдеся́т дóлларов.	I had fifty dollars.
Ей тогдá бы́ло три гóда.	She was three years old then.
Пришлó пять человéк.	Five people came.

But note the following details:

– Plural verbs are quite common if the subject is animate (i.e. people):

Пришлó (Пришлй) дéсять америкáнцев. Ten Americans came.

– Plural verbs are *normal* with animate subjects if (a) the number is **два,
три, четы́ре**, or the collective numerals **двóе, трóе, чéтверо**, and/or (b)
the subject comes before the verb:

Её три сы́на жда́ли (not **жда́ло**) **нас на вокза́ле.**
Her three sons were waiting for us at the station.

Де́сять-пятна́дцать тури́стов хотя́т (not **хо́чет**) **пойти́ в теа́тр.**
Ten or fifteen tourists want to go to the theatre.

Приду́т дво́е. Two men will come.

В ваго́не-рестора́не сиде́ли/сиде́ло тро́е америка́нцев.
There were three American men sitting in the restaurant car.

EXERCISE 22/5

Say in Russian:

1 We have two children. 2 There are three of us. 3 You have to travel for three days and three nights (use **су́тки**). 4 Two men were waiting for us. 5 I had more than (**бо́лее** + gen.) a hundred dollars.

22.13 Fractions

You should already know the feminine nouns **полови́на** 'half' and **че́тверть** 'a quarter'. Notice also **треть** (f) 'a third'. The other fractions are all feminine adjectives, with the usual adjective endings after numbers:

одна́ пя́тая	one-fifth
одна́ шестна́дцатая	one-sixteenth
две пя́тых (gen. pl.)	two-fifths
три и пять деся́тых	3.5 (three and five-tenths)

Both decimal fractions and vulgar fractions are read in the same way. So 4,3 and $4^3/_{10}$ are read as **четы́ре и три деся́тых**[‡]. After fractions, adjectives and nouns are in the genitive *singular*:

56,8%	**пятьдеся́т шесть и во́семь деся́тых проце́нта** fifty-six and eight-tenths of a per cent (**проце́нт** is a masculine noun)
2,6 ребёнка	2.6 children (two and six-tenths of a child)

[‡]A note on halves. 'Half' is **полови́на** in everyday contexts and **пять**

279

деся́тых ('five-tenths') in statistical contexts. In everyday speech 'two/three/four etc. and a half' is **два/три/четы́ре** etc. **с полови́ной** ('with a half'); the form of the following noun is then governed by the integer (the whole number), not by the fraction. For example:

пять с полови́ной ме́тров (gen.pl. after 5)   five and a half metres

But in a more mathematical/statistical/official context ('5.5 metres'):

пять и пять деся́тых (5,5) ме́тра (gen.sg. after a decimal fraction)

Remember that 'one and a half' is **полтора́** (see above 22.5).

Note that Russians use a decimal comma (5,5), not a decimal point.

22.14 **Текст. Стати́стика** ('Statistics')

As a difficult and entirely optional exercise, you can try reading out the numbers. They are written out in words immediately following the text.

В 1982 году́ в Сове́тском Сою́зе прожива́ло бо́лее 268.000.000 челове́к, из них о́коло 5.000.000 студе́нтов, кото́рые учи́лись в 900 университе́тах и институ́тах. В 1982 году́ бы́ло о́коло 1.000.000 враче́й. В то́м же году́ в Москве́ бы́ло бо́лее 8.350.000 жи́телей, кото́рые смотре́ли спекта́кли в 26 теа́трах. Моско́вские де́ти ходи́ли в 1.000 шко́л.

Answers to the numbers exercise: <u>**1982**</u> **ты́сяча девятьсо́т во́семьдесят второ́м** – '1982nd year' (17.11); <u>**268.000.000**</u> **двухсо́т шести́десяти восьми́ миллио́нов** – **бо́лее** = **бо́льше** + gen. 'more than' (18.2); <u>**5.000.000**</u> **пяти́ миллио́нов** – gen. after **о́коло** 'about'; <u>**900**</u> **девятиста́х** – prep.; <u>**1.000.000**</u> **(одного́) миллио́на**; <u>**8.350.000**</u> **восьми́ миллио́нов трёхсо́т пяти́десяти ты́сяч** – gen.; <u>**26**</u> **двадцати́ шести́** – prep.; <u>**1.000**</u> **ты́сячу** – acc.

COMPREHENSION EXERCISE 22/6

Russian Divorce Statistics

Find the answers to the following questions:

1 What percentage of married couples get divorced in any one year?

2 How do the divorce figures for 1950 compare with those for 1977?

3 At the time of writing what proportion of marriages break up within five years of the wedding?

4 What proportion of divorcing couples have no children?

Éсли сравни́ть число́ разво́дов за́[‡] год с число́м бра́чных[‡] пар, кото́рые существова́ли в нача́ле го́да, то́ за́ год разво́дится всего́ о́коло полу́тора[‡] проце́нтов супру́гов, то́ есть за́ год распада́ется[‡] всего́ о́коло пятна́дцати из ты́сячи семе́й.

В 1950 году́ на ты́сячу сва́деб бы́ло три́дцать два разво́да. В 1977 году́ на ты́сячу сва́деб бы́ло уже́ три́ста два́дцать три разво́да.

Иссле́дования[‡] показа́ли, что́ треть всех разво́дов происхо́дит на пе́рвом году́ семе́йной жи́зни, ещё треть прихо́дится[‡] на се́мьи, существу́ющие[‡] от одного́ до пяти́ лет. Из ста но́вых семе́йных пар на пе́рвом году́ жи́зни распада́ется оди́ннадцать, до пяти́ лет распада́ется два́дцать две семьи́.

Изве́стно, что́ в тех слу́чаях, когда́ в семье́ ещё нет дете́й (их нет у че́тверти разводя́щихся пар), мужья́ выступа́ют[‡] инициа́торами[‡] в полови́не слу́чаев. А в се́мьях с детьми́ инициа́торами ча́ще выступа́ют[‡] же́нщины – две тре́ти всех исковы́х[‡] заявле́ний[‡] в се́мьях с одни́м-двумя́ детьми́ по́дали же́нщины (таки́х се́мьдесят проце́нтов от всех распада́ющихся[‡] семе́й, с бо́льшим коли́чеством дете́й – всего́ пять проце́нтов). Тем са́мым[‡] же́нщины стремя́тся[‡] защити́ть дете́й от конфли́ктов семе́йной жи́зни. Они́ счита́ют, что́ де́тям бу́дет лу́чше без отца́, чем с плохи́м отцо́м.

(Based on figures quoted by the demographer **В. Переве́денцев** in 1981.)

22.15 **Vocabulary**

([‡]Words marked with a [‡] are less common and probably not worth learning at this stage.)

бо́лее (bookish) (gen.) more (than) (18.2) (same as more colloquial	**бо́льше** + gen.) **брак** marriage

‡**бра́чная па́ра** married couple

‡**выступа́ть инициа́тором** to initiate (divorce proceedings)

дво́е two, a twosome

заявле́ние application

‡**за́ год** (note stress on prep.) during the year

защити́тьᵖ **защищу́, защити́шь (защища́ть** like **знать)** (+ acc.) to defend, protect (someone)

изве́стно it is known

‡**инициати́ва** initiative

‡**инициа́тор** initiator

‡**исково́е заявле́ние** divorce application

иссле́дование investigation, research

коли́чество quantity

‡**конфли́кт** conflict

миллиа́рд a thousand million (US billion)

о́ба/о́бе both (22.4)

па́ра couple

пода́тьᵖ (like **дать)** (+ acc.) **(подава́ть** like **дава́ть)** to serve, hand in, lodge

полтора́ one and a half (22.5)

полу́тора gen. of **полтора́** one and a half

получи́тьᵖ **получу́, полу́чишь** (+ acc.) **(получа́ть)** to receive, get

‡**прихо́дится на се́мьи** happens to families

прожива́ть (like **знать)** to reside

происходи́ть (like **ходи́ть)**

(произойти́ᵖ like **идти́)** to occur

проце́нт a per cent

‡**разводя́щийся** divorcing

‡**распада́ющийся** breaking up

‡**распада́ться** to break up

рука́ acc. **ру́ку** pl. **ру́ки, рука́м** hand, arm

сва́дьба gen.pl. **сва́деб** wedding

семе́йный family

слу́чай gen.pl. **слу́чаев** case

Сове́тский Сою́з Soviet Union

спекта́кль (m) performance, show

сравни́тьᵖ **сравню́, сравни́шь (сра́внивать** like **знать)** to compare

е́сли сравни́ть if one compares

‡**стреми́ться** to strive, try

студе́нт student

‡**супру́ги** (pl.) husband and wife (from **супру́г** 'm spouse', **супру́га** 'f spouse')

существова́ть **существу́ю существу́ешь (про-**ᵖ**)** to exist

‡**существу́ющий** existing (Lesson 29)

‡**тем са́мым** in this way ('by that very')

то́ есть that is

треть (f) a third (22.13)

тро́е three, a threesome

че́тверо four, a foursome

че́тверть (f) quarter (22.12)

число́ pl. **чи́сла** gen.pl. **чи́сел** number

23

УРÓК НÓМЕР ДВÁДЦАТЬ ТРИ

TIME EXPRESSIONS

23.1 Key Phrases

вчерá вéчером	yesterday evening/last night
в прóшлую срéду	last Wednesday
в тóт день	that day
в двадцáтом вéке	in the twentieth century
в шестидесятых годáх	in the sixties
за час до начáла	an hour before the start
Я éду в Москвý на недéлю.	I'm going to Moscow for a week.
Мы шли до теáтра дéсять минýт.	It was a ten-minute walk to the theatre.
Мы дошлú до теáтра за пять минýт.	We reached the theatre in five minutes.

23.2 Grammar of Time Expressions

The main structures for telling the time and giving the date are in Lesson 17. This lesson gives you more information on the grammatical patterns and also deals with the question of duration ('How long?'). There are several types of time meanings. Three basic types answer the following questions:

(1) When?
(2) How long does something go on? 'He worked *for* three days.'
(3) How long does something take to finish? 'He did it *in* three days.'

283

23.3 When?

The 'when' type is the commonest and the one with the biggest variety of answers. Notice that in English, when answering the question 'When did she arrive?', possible answers are *on* Wednesday, *at* three o'clock, *in* the morning. The use of 'on', 'at' or 'in' depends on what the noun is. In Russian too there are several different constructions, depending on the noun.

(a) The first regularity to notice is the common use of **в** to mean in/at/on with time words: **в среду** 'on Wednesday', **в два часа** 'at two o'clock'. We met such examples in Lesson 17.

(b) If the word denotes a day or shorter (e.g. hour, second etc.), **в** is used with the *accusative* case:

в среду	on Wednesday
в час	at one o'clock/in an hour
в любой день	on any day

(c) if the time word is longer than a day (e.g. week, month, year etc.), **в** is used with the *prepositional* case:

в январе	in January
в этом году	this year
в девятнадцатом веке	in the nineteenth century

Exception: **неделя** 'week' is used with **на** (+ prep.) instead of **в**:

на прошлой неделе	last week
на этой неделе	this week
на следующей (будущей) неделе	next week

(d) The parts of the day and the seasons are in the instrumental with no preposition: **утром** 'in the morning', **весной** 'in spring' (see 16.5).

(e) Words which denote activities (e.g. **война** 'war', **урок** 'lesson') or indefinite periods (e.g. **эпоха** 'era' and **время** 'time' itself) rather than specific time periods (e.g. **неделя** 'week') are used with **в** and the *accusative*:

в э́то вре́мя	at that time
в войну́	in the war
в на́шу эпо́ху	in our epoch/era

(f) In the plural, *all* time words normally take **в** + acc.:

| в э́ти дни/ме́сяцы/го́ды | during these days/months/years |

(g) Decades

The nineties are **девяно́стые го́ды** 'the ninetieth years', the eighties are **восьмидеся́тые го́ды** and so on. In this context, the genitive plural of **го́ды** is <u>годо́в</u> (not **лет**):

| в конце́ шестидеся́тых годо́в | at the end of the sixties |

'In a decade' is *either* the prepositional or the accusative. So 'in the seventies' is **в семидеся́тых года́х** (prep. – slightly commoner) or **в семидеся́т<u>ые</u> го́ды** (acc. – in accordance with (f) above).

(h) During

To indicate that something took place over a period of time (rather than momentarily), the two commonest equivalents of English 'during' are:

во вре́мя (+ gen.) with activity words, and
в тече́ние (+ gen.) with specific time words

во вре́мя войны́/уро́ка/	during the war/the lesson/the
револю́ции	revolution
в тече́ние неде́ли	during the week, in the course of a week

(i) From . . . until (see 17.12)

Both 'since' and 'from' are **с** with the genitive:

| с четверга́ | since/from Thursday |
| с со́рок четвёртого го́да | since (nineteen) forty-four |

'Until' is **до** with the genitive:

| до среды́ | until Wednesday |
| до двухты́сячного го́да | until the year 2000 |

'From . . . to' is **с . . . до** (or **с . . . по** with the accusative in the meaning 'inclusive'):

с шести́ часо́в до девяти́	from six o'clock to nine
с деся́того по трина́дцатое	from the tenth to the thirteenth inclusive

(j) A month before /A week after

These structures involve *two* prepositions in Russian:

before: **за** + acc . . . **до** + gen.

За ме́сяц до пое́здки о́н сходи́л^р в посо́льство.
A month before the trip he went to the embassy.

after: **че́рез** + acc . . . **по́сле** + gen.

Че́рез неде́лю по́сле экза́менов мы уе́хали на мо́ре.
A week after the exams we left for the seaside.

(k) Before

до + gen. means 'before'; **перед** + inst. means 'immediately before':

до войны́	before the war
пе́ред войно́й	just before the war

(l) Once

'Once' in the meaning 'one day' is **одна́жды**:

Одна́жды весно́й я гуля́л по на́бережной.
One day in spring I was strolling on the embankment.

одна́жды ве́чером	one evening

'Once' meaning 'one time' is **раз** (or **оди́н раз**):

ско́лько раз (m)? how often?

'Twice' is **два ра́за** (gen. sg.). 'Five times' is **пять раз** (gen. pl.). If you want to say 'twice a week', 'a' translates as **в** *with the accusative*:

twice a week	**два ра́за в неде́лю**
five times a year	**пять ра́з в го́д**
three times a month	**три ра́за в ме́сяц**

EXERCISE 23/1

Translate the words in brackets:

1 **Éва придёт** (on Saturday at seven). 2 (This year) **мы бу́дем отдыха́ть в Крыму́.** 3 **Ми́стер По́уп был здесь** (last week). 4 (During the war) **мы жи́ли в Сиби́ри.** 5 **Мэ́ри встреча́ется с Воло́дей** (four times a week).

23.4 **How Long?**

(a) If the question is about duration (**Ско́лько вре́мени?/Как до́лго?** – both meaning 'How long?'), the answer is simply the accusative with no preposition:

Ско́лько вре́мени вы бу́дете здесь? or **Как до́лго вы бу́дете здесь?**	How long will you be here?
Я бу́ду здесь одну́ неде́лю.	I shall be here (for) a week.
Мы жи́ли в Сиби́ри три го́да.	We lived in Siberia (for) three years.
Подожди́те мину́точку.	Wait a moment ('a little minute' – see Lesson 25).

(b) 'For' in the meaning 'in order to spend' ('We're going to Moscow for a month') is **на** with the accusative: **Мы е́дем в Москву́ на ме́сяц.**

Она́ прие́хала <u>на</u> неде́лю.	She's come for a week.
Дире́ктор вы́шел <u>на</u> пять мину́т.	The director has gone out for five minutes.
Он прие́дет всего́ <u>на</u> оди́н день.	He'll come for just one day.

Rule of Thumb: 'for' in time expressions

If 'for' can be omitted in English ('He waited (for) ten minutes'), it must be omitted in Russian (**Он ждал де́сять мину́т**). If 'for' cannot be omitted in an English time expression ('He's coming for a week'), then it is **на** + acc. in Russian (**Он приезжа́ет <u>на</u> неде́лю**).

23.5 **How Long Did It Take?**

If the question concerns how long something took to finish, then the preposition **за** *with the accusative* is used:

Я прочитáла «Войнý и мир»   I read *War and Peace* in a month.
  за мéсяц.

Мы всё сдéлаем за недéлю.   We'll do everything in a week.

Note the use of perfective verbs because the meaning involves completion.

EXERCISE 23/2

Translate the words in brackets:

1 **Мы ждáли** (twenty minutes). 2 **Мэ́ри бýдет в Киéве** ((for) a week).
3 **Мы éдем в Москвý** (for three months). 4 **Дирéктор вы́шел** (for five
minutes). 5 **Мэ́ри прочитáла «Áнну Карéнину»** (in two weeks). 6 **Éва
доéхала до дóма** (in an hour).

23.6 **Until/After/Before with Verbs**

'Before' with a verb is **до тогó как** (or **пéред тем как** 'immediately
before'):

До тогó как Мэ́ри поéхала в Москвý, онá учи́лась в Бри́столе.
Before Mary went to Mosow, she studied in Bristol.

До is a preposition[1], so it cannot be immediately followed by a verb. If you
don't like the complex conjunction **до тогó как**, use **до** with a noun in
the genitive. The above sentence could thus be **До поéздки в Москвý
Мэ́ри учи́лась в Бри́столе** ('Before her trip . . .').

  Similarly, 'after' with a verb is **пóсле тогó как**:

Пóсле тогó как мы вернёмся из Ки́ева, мы поéдем в Сиби́рь.
After we return from Kiev, we'll go to Siberia.

But notice that the simpler **Когдá** ('When') **мы вернёмся из Ки́ева . . .**
has the same meaning.

'Until' with a verb is **пока́ . . . не**:

Я бу́ду ждать в ба́ре, пока́ она́ не вернётся.

I'll wait in the bar until she returns (= will return).

Пока́ вы не дади́те мне биле́т, я не уйду́.

Until you give me a ticket I won't leave.

EXERCISE 23/3

Translate the words in brackets:

1 (After I master Russian), **я прочита́ю «А́нну Каре́нину».** 2 **Вади́м бу́дет сиде́ть до́ма,** (until Eva rings). 3 **Вы должны́ спря́тать буты́лку,** (before Eva comes home),

EXERCISE 23/4

Say in Russian:

1 We went to Russia last year. 2 Life will be better in the twenty-first century. 3 Next week we'll go to Siberia. 4 In the summer Eva and Vadim will go to Yalta for a month. 5 That day we got up at 6 a.m. 6 Ivan Petrovich lived in America for two years. 7 He'll be working all week. 8 I've been there twice. 9 Mary read *War and Peace* in sixty-two hours. 10 During the war they worked eighty hours a week.

23.7 **Vocabulary**

акце́нт accent
библиоте́ка library
ближа́йший next, nearest
бу́дние дни (or **бу́дни** pl.)
    weekdays
быва́тьᵢ (like **знать**) to be
    (repeatedly/often)
век pl. **века́** century
ви́за visa

встре́ча meeting
дире́ктор pl. **директора́** director
дово́льно rather
зави́доватьᵢ **(по-ᵖ)** (+ dat.)
    зави́дую, зави́дуешь to envy
    (someone)
зае́хатьᵖ **зае́ду, зае́дешь к** (+ dat.)
    (заезжа́тьᵢ like **знать)** to call
    on someone (by transport)

зака́зывать¹ (like **знать**) (+ acc.)
(**заказа́ть**ᵖ **закажу́**,
зака́жешь) to order
(something)

замести́тель (m) deputy

звуча́ть¹ (like **говори́ть**) to sound
э́то звучи́т смешно́ that
sounds funny

изда́тельство publishing house

конта́кт contact

контра́кт contract

коро́ткий short

меня́ть(ся)¹ **меня́ю(сь)**,
меня́ешь(ся) to change – for
-ся see 11.6 (end)

министе́рство ministry

одна́жды once, one day

отту́да from there

парикма́херская (f adj)
hairdresser's, barber's

переговоры (m pl.) negotiations,
talks
вести́ переговоры to conduct
negotiations

по (+ acc.) up to and including
(17.12)

подписа́тьᵖ **подпишу́**,
подпи́шешь (**подписыва́ть**¹
like **знать**) (+ acc.) to sign

поздра́витьᵖ (+ acc.) **поздра́влю**,
поздра́вишь (**поздравля́ть**¹
like **знать**) to congratulate

посыла́ть¹ (like **знать**) (+ acc.)
(**посла́ть**ᵖ **пошлю́**, **пошлёшь**)
to send (someone or something)

поэ́зия poetry

поэ́т poet

прерва́тьᵖ **прерву́**, **прервёшь**
(+ acc.) (**прерыва́ть**¹ like
знать) to interrupt

престаре́лый aged

прие́зд arrival

при́нцип principle

распространённый common,
widespread

смешно́ (it's) funny

срок period of time; time limit

стихи́ (pl. of **стих**) gen.pl. **стихо́в**
poetry

су́тки (f pl.) gen.pl. **су́ток** twenty-
four hours (22.10)

свято́й (m adj) saint

тогда́шний (coll) then (adj)

учрежде́ние institution; office

умира́ть¹ (like **знать**) (**умере́ть**ᵖ)
to die

фи́рма firm, company

хоть even

шути́ть¹ (**по-**ᵖ) **шучу́**, **шу́тишь**
to joke

экза́мен examination

эмигри́ровать¹ᐟᵖ **эмигри́рую**
эмигри́руешь to emigrate

эпо́ха era, epoch

23.8 **Разгово́р**

Вади́м: Поздра́вь меня́! Че́рез ме́сяц меня́ посыла́ют в командиро́вку в Ло́ндон.

Ёва: Поздравля́ю – и зави́дую. Ско́лько вре́мени ты бу́дешь в А́нглии?

Вади́м: С два́дцать девя́того ма́я по пе́рвое ию́ня. К сожале́нию, я е́ду всего́ на четы́ре дня.

Ёва: Что́ ты успе́ешь уви́деть за тако́й коро́ткий сро́к?

Вади́м: Наве́рное, то́лько Си́ти, собо́р свято́го Па́вла и, мо́жет быть, Биг Бен. Ведь я бу́ду весь день вести́ перегово́ры в ра́зных учрежде́ниях.

Ёва: Ты е́дешь по́ездом и́ли лети́шь?

Вади́м: Лечу́, коне́чно. На по́езде на́до е́хать почти́ дво́е су́ток, а на самолёте я долечу́ за три с полови́ной часа́. Биле́т я до́лжен заказа́ть уже́ сего́дня, до пяти́ часо́в. А каки́е у тебя́ пла́ны на сего́дня?

Ёва: Я е́ду в библиоте́ку. Пото́м я зае́ду к Ви́ктору Па́вловичу в институ́т на полчаса́. Отту́да я иду́ в парикма́херскую. Я тебе́ позвоню́ о́коло шести́, по́сле того́ как верну́сь.

Вади́м: Я верну́сь из го́рода не ра́ньше полови́ны шесто́го. Ме́ньше чем за три часа́ я биле́т не доста́ну. Пото́м зайду́ к Воло́де. Но я не уйду́, пока́ ты не позвони́шь.

Ёва: Ты идёшь к Воло́де?

Вади́м: Не беспоко́йся. Ты же зна́ешь, что в бу́дние дни мы совсе́м не пьём.

COMPREHENSION EXERCISE 23/5

Two Businessmen Meet

1 What is Mr Pope's Russian background?
2 Why did his father change his name?
3 What leads him to believe that the business atmosphere in Russia has changed?

КИ: Здра́вствуйте, меня́ зову́т Кузнецо́в, Константи́н Ива́нович. Я заместитель директора по контактам с зарубежными издательскими[‡] фирмами.

РП: Здравствуйте, Константин Иванович. Моя фамилия Поуп. Ричард Поуп.

КИ: Вы говорите по-русски почти без акцента. Вы часто бываете в России?

РП: Нет. За последние двадцать лет я был здесь только три раза. Но я говорю по-русски с детства. Мой отец эмигрировал из России в начале двадцатых годов, во время гражданской[‡] войны. Его фамилия тогда была Попов, но через два года после приезда в Англию он решил стать Поупом.

КИ: Почему? Ведь «Поуп» – это папа[‡] римский.

РП: Хотя в России Попов – одна из самых распространённых фамилий, в Англии она звучит смешно. Например, когда в восьмидесятых годах престарелые советские лидеры[‡] – Брежнев, Андропов, Черненко – умирали один за другим, англичане шутили, что следующего будут звать Попов, а после него будет Абауттупопов. А что касается фамилии Поуп, то мой отец хорошо знал стихи английского поэта восемнадцатого века Александра Поупа. Конечно, большинство англичан довольно холодно относится к поэзии, а отец, как настоящий русский, очень уважал поэтов, и своих, и зарубежных.

КИ: Очень интересно. Но я должен вас прервать. Уже пора идти к директору. Он обычно бывает здесь только во второй половине дня[‡], но сегодня утром он приехал из министерства специально для того, чтобы встретиться с вами. Он очень надеется, что мы сможем подписать контракт с вашей фирмой в течение ближайших двух–трёх дней.

РП: Как времена меняются! Когда я был в России прошлый раз, в конце семидесятых годов, я звонил тогдашнему директору этого издательства три раза в день, но он совсем не хотел встречаться со мной.

‡Additional Vocabulary

втора́я полови́на дня afternoon
('second half of the day')
гражда́нская война́ civil war
изда́тельский publishing (adj)

ли́дер leader
па́па ри́мский the Pope ('Father Roman')

24

УРÓК НÓМЕР ДВÁДЦАТЬ ЧЕТЫ́РЕ

NEGATION; PLACE OF **НЕ**

24.1 **Key Phrases**

Я э́того не знáл(а).	I didn't know that.
Не обращáйте внимáния.	Pay no attention.
Я не понимáю ни одногó слóва.	I don't understand a single word.
Нéчего дéлать.	There is nothing to do.

24.2 **Genitive or Accusative after a Negated Verb**

There is a general rule which says: if a transitive¹ verb (a verb which takes the accusative case) has **не** in front of it, the object is in the genitive, not the accusative:

Óн знáет рýсский язы́к.	He knows Russian.
Óн не знáет рýсского языкá.	He doesn't know Russian.
Онá читáла рýсские кни́ги.	She read Russian books.
Онá не читáла рýсских книг.	She didn't read Russian books.

Notice these set phrases:

игрáть рóль (f acc.)	to play a role
Это не игрáет рóли (gen.).	That doesn't matter/plays no part.
обращáть/обрати́ть внимáние (acc.)	to take note/pay attention
Óн не обращáет внимáния (gen.).	He pays no attention.

294

име́ть значе́ние (acc.)	to have meaning/significance
Э́то не име́ет значе́ния (gen.).	It's of no importance.

However, this genitive rule often does not apply, particularly in conversational Russian. If the negation relates to the verb more than the noun, the accusative is preferred:

Не открыва́йте окно́ (acc.).	Don't open the window (emphasis on 'Don't open').
Я не зна́ю э́ту же́нщину (acc.).	I don't know that woman (stressing 'don't know').
Кузнецо́в не по́нял шу́тку (acc.) **ми́стера По́упа.**	Kuznetsov didn't understand Mr Pope's joke (stressing 'didn't understand').

Rules of Thumb

1 If the object is strongly negated, the object must be in the genitive, particularly if a word such as **никако́й** 'no kind of' (see 24.7) or **ни оди́н** 'not a single' is present, or if in English you would use 'any' ('I didn't buy *any* souvenirs'):

Я не понима́ю ни одного́ сло́ва.	I don't understand a single word.
Я не купи́л никаки́х сувени́ров.	I didn't buy any souvenirs (at all).

2 Use the *genitive* if the object is an abstract noun, something indefinite or the word **э́то**:

Не обраща́йте внима́ния (gen.).	Pay no attention.
Я не чита́ю газе́т (gen.).	I don't read newspapers.
Я э́того (gen.) **не говори́л(а).**	I didn't say that.

3 Use the *accusative* if the object is a definite person or definite thing (e.g. with 'the' in front of it):

Я Е́ву не люблю́ (acc.).	I don't like Eva.
Я не чита́л газе́ту (acc.).	I haven't read *the* newspaper.

4 If in doubt, use the genitive.

24.3 **EXTRA: Explanation**

There is a connection between the use of the genitive after a negated verb
and the use of the genitive after **нет** meaning 'there isn't' (10.5 **Нет газе́т**
'There are no newspapers'). If you say **Я не чита́ю газе́т** (gen.), the statement is akin to 'There are no newspapers which I read'. But in a sentence
such as **Не открыва́йте окно́** (acc.) 'Don't open the window', you are *not*
saying that there is no window, so the accusative is used.

Я не ви́жу письмо́ (acc.).	I can't see the letter
	(but I know it's there somewhere).
Я не ви́жу письма́ (gen.).	I can't see a (any) letter
	(maybe there isn't one).

24.4 **Place of не**

Не is placed in front of what it negates. Usually that is the verb, but it can
be other parts of the sentence, depending on the meaning.

Е́ва не купи́ла анана́са (gen.).	Eva didn't buy a pineapple.
Е́ва купи́ла не анана́с (acc.),	Eva bought not a pineapple,
а то́рт.	but a cake.
Анана́с купи́ла не Е́ва (nom.), **а**	It wasn't Eva who bought the
Вади́м (for word order see 26.8).	pineapple, but Vadim.

Notice that the genitive instead of accusative rule (24.2) only applies when
не goes with the *verb*.

Note the construction **Я не могу́ не** + infinitive, which is the equivalent of 'I can't help' or 'I can't avoid':

Я не могу́ не купи́ть	I can't not (= I must) buy a present.
пода́рок (acc.).	

The meaning is positive, because the two **не**'s cancel each other, so the
noun is accusative.

296

24.5 **EXTRA: Another Negative Oddity**

Phrases which are equivalent in meaning to **нет** 'there isn't' sometimes have the *genitive* instead of the *nominative* (and the verb is singular):

Си́них анана́сов (gen.) **не существу́ет.** Blue pineapples don't exist (**существова́ть** 'to exist') = **Си́них анана́сов нет.** There are no blue pineapples.

Не нашло́сь ни одного́ интере́сного мужчи́ны (gen.).
There wasn't a single interesting man (**найти́сь** 'to find itself').

Sometimes this structure is overused, as in this comic example:

(*Someone is attacking a queue-jumper*) **Вас** (gen.) **здесь не стоя́ло!** 'You weren't standing here!' (by analogy with **Вас** (gen.) **здесь не́ было** 'You weren't here'). Normal would be **Вы** (nom.) **здесь не стоя́ли.**

EXERCISE 24/1

Put the nouns in the genitive and translate:

1 **Не обраща́йте на них (внима́ние).** 2 **Я не купи́л (ни оди́н пода́рок).** 3 **Мы не хоти́м (э́то).** 4 **Турге́нев не разделя́л (взгля́ды) База́рова** (Ex. 21/5).

EXERCISE 24/2

Say in Russian:

1 I won't give (p) you (pol.) a single kopeck. 2 Why didn't you (f fam) buy (p) any wine? 3 Don't buy that book. 4 It wasn't Vadim who bought (p) the wine. 5 I'll come (p) not on Friday but on Saturday.

EXTRA: Exercise 24/3

Choose between the accusative and the genitive:

1 **Я не пью вино́/вина́** 'I don't drink wine'. 2 **Она́ не доста́ла билéт/билéта** 'She didn't manage to get a ticket'. 3 **А́ню/А́ни мы сего́дня не ви́дели** 'We didn't see Anya today'. 4 **Не теря́й врéмя/врéмени** 'Don't waste any time' (**теря́ть** 'to lose').

24.6 **Nothing, Nobody, Never**

You have already met negative words such as **никогда́** 'never' (16.10) and **я <u>ничего́</u> не ви́дел** 'I saw nothing' (11.8). The common ones are:

никто́	nobody
ничто́ (gen. **ничего́**)	nothing
нигдé	nowhere (place)
никуда́	nowhere (motion)
ника́к	in no way

Any sentence with one (or more) of these words always has **не** before the verb. A Russian negative sentence *must* have a **не** in it somewhere.

Никто́ не зна́ет.	Nobody knows.
Мы никуда́ не ходи́ли.	We didn't go anywhere/We went nowhere.
Я ника́к не могу́ откры́ть дверь.	I just can't open the door.
О́н никогда́ ничего́ не покупа́ет.	He never buys anything ('He never nothing doesn't buy').

Note that **никто́** 'nobody' and **ничто́** 'nothing' have the same declensions as **кто́** 'who' and **что́** 'what' (Table 4):

Я никого́ (gen./acc.) **не зна́ю.**	I don't know anybody.
В магази́не ничего́ (gen.) **нет.**	There's nothing in the shop (**нет** 'there isn't' from **не + есть**).

If there is a preposition, it comes *between* the **ни** and the rest of the word:

Вади́м ни с кем (inst.) **не говори́л.** Vadim didn't talk to (with) anyone.

Ве́ра ни за что́ (acc.) **не пла́тит.** Vera doesn't pay for anything.

EXERCISE 24/4

Translate the negative words in brackets:

1 **Воло́дя** (never) **помога́ет жене́** 'Volodia never helps his wife.' 2 **Мы** (nothing) **понима́ем** 'We don't understand anything.' 3 **Она́ не занима́ется** (anything – inst.) 'She doesn't do anything.' 4 **Я не получа́ю пи́сем от** (anybody). 5 **В кни́ге** (there was nothing) **интере́сного.** 6 **Бана́нов** (there aren't anywhere).

24.7 **Никако́й: 'по'**

Никако́й 'no' (= 'none at all') is declined like **како́й** (7.8). Any preposition comes between **ни** and **како́й**:

У нас нет никаки́х прав.	We have no rights (at all).
Он не остано́вится ни перед каки́ми тру́дностями.	No difficulties of any kind will stop him.
ни при каки́х обстоя́тельствах	in no circumstances (of any kind)

24.8 **Не́кого, не́чего: There is No One/Nothing**

Russian has another set of negative words which all begin with stressed **не́** and which translate as 'there is no one/nothing etc.'

Не́кого спроси́ть.	There is no one to ask.
Не́чего де́лать.	There is nothing to do.

The verb is always in the infinitive (i or p depending on meaning). You may add the person affected – in the *dative* case:

Мне не́кого спроси́ть.	There is no one for me to ask (I have no one to ask).
Им не́чего де́лать.	There is nothing for them to do (They have nothing to do).

Remember that a Russian negative sentence contains *one* **не**, so do not try to put another **не** before the verb.

As with **никто́** etc., the other case forms are based on the forms of **кто́** and **что́** (see 24.6) and any preposition comes between the **не́** and the form of **кто́** or **что́**:

Не́ с кем поговори́ть.	There is no one to talk to (with).
Не́ от кого́ получа́ть пи́сем.	There is no one from whom (I) could receive letters.

The future is formed with **бу́дет** and the past with **бы́ло**:

Нам не́ о чем бы́ло говори́ть.	We had nothing to talk about.
	(No dots on **чем** because stress on **не́**)

The other words in the set are **не́где** 'there is nowhere' (place), **не́куда** 'there is nowhere' (motion) and **не́когда** 'there is no time', based on **где** 'where', **куда́** 'where'/'whither', and **когда́** 'when'.

Не́где сесть.	There is nowhere to sit down.
Нам не́куда идти́.	There is nowhere for us to go.
	(We have nowhere to go.)
Идти́ бы́ло не́куда.	There was nowhere to go.
Мне не́когда.	I haven't got time.

EXERCISE 24/5

Translate:

1 В э́том го́роде не́чего де́лать ве́чером. Не́куда пойти́. Не́где пить ко́фе и́ли пи́во ('beer'). Нам ску́чно. 2 Вади́м не зна́ет, Ве́ра не зна́ет, Мари́на и Ви́ктор то́же не зна́ют. Бо́льше не́кого спроси́ть. 3 Извини́те, я не могу́ вам помо́чь. Мне не́когда, я о́чень спешу́ (спеши́ть' 'to hurry'). 4 В кафе́ не́ было никого́. Не́ с кем бы́ло поговори́ть. 5 Мэ́ри прочита́ла Турге́нева до́ма в А́нглии, потому́ что она́ зна́ла, что́ в Москве́ чита́ть ей бу́дет не́когда.

24.9 **Vocabulary**

(See also list of **не-** and **ни-** words 24.6, 24.8.)

ананáс pineapple

валю́та currency, hard currency

влáсти gen.pl. **властéй** pl. of
влáсть (f) power, authorities

внимáние attention
обращáтьⁱ (like **знать**)/
обрати́тьᵖ (**обращу́,**
обрати́шь) **внимáние на**
(+ acc.) to pay attention to

грýппа group

значéние meaning, significance

ни . . . ни neither . . . nor

нигдé nowhere

никакóй no; none at all; any (24.7)

обстоя́тельство circumstance

пережива́тьⁱ (like **знать**) to be
upset, worry
не пережива́й(те) don't be upset

плати́тьⁱ (**за-**ᵖ) **плачý, плáтишь**
(**за** + acc.) to pay (for)

побывáтьᵖ (no i) (like **знать**)
(+ prep.) to visit (somewhere)

подари́тьⁱ **подарю́, подáришь**
(**дари́ть**ᵖ) to give, present

прáво pl. **правá** right

прекрáсный beautiful, fine

придýматьᵖ (like **знать**) (+ acc.)
(**придýмывать**ⁱ like **знать**) to

think up, invent

продáжа sale

расти́ⁱ (**вы́-**ᵖ) **растý, растёшь**
(past **рóс, рослá, рослó,**
росли́) to grow

самостоя́тельно independently
('self standing')

случáйно by chance

спекуля́нт speculator (black
marketeer)

спеши́тьⁱ (**по-**ᵖ) **спешý, спеши́шь**
спешáт (Spelling Rules 3 and 4)
to hurry

спрáвка gen.pl. **спрáвок** (piece
of) information

стóитьⁱ to cost, be worth
не стóит (+ i inf) it's not worth

сýмка gen.pl. **сýмок** bag, shopping bag

торгóв(е)ц (+ inst.) trader
(dealing in)

трýдность (f) difficulty

ужé не no longer

цéрковь (f) gen./dat./prep.
цéркви, inst. **цéрковью,** pl.
цéркви, церквáх, церквéй,
церквáм, церквáми church

24.10 A Pineapple, but No Bananas

Ева: Это‡ вы принесли ананас?

ВП: Нет, я никакого ананаса не приносил. Где вы видели ананас?

Ева: Таня говорит, что на кухне в сумке лежит ананас.

ВП: Не обращайте внимания на то, что говорит Таня. Она никогда в жизни не видела ананаса. Она даже не знает, что это такое‡.

*

Вадим: Ева, почему ты сказала Марине, что на кухне лежит ананас?

Ева: Это‡ не я сказала, а Таня. Это‡ она придумала.

Вадим: Нет, она этот ананас не придумала. Я его купил случайно на рынке. Я хотел подарить его Марине и Виктору. Теперь это уже не сюрприз.

Ева: Не переживай. Это не имеет значения. Всё равно‡ это прекрасный подарок.

‡**Это** is used colloquially for emphasis: 'Was it *you* who brought the pineapple?' 'It wasn't *I* who said it, it was *Tanya*.'

‡**что это такое** what it is

‡**Всё равно** (11.8) All the same.

*

Мэри: Я не могу купить бананов. Их нигде нет.

Володя: И не стоит их искать. Я никогда нигде не видел в России бананов, ни на рынке, ни у спекулянтов. Бананы здесь не растут.

Мэри: И вы думаете, что их никогда не будет ни при каких обстоятельствах?

Володя: Нет, я этого не говорю. Раньше у нас не было валюты, не на что было их покупать. Но скоро у всех будет валюта, тогда прохода‡ не будет от торговцев бананами.

‡**прохода не будет от** + gen. there will be no way of avoiding

COMPREHENSION EXERCISE 24/6

A Tourist Negotiates with Intourist

1 A tourist (**T**) wants to go to the religious centre in the town of Sergievskii Posad (formerly Zagorsk), 74 km NE of Moscow. Why is the Intourist woman (**И**) initially unwilling to assist?
2 Why does the tourist reject her offer of the Friday excursion?
3 If he accepts her second proposal, how much notice must he give?
4 Why shouldn't he go at the weekend?

Т: Скажи́те, пожа́луйста, вы не мо́жете подсказа́ть[‡], как мне
поéхать в Сéргиевский Поса́д? Я слы́шал, что там мно́го
краси́вых церквéй. Я хочу́ поéхать оди́н, без ги́да.

И: К сожалéнию, я не могу́ вам помо́чь. Мы продаём билéты
то́лько на экску́рсии. Спра́вок мы не даём. А éсли вы хоти́те
поéхать самостоя́тельно, то, к сожалéнию, я не могу́ вам
ничéм помо́чь.

Т: Я хочу́ поéхать в Сéргиевский Поса́д, и никто́ мне не мо́жет
помо́чь, и да́же не мо́гут подсказа́ть, как мне проéхать туда́.

И: На вокза́ле вам всё ска́жут. А мы коммéрческая[‡] организа́ция
и занима́емся прода́жей услу́г[‡] и билéтов на экску́рсии.

Т: Поня́тно. Но всё равно́ я хочу́ побыва́ть в Сéргиевском Поса́де.

И: Пожа́луйста, вы мо́жете поéхать с гру́ппой в пя́тницу.

Т: Спаси́бо. Но я не хочу́ éхать с гру́ппой. Я хочу́ поéхать сам,
самостоя́тельно.

И: Тогда́ вы мо́жете заказа́ть маши́ну и ги́да за су́тки до поéздки.

Т: Мо́жно поéхать туда́ с ги́дом в любо́й день?

И: В любо́й день, кро́ме суббо́ты и воскресéнья.

Т: Скажи́те, а почему́ нельзя́ в суббо́ту и воскресéнье?

И: В при́нципе мо́жно, но церко́вные[‡] вла́сти[‡] попроси́ли, чтобы
мы не посыла́ли тури́стов по суббо́там и воскресéньям. Они́
бы не хотéли, чтобы их беспоко́или во врéмя богослужéний.[‡]

Т: Поня́тно. Спаси́бо.

И: Пожа́луйста.

One often gets the impression in Russia that officials are programmed to be unhelpful. But if you are politely insistent and always take the trouble

303

to ask three times for what you want, they will often soften up. In Russia, never expect to do business quickly.

‡Additional Vocabulary

богослуже́ние (church) service
комме́рческий commercial
подсказа́ть to suggest

услу́га service
церко́вный church (adj)

25

УРÓК НÓМЕР ДВÁДЦАТЬ ПЯТЬ

DIMINUTIVES; PROPER
NAMES; POLITENESS

25.1 Key phrases

Возьмúте стакáнчик.	Take a glass.
Хотúте чайкý?	Would you like a little tea?
Дáйте копéечку, пожáлуйста?	Would you have a one-kopeck coin?

25.2 Diminutives

In informal conversations with Russians, you begin to notice that large numbers of everyday words are given suffixes such as **-ик** and **-чка**. These forms are known collectively as 'diminutives', denoting smallness, like -let in English (booklet, coverlet). So, **стóлик** is literally 'small table' and **собáчка** is 'small dog'. In most cases, however, the intended meaning is not smallness but politeness, tenderness or some related emotion. English has a similar phenomenon in the use of the ending -ie ('a doggie', 'Johnny', 'Annie'), but relatively few words, other than personal names, can have endings such as -ie or -let, at least in standard English. In Russian, as well as personal names, *every* noun can be made into a diminutive. Where in English you might offer a friend 'a nice cup of tea', a Russian offers **чайкý**, 'some little tea', forming the partitive ('some') genitive of **ча(ё)к**, the 'diminutive' of **чай** 'tea'. And the tea may come in a **стакáнчик** 'a little glass' from **стакáн** 'glass'. Diminutives are an important part of friendliness and politeness in everyday Russian.

They are also essential if you have to deal with Russian children, or read a children's story. All hands are little hands, all foxes are little foxes, and many of the words may be hard to find in your pocket dictionary unless you know the basic rules for forming diminutives. The rules are fairly simple, which is why dictionaries do not normally list diminutives.

Here are some examples of diminutives. Look for the patterns.

		Diminutive form	
брат	brother	**бра́тик**	little brother
вода́	water	**води́чка**	a little water
во́дка	vodka	**во́дочка**	a little vodka
до́м	house	**до́мик**	cottage
изба́	peasant cottage	**избу́шка**	little cottage
кни́га	book	**кни́жка**	small book
ко́мната	room	**ко́мнатка**	little room
неде́ля	week	**неде́лька**	little week
нога́	foot, leg	**но́жка**	little foot, little leg
окно́	window	**око́шко**	little window
письмо́	letter	**письмецо́**	little letter
пло́щадь	square	**площа́дка**	piece of ground; staircase landing
река́	river	**ре́чка**	stream, rivulet
рука́	hand, arm	**ру́чка**	little hand, little arm
сестра́	sister	**сестри́чка**	little sister
стака́н	glass	**стака́нчик**	little glass
стена́	wall	**сте́нка**	partition; a set of wall units (shelves and cupboards)
сто́л	table	**сто́лик**	small table; restaurant table
стул	chair	**сту́льчик**	small chair
ча́шка	cup	**ча́шечка**	little cup

'Diminutives' suggest smallness, and **сто́лик** is indeed a small table, for example a restaurant table as distinct from a domestic dining-table. However, much of the time, so-called 'diminutives' have little to do with size. Their main stylistic colourings are tenderness, familiarity or politeness.

If someone offers you **стака́нчик со́ка** ' a little glass of juice', it will be no smaller than a normal **стака́н** 'glass'.

Some diminutives are particularly frequent. People commonly call a kopeck coin **копе́ечка** 'little kopeck', rather than **копе́йка**. Within families **до́чка** 'little daughter' is much commoner than **дочь**, and forms such as **ма́мочка** (from **ма́ма**) and **па́почка** (from **па́па**) are much used. **Де́душка** 'granddad' is commoner than **дед** 'grandfather', and the originally diminutive **ба́бушка** 'granny' (**ба́ба** 'old woman') is now the standard word for 'grandmother'.

Foreign learners need to be able to recognize diminutives rather than to form and use them. If you do bother to add the common ones to your active vocabulary, it is worth noting that diminutives have the advantage of regular grammatical endings and predictable stress. So a difficult word like **сестра́** (pl. **сёстры, сестёр, сёстрам**) becomes quite regular if you use the form **сестри́ца** (pl. **сестри́цы, сестри́ц, сестри́цам**).

Some general points:

(1) Any noun can have several diminutives. To the 'everyday' diminutive (examples above), further suffixes can be added – with further nuances of greater tenderness, familiarity, derision and so on. For example, from **сестри́ца** 'little sister' can be formed the more affectionate 'double diminutive' **сестри́чка**, and from **сестри́чка** comes the colloquial 'triple diminutive' **сестри́чушка** 'darling little sisterlet' (diminutives are notoriously hard to translate). There are other variants too, e.g. **сестрёнка** and **сестрёночка. Избу́шка** (from **изба́** 'peasant cottage') produces the even more affectionate form **избу́шечка**. Here we shall restrict ourselves to 'everyday' diminutives.

(2) 'Everyday' diminutives normally keep the same gender as the base noun.

Feminine diminutives normally end **-ка** (always unstressed):

голова́	head	**голо́вка**	little head
дочь	daughter	**до́чка**	little daughter
печь	stove	**пе́чка**	little stove

Nouns whose normal forms end with **-ка** or a group of consonants have **-чка**:

звезда́	star	**звёздочка**	little star; asterisk
игру́шка	toy	**игру́шечка**	little toy

307

копе́йка	kopeck	копе́ечка	one-kopeck coin
ла́мпа	lamp	ла́мпочка	little lamp; bulb
рука́	hand, arm	ру́чка	little hand or arm

The last consonant before the **-a** often changes:

доро́га	road	доро́жка	little road; path
нога́	leg, foot	но́жка	little leg or foot
стару́ха	old woman	стару́шка	little old woman

Other variations:

дверь	door	две́рца	little door, car door
икра́	caviare	ико́рка	nice caviare
ку́рица	hen	ку́рочка	little hen
у́лица	street	у́лочка	little street, lane

Masculine nouns add **-ик** (unstressed) or **-(о́)к**:

го́род	town, city	город(о́)к	small town
слова́рь	dictionary	слова́рик	small dictionary
сто́л	table	сто́лик	small table

Some nouns (with **-л, -м, -н, -р**) add **-чик**:

| бока́л | wineglass | бока́льчик | little wineglass |
| стака́н | glass, tumbler | стака́нчик | little glass |

Sometimes there are consonant changes:

| друг | friend | друж(о́)к | pal |
| стари́к | old man | старич(о́)к | little old man |

Neuter nouns have a variety of (neuter) endings:

де́ло	matter, piece of business	де́льце	small matter
де́рево	tree	деревцо́/де́ревце	little tree
заявле́ние	application	заявле́ньице	small application
лицо́	face	ли́чико	little face
ме́сто	place	месте́чко	little place
окно́	window	око́нце/око́шко	little window
письмо́	letter	письмецо́	little letter

пла́тье	dress	пла́тьице	little dress
сло́во	word	словцо́	little word
со́лнце	sun	со́лнышко	little sun
у́хо	ear	у́шко	little ear
я́блоко	apple	я́блочко	little apple

EXAMPLES

Да́йте, пожа́луйста, стака́нчик ча́я. (стака́н 'glass')	Could I trouble you for a glass of tea?
Хоти́те ча́шечку ко́фе? (ча́шка 'cup')	Would you like a nice cup of coffee?
Приходи́те че́рез неде́льку. (неде́ля 'week')	Could I ask you to come back in a week or so?
Пожа́луйста, пиши́те заявле́ньице. (заявле́ние 'application')	Would you mind writing an official request?

EXERCISE 25/1

Find the non-diminutive forms of the diminutives in the following and suggest translations of the phrases:

1 Sales assistant: **У вас нет копе́ечки?** 2 Elderly theatre usher: **Ваш биле́тик, пожа́луйста.** 3 Polite customer: **Да́йте одну́ буты́лочку минера́льной воды́, пожа́луйста.** 4 Mother: **Та́нечка, наде́нь** (put on) **ша́почку.** 5 Fond aunt: **Посмотри́ на Ле́ночку. Како́е краси́вое пла́тьице!** 6 Mother to child: **Дай ко́шке** (cat) **води́чки.** 7 Hostess: **Хоти́те чайку́?** 8 Street trader: **Ико́рки не жела́ете?** 9 Grandmother to child: **Каки́е у тебя́ гря́зные ру́чки!** 10 Taxi driver: **Закро́йте две́рцу.** 11 To a friend: **Подожди́ мину́точку, пожа́луйста.** 12 Mother to son: **Посмотри́ в око́шко. Мо́жет быть, до́ждь уже́ прошёл.**

25.3 **Proper Names**

As mentioned in 6.10, 'diminutive' (or 'intimate') forms of proper names are very popular in Russia as ways of indicating affection, familiarity and so on. Here are examples of the large range of possibilities. (There is also scope for individual creativity.)

From **Мари́я**:

(Commoner forms) **Мару́ся, Мару́сенька, Мару́сечка, Мару́ська, Мари́йка, Ма́рьюшка, Марья́ша, Ма́ша, Ма́шенька, Ма́шка, Ма́ня, Ма́нечка, Ма́нька, Му́ся, Му́сенька, Му́сечка, Му́ська, Ма́ра, Му́ра, Му́рочка, Маря́та.** (Rarer forms) **Ма́шечка, Мари́ша, Ма́ря, Марю́ня, Мару́ня, Мару́ля, Му́ля, Ма́ся, Мася́та, Марю́та, Марю́ха, Мару́ха, Марю́ша, Мару́ша, Му́ша, Маню́ня, Маню́ра, Маню́ся, Маню́та, Маню́ха, Маню́ша, Маня́тка, Ма́ка, Маня́ша, Маша́ня, Машо́ня, Машу́ка, Машу́ня, Му́ня, Машу́ра, Маша́ра, Машу́та, Му́та, Машу́ха, Мо́ря.**

From **Влади́мир**:

Влади́мирушка, Вла́дя, Ла́дя, Ва́дя, Ва́ва, Ваву́ля, Ваву́ся, Воло́дя, Володю́ка, Володю́ха, Володю́ша, Володя́ка, Володя́ха, Володя́ша, Во́ва, Вову́ля, Вову́ня, Вову́ся, Вову́ша, Во́ля.

25.4 **'Diminutive' Adjectives**

Adjectives can be given the same connotation of affection or 'niceness' by replacing the final **-ый/-ой** or **-кий** with **-енький**. So **молодо́й** 'young' becomes **моло́денький** 'nice and young'; **худо́й** 'thin' becomes **ху́денький** 'thin in a nice way' (slim);[1] **ста́рый** 'old' becomes

---

1 In a culture where fat tends to be regarded as a good thing (it keeps the cold out), there are some features of the Russian language which should intrigue westerners obsessed with slimming. Note that **худо́й** 'thin' also means 'bad', **попра́виться** 'to get fatter' also means 'to get better', **жи́рный** 'fat' has associations with richness (**жи́рный кусо́к** 'fatty piece' is used of something tempting), and the phrase **с жи́ру беси́ться** 'to be in a rage because of fat' means 'to be too well off'.

ста́ренький 'attractively old'. An equivalent feature of English is the use of 'small' and 'little'. 'Small' is a neutral description of size ('a small dog') while 'little' means 'attractively small' ('a little dog'). Note, however, that the adjective **ма́ленький** 'small', originally formed from **ма́лый** 'small' with the same ending **-енький**, has lost its positive connotation of niceness and is now a neutral word. Its hypocoristic (affectionate) equivalent is **малю́сенький** 'little'/'little tiny' or **ма́сенький**, a children's nursery word.

Я люблю́ таки́е до́мики, как ваш, ста́ренькие да тёпленькие.
I'm very fond of little houses like yours, nice and old, nice and warm.

25.5 Politeness Phrases

Apologies

Извини́те (за + acc.) . . .	Excuse me/I'm sorry (for) . . .
Прости́те (за + acc.) . . .	Excuse me/I'm sorry (for) . . .
Я до́лжен (должна́) извини́ться.	I must apologize (more formal).
Извини́те/Прости́те за опозда́ние.	I'm sorry I'm late.
Извини́те за беспоко́йство.	Sorry for troubling you.
Прости́те, я неча́янно.	I'm sorry, it was accidental.
Извини́те, я совсе́м не хоте́л(а) вас оби́деть.	I'm sorry. I didn't mean to offend you.
Разреши́те пройти́.	Excuse me (when you want someone to let you pass).

Responses to Apologies

Пожа́луйста.	That's all right.
Ничего́ [nee-chye-vó]	It doesn't matter (lit. 'nothing').
Не сто́ит.	There's no need to.
Ну что́ вы!	Forget it (informal).
Пустяки́!	It's nothing.
Ничего́ стра́шного!	Nothing to worry about.

311

Requests

Извини́те за беспоко́йство.	Excuse me for troubling you.
Бу́дьте добры́ . . .	Would you mind . . . ('Be so good . . .').
Е́сли вам не тру́дно . . .	If it isn't too much trouble . . .
Сде́лайте одолже́ние . . .	Could you do me a favour?

Прости́те, у вас не бу́дет двух копе́ек, что́бы позвони́ть?
Excuse me, could you let me have two kopecks to make a phone call?

Note how the Russian polite negative ('you won't have two kopecks?')
often corresponds to the English use of the conditional.

EXERCISE 25/2

Translate:

1 **Прости́те, я не хоте́л вас оби́деть.** 2 **Извини́те, я, ка́жется, за́нял ва́ше ме́сто.** 3 **Прости́те, пожа́луйста, я вам не помеша́л?** 4 **Извини́те, е́сли не тру́дно, принеси́те чи́стый стака́н.** 5 **Бу́дьте добры́, вы не ска́жете, где здесь по́чта?**

25.6 **Acceptance**

Я ничего́ не име́ю про́тив.	I've nothing against (it).
Я не про́чь!	I'm willing ('I'm not averse').
Охо́тно.	Willingly.
С удово́льствием.	With pleasure.
С ра́достью!	With pleasure ('With joy').
С велича́йшим удово́льствием.	With the greatest of pleasure.

25.7 **Refusal**

Извини́те, не могу́.	I'm sorry but I can't
Ника́к не могу́.	It's quite impossible.
Я за́нят(а́).	I'm busy.

Что́-то мне не хо́чется.	I don't feel like it.
Ни в ко́ем слу́чае!	On no account/Out of the question.
Ни за что́!	Not for anything.
Нет уж!	I do mean no ('No really').
Отка́зываюсь наотре́з.	I absolutely refuse.

EXERCISE 25/3

Translate the three dialogues:

(a) B Accidentally Bumps into A

А: О́й!
Б: Извини́те, я нечаянно.
А: Пожа́луйста, пожа́луйста.

(b) Acceptance

Андре́й: Дава́йте пое́дем ко мне. У меня́ до́ма хоро́ший конья́к.
Бо́ря: Я не про́чь!
Ва́ся: Я то́же ничего́ не име́ю про́тив.
Андре́й: Серёжа, ты пое́дешь с на́ми? Жена́ приго́товит нам у́жин.
Серёжа: С удово́льствием. С велича́йшим удово́льствием.
Андре́й: А ты, Воло́дя?
Воло́дя: С ра́достью! Охо́тно.
Андре́й: Ну что́ же‡, пое́дем.

‡ **ну что́ же** well then.

(c) Refusal (A Telephone Conversation)

Андре́й: Вади́м, э́то ты? Мы все собрали́сь у меня́, отмеча́ем день
рожде́ния одного́ това́рища. Заходи́.
Вади́м: Ника́к не могу́. Я о́чень за́нят.
Андре́й: Ну вы́пей с на́ми хотя́ бы сто́ грамм‡.
Вади́м: Ни в ко́ем слу́чае! Ни за что́! Ты же зна́ешь, что Е́ва не
разреша́ет.
Андре́й: Ну, вы́пей чайку́.
Вади́м: Что́-то мне не хо́чется. Дава́й лу́чше за́втра.

Андрей: Слушай, не обращай внимания на Éву. Подумай о нас. Не забывай друзей. Возьми такси и приезжай!

Вадим: Нет уж! Не хочу обидеть Éву.

Андрей: Отказываешься наотрез? Жалко.

‡**сто грамм** 100 grams – a generous glass of vodka (Russians measure vodka in grams, not glasses, treating half a litre as 500 grams).

25.8 Vocabulary

(See also diminutive list 25.2 and phrases 25.6–25.7)

броситьᵖ **брошу, бросишь (бросать**' like **знать)** (+ acc.) to throw, throw away

всё (всё время) all the time

вскочитьᵖ **вскочу, вскочишь (вскакивать**' like **знать)** to jump in/up

выскочитьᵖ **выскочу, выскочишь (выскакивать**' like **знать)** (**из** + gen.) to jump out (out of)

глаз pl. **глаза** gen.pl. **глаз** (dim **глаз(ó) к** pl. **глазки)** eye

глядеть' (**по-) гляжу, глядишь** (**на** + acc.) to look (at)

дéвочка dim of **дéва** 'maid' little girl

дéлать' **нéчего** there was nothing to be done, there was nothing for it

дорóга (dim **дорóжка)** road

жáлко (dat. of person + inf 14.6) it's a pity; to grudge

зáнят (m)/**занятá** (f)/**зáняты** (pl.) busy

избá pl. **йзбы** peasant cottage

икрá (dim **икóрка)** caviar(e)

испугáтьсяᵖ (**пугáться**') (+ gen.) (like **знать)** to take fright (at)

коньяк gen. **коньякá** cognac, brandy

леглá see **лечь**ᵖ

лечьᵖ **лягу, ляжешь** past **лёг, леглá** imper **ляг(те) (ложиться**' **ложусь, ложишься)** to lie down

лягу see **лечь**ᵖ

мешáть' (**по-**ᵖ) (like **знать)** (+ dat.) to hinder (someone)

меш(ó)к bag, sack

мужйк gen. **мужикá** peasant man (orig. dim of **муж** 'man')

ничегó не подéлаешь there's nothing one can do (idiom)

ногá pl. **нóги** (dim **нóжка)** leg, foot

ну well

обидетьᵖ **обижу, обидишь** (+ acc.) (**обижáть**' like **знать)** to offend, hurt

отдавáть' (like **давáть)** to give up

отда́тьᵖ (like **дать**) to give away

отка́зыватьсяⁱ (like **знать**) (+ inf)
(**отказа́ться**ᵖ **откажу́сь,
отка́жешься**) to refuse

охо́тно willingly

печь (f) gen.pl. **пече́й** (dim **пе́чка**)
stove

переночева́тьᵖ (**ночева́ть**ⁱ) пере-
ночу́ю, переночу́ешь to
spend the night

пе́сня gen.pl. **пе́сен** song

под (+ acc.) under (motion)

подня́тьᵖ **подниму́, подни́мешь**
(**поднима́ть**ⁱ like **знать**) to lift,
pick up

пой! (imper of **петь**ⁱ) sing!

положи́тьᵖ **положу́, поло́жишь**
(**класть**ⁱ **кладу́, кладёшь**)
(+ acc.) to put

постуча́тьᵖ **постучу́, постучи́шь**
(**стуча́ть**ⁱ) (**в** + acc.) to knock (at)

прийти́сьᵖ (+ dat. of person + inf)
like **прийти́** (**приходи́ться**ⁱ like

приходи́ть) to be forced to

пришло́сь see **прийти́сь**ᵖ

пусти́тьᵖ **пущу́, пу́стишь** (+ acc.)
(**пуска́ть**ⁱ like **знать**) to let, permit; to let in/out

сестра́ pl. **сёстры сестёр
сёстрам сёстрами сёстрах**
sister

стака́н glass, tumbler

схвати́тьᵖ (+ acc. **за** + acc.)
схвачу́, схва́тишь (**хвата́ть**ⁱ or
схва́тыватьⁱ both like **знать**)
to seize (someone by something)

те́сно crowded; tight

това́рищ comrade, friend

тут here (= **здесь**)

у́хо pl. **у́ши** (dim **у́шко** pl. **у́шки**)
ear

хозя́ин pl. **хозя́ева** gen.pl.
хозя́ев host, owner, master

COMPREHENSION EXERCISE 25/4

Note the diminutives in this well-known Russian folk tale 'The Fox and
the Rolling-Pin' (or, literally, 'The Little Fox and the Little Rolling-Pin').

1 The rules of peasant hospitality allow travellers to ask for a bed for the
night at the first house they come to. However, the fox is not a very welcome guest. How does the peasant try to turn the fox away?

2 How does she counter this objection?

3 If a guest loses something, the host has to make good the loss. How
does the fox acquire a hen?

4 What happens to the hen?

5 What does the fox want for the goose and what does she get?
6 How does the surreal conversation in the burrow under the tree-stump
   lead to punishment for the fox?

Шла лиси́чка[‡] по доро́жке, нашла́ ска́лочку[‡]. Подняла́ её и
пошла́ да́льше. Пришла́ в дере́вню и постуча́ла в дверь пе́рвой
избы́:

— Стук-стук-стук[‡]!

— Кто там?

— Я, лиси́чка-сестри́чка[‡], пусти́те переночева́ть.

— У нас и[‡] без тебя́ те́сно.

— Да[‡] я не потесню́[‡] вас: сама́ ля́гу на ла́вочку[‡], хво́стик[‡] под
ла́вочку, ска́лочку под пе́чку.

Её пусти́ли.

Она́ легла́ сама́ на ла́вочку, хво́стик под ла́вочку, ска́лочку под
пе́чку.

Ра́но у́тром лиси́чка вста́ла, сожгла́[‡] свою́ ска́лочку, а пото́м
спроси́ла:

— Где же моя́ ска́лочка? Дава́йте мне за неё ку́рочку[‡]!

Мужи́к - де́лать не́чего! - о́тдал ей за ска́лочку ку́рочку. Взяла́
лиси́чка ку́рочку, идёт и поёт:

      — Шла лиси́чка по доро́жке,
        Нашла́ ска́лочку.
        За ска́лочку взяла́ ку́рочку!

Пришла́ она́ в другу́ю дере́вню:

— Стук-стук-стук!

— Кто там?

— Я, лиси́чка-сестри́чка, пусти́те переночева́ть.

— У нас и без тебя́ те́сно.

— Да я не потесню́ вас: сама́ ля́гу на ла́вочку, хво́стик под
ла́вочку, ку́рочку под пе́чку.

Её пусти́ли.

Лиси́чка легла́ сама́ на ла́вочку, хво́стик под ла́вочку, ку́рочку
под пе́чку.

Ра́но у́тром лиси́чка потихо́ньку[‡] вста́ла, схвати́ла ку́рочку,
съе́ла, а пото́м и говори́т:

— Где же моя́ ку́рочка? Дава́йте мне за неё гу́сочку[‡]!

Ничего́ не поде́лаешь, пришло́сь хозя́ину отда́ть ей за ку́рочку гу́сочку. Взяла́ лиси́чка гу́сочку, идёт и поет:

> – Шла лиси́чка по доро́жке,
> Нашла́ ска́лочку,
> За ска́лочку взяла́ ку́рочку,
> За ку́рочку взяла́ гу́сочку!

Пришла́ она́ ве́чером в тре́тью дере́вню:

– Стук-стук-стук!

– Кто́ там?

– Я, лиси́чка-сестри́чка! Пусти́те переночева́ть!

– У нас и без тебя́ те́сно.

– А я не потесню́ вас: сама́ ля́гу на ла́вочку, хво́стик под ла́вочку, гу́сочку под пе́чку.

Её пусти́ли.

Она́ легла́ сама́ на ла́вочку, хво́стик под ла́вочку, гу́сочку под пе́чку. У́тром лиси́чка вскочи́ла, схвати́ла гу́сочку, съе́ла, пото́м и говори́т:

– А где же моя́ гу́сочка? Дава́йте мне за неё де́вочку!

А мужику́ де́вочку жа́лко отдава́ть. Положи́л он в мешо́к большу́ю соба́ку и о́тдал лисе́:

– Бери́, лиса́[‡], де́вочку!

Вот лиса́ взяла́ мешо́к, вы́шла на доро́гу и говори́т:

– Де́вочка, пой[‡] пе́сни!

А соба́ка в мешке́ зарыча́ла[‡]!

Лиси́чка испуга́лась, бро́сила мешо́к, побежа́ла.

Тут соба́ка вы́скочила из мешка́ – и за ней!

Лиса́ от соба́ки бежа́ла-бежа́ла да под пенёк[‡] в но́ру[‡] забежа́ла. Сиди́т там и говори́т:

– У́шки мои́, у́шки! Что́ вы де́лали?

– Мы всё слу́шали.

– А вы, но́жки, что де́лали?

– Мы всё бежа́ли.

– А вы, гла́зки?

– Мы всё гляде́ли.

– А ты, хвост[‡]?

– А я всё меша́л тебе́ бежа́ть.

317

– А, ты всё меша́л! Ну посто́й же‡, во́т я покажу́ тебе‡! – И вы́сунула‡ хвост из норы́: – Ешь его, соба́ка!

Тут соба́ка схвати́ла лиси́цу за хвост, вы́тащила‡ нз норы́ и начала́ её терза́ть‡!

‡Extra Vocabulary for Comprehension Exercise

вы́сунутьᵖ to thrust out

вы́тащитьᵖ to drag out (**вы** + **тащи́ть** 20.4 + 20.2)

гу́сочка (dim from **гусы́ня** coll) little goose

да (coll) (30.4) and/but

зарыча́тьᵖ to start growling

ку́рица (dim **ку́рочка**) hen

ла́вка (dim **ла́вочка**) bench in peasant hut

лиса́ pl. **ли́сы** fox

лиси́чка-сестри́чка little fox-little sister (standard rhyming name for the fox in folk tales)

лиси́ца (dim **лиси́чка**) fox, vixen

нора́ burrow; lair

п(е)нь (m) (dim **пен(ё)к**) tree stump

Во́т я покажу́ тебе́! I'll show you!

посто́й же hang on a moment

потесни́тьᵖ (+ acc.) to constrict (someone); to get in (someone's) way

потихо́ньку (coll) noiselessly (dim. from **ти́хо** 'quiet')

ска́лка (dim **ска́лочка**) little rolling-pin (for rolling pastry)

сожгла́ burnt past of **сжечь**ᵖ (+ acc.) to burn (something)

стук-стук-стук knock-knock-knock

терза́ть' to pull about, torment

хвост tail

EXERCISE 25/5
REVISION OF LESSONS 21–25

Put the words in brackets in the correct form and translate:

1 За шесть дней мы побыва́ли в (шесть городо́в). 2 Мы разгова́ривали с (три ру́сских студе́нта). 3 Я вам дам не бо́льше (четы́ре до́ллара). 4 Мы бу́дем в Петербу́рге (одна́ неде́ля).

Translate:

5 She loves only herself. 6 They are in their hotel room. 7 We have come to Russia in order to speak Russian. 8 I want him to apologize. 9 She is

here alone. 10 They have three children. 11 There are four of us. 12 I don't know anybody in Irkutsk. 13 She doesn't understand a single word. 14 There's no one to ask (p). 15 There was no one for her to talk to (i).

Translate the English into Russian and Russian into English:

А: Ми́стер Смит, мы с жено́й хоти́м вас пригласи́ть к себе́ домо́й.

Б: With pleasure.

А: Вы смо́жете прийти послезавтра, в пя́тницу?

Б: Unfortunately, I can't. I shall be in Kiev for three days.

А: Тогда́ приходи́те два́дцать седьмо́го.

Б: On that day I'm busy.

А: А тридца́того?

Б: I think I have no meetings (**встре́ча**) at all after the twenty-ninth.

А: Прекра́сно. Мы вас ждём тридца́того, по́сле семи́ часо́в.

26

УРÓК ДВÁДЦАТЬ ШЕСТЬ

INDEFINITE PRONOUNS;
WORD ORDER;
WRITING LETTERS

26.1 **Useful Expressions**

Ктó-нибудь звонúл?	Did anyone ring?
Ктó-то звонúл.	Someone rang.
Онá ушлá кудá-то.	She's gone off somewhere.
Расскажúте чтó-нибудь о себé.	Tell me something about yourself.

26.2 Someone **ктó-то**

Ктó-то 'someone' means someone definite, though the speaker may not know who. It is declined like **ктó**:

Ктó-то стучúт в дверь.	Someone is knocking at the door.
Я вúдел когó-то.	I saw someone.

26.3 Anyone **ктó-нибудь**

Ктó-нибудь 'anyone' means that no specific person is meant:

Éсли ктó-нибудь придёт, скажú, что меня нет.	If anyone comes, say I'm out.

For most uses of someone/anyone, English and Russian usage coincide:

Кто́-то пришёл.	Someone has come.
Éсли ты кому́-нибудь ска́жешь,	If you tell anyone, I'll divorce you.
я с тобо́й разведу́сь.	

But note the following differences:

(1) The distinction between definite person (**-то**) and no specific person (**-нибудь**) tends to be stricter than in English, so an English sentence such as 'If someone rings, tell them I'm out' should be **Éсли кто́-<u>нибудь</u> позвони́т** if you do not know who is going to ring. This means that future and imperative sentences will nearly always have **-нибудь**.

Спроси́те кого́-нибудь.	Ask someone (I have no specific person in mind).

(2) When English 'anyone' means 'no one', i.e. in negative sentences, forms of the Russian word **никто́** ('no one', 'nobody' 24.6) are used:

I don't know anyone.	**Я никого́ не зна́ю** (= I know no one).
Don't tell anyone.	**Не говори́те никому́**
	(= Tell no one). (See Lesson 24.)

26.4 Somewhere, Anywhere, Sometime, Anytime etc.

The rules for other **-то** and **-нибудь** words are exactly the same:

something **что́-то**	anything **что́-нибудь**
somewhere **где́-то**	anywhere **где́-нибудь**
somehow **ка́к-то**	anyhow **ка́к-нибудь**
(to) somewhere **куда́-то**	(to) anywhere **куда́-нибудь**
sometime **когда́-то**	anytime **когда́-нибудь**
for some reason **почему́-то**	for any reason **почему́-нибудь**

Я вас где́-то ви́дел.	I've seen you somewhere (somewhere specific, though I can't remember where).
Éсли вы бу́дете когда́-нибудь в Москве́, позвони́те нам.	If you are ever (anytime) in Moscow, telephone us.

321

Он куда́-то ушёл.	He's gone off somewhere.
Дава́йте пое́дем куда́-нибудь.	Let's go somewhere (I have nowhere specific in mind).
Она́ что́-то купи́ла.	She's bought something.
Она́ что́-нибудь купи́ла?	Has she bought anything/something?
Она́ ничего́ не купи́ла.	She hasn't bought anything.
Они́ никуда́ не ходи́ли.	They didn't go anywhere.

26.5 Како́й-то/како́й-нибудь

Notice also the adjectives **како́й-то** 'some (or other)', 'some kind of' and **како́й-нибудь** 'any', 'any kind of':

Вам звони́ла кака́я-то же́нщина.	Some woman rang you.
Он и́щет каку́ю-нибудь рабо́ту.	He's looking for any kind of job.
Мы найдём каку́ю-нибудь гости́ницу.	We'll find some kind of hotel.

EXERCISE 26/1

Translate the words in brackets:

1 **Она́ купи́ла** (something). 2 **Вы купи́ли** (anything)? 3 **Мы не купи́ли** (anything). 4 **Расскажи́те нам** (something) **о жи́зни в Сиби́ри**. 5 **Éсли** (anybody) **позвони́т, скажи́те, что́ я бу́ду по́сле семи́**. 6 **Она́ ушла́** (somewhere) **с** (some) **молоды́м челове́ком**. 7 (For some reason) **она́ не мо́жет прийти́**. 8 **Вы жи́ли** (ever/at any time) **в дере́вне?**

26.6 Rules of Thumb for 'Some-/Any-' Words

(a) **-то** is 'some'.

(b) **-нибудь** is 'any'.

(c) Use **-нибудь** for 'some' in sentences about the future, in orders and questions.

(d) Use **никто́/ничто́/нигде́** (24.6) etc. for 'any' in negative sentences.

Key examples:

Кто́-то вас и́щет.	Someone is looking for you.
Вы купи́ли что́-нибудь?	Have you bought anything?
Спроси́те кого́-нибудь.	Ask someone.
Мы никого́ не зна́ем.	We don't know anyone.

26.7 EXTRA: -либо and ко́е-

There is another suffix **-либо**, which is similar to **-нибудь** but implies even more unrestricted choice:

Е́сли вам что́-либо ну́жно . . .   If you need anything (whatever) . . .

It is also a little more formal than **-нибудь** so it is not common in conversation.

Note also the prefix **ко́е-**, which generally has a distributive meaning:

ко́е-где́	in several places/here and there
ко́е-кто́	a number of people (declines like **кто́**)
ко́е-куда́	to several places
ко́е-что́	certain things (declines like **что́**)

Ко́е-где лежа́л снег.	Snow lay here and there.
Ко́е-кому́ (dat.) **э́то не** **понра́вится.**	A number of people won't like this.

Prepositions with **ко́е-кто́** and **ко́е-что́** generally come between the two parts:

Она́ уже́ <u>ко́е с кем</u> **познако́милась.**	She's already met a few people.

However, **ко́е-** can also be an equivalent of **-то**, but with the *extra* nuance that the speaker is concealing the identity of the person, thing or place. So **ко́е-кто́** can mean 'someone' in the sense 'a certain person whom I am not naming'. **Я привёз ей ко́е-что́** 'I've brought her something (which I'm not naming)'; **Я иду́ ко́е-куда́** 'I'm going to a certain place' (a euphemism for the toilet).

Note that **кóе-кáк** means 'badly', 'sloppily' or 'with difficulty', *not* 'in several ways'/'in a certain way': **Óн всё дéлает кóе-кáк** 'He does everything sloppily.' **Пробавля́емся кóе-кáк** 'We manage to get by' (30.5).

26.8 Word Order

You will have noticed that Russian word order is very flexible. The endings of words show the relationships between parts of the sentence so these parts can go in almost any order without causing misunderstandings. The basic rule for written Russian is that new information (or emphasized information) comes at the end of the sentence.

Здесь был Вáся. Vasia was here (emphasis on Vasia).

Óн свобóдно говори́т по-рýсски и по-немéцки. He speaks fluent Russian and German (emphasis on the languages, not the fluency).

Óн говори́т по-рýсски свобóдно. He speaks Russian flúently (emphasis on the fluency).

В апрéле мы бы́ли в Сóчи. In April we were in Sochi (emphasis on *where*). **В Сóчи мы бы́ли в апрéле** (emphasis on *when*).

As general rules, note that *unemphasized* time and place expressions come first in the sentence and that unemphasized adverbs come before the verb.

For the beginner in Russian there is nothing very important to remember about Russian word order – other than the fact that it is very flexible. However, it is worth noting that some things which are complicated in English are simpler in Russian because of this flexibility. An English sentence such as 'It was Tolstoi who wrote *Resurrection*' (emphasizing 'Tolstoi') can be in Russian **«Воскресéние» написáл Толстóй**.

EXERCISE 26/2

Translate, paying attention to the word order:

1 **Some woman** rang you (fam) (emphasis on 'some woman'). 2 She

bought something (emphasis on 'bought'). 3 There are **no bananas** in Moscow (emphasis on 'no bananas'). 4 There was a **Russian book** lying (**лежа́ть**) on the table (emphasis on 'Russian book'). 5 It was **Mary** who brought the book (emphasis on 'Mary'). 6 I'll **phone** you (fam) **tomorrow** (main emphasis on 'tomorrow', some emphasis on 'phone'). 7 I'll phone **Vadim** tomorrow (emphasis on 'Vadim').

26.9 **EXTRA: Word Order in Speech**

Different rules apply in informal conversation, where intonation and stress play important roles. For example, important information is likely to come *first* and to be pronounced with extra emphasis:

Терпе́ть не могу́ когда́ руга́ются! 'I **can't stand** people swearing!'

26.10 **Russian Addresses**

A Russian address (**а́дрес** pl. **адреса́**) runs backwards (from a western point of view), starting with the town and ending with the name of the resident. Here is an example:

Москва 127436	(Moscow + six-figure postcode)
ул. Новаторов	(**у́лица** 'Street of the Innovators')
д. 35, корп. 2, кв. 236	(**до́м** 'house' 35, **ко́рпус** 'block' 2, **кварти́ра** 'flat' 236, which can also be written 35/2/236)
Смирно́ву В.С.	(to Mr V. S. Smirnov - dative case)

Most city dwellers live in blocks of flats. The street number, 35 in the example above, may cover several buildings one behind the other, each of which is called a **ко́рпус**. Blocks of flats are often built round an open space called a **дво́р** 'yard', which may contain benches, a children's playground, trees, a kindergarten and sometimes a parking lot. The entrances (**подъе́зд** 'porch', 'entrance') to the blocks are usually on the **дво́р** side of the building, not on the street.

26.11 Writing Letters

In English we begin 'Dear . . .', whether writing to a friend or the tax inspector. In Russian, the greeting depends on the degree of formality. If you are writing to someone you call **ты**, you can use:

Дорогóй ('Dear') **Вáня!**

or **Дорогáя Мáша!**

or **Здрáвствуй, Вáня/Мúша!**

The ending of the letter can be **Целýю тебя́** ('I kiss you'), **Обнимáю тебя́** ('I embrace you'), **До свидáния** or **До скóрой встрéчи** ('See you soon').

If writing to someone you call **вы**, use **уважáемый** 'respected':

Уважáемый Пётр Ивáнович!

Уважáемая Марúя Владúмировна!

An even more honorific form of address is **мнóгоуважáемый** 'much respected':

Мнóгоуважáемый профéссор Мирчáнов!

The ending of the letter should be:

С уважéнием ('With respect')

26.12 Vocabulary

áдрес pl. **адресá** address

атмосфéра atmosphere

весёлый cheerful, jolly

возвращéние return

гастрóли (f.pl.) gen.pl. **гастрóлей** (theatre) tour ('guest roles')

дéрево pl. **дерéвья** gen.pl. **дерéвьев** tree

дéтская площáдка children's playground

застóлье party (round a table, with food and drink)

здорóвье health

знакóмая (f adj) female acquaintance

знакóмый (m adj) male acquaintance

знакóмство acquaintanceship, first meeting

качéли (pl.) gen.pl. **качéлей** swings

кóе-какúе certain, a number of (26.7)

крéпко firmly, strongly

материáл material

мысль (f) thought
национа́льный national
неожи́данный unexpected
несмотря́ на то́, что́ in spite of the fact that
нового́дний New Year (adj)
оказа́тьсяᵖ **окажу́сь, ока́жешься (ока́зываться** like **знать)** to find oneself; to turn out
осо́бый special
отли́чный excellent
отъе́зд departure
печа́ль (f) sadness
повторя́ть (like **знать)** **(повтори́ть**ᵖ **повторю́, повтори́шь)** (+acc.) to repeat
поздравле́ние greeting, congratulation
поколе́ние generation
понра́витьсяᵖ to please
кни́га мне понра́вилась I liked the book
посели́тьсяᵖ **поселю́сь, посели́шься (поселя́ться** like **знать)** to settle, take up residence
пре́жде всего́ first of all, primarily
приступи́тьᵖ **приступлю́, присту́пишь (приступа́ть** like **знать) (к** +dat.) to get down to, to start on

приве́т greetings (informal usage)
пятиэта́жный five-floor
рабо́та над (+ inst.) work on something
середи́на middle
скаме́йка gen.pl. **скаме́ек** bench (dim. of **скамья́** 'bench')
собира́ться (+ inf) to intend to
собра́тьᵖ **соберу́, соберёшь (собира́ть** like **знать)** to gather
стари́к old man
стару́шка old woman (dim 25.2)
статья́ article
сча́стье happiness, luck
так что́ so, so that
то́, что́ the fact that
труд gen.sg **труда́** work
уважа́емый respected
уваже́ние respect
удивлённо with surprise
удивля́ться (like **знать)** (+ dat.) **(удиви́ться**ᵖ **удивлю́сь, удиви́шься)** to be surprised (at)
улы́бка gen.pl. **улы́бок** smile
у́ров(е)нь (m) level
целова́ть **целу́ю, целу́ешь (по-**ᵖ**)** to kiss
что́-либо anything whatever (26.7)
шу́мный noisy

26.13 Письмо́, Запи́ска, Поздравле́ние

Уважа́емый профе́ссор Ники́форов!

Извини́те за то́, что я так до́лго не писа́ла. Я собира́лась написа́ть Вам сра́зу же по́сле возвраще́ния из Москвы́, но дел бы́ло сли́шком мно́го.

На про́шлой неде́ле я прочита́ла Ва́шу прекра́сную кни́гу о Большо́м теа́тре. Она́ мне о́чень понра́вилась.

Че́рез па́ру неде́ль по́сле возвраще́ния в Бри́столь я позвони́ла в наш Национа́льный теа́тр и говори́ла с Ва́шей знако́мой. Она́ сказа́ла, что ко́е-каки́е материа́лы для Вас она́ уже́ собрала́, так что, когда́ Вы бу́дете в Ло́ндоне в а́вгусте, Вы смо́жете сра́зу приступи́ть к рабо́те над статьёй о гастро́лях Большо́го теа́тра в А́нглии.

Е́сли ничто́ не помеша́ет, то́ мы с Ри́чардом сно́ва ока́жемся в Москве́ где́-то в середи́не ию́ля. Е́сли я смогу́ Вам чем-нибудь помо́чь (что́-то переда́ть от Ва́шей знако́мой и́ли что-ли́бо ещё), звони́те мне.

Ещё раз спаси́бо за отли́чную кни́гу.

Всего́ Вам до́брого‡.

С уваже́нием

Ба́рбара По́уп

‡Best wishes (short for **Я жела́ю Вам всего́ до́брого** (gen.) 'I wish to you all good').

Запи́ска (A Note)

Дорога́я моя́ А́ннушка!

Приве́т тебе́ из Пари́жа. Здесь сто́лько интере́сного, что не́когда писа́ть пи́сьма. Я верну́сь в четве́рг, по́сле шести́. Приходи́ в го́сти, я тебе́ всё расскажу́.

Целу́ю кре́пко,

Ю́ра

Новогóднее поздравлéние (New Year Greetings)

Уважáемый Пётр Ивáнович!

Пусть печáли остáнутся в прóшлом годý. Пусть в Вáшем дóме посели́тся счáстье! Желáю Вам весёлого застóлья, улы́бок, рáдости, здорóвья. Желáю Вам успéхов в жи́зни и в трудé. Желáю Вам тогó, чтó Вы желáете себé.

С уважéнием

    Éва Антóнова

Note that in letters (a) the first line is positioned towards the middle of the page, (b) the name is followed by an exclamation mark, and (c) all forms of **Вы** are written with a capital letter.

EXERCISE 26/3

Translate:

Note the word order: in eleven cases the subject (noun in the nominative case) comes *after* the verb (see 26.8).

Двóр ('The Courtyard' – see 26.10)

Волóдя и Мэ́ри вошли́ во двóр пятиэтáжного дóма. Хотя́ шýмный проспéкт был недалекó, во дворé бы́ло ти́хо, росли́ большúе стáрые дерéвья, а в сáмом цéнтре былá дéтская площáдка с качéлями. На скамéйках сидéли старики́ и старýшки, пéред ни́ми игрáли дéти.

– Здрáвствуйте! Здрáвствуйте - повторя́л Волóдя.

– Ты всех здесь знáешь? - удивлённо спроси́ла Мэ́ри.

– Конéчно. Я ведь вы́рос в э́том дворé. В стáрых москóвских домáх осóбая атмосфéра. В них иногдá живýт два-три поколéния. Вóт э́ти старýшки знáли мои́х дéдушку и бáбушку, ви́дели, как рóс мóй пáпа как рóс я, как рослá моя́ сестрá Мáша. Здесь прошлá их жизнь. И они́ лю́бят и э́тот дóм, и всех, ктó в нём живёт.

COMPREHENSION EXERCISE 26/4

1 Where exactly did Vera Petrishcheva and Barbara Pope meet?
2 **У меня возни́кла мысль . . .** What is Vera's idea?
3 What two reasons does she give for considering this idea realistic?
4 What does she want Mrs Pope to do?

> **Здра́вствуйте,**
>
> **уважа́емая ми́ссис По́уп!**

Не удивля́йтесь, пожа́луйста, моему́ неожи́данному письму́, несмотря́ на то́, что со дня на́шего знако́мства уже́ прошло́ во́семь ме́сяцев.

Де́ло в то́м, что‡ то́лько Вы смо́жете помо́чь мне и мои́м друзья́м. Но для нача́ла я напо́мню немно́го о себе́.

Меня́ зову́т Ве́ра. Я из го́рода Минуси́нска. Того́ ма́ленького провинциа́льного‡ сиби́рского городка́‡, где Вы со свои́м му́жем бы́ли в командиро́вке в ма́е про́шлого го́да.

Я о́чень сожале́ю, что э́то письмо́ я не написа́ла сра́зу по́сле Ва́шего отъе́зда, но, как у нас говоря́т, «Лу́чше по́зже‡, чем никогда́».

По́сле знако́мства с Ва́ми в на́шем музе́е у меня́ возни́кла‡ мысль, кото́рая не покида́ла‡ меня́ уже́ никогда́. Она́ заключа́ется‡ в то́м, что я хочу́ как-то побли́же познако́миться с Ва́шей страно́й, с её обы́чаями‡ и людьми́.

Тепе́рь э́то ста́ло бо́лее реа́льно‡, чем ра́ньше. Наве́рное, э́то свя́зано‡ пре́жде всего́ с о́ттепелью‡ в полити́ческих‡ и культу́рных‡ отноше́ниях‡ ме́жду на́шими стра́нами, а, кро́ме того́, я поступи́ла в институ́т, где я начала́ занима́ться англи́йским языко́м, кото́рый преподаётся‡ на неплохо́м‡ у́ровне.

Поэ́тому я бы хоте́ла, что́бы Вы помогли́ мне связа́ться‡ с ке́м-нибудь из университе́та в Бри́столе, кто́ интересу́ется исто́рией Сиби́ри.

Е́сли я смогу́ че́м-нибудь помо́чь Вам, бу́ду о́чень ра́да‡.

С нетерпе́нием‡ жду Ва́шего письма́.

Мо́й а́дрес:
660022 г. Краснoя́рск,
ул. Абака́нская 33/2/315
Петри́щевой Ве́ре

Извини́те за беспоко́йство.

С уваже́нием

Ве́ра

‡**Extra Vocabulary**

возни́кнутьᴾ past **возни́к,**
  возни́кла to arise
  у меня́ возни́кла мысль
  I had an idea
горо́д(о́)к small town (dim 25.2)
де́ло в то́м, что́ the thing is that
заключа́тьсяⁱ **(в** + prep.) to consist
  of, to be
знако́мство acquaintance with,
  first meeting
культу́рный cultural
неплохо́й (adj) not bad
нетерпе́ние impatience
  с нетерпе́нием impatiently
обы́чай custom
отноше́ние relation

о́ттепель (f) thaw
побли́же (comp of **бли́зкий** 18.3)
  a bit closer
покида́тьⁱ to leave
полити́ческий political
по́зже later (comp of **по́здно**)
преподава́тьсяⁱ to be taught
провинциа́льный provincial
ра́да (f adj – 29.7) glad
реа́льно realistic
связа́тьсяᴾ **с** (+ inst.) to make
  contact with
  свя́зано с (+ inst.) connected
  with
сожале́тьⁱ to regret

27

УРÓК НÓМЕР ДВÁДЦАТЬ СЕМЬ

PARTICIPLES:
TYPES AND STRESS

27.1 **Key Examples**

Всё бýдет сдéлано.	Everything will be done.
Все билéты прóданы.	All the tickets have been sold.
Мы бы́ли удивлены́.	We were surprised.
Э́то мéсто зáнято?	Is this seat occupied?

27.2 **Participles¹**

In Russian, there are six other verbal forms which you need to know, or at least to recognize, if you want to read Russian. These six forms are different types of *participle*¹, that is, verb forms which have some of the features of adjectives or adverbs. Equivalent participles in English are 'murdered', 'exhausted', 'sitting' in 'Was Stalin *murdered*?', '*Exhausted* by participles, I needed a large whisky', 'I know the girl *sitting* in the corner'. Four types of Russian participles are verbal adjectives, dealt with in this lesson and in Lesson 29. Two are verbal adverbs, dealt with in Lesson 28.

The most important of these participles is the past passive participle (PPP), corresponding to 'done', 'exhausted' etc. in English.

27.3 **Past Passive Participle (PPP) or Past Passive Verbal Adjective**

Всё бу́дет сде́лано.   Everything will be done.

The participle **сде́лано** 'done' is from **сде́лать**[º] 'to do'. The neuter ending **-но** agrees with the subject **всё**. The linking verb is always a form of **быть** 'to be'.

These participles are quite common, though more so in bookish style. They correspond to 'murdered', 'surprised' in such sentences as 'Stalin was murdered' and 'He was very surprised'. They are formed only from transitive[t] verbs (i.e. verbs which can be followed by a noun in the accusative case) and normally only from *perfective* verbs (since PPPs denote completed actions).

27.4 **Formation of Past Passive Participles (PPPs)**

There are three categories, based on the endings of the infinitive. Under each category, note that there are two separate rules to remember, namely (a) how to form the participle, and (b) where to put the stress.

(1) *Fairly Simple:* **-ать**-type Verbs

(a) *Ending.* If the verb ends **-ать**, take off the **ть** and add **-н** (m)/**-на**(f)/ **-но**(n)/**-ны** (pl.) It doesn't matter what the future conjugation[t] of the verb is or how irregular it is. So:

дать 'to give' has the PPP: **дан/дана́/дано́/даны́** 'given'

(b) *Stress.* If the verb ends **-а́ть**, the stress moves back a syllable. So:

прочита́ть 'to read' has: **прочи́тан/прочи́тана/прочи́тано/**
  прочи́таны 'read'

A one-syllable verb such as **дать** 'to give' always has the stress on the last vowel, so the endings are **дан, дана́, дано́, даны́** 'given'. Where the stress moves back a syllable on to a prefix, the stress is often on the ending in the feminine form: **о́тдан, отдана́, о́тдано, о́тданы** 'given back'.

Common phrases with PPPs ending **-ан/-ана/-ано/-аны**:

сде́латьᵖ 'to do'

Всё сде́лано.	Everything's done.
Бу́дет сде́лано.	(It)'ll be done.

показа́тьᵖ 'to show'

Фильм бу́дет пока́зан за́втра.   The film will be shown tomorrow.

прода́тьᵖ 'to sell'

Все биле́ты про́даны.   All the tickets have been (are) sold.

Note that the missing present tense form of **быть** 'to be' can correspond to the English perfect tense 'has/have been', as in the last example.

(2) *Trickier*: **-ить** and **-ти** Verbs (and **-еть** verbs of Type 2, i.e. with conjugation **-ю, -ишь**)

(a) *Ending*. To find the PPP of these verbs, you need to know the first person **я** ('I') form of the future conjugation. Take off the **-у** or **-ю** and add **-ен** or **-ён**, depending on the stress. Examples:

оби́деть 'to offend' **я оби́жу**, PPP: **оби́жен** 'offended'
пригласи́ть 'to invite' **я приглашу́**, PPP: **приглашён** 'invited'
предста́вить 'to present' **я предста́влю**, PPP: **предста́влен** 'presented'
привести́ 'to bring' **я приведу́**, PPP: **приведён** 'brought'

(b) *Stress*. If the verb is stressed on the stem (i.e. not on the **-ить**), the stress is on the stem in all forms, so:

предста́вить 'to present' has **предста́влен** (m), **предста́влена** (f),
  предста́влено (n), **предста́влены** (pl) 'presented'

If the m form is **-ен**, the f, n and plural forms are always *un*stressed **ена, ено, ены.**

If the verb has fixed stress on the ending in the future, then the PPP always ends **ён/ена́/ено́/ены́**:

пригласи́ть 'to invite' **(я приглашу́, ты пригласи́шь)**, PPP: **приглашён** 'invited'. The f, n and plural are **приглашена́, приглашено́, приглашены́.**

Note that if the m form ends **-ён**, the other three endings are always **ена́, ено́, ены́.**

If the stress of the future shifts back from the ending to the root, the stress of the PPP is *likely* to match the stress of the **ты** form (though there are exceptions). Examples:

купи́ть 'to buy' (я куплю́, ты ку́пишь). The PPP is ку́пл<u>ен</u>/ку́плена/
ку́плено/ку́плены 'bought').

объяви́ть 'to announce' я объявлю́, ты объя́вишь, PPP: объя́влен
'announced'.

Examples:

Вопро́с бу́дет решён.	The question will be dealt with ('solved', 'decided').
Биле́ты уже́ ку́плены.	The tickets have already been bought.

(3) *Easy Ones*: Verbs with Unusual Infinitives -оть, -уть, -ять, -ыть, -еть
(if not Type 2)

(a) *Endings*. Simply take off the soft sign. The four endings are then
-т/та/то/ты. Example:

закры́ть 'to close' PPP: закры́т, закры́та, закры́то, закры́ты 'closed'

(b) *Stress*. Verbs in -ы́ть have fixed stress on the -ы́. Verbs in -о́ть and
-у́ть shift the stress to the stem like -а́ть verbs (see 1(b) above). Verbs in
-я́ть also shift the stress forward, but the feminine form tends to be
stressed on the -а́. Examples:

затяну́ть 'to tighten': PPP затя́нут, затя́нута 'tightened'
проколо́ть 'to pierce': PPP проко́лот, проко́лота 'pierced'
заня́ть 'to occupy': PPP за́нят, занята́, за́нято, за́няты 'occupied', 'busy'
отня́ть 'to take away': PPP о́тнят, отнята́, о́тнято, о́тняты 'taken away'
оде́ть 'to dress': PPP оде́т, оде́та, оде́то, оде́ты 'dressed' (в + acc. 'in')
Она́ была́ оде́та в кра́сное пла́тье. She was wearing a red dress.

Notice that вы́пить 'to drink' belongs to type 3:

вы́пит, вы́пита, вы́пито, вы́питы 'drunk' (of a liquid, not a human)
Вчера́ бы́ло вы́пито мно́го. A lot was drunk yesterday.

27.5 Use of PPPs

Рабо́та сде́лана.	The work is/has been done.
Рабо́та была́ сде́лана.	The work was done.
Рабо́та бу́дет сде́лана.	The work will be done.
Рабо́та была́ бы сде́лана.	The work would be/ would have been done.

If you want to say who did it, use the instrumental, meaning 'by':

Рабо́та была́ сде́лана Ма́шей.   The work was done by Masha.

(**Ма́шей** is the instrumental case of **Ма́ша**.)

27.6 **EXTRA: Exceptional Cases**

Найти́ 'to find', PPP **на́йден, на́йдена, на́йдено, на́йдены** 'found' (note stress). **Вы́нудить (я вы́нужу, ты вы́нудишь)** 'to force', PPP **вы́нужден** 'forced'. **Уви́деть** 'to see', PPP **уви́ден** 'seen'. **Нача́ть** 'to begin', PPP **на́чат, начата́, на́чато, на́чаты** 'begun'.

27.7 **PPPs with -ый-adjective Endings**

In dictionaries you will find PPPs given with a long-form adjective ending, i.e. **-нный** (types 1 and 2 – note the two **нн**'s) or **-тый** (type 3). For example **напи́санный** 'written' or **взя́тый** 'taken'. These long forms, which have all the case endings of an adjective, are used in certain bookish constructions which you will meet when you read technical books or literature and newspapers. Examples:

Во всех кни́гах, напи́санных (prep. pl.) **э́тим а́втором до 39-го го́да, есть интере́сные же́нщины.**

In all the books written by this author before 1939 there are interesting women.

In more neutral style, you would say:

Во всех кни́гах, кото́рые бы́ли напи́саны э́тим а́втором до 39-го го́да, есть интере́сные же́нщины (or **Во всех кни́гах, кото́рые написа́л э́тот а́втор . . .**).

These 'long' participles replace a clause beginning **кото́рый** 'which', just as in English you can say either 'all the books written by this author' or 'all the books *which were* written by this author'. Notice that it is easier and less bookish to use **кото́рый** + the short participle in Russian; if you

336

choose to miss out the **кото́рый**, then you must use the long participle and make its adjective ending agree with the noun to which it refers.

Во́т пять биле́тов, кото́рые бы́ли ку́плены вчера́
or **Во́т пять биле́тов, ку́пленных** (gen. pl.) **вчера́.**
Here are five tickets (which were) bought yesterday.

Рабо́ту, кото́рая была́ сде́лана Ма́шей, до́лжен был сде́лать Ва́ня.
The work which was done by Masha should have been done by Vanya.
Рабо́ту, сде́ланную (f acc. sg.) **Ма́шей, до́лжен был сде́лать Ва́ня.**
The work done by Masha should have been done by Vanya.

If you miss out the 'which' in the participial clause, then you have to use the long form of the participle and make it agree in case with the noun to which it relates (in this instance **рабо́ту** in the accusative).

In bookish style you will also meet constructions in which the *long* participle is placed in front of its noun, often with words inserted between them, e.g.:

Напи́санные Достое́вским в э́то вре́мя рома́ны ста́ли о́чень популя́рными.
'The written-by-Dostoevsky-at-this-time novels became very popular'
(i.e. 'The novels written by Dostoevsky at this time . . .').
В на́званных кни́гах мо́жно найти́ мно́го интере́сного.
In the named books one can find much of interest.

The forms given in section 27.4 above (**сде́лан/а/о/ы** etc.) are the ones you will normally meet and use. Do not mix up the short and long forms of the participles! In a sentence of the type 'Something is/was/will be done', you *must* use the short form. For 'The work is done' it is wrong to say **Рабо́та сде́ланная**. Correct is **Рабо́та сде́лана**.

EXERCISE 27/1

Translate:

1 **Всё бу́дет сде́лано.** 2 **Магази́н ГУМ был постро́ен в девятна́дцатом ве́ке.** 3 **Э́тот рома́н был напи́сан Толсты́м.** 4 **Никто́ не забы́т, ничто́ не забы́то** (quotation from the poet **Ве́ра И́нбер** at the

main Petersburg war cemetery). 5 **Фестива́ль был организо́ван студе́нтами.** 6 **Мы бы́ли приглашены́ на ве́чер в До́ме дру́жбы.** 7 **Не все вопро́сы бы́ли решены́.** 8 **Рабо́та ко́нчена.** 9 **Апельси́ны бы́ли привезены́ из А́фрики.** 10 **В переда́че** (programme) **бу́дет расска́зано о жи́зни в Сиби́ри.** 11 **Две тре́ти всех фи́льмов, пока́занных на фестива́ле, бы́ли ку́плены америка́нцами.** 12 **Мно́гие из при́нятых в институ́т студе́нтов – иностра́нцы.**

EXERCISE 27/2

Put the correct endings on the words in brackets:

1 **Фильм бу́дет (показа́ть) за́втра** The film will be shown tomorrow. 2 **Все места́ бы́ли (заня́ть)** All the seats were occupied. 3 **Вопро́с уже́ (реши́ть)** The matter has already been dealt with. 4 **Э́тот вопро́с был (зада́ть) (ру́сский журнали́ст)** This question was asked by a Russian journalist. 5 **Магази́н (закры́ть)** The shop is closed. 6 **Бы́ло (объяви́ть), что конце́рт начнётся в семь часо́в** It was announced that the concert would begin at seven. 7 **Ваш зака́з (приня́ть)** Your order has been accepted.

EXERCISE 27/3

Say in Russian:

1 All the tickets have been sold. 2 The museums will be closed tomorrow. 3 Is this seat (**ме́сто**) occupied? 4 The tickets will be ordered (**заказа́ть**ᵖ) tomorrow. 5 In our shops it is difficult to find (p) books written by modern Russian writers.

27.8 EXTRA: The Present Passive Participle (or Present Verbal Adjective)

This participle is very rare. You may find examples if you read scientific Russian and other texts in 'bookish' style. Its meaning is 'being V-ed' (V being any transitive' verb), e.g. **уважа́емый** 'being respected' from **уважа́ть** 'to respect'. Here is an example:

Она́ челове́к, уважа́емый все́ми.   She is a person who is respected
(being respected) by everybody.

These participles are formed from the first person plural (the **мы** form) of *imperfective* transitive' verbs by adding the adjective ending **-ый**:

уважа́ть' 'to respect': **мы уважа́ем: уважа́емый** '(being) respected'
чита́ть' 'to read': **мы чита́ем: чита́емый** '(being) 'read'
организова́ть/ᴾ 'to organize': **мы организу́ем: организу́емый**
  '(being) organized'
обсужда́ть' 'to discuss': **мы обсужда́ем: обсужда́емый** 'being
  discussed'

The stress is generally the same as the infinitive:

люби́ть' 'to love': **мы лю́бим: люби́мый** '(being) loved'

Special cases:

ведо́мый 'being led' (from **вести́** 'to lead'), **несо́мый** 'being carried'
(from **нести́** 'to carry')

Like past passive participles, present passive participles match the nouns to which they relate in number, gender and case.

**Профе́ссор Мирча́нов давно́ занима́ется вопро́сами,
обсужда́емыми на э́той конфере́нции.**   Professor Mirchanov has long been concerned with the questions being discussed at this conference.

These participles are sometimes used as adjectives:

<u>**Уважа́емая**</u> **Ли́дия Никола́евна!**   Respected Lidiia Nikolaevna!
(start of a formal letter – see Lesson 26)
Э́то пода́рок для мое́й <u>люби́мой</u> сестри́чки.
This is a present for my beloved ('being loved') little sister.

EXERCISE 27/4

A text with and without PPPs. Translate:

(a) **В сре́ду бы́ло объя́влено, что́ все биле́ты уже́ про́даны. Мы бы́ли о́чень удивлены́, потому́ что в письме́ дире́ктора бы́ло напи́сано, что́ биле́ты для нас бу́дут ку́плены в четве́рг.**

(b) **В сре́ду объяви́ли, что́ все биле́ты уже́ про́дали. Мы о́чень удиви́лись, потому́ что в своём письме́ дире́ктор написа́л, что́ биле́ты для нас ку́пят в четве́рг.**

27.9 Vocabulary

аге́нт agent

актёр actor

актри́са actress

аплоди́роватьᶦ **(за-**ᵖ**)**
аплоди́рую, аплоди́руешь
(+ dat.) to applaud someone

А́фрика Africa

Великобрита́ния Great Britain

ве́т(е)р wind

включи́тьᵖ **включу́, включи́шь**
(включа́тьᶦ like **знать) (в**
+ acc.) to include (in)

возмо́жный possible

вопро́с question

впервы́е for the first time

вы́братьᵖ **вы́беру, вы́берешь**
(выбира́тьᶦ like **знать) (+ acc.)**
to choose

вы́нудитьᵖ **вы́нужу, вы́нудишь**
(PPP **вы́нужден) (вынужда́ть**ᶦ
like **знать) (+ acc. + inf.)** to
force (someone to do something)

вы́сказатьсяᵖ **вы́скажусь**
вы́скажешься (за + acc.)

(выска́зываться like **знать)** to
speak for/in favour of

генера́л general

еди́нственно only

журнали́стка gen.pl.
журнали́сток female journalist

зада́тьᵖ (like **дать** 12.7) **(задава́ть**
задаю́, задаёшь) to set, pose
зада́ть вопро́с (+ dat.) to ask
(someone) a question

изве́стный well-known

исключи́тьᵖ **исключу́,**
исключи́шь (исключа́тьᶦ like
знать) + acc. to exclude

кампа́ния campaign

кинофестива́ль (m) film festival

коро́ль (m) gen.sg. **короля́** king

междунаро́дный international

облада́тьᶦ (like **знать) (+ inst.)** to
possess

обсужда́тьᶦ (like **знать) (+ acc.)**
(обсуди́тьᵖ **обсужу́,**
обсу́дишь) to discuss

объяви́тьᵖ **объявлю́, объя́вишь**

(**объявля́ть**' **объявля́ю,
объявля́ешь**) (+ acc.) to
announce
опро́с survey
организова́ть[i/p] **организу́ю,
организу́ешь** (+ acc.) to
organize
покло́нник admirer
предста́вить[p] **предста́влю пред-
ста́вишь** (**представля́ть**' like
знать) (+ acc. + dat.) to
present something/someone
to someone
президе́нт president
премье́ра première
премье́р-мини́стр prime minister
приня́ть[p] **приму́, при́мешь** past
при́нял, приняла́, при́няли
(**принима́ть**' like **знать**) (+ acc.)
to accept
приня́ть реше́ние to take a
decision
приобрести́[p] **приобрету́,
приобретёшь** past **приобрёл,
приобрела́, -ло́, -ли́**

(**приобрета́ть**' like **знать**)
(+ acc.) to acquire
програ́мма programme
разведённый divorced (originally
a PPP)
реа́льный real, real-life
результа́т result
в результа́те (+ gen.) as a
result of
реше́ние decision
содержа́ние content, contents
спо́рить' **спо́рю, спо́ришь**
(**по-**[p]) to argue, dispute
суперзвезда́ superstar
театра́льный theatre (adj.)
уча́ствовать' **уча́ствую, уча́ству-
ешь в** (+ prep.) to participate in
удиви́ть[p] **удивлю́, удиви́шь**
(+ acc.) (**удивля́ть**' like **знать**)
to surprise (someone)
унести́[p] (like **нести́** 20.2) (**уноси́ть**'
like **носи́ть**' 20.2) to carry away
чино́вник bureaucrat
число́ number
в числе́ (+ gen.) among

COMPREHENSION EXERCISE 27/5

«Унесённые ве́тром»

1 What is the English name of this film?
2 The film was made in 1939. What reason is suggested for its absence
   from Soviet screens until 1990?
3 What main principle determines how English or American names are
   spelt in Russian transcription?
4 Translate the eight underlined PPPs.

В 1937 году, после того как было <u>принято</u> решение сделать фильм по роману «Унесённые ветром», агент продюсера Дэвида Селзника, Рассел Бёрдвелл, начал кампанию в Америке – поклонникам романа был <u>задан</u> вопрос: кто же должен играть Скарлетт и Ретта?

Люди перестали обсуждать реальную драму – роман английского короля Эдуарда VIII с разведённой американкой Уоллес Симпсон (в результате которого король Англии был <u>вынужден</u> отречься‡ от престола). В каждой семье за обедом спорили о том, что, может быть, Гари Купер . . . А если Эррол Флинн? . . . Но Кларк Гейбл! . . . Девяносто пять процентов тех, кто участвовал в опросе, назвали Кларка Гейбла единственно возможным Реттом Батлером. Что касается Скарлетт О'Хары – сорок пять процентов высказались за Бетт Дэвис, которая уже обладала двумя «Оскарами». Но она отказалась. Селзник выбрал английскую театральную актрису Вивьен Ли.

Фильм сделал Вивьен Ли суперзвездой. В 1943 году, через четыре года после премьеры, во время её концертов в северной Африке ей аплодировали американский генерал Эйзенхауер и британский генерал Монтгомери.

Фильм «Унесённые ветром» был <u>показан</u> впервые в России в октябре 1990 года. Раньше он был <u>включён</u> в программу одного из московских международных кинофестивалей, но почему-то <u>исключён</u> в последнюю минуту. Наверное, каким-то чиновникам содержание фильма не понравилось.

Права показывать «Унесённых ветром» были <u>приобретены</u> у американской компании «Юнайтед Интернэшнл Пикчерз». На премьере в кинотеатре «Октябрь» фильм был <u>представлен</u> президентом «Ю.И.П.», Тедом Тёрнером. Было много гостей, в числе которых – Джейн Фонда, известный английский актёр Бен Кингсли с женой, журналистка Кэрол Тэтчер, дочь тогдашнего премьер-министра Великобритании.

‡**отречься от престола** to abdicate ('renounce from throne')

28

УРÓК НÓМЕР ДВÁДЦАТЬ ВÓСЕМЬ

VERBAL ADVERBS

28.1 Key Examples

Уходя́, гаси́те свет.   As you leave, put out the light.

Óн ушёл, не сказáв ни слóва.   He left without saying a word.

28.2 Verbal Adverbs ('Gerunds')

Russian has two types of verbal adverb (sometimes called 'gerunds' in old-fashioned grammars of Russian). They are fairly common in writing, and you may occasionally hear one used in conversation.

28.3 Imperfective Verbal Adverb

The basic meaning of this verb form is 'while doing something'; it generally corresponds to English verbs with the ending '-ing'. So **уходя́** (from **уходи́ть¹**) is 'while leaving'. As its name tells you, it is formed only from imperfective verbs. The characteristic ending is **-я**.

Formation

Take the third person plural form of the present tense (the **они́** form), take off the last two letters and add **-я**:

говори́ть[1] 'to speak' **(они́ говоря́т) говор + я́ = говоря́** '(while) speaking'
знать[1] 'to know' **(они́ зна́ют) зна́ + я = зна́я** '(while) knowing'
идти́[1] 'to go' **(они́ иду́т) ид + я́ = идя́** '(while) going'

Verbs with the stress pattern of **кури́ть: я курю́, ты ку́ришь** (see 4.9) stress the verbal adverb on the end:

уходи́ть[1] 'to leave' **ухожу́, они́ ухо́дят: уход + я = уходя́** '(while) leaving'

If the verb is reflexive[1], add **-сь** after the **я**:

улыба́ться 'to smile' **они́ улыба́ются: улыба́ + я + сь = улыба́ясь**
  '(while) smiling'

Note. Don't forget the 'spelling rule' which says that after **г, к, х, ж, ч, ш, щ, ц** you find **а** instead of **я** (see 12.11). So:

спеши́ть 'to hurry' **(они́ спеша́т) спеш + а** (not **я**) **= спеша́** 'while hurrying'
учи́ться 'to study' **(я учу́сь, они́ у́чатся) уч + а** (not **я**) **+ сь = уча́сь**
  'while studying'

28.4 EXTRA: Exceptions

(a) Verbs ending **-авать**, e.g. **дава́ть**[1] 'to give', keep the **-ав-** of the infinitive in the verbal adverb:

дава́ть 'to give': **дава́я** 'while giving' (not **дая́** from **они́ да́ют**)
встава́ть 'to get up': **встава́я** 'while getting up' (not **встая́** from **они́ встаю́т**)

(b) Some verbal adverbs are unexpectedly stressed on the stem:

стоя́ть 'to stand': **сто́я** 'while standing' (preferred to **стоя́**)
сиде́ть 'to sit': **си́дя** 'while sitting' (not **сидя́**)

(c) Some, generally short, verbs have *no* verbal adverb. The ones to note are **есть** 'to eat', **пить** 'to drink' (**пия́** is archaic), **писа́ть** 'to write', **е́хать** 'to travel' (but see (d) below), verbs ending **-нуть** (e.g. **тяну́ть** 'to drag')

(d) There is an alternative ending **-учи**, which is used with **быть**: 'to be':

бу́дучи 'being'. Colloquially, this ending can be used with **е́хать** 'to travel': **е́дучи** 'while travelling'. **Йдучи** 'while going' is a colloquial equivalent of **идя́**.

28.5 Use of Imperfective Verbal Adverbs (IVAs)

Although we suggest the translation 'while Verb-ing' ('while going' etc.), the actual translation in context will vary.

Уходя́, гаси́те свет (common notice).
As you leave/When leaving, put out the light.
Она́ у́чит слова́, сто́я на голове́. (голова́ 'head')
She learns words standing on her head.
Возвраща́ясь домо́й, мы пе́ли ру́сские пе́сни.
On our way home (While returning home), we sang Russian songs.

The negated IVA (with **не**) can be translated 'without V-ing':

По́езд идёт в Хе́льсинки, не заходя́ в Петербу́рг.
The train goes to Helsinki without calling at St Petersburg.
Не доезжа́я до светофо́ра, сверни́те напра́во.
Before you reach (Without going as far as) the lights, turn right.

Notice that it is more important to be able to recognize IVAs than to be able to form them. You can always avoid an IVA by using a clause beginning with **когда́** 'when' or some equivalent conjunction:

Уча́сь в Москве́, Йгорь жил в Тёплом Ста́не
means the same as
Когда́ он учи́лся в Москве́, Йгорь жил в Тёплом Ста́не.
Studying/When he studied/in Moscow, Igor lived in Tëplyi Stan.

Basically, the IVA describes an action or state which is simultaneous with the action expressed by the verb in the main clause. As in English, the subject of the verbal adverb is the subject of the verb in the main clause, i.e. in the last example the person studying is the person living in Tëplyi Stan.

Common phrases based on verbal adverbs:

су́дя по (+ dat.)   judging by (**суди́ть** 'to judge')

345

Су́дя по ва́шей фами́лии, вы украи́нец.	Judging by your surname, you're Ukrainian.
несмотря́ на (+ acc.)	despite (not looking at)
Несмотря́ на плоху́ю пого́ду, мы пошли́ в парк.	Despite the bad weather, we went to the park.
не говоря́ (уж) о (+ prep.)	not to speak of (not talking about)
начина́я с (+ gen.)	beginning with

EXERCISE 28/1

Translate:

1 Зна́я, что Éва вернётся по́здно, Ва́дим вы́пил стака́н во́дки.
2 Проезжа́я ми́мо теа́тра, мы узна́ли, что идёт пье́са «Три сестры́». 3 Отдыха́я в Крыму́, Мэ́ри познако́милась с интере́сным профе́ссором. 4 Мы шли не спеша́, вре́мени бы́ло мно́го. 5 Занима́ясь три часа́ ка́ждый день, Воло́дя вы́учил англи́йский язы́к за два го́да.

28.6 Perfective Verbal Adverb (PVA)

The closest English equivalent of the perfective verbal adverb (PVA) is 'having Verb-ed', e.g. 'having said'. PVAs are formed from perfective verbs and have the characteristic endings -в, or, for reflexive verbs, -вшись.

Formation

If the infinitive ends -ть, replace the ть with в:

сказа́ть[p] 'to say'	сказа́в 'having said'
дать[p] 'to give'	дав 'having given'

If the infinitive does not end -ть, form the PVA using the rules for the *imperfective* VA, i.e. replace the third-person plural ending with -я:

уйти́[p] 'to go away' они́ уйду́т: уйд + я = уйдя́ 'having left'
вы́йти[p] 'to go out' они́ вы́йдут: вы́йд + я = вы́йдя 'having gone out'
принести́[p] 'to bring' они́ принесу́т: принес + я = принеся́ 'having brought'

In both cases the stress is the same as on the infinitive.

Most non-**ть** verbs are verbs of motion based on **идти́** 'to go', **вести́** 'to lead', **нести́** 'to carry' and **везти́** 'to transport', e.g. **уйти́**ᴾ 'to go away', **увести́**ᴾ 'to lead away', **привезти́**ᴾ 'to bring by transport'. If you should ever want to form a PVA from a verb ending **-ти/-чь** which is not a verb of motion, e.g. **лечь** 'to lie down', use the rule given in EXTRA (a) below.

Reflexive verbs have **-вшись**:

улыбну́ться 'to smile': **улыбну́вшись** 'having smiled'

Прочита́в письмо́, она́ сра́зу же позвони́ла ма́тери.
Having read the letter, she immediately phoned her mother.

The 'having done something' structure often sounds stilted in English. Simpler translations are possible in context.

Войдя́ в ко́мнату, он сел у окна́.
Coming into the room (rather than 'Having come into'), he sat down by the window.

Прожи́в в Сиби́ри три ме́сяца, он верну́лся в Ки́ев.
After spending (rather than 'Having lived') three months in Siberia, he went back to Kiev.

Он ушёл, ничего́ не сказа́в.
He left without saying anything (having said nothing).

Basically, the perfective VA describes an action completed (that's why it's perfective) before the action described in the main clause.

EXERCISE 28/2

Translate:

1 **Прое́хав три остано́вки, Мэ́ри вы́шла на ста́нции «Университе́т».**
2 **Ничего́ не купи́в в магази́не, Ве́ра реши́ла пойти́ на ры́нок.**
3 **Заинтересова́вшись чеки́стами, Воло́дя на́чал проводи́ть всё свобо́дное вре́мя в библиоте́ках.** 4 **Не дойдя́ до проспе́кта, мы сверну́ли нале́во.** 5 **Вади́м ушёл, не закры́в окна́.**

28.7 EXTRA: on PVAs

(a) Non-**ть** verbs can also form the PVA by adding -**ши** to the masculine form of the past tense:

унести 'to take/carry away': past **унёс**, PVA **унёсши** 'having taken away'
лечь 'to lie down': past **лёг**, PVA **лёгши** 'having lain down'

(b) But note that verbs based on **идти** (**уйти**, **выйти** etc.) have PVAs ending -**шедши** (not -**шёлши**):

уйти 'to go away': **ушедши** 'having gone away'
выйти 'to go out' **вышедши** 'having gone out'

(c) Some writers form perfective VAs from -**ть** verbs using the formation rule for imperfective VAs. So you may meet forms such as **увидя** 'having seen' (instead of the more normal **увидев**).

(d) Note also that in nineteenth-century literature you may also meet -**вши** where the modern language has -**в**. So **сказавши** 'having said' is simply an older version of **сказав**.

EXERCISE 28/3

Translate the words in brackets, with or without verbal adverbs (your choice):

1 (Not knowing) **русского языка, Кэрол не могла найти свою гостиницу.** 2 **Ева ушла,** (without saying), **куда она идёт.**
3 (After drinking) **два стакана водки, Вадим решил зайти к Вере.**
4 (After getting dressed – **одеться**), **мы с братьями идём завтракать.**

28.8 Vocabulary for 'Peter the Great'

беспощадно mercilessly
борода acc. **бороду** pl. **бороды** beard

боярин pl. **бояре** gen.pl. **бояр** (9.8n) boyar (powerful landowner)

брить[i] **(по-**[р]**) бре́ю, бре́ешь** to shave

быт way of life

вое́нно-морско́е де́ло naval matters, naval science ('war-sea matter')

вое́нный military

восста́ние uprising

вско́ре soon

выдаю́щийся outstanding (29.3)

вы́ехать[р] **(выезжа́ть**[i]**)** (20.4) to depart (by transport)

вы́яснить[р] **вы́ясню, вы́яснишь (выясня́ть**[i] **like знать)** to find out, establish

глава́ pl. **гла́вы** chief, head; chapter

во главе́ (+ gen.) at the head of

Голла́ндия Holland

госуда́рственный state, belonging to the state

грани́ца border

за грани́цу abroad (motion)

за грани́цей abroad (place)

дворяни́н pl. **дворя́не** gen.pl. **дворя́н** nobleman, member of gentry

добива́ться[i] **(like знать)** (+ gen.) **(доби́ться**[р] **добью́сь, добьёшься)** to work for, get, obtain

европеиза́ция Europeanization

европе́(е)ц (8.6) European (noun)

жени́ться[i/p] **женю́сь, же́нишься** (**на** + prep.) to marry (of a man) ('to wife on')

за́говор plot

заседа́ние meeting, sitting

на заседа́нии at a meeting, sitting

изда́ть[р] **(like дать) (издава́ть**[i]**)** (+ acc.) to publish

казни́ть[i/p] **казню́, казни́шь** to execute

ка́чество quality

в ка́честве (+ gen.) as ('in the quality of')

коле́но pl. **коле́ни** gen.pl. **коле́ней** knee

по коле́ни (acc. pl.) up to one's knees

кора́бль (m) gen.sg. **корабля́** ship

крепостни́чество serfdom

крепостно́й (m adj) serf, semi-slave in pre-1861 Russia

культу́рный cultural

куп(е́)ц gen.pl. **купцо́в** merchant

медици́на medicine

нало́г tax

напра́вить[р] **напра́влю, напра́вишь (направля́ть** like **знать)** (+ acc.) to direct

научи́ться[р] (+ inf) **(учи́ться**[i]**)** to learn to do sth

необходи́мость (f) (+ gen.) necessity (for)

непоси́льный excessive, over-demanding

но́жницы (pl.) gen.pl. **но́жниц** scissors

носи́ть[i] (20.2) to carry around; to wear

обре́зать[р] **обре́жу, обре́жешь (обреза́ть**[i] like **знать)** to clip, cut

обсервато́рия observatory

обы́чай gen.pl. **обы́чаев** custom

обя́зыватьⁱ (like **знать**) (+ acc.)
(**обяза́ть**ᵖ **обяжу́, обя́жешь**)
to compel, oblige

одновреме́нно at the same time

организа́тор organizer

остана́вливатьсяⁱ to stop

отстава́тьⁱ **отстаю́, отстаёшь**
(**отста́ть**ᵖ like **стать**) (от +
gen.) to be backward, lag
behind (s.o.)

отста́лость (f) backwardness

парла́мент parliament

передово́й advanced, progressive

пло́тник carpenter

по-европе́йски in European style
('Europeanly')

поги́бнутьᵖ past **поги́б, поги́бла**
to perish

пощади́тьᵖ **пощажу́, пощади́шь**
(**щади́ть**ⁱ) (+ acc.) to spare

посеща́тьⁱ (like **знать**) (+ acc.)
(**посети́ть**ᵖ **посещу́,
посети́шь**) to visit (a place)

поспеши́тьᵖ **поспешу́, поспе-
ши́шь (спеши́ть**ⁱ) to hurry

по́лностью completely

предприя́тие firm, company,
business

преобразова́ние reform
(= **рефо́рма**)

преодоле́тьᵖ **преодоле́ю,
-оле́ешь (преодолева́ть**ⁱ like
знать) (+ acc.) to overcome

при (+ prep. (5.4)) at the time of,
under

прибега́тьⁱ (**прибежа́ть**ᵖ) (к
+ dat.) to resort to

пригоня́тьⁱ (like **гоня́ть** 20.2)
(**пригна́ть**ᵖ like **гнать** 20.2) to
drive (to somewhere)

приговори́тьᵖ (к + dat.)
(**пригова́ривать**ⁱ like **знать**) to
condemn to, sentence to

прика́з order

приобща́тьⁱ (like **знать**) (к + dat.)
(**приобщи́ть**ᵖ **приобщу́,
-общи́шь**) to introduce to
(something)

проведённый (PPP of **провести́**)
conducted, passed, executed,
carried out

промы́шленность (f) industry

промы́шленный industrial

проти́вник opponent

рабо́чий (m adj) worker

расправля́тьсяⁱ (like **знать**) (с +
inst.) (**распра́виться**ᵖ **распра́-
влюсь, распра́вишься**) to
deal with

ре́зко sharply

рефо́рма reform

реши́тельно resolutely, with
determination

родно́й own (of family
relationships); native

самодержа́вие autocracy

согла́сие agreement
с согла́сия (+ gen.) with
('from') the agreement of

созда́ние creation

спосо́бность (f) ability

спосо́бствоватьⁱ **спосо́бствую,**

способствуешь (+ dat.) to assist, facilitate

спустя later, after (a period of time)

стрел(е́)ц gen.pl. **стрельцо́в** strelets (member of privileged military corps in sixteenth/seventeeth century Russia)

торго́вля trade

тяжёлый heavy, hard

уделя́тьⁱ (**уделя́ю, уделя́ешь**) (**удели́ть**ᵖ **уделю́, удели́шь**) (+ acc.) to give, devote

уделя́ть внима́ние (+ dat.) to give attention to

узна́тьᵖ (like **знать**) (**узнава́ть**ⁱ **узнаю́, узнаёшь**) to find out

укрепле́ние strengthening

у́мственный mental

уничтоже́ние annihilation

усло́вие condition

уху́дшитьсяᵖ (**ухудша́ться**ⁱ) to get worse

физи́ческий physical

царе́вич son of the tsar

цель (f) goal, aim

цивилиза́ция civilization

экономи́ческий economic

эне́ргия energy

28.9 Пётр Вели́кий Peter the Great (Translation in Key)

Пётр роди́лся 30 ма́я 1672 го́да[1]. В 1689 году́[2] он жени́лся на до́чери моско́вского боя́рина Евдоки́и Лопухино́й. Царём он стал в 1696 году́[3]. Облада́я выдаю́щимися у́мственными спосо́бностями и огро́мной эне́ргией, он постоя́нно учи́лся. Зна́я, что Росси́я отстаёт от передовы́х стран За́пада, он хорошо́ понима́л необходи́мость экономи́ческих, вое́нных и культу́рных преобразова́ний. В 1697 году́[4] он вы́ехал за грани́цу. В Голла́ндии он научи́лся стро́ить корабли́, рабо́тая просты́м пло́тником. Он посеща́л заво́ды, шко́лы, интересова́лся медици́ной. В А́нглии он изуча́л вое́нно-морско́е де́ло, посети́л обсервато́рию, побыва́л на заседа́нии парла́мента. В а́вгусте 1698 го́да[5], узна́в о восста́нии стрельцо́в в Москве́, Пётр до́лжен был поспеши́ть на ро́дину.

---

1 тридца́того ма́я ты́сяча шестьсо́т се́мьдесят второ́го го́да (17.11).

2 в ты́сяча шестьсо́т во́семьдесят девя́том году́.

3 в ты́сяча шестьсо́т девяно́сто шесто́м году́.

4 в ты́сяча шестьсо́т девяно́сто седьмо́м году́.

5 в а́вгусте ты́сяча шестьсо́т девяно́сто восьмо́го го́да.

За грани́цей Пётр познако́мился с бы́том и обы́чаями европе́йцев. Верну́вшись в Москву́, он стал реши́тельно приобща́ть ру́сских дворя́н и купцо́в к европе́йской цивилиза́ции. Когда́ боя́ре и дворя́не пришли́ поздра́вить Петра́ с прие́здом, он но́жницами обре́зал у них бо́роды. Вско́ре был и́здан прика́з, кото́рый обя́зывал дворя́н одева́ться по-европе́йски и брить бо́роды. Купца́м Пётр разреши́л носи́ть бо́роду, но за э́то они́ плати́ли нало́г.

Пётр уделя́л мно́го внима́ния вопро́сам разви́тия промы́шленности и торго́вли. Дава́я купца́м де́ньги для созда́ния промы́шленных предприя́тий, он пригоня́л госуда́рственных крестья́н в города́ в ка́честве крепостны́х рабо́чих.

Добива́ясь свои́х це́лей, он ни пе́ред чем не остана́вливался. Стро́я го́род Петербу́рг, он не обраща́л внима́ния на тяжёлые усло́вия. Рабо́тая в хо́лоде, под дождём, сто́я по коле́ни в воде́ и грязи́, ты́сячи крестья́н поги́бли от боле́зней, го́лода и непоси́льного труда́. Со свои́ми проти́вниками Пётр расправля́лся беспоща́дно, иногда́ прибега́я к их физи́ческому уничтоже́нию. В 1698 году́, вы́яснив, что во главе́ восста́ния стрельцо́в стоя́ли боя́ре Милосла́вские, он казни́л организа́торов и бо́лее ты́сячи стрельцо́в. Не́которое вре́мя спустя́ Пётр не пощади́л родно́го сы́на Алексе́я, узна́в, что царе́вич уча́ствует в за́говоре. В 1718 году́ с согла́сия отца́ Алексе́й был приговорён к сме́рти.

Рефо́рмы, проведённые Петро́м, спосо́бствовали европеиза́ции Росси́и. Одна́ко он не смог по́лностью преодоле́ть отста́лость страны́, так как его́ рефо́рмы бы́ли одновреме́нно напра́влены на укрепле́ние самодержа́вия и крепостни́чества. При Петре́ жизнь наро́да ре́зко уху́дшилась.

28.10 Vocabulary for Solianka Recipe

бе́лый гриб boletus

вы́ложить᷎ (выкла́дывать᷎) to spread out

голо́вка little head (dim)

  голо́вка лу́ка an onion

грибно́й mushroom (adj)

доба́вить᷎ (добавля́ть᷎) to add

духово́й шкаф oven

жир fat, grease

замени́ть᷎ (заменя́ть᷎) to replace

запека́ние baking
кастрю́ля gen.pl. **кастрю́ль**
saucepan
ква́шеный sour, fermented
кипя́щий boiling
лавро́вый лист bay leaf
ло́мтик slice
лу́к onions
масли́на olive
ми́ска bowl
наре́зать^p **(нареза́ть')** to cut, slice
обжа́рить^p **(обжа́ривать')** to fry
all over
огур(е́)ц cucumber
оконча́ние end
оста́вшийся remaining
очи́стить^p **(очища́ть')** to clean
пер(е)ц pepper
пода́ча serving
подберёзовик brown mushroom
поджа́рить^p **(поджа́ривать')** to
brown
покры́ть^p **(покрыва́ть')** to cover
посы́пать^p **(посыпа́ть')** to
sprinkle (with sth solid)

приба́вить^p **(прибавля́ть')** to add
промы́ть^p **(промыва́ть')** to wash
thoroughly
ры́жик saffron milk-cap
сбры́знуть^p to sprinkle (with liquid)
сковорода́ frying-pan
сма́зать^p **(сма́зывать')** to grease
sth with sth
сма́занный greased (27.7)
смеша́ть^p **(сме́шивать')** to mix
солёный salted, pickled
со́ль (f) salt
соля́нка solianka (spicy cabbage
dish)
столо́вый table (adj)
суха́рь (m) rusk
сушёный dried
тома́т-пюре́ tomato purée
то́т же the same
туше́ние stewing
тушёный stewed
туши́ть' **(по-^p)** to stew
у́ксус vinegar

COMPREHENSION EXERCISE 28/4

1 Does this dish contain any meat?
2 What does the recipe tell you to do with the cabbage?
3 Apart from the choice of type of mushrooms, three instructions involve
options. What are the three options?
4 Translate literally the seven underlined verbal adverbs.

Соля́нка грибна́я A Recipe for Mushroom Solianka

(Note how the recipe uses infinitives as impersonal commands)

На 500 г (пятьсо́т гра́ммов) све́жих грибо́в – 1 кг (оди́н килогра́мм) све́жей капу́сты, 1 (оди́н) солёный огуре́ц, 1 (одна́) голо́вка лу́ка, 2 ст. (две столо́вые) ло́жки тома́та-пюре́, 1-2 (одна́-две) ча́йные ло́жки са́хара, 2 ст. (две столо́вые) ло́жки ма́сла.

Капу́сту наре́зать, положи́ть в кастрю́лю, доба́вить ма́сло и немно́го воды́. Туши́ть о́коло ча́са. За 15-20 мину́т до оконча́ния туше́ния приба́вить тома́т-пюре́, са́хар, со́ль, пе́рец, лавро́вый лист, у́ксус.

Очи́стив и промы́в грибы́ (бе́лые, подберёзовики, ры́жики и други́е), положи́ть их на 10-15 мину́т в кипя́щую во́ду. Зате́м наре́зав ло́мтиками, обжа́рить в ма́сле. Положи́в грибы́ в ми́ску, на то́й же сковороде́ поджа́рить лук и зате́м смеша́ть его́ с гриба́ми, доба́вив наре́занный огуре́ц, со́ль, пе́рец.

Полови́ну тушёной капу́сты положи́ть на сма́занную жи́ром сковороду́, на капу́сту вы́ложить приготовле́нные грибы́ и покры́ть оста́вшейся капу́стой. Посы́пав капу́сту сухаря́ми и сбры́знув ма́слом, поста́вить в духово́й шкаф для запека́ния. Пе́ред пода́чей на соля́нку мо́жно положи́ть ло́мтик лимо́на и́ли масли́ны.

Грибну́ю соля́нку мо́жно пригото́вить та́кже из ква́шеной капу́сты, не добавля́я в э́том слу́чае у́ксуса. Све́жие грибы́ мо́жно замени́ть солёными и́ли сушёными.

29

УРÓК НÓМЕР ДВÁДЦАТЬ ДÉВЯТЬ

'BOOKISH' STYLE; ACTIVE PARTICIPLES; PUNCTUATION; SHORT-FORM ADJECTIVES

29.1 Key Examples of Active Participles

слéдующий	following, next
начинáющий	beginner ('one who is beginning')
выдаю́щийся	outstanding
пи́шущая маши́нка	typewriter ('writing machine')
желáющий	wishing; person who wants to
опоздáвший	latecomer ('who has come late')
В э́той дерéвне живу́т лю́ди, говоря́щие по-рýсски.	In this village live people who speak Russian.
Мы говори́ли со студéнтами, приéхавшими из Иркýтска.	We talked to the students who had arrived from Irkutsk.

29.2 Active Participles

Russian has two active participles, whose use is restricted to formal, bookish Russian (novels, scholarly works, some newspaper writing). The present active participle corresponds to English '-ing' verb forms in such sentences as 'The man read*ing* the newspaper is a spy'.

The past active participle, which has both imperfective and perfective forms, corresponds to 'who/which + the past tense' ('The woman *who gave* you all this money is a spy').

355

Both participles are met quite frequently in written Russian (particularly in newspapers and scientific writing) but they are not used in the spoken language. They can always be replaced with a clause beginning **кото́рый** followed by the present or past tense.

Like the passive participles you met in Lesson 27, active participles are formed from verbs and have adjective endings. In some grammar books, these participles are called 'verbal adjectives'.

29.3 Present Active Participle (Who/Which is VERB-ing)

These participles are easily recognized by their characteristic **-щ-** followed by the adjective ending **-ий**. To form them, take any imperfective verb in its **они́** form (e.g. **чита́ют**), take off the **-т** and add **-щий**:

чита́ть (они́ чита́ют) - чита́ю + щий = чита́ющий 'reading'
говори́ть (они́ говоря́т) - говоря́ + щий = говоря́щий 'speaking'

These adjectival forms agree with the noun to which they relate. The endings are the same as those of the adjective **хоро́ший** (see Table 5.)

Я зна́ю де́вушку, чита́ющую (f. acc. sg.) **газе́ту.**
I know the girl reading the newspaper.

Notice that this sentence means exactly the same as:

Я зна́ю де́вушку, кото́рая чита́ет газе́ту.
I know the girl who is reading the newspaper (see 18.9 for **кото́рый**).

If the verb is reflexive, add **-ся** (*which is never shortened to* **-сь** *in participles*):

Де́вушка, занима́ющаяся ру́сским   The girl study*ing* Russian
языко́м, подру́га Ве́ры.   is a friend of Vera.
(занима́ться 'to study': **занима́ю + щий + ся** 'studying')

There are no exceptions to these rules for forming present active participles. Occasionally the stress is hard to predict (e.g. participles from **-ить** verbs with the stress pattern of **кури́ть (курю́, ку́ришь, ку́рят)** tend to have the stress of the first person, i.e. **куря́щий** 'smoking', not **ку́рящий**), but the stress is of little importance since you will rarely have to use them in speech.

EXERCISE 29/1

Find the infinitives from which the participles are formed and translate the sentences:

1 Мы шли по доро́ге, <u>веду́щей</u> в лес. 2 Все уважа́ют писа́телей, <u>пи́шущих</u> пра́вду о коммуни́зме. 3 Ми́стер По́уп встреча́ется с бизнесме́ном ('businessman'), <u>стро́ящим</u> но́вые заво́ды в Сиби́ри. 4 Для на́шего магази́на мы и́щем же́нщин, <u>уме́ющих</u> одева́ться краси́во. 5 В э́том сиби́рском го́роде, <u>существу́ющем</u> всего́ де́сять лет, уже́ бо́лее пяти́ ты́сяч жи́телей. 6 Дире́ктор встреча́ется с рабо́чими, <u>отка́зывающимися</u> рабо́тать в воскресе́нье.

29.4 Past Active Participles (Who/Which VERB-ed/was VERB-ing

These participles have the characteristic ending **-вший**, an adjective ending which agrees in number, gender and case with the noun to which it relates. It means 'who (or which) VERB-ed or was VERB-ing'.

изуча́вшийⁱ	who was studying
изучи́вшийᵖ	who mastered

They are formed from both imperfective and perfective verbs using this rule: take off the **-л** of the past tense and add **-вший**:

изуча́тьⁱ 'to study' (past **изуча́л**) – **изуча́вший**:

Студе́нты, изуча́<u>вшие</u>ⁱ ру́сский язы́к, нашли́ интере́сную рабо́ту.
The students who studied Russian found interesting work.

изучи́тьᵖ 'to master' (past **изучи́л**) – **изучи́вший**:

Бизнесме́нов, изучи́<u>вших</u>ᵖ (gen.pl) ру́сский язы́к, о́чень ма́ло.
There are very few businessmen who have mastered Russian.

If the verb is reflexive, add **-ся** (never **-сь**).

занима́тьсяⁱ 'to study' (past **занима́лся**) – **занима́вшийся**:

Все де́вушки, занима́вшиесяⁱ **ру́сским языко́м, вы́шли за́муж за ру́сских.**
All the girls who studied Russian married Russians.

If the past tense of the verb does not end **-л**, add **-ший** (without the **в**) to the masculine singular of the past tense:

принестиᴾ 'to bring' (past **принёс**) – **принёсший**ᴾ 'who brought'

Exceptions

The main one is **идти** (and all its prefixed forms) which has the past participle form **шёдший**:

войтиᴾ	**вошёдший**ᴾ 'who went in'
пройтиᴾ	**прошёдший**ᴾ 'who went through'

Note also:

вести' (to lead)	**вёдший**' 'who/which led'
приобрестиᴾ (to acquire)	**приобрётший**ᴾ 'who acquired'

These participles always correspond in meaning to **который** + the past tense:

Бизнесме́нов, изучи́вших ру́сский язы́к, о́чень ма́ло = Бизнесме́нов, кото́рые изучи́ли ру́сский язы́к, о́чень ма́ло.

EXERCISE 29/2

Translate:

1 **Студе́нты, <u>опозда́вшие</u>ᴾ на экза́мен, о́чень беспоко́ились.** 2 **Люде́й, <u>ви́девших</u>' Ле́нина, тепе́рь о́чень ма́ло.** 3 **Же́нщину, <u>нашёдшую</u>ᴾ су́мку, про́сят подойти́ к администра́тору теа́тра.**

29.5 Participles as Adjectives: 'Has been Wife'

A number of active participles, mainly present ones, are commonly used as adjectives (i.e. they are used in front of a noun and have little or no verbal meaning of action). They are listed in dictionaries.

Examples:

<u>сле́дующий</u> день	the following day (from **сле́довать** 'to follow')
<u>пи́шущая</u> маши́нка	typewriter ('little writing machine') (from **писа́ть** 'to write')
<u>веду́щая</u> ро́ль	leading role (from **вести́** 'to lead')
<u>блестя́щая</u> кни́га	brilliant ('shining') book (from **блесте́ть** 'to shine')
<u>кипя́щая</u> вода́	boiling water (from **кипе́ть** 'to boil')
<u>выдаю́щиеся</u> писа́тели	outstanding writers (from **выдава́ться** 'to stand out')
<u>непью́щий</u>	non-drinking, abstemious (from **пить** 'to drink')
<u>бы́вшая</u> жена́	former ('has been') wife (**бы́вший** is the past active participle of **быть** 'to be')
<u>проше́дшее</u> вре́мя	past time, past tense (**проше́дший**ᵖ from **пройти́**ᵖ 'to pass')

Some are used as nouns:

Мы приглаша́ем всех жела́ющих.	We invite all those who want to come (**жела́ющий** 'who wishes' from **жела́ть**).
Он рабо́тает с начина́ющими.	He works with beginners (**начина́ющий** 'beginning' from **начина́ть** 'to begin').
Опозда́вших про́сят подожда́ть.	Latecomers are asked to wait (**опозда́вший**ᵖ 'who was late' from **опозда́ть**ᵖ 'to be late').

EXERCISE 29/3

Translate the words in brackets, using a participle or **кото́рый** (your choice):

1 **Студе́нтов,** (who wish – **жела́ть**) **изуча́ть англи́йский язы́к, о́чень мно́го.** 2 **В институ́те мы разгова́ривали со студе́нтами,** (who are studying – **занима́ться**) **ру́сским языко́м.** 3 **Профе́ссор Мирча́нов чита́ет ле́кции о поэ́тах,** (who wrote) **при Ста́лине.** 4 **Дире́ктор пригласи́л на ве́чер всех студе́нтов,** (who had arrived ᵖ) **из Владивосто́ка.**

29.6 **EXTRA: Punctuation**

You may have noticed above that an active participle is always separated from its preceding noun by a comma. Russian has very strict rules for the use of commas. In English, we tend to insert a comma when we pause; in Russian, on the other hand, the placing of commas is determined primarily by grammatical structure and only secondarily by meaning or intonation. The main rule: a comma is always used to separate a main clause¹ from a subordinate¹ or participial clause, e.g.:

Вади́м сказа́л, что́ ско́ро придёт. Vadim said he would come soon.
/main clause/   subordinate clause/

A comma would look most unnatural in this English sentence, but in Russian it is compulsory. If you miss it out, you look uneducated. Russian school-children are not considered literate if they don't put the main commas in.

Кварти́ра, в кото́рой о́н живёт, о́чень больша́я. 'The flat he lives in is very large.' The main clause is **Кварти́ра о́чень больша́я** and the subordinate clause, separated by commas, is **в кото́рой о́н живёт**.

Note the number of commas in the following (all compulsory):

Ка́жется, те, кто́ пришёл в во́семь, смогли́ купи́ть биле́ты, а тем, кто́ пришёл в де́вять, дире́ктор сказа́л, что́ все биле́ты про́даны.
It seems that those who came at eight were able to buy tickets, while those who came at nine were told by the director that all the tickets had been sold.

By contrast, note that Russian does not use commas to separate time and place phrases from the rest of the clause. In English you can write 'In 1937, we lived . . .' but in Russian there is no comma: **В 1937 году́ мы жи́ли . . .**

There are other differences between Russian and English punctuation, particularly in representing direct speech, but the use of commas is the only one likely to be noticed.

29.7 Long- and Short-Form Adjectives

This grammar aims to be complete. That is, it deals with all the basic structures of Russian grammar, even with those which you are unlikely to use, because you will meet them in the speech or writing of Russians. One of these minor topics is the choice between the long and short forms of adjectives. You have met some short-form adjectives simply as vocabulary items, e.g. **до́лжен/должна́/должно́/должны́** 'obliged' (19.4), **рад, ра́да, ра́до, ра́ды** 'glad' (26). What has not been mentioned is the fact that most adjectives of the **но́вый/молодо́й/вели́кий** types (7.2), but *not* those ending **-ский**, can have the short endings **-/а/о/ы** in certain circumstances.

Short-form adjectives are met only in sentences of the type 'The film is interesting', 'She was grateful', in which an adjective used predicatively (i.e. with no noun after it) is linked to the subject by a form of the verb 'to be'. These short-form adjectives have only one case, the nominative, and therefore only four possible endings, namely masculine, feminine, neuter and plural. They are called 'short-form' adjectives because their endings are truncated versions of the nominative 'long-form' adjective endings you met in 7.2. Here are the two sets of endings compared.

m	f	n	pl	
но́вый	**но́вая**	**но́вое**	**но́вые** 'new'	long forms
но́в	**нова́**	**но́во**	**но́вы** 'new'	short forms

You will see that short-form adjectives have the endings you associate with nouns (consonant ending: masculine; **-а**: feminine; **-о**: neuter; **-ы**: plural).

If you want to say 'a new house', using the adjective 'new' attributively (i.e. in front of a noun), the only possible form is **но́вый до́м**. But if you want to say 'The house is new', you have a choice between **До́м но́вый** and **До́м но́в**. The difference is a stylistic one: in most cases, the long form is normal, neutral Russian, while the short form is bookish. This means that the long form is the one you have been using, but when reading bookish Russian (formal articles, speeches, scientific writing, poetry) you will meet many examples of short forms.

Here are examples of short forms you may meet:

ве́рный	true	ве́р<u>ен</u>, верна́, ве́рно, ве́рны
краси́вый	beautiful	краси́в, краси́ва, краси́во, краси́вы
интере́сный	interesting	интере́с<u>ен</u>, интере́сна, интере́сно, интере́сны
холо́дный	cold	хо́лод<u>ен</u>, холодна́, хо́лодно, хо́лодны
ну́жный	necessary	ну́жен, нужна́, ну́жно, нужны́ (ну́жны also occurs)
дорого́й	dear/expensive	до́рог, дорога́, до́рого, до́роги
кра́ткий	short	кра́т<u>ок</u>, кратка́, кра́тко, кра́тки
лёгкий	light/easy	лёгок, легка́, легко́, легки́ (г pronounced х before к)
тру́дный	difficult	тру́ден, трудна́, тру́дно, тру́дны
вели́кий	great	вели́к, вели́ка, вели́ко, вели́ки
хоро́ший	good	хоро́ш, хороша́, хорошо́, хоро́ший

You may notice that the neuter forms are the same as adverbs (7.16).

Special cases

большо́й	large	вели́к, велика́, велико́, велики́
ма́ленький	small	мал, мала́, мало́, малы́

Examples:

Э́то до́рого.	That's expensive.
Я бу́ду кра́ток/кратка́.	I shall be brief.
Э́то легко́.	That's easy.
Ва́ша до́чь о́чень краси́ва.	Your daughter is very pretty.
Вопро́сы бы́ли сли́шком тру́дны для нас.	The questions were too difficult for us.
Э́тот стул вам ну́жен?	Do you need this chair? ('Is this chair to you necessary?')

Points to note:

Short-form adjectives are harder to form than long-form ones. While long-form adjectives are very regular and have fixed stress (see 7.2), short forms involve irregularities. Although the basic rule for forming short-forms is 'Take off the last two letters of the masculine form (**но́вый** becomes **нов**) and the last letter of the other three forms (**но́вая** becomes **нова́**, **но́вое** becomes **но́во**, **но́вые** becomes **но́вы**)', there is a general tendency for the stress of two-syllable adjectives to shift to the end in the feminine (and sometimes in the plural as well). Many adjectives have other stress shifts, e.g. **молодо́й** 'young' has the short forms **мо́лод**, **молода́**, **мо́лодо**, **мо́лоды**. Adjectives with a consonant group before the ending, e.g. **интере́сный**, usually add **-е-** (or **-о-**) between the con-sonants in the masculine form only (**фильм интере́сен** 'The film is interest-ing'). Many adjectives, particularly all those ending **-ский** and most soft adjectives (e.g. **после́дний** 'last'), have no short forms at all.

Usage

(1) As mentioned above, you can manage without short adjectives most of the time because they tend to be bookish, while the forms you learnt in Lesson 7 are normal everyday Russian. However, there are a few adjec-tives (such as **рад** 'glad' – see above) which, when predicative (used with no following noun), are *always* in the short form. Here are the main ones:

Гото́вый 'ready' is only used in the short form **гото́в, гото́ва, гото́во, гото́вы** in sentences such as 'I am/was/will be/would be ready':

Я гото́в/гото́ва.	I'm ready.
Когда́ вы бу́дете гото́вы?	When will you be ready? (*Note:* With **вы**, short-form adjectives are always plural (ending **-ы**), even when you are talking to one person.)
Бу́дьте добры́	Be so good (in polite requests).

Рад, ра́да, ра́до, ра́ды 'glad'. (Notice that in English, too, 'glad' is nearly always used predicatively: 'She is glad' is much more likely than 'She is a glad person'.)

Я так ра́да вас ви́деть.	I'm so glad to see you (woman speaking).
Мы бу́дем ра́ды.	We'll be glad.

Похо́жий 'similar': **похо́ж, похо́жа, похо́же, похо́жи:**

Вы похо́жи на Кла́рка Ге́йбла.	You look like Clark Gable.

Ну́жный 'necessary' always has the forms **ну́жен, нужна́, ну́жно, нужны́** if it is used predicatively:

Ва́ня – ну́жный челове́к.	Vanya is a useful ('necessary') person.

But

Ва́ня нам ну́жен.	We need Vanya ('Vanya to us is necessary').
Мне нужна́ ва́ша по́мощь.	I need your help ('To me is necessary your help').

(2) If the subject is **э́то** 'this/that/it' or **всё** 'everything', the predicative adjective *must* be short:

Э́то до́рого (not **дорого́е**).	That's expensive.
Всё здесь интере́сно.	Everything here is interesting.

(3) As well as sounding more bookish, the short form may carry other connotations, depending on the situation: it may sound more categorical/emphatic, or it may restrict the description to a particular situation – see (4).

Она́ така́я глу́пая.	She's so silly (long form).
Она́ так глупа́.	She's so stupid (short form – more emphatic).

Note that 'so' is **так** with short adjectives (and adverbs) and **тако́й** 'such' with 'normal' (long form) adjectives.

(4) If the adjective has a dependent phrase such as 'difficult *for me*', '(too) big *for you*', then the short form should be used:

Пого́да хоро́шая.	The weather is good.

But

Пого́да хороша́ для лыж.	The weather is good for skiing.
Э́то пальто́ ему́ велико́.	That coat is (too) big for him.

EXERCISE 29/4

Translate:

A Conversation with Short Forms

ИЕ: Здра́вствуйте, Ве́ра Петро́вна. Рад вас ви́деть.
ВП: Я то́же ра́да, Илья́ Его́рович.
ИЕ: Вы гото́вы?
ВП: Уже́ гото́ва.
ИЕ: Бу́дьте добры́, переда́йте портфе́ль, он мне ну́жен.
ВП: Ваш портфе́ль похо́ж на чемода́н.
ИЕ: Э́то ве́рно. Но ва́ша су́мка то́же была́ бы похо́жа на чемода́н, е́сли бы вы бы́ли так же за́няты, как я.

EXERCISE 29/5

Translate, using short forms:

1 I was glad. 2 She looks like her father. 3 That's good. 4 That's expensive. 5 They need dollars. 6 Tania, are you ready? 7 We'll be ready in (**че́рез**) five minutes. 8 The hat (**ша́пка**) is too big for ('to') her.

29.8 Vocabulary

Адмиралте́йство Admiralty
анса́мбль (m) ensemble
арка́да arcade
архитекту́рный architectural
баро́кко (n indecl) baroque
бога́тство richness, wealth
воро́та (n pl.) gen.pl. **воро́т** gates
великоле́пный magnificent
вели́чественно-прекра́сный majestically beautiful
ве́рный true; faithful

возвыша́ться¹ (like **знать**) to tower
впечатля́ющий impressive (from **впечатля́ть**¹ (coll) to impress)
въездны́е воро́та entrance gates
выдава́ться¹ (**вы́даться**ᵖ) to project, stand out
выступа́ющий projecting
выступа́ть¹ to project, stick out
выходи́ть¹ **на** (+ acc.) to look out on

365

вы́садитьсяᵖ (**выса́живаться**ⁱ)
to disembark, land

гармони́чный harmonious

глу́пый stupid, silly

гото́в/а/о/ы ready (29.7)

деко́р decoration

двор(е́)ц palace

Дворцо́вая пло́щадь Palace
Square

за́муж

выходи́тьⁱ/**вы́йти**ᵖ **за́муж** (**за**
+ acc.) to marry (of the woman)
('to go out after a husband')

испо́лненный executed, carried
out PPP of **испо́лнить**ᵖ to carry
out, execute, perform

коло́нна column, pillar

крыло́ pl. **кры́лья** wing

ландша́фт landscape

лы́жи (pl.) gen.pl. **лы́ж** skis

масшта́б scale

матро́с sailor

моде́ль (f) model

музе́йный museum (adj)

на́бережная (f adj) embankment,
quay

наибо́лее most

необыча́йно extraordinarily

неповтори́мый unique

ну́жный necessary

о́браз form; image; manner

обращён PPP of **обрати́ть**ᵖ
turned

океа́н ocean

опозда́тьᵖ **опозда́ю, опозда́ешь**
(**опа́здывать**ⁱ like **знать**) (**на**
+ acc.) to be late (for)

определи́тьᵖ **определю́, -ли́шь**
(**определя́ть**ⁱ like **знать**) (+ acc.)
to determine, define

основа́тьᵖ **осную́, оснуёшь**
(+ acc.) (**осно́вывать**ⁱ like
знать) to found

пара́дный grand

полуо́стров peninsula

портфе́ль (m) briefcase

представля́тьⁱ (**предста́вить**ᵖ)
себе́ to imagine

прое́кт plan, project

пропо́рция proportion

разнообра́зие variety

располага́тьсяⁱ (like **знать**) to be
situated, placed

располо́жен/а/о/ы situated

решётка gen.pl. **решёток** grille,
railing, decorated ironwork

склон slope

стул pl **сту́лья,** gen.pl **сту́льев**
chair

субтропи́ческий subtropical

торже́ственный grand, splendid,
majestic

тройно́й triple

укра́ситьᵖ **укра́шу, укра́сишь**
(**украша́ть**ⁱ like **знать**) (+ acc.)
to adorn

фаса́д façade

чемода́н suitcase

29.9 **Владивосто́к** Vladivostok (bookish style)

Владивосто́к располо́жен на полуо́строве, выдаю́щемся в
Ти́хий океа́н. Э́то огро́мный по́рт. Са́мая интере́сная часть го́рода –
на́бережная. Здесь возвыша́ется коло́нна с моде́лью корабля́, с
кото́рого вы́садились матро́сы, основа́вшие Владивосто́к в 1880
году́. Го́род, спуска́ющийся по скло́нам к мо́рю, о́чень краси́в. Его́
необыча́йно украша́ют неповтори́мый ландша́фт, субтропи́ческая
приро́да.

COMPREHENSION EXERCISE 29/6

1 What is the connection between the Hermitage Museum and the Winter
Palace?
2 What are we told about the location of the Winter Palace in relation to its
Petersburg surroundings?
3 Find and translate the four active participles, the one verbal adverb and
the four past passive participles.

Зи́мний дворе́ц The Winter Palace (Another bookish text, not easily
translated)

Ка́ждый, хоть оди́н раз побыва́вший в Эрмита́же, вспомина́ет
о нём, представля́я себе́ вели́чественно-прекра́сный Зи́мний
Дворе́ц – са́мое замеча́тельное и наибо́лее впечатля́ющее из пяти́
музе́йных зда́ний. Постро́енный в 1754–1762 года́х по прое́кту
Франче́ско Бартоломе́о Растре́лли (1700–1771), он определи́л
великоле́пный архитекту́рный анса́мбль на берегу́ Невы́.

Масшта́бами, бога́тством, разнообра́зием архитекту́рного
деко́ра, а та́кже пропо́рцией часте́й Зи́мний дворе́ц, испо́лненный
в сти́ле ру́сского баро́кко, создаёт гармони́чный и торже́ствен-
ный о́браз.

Два крыла́ с за́падной стороны́ обращены́ к Адмиралте́йству;
гла́вный фаса́д, выходя́щий на Дворцо́вую пло́щадь, – наибо́лее
пара́дный. В сре́дней, выступа́ющей, ча́сти располага́ется
тройна́я арка́да въездны́х воро́т, укра́шенных великоле́пной
решёткой.

30

УРÓК НÓМЕР ТРИ́ДЦАТЬ

ABBREVIATIONS;
NAMES OF RUSSIAN LETTERS;
PARTICLES

30.1 **What's Left?**

You have now covered all the basic grammar you need to speak correctly and to work your way through written Russian texts. Your main task now is to build up your working vocabulary sufficiently to be able to follow Russian speech and read Russian books and newspapers without constantly hunting in dictionaries.

This lesson deals with a few vocabulary points and then tests your mastery of Russian with a complete classic short story.

30.2 **Dictionaries**

You will need the largest Russian–English/English–Russian dictionary you can afford. The best three currently available are those published by Collins, Oxford University Press and Penguin Books. If you want a pocket dictionary, the best is the *Oxford Pocket Russian–English/English–Russian Dictionary*.

30.3 **Russian Abbreviations**

A feature of post-1917 Russian has been the widespread use of abbreviations, including acronyms such as **TACC** 'TASS' and 'stump compounds' (made up of parts of words) such as **универма́г** 'department store' from **универса́льный магази́н** 'universal shop'). Good dictionaries, such as those mentioned above, include the commonest ones.

To read abbreviations such as **МГУ** (Moscow State University **Моско́вский госуда́рственный университе́т**), you need to know the names of the letters – see 1.5.

МГУ (MGU)	**[em-ge-oó]**
ЦРУ (CIA)	**[tse-er-oó]**
СССР (USSR)	**[es-es-es-ér]**
КГБ (KGB)	**[ka-ge-bé]**
Note **США** (USA)	Though the letters are **[es-sha-á]** the pronunciation is usually **[se-she-á]**

However, if the letters form a pronounceable word, they are read as a word (like Unesco or Nato in English):

ТАСС	pronounced **[tas]**
ЮНЕСКО	pronounced as in English **[yoo-né-sko]**

Note the Russian predilection for abbreviations constructed out of parts of words (stump compounds), particularly for the names of companies and trading organizations. That is, rather than names of the type IBM (from International Business Machines) or BBC (from British Broadcasting Corporation), Russians prefer the type we find in Natwest (from National Westminster Bank).

Уралма́ш [oo-ral-má sh] (from **Ура́льский заво́д тяжёлого машино-строе́ния)** Urals Heavy Machinery Works in Ekaterinburg.

совми́н (сове́т мини́стров) Council of Ministers

Минлегпро́м (Министе́рство лёгкой промы́шленности)
Ministry of Light Industry

Минмясомолпро́м (Министе́рство мясно́й и моло́чной промы́ш-ленности)
Ministry of the Meat and Milk Industry

Гостелера́дио (Госуда́рственное телеви́дение и ра́дио)
State Television and Radio (an analogy would be 'Britbroadcorp' for the BBC)

**Главсахалинбумпро́м (Гла́вное управле́ние бума́жной промыш-
ленности на Сахали́не)** Chief Administration of the Sakhalin
Paper Industry

30.4 **Particles**

Some of the trickiest words to translate are the so-called 'particles"
(**части́цы**). A particle is a (usually short) word, such as **же** (5.2), which
occurs only with other words, never on its own, to indicate such things as
emphasis (**же**), speaker's attitude (**ведь**), emotion, or, sometimes, grammatical structure (e.g. **ли**, indicating a yes–no question **Зна́ете ли вы . . .?**
'Do you know . . .?').

Где Ива́н?	Where is Ivan?
Где же Ива́н?	**Where** is Ivan?

Other particles you have met are **ведь**, indicating that the speaker expects
you to agree with his statement or to know the information already (**Ведь
она́ уе́хала!** She's left, you know); **бы** indicating doubt or hypothesis (**Я
бы купи́л два** I would buy two/I would like to buy two); **вот** here/there is,
used to draw attention to what follows (**Вот почему́** That's why); **ну**
corresponding to the English hesitation word 'well' (**Ну, я то́чно не зна́ю**
Well, I'm not quite sure).

Other particles to note are:

-то which (apart from its use in words like **кто́-то** 'someone' (26.2)) is a
colloquial and weaker equivalent of **же**

В то́м-то и де́ло.	That's just it/That's just the point.
Наро́ду-то!	Such crowds!

-ка which softens imperatives, making them friendlier or more like invitations. **Скажи́-ка** . . . Do tell me . . . **Подойди́-ка** Come here, won't
you? **Не шуми́те-ка** You'd better stop making a noise.

-ка with verbs in the first person future indicates tentative intentions:

Зае́ду-ка к нему́. I think I might call on him (example from *The Penguin
Russian Dictionary*).

да which apart from meaning 'yes' is a weaker, colloquial equivalent of **а**
('and/but')

Принеси́те мне во́дки, да поскоре́е! Bring me some vodka, and quick about it! (example from *The Oxford Russian Dictionary*)

и 'even', 'too', emphasizes the following word:

Она́ не зна́ла, что́ и он отка́жется. She didn't know that even he would refuse.

More examples:

Вот не ожида́л!	I didn't expect this!
Вот сюрпри́з!	What a surprise!
Да кни́гу же забы́л я ему́ переда́ть-то!	Oh, but I've gone and forgotten to give him the book though!
Ну, да погляди́ же на меня́!	Well, but just take a look at me then!
Ну, что́ же ты?	Well, how are you then?
Ну да бог с ним!	Well but what does it matter? (**бог** 'God')
То́-то и оно́!	That's it!
Ну да?!	Really? (astonishment with a note of distrust)
Да ну!	Oh, no! (disagreement, unwillingness, refusal)
Как бы не так!	Not at all. On the contrary.

30.5 **Vocabulary for Chekhov's То́лстый и то́нкий** 'Fat and Thin'

ба́тюшки! good gracious!

благогове́ние reverence

бог [boh] pl. **бо́ги** gen.pl. **бого́в** God; god

бог с ним/ней good luck to him/her; what does it matter?

бога́тый (short form **бога́т**) rich

не бо́йся (from **боя́ться**) don't be afraid

ве́домство department

вельмо́жа grandee, big shot

ветчина́ ham

ви́шня gen.pl. **ви́шен** cherry

воскли́кнутьᵖ **воскли́кну, -кнешь (восклица́ть** like **знать)** to exclaim

восто́рженно enthusiastically

вро́де (+ gen.) like

выгля́дывать (like **знать) (вы́глянуть**ᵖ **вы́гляну, вы́глянешь)** to look out

вы́тянутьсяᵖ **вы́тянусь, -нешься** to stretch; to stand erect

вы́тянутьсяᴾ **во фрунт** to stand to attention

Геростра́т Herostratus (who burnt down the temple of Artemis at Ephesus)

гимнази́ст grammar-school boy

гимна́зия grammar school

гляде́тьⁱ **(по-**ᴾ**) гляжу́, гляди́шь (на** + acc.) to look (at)

голу́бчик dear friend, my dear

го́споди! good heavens! good Lord!

    ах ты го́споди! oh, good heavens!

губа́ pl. **гу́бы** dat.pl. **губа́м** lip

гу́ща grounds, dregs

департа́мент (old word) (government) department

де́рево wood (also 'tree')

дли́нный long

дослужи́тьсяᴾ **дослужу́сь, дослу́жишься (до** + gen.) **(дослу́живаться**ⁱ like **знать)** to reach a position, the top

дразни́тьⁱ **дразню́, дра́знишь** (+ acc.) to tease, (+ inst.) to call someone a name (in order to tease)

друг дру́га each other

друг на дру́га at each other (30.6 note 3)

душо́н(о)к swell, smart lad

жа́лованье (old word) salary

желе́зная доро́га railway ('iron road')

жена́т (short adj) married (of a man)

живи́тельная вла́га (coll) intoxicating liquor

застегну́тьᴾ **застегну́, застегнёшь (застёгивать**ⁱ**)** like **знать)** (+ acc.) to fasten

захихи́катьᴾ (like **знать**) to start giggling (**хихи́кать**ⁱ to giggle)

звезда́ pl. **звёзды,** gen.pl. **звёзд** star

из-за (+ gen.) from behind

изуми́тьсяᴾ **изумлю́сь, изуми́шься (изумля́ться**ⁱ **изумля́юсь, -я́ешься)** to be astonished

и́скра spark

искриви́тьсяᴾ **искривлю́сь, искриви́шься (искривля́ться**ⁱ **искривля́юсь, -я́ешься)** to become distorted, to twist

казённый state, belonging to the state

как бы as it were

карто́нка gen.pl. **карто́нок** cardboard box

кислота́ pl. **кисло́ты** acidity, sourness

кита́(е)ц Chinese (noun)

класс class, form

    тре́тьего кла́сса of the third form

кни́жка (dim 25.2) gen.pl. **кни́жек** book, small book, some book (fam)

ко́е-ка́к (26.7) somehow, just, with difficulty

колле́жский асе́ссор collegiate assessor (eighth grade in fourteen-grade tsarist civil service)

кофе́йный coffee (adj)

краса́в(е)ц handsome man

лобыза́ние (old word) kiss

лосни́ться' **лосню́сь, лосни́шься** to shine, gleam

лютера́нка gen.pl. **лютера́нок** Lutheran (Protestant)

ми́лостивый (old word) gracious, kind

ми́лый мо́й! my dear

мунди́р uniform

навью́читьᴾ **навью́чу, навью́чишь (навью́чивать**' like **знать)** (+ inst.) to load (with)

небо́сь (coll) probably

не́которым о́бразом somehow; so to speak

Никола́евская желе́зная доро́га The Moscow–St Petersburg line (named after Tsar Nicholas I)

облобыза́тьсяᴾ (like **знать) (лобыза́ться**') (old word) to kiss each other

окамене́тьᴾ **окамене́ю, -не́ешь (камене́ть**') to turn to stone

отверну́тьсяᴾ **отверну́сь, -нёшься (отвора́чиваться**' like **знать) (от** + gen.) to turn away (from)

отку́да from where

отку́да ты взя́лся? where have you sprung from?

ошеломи́тьᴾ **ошеломлю́, -ми́шь (ошеломля́ть**' **-мля́ю, -я́ешь)** to stun, astound

папиро́ска (dim of **папиро́са**) Russian-style cigarette

па́хло (past of **па́хнуть**' to smell) it smelled

па́хло от него́ (+ inst.) he smelled of

переведён (PPP of **перевести́**) transferred

побледне́тьᴾ **побледне́ю, -не́ешь (бледне́ть**') to turn pale

погляде́тьᴾ (see **гляде́ть**') (**на** + acc.) to take a look at

пода́тьᴾ **ру́ку** to hold out one's hand

подборо́д(о)к chin

подёрнут(ый) (PPP of **подёрнуть**) covered, coated

поду́матьᴾ (**ду́мать**') (like **знать**) to think for a moment

пожа́тьᴾ **пожму́, пожмёшь (пожима́ть**' like **знать) (ру́ку)** to press, squeeze, shake (hands)

поклони́тьсяᴾ **поклоню́сь, покло́нишься (поклоня́ться**' **поклоня́юсь, -я́ешься)** to bow

по́лно! (coll) enough of that!

по́лный (+ gen.) full (of)

поми́луйтеᴾ pardon me

помо́рщитьсяᴾ **помо́рщусь помо́рщишься (мо́рщиться**') to crease, wrinkle; to frown

портсига́р cigarette-case, cigar-case

посы́патьсяᴾ **посы́плется** to rain down

почти́тельный respectful, deferential

превосходи́тельство Excellency (title of general and equivalent ranks)

прива́тно (old word) privately

прищу́ренный half-closed (of eyes)

прия́тель (m) friend

пробавля́ться' -ля́юсь, -ля́ешься to get by, make do (coll)

прожéчьᵖ **прожгу́, прожжёшь прожгу́т** past **прожёг, прожгла́ (прожига́ть'** like **знать)** to burn through

проща́ние farewell, parting **на проща́ние** in farewell

проти́вно disgusting, disgusted

пу́говка gen.pl. **пу́говок** button

сго́рбитьсяᵖ **сго́рблюсь, -бишься (го́рбиться')** to hunch up, become bent

сла́дость (f) sweetness

слеза́ pl **слёзы,** gen.pl. **слёз,** dat.pl. **слеза́м** tear, teardrop

служи́ть' служу́, слу́жишь (+ inst.) **(по-**ᵖ**)** to serve, to work (as)

снятьᵖ **сниму́, сни́мешь** (+ acc.) **(снима́ть'** like **знать)** to take off

спе́лый ripe

спина́ acc. **спи́ну,** pl. **спи́ны** back

спря́татьсяᵖ **спря́чусь, -чешься (пря́таться')** (за + acc.) to hide (oneself) behind

Станисла́в Order of St Stanislas (tsarist civil-service medal)

ста́тский (сове́тник) Councillor of State (fifth highest civil-service rank)

столонача́льник (old word) head of a civil-service section

су́зитьсяᵖ **су́зится (су́живаться'** like **знать)** to become narrow

съёжитьсяᵖ **съёжусь, съёжишься (съёживаться'** like **знать)** to shrivel, shrink

та́йный (сове́тник) Privy Councillor (third highest civil-service rank)

то́лстый fat

то́н tone

то́нкий thin

троекра́тно thrice, three times

ту́ловище body, torso

у́з(е)л pl. **узлы́** bundle

урождённая née (indicating maiden name)

урони́тьᵖ **уроню́, уро́нишь** (+ acc.) **(роня́ть'** **роня́ю, роня́ешь)** to drop

устреми́тьᵖ **устремлю́, устреми́шь (устремля́ть'** -ля́ю, -ля́ешь) **(глаза́ на** + acc.**)** to direct, fasten (one's gaze on)

усту́пка gen.pl. **усту́пок** price reduction; concession

учени́к gen.sg. **ученика́** pupil

флёрдора́нж orange blossom (scent)

фура́жка gen.pl. **фура́жек** peaked cap

хе́рес sherry

хороше́нько properly, well and truly (25.4)

хо́-хо́ ho-ho!

ху́денький thin (25.4)

чемода́н suitcase

чинопочита́ние respect for rank, kowtowing, boot-licking

ша́ркунтьᵖ **ша́ркну, ша́ркнешь** (**ша́ркать**¹ like **знать**) (+ inst.) to shuffle

ша́ркнутьᵖ **ного́й** to click one's heels (**нога́** 'foot')

широча́йший widest (18.8)

шту́ка thing, piece

щёголь (m) dandy

Эфиа́льт Ephialtes (Greek traitor)

я́бедничать¹ (**на-**ᵖ) (like **знать**) to tell tales, sneak

30.6 A taste of Russian nineteenth-century literature, a complete early comic-satirical Chekhov story from 1883:

То́лстый и то́нкий The Fat One and the Thin One

На вокза́ле Никола́евской желе́зной доро́ги встре́тились два прия́теля: оди́н то́лстый, друго́й то́нкий. То́лстый то́лько что́ пообе́дал на вокза́ле, и гу́бы его́, подёрнутые ма́слом, лосни́лись, как спе́лые ви́шни. Па́хло от него́ хе́ресом и флёрдора́нжем. То́нкий же¹ то́лько что́ вы́шел из ваго́на и был навьючен чемода́нами, узла́ми и карто́нками. Па́хло от него́ ветчино́й и кофе́йной гу́щей. Из-за его́ спины́ выгля́дывала ху́денькая же́нщина с дли́нным подборо́дком – его́ жена́, и высо́кий гимнази́ст с прищу́ренным гла́зом – его́ сын.

– Порфи́рий! – воскли́кнул то́лстый, уви́дев то́нкого. – ты ли э́то? Голу́бчик мой! Ско́лько зим, ско́лько лет²!

– Ба́тюшки! – изуми́лся то́нкий. – Ми́ша! Друг де́тства! Отку́да ты взя́лся?

Прия́тели троекра́тно облобыза́лись и устреми́ли друг на дру́га³ глаза́, по́лные слёз. О́ба бы́ли прия́тно ошеломлены́.

– Ми́лый мой! – на́чал то́нкий по́сле лобыза́ния. – Во́т не ожида́л⁴! Во́т сюрпри́з! Ну, да погляди́ же⁵ на меня́ хороше́нько! Тако́й же краса́вец, как и бы́л⁶! Тако́й же душо́нок и щёголь! Ах ты го́споди! Ну, что́ же ты⁷? Бога́т? Жена́т? Я уже́ жена́т, как ви́дишь . . . Это во́т моя́ жена́, Луи́за, урождённая Ва́нценбах . . .

лютера́нка . . . А э́то сын мо́й, Нафана́йл, учени́к тре́тьего кла́сса. Э́то, Нафа́ня, друг моего́ де́тства! В гимна́зии вме́сте учи́лись!

Нафана́йл немно́го поду́мал и снял ша́пку.

– В гимна́зии вме́сте учи́лись! – продолжа́л то́нкий. – По́мнишь, как тебя́ дразни́ли? Тебя́ дразни́ли Геростра́том за то́, что ты казённую кни́жку папиро́ской прожёг, а меня́ Эфиа́льтом за то́, что я я́бедничать люби́л. Хо́-хо́ . . . Детьми́ бы́ли! Не бо́йся, Нафа́ня! Подойди́ к нему́ побли́же . . . А э́то моя́ жена́, урождённая Ва́нценбах . . . лютера́нка.

Нафанаи́л немно́го поду́мал и спря́тался за спи́ну отца́.

– Ну, как живёшь, друг? – спроси́л то́лстый, восто́рженно гля́дя на дру́га. – Слу́жишь где? Дослужи́лся?

– Служу́, ми́лый мо́й! Колле́жским асе́ссором уже́ второ́й го́д и Станисла́ва име́ю. Жа́лованье плохо́е . . . ну да бо́г с ним[8]! Жена́ уро́ки му́зыки даёт, я портсига́ры прива́тно из де́рева де́лаю. Отли́чные портсига́ры! По рублю́[9] за шту́ку продаю́. Е́сли кто́[10] берёт де́сять штук и бо́лее, тому́[11], понима́ешь, усту́пка. Пробавля́емся ко́е-ка́к. Служи́л, зна́ешь, в департа́менте, а тепе́рь сюда́ переведён столонача́льником[12] по тому́ же[13] ве́домству . . . Здесь бу́ду служи́ть. Ну, а ты как? Небо́сь, уже́ ста́тский? А[14]?

– Нет, ми́лый мо́й, поднима́й повы́ше, – сказа́л то́лстый. – Я уже́ до та́йного дослужи́лся . . . Две звезды́ име́ю.

То́нкий вдруг побледне́л, окамене́л, но ско́ро лицо́ его́ искриви́лось во все сто́роны широча́йшей улы́бкой; каза́лось, что́ от лица́ и глаз его́ посы́пались и́скры. Сам о́н съёжился, сго́рбился, су́зился . . . Его́ чемода́ны, узлы́ и карто́нки съёжились, помо́рщились . . . Дли́нный подборо́док жены́ стал ещё длинне́е; Нафанаи́л вы́тянулся во фрунт и застегну́л все пу́говки своего́ мунди́ра . . .

– Я, ва́ше превосходи́тельство . . . О́чень прия́тно-с[15]! Друг, мо́жно сказа́ть, де́тства и вдруг вы́шли[16] в таки́е вельмо́жи-с! Хи-хи́-с.

– Ну, по́лно! – помо́рщился то́лстый. – Для чего́ э́тот то́н? Мы с тобо́й друзья́ де́тства – и к чему́[17] тут э́то чинопочита́ние!

– Поми́луйте . . . Что́ вы-с . . . – захихи́кал то́нкий, ещё бо́лее съёживаясь. – Ми́лостивое внима́ние ва́шего превосходи́тельства . . . вро́де как бы живи́тельной вла́ги . . . Э́то во́т, ва́ше превосходи́тельство, сын мо́й Нафанаи́л . . . жена́ Луи́за, лютера́нка, не́которым о́бразом . . .

То́лстый хоте́л бы́ло[18] возрази́ть что́-то, но́ на лице́ у то́нкого[19] бы́ло напи́сано сто́лько благогове́ния, сла́дости и почти́тельной кислоты́, что́ та́йному сове́тнику ста́ло проти́вно. О́н отверну́лся от то́нкого и по́дал ему́ на проща́ние ру́ку.

То́нкий пожа́л три па́льца, поклони́лся всем ту́ловищем и захихи́кал, как кита́ец: «хи-хи-хи́». Жена́ улыбну́лась. Нафанаи́л ша́ркнул ного́й и урони́л фура́жку. Все тро́е бы́ли прия́тно ошеломлены́.

Notes:

[1]**То́нкий же** (emphatic particle) 'As for the thin one, he . . .' [2]**Ско́лько зим, ско́лько лет!** 'How many winters, how many summers' = 'Long time no see!' [3]**друг на дру́га** 'at each other'; in the structure **друг дру́га** 'each other', the first **друг** is indeclinable, while the second declines like **друг** 'friend'. Prepositions come between the two **друг** words. [4]**Во́т** (30.4) **не ожида́л** 'I didn't expect this.' [5]See the particles section 30.4. The meaning here is 'Look straight at me so that I can have a good look at you.' [6]**Тако́й же краса́вец, как и был** (30.4) 'The same handsome fellow that you (always) were.' [7]**Ну, что́ же ты?** 'Well how are you doing then?' [8]See particles, section 30.4 [9]**По рублю́ за шту́ку** 'at a rouble each.' [10]**Е́сли кто́** . . . 'If anyone . . .' [11]**тому́ . . . усту́пка** 'he gets a reduction' ('to that (one) a reduction'). [12]**столонача́льником** (inst.) 'as a section head.' [13]**по тому́ же ве́домству** 'In the same ('that very') department.' [14]**А?** Eh? [15]The **-с** suffix is short for **су́дарь** 'sir.' [16]**вы́шли в таки́е вельмо́жи-с!** . . . 'you've become such a VIP, sir!' Note the change to **вы.** [17]**к чему́** 'why.' [18]**хоте́л бы́ло** 'was about to.' [19]**на лице́ у то́нкого** 'on the thin one's face.'

GRAMMATICAL TABLES

Declension of Nouns. N = nominative, A = accusative, anim = animate accusative, inanim = inanimate accusative, G = genitive, D = dative, I = instrumental, P = prepositional

1 **Masculine Nouns**

	table		writer	
	singular	plural	singular	plural
N	**стол**	**столы́**	**писа́тель**	**писа́тели**
A	**стол**	**столы́**	**писа́теля**	**писа́телей**
G	**стола́**	**столо́в**	**писа́теля**	**писа́телей**
D	**столу́**	**стола́м**	**писа́телю**	**писа́телям**
I	**столо́м**	**стола́ми**	**писа́телем**	**писа́телями**
P	**столе́**	**стола́х**	**писа́теле**	**писа́телях**

	museum		Englishman	
	singular	plural	singular	plural
N	**музе́й**	**музе́и**	**англича́нин**	**англича́не**
A	**музе́й**	**музе́и**	**англича́нина**	**англича́н**
G	**музе́я**	**музе́ев**	**англича́нина**	**англича́н**
D	**музе́ю**	**музе́ям**	**англича́нину**	**англича́нам**
I	**музе́ем**	**музе́ями**	**англича́нином**	**англича́нами**
P	**музе́е**	**музе́ях**	**англича́нине**	**англича́нах**

	boy		grandfather	
	singular	plural	singular	plural
N	ма́льчик	ма́льчики	де́душка	де́душки
A	ма́льчика	ма́льчиков	де́душку	де́душек
G	ма́льчика	ма́льчиков	де́душки	де́душек
D	ма́льчику	ма́льчикам	де́душке	де́душкам
I	ма́льчиком	ма́льчиками	де́душкой	де́душками
P	ма́льчике	ма́льчиках	де́душке	де́душках

2 Feminine Nouns

	newspaper		week	
	singular	plural	singular	plural
N	газе́та	газе́ты	неде́ля	неде́ли
A	газе́ту	газе́ты	неде́лю	неде́ли
G	газе́ты	газе́т	неде́ли	неде́ль
D	газе́те	газе́там	неде́ле	неде́лям
I	газе́той	газе́тами	неде́лей	неде́лями
P	газе́те	газе́тах	неде́ле	неде́лях

	square		surname	
	singular	plural	singular	plural
N	пло́щадь	пло́щади	фами́лия	фами́лии
A	пло́щадь	пло́щади	фами́лию	фами́лии
G	пло́щади	площаде́й	фами́лии	фами́лий
D	пло́щади	площадя́м	фами́лии	фами́лиям
I	пло́щадью	площадя́ми	фами́лией	фами́лиями
P	пло́щади	площадя́х	фами́лии	фами́лиях

3 Neuter Nouns

	matter, business		exercise	
	singular	plural	singular	plural
N	де́ло	дела́	упражне́ние	упражне́ния
A	де́ло	дела́	упражне́ние	упражне́ния
G	де́ла	дел	упражне́ния	упражне́ний
D	де́лу	дела́м	упражне́нию	упражне́ниям
I	де́лом	дела́ми	упражне́нием	упражне́ниями
P	де́ле	дела́х	упражне́нии	упражне́ниях

	name, first name	
	singular	plural
N	и́мя	имена́
A	и́мя	имена́
G	и́мени	имён
D	и́мени	имена́м
I	и́менем	имена́ми
P	и́мени	имена́х

4 Pronouns

	who	what	I	you	he	she	it	we	you	they
N	кто́	что́	я	ты	о́н	она́	оно́	мы	вы	они́
A	кого́	что́	меня́	тебя́	его́	её	его́	нас	вас	их
G	кого́	чего́	меня́	тебя́	его́	её	его́	нас	вас	их
D	кому́	чему́	мне	тебе́	ему́	ей	ему́	нам	вам	им
I	кем	чем	мно́й	тобо́й	им	ей	им	на́ми	ва́ми	и́ми
P	ко́м	чём	мне	тебе́	нём	ней	нём	нас	вас	них

	this				that			
	m	f	n	pl	m	f	n	pl
N	э́тот	э́та	э́то	э́ти	то́т	та	то́	те
A	э́тот	э́ту	э́то	э́ти	то́т	ту	то́	те
A anim	э́того	э́ту	э́то	э́тих	того́	ту	то́	тех
G	э́того	э́той	э́того	э́тих	того́	то́й	того́	тех
D	э́тому	э́той	э́тому	э́тим	тому́	то́й	тому́	тем
I	э́тим	э́той	э́тим	э́тими	тем	то́й	тем	те́ми
P	э́том	э́той	э́том	э́тих	то́м	то́й	то́м	тех

380

	all				self			
	m	f	n	pl	m	f	n	pl
N	весь	вся	всё	все	сам	сама́	само́	са́ми
A	весь	всю	всё	все	сам	самоё*	само́	са́ми
A anim	всего́	всю	всё	всех	самого́	самоё*	само́	сами́х
G	всего́	всей	всего́	всех	самого́	само́й	самого́	сами́х
D	всему́	всей	всему́	всем	самому́	само́й	самому́	сами́м
I	всем	всей	всем	все́ми	сами́м	само́й	сами́м	сами́ми
P	всём	всей	всём	всех	само́м	само́й	само́м	сами́х

*or саму́

5 Adjectives

	new			
	m	f	n	pl
N	но́вый	но́вая	но́вое	но́вые
A	но́вый	но́вую	но́вое	но́вые
A anim	но́вого	но́вую	но́вое	но́вых
G	но́вого	но́вой	но́вого	но́вых
D	но́вому	но́вой	но́вому	но́вым
I	но́вым	но́вой	но́вым	но́выми
P	но́вом	но́вой	но́вом	но́вых

	Russian			
	m	f	n	pl
N	ру́сский	ру́сская	ру́сское	ру́сские
A	ру́сский	ру́сскую	ру́сское	ру́сские
A anim	ру́сского	ру́сскую	ру́сское	ру́сских
G	ру́сского	ру́сской	ру́сского	ру́сских
D	ру́сскому	ру́сской	ру́сскому	ру́сским
I	ру́сским	ру́сской	ру́сским	ру́сскими
P	ру́сском	ру́сской	ру́сском	ру́сских

good

	m	f	n	pl
N	хоро́ший	хоро́шая	хоро́шее	хоро́шие
A	хоро́ший	хоро́шую	хоро́шее	хоро́шие
A anim	хоро́шего	хоро́шую	хоро́шее	хоро́ших
G	хоро́шего	хоро́шей	хоро́шего	хоро́ших
D	хоро́шему	хоро́шей	хоро́шему	хоро́шим
I	хоро́шим	хоро́шей	хоро́шим	хоро́шими
P	хоро́шем	хоро́шей	хоро́шем	хоро́ших

last

	m	f	n	pl
N	после́дний	после́дняя	после́днее	после́дние
A	после́дний	после́днюю	после́днее	после́дние
A anim	после́днего	после́днюю	после́днее	после́дних
G	после́днего	после́дней	после́днего	после́дних
D	после́днему	после́дней	после́днему	после́дним
I	после́дним	после́дней	после́дним	после́дними
P	после́днем	после́дней	после́днем	после́дних

third

	m	f	n	pl
N	тре́тий	тре́тья	тре́тье	тре́тьи
A	тре́тий	тре́тью	тре́тье	тре́тьи
A anim	тре́тьего	тре́тью	тре́тье	тре́тьих
G	тре́тьего	тре́тьей	тре́тьего	тре́тьих
D	тре́тьему	тре́тьей	тре́тьему	тре́тьим
I	тре́тьим	тре́тьей	тре́тьим	тре́тьими
P	тре́тьем	тре́тьей	тре́тьем	тре́тьих

6 Possessives

	my (same endings for твой 'your', свой 'own')				our (same endings for ваш 'your')			
	m	f	n	pl	m	f	n	pl
N	мой	моя	моё	мои	наш	наша	наше	наши
A	мой	мою	моё	мои	наш	нашу	наше	наши
A anim	моего	мою	моё	моих	нашего	нашу	наше	наших
G	моего	моей	моего	моих	нашего	нашей	нашего	наших
D	моему	моей	моему	моим	нашему	нашей	нашему	нашим
I	моим	моей	моим	моими	нашим	нашей	нашим	нашими
P	моём	моей	моём	моих	нашем	нашей	нашем	наших

7 Numbers (See 22.3 for declensions of два/две, три, четыре, пять, шесть, восемь, сорок, пятьдесят, восемьдесят, девяносто, сто, двести, пятьсот)

	one				twenty	three hundred
	m	f	n	pl		
N	один	одна	одно	одни	двадцать	триста
A	один	одну	одно	одни	двадцать	триста
A anim	одного	одну	одно	одних	двадцать	триста
G	одного	одной	одного	одних	двадцати	трёхсот
D	одному	одной	одному	одним	двадцати	трёмстам
I	одним	одной	одним	одними	двадцатью	тремястами
P	одном	одной	одном	одних	двадцати	трёхстах

8 Verbs

The references are to lesson numbers

active participles, 29

aspects (perfective and
  imperfective), 12, 13, 14, 15

conditional, 19

future tense, 12, 14

imperatives, 15

infinitive, 4

passive participles, 27

past tense, 11, 13

present tense, 4

reflexives, 11

verbal adverbs, 28

Verb types

Type 1   **знать**' 'to know' (imperfective example), stem **зна́-**

	present	past	future	imperative
я	зна́ю	зна́л(а)	бу́ду знать	
ты	зна́ешь	зна́л(а)	бу́дешь знать	зна́й
о́н	зна́ет	зна́л	бу́дет знать	пусть зна́ет
она́	зна́ет	зна́ла	бу́дет знать	пусть зна́ет
оно́	зна́ет	зна́ло	бу́дет знать	пусть зна́ет
мы	зна́ем	зна́ли	бу́дем знать	дава́й(те) знать
вы	зна́ете	зна́ли	бу́дете знать	зна́йте
они́	зна́ют	зна́ли	бу́дут знать	пусть зна́ют

pres. active participle	зна́ющий
past active participle	зна́вший
verbal adverb	зна́я

Type 1   **прочита́ть**ᵖ 'to read' (perfective example)

	past	future	imperative
я	прочита́л(а)	прочита́ю	
ты	прочита́л(а)	прочита́ешь	прочита́й
о́н	прочита́л	прочита́ет	пусть прочита́ет
она́	прочита́ла	прочита́ет	пусть прочита́ет
оно́	прочита́ло	прочита́ет	пусть прочита́ет
мы	прочита́ли	прочита́ем	дава́й(те) прочита́ем
вы	прочита́ли	прочита́ете	прочита́йте
они́	прочита́ли	прочита́ют	пусть прочита́ют

past passive participle	прочи́тан(ный)
past active participle	прочита́вший
verbal adverb	прочита́в

Type 1 with stress on the end: same endings, except that stressed **e** turns into **ё**

встава́ть[1] 'to get up'; present tense stem **вста-**

	present	past	future	imperative
я	встаю́	встава́л(а)	бу́ду встава́ть	
ты	встаёшь	встава́л(а)	бу́дешь встава́ть	встава́й
о́н	встаёт	встава́л	бу́дет встава́ть	пусть встаёт
она́	встаёт	встава́ла	бу́дет встава́ть	пусть встаёт
оно́	встаёт	встава́ло	бу́дет встава́ть	пусть встаёт
мы	встаём	встава́ли	бу́дем встава́ть	дава́й(те) встава́ть
вы	встаёте	встава́ли	бу́дете встава́ть	встава́йте
они́	встаю́т	встава́ли	бу́дут встава́ть	пусть встаю́т

pres. active participle	**встаю́щий**
past active participle	**встава́вший**
verbal adverb	**встава́я**

Type 1B **жить**[1] 'to live', with stem ending in consonant **жив-**

	present	past	future	imperative
я	живу́	жил(а́)	бу́ду жить	
ты	живёшь	жил(а́)	бу́дешь жить	живи́
о́н	живёт	жил	бу́дет жить	пусть живёт
она́	живёт	жила́	бу́дет жить	пусть живёт
оно́	живёт	жи́ло	бу́дет жить	пусть живёт
мы	живём	жи́ли	бу́дем жить	дава́й(те) жить
вы	живёте	жи́ли	бу́дете жить	живи́те
они́	живу́т	жи́ли	бу́дут жить	пусть живу́т

pres. active participle	**живу́щий**
past active participle	**жи́вший**
verbal adverb	**живя́**

Type 2 **говори́ть** 'to speak' (imperfective example), stem **говор-**

	present	past	future	imperative
я	говорю́	говори́л(а)	бу́ду говори́ть	
ты	говори́шь	говори́л(а)	бу́дешь говори́ть	говори́
óн	говори́т	говори́л	бу́дет говори́ть	пусть говори́т
она́	говори́т	говори́ла	бу́дет говори́ть	пусть говори́т
оно́	говори́т	говори́ло	бу́дет говори́ть	пусть говори́т
мы	говори́м	говори́ли	бу́дем говори́ть	дава́й(те) говори́ть
вы	говори́те	говори́ли	бу́дете говори́ть	говори́те
они́	говоря́т	говори́ли	бу́дут говори́ть	пусть говоря́т

pres. active participle	говоря́щий
past active participle	говори́вший
verbal adverb	говоря́

THE FOUR SPELLING RULES

Rule 1 (8.3)   и instead of ы after   г, к, х, ж, ш, ч, щ

So кни́г**и** (not кни́гы) 'books'

Rule 2 (8.10)   е instead of *un*stressed о after   ж, ш, ч, щ, ц

So **с Са́шей** (not Са́шой) 'with Sasha'
(but **в Большо́м теа́тре**)

Rule 3 (12.11)   а instead of я after   г, к, х, ж, ш, ч, щ, ц

So **Они́ у́чат** (not у́чят) **ру́сский язы́к.**
They're learning Russian.

Rule 4 (12.11)   у instead of ю after   г, к, х, ж, ш, ч, щ, ц

So **Я учу́** (not учю́) **ру́сский язы́к.**
I'm learning Russian.

RUSSIAN–ENGLISH VOCABULARY

In alphabetical order: **а б в г д е ё** (**е** and **ё** are treated as one letter in dictionaries) **ж з и й к л м н о п р с т у ф х ц ч ш щ ъ ы ь э ю я**.

This is a complete list of all the words given in the main lesson vocabularies, together with other words used in examples and exercises. Its main purpose is to enable you to find words whose meaning or grammatical forms you may have forgotten or want to check. The bracketed number refers to the lesson in which the word is first used or in which there is further information.

Nouns. Gender is shown (as m, f or n) only when it is not obvious from the ending (see Lesson 3). Mobile vowels are shown in brackets, e.g. **от(é)ц**. Irregular plurals are also shown. If the noun is unpredictably used with **на** (+ prep. 'in', 'at'; + acc. 'to'), this is shown as (**на**).

Stress of nouns. Where no other information is given, e.g. **ананáс**, the stress on all forms of the words is on the same syllable as in the nominative. Where the genitive singular (gen.sg.) of a masculine noun is given (e.g. **стóл** gen.sg. **столá**), the stress is always on the *ending* of all forms. If the nominative plural (pl.) of a noun is given, with no other forms, then the singular forms have the same stress as the nominative singular and all the plural forms have the same stress as the nominative plural. For example, **гóрод** pl. **городá** means that the dative singular (dat.sg.) is **гóроду** and the dative plural (dat.pl.) is **городáм**. If only the genitive plural (gen.pl.) is shown, then the dat.pl, instrumental plural (inst.pl.) and prepositional plural (prep.pl.) have the same stress as the gen.pl., while all other forms have the same stress as the nominative singular (e.g. **звéрь** gen.pl. **звéрéй** means that the stress is on the first **е**, except in the forms **зверéй**, **зверя́м**, **зверя́ми**, **зверя́х**). A very few nouns, e.g. **лю́ди**, have different stresses in the gen.pl., dat.pl., inst.pl. and prep.pl.; for these nouns, all plural forms are given. Some f nouns (e.g. **рука́** 'hand') are stressed on the end in all forms except the accusative singular (acc. sg.) and the nom./acc.pl. They are shown thus: **рука́** acc.sg. **ру́ку**, pl. **ру́ки**.

Verbs (see Lessons 4, 11, 12, 13, 14, 15). The first and second person singular pres./fut. (the **я** and the **ты** forms) are given. The other four forms will have the same stem and stress as the **ты** form. If a verb is not normally used in the first or second person (e.g. **приходи́ться**), the third person singular (the **óн/онá/онó** form) is given instead. Any exceptions to this pattern, e.g. **мóгут** 'they can' (from **мóчь**), are also given. Unpredictable past tense and imperative forms are shown. Where the stress of the past tense is on the *ending* of *all four* forms (m, f, n and pl.), the m, f and n are given (the stress of the pl. is always the same as the n). If only the m and f forms are given, the stress of the n and pl. is the same as the f form. If only the f form is given, then the m, n and pl. forms have the same stress as the infinitive. The perfective[p] or imperfective[i] equivalent, if one exists, is given in brackets.

Abbreviations:

acc.	accusative	IVA	imperfective verbal adverb
adj	adjective	m	masculine
adv	adverb	mv	multidirectional verb (20)
anim	animate	n	neuter
coll	colloquial usage	nom.	nominative
comp	comparative	past	past tense
dat.	dative	p	perfective
dim	diminutive	pl.	plural
f	feminine	pol	polite
fam	familiar	PPP	past passive participle
fut.	future tense	prep.	prepositional
gen.	genitive	pres.	present tense
i	imperfective	PVA	perfective verbal adverb
imper	imperative	sg.	singular
inanim	inanimate	s.o.	someone
indecl	indeclinable	sth	something
inf	infinitive	T	Grammatical Table
inst.	instrumental		(see pages 378–86)
intrans	intrans	u	unidirectional verb (20)

Main list

a (3) and/but (slight contrast)

а́вгуст (17) August

авиаконве́т (10) airmail envelope

авто́бус (4) bus

а́втор (21) author

аге́нт (27) agent

администра́тор (21) administrator; hotel manager

Адмиралте́йство (29) Admiralty

а́дрес (26) pl. **адреса́** address

А́зия (18) Asia

актёр (27) actor

актри́са (27) actress

акце́нт (23) accent

Аме́рика (13) America

америка́н(е)ц (8) American (man)

америка́нка (18) gen.pl. **америка́нок** American (woman)

америка́нский (7) American (adj)

анана́с (24) pineapple

англи́йский (10) English

англича́нин (5) pl. **англича́не**, gen.pl. **англича́н** Englishman (T1)

англича́нка (3) gen.pl. **англича́нок** Englishwoman

А́нглия (5) England (also, loosely, 'Britain')

анекдо́т (18) joke, anecdote

анса́мбль (m) (29) ensemble

апельси́н (8) orange

аплоди́р/овать (27) **-ую, -уешь** (+ dat.) to applaud someone

апре́ль (m) (17) April

арка́да (29) arcade

архитекту́рный (29) architectural

атмосфе́ра (26) atmosphere

А́фрика (27) Africa

ах (18) oh

ба́бушка (19) gen.pl. **ба́бушек** grandmother

Байка́л (18) Lake Baikal

Балти́йское мо́ре (11) Baltic Sea

бана́н (10) banana

бар (18) bar

баро́кко (n indecl) (29) baroque

ба́тюшки! (30) good gracious!

ба́шня (16) gen.pl. **ба́шен** tower

бе́гать (mv) (20) **бе́гаю, бе́гаешь** to run

бегу́ see **бежа́ть**

бежа́ть (u) (20) **бегу́, бежи́шь, бегу́т** (**по-**ᵖ) to run

без (10) (+ gen.) without

бе́лый (8) white

бе́рег (18) prep. **на берегу́**, pl. **берега́** bank, shore

беспоко́иться (14) **-ко́юсь, -ко́ишься** to worry

беспоща́дно (28) mercilessly

библиоте́ка (23) library

бизнесме́н (29) businessman

биле́т (10) ticket

бифште́кс (12) **[-shteks]** meat rissole, hamburger

благогове́ние (30) reverence

ближа́йший (18) (23) next, nearest

бли́же (18) nearer

бли́зкий (18) near

блин (8) pl. **блины́** pancake

блю́до (12) pl. **блю́да** dish, course of a meal

бога́тство (29) richness, wealth

бога́тый (18) rich

бога́че (18) (comp of **бога́тый**) richer

не бо́йся see **боя́ться** don't be afraid

бока́л (21) wineglass

бо́лее (18) (22) more (forms comp of adj/adv); (+ gen.) more than (= **бо́льше**)

боле́знь (f) (11) disease

бо́льше (9) (18) (+ gen.) more; more than

бо́льше не (+ verb) no longer, no more

бо́льший (18) bigger

большинство́ (17) majority

большо́й (7) large

борода́ (28) acc. **бо́роду**, pl. **бо́роды**, gen.pl. **боро́д** beard

борщ (3) gen.sg. **борща́** beetroot soup

боя́рин (28) pl. **боя́ре** gen.pl. **бояр** boyar (powerful landowner)

боя́ться (15) **бою́сь, бои́шься** (+ gen.) to be afraid (of)

брак (22) marriage

брат (3) pl. **бра́тья** gen.pl. **бра́тьев** brother

брать (10) **беру́, берёшь** f past **брала́ (взять**ᵖ**)** to take

бра́чная па́ра (22) married couple

брести́ (u) (20) **бреду́, бредёшь** past **брёл, брела́, брело́ (по-**ᵖ**)** to plod along

брита́нский (7) British

брить (28) **бре́ю, бре́ешь (по-**ᵖ**)** to shave

бри́ться (11) **бре́/юсь, -ешься (по-**ᵖ**)** to shave oneself

броди́ть (mv) (20) **брожу́, бро́дишь** to wander

броса́/ть (25) **-ю, -ешь (бро́сить)** (+ acc.) to throw, throw away

бро́ситьᵖ (25) **бро́шу, бро́сишь (броса́ть)** (+ acc.) to throw, throw away

брю́ки (pl.) (22) gen.pl. **брюк** trousers

бу́дни (pl) (23) gen.pl. **бу́дней** weekdays

бу́дний д(е)нь (23) weekday

бу́ду, бу́дешь – see **быть**

бу́дущий (17) future (adj)

бу́дьте добры́ (12) be so good (introducing request)

бума́га (21) paper

бутербро́д (8) open sandwich

буты́лка (9) gen.pl. **буты́лок** bottle

буфе́т (10) snack bar

бы (19) (conditional particle 'would')

быва́/ть (23) **-ю, -ешь** to be (repeatedly/often)

бы́вший (16) former

бы́стро (13) quickly, fast

бы́стрый (18) quick

быт (28) way of life, everyday life

быть (11) (only pres. form **есть**; fut **бу́ду, бу́дешь**, imper **бу́дь(те)**; past **был, была́, бы́ло** to be

бюро́ (17) (n indecl) office

в (4) + prep.; + acc. (+prep.) in; (+ acc.) to (a place)

ваго́н (20) carriage

ва́жный (13) important

валю́та (24) currency, hard currency

валю́тный (9) currency, foreign currency (adj)

вам, ва́ми – see **вы** (T4) you

ва́нная (f adj) (7) bathroom

Ва́ня (m) (3) Vanya (familiar form of Ivan)

варе́нье (16) jam, preserves

вас – see **вы** (T4) you

ваш (6) your (T6)

вдруг (13) suddenly

вегетариа́н(е)ц (12) (male) vegetarian

вегетариа́нка (9) g.pl. **вегетариа́нок** (female) vegetarian

вегетариа́нский (12) vegetarian (adj)

ве́домство (30) department

веду́, веде́шь see **вести́** lead

ведь (9) you know/isn't it/aren't you etc. (indicating that the speaker expects agreement)

вез/ти́ (u) (20) **-зу́, -ёшь**, past **вёз, везла́, везло́ (по-ᵖ)** to transport

век pl. **века́** (17) century

вёл, вела́ – see **вести́** led

вели́кий (11) great

Великобрита́ния (27) Great Britain

великоле́пный (29) magnificent

вели́чественно-прекра́сный (29) majestically beautiful

вельмо́жа (30) grandee, big shot

ве́рить (21) **ве́рю, ве́ришь (по-ᵖ)** to believe (+ dat. = s.o.) (**в** + acc. = in s.o. or sth)

верн/у́тьсяᵖ (14) **-у́сь, -ёшься** (**возвраща́ться**) to return, come back

ве́рный (29) true; faithful

весёлый (18) cheerful

весна́ pl. **вёсны** gen.pl. **вёсен** spring

вести́ (u) (20) **веду́, веде́шь**, past **вёл, вела́, вело́ (по-ᵖ)** to lead

весь (11) (see T4) all

ве́т(е)р (27) gen.sg. **ве́тра** wind

ветчина́ (30) ham

ве́чер (16) pl. **вечера́** evening; evening party

вече́рний (7) evening (adj)

ве́чером (15) in the evening

вещь (f) (10) gen.pl. **веще́й** thing

взгляд (21) view, opinion; look

взятьᵖ (12) **возьму́, возьме́шь** past **взял, взяла́, взя́ло (брать)** to take

вид (18) view; form

ви́деть (11) **ви́жу, ви́дишь (у-ᵖ)** to see

ви́за (23) visa

вино́ (3) pl. **ви́на** wine

ви́шня (30) gen.pl. **ви́шен** cherry

включа́/ть (21) **-ю, -ешь** (**включи́ть**ᵖ) (+ acc.) to switch on, plug in; to include

включ/и́тьᵖ (21) (27) **-у́, -и́шь** see **включа́ть**

вку́сный (8) tasty

вла́сть (f) (24) gen.pl. **власте́й** power

вла́сти (24) gen.pl. **власте́й** authorities

влета́/ть (20) **-ю, -ешь** (**влете́ть**ᵖ) to fly in

влете́тьᵖ (20) **влечу́, влети́шь** – see **влета́ть**

вме́сте (16) (**с** + inst.) together (with)

вме́сто (16) (+ gen.) instead of

вме́сто того́ чтобы (21) (+ inf) instead of (doing something)

вниз (15) down

внима́ние (24) attention

во вре́мя (17) (+ gen.) during

во = **в** before **в/ф** + consonant (+ prep.) in; (+ acc.) to (a place)

вода́ (8) acc.sg. **во́ду**, pl. **во́ды**, dat.pl. **вода́м** water

води́ть (mv) (20) **вожу́, во́дишь** to take on foot, lead

во́дка (3) vodka

вое́нно-морско́е де́ло (28) naval matters, naval science

вое́нный (28) military

возвраща/тьсяᶦ (14) **-юсь, -ешься**
  (**верну́ться**ᵖ) to return, come back
возвраще́ние (26) return
возвыша́/тьсяᶦ (29) **-ется** to tower
вози́тьᶦ (mv) (20) **вожу́, во́зишь** to
  transport
возмо́жность (f) (13) possibility,
  opportunity
возмо́жный (27) possible
возража́/тьᶦ (14) **-ю, -ешь**
  (**возрази́ть**ᵖ) to object
возра/зи́тьᵖ (14) **-жу́, -зи́шь** – see
  возража́тьᶦ
война́ (14) pl. **во́йны** war
войти́ᵖ (13) **войду́, войдёшь** past
  вошёл, вошла́, вошло́ (входи́тьᶦ**)**
  to enter
вокза́л (5) **(на)** station, terminus
Воло́дя (m) (3) Volodia (fam form of
  Vladimir)
во́н там (5) over there
вообще́ (13) altogether, totally
вопро́с (27) question
воро́та (n.pl.) (29) gen.pl. **воро́т** gates
восемна́дцать (22.3) eighteen
во́семь (22.3) eight
во́семьдесят (22.3) eighty
восемьсо́т (22.3) eight hundred
восклѝкн/утьᵖ (30) **-у, -ешь**
  (**восклица́ть**ᶦ) to exclaim
воскресе́нье (17) gen.pl.
  воскресе́ний Sunday
воспи́тыва/тьᶦ (19) **-ю, -ешь** (+ acc.)
  to bring up (s.o.)
восста́ние (28) uprising
восто́к (18) **(на)** east
восто́рженно (30) enthusiastically
восто́чный (18) eastern
во́т (3) here/there (when pointing)

во́т почему́ (13) that is why
вошёл, вошла́ – see **войти́** entered
впервы́е (27) for the first time
вперёд (20) forward
впечатля́ющий (29) impressive
врач (16) gen.sg. **врача́** doctor
вре́дно (14) harmful, it's harmful
вре́мя (9) gen.sg. **вре́мени**, gen.pl.
  времён time
вро́де (30) (+ gen.) like
вряд ли (21) hardly, unlikely
все (11) (pl. of **весь** 'all' T4) everybody
всё (10) (see **весь** 'all' T4) everything
всё (25) (**всё вре́мя**) all the time
всё равно́ (11) all the same; it's all the
  same
всегда́ (18) always
всего́ (10) (also gen. of **весь** T4) in
  all/only
всё-таки (19) nevertheless
вска́кива/тьᶦ (25) **-ю, -ешь**
  (**вскочи́ть**ᵖ) to jump in/up
вско́ре (28) soon
вскочи́тьᵖ (25) **вскочу́, вско́чишь**
  (**вска́кивать**ᶦ) to jump in/up
вспомина́/тьᶦ (13) **-ю, -ешь**
  (**вспо́мнить**ᵖ) (+ acc. or **о** + prep.)
  to recall
вспо́мн/итьᵖ (13) **-ю, -ишь** see
  вспомина́тьᶦ
встава́тьᶦ (16) **встаю́, встаёшь**,
  imper **встава́й(те)** (**встать**ᵖ) to get
  up
встатьᵖ (16) **вста́ну, вста́нешь**
  (**встава́ть**ᶦ) to get up
встре́/титьсяᵖ (19) **-чусь, -тишься**
  (**встреча́ться**ᶦ) (**с** + inst.) to meet
  (s.o.)
встре́ча (23) meeting

встреча/ться¹ (19) **-юсь, -ешся**
(встре́титься¹) (**с** + inst.) to meet
(s.o.)

вто́рник (17) Tuesday

второ́й (7) second

вхо́д (19) (**в** + acc.) entrance (to)

входи́ть¹ (13) **вхожу́, вхо́дишь**
(войти́ᵖ) to enter

вчера́ (10) yesterday

въездны́е воро́та (n pl.) (29)
entrance gates

вы (4) (see T4) you

выбега/ть¹ (20) **-ю, -ешь**
(вы́бежать⁰) to run out

вы́бежать⁰ (20) **вы́бегу, вы́бежишь,**
вы́бегут – see выбега́ть¹

вы́брать⁰ (27) **вы́беру, вы́берешь**
(выбира́/ть¹ **-ю, -ешь**) (+ acc.) to
choose

выгля́дыва/ть¹ (30) **-ю, -ешь**
(вы́глян/уть⁰ **-у, -ешь**) to look out

выда/ва́ться¹ (29) **-юсь, -ёшься**
(вы́даться⁰) to project, stand out

выдаю́щийся (28) outstanding;
projecting

вы́ехать⁰ (28) **вы́еду, вы́едешь**
(выезжа́ть¹) to leave (by transport)

вы/звать⁰ (21) **-зову, -зовешь**
(вызыва́ть¹) to summon

вызыва́/ть¹ (21) **-ю, -ешь** (вы́звать⁰)
(+ acc.) to summon

вы́йти⁰ (15) **вы́йду, вы́йдешь** past
вы́шел, вы́шла, imper **вы́йди(те)**
(выходи́ть¹) to go out

вылета́/ть¹ (20) **-ю, -ешь** (вы́лететь⁰)
to fly out

вы́ле/теть⁰ (20) **-чу, -тишь** – see
вылета́ть¹

вы́ложить⁰ (28) **-у, -ишь**

(выкла́дывать¹) to spread out

вы́нудить⁰ (27) **вы́нужу, вы́нудишь,**
(вынужда́/ть¹ **-ю, -ешь**) to force

вы́нужден (27) PPP of **вы́нудить**
forced

вы́пить⁰ (12) **вы́пью, вы́пьешь**
(пить¹) (+ acc.) to have a drink

выраже́ние (21) expression

вы́са/диться⁰ (29) **-жусь, -дишься**
(выса́живаться¹ (29)) to
disembark, land

выса́жива/ться¹ (29) **-юсь, -ешься** –
see вы́садиться⁰

вы́ска/заться⁰ (27) **-жусь, -жешься**
(выска́зыва/ться¹ **-юсь, -ешься**)
(**за** + acc.) to speak for/in favour of

выска́кива/ть¹ (25) **-ю, -ешь**
(вы́скочить⁰) to jump out

вы́скоч/ить⁰ (25) **-у, -ишь**
(выска́кивать¹) to jump out

высо́кий (18) tall

выступа́/ть¹ (29) **-ю, -ешь**
(вы́ступить⁰) to project, stick out,
step out

выступа́ющий (29) projecting

вы́тян/уться⁰ (30) **-усь, -ешься** to
stretch; to stand erect

вы́учить⁰ (13) **вы́учу, вы́учишь**
(учи́ть¹) (+ acc.) to master

выходи́ть¹ (15) **выхожу́, выхо́дишь**
(вы́йти⁰) to go out

вы́ход (15) exit

выходно́й день (17) day off

вы́ше (18) taller

вы́ясн/ить⁰ (28) **-ю, -ишь**
(выясня́ть¹) to find out, establish

газе́та (3) newspaper

гармони́чный (29) harmonious

гастро́ли (f pl.) (26) **гастро́лей** (theatre) tour

гастроно́м (17) food shop

где (3) where

где́-нибудь (26) anywhere

где́-то (26) somewhere

генера́л (27) general

Герма́ния (20) Germany

геро́й (21) gen.pl. **геро́ев** hero

гид (16) guide (person)

гимнази́ст (30) grammar-school boy

гимна́зия (30) grammar school

гита́ра (16) guitar

глава́ (28) pl. **гла́вы** chief, chapter

гла́вный (7) main

глаз (25) pl. **глаза́** gen.pl. **глаз** eye

глаз(о́)к (25) pl. **гла́зки** little eye

глу́бже (18) comp of **глубо́кий** deeper

глубо́кий (18) deep

глу́пый (29) stupid, silly

гля/де́ть (25) **-жу́, -ди́шь (по-ᴾ) (на** + acc.) to look (at)

гнать (u) (20) **гоню́, го́нишь,** past **гнала́ (по-ᴾ)** (+ acc.) to chase, drive

гне́вный (21) angry

говори́ть (4) **-ю, -и́шь (по-ᴾ; сказа́тьᴾ)** to speak, say

год (6) prep. **в году́,** gen.pl. **лет,** dat.pl. **года́м** year

годовщи́на (14) anniversary

Голла́ндия (28) Holland

голова́ (28) acc. **го́лову,** pl. **го́ловы,** gen.pl. **голо́в** head

голо́вка (28) gen.pl. **голо́вок** little head

голо́вка лу́ка (28) an onion (**лук** onion, onions)

го́лос (14) pl. **голоса́** voice

голу́бчик (30) dear friend, my dear

гоня́/ть (mv) (20) **-ю, -ешь** (+ acc.) to chase, drive

гора́ (18) acc. **го́ру,** pl. **го́ры,** dat.pl. **гора́м** hill; mountain

гора́здо (18) much (with comparatives)

го́рничная (f adj) (21) maid

го́род (7) pl. **города́** town, city

горя́чий (8) hot

го́споди! (30) good heavens! good Lord!

гости́ница (4) hotel

гость (m) (12) gen.pl. **госте́й** guest **быть в гостя́х у** (+ gen.) to be visiting s.o. **идти́ в го́сти к** + dat., to go to visit s.o.

госуда́рственный (28) state, belonging to the state

гото́в/а/о/ы (29) (short adj) ready

гото́в/ить (16) **-лю, -ишь (при-ᴾ)** (+ acc.) to prepare; to cook

грамм (9) gen.pl. **гра́ммов** or **грамм** gram(me)

грани́ца (18) border **за грани́цей** (21) (28) abroad (place) **за грани́цу** (21) (28) abroad (motion)

гриб (12) pl. **грибы́** mushroom

грибно́й (28) mushroom (adj)

гро́мкий (14) loud

гру́ппа (24) group

гря́зный (20) dirty

грязь (f) (11) prep. sg. **в грязи́** mud

губа́ (30) pl. **гу́бы,** dat. pl. **губа́м** lip

гуля́/ть (17) **-ю, -ешь (по-ᴾ)** to take a walk

гу́ща (30) grounds, dregs

да (3) yes

дава́ть' (12) **даю́, даёшь,** imper
дава́й(те) (датьᵖ**)** to give

давно́ (13) long ago, since long ago

да́же (14) even

да́йте (8) give (imperative')

далёкий (18) far

далеко́ (12) (**от** + gen.) far (from)

да́льше (16) further, onwards

датьᵖ (12) **дам, дашь, даст, дади́м,
дади́те, даду́т,** past **дал, дала́,
да́ло (дава́ть')** to give

два (m and n)/**две** (f) (22.3) two

два́дцать (22.3) twenty

двена́дцать (22.3) twelve

дверь (f) (3) prep.sg. **в двери́,** gen.pl.
двере́й door

две́сти (22.3) two hundred

дво́е (22.10) two

двор (26) gen.sg. **двора́** yard,
courtyard; royal court

двор(е́)ц (29) gen.pl. **дворцо́в**
palace

Дворцо́вая пло́щадь (29) Palace
Square

дворяни́н (28) pl. **дворя́не** gen.pl.
дворя́н member of nobility or gentry

двух – gen. of **два/две**

де́вочка (25) dim of **де́ва** 'maid' little
girl

де́вушка (9) gen.pl. **де́вушек** girl

девяно́сто (22.3) ninety

девятна́дцать (22.3) nineteen

де́вять (22.3) nine

девятьсо́т (22.3) nine hundred

де́душка (m) (6) gen.pl. **де́душек**
grandfather

дека́брь (m) gen.sg. **декабря́**
December

дека́н (19) dean (of university or
insititute)

деко́р (29) decoration

де́ла/ть' (8) **-ю, -ешь (с-**ᵖ**)** (+ acc.)
to do; to make

де́ло (19) pl. **дела́** matter

де́ло в то́м, что́ . . . (13) the thing is
that . . .

д(е)нь (m) (3) day

день рожде́ния (17) birthday

де́ньги (pl.) (8) gen.pl. **де́нег,** dat.pl.
деньга́м money

департа́мент (30) (old word)
(government) department

дере́вня (19) gen.pl. **дереве́нь**
village; country (opposite of town)

де́рево (26) pl. **дере́вья** gen.pl.
дере́вьев tree; wood (material)

де́сять (22.3) ten

де́ти (10) (sg. **ребён(о)к**) gen. **дете́й,**
dat. **де́тям,** inst. **детьми́,** prep.
де́тях children

де́тская площа́дка (26) children's
playground

де́тство (17) childhood

деше́вле (18) cheaper

дешёвый (18) cheap

дире́ктор (23) pl. **директора́**
director

дли́нный (18) long

для (10) (+ gen.) for (benefit, purpose)

до (9) (+ gen.) as far as; until

до свида́ния (3) goodbye

до тако́й сте́пени to such a degree

доба́в/итьᵖ (28) **-лю, -ишь
(добавля́ть')** (+ acc.) to add

добавля́/ть' **-ю, -ешь** – see
доба́витьᵖ

добива́/ться' (28) **-юсь -ешься**

(**доби́ться**ᴾ) (+ gen.) to work for, achieve

доби́тьсяᴾ (28) **добью́сь, добьёшься** – see **добива́ться**

до́брый (7) good, kind

до́брый день (3) good day

дово́льно (15) fairly, quite

догова́рива/тьсяᴵ (19) **-юсь, -ешься** (**с** + gen.) to reach an agreement (with s.o.)

договор/и́тьсяᴾ (19) **-ю́сь, и́шься** (**с** + inst.) – see **догова́риваться**ᴵ

доезжа́/тьᴵ (20) **-ю, -ешь** (**дое́хать**ᴾ) (**до** + gen.) to reach, go as far as

дое́хатьᴾ (20) **дое́ду, дое́дешь** – see **доезжа́ть**ᴵ

до́ждь (11) (m) gen.sg. **дождя́** rain

дойти́ᴾ (15) **дойду́, дойдёшь,** past **дошёл, дошла́, дошло́** (**доходи́ть**ᴵ) (**до** + gen.) to reach (on foot)

до́лго (11) for a long time

долета́/тьᴵ (20) **-ю, -ешь** (**долете́ть**ᴾ) to reach by flying

долете́тьᴾ (20) **долечу́, долети́шь** – see **долета́ть**ᴵ

до́лжен/должна́/должно́/должны́ (19) obliged, must

должно́ быть (19) probably ('must be')

до́ллар (9) dollar

до́м (3) pl. **дома́** house

до́ма (7) at home

домо́й (4) home, to one's home

доро́га (25) road

дорого́й (8) dear, expensive

доро́жка (25) (dim of **доро́га**) gen.pl. **доро́жек** little road

дос/лужи́тьсяᴾ (30) **-ужу́сь, -у́жишься**

to reach a position, reach the top

достава́тьᴵ (18) **достаю́, достаёшь** – see **доста́ть**ᴾ

доста́точно (19) (+ gen.) enough (of something)

доста́/тьᴾ (18) **-ну, -ешь** (**достава́ть**ᴵ) (+ acc.) to get hold of, obtain; to reach

дох/оди́тьᴵ (15) **-ожу́, -о́дишь** (**дойти́**ᴾ) (**до** + gen.) to reach

до́чка (16) gen.pl. **до́чек** (little) daughter

до́чь (f) (5.6) gen.sg. **до́чери** gen.pl. **дочере́й**, inst.pl. **дочерьми́** daughter

дошёл, дошла́ – see **дойти́** reached

дразн/и́тьᴵ (30) **-ю, -и́шь** (+ acc.) to tease (s.o.)

дре́вний (18) ancient

дру́г (8) pl. **друзья́,** gen.pl. **друзе́й** friend

дру́г дру́га (30) each other

дру́жба (1) friendship

друзья́ pl. of **дру́г** friends

ду́ма/тьᴵ (19) **-ю, -ешь** (**по-**ᴾ) to think

душо́н(о)к (30) swell, smart lad

духово́й шкаф (28) oven

дя́дя (m) (3) gen.pl. **дя́дей** uncle

европе́(е)ц (28) European (noun)

европеиза́ция (28) Europeanization

европе́йский (21) European

его́ (indecl) (6) **[ye-vó]** his/its

его́, ему́ – see **о́н** (T4) him

еди́м, еди́те, едя́т see **е́сть**ᴵ eat

еди́нственно (27) only

е́ду, е́дешь see **е́хать**

её (indecl) (6) her (possessive)

её, ей see **она́** (T4) her (pronoun)

е́здить' (mv) (20) **е́зжу, е́здишь** to go
(by transport)

ем, ешь, ест see **есть**' eat

е́сли (8) if

есть (7) (8) is/are

есть' (12) **ем ешь ест еди́м еди́те
едя́т** past **ел, е́ла,** imper **е́шь(те)
(съесть**ᵖ**)** (+ acc.) to eat

е́хать' (u) (4) (2) **е́ду, е́дешь (по-**ᵖ**)** to
go (by transport)

ещё (9) yet; still; more

ещё раз (15) again

жа́лко (14) it's a pity; to grudge

жа́лованье (30) (old word) salary

жа́л/оваться' (21) **-уюсь, -уешься
(по-**ᵖ**) (на** + acc.) to complain
(about)

жаль (14) it's a pity

жа́рко (14) hot (of weather), it's hot

жда́ть' (15) **жду, ждёшь,** f past
ждала́ (подо-ᵖ**)** (+ acc./+ gen.) to
wait (for s.o./sth)

же (5) (emphasizes previous word)

жела́/ть' (21) **-ю, -ешь (по-**ᵖ**)** (+ gen.)
to wish

желе́зная доро́га (30) railway ('iron
road')

жена́ (6) pl. **жёны,** gen.pl. **жён** dat.pl.
жёнам wife

жена́т (30) (short adj) married (of a
man)

жени́ться'/ᵖ (28) **женю́сь, же́нишься**
to marry (of a man)

же́нский (15) female

же́нщина (14) woman

живи́тельная вла́га (30) (coll)
intoxicating liquor

жизнь (f) (19) life

жир (28) prep.sg. **в жиру́,** pl. **жиры́**
fat, grease

жи́тель (m) (9) inhabitant

жить' (4) **живу́, живёшь,** f past **жила́
(прожи́ть**ᵖ**)** to live

журна́л (1) magazine

журнали́ст (13) journalist

журнали́стка (27) gen.pl.
журнали́сток female journalist

за (+ acc.) (6) for (in return for);
behind (motion)

за (+ inst.) (16) behind (place),
beyond; for (to fetch)

Забайка́лье (19) region beyond (**за**)
Lake Baikal

забега́/ть (20) **-ю, -ешь (забежа́ть**ᵖ**)**
to call in (running)

забежа́тьᵖ (20) **забегу́, забежи́шь,
забегу́т** – see **забега́ть**'

забыва́/ть' (13) **-ю, -ешь (забы́ть**ᵖ**)**
(+ acc.) to forget

забы́тьᵖ (13) **забу́ду, забу́дешь
(забыва́ть**'**)** (+ acc.) to forget

заверн/у́тьᵖ (19) **-у́, -ёшь
(завора́чива/ть**' **-ю, -ешь) (за** +
acc.) to turn (round sth)

зави́довать' (23) **зави́ду/ю, -ешь
(по-**ᵖ**)** (+ dat.) to envy (someone)

зави́/сеть' (19) **-шу́, -сишь (от** + gen.)
to depend (on)

заво́д (16) **(на)** factory

завора́чива/ть' (19) **-ю, -ешь
(заверну́ть**ᵖ**)** to turn (a corner); to
wrap

за́втра (6) tomorrow

за́втрак (16) breakfast

за́втрака/ть' (16) **-ю, -ешь (по-**ᵖ**)** to
breakfast

за́говор (28) plot

задава́тьᶦ (27) **задаю́, задаёшь
(зада́ть**ᵖ**)** to set, pose

зада́тьᵖ (27) like **дать,** past **за́дал,
задала́, за́дало (задава́ть**ᶦ**)** to set,
pose

зада́ть вопро́с (27) to ask a question

заезжа́тьᶦ (23) **-ю, -ешь** – see
зае́хатьᵖ

зае́хатьᵖ (23) **зае́ду, зае́дешь
(заезжа́ть**ᶦ**) (к** + dat.) to call on
someone (by transport)

заинтересова́тьсяᵖ – see
интересова́тьсяᶦ

зай/ти́ᵖ (20) **-ду́, дёшь,** past **зашёл,
зашла́, зашло́ (заходи́ть**ᶦ**)** to call in

зака́з (27) order (for goods or
services)

заказа́тьᵖ (23) **закажу́, зака́жешь
(зака́зывать**ᶦ**)** (+ acc.) to order (sth)

зака́зыва/тьᶦ (23) **-ю, -ешь** – see
заказа́тьᵖ

закрич/а́тьᵖ (20) **-у́, -и́шь (крича́ть**ᶦ**)**
to shout, start shouting

закрыва́/тьᶦ (17) **-ю, -ешь (закры́ть**ᵖ**)**
to close

закр/ы́тьᵖ (17) **-о́ю, -о́ешь** – see
закрыва́тьᶦ

закури́тьᵖ (15) **закурю́, заку́ришь
(кури́ть**ᶦ**)** to smoke, light a cigarette

замени́тьᵖ (28) **заменю́, заме́нишь
(заменя́/ть**ᶦ **-ю, -ешь)** to replace

замести́тель (m) (23) deputy

замеча́тельный (17) remarkable

за́муж (29): **выходи́ть/вы́йти**ᵖ
за́муж за (+ acc.) to marry (of a
woman)

занима́/тьᶦ (18) **-ю, -ешь (заня́ть**ᵖ**)** to
occupy (something)

занима́/тьсяᶦ (16) **-юсь, -ешься**
(+ inst.) to study (something)

за́нят (25) (m)**/занята́** (f)**/за́нято**
(n)**/за́няты** (pl.) occupied, busy

заня́тьᵖ (18) **займу́, займёшь,** past
за́нял, заняла́, за́няло (+ acc.) to
occupy

за́пад (18) **(на)** west

за́падный (7) western

запа́с (18) stock, reserve

запека́ние (28) baking

записа́тьᵖ (19) **запишу́, запи́шешь
(запи́сывать**ᶦ**)** (+ acc.) to note down

запи́ска (15) gen.pl. **запи́сок** note

запи́сыва/тьᶦ (19) **-ю, -ешь
(записа́ть**ᵖ**)** (+ acc.) to note down

запла́катьᵖ – see **пла́кать**ᶦ to start
crying

зарубе́жный (17) foreign

заседа́ние (28) **(на)** meeting, sitting

засме/я́тьсяᵖ (13) **-ю́сь, -ёшься
(смея́ться**ᶦ**)** to start laughing

застегн/у́тьᵖ (30) **-у́, -ёшь
(застёгивать**ᶦ**)** (+ acc.) to fasten

засто́лье (26) party

зате́м (17) then, next

захихи́ка/тьᵖ (30) **-ю, -ешь
(хихи́кать**ᶦ**)** to giggle, start giggling

заходи́тьᶦ (20) **захожу́, захо́дишь
(зайти́**ᵖ**)** to call in

захоте́тьᵖ see **хоте́ть**ᶦ to begin to
want

защи/ти́тьᵖ (22) **-щу́, -ти́шь
(защища́ть**ᶦ**)** (+ acc.) to defend
(s.o.)

защища́/тьᶦ (22) **-ю, -ешь (защити́ть**ᵖ**)**
(+ acc.) to defend (s.o.)

заяви́тьᵖ (21) **заявлю́, зая́вишь
(заявля́ть**ᶦ**)** to announce

заявля/ть¹ (21) **-ю, -ешь (заяви́ть**ᵖ**)** to announce

заявле́ние (22) application

звать¹ (4) **зову́, зовёшь,** f past **звала́ (по-**ᵖ**)** (+ acc.) to call (s.o.)

звезда́ (30) pl. **звёзды,** gen.pl. **звёзд** star

зверь (m) (18) gen.pl. **звере́й** (wild) animal

звон/и́ть¹ (12) **-ю́, -и́шь (**coll **зво́нишь) (по-**ᵖ**)** (+ dat.) to telephone (s.o.)

звуча́ть¹ (23) **звучи́т** to sound

зда́ние (15) building

здесь (4) here

здоро́вье (26) health

здра́вствуй(те) (3) hello

земля́ (2) acc. sg. **зе́млю,** pl. **зе́мли,** gen.pl. **земе́ль,** dat.pl. **зе́млям** earth, land

зима́ (16) acc. sg. **зи́му,** pl. **зи́мы,** dat.pl. **зима́м** winter

зи́мний (7) winter

знако́мая (f adj) (26) female acquaintance

знако́м/ить (16) **-лю, -ишь (по-**ᵖ**)** (+ acc. + inst.) to acquaint someone with, to introduce someone to

знако́м/иться¹ (по-ᵖ**) -люсь, -ишься** + inst. to become acquainted with, to meet

знако́мство (26) acquaintanceship, first meeting

знако́мый (m adj) (26) male acquaintance

знамени́тый (7) famous

знать¹ (4) **зна́ю, зна́ешь** (+ acc.) to know

значе́ние (24) meaning, significance

зна́чит (10) so (that means)

зову́т see **звать** (they) call

зо́лото (18) gold

и (4) and

игра́ть¹ (16) **-ю, -ешь (сыгра́ть**ᵖ**)** to play

идти́¹ (u) (6) **иду́, идёшь,** past **шёл, шла (пойти́**ᵖ**)** to go (on foot)

из (10) (+ gen.) out of, from

изба́ (25) pl. **и́збы,** gen.pl. **изб** peasant cottage

изве́стно (22) it is known

изве́стный (27) well-known

извини́те (11) **за** (+ acc.) excuse me for

извин/и́тьсяᵖ (19) **-ю́сь, -и́шься (извиня́ться¹) (за** + acc.) to apologize (for)

извиня́/ться¹ (19) **-ю́сь, -ешься (извини́ться**ᵖ**) (за** + acc.) to apologize (for)

изда/ва́ть (28) **-ю́, -ёшь (и́зда́ть**ᵖ (+ acc.) to publish

изда́тельство (23) publishing house

изда́тьᵖ (28) (like **дать**) **(издава́ть¹)** (+ acc.) to publish

из-за (11) (30) (+ gen.) because of; from behind

изум/и́тьсяᵖ (30) **-лю́сь, -и́шься (изумля́/ться**ᵖ **-ю́сь, -ешься)** to be astonished

изуча́/ть¹ (4) (13) **-ю, -ешь (изучи́ть**ᵖ**)** (+ acc.) to study

изучи́тьᵖ (13) **изучу́, изу́чишь (изуча́ть¹)** (+ acc.) to master

ико́рка (25) dim of **икра́**

икра́ (25) caviare (fish roe)

и́ли (9) or

име́/ть[i] (10) **-ю, -ешь** (+ acc.) to have (+ abstract noun)

и́мя (n) (6) gen.sg. **и́мени**, pl. **имена́** (T4) forename, first name

инжене́р (16) engineer

инициати́ва (22) initiative

инициа́тор (22) initiator

иногда́ (9) sometimes

иностра́н(е)ц (16) foreigner

иностра́нный (10) foreign

институ́т (5) institute

интере́с (16) interest

интере́сно (14) (it's interesting

интере́сный (7) interesting

интерес/ова́ться[i] (16) **-у́юсь, -у́ешься** (за-[p]) (+ inst.) to be interested (in)

иска́ть[i] (11) **ищу́, и́щешь (по-**[p]**)** (+ acc. or gen.) to look for, to seek

исключ/и́ть[p] (27) **-у́, -и́шь** (**исключа́ть**[i]) to exclude

и́скра (30) spark

искрив/и́ться[p] (30) **-лю́сь, -и́шься** (**искривля́ться**[i]) to become distorted, to twist

испо́лненный (29) executed, carried out

испуга́/ться[p] (25) **-юсь, -ешься** (**пуга́ться**[i]) (+ gen.) to take fright (at)

иссле́дование (22) investigation, research

исто́рия (16) history

их (indecl) (6) their

их, им, и́ми see **они́** (T4) them

ищу́, и́щешь see **иска́ть**

ию́ль (m) (17) July

ию́нь (m) (17) June

к (12) (+ dat.) to (a person), towards

ка́ждый (9) each, every

ка́жется (11) (from **каза́ться**) it seems, I think

каза́ться[i] (11) **кажу́сь, ка́жешься** (**по-**[p]) to seem

казённый (30) state, state-owned

казни́ть[i]/[p] (28) to execute

как (4) how

как бы (30) as it were

как раз (20) exactly, just

како́й (7) what kind of

како́й-нибудь (26) any kind of

како́й-то (26) some kind of

ка́к-то (26) somehow

кампа́ния (27) campaign

капу́ста (12) (no pl.) cabbage

каранда́ш (16) gen.sg. **карандаша́** pencil

ка́рта (10) map

карто́нка (30) gen.pl. **карто́нок** cardboard box

карто́фель (m) (no pl.) potatoes

каса́/ться[i] (21) **-юсь, -ешься** (**косну́ться**[p]) (+gen.) to touch (sth); to concern

что́ каса́ется (+ gen.) as for ('what concerns')

ка́сса (1) cash desk/ticket office

кастрю́ля (28) gen.pl. **кастрю́ль** saucepan

ката́/ть[i] (mv)(20) **-ю, -ешь** to roll

кати́ть[i] (u) (20) **качу́, ка́тишь (по-**[p]) to roll

каче́ли (pl) (26) gen.pl. **каче́лей** swings

ка́чество (28) quality

в ка́честве (28) (+ gen.) as ('in the quality of')

ка́ша (16) kasha, Russian porridge

кварти́ра (7) flat, apartment

ква́шеный (28) sour, fermented

кем – see **кто**

кефи́р (8) fermented milk drink

кило́ (n indecl) (8) kilo (gram)

килогра́мм (8) kilogram

кино́ (n indecl) (11) cinema

кинотеа́тр (20) cinema

кинофестива́ль (m) (27) film festival

кио́ск (1) kiosk

кипят(о́)к (21) boiling water

кипя́щий (28) boiling

кислота́ (30) pl. **кисло́ты** acidity, sourness

кита́(е)ц (30) pl. **кита́йцы** Chinese (n.)

Кита́й (18) China

класс (30) class, form

клие́нт (15) client

кни́га (7) book

кни́жка (30) (dim of **кни́га**) gen.pl. **кни́жек** small book, some book

ко = **к** before **к** + consonant, **мне** and **всей/всем/всему́**

когда́ (5) when

когда́-нибудь (26) ever; sometime (in the future)

когда́-то (26) sometime

кого́ [ka-vó] – acc./gen. of **кто**

ко́е-где (26) here and there

ко́е-как (26) (30) badly, sloppily; with difficulty

ко́е-каки́е (pl.) (26) certain, some

ко́е-что (26) something, some things

колбаса́ (8) (no pl.) salami

коле́но (28) pl. **коле́ни** gen.pl. **коле́ней** knee

коли́чество (22) quantity

колле́жский асе́ссор (30) collegiate assessor (eighth grade in fourteen-grade tsarist civil sevice)

коло́нна (29) column, pillar

ко́м - prep. of **кто**

командиро́вка (19) (**в** 'on') gen.pl. **командиро́вок** business or study trip, assignment

коммуни́зм (29) Communism

ко́мната (14) room

компа́ния (14) (27) company; company, firm

кому́ – dat. of **кто**

конве́рт (10) envelope

кон(е́)ц (18) gen.sg. **конца́** end

коне́чно (10) **[ka-nyésh-na]** of course

конта́кт (23) contact

контра́кт (23) contract

конфли́кт (22) conflict

конце́рт (11) **(на)** concert

конча́/ть (13) **-ю, -ешь (ко́нч/ить**[р] **-у, -ишь)** to finish

конья́к (25) gen.sg. **коньяка́** cognac, brandy

копе́йка (9) gen.pl. **копе́ек** kopeck (1/100th of a rouble)

кора́бль (m) (28) gen.sg. **корабля́** ship

коро́ль (m) (27) gen.sg. **короля́** king

коро́ткий (18) (23) short

коро́че (18) shorter

косн/у́ться[р] (21) **-ну́сь, -ёшься (каса́ться')** (+ gen.) to touch

котле́ты по-ки́евски (12) Chicken Kiev (**котле́та** cutlet)

кото́рый (18) who/which

ко́фе (m indecl) (5) coffee

кофе́йный (30) coffee (adj)

краса́в(е)ц (30) handsome man

краси́во (14) it's attractive

краси́вый (7) beautiful, attractive

кра́сный (7) red

красота́ (11) beauty

Кремль (m) (7) g.sg. **Кремля** the Kremlin (fortress)

крепкий (18) strong

крепко (26) firmly, strongly

крепостничество (28) serfdom

крепостной (m adj) (28) serf

крепче (18) stronger

крестьянин (11) pl **крестьяне** gen.pl. **крестьян** peasant

крич/ать' (20) -**ý**, -**ишь** (за-ᴾ) to shout

кровать (f) (21) bed

кроме (10) (+ gen.) apart from, except

кроме того (12) also, in addition

крыло (29) pl. **крылья**, gen.pl. **крыльев** wing

Крым (5) prep. **в Крыму** Crimea

крымский (12) Crimean

кто (5) (T4) who

кто-нибудь (26) anyone

кто-то (26) someone

куда (4) (to) where (whither)

куда-нибудь (26) anywhere (motion)

куда-то (26) somewhere (motion)

культура (21) culture

культурный (28) cultural

куп(é)ц (28) gen.sg. **купца** merchant

купитьᴾ (12) **куплю**, **купишь** (**покупать**') (+ acc.) to buy

курить' (4) **курю**, **куришь** (**по-**ᴾ, **за-**ᴾ) to smoke

курсы (pl. of **курс**) (13) classes, a course of study

кухня (7) (**в** or **на**) gen.pl. **кухонь** kitchen

лавровый лист (28) bay leaf

лазить' (mv) (20) **лажу**, **лазишь** to climb, clamber

ландшафт (29) landscape

лёг – see **лечь**

лёгкий (18) easy

легла see **лечь**ᴾ

легче (18) easier

лежать' (30) **лежу**, **лежишь** (**по-**ᴾ) to lie, be in a lying position

лезть' (u) (20) **лезу**, **лезешь** past **лез**, **лезла** (**по-**ᴾ) to climb, clamber

лекция (18) (**на**) lecture

лес (5) prep. **в лесу**, pl. **леса** wood, forest

лестница (20) staircase

лет (9) gen.pl. of **год** and **лето** years; summers

лета/ть' (mv) (20) -**ю**, -**ешь** to fly

лететь' (u) (20) **лечу**, **летишь** (**по-**ᴾ) to fly

летний (7) summer

лето (16) pl. **лета** summer

летом (14) in summer

лечьᴾ (25) **лягу**, **ляжешь** past **лёг**, **легла**, **легло**, imper **ляг(те)** (**ложиться**') to lie down

ли (10) (13) (yes–no question word); whether

лимон (16) lemon

линия (12) line

литература (13) literature

лицо (21) pl. **лица** face; person

лобызание (30) (old word) kiss

ложиться' (25) **ложусь**, **ложишься** (**лечь**ᴾ) to lie down; to go to bed

ложка (16) gen.pl. **ложек** spoon

ломтик (28) slice

Лондон (4) London

лосн/иться' (30) -**юсь**, **ишься** to shine, gleam

лук (28) (no pl.) onions

лучше (18) better

лучший (18) best

лы́жи (pl) (29) gen.pl. **лыж** skis

люби́мый (16) beloved; favourite

люби́ть (6) **люблю́, лю́бишь (по-ᵖ)** (+ acc.) to love, be fond of

любо́й (15) any (any one you like)

лю́ди (16) gen.pl. **люде́й,** dat. **лю́дям,** inst. **людьми́,** prep. **лю́дях** people (pl. of **челове́к** 'person')

лютера́нка (30) gen.pl. **лютера́нок** Lutheran (Protestant)

ля́гу see **лечь**ᵖ

магази́н (6) shop

магнитофо́н (13) tape recorder

май (17) May

ма́ленький (7) small

ма́ло (9) (+ gen.) little, not much

ма́льчик (13) boy

ма́ма (11) mother, mum (my)

ма́рка (10) gen.pl. **ма́рок** stamp

март (17) March

масли́на (28) olive

ма́сло (8) butter; oil

ма́стер (21) pl. **мастера́** skilled workman

масшта́б (29) scale

материа́л (26) material

матро́с (29) sailor

мать (f) (3) (5.6) gen.sg. **ма́тери,** gen.pl. **матере́й** mother

маши́на (10) car; machine

медици́на (28) medicine

ме́дленный (18) slow

ме́жду (16) (+ inst.) between

междунаро́дый (27) international

ме́нее (18) less

ме́ньше (9) (18) (+ gen.) less; less than

меню́ (n indecl) (3) menu

меня́ – see **я** (T4) me

меня́/тьсяⁱ (23) **-юсь, -ешься** to change (intrans)

ме́сто (8) pl. **места́** place, seat

ме́сяц (9) gen.pl. **ме́сяцев** month

метро́ (n indecl) (5) metro, underground

меша́/тьⁱ (25) **-ю, -ешь (по-ᵖ)** (+ dat.) to hinder (someone)

меш(о́)к (25) gen.sg. **мешка́** bag, sack

мили́ция (21) police

миллиа́рд (22) a thousand million (US billion)

миллио́н (22) million

ми́лостивый (30) (old word) gracious, kind

ми́лый (30) dear, sweet, lovable

ми́мо (10) (+ gen.) past

минера́льный (12) mineral (adj)

министе́рство (23) ministry

мину́та (6) minute

мир (12) (18) peace; world

ми́ска (28) gen.pl. **ми́сок** bowl

мла́дший (18) younger; junior

мне, мно́й – see **я** me

мно́гие (pl. adj) (13)) many (people)

мно́го (9) (+ gen.) much, many

могу́, мо́гут, мо́г, могла́, могло́, могли́ – see **мо́чь**

моде́ль (f) (29) model

мо́жет, мо́жешь, мо́жем, мо́жете – see **мо́чь**

мо́жет быть (9) perhaps

мо́жно (14) it's possible, one may

мой (6) (T6) my

молодо́й (13) young

молодо́й челове́к (18) young man

моло́же (18) younger

молоко́ (8) milk

моло́чный (8) milk, dairy (adj)

молча́тьⁱ (16) **молчу́, молчи́шь (за-**ᵖ**)** to keep silent, say nothing

Монго́лия (18) Mongolia

монтёр (21) electrician

мо́ре (5) gen.pl. **море́й** sea

Москва́ (3) Moscow

москви́ч (17) gen.sg. **москвича́** Muscovite

моско́вский (17) Moscow (adj)

мо́ст (7) prep. **на мосту́**, pl. **мосты́** bridge

мо́чьⁱ (11) (13) (15) **могу́, мо́жешь, мо́гут** past **мо́г, могла́, могло́, могли́ (с-**ᵖ**)** to be able

муж (6) pl. **мужья́** husband

мужи́к (25) gen.sg. **мужика́** peasant man

мужско́й (14) male

мужчи́на (m) (18) man

музе́й (5) gen.pl. **музе́ев** museum

музе́йный (29) museum (adj)

му́зыка (6) music

музыка́нт (16) musician

мунди́р (30) uniform

мы (4) we (T4)

мысль (f) (26) thought

мя́со (8) meat

на (4) on

на́бережная (f adj) (29) embankment, quay

наве́рное (21) probably

навью́ч/итьᵖ (30) **-у, -ишь (навью́чивать**ⁱ**)** (+ inst.) to load (with)

над (16) (+ inst.) above

наде́ятьсяⁱ (11) **наде́юсь, наде́ешься** to hope

на́до (14) it's necessary, one must

надоеда́/тьⁱ **-ю, -ешь (надое́сть**ᵖ**)** (+ dat.) to bore (s.o.)

надое́ло (15) past of **надое́сть**ᵖ that's enough, I'm tired (of it)

наза́д (13) ago; back

назва́ние (16) name

называ́/тьⁱ (11) **-ю, ешь (назва́ть**ᵖ**)** (+ acc.) to name (s.o./sth)

называ́/тьсяⁱ (11) **-ется** (+ inst.) to be called (of thing, not person)

наи- (18) most (forms superlatives)

наибо́лее (29) most

найти́ᵖ (13) **найду́, найдёшь** past **нашёл, нашла́, нашло́ (находи́ть**ⁱ**)** (+ acc.) to find

наказа́тьᵖ (15) **накажу́, нака́жешь (нака́зывать**ⁱ**)** (+ acc.) to punish

нака́зыва/тьⁱ (15) **-ю, -ешь (наказа́ть**ᵖ**)** (+ acc.) to punish

нале́во (5) to the left

нало́г (28) tax

намно́го (18) much (with comparatives)

напива́/тьсяⁱ (14) **-юсь, -ешься (напи́ться**ᵖ**)** to get drunk

написа́тьᵖ (13) **напишу́, напи́шешь (писа́ть**ⁱ**)** to write

напи́тьсяᵖ (14) **напью́сь, напьёшься (напива́ться**ⁱ**)** to get drunk

напомина́/тьⁱ (15) **-ю, -ешь (напо́мнить**ᵖ**)** (+ dat.) to remind (someone)

напо́мн/итьᵖ (15) **-ю, -ишь (напомина́ть**ⁱ**)** (+ dat.) to remind (someone)

напра́в/итьᵖ (28) **-лю, -ишь (направля́ть**ⁱ**)** (+ acc.) to direct

напра́во (5) to the right

наприме́р (18) for example

напро́тив (10) opposite (adv of place)

наре́/затьᵖ (28) **-жу, -жешь (нареза́ть**ⁱ**)** to cut, slice

наро́д (13) people, nation

наро́чно (21) deliberately

наста́ива/ть (21) **-ю, -ешь** (**на** + prep.) to insist (on)

настоя́щий (16) real, genuine

настрое́ние (14) mood

научи́ться[р] (28) **научу́сь, нау́чишься** (**учи́ться**[¹]) (+ inf.) to learn to do sth

находи́ть[¹] (13) **нахожу́, нахо́дишь** (**найти́**[р]) (+ acc.) to find

находи́ться[¹] (15) **нахо́дится** to be situated

национа́льный (26) national

нача́ло (18) beginning

нач/а́ть[р] (13) **-ну́, -нёшь** past **на́чал, начала́, на́чало** (**начина́ть**[¹]) (+ acc.) to begin sth

начина́/ть (11) **-ю, -ешь** (**нача́ть**[р]) (+ acc.) to begin sth

начина́/ться (11) **-ется** to begin

наш (6) our (T6)

нашёл, нашла́ – see **найти́**

не (4) not

небо́сь (30) (coll) probably

Нева́ (11) Neva River

невозмо́жно (14) (+ [р] inf) it's impossible (to do sth)

не́где (24) there is nowhere (place)

него́ – form of **он, оно́** (T4) him, it

неда́вно (11) recently

недалеко́ (14) not far

неде́ля (6) gen.pl. **неде́ль** week

недоста́точно (27) insufficiently

ней, неё – forms of **она́** (T4) her

не́когда (24) there is no time

не́кого (24) there is no one

не́который (17) some, certain

не́куда (24) there is nowhere (motion)

нельзя́ (14) it's not allowed, it's impossible

неме́цкий (18) German (adj)

немно́го (13) (+ gen.) a little

немно́жко (14) (dim of **немно́го**) (+ gen.) a little

нему́, нём – forms of **он, оно́** (T4) him, it

необходи́мо (14) it's essential

необходи́мость (f) (28) (+ gen.) necessity (for)

необыча́йно (29) extraordinarily

неожи́данный (26) unexpected

неплохо́ (6) not bad, not badly

неповтори́мый (29) unique

непоси́льный (28) excessive, over-demanding

не́сколько (9) (+ gen.) several, a few

несмотря́ на (+ acc.) (26) in spite of

нести́[¹] (u) (20) **несу́, несёшь** past **нёс, несла́, несло́** (**по-**[р]) to carry

нет (3) no

нет (10) (+ gen.) there isn't/there aren't

неудо́бно (10) it's awkward

не́чего (24) **[nyé-chye-va]** there is nothing

ни . . . ни (24) neither . . . nor

нигде́ (24) nowhere (place)

ни́же (18) lower

ни́зкий (18) low

ника́к (24) in no way

никако́й (24) no; none at all; any

никогда́ (16) (24) never

никто́ (24) nobody

никуда́ (24) nowhere (motion)

ним, ни́ми, них – forms of **он, оно́, они́** (T4)

ничего́ (11) **[nee-chye-vó]** see **ничто́** nothing; it doesn't matter/ that's all right

ничто́ (24) nothing

но́ (4) but

нового́дний (26) New Year (adj)

но́вый (7) new

нога́ (25) acc. **но́гу**, pl. **но́ги**, dat. **нога́м** leg, foot

но́жка (25) (dim of **нога́**) gen.pl. **но́жек** little leg, little foot

но́жницы (pl.) (28) gen.pl. **но́жниц** scissors

но́мер (5) (21) pl. **номера́** number; hotel room

носи́ть (mv) (20) (28) **ношу́, но́сишь** to carry; to wear

ноч/ева́ть (25) **-у́ю, -у́ешь (пере-**р**)** to spend the night

но́чь (f) (9) gen.pl. **ноче́й** night

но́чью (16) at night

ноя́брь (m) (17) gen.sg. **ноября́** November

нра́в/иться (12) **-люсь, -ишься (по-**р**)** to please

ну (25) well

ну́жен/нужна́/нужно́, нужны́ (short adj) (29) necessary

ну́жно (11) it's necessary

ну́жный (29) necessary

о (5) (+ prep.) about, concerning

об = о before **а, и, о, у, э**

о́ба (m/n) **о́бе** (f) (22.4) both

обе́д (12) dinner; meal

обе́да/ть (12) **-ю, -ешь (по-**р**)** to dine, have a meal

обжа́р/итьр **(28) -ю, -ишь (обжа́ривать)** to fry all over

оби́детьр **(25) оби́жу, оби́дишь (обижа́ть)** (+ acc.) to offend, hurt

обижа́/ть (25) **-ю, -ешь (оби́деть**р**)** (+ acc.) to offend, hurt

облада́/ть (27) **-ю, -ешь** (+ inst.) to possess

облобыза́тьсяр (30) (old word) to kiss each other

обо́и (m pl.) (21) gen.pl. **обо́ев** wallpaper

о́браз (29) form; image; manner

обрати́ть (29) **(обраща́ть**) (+ acc.) to turn

обраща́/ть **-ю, -ешь (обра/ти́ть**р **-щу́, -ти́шь) внима́ние** (24) **на** (+ acc.) to pay attention to, note sth

обре́затьр (28) **обре́жу, обре́жешь (обреза́/ть -ю, -ешь)** to clip, cut

обреза́ть (28) see **обре́зать**р

обсервато́рия (28) observatory

обстоя́тельство (24) circumstance

обсужда́/ть (27) **-ю, -ешь (обсуди́ть**р**)** (+ acc.) to discuss

объяви́тьр (27) **объявлю́, объя́вишь (объявля́ть)** to announce

объявле́ние (2) announcement

объявля́/ть (27) **-ю, -ешь (объяви́ть**р**)** to announce

обы́чай (28) gen.pl. **обы́чаев** custom

обы́чно (13) usually

обяза́тельно (15) definitely, without fail

обя́зыва/ть (28) **-ю, -ешь (обяза́ть**р **обяжу́, обя́жешь)** to compel

о́вощи (9) gen.pl. **овоще́й** vegetables

огро́мный (18) enormous

огур(е́)ц (28) gen.sg. **огурца́** cucumber

одева́/ть(ся) (11) **-ю(сь), -ешь(ся) (оде́ть(ся)**р**)** to dress (oneself)

оде́/ть(ся)р **-ну(сь) -ешь(ся)** – see **одева́ть(ся)**

оди́н (m)/**одна́** (f)/**одно́** (n) (T7) one

одина́ковый (21) identical

оди́ннадцать (22.3) eleven

одна́жды (23) once, one day

одновреме́нно (28) at the same time

ожида́/ть' (11) **-ю, -ешь** (+ gen.) to expect (sth/s.o.)

о́зеро (18) pl. **озёра**, gen.pl. **озёр** lake

оказа́тьсяᵖ (20) (26) **окажу́сь, ока́жешься** (**ока́зываться**') to find oneself; to turn out

ока́зыва/ться' (26) **-юсь, -ешься** – see **оказа́ться**ᵖ

окамене́/тьᵖ (30) **-ю, -ешь** (**камене́ть**') to turn to stone

ока́нчива/ть' (13) **-ю, -ешь** (**око́нчить**ᵖ) (+ acc.) to finish, graduate from

океа́н (29) ocean

окно́ (3) pl. **о́кна**, gen.pl. **о́кон** window

о́коло (10) + gen. near; approximately

оконча́ние (28) end

око́нч/итьᵖ (13) **-у, -ишь** (**ока́нчивать**') (+ acc.) to finish, graduate from

октя́брь (m) (17) gen.sg. **октября́** October

о́н (3) (T4) he

она́ (3) (T4) she

они́ (4) (T4) they

оно́ (3) (T4) it

опозда́ние (11) lateness

определ/и́тьᵖ (29) **-ю, -и́шь** (**определя́ть**') (+ acc.) to determine, define

определя́/ть' (29) **-ю, -ешь** – see **определи́ть**ᵖ

опро́с (27) survey

опя́ть again

организа́тор (28) organizer

организа́ция (16) organization

организ/ова́ть'/ᵖ (27) **-у́ю, уешь** (+ acc.) to organize

оригина́л (13) original (noun)

освобо/ди́тьсяᵖ (15) **-жу́сь, -ди́шься** (**освобожда́ться**') to become free

освобожда́/ться' (15) **-юсь, -ешься** – see **освободи́ться**ᵖ

о́сень (f) (16) autumn

о́сенью (14) in autumn

основа́тьᵖ (29) **осную́, оснуёшь** (**осно́вывать**') (+ acc.) to found

осно́выва/ть' (29) **-ю, -ешь** – see **основа́ть**ᵖ

осо́бенно specially

осо́бый (26) special

остава́ться' (14) **остаю́сь, остаёшься** (**оста́ться**ᵖ) to remain

оста́в/итьᵖ (15) **-лю, -ишь** (**оставля́ть**') (+ acc.) to leave (sth)

оставля́/ть' (15) **-ю, -ешь** – see **оста́вить**ᵖ

оста́вшийся (28) remaining

остана́влива/ть(ся)'(13) (28) **-ю(сь), -ешь(ся)** to stop

остан/ови́ть(ся)ᵖ (13) (28) **-овлю́(сь), -о́вишь(ся)** to stop

остано́вка (20) gen.pl. **остано́вок** stop

оста́тьсяᵖ (14) **оста́нусь, оста́нешься** (**остава́ться**') to remain, stay

о́стров (18) pl. **острова́** island

от (9) (+ gen.) from (a person), away from

отвез/ти́ᵖ (20) **-у́, ёшь**, past **отвёз, отвезла́, отвезло́** (**отвози́ть**') to take somewhere (by transport)

отверну́/тьсяᵖ (30) **-у́сь, -ёшься** (**отвора́чиваться**') (**от** + gen.) to turn away from

отве́/тить᷾ (13) **-чу, -тишь**
(**отвеча́ть**') (+ dat./**на** + acc.) to
answer (s.o./sth)

отвеча́/ть' (13) **-ю, -ешь** see **отве́/тить**᷾

отвози́ть' (20) **отвожу́, отво́зишь** –
see **отвезти́**᷾

отдава́ть' (25) **отдаю́, отдаёшь**
(**отда́ть**᷾) (+ acc.) to give away

отда́ть᷾ (25) like **дать**, past **о́тдал,
отдала́, о́тдало** (**отдава́ть**')
(+ acc.) to give away

отде́л (8) section (of a shop)

отде́льный (18) separate

отдохн/у́ть᷾ (12) **-у́, нёшь** – see
отдыха́ть

отдыха́/ть' (12) **-ю, -ешь**
(**отдохну́ть**᷾) to rest

от(е́)ц (6) gen.sg. **отца́** father

отказа́ться᷾(25) **откажу́сь,
отка́жешься** (**отка́зываться**')
(+ inf) to refuse (to do sth)

отка́зыва/ться' (25) **-юсь, -ешься** –
see **отказа́ться**᷾

открыва́/ть'(14) **-ю, -ешь** (**откры́ть**᷾)
(+ acc.) to open (sth)

открыва́/ться' (11) **-ется**
(**откры́ться**᷾) to open

откр/ы́ть᷾ (14) **-о́ю, -о́ешь** – see
открыва́ть'

откры́ться᷾ – see **открыва́ться**'

отку́да (30) from where

отли́чный (26) excellent

отме́/тить᷾ (14) **-чу, -тишь** – see
отмеча́ть'

отмеча́/ть' (14) **-ю, -ешь** (**отме́тить**᷾)
(+ acc.) to mark, to celebrate

отнес/ти́᷾ (20) **-у́, -ёшь**, past **отнёс,
отнесла́, отнесло́** – see **относи́ть**'

относи́ть' (20) **отношу́, отно́сишь**

(**отнести́**᷾) (+ acc.) to take away
somewhere (by carrying)

относи́ться' (13) **отношу́сь,
отно́сишься** (**к** + dat.) to relate to,
regard, treat (s.o./sth)

отноше́ние (21) attitude

отой/ти́ (20) **-ду́, дёшь**, past **отошёл,
отошла́, отошло́** (**отходи́ть**') to
move away; to depart (of trains)

отста/ва́ть' (28) **-ю́, -ёшь** (**отста́ть**᷾)
(**от** + gen.) to be backward, lag
behind (s.o./sth)

отста́лость (f) (28) backwardness

отста́/ть᷾ (28) **-ну, -нешь** – see
отставать'

отсю́да from here

отту́да (23) from there

отходи́ть' (20) **отхожу́, отхо́дишь**
(**отойти́**᷾) to move away; to depart
(of trains)

о́тчество (6) patronymic

отъе́зд (26) departure

официа́нт (12) waiter

официа́нтка (12) gen.pl.
официа́нток waitress

охо́тно (25) willingly

о́чень (4) very

очи́/стить᷾ (28) **-щу, -стишь**
(**очища́ть** '**-ю, -ешь**) (+ acc.) to clean

ошелом/и́ть᷾ (30) **-лю́, -и́шь**
(**ошеломля́/ть**' **-ю, -ешь**) + acc. to
stun, astound

па́л(е)ц (16) gen.sg. **па́льца** finger, toe

пальто́ (n indecl) (7) overcoat

па́мять (f) (17) memory

па́па (m) (3) father, dad

папиро́са (30) (dim **папиро́ска**)
Russian-style cigarette

пáра (22) couple

парáдный (29) grand

парикмáхерская (f adj) (23) hairdresser's, barber's

парк (20) park; depot (taxis, trams)

парлáмент (28) parliament

пáхнуть (30) **пáхнет,** past **пáхло** (+ inst.) to smell (of)

пéрвый (7) first

переве/стúᵖ (21) **-дý, -дёшь** past **перевёл, перевелá, перевелó** (**переводúть**) (+ acc.) to take across; to shift; to translate

пере/водúть (13) **-вожý, -вóдишь-** see **перевестú**ᵖ

перевóдчик (21) translator

переговóры (m pl.) (23) gen.pl. **переговóров** negotiations, talks

пéред (16) (+ inst.) before, in front of

переда/вáть (15) **-ю, -ёшь** (+ acc. + dat.) to pass (sth to s.o.), give a message

передáтьᵖ (15) like **дать,** past **пéредал, передалá, пéредало** – see **передавáть**

передовóй (28) advanced, progressive

переезжá/ть (13) **-ю, -ешь** (**переéхать**ᵖ) to move (house); to drive across

пере/éхатьᵖ (13) **-éду, -éдешь** – see **переезжáть**

переживá/ть (24) **-ю, -ешь** to be upset, worry

перейтúᵖ (19) **перейдý, перейдёшь,** past **перешёл, перешлá, перешлó** (**переходúть**) (**через**) (+ acc.) to cross

перенес/тúᵖ (21) **-у, ёшь** (**переносúть**) (+ acc.) to carry across; to transfer

пере/носúть (21) **-ношý, -нóсишь** – see **перенестú**ᵖ

переноч/евáтьᵖ (25) **-ýю, -ýешь** (**ночевáть**) to spend the night

перерýв (17) break, interval

пересáжива/ться (15) **-юсь, -ешься** (**на** + acc.) see **пересéсть**ᵖ

пересел/úтьᵖ (21) **-ю, -úшь** (**переселя́ть**) (+ acc.) to move, resettle (s.o.)

переселя́/ть (21) **-ю, -ешь** – see **переселúть**ᵖ

пере/сéстьᵖ (15) **-ся́ду, -ся́дешь,** past **пересéл, пересéла** (**пересáживаться**) to change from one form of transport to another

переста/вáть (15) **-ю, -ёшь** see **перестáть**ᵖ

перестá/тьᵖ (15) **-ну, -нешь** (**перестá/вáть**) (+ inf) to stop (doing sth)

перехóд (15) street crossing

пере/ходúть (19) **-хожý, -хóдишь** (**перейтú**ᵖ) (**через**) (+ acc.) to cross

пéр(е)ц (28) gen.sg. **пéрца** pepper

перешёл, перешлá – see **перейтú**

пéсня (25) gen.pl. **пéсен** song

петербýргский (17) Petersburg (adj)

петь (16) **пою, поёшь (с-**ᵖ**)** (+ acc.) to sing (sth)

печáль (f) (26) sadness

печь (f) (25) gen.pl. **печéй** (dim **пéчка**) stove

пешкóм (20) on foot

пúво (20) beer

пирóг (10) gen.sg. **пирогá** (large) pie

пирож(ó)к (8) gen.sg. **пирожкá** small pie

писáтель (m) (17) writer

писáть (13) **пишý, пúшешь (на-**ᵖ**)** (+ acc.) to write

письмо́ (5) pl. **пи́сьма**, gen.pl. **пи́сем**
letter

питьˈ (12) **пью, пьёшь**, f past **пила́**,
imper **пей(те) (вы́-**ᴾ**)** (+ acc.) to drink

пла́ва/тьˈ (mv) (20) **-ю, -ешь** to swim; to
sail

пла́катьˈ (15) **пла́чу, пла́чешь (за-**ᴾ**)** to
cry

план (7) plan, street map

плати́тьˈ (24) **плачу́, пла́тишь (за-**ᴾ**)**
(за + acc.**)** to pay (for)

пла́тье (25) gen.pl. **пла́тьев** dress

пло́тник (28) carpenter

плохо́й (8) bad

пло́щадь (f) (5) gen.pl. **площаде́й (на)**
square

плытьˈ (u) (20) **-ву́, -вёшь**, f past **плыла́**
(по-ᴾ**)** to swim; to sail

по (12) (+ dat.) along; according to; on;
round

по (17.12) (23) (+ acc.) up to and
including

по-англи́йски (4) in English

побе́га/тьᴾ (mv) (20) **-ю, -ешь (бе́гать**ˈ**)**
to run about

побежа́тьᴾ (u) (20) **побе/гу́, -жи́шь,**
-гу́т (бежа́тьˈ**)** to run, start running

побледне́/тьᴾ (30) **-ю, -ешь**
(бледне́тьˈ**)** to turn pale

побли́же (18) a bit closer

побыва́/тьᴾ (24) **-ю, -ешь** (+ prep.)
to visit, spend time (somewhere)

повезло́ (13) (+ dat. of person) (s.o.)
was lucky
мне повезло́ I was lucky

повезти́ᴾ – see **везти́**ˈ

поверн/у́тьᴾ (15) **-у́, -ёшь**
(повора́чиватьˈ**)** to turn (change
direction)

повести́ᴾ – see **вести́**ˈ

по́вод (21) (**для** + gen.) cause,
grounds (for)

повора́чива/тьˈ (15) **-ю, -ешь** – see
поверну́тьᴾ

повтор/и́тьᴾ (26) **-ю, -и́шь (повторя́ть**ᴾ**)**
(+ acc.) to repeat

повторя́/тьˈ (26) **-ю, -ешь (повтори́ть**ᴾ**)**
(+ acc.) to repeat

поги́бнутьᴾ (28) – past **поги́б, поги́бла**
(погиба́/тьˈ **-ю, -ешь)** to perish

погля/де́тьᴾ (30) **-жу́, -ди́шь**
(гляде́тьˈ**) (на** + acc.) to take a
look at

поговор/и́тьᴾ (15) **-ю, -и́шь (говори́ть**ˈ**)**
to talk for a while

пого́да (7) weather

под (16) (25) (+ inst. + acc. + inst.)
under (place); (+ acc.) under (motion)

пода/ва́тьˈ (22) **-ю, -ёшь** – see **пода́ть**ᴾ

подари́тьᴾ (24) **подарю́, пода́ришь**
(дари́тьˈ**)** to give, present

пода́р(о)к (19) gen.sg. **пода́рка**
present, gift

пода́тьᴾ (22) (like **дать**), past **по́дал,**
подала́, по́дало (подава́тьˈ**)**
(+ acc.) to serve, hand in

пода́тьᴾ **ру́ку** (30) to hold out
one's hand

пода́ча (28) serving

подберёзовик (28) brown mushroom

подборо́д(о)к (30) gen.sg.
подборо́дка chin

подёрнут/ый (PPP) (30) covered,
coated

поджа́р/итьᴾ (28) **-ю, -ишь**
(поджа́рива/тьˈ **-ю, -ешь)** (+ acc.) to
brown

подзе́мный (15) underground

411

поднима́ть[¹] (25) **-ю, -ешь** – see
  подня́ть[ᵖ]

поднима́ться[¹] (19) **-юсь, -ешься** – see
  подня́ться[ᵖ]

под/ня́ть[ᵖ] (25) **-ниму́, -ни́мешь**, past
  по́днял, подняла́, по́дняло (+ acc.)
  (**поднима́ть**[¹]) to lift, pick up

под/ня́ться[ᵖ] (19) **-ниму́сь, -ни́мешься,**
  past **-ня́лся, -няла́сь, -няло́сь**
  (**поднима́ться**[¹]) to climb; to rise

подожд/а́ть[¹] (15) **-у́, -ёшь**, f past
  подождала́ (**ждать**[¹]) to wait

подожди́те (6) see **подожда́ть** wait
  (imper)

под/писа́ть[ᵖ] (23) **-пишу́, -пи́шешь**
  (**подписыва́ть**[¹]) (+ acc.) to sign

подписыва́ть[¹] (23) **-ю, -ешь** – see
  подписа́ть[ᵖ]

подру́га (4) (female) friend

поду́м/ать[ᵖ] (30) **-ю, -ешь** (**ду́мать**[¹]) to
  think for a moment

подъе́зд (19) entrance, doorway

по-европе́йски (28) in European style
  ('Europeanly')

по́езд (17) pl. **поезда́** train

пое́здка (21) gen.pl. **пое́здок** journey

поёт see **петь** (16) (he) sings

пое́хать[ᵖ] (12) **пое́ду, пое́дешь** (**е́хать**[¹])
  to go (by transport)

пожа́луйста (3) [pa-zhál-sta] please/
  don't mention it/here you are/go ahead

пожа́ть[ᵖ] (30) **пожму́, пожмёшь**
  (**пожима́ть**[¹] **-ю, -ешь**) (**ру́ку**) to
  press, squeeze, shake (hands)

пожива́ть[¹] (6) **-ю, -ешь** to live, get along

позавчера́ (18) the day before
  yesterday

по́здно (16) [pó-zna] late

поздра́в/ить[ᵖ] (23) **-лю, -ишь**

(**поздравля́ть**[¹]) (+ acc.) (**с** + inst.) to
  congratulate s.o. on sth

поздравле́ние (26) greeting,
  congratulation

поздравля́ть[¹] (23) **-ю, -ешь**
  (**поздра́вить**[ᵖ]) (+ acc.) (**с** + inst.) to
  congratulate s.o. on sth

поздравля́ю! (6) congratulations!
  (= I congratulate)

познако́миться[ᵖ] (16) – see
  знако́миться[¹]

познако́мьтесь (imper) (6) meet
  (become acquainted)

позови́те (6) (imper of **позва́ть**[ᵖ]) call

пой(те) (25) (imper of **петь**[¹]) sing

пой/ти́[ᵖ] (u) (12) **-ду́, -дёшь**, past,
  пошёл, пошла́, пошло́ (**идти́**[¹]) to
  go, set off

пока́ . . . не (14) until

пока́ нет (15) not yet

показа́ть[ᵖ] (12) **покажу́, пока́жешь**
  (**пока́зывать**[¹]) to show

пока́зыва/ть[¹] (7) **-ю, -ешь** (**показа́ть**[ᵖ])
  (+acc. + dat.) to show (sth to s.o.)

покл/они́ться[ᵖ] (30) **-оню́сь, -о́нишься**
  (**кла́ня/ться**[¹] **-юсь, -ешься**) to bow

покло́нник (27) admirer

поколе́ние (26) generation

покр/ы́ть[ᵖ] (28) **-о́ю, -о́ешь** (**покрыва́/
  ть**[¹] **-ю, -ешь**) (+ acc.) to cover

покупа́тель (m) (10) customer

покупа́/ть[¹] (8) **-ю, -ешь** (**купи́ть**[ᵖ])
  (+ acc.) to buy

по́лдень (17) gen. **полу́дня** midday

по́лза/ть[¹] (mv) (20) **-ю, -ешь** to crawl

полз/ти́[¹] (u) (20) **-у́, -ёшь**, past **по́лз,
  ползла́, ползло́** (**по-**[ᵖ]) to crawl

по́лкило́ (n indecl) (9) half a kilo

по́лно! (30) (coll) enough of that!

по́лностью (28) completely

по́лночь (17) gen. **полу́ночи** midnight

по́лный (30) (+ gen.) full (of)

полови́на (17) half

положи́тьᵖ (25) **положу́, поло́жишь** (**кла/сть**ᶦ **-ду, -дёшь**) (+ acc.) to put

полтора́ (22) one and a half

полуо́стров (29) pl. **полуострова́** peninsula

полу́тора (22) gen. of **полтора́** one and a half

получа́/тьᶦ (9) **-ю, -ешь (получи́ть**ᵖ) (+ acc.) to receive, get

получи́тьᵖ (22) **получу́, полу́чишь** see **получа́ть**ᶦ.

полчаса́ (20) half an hour

по́льз/оватьсяᶦ (21) **-уюсь, -уешься** (**вос-**ᵖ) (+ inst) to use (sth)

помидо́р (12) tomato

поми́луйтеᵖ (30) pardon me

по́мн/итьᶦ (18) **-ю, -ишь** (+ acc.) to remember

помога́/тьᶦ (12) **-ю, -ешь (помо́чь**ᵖ) (+ dat.) to help (someone)

по-мо́ему (13) in my opinion

помо́рщ/итьсяᵖ (30) **-усь, -ишься** (**мо́рщиться**ᵖ) to crease, wrinkle; to frown

помо́чьᵖ (12) **помогу́, помо́жешь, помо́гут**, past **помо́г, помогла́, помогло́ (помога́ть**ᶦ) (+ dat.) to help (s.o.)

по́мощь (f) (19) help

понеде́льник (17) Monday

по-неме́цки (13) in German

понима́/тьᶦ (4) **-ю, -ешь (поня́ть**ᵖ) to understand

понра́в/итьсяᵖ (26) **-ится** (**нра́виться**ᶦ) (+ dat.) to please (s.o.)

поня́тно (14) comprehensible (= I see)

поня́тьᵖ (13) **пойму́, поймёшь**, past **по́нял, поняла́, по́няло (понима́ть**ᶦ) to understand, realize

пообе́да/тьᵖ (12) **-ю, -ешь (обе́дать**ᶦ) to dine, have a meal

попр/оси́тьᵖ (15) **-ошу́, -о́сишь** (**проси́ть**ᶦ) (+ acc. + inf) to ask s.o. to do sth

популя́рный (13) popular

пора́ (14) (+ inf) it's time (to do sth)

по́рт (11) prep. **в порту́**, gen.pl. **порто́в** port

портсига́р (30) cigarette-case, cigar-case

портфе́ль (29) (m) briefcase

по-ру́сски (4) in Russian

посел/и́тьсяᵖ (26) **-ю́сь, -и́шься** (**поселя́/ться**ᶦ **-юсь, -ешься**) to settle, take up residence

посети́тель (m) (12) customer

посе/ти́тьᵖ (28) **-щу́, -ти́шь (посеща́ть**ᶦ) (+ acc.) to visit (a place)

посеща́/тьᶦ (28) **-ю, -ешь** (+ acc.) (**посе/ти́ть**ᵖ) to visit (a place)

поси/де́тьᵖ **-жу́, -ди́шь (сиде́ть**ᶦ) to sit for a while

посла́тьᵖ (23) **пошлю́, пошлёшь** (**посыла́ть**ᶦ) (+ acc.) to send

по́сле (10) (+ gen.) after

после́дний (7) last

послу́ша/тьᵖ (12) **-ю, -ешь (слу́шать**ᶦ) (+ acc.) to listen to

посм/отре́тьᵖ (13) **-отрю́, -о́тришь** (**смотре́ть**ᶦ) to watch; (**на** + acc.) to look at

посо́льство (7) embassy

поспеш/и́тьᵖ (28) **-у́, -и́шь (спеши́ть**ᶦ) to hurry

постро́/итьᵖ **-ю, -ишь** – see **стро́ить**ᶦ

413

поступа́/ть' (13) -ю, ешь – see
   поступи́ть^р
пост/упи́ть^р (13) -уплю́, -у́пишь
   (поступа́ть') (в + асс.) to enter
   (university)
постуч/а́ть^р(25) -у́, -и́шь (стуча́ть')
   (в + асс.) to knock (at)
посыла́/ть' (23) -ю, -ешь (посла́ть^р)
   (+ асс.) to send (s.o./sth)
посы́п/ать' -лю, -лешь (28)
   (посыпа́/ть' -ю, -ешь) (+ inst.) to
   sprinkle (with sth solid)
посы́паться^р (30) посы́плется to rain
   down
пото́м (12) then, next
потому́ что (12) because
потре́б/овать^р (21) -ую, -уешь
   (тре́бовать') (+ gen.) to demand
   (sth)
по-францу́зски (4) in French
пох/оди́ть^р (mv) (20) -ожу́, -о́дишь
   (ходи́ть') to walk about for a while
почему́ (4) why
почему́-то (26) for some reason
по́чта (5) (на) post office
почти́ (13) almost
почти́тельный (4) respectful,
   deferential
почто́вый (10) postage (adj)
поща/ди́ть^р (28) -жу́, -ди́шь (ща/ди́ть^р)
   (+ асс.) to spare
пое́зия (23) poetry
поэ́т (23) poet
поэ́тому (9) so, consequently
пра́вда (11) truth
пра́вда? (11) is that so?
пра́во (24) pl. права́ right
пра́здник (17) [práz-neek] national
   holiday; festival

превосходи́тельство (30) Excellency
предприя́тие (28) (на) firm, company,
   business
председа́тель (16) (m) chairman
предста́в/ить^р (27) -лю, -ишь
   (представля́ть') (+ асс. + dat.) to
   present (s.o./sth to s.o.)
предста́вить себе́ (29) (+ асс.) to
   imagine (sth)
представля́/ть' (29) -ю, -ешь – see
   предста́вить
предупрежда́/ть' (12) -ю, -ешь
   (предупре/ди́ть^р -жу́, -ди́шь)
   (+ асс.) to warn (s.o.)
пре́жде (26) before
пре́жде всего́ (26) first of all, primarily
президе́нт (27) president
прекра́сный (24) beautiful, fine
премье́ра (27) premiere
премье́р-мини́стр (27) gen.sg.
   премье́р-мини́стра prime minister
преобразова́ние (28) reform
   (= рефо́рма)
преодоле́/ть^р (28) -ю, -ешь
   (преодолева́/ть' -ю, -ешь) (+ асс.)
   to overcome
преподава́тель (m) (13) teacher,
   lecturer
препода/ва́ть' (13) -ю́, -ёшь (+ асс.) to
   teach (sth)
прерв/а́ть^р (23) -у́, -ёшь, f past
   прервала́ (прерыва́ть' (+ асс.) to
   interrupt
прерыва́/ть' (23) -ю, -ешь – see
   прерва́ть^р
престаре́лый (23) aged
при (5) (28) (+ prep.) attached to; at the
   time of, under
приба́в/ить^р (28) -лю, -ишь

(прибавля/ть' -ю, -ешь) to add

прибега/ть' (20) **-ю, -ешь (прибежа́ть^р)** to arrive (running)

прибега́/ть^р (28) **-ю, -ешь (прибе́гн/уть^р -у, -ешь) (к +** dat.**)** to resort to

прибе/жа́ть^р (20) **-гу́, -жи́шь, -гу́т (прибега́ть')** to arrive (running)

прива́тно (30) (old word) privately

привез/ти́^р (20) **-у́, -ёшь,** past **привёз, привезла́ (привози́ть')** to bring by transport

привёл – see **привести́**

приве/сти́^р (20) **-ду́, -дёшь,** past **привёл, привела́, привело́ (приводи́ть')** to bring (by leading)

приве́т (26) greetings (informal usage)

при/води́ть' (20) **-вожу́, -во́дишь (привести́^р)** to bring (by leading)

при/вози́ть' (20) **-вожу́, -во́зишь (привезти́^р)** to bring (by transport)

привы́чка (16) gen.pl. **привы́чек** habit

пригла/си́ть^р (18) **-шу́, -си́шь (приглаша́ть')** (+ acc.) to invite (someone)

приг/на́ть^р (28) **-оню́, -о́нишь (пригоня́ть')** (+ acc.) to drive

приговор/и́ть^р (28) **-ю́, -и́шь (пригова́рива/ть' -ю, -ешь) (к +** dat.**)** to condemn to, sentence to

пригоня́/ть' (28) **-ю, -ешь** (+ acc.) to drive

пригото́в/ить^р (16) **-лю, -ишь (гото́вить')** (+ acc.) to prepare; to cook

придётся^р (20) (see **прийти́сь^р**) it will be necessary

приду́, придёшь – see **прийти́^р**

придума́/ть^р (24) **-ю, -ешь**

(придумывать') (+ acc.) to think up, invent

придумыва/ть' (24) **-ю, -ешь (приду́мать^р)** (+ acc.) to think up, invent

прие́зд (23) arrival (by transport)

прие́/хать^р (13) **-ду, -дешь (приезжа́ть')** to arrive (by transport)

приезжа́/ть' (13) **-ю, -ешь** – see **прие́хать^р**

прийти́^р (12) **приду́. придёшь,** past **пришёл пришла́, пришло́ (приходи́ть')** to arrive, come

прийти́сь^р (25) **придётся,** past **пришло́сь (приходи́ться')** (+ dat. of person + inf.) to be necessary, to be forced to

прика́з (28) order

приказа́ть^р (13) **прикажу́, прика́жешь (прика́зывать')** (+ dat. + inf) to order someone to do sth

прика́зыва/ть' (13) **-ю, -ешь (приказа́ть^р)** (+ dat. + inf.) to order someone to do sth

прилета́/ть' (20) **-ю, -ешь (прилете́ть^р)** to arrive (by air)

приле/те́ть^р (20) **-чу́, ти́шь** – see **прилета́ть'**

приме́рно (22) approximately

принес/ти́^р (12) **-у́, -ёшь,** past **принёс, принесла́, принесло́ (приноси́ть')** to bring (by carrying)

принима́/ть' (27) **-ю, -ешь (приня́ть^р)** (+ acc.) to accept

при/носи́ть' (20) **-ношу́, -но́сишь (принести́^р)** to bring (by carrying)

при́нцип (23) principle

приня́ть^р (27) **приму́, при́мешь,** past **при́нял, приняла́, при́няло**

(принима́ть') (+ acc.) to accept

приобре/сти́ᴾ (27) **-ту́, -тёшь,** past
приобрёл, -обрела́, -обрело́
(приобрета́ть') (+ acc.) to acquire

приобрета́/ть' (27) **-ю, -ешь**
(приобрести́ᴾ**)** (+ acc.) to acquire

приобща́/ть' (28) **-ю, -ешь (приобщ/и́ть**ᴾ
-у́, -и́шь) (к + dat.) to introduce (to sth)

приро́да (17) nature, scenery

прист/упи́тьᴾ (26) **-уплю́, -у́пишь**
(приступа́ть' -ю, -ешь) (к + dat.) to
get down to, to start on

при/ходи́ть (20) **-хожу́, -хо́дишь**
(прийти́ᴾ**)** to arrive

приходи́ться' (25) **прихо́дится,** past
приходи́лось (прийти́сьᴾ**)** (+ dat. of
person + inf) to be necessary, to be
forced to

причи́на (21) (+ gen.) reason (for),
cause (of)

пришёл, пришла́ – see **прийти́** ᴾ

пришло́сь see **прийти́сь**ᴾ

прищу́р/итьᴾ (30) **-ю, -ешь**
(прищу́рива/ть' -ю, -ешь) to half-
close (one's eyes)

прия́тель (m) (30) friend

прия́тно (4) pleasant (adv)

прия́тный (10) pleasant (adj)

пробавля́/ться' (30) **-юсь, -ешься** to
get by, make do

пробле́ма (21) problem

проведён/ный (PPP) (28) conducted,
passed, executed

провёл – see **провести́**

прове́р/итьᴾ (21) **-ю, -ишь (проверя́ть')**
(+ acc.) to check

проверя́/ть' (21) **-ю, -ешь (прове́рить**ᴾ**)**
(+ acc.) to check

прове/сти́ᴾ (21) **-ду́, -дёшь,** past

провёл, провела́, провело́
(проводи́ть') to conduct; to spend
(time)

про/води́ть' (17) **-вожу́, -во́дишь**
(провести́ᴾ**) вре́мя** to conduct; to
spend time

програ́мма (27) programme

прогу́лка (17) gen.pl. **прогу́лок** walk

прода/ва́ть' (8) **-ю́, -ёшь (прода́ть**ᴾ**)**
(+ acc.) to sell

продав(е́)ц (8) gen.sg. **продавца́**
sales assistant

прода́жа (24) sale

прода́ть like **дать,** past **про́дал,**
продала́, про́дало (продава́ть')
(+ acc.) to sell

продово́льственный (17) food (adj),
grocery

продолжа́/ть' (11) **-ю, -ешь** (+ acc.) to
continue sth

продолжа́/ться' (11) **-ется** to continue

проду́кты (m.pl) (8) gen.pl. **проду́ктов**
groceries, food

проезжа́/ть' (15) (20) **-ю, -ешь**
(прое́хатьᴾ**)** to travel to/through/past

прое́кт (29) plan, project

про/е́хатьᴾ (15) (20) **-е́ду, -е́дешь**
(проезжа́ть') to travel to/through/past

про/же́чьᴾ (30) **-жгу́, -жжёшь, -жгу́т**
past **прожёг, прожгла́, прожгло́**
(прожига́/тьᴾ **-ю, -ешь)** to burn
through

прожива́/ть' (22) **-ю, -ешь** to reside

прожива́ющий (21) (m adj) resident

прожи́/ть' (13) **-ву́, -вёшь,** past
про́жил, прожила́, про́жило to live
(for a specified period)

произой/ти́ᴾ (22) **-дёт** past **произошло́**
(происходи́ть') to occur

проис/ходи́ть' (22) **-хо́дит** – see
   произойти́ᵖ
пройти́ᵖ (19) **пройду́, пройдёшь,** past
   про/шёл, -шла́, -шло́ (проходи́ть')
   to go through/past
пролета́/ть' (20) **-ю, -ешь**
   (проле/те́тьᵖ) to fly past or through
пролете́тьᵖ (20) **-чу́, -ти́шь** – see
   пролета́/ть'
про́мтова́рный магази́н (17) non-food
   goods shop
пром/ы́тьᵖ (28) **-о́ю, -о́ешь**
   (промыва́/ть' **-ю, -ешь)** to wash
   thoroughly
промы́шленность (f) (28) industry
промы́шленный (28) industrial
пропо́рция (29) proportion
проси́ть' (15) **прошу́, про́сишь (по-**ᵖ)
   (+ acc. + inf) to ask s.o. to do sth
проспе́кт (4) avenue, prospect (wide
   street)
прости́те (3) excuse me/I'm sorry
про́сто (10) simply
просто́й (18) simple
про́сьба (21) gen.pl. **про́сьб** request
про́тив (10) (+ gen.) opposite
проти́вник (28) opponent
проти́вно (30) disgusting, disgusted
противополо́жный (20) opposite (adj)
профессиона́л (16) professional
   (noun)
профе́ссор (19) pl **профессора́**
   professor
прох/оди́ть' (20) **-ожу́, -о́дишь**
   (пройти́ᵖ) to go through/past
проце́нт (22) per cent
прочита́/тьᵖ (13) **-ю, -ешь (чита́ть**')
   (+ acc.) to read
про́шлый (11) previous, last

проща́ние (30) farewell, parting
про́ще (18) simpler
пря́мо (5) straight on
прямо́й (12) direct, straight
пря́тать' (28) **пря́чу, пря́чешь (с-**ᵖ)
   (+ acc.) to hide
пти́ца (18) bird
пуска́/ть' (25) **-ю, -ешь** – see **пусти́ть**ᵖ
пусти́тьᵖ (25) **пущу́, пу́стишь**
   (пуска́/ть') (+ acc.) to permit; to let in/out
пусть (15) let
путеводи́тель (m) (10) guidebook
путеше́ств/овать' (21) **-ую, -уешь** to
   travel
путь (m) (20) gen./dat./prep./sg. **пути́**,
   inst.sg. **путём**, pl. **пути́**, gen.pl. **путе́й**
   way
пу́говка (30) gen.pl. **пу́говок** button
пья́ный (14) drunk
пятиэта́жный (26) five-floor
пятна́дцать (22.3) fifteen
пя́тница (17) Friday
пять (22.3) five
пятьдеся́т (22.3) fifty
пятьсо́т (22.3) five hundred

рабо́та (6) work
рабо́та/ть' (4) **-ю, -ешь (по-**ᵖ) to work
рабо́чий (m adj) (28) worker
равно́ – see **всё равно́**
равноду́шно (13) with indifference
ра́д/а/о/ы (29) glad
ра́ди (10) (+ gen.) for the sake of
ра́дио [о] (n indecl) (5) radio
ра́дость (f) (13) joy
ра́з (9) gen.pl. **раз** a time
разведённый (27) divorced
разве/сти́сьᵖ (19) **-ду́сь, -дёшься,** past
   развёлся, развела́сь

(разводи́ться´) to get divorced
разви́тие (21) development
разво́д (14) divorce
раз/води́ться´ (19) **-вожу́сь,**
-во́дишься, (развести́сьр**)** to get
divorced
разгова́рива/ть´ (16) **-ю, -ешь** to
converse, talk
разгово́р (10) conversation
раздева́йтесь (11) take your coat off;
undress
раздели́тьр (21) **разделю́,**
разде́лишь (разделя́ / ть´ -ю, -ешь)
(+ acc.) to share, to divide up
разме́р (10) size, dimension
разнообра́зие (29) variety
ра́зный (9) various
разреша́/ть´ (15) **-ю, -ешь (разреши́ть**р**)**
(+ dat.) to allow (someone)
разреш/и́ть´ (15) **-у́, -и́шь** (+ dat.) – see
разреша́ть´
ра́но (16) early
ра́ньше (16) before; earlier
распада́/ться´ (22) **-ется (распа́сться**р
распадётся, past **распа́лся,**
распа́лась) to break up
располага́/ться´ (29) **-ется** to be
situated, placed
расположен/а/о/ы (29) situated
расправля́/ться´ (28) **-юсь, -ешься**
(распра́в/иться -люсь, -ишься)
(**с** + inst.) to deal with
распространённый (23) common,
widespread
рассерди́тьсяр – see **серди́ться´** to
get angry
рассе́янный (19) absent-minded
расск/аза́тьр (12) **-ажу́, -а́жешь**
(расска́зывать´) to tell, talk

расска́зыва/ть´ (12) **-ю, -ешь**
(рассказа́тьр**)** to tell, talk
рас/ти́´ (24) **-ту́, -тёшь,** past **рос,**
росла́, росло́ (вы́-р**)** to grow
реа́льный (27) real, real-life
ребён(о)к (10) pl. – see **де́ти** child
революционе́р (16) revolutionary
револю́ция (16) revolution
ре́дкий (18) rare
ре́зко (28) sharply
результа́т (27) result
река́ (7) acc. **ре́ку,** pl. **ре́ки,** dat. pl.
река́м river
рекла́ма (27) advertising, publicity
ремо́нт (21) repair(s), maintenance
рестора́н (5) restaurant
рефо́рма (28) reform
реша́/ть´ (13) **-ю, -ешь (реши́ть**р**)**
(+ acc.) to decide; to solve
реше́ние (27) decision
решётка (29) gen.pl. **решёток** grille,
railing, decorated ironwork
реши́тельно (28) resolutely, with
determination
реш/и́тьр (13) **-у́, -и́шь (реша́ть´)** (+ acc.)
decide; to solve
ро́вно (17) precisely; evenly
ро́дина (21) **(на)** homeland
роди́тели (9) (sg. **роди́тель** m)
parents
роди́тьсяр (13) past **роди́лся,**
родила́сь, роди́ли́сь to be born
родно́й (28) own (of family relationships);
native
рожде́ние (17) birth
розе́тка (21) gen.pl. **розе́ток** elecricity
socket, power point
ро́ль (f) (24) gen.pl. **роле́й** role
рома́н (13) novel; love affair

Росси́я (4) Russia

рубль (m) (3) gen.sg. **рубля́** rouble

рука́ (22) acc. **ру́ку** pl. **ру́ки, рука́м** hand, arm

ру́сская (f adj) a Russian woman

ру́сский (7) (9) Russian; a Russian (man)

ры́ба (10) fish

ры́бный (10) fish (adj)

ры́жик (28) saffron milk-cap (mushroom)

ры́н(о)к (8) **(на)** market

ря́дом (7) (16) **(с** + inst.) nearby; beside

с (10) + gen.; (16) + inst.; + gen. off, from; + inst. with

сад (5) prep. **в саду́**, pl. **сады́** garden, orchard

сади́тьсяᶦ (15) **сажу́сь, сади́шься (сесть**ᵖ**)** to sit down; to take (transport)

сала́т (12) salad

сам (m)**/сама́** (f)**/само́** (n)**/са́ми** (pl) (13) (T4) oneself (emphatic)

самова́р (21) samovar, urn

самодержа́вие (28) autocracy

самолёт (20) aeroplane

самостоя́тельно (24) independently ('self standing')

са́мый (18) very; most (forms superlative)

са́хар (8) sugar

сбе́га/тьᵖ (20) **-ю, -ешь (бе́гать**ᶦ**)** to run there and back

сбры́знутьᵖ (28) to sprinkle (with liquid)

сва́дьба (22) (gen.pl.) **сва́деб** wedding

све́жий (8) fresh

сверну́тьᵖ (20) **сверну́, сверне́шь (свора́чивать**ᶦ**)** to turn

светофо́р (19) traffic light

свида́ние (9) meeting, rendezvous

свобо́дный (10) free

свой (21) own

свора́чива/тьᶦ (20) **-ю, -ешь (сверну́ть**ᵖ**)** to turn

свято́й (23) (m adj) saint; holy, sacred

сго́рб/итьсяᵖ (30) **-люсь, -ишься (го́рбиться**ᶦ**)** to hunch up

сда́ча (9) change (money returned)

сде́ла/тьᵖ (12) **-ю, -ешь (де́лать**ᶦ**)** (+ acc.) to do; to make

себя́ (21) self

се́вер (18) **(на)** north

се́верный (18) northern

сего́дня (7) **[sye-vód-nya]** today

сейча́с (6) now, at the moment

секрета́рь (m) (15) gen.sg. **секретаря́** secretary (male or female)

семе́йный (22) family (adj)

семна́дцать (22.3) seventeen

семь (22.3) seven

се́мьдесят (22.3) seventy

семьсо́т (22.3) seven hundred

семья́ (12) pl. **се́мьи**, gen.pl. **семе́й**, dat.pl. **се́мьям** family

сентя́брь (m) (17) gen.sg. **сентября́** September

серди́тьсяᶦ (11) **сержу́сь, се́рдишься (рас-**ᵖ**)** to be angry

се́рдце (15) gen.pl. **серде́ц** heart

середи́на (26) middle

серьёзно (19) seriously

сестра́ (14) pl. **сёстры сестёр сёстрам сёстрами сёстрах** sister

сестьᵖ (15) **ся́ду, ся́дешь** past **сел, се́ла (сади́ться**ᶦ**)** to sit down; **(на** + acc.) to take (transport)

сеть (f) (21) gen.pl. **сете́й** network; circuit

Сиби́рь (f) (3) Siberia

сиде́ть (14) **сижу́, сиди́шь (по-ᵖ)** to sit, be sitting

скажи́те (4) see **сказа́ть** tell/say (imperative¹ form)

сказа́тьᵖ (12) **скажу́, ска́жешь (говори́ть¹)** to say

скаме́йка (26) gen.pl. **скаме́ек** bench (dim, of **скамья́** 'bench')

скло́н (29) slope

сковорода́ (28) pl. **ско́вороды**, gen.pl. **сковоро́д**, dat.pl. **сковорода́м** frying-pan

ско́лько (9) (+ gen.) how much, how many

ско́ро (20) soon

ску́чно (14) [sko´o-shna] boring, it's boring

сла́дость (f) (30) sweetness

сле́ва (15) on the left

сле́дующий (8) following, next

слеза́ (30) pl. **слёзы** gen.pl. **слёз**, dat.pl. **слеза́м** tear

сли́шком (10) too (excessively)

слова́рь (m) (10) gen.sg. **словаря́** dictionary

сло́во (8) pl. **слова́** word

служи́ть (30) **служу́, слу́жишь (по-ᵖ)** to serve

слу́чай (22) gen.pl. **слу́чаев** case

случа́йно (24) by chance

случи́тьсяᵖ (16) **-и́тся (случа́ться¹ -ется) (с** + inst.) to happen (to)

слу́шать¹ (12) **-ю, -ешь (по-ᵖ)** (+ acc.) to listen to

слы́шать¹ (11) **-у, -ишь (у-ᵖ)** (+ acc.) to hear

слы́шно (14) audible

сма́затьᵖ (28) **-жу, -жешь (сма́зыва/ть¹ -ю, -ешь)** to grease

смерть (f) (17) gen.pl. **смерте́й** death

смета́на (3) sour cream

смеша́/тьᵖ (28) **-ю, -ешь (сме́шива/ть¹ -ю, ешь)** to mix

смешно́ (23) (it's) funny

смея́ться¹ (11) **смею́сь, смеёшься (за-ᵖ)** to laugh

смотре́ть¹ (11) **смотрю́, смо́тришь (по-ᵖ) ((на** + acc.) to watch; look (at)

смо́чь¹ (13) **смогу́, смо́жешь, смо́гут,** past **смог, смогла́, смогло́, смогли́ (мо́чь¹)** to be able (to), manage (to)

снача́ла (16) first, at first

снег (20) prep. **в снегу́**, pl. **снега́** snow

снима́/ть¹ (30) **-ю, -ешь (снять**ᵖ**)** to take off

сно́ва (17) again

сно́м – see **со́н**

снятьᵖ (30) **сниму́, сни́мешь,** f past **сняла́ (снима́ть¹)** (+ acc.) to take off

со = **с** before **с** + consonant, **мно́й, всего́, всем, все́ми, всех**

соба́ка (10) dog

собира́/ть¹ (26) **-ю, -ешь (собра́ть**ᵖ**)** to collect, gather

собира́/ться¹ (26) **-юсь, -ешься** (+ inf) to intend to

собо́й – see **себя́** self

собо́р Васи́лия Блаже́нного (15) St Basil's on Red Square ('the Cathedral of Vasilii the Blessed')

собра́тьᵖ (26) **соберу́, соберёшь** f past **собрала́ (собира́ть¹)** to gather

со́бственный (21) own, personal

сове́тник (30) adviser

Сове́тский Сою́з (22) Soviet Union

совреме́нный (13) modern, contemporary

совсе́м (10) completely

совсе́м нет (+ gen.) none at all

согла́сие (28) agreement

с согла́сия (28) (+ gen.) with the agreement of

содержа́ние (27) content(s)

Соединённые Шта́ты Аме́рики (12) United States of America

сожале́ние (10) regret

к сожале́нию (10) unfortunately

созда/ва́ть (17) **-ю́, -ёшь (созда́ть**[р]**)** (+ acc.) to create

созда́ние (28) creation

созда́ть[р] (17) like **дать**, past **со́здал, создала́, со́здало (создава́ть**) to create

сой/ти́[р] (20) **-ду́, -дёшь,** past **сошёл, сошла́, сошло́ (сходи́ть**) (20) (**с** + gen.) to get off, down

со́к (10) juice

солёный (28) salted, pickled

со́ль (f) (28) gen.pl. **соле́й** salt

соля́нка (28) solianka (spicy cabbage dish)

с(о́)н (17) sleep, dream

со́рок (22.3) forty

сосе́д (11) pl. **сосе́ди** gen.pl. **сосе́дей** neighbour

сосе́дний (20) neighbouring, next

спа́льня (7) gen.pl. **спа́лен** bedroom

спаси́бо (3) (**за** + acc.) thank you (for)

спать (16) **сплю, спишь (по-**[р]**)** to sleep

спекта́кль (m) (22) performance, show

спекуля́нт (24) speculator (black marketeer)

спе́лый (30) ripe

специали́ст (18) specialist

специа́льно (18) specially

спеш/и́ть (24) **-у́, -и́шь (по-**[р]**)** to hurry

спина́ (30) acc. **спи́ну,** pl. **спи́ны** back

спо́р/ить (27) **-ю, -ишь (по-**[р]**)** to argue, dispute

спосо́бность (f) (28) ability

спосо́бствовать (28) (+ dat.) to assist, facilitate

спра́вка (24) gen.pl. **спра́вок** (piece of) information

спра́шива/ть (13) **-ю, -ешь (спроси́ть**[р]**)** to ask (a question)

спроси́ть[р] (13) **спрошу́, спро́сишь** – see **спра́шивать**

спря́/тать[р] (21) **-чу, -чешь (пря́тать**) (+ acc.) to hide

спря́/таться[р] (30) **-чусь, -чешься (пря́таться**) (**за** + acc.) to hide behind

спуска́/ться (15) **-юсь, -ешься (спусти́ться**[р]**)** to go down

спусти́ться[р] (29) **спущу́сь, спу́-стишься (спуска́ться**) to go down

спустя́ (28) later

спу́тник (16) travelling companion

сравн/и́ть[р] (22) **-ю́, -и́шь (сра́внива/ть -ю, -ешь)** to compare

сра́зу (же) (21) immediately

среда́ (17) acc. **сре́ду,** pl. **сре́ды,** dat.pl. **среда́м** Wednesday

среди́ (17) (+ gen.) among

сре́дний (10) average; middle

сро́к (23) period of time; time limit

сро́чно (21) urgently

сро́чный (19) urgent

стадио́н (20) **(на)** stadium

стака́н (25) glass, tumbler

стан/ови́ться (16) **-овлю́сь, -о́вишься (стать**[р]**)** (+ inst.) to become

ста́нция (7) **(на)** station (on metro or in country)

стари́к (26) gen.sg. **старика́** old man

стару́шка (26) gen.pl. **стару́шек** old woman

ста́рший (18) elder; senior

ста́рый (7) old

ста́тский сове́тник (30) Councillor of State

статьᵖ (16) **ста́ну, ста́нешь (станови́ться**') (+ inst.) to become; to start (P only)

статья́ (26) gen.pl. **стате́й** article

стена́ (16) acc. **сте́ну**, pl. **сте́ны**, dat.pl. **стена́м** wall

сте́пень (f) (17) gen.pl. **степене́й** degree, extent

стиль (m) (21) style

стихи́ (23) (pl. of **стих**) gen.pl. **стихо́в** poetry

сто́ (22.3) hundred

сто́ить' (9) (24) **сто́ит, сто́ят** to cost; to be worth

не сто́ит (+ inf) it's not worth

стол (16) gen.sg. **стола́** table

столо́вый (28) table (adj)

столонача́льник (30) (old word) head of civil-service section

сто́лько (10) (+ gen.) so much, so many

сторона́ (15) acc. **сто́рону**, pl. **сто́роны** gen.pl. **сторо́н** side, direction

стоя́ть' (11) **стою́, стои́шь (по-**ᵖ**)** to stand

страна́ (12) pl. **стра́ны** country

стра́нно (20) strange; it's strange

стрел(ё)ц (28) gen.sg. **стрельца́** strelets

стрем/и́ться' (22) **-лю́сь, -и́шься** (к + dat.) to strive, try for

стро́ить (11) **стро́ю, стро́ишь (по-**ᵖ**)** to build

стро́иться' (11) **стро́ится** to be built ('build itself')

студе́нт (22) student

стул (29) pl. **сту́лья**, gen.pl. **сту́льев** chair

стуч/а́ть' (25) **-у́, -и́шь (по-**ᵖ**)** (в + acc) to knock (at)

сты́дно (14) shameful, it's shameful

суббо́та (14) Saturday

субтропи́ческий (29) subtropical

су́зитьсяᵖ (30) **су́зится (су́жива/ться**' **-ется)** to become narrow

су́мка (24) gen.pl. **су́мок** bag, shopping bag

суперзвезда́ (27) superstar

супру́г (22) male spouse, husband (formal word)

супру́га (27) female spouse, wife (formal word)

су́тки (f pl.) (23) gen.pl. **су́ток** twenty-four hours

суха́рь (m) (28) gen.sg. **сухаря́** rusk

сушёный (28) dried

существ/ова́ть' (22) **-у́ю, -у́ешь (про-**ᵖ**)** to exist

схвати́тьᵖ (25) **схвачу́, схва́тишь (хвата́/ть**' or **схва́тыва/ть**' **-ю, -ешь)** (+ acc. **за** + acc.) to seize (s.o. by sth)

сходи́тьᵖ (20) **схожу́, схо́дишь (сходи́ть**') to go on foot (there and back)

сходи́ть' (20) **схожу́, схо́дишь (сойти́**ᵖ**)** (+ gen.) to get off, go down from

сча́стье (12) (26) **[shshá-]** happiness, luck

к сча́стью (12) fortunately

счита́/ть' (13) **-ю, -ешь** (+ acc. + inst.)

to consider, count (sth as sth)

съёж/итьсяᴾ (30) **-усь, -ишься**
  (**съёжива/ться**ⁱ **-юсь, -ешься**) to
  shrivel, shrink

съе́здитьᴾ (20) **съе́зжу, съе́здишь**
  (**е́здить**ⁱ) to travel (there and back)

съестьᴾ – see **есть**ⁱ to eat

сын (6) pl. **сыновья́**, gen.pl. **сынове́й**,
  dat.pl. **сыновья́м** son

сыр (8) cheese

сюда́ (17) here (motion)

сюрпри́з (10) surprise

та́йный сове́тник (30) Privy Councillor

так (6) so

так как (10) since (because)

так что (26) so, so that

та́кже (7) also, in addition

тако́й (10) such

такси́ (n) (3) taxi

там (5) there

та́почки (11) gen.pl. **та́почек** slippers

таре́лка (20) gen.pl. **таре́лок** plate

таска́/тьⁱ (mv) (20) **-ю, -ешь** to drag

тащи́тьⁱ (u) (20) **тащу́, та́щишь (по-**ᴾ**)**
  to drag

твой (6) (T6) your

теа́тр (7) theatre

театра́льный (27) theatre (adj)

тебя́ see **ты** (T4) you

телеви́зор (13) television set

телефо́н (15) telephone

тем – inst. of **тот**

те́ма (16) theme, topic

тепе́рь (4) now

тепло́ (14) it's warm

тёплый (7) warm

терпе́тьⁱ (21) **терплю́, те́рпишь** to
  endure; to be patient

террито́рия (18) territory

те́сно (25) crowded; tight

тех – gen.pl. of **тот**

тёща (19) mother-in-law (wife's mother)

ти́хий (18) quiet

ти́хо (14) quiet, it's quiet

ти́ше (18) quieter

тишина́ (17) silence, quiet

то (12) then (in that case)

то есть (22) that is

то, что (26) the fact that

тобо́й see **ты** (T4) you

това́рищ (25) comrade, friend

тогда́ (12) at that time, in that case

тогда́шний (23) (coll) then (adj)

то́же (4) too

то́лстый (30) fat

то́лько (8) only

то́лько что (15) (+ past) just (= very
  recently)

тома́т-пюре́ (28) tomato purée

тон (30) tone

то́нкий (30) thin

торго́в(е)ц (24) (+ inst.) trader (dealing
  in)

торго́вля (28) trade

торже́ственный (29) grand, splendid,
  majestic

тот (7) (T4) that

тот же (28) (T4) the same

то́чно (9) exactly

трамва́й (15) gen.pl. **трамва́ев** tram

тре́б/оватьⁱ (21) **-ую, -уешь (по-**ᴾ**)**
  (+ gen.) to demand

тре́тий (7) third (T6)

треть (f) (22) gen.pl. **трете́й** a third

трёх – gen. of **три**

три (22.3) three

три́дцать (22.3) thirty

трина́дцать (22.3) thirteen

три́ста (22.3) three hundred

тро́га/тьᴵ (16) **-ю, -ешь (тро́н/уть**ᴾ **-у -ешь)** (+ acc.) to touch (s.o./sth)

тро́е (22.10) three

троекра́тно (30) thrice, three times

тройно́й (29) triple

тролле́йбус (4) trolley bus

труд (26) gen.sg. **труда́** work

тру́дно (14) difficult, it's difficult

тру́дность (f) (24) difficulty

тру́дный (13) difficult

туале́т (5) toilet

туале́тная бума́га (21) toilet paper

туда́ (9) there (motion 'thither')

ту́ловище (30) body, torso

тума́н (11) mist, fog

тургру́ппа (21) tourist group

тури́ст (15) tourist

тут (25) here

ту́фли (21) (f pl.) gen.pl. **ту́фель** shoes, house shoes

туше́ние (28) stewing

тушёный (28) stewed

туши́тьᴵ (28) **тушу́, ту́шишь (по-**ᴾ**)** to stew

ты (4) you (T4)

ты́сяча (9) (22) thousand

тяжёлый (28) heavy, hard

у (10) (+ gen.) near; by; at the house of; chez

убега́/тьᴵ (20) **-ю, -ешь (убежа́ть**ᴾ**)** to run away

убе/жа́тьᴾ (20) **-гу́, -жи́шь, -гу́т (убега́/ть**ᴵ**)** to run away

уважа́емый (26) respected

уважа́/тьᴵ (21) **-ю, -ешь** (+ acc.) to respect

уваже́ние (26) respect

уви́/детьᴾ (12) **-жу, -дишь (ви́деть**ᴵ**)** (+ acc.) to see, (past) to catch sight of

увлека́/тьсяᴵ (16) **-юсь, -ешься** (+ inst.) to be keen on, enthusiastic about

у́г(о)л (19) prep. **в/на углу́**, gen.sg. **угла́** corner

уделя́/тьᴵ (28) **-ю, -ешь (удел/и́ть**ᴾ **-ю́, -и́шь) внима́ние** (+ dat.) to pay attention to

удив/и́тьᴾ (27) **-лю́, -и́шь (удивля́ть**ᴵ**)** (+ acc.) to surprise (s.o.)

удив/и́тьсяᴾ (26) **-лю́сь, -и́шься (удивля́ться**ᴵ**)** to be surprised

удивлённо (26) with surprise

удивля́/тьᴵ (27) **-ю, -ешь** – see **удиви́ть**ᴾ

удивля́/тьсяᴵ (26) **-юсь, -ешься** (+ dat.) – see **удиви́ться**ᴾ

удово́льствие (16) pleasure, satisfaction

уезжа́/тьᴵ (14) **-ю, -ешь (уе́хать**ᴾ**)** to leave (by transport)

уе́хатьᴾ (14) **уе́ду, уе́дешь** – see **уезжа́ть**ᴵ

уже́ (6) already

уже́ не (24) no longer

уже́ нет (11) (+ gen.) there is/are no more

у́жин (16) supper

у́жина/ть (16) **-ю, -ешь (по-**ᴾ**)** to have supper

у́з(е)л (30) gen.sg. **узла́** bundle

узна/ва́тьᴵ (28) **-ю́, -ёшь (узна́ть**ᴾ**)** to find out; to recognize

узна́/тьᴾ (28) **-ю, -ешь (узнава́ть**ᴵ**)** to find out; to recognize

уйти́ᴾ (12) **уйду́, уйдёшь**, past **ушёл, ушла́, ушло́ (уходи́ть**ᴵ**)** to leave

Украи́на (5) **(на)** Ukraine

укра́/ситьᴾ (29) **-шу, -сишь**
(**украша́/ть**ⁱ **-ю, -ешь**) to adorn

укрепле́ние (28) strengthening

у́ксус (28) vinegar

у́лица (4) **(на)** street

улыба́/тьсяⁱ (11) **-юсь, -ешься**
(**улыбн/у́ться**ᴾ **-у́сь, -ёшься**) to
smile

улы́бка (26) gen.pl. **улы́бок** smile

уме́/тьⁱ (13) **-ю, -ешь** (+ inf) to know how to

умира́/тьⁱ (23) **-ю, -ешь** (**умере́ть**ᴾ) to
die

у́мный (18) clever

у́мственный (28) mental

унес/ти́ᴾ (27) **-у́, -ёшь**, past **унёс,**
унесла́, унесло́ (**уноси́ть**ⁱ) (+ acc.)
to carry away

университе́т (5) university

уничтоже́ние (28) annihilation

уноси́тьⁱ (27) **уношу́, уно́сишь**
(**унести́**ᴾ) (+ acc.) to carry away

упади́ (15) – see **упа́сть**

упа́стьᴾ **упаду́, упадёшь**, past **упа́л,**
упа́ла (**па́дать**ⁱ **-ю, -ешь**) to fall

упражне́ние (3) exercise

Ура́л (17) **(на)** the Urals

у́ров(е)нь (m) (26) gen.sg. **у́ровня** level

урождённая (30) née (indicating
maiden name)

уро́к (16) **(на)** lesson

урони́тьᴾ (30) **уроню́, уро́нишь**
(**роня́/ть**ⁱ **-ю, -ешь**) (+ acc.) to drop

усло́вие (28) condition

услы́ш/атьᴾ (20) **-у, -ишь** (**слы́шать**ⁱ)
(+ acc.) to hear

успева́/тьⁱ (15) **-ю, -ешь** (**успе́ть**ᴾ)
(+ inf) to have time (to do sth)

успе́/тьᴾ **-ю, -ешь** – see **успева́ть**ⁱ

устава́тьⁱ (15) **устаю́, устаёшь**
(**уста́ть**ᴾ) to get tired

уста́/тьᴾ (15) **-ну, -нешь** – see **устава́ть**ⁱ

устра́ива/тьⁱ (21) **-ю, -ешь** (**устро́ить**ᴾ)
(+ acc.) to organize (sth); to suit (s.o.)

устрем/и́тьᴾ (30) **-лю́, и́шь**
(**устремля́/ть**ⁱ **-ю, -ешь**) to direct,
fasten (one's gaze)

устро́/итьᴾ (21) **-ю, -ишь** – see
устра́иватьⁱ

усту́пка (30) gen.pl. **усту́пок** price
reduction; concession

у́тро (3) gen.sg. **у́тра**, but **до/с утра́**, pl.
у́тра, gen.pl. **утр**, dat.pl. **у́трам** but
по утра́м morning

у́тром (16) in the morning

у́хо (25) pl. **у́ши** ear

уходи́тьⁱ (12) **ухожу́, ухо́дишь** (**уйти́**ᴾ)
to go away

уху́дш/итьсяᴾ (28) **-ится**
(**ухудша́/ться**ⁱ **- ется**) to get worse

уча́ств/оватьⁱ (27) **-ую, -уешь**
(**в** + prep.) to participate in

учени́к (30) gen.sg. **ученика́** pupil

учи́тель (m) (16) pl. **учителя́** teacher,
schoolteacher

учи́тьⁱ (13) **учу́, у́чишь** (**вы́-**ᴾ) to learn

учи́тьсяⁱ (13) **учу́сь, у́чишься** to study
(somewhere)

учрежде́ние (23) institution; office

у́шко (25) pl. **у́шки**, gen.pl. **у́шек** little ear

фами́лия (6) surname

фаса́д (29) façade

февра́ль (m) (17) gen.sg. **февраля́**
February

физи́ческий (28) physical

фильм (11) film

фи́рма (23) firm, company

флёрдора́нж (30) orange blossom (scent)

францу́зский (18) French

фрукт (8) a piece of fruit

фу́нт (9) pound (weight and currency)

фура́жка (30) gen.pl. **фура́жек** peaked cap

хе́рес (30) sherry

хлеб (8) bread

ходи́ть' (mv) (9) (20) **хожу́, хо́дишь** to go on foot (there and back)

хозя́ин (25) pl. **хозя́ева** gen.pl. **хозя́ев** host, owner, master

хо́лод (11) cold

холоди́льник (13) refrigerator

хо́лодно (14) it's cold; coldly

холо́дный (7) cold

хороше́нько (30) properly, well and truly

хоро́ший (8) good

хорошо́ (4) well

хоте́ть' (12.5) **хочу́, хо́чешь, хо́чет, хоти́м, хоти́те, хотя́т (за-ᴾ)** to want

хо́ть (23) even

хотя́ (16) although

ху́денький (30) thin

худо́й (18) thin

ху́же (18) worse

царе́вич (28) son of a tsar

царь (m) (5) gen.sg. **царя́** tsar (emperor)

цвет (21) pl. **цвета́** colour

цел/ова́ть' (26) **-у́ю, -у́ешь (по-ᴾ)** (+ acc.) to kiss

цель (f) (28) goal, aim

цена́ (10) acc. **це́ну**, pl. **це́ны** price

центр (5) centre

центра́льный (20) central

це́рковь (f) (24) gen./dat./prep.sg. **це́ркви**, inst. **це́рковью**, pl. **це́ркви, церкве́й, церква́м, церква́ми, церква́х** church

цивилиза́ция (28) civilization

чай (3) tea

ча́йник (21) kettle; teapot

час (6) gen.sg. **ча́са** but **два/три/четы́ре часа́**, pl. **часы́** hour

ча́сто (12) often

ча́стый (21) frequent

часть (f) (18) gen.pl. **часте́й** part

часы́ (17) (pl. of **час**) watch; clock

ча́шка (21) gen.pl. **ча́шек** cup

ча́ще (18) more often

чего́ [chye-vó] gen. of **что́**

челове́к (18) – pl. see **лю́ди** person

чем (18) than; also inst. of **что́**

чём – prep. of **что́**

чемода́н (29) suitcase

чему́ – dat. of **что́**

че́рез (6) (+ acc.) through; across; after (a period of time)

чёрный (8) black

четве́рг (17) gen.sg. **четверга́** Thursday

че́тверо (22.10) four

четвёртый (15) fourth

че́тверть (f) (22) quarter

четы́ре (22.3) four

четы́реста (22.3) four hundred

четы́рнадцать (22.3) fourteen

чино́вник (27) bureaucrat

чинопочита́ние (28) respect for rank, boot-licking

число́ (17) (22) pl. **чи́сла** gen. pl. **чи́сел** number; date

в числе́ (27) (+ gen.) among

чи́стый (18) pure, clean

чита́/ть˙ (12) **-ю, -ешь (про-ᵖ)** (+ acc.)
to read

что́ (3) (5.8) (T4) **[shto]** what; that

что́ ли? (10.15) am I? is it? etc.

что́бы (21) **[shtó-bi̇]** (in order) to

что́-либо (26) anything whatever

что́-нибудь (9) anything

что́-то (26) something

чу́вств/овать˙ (21) **-ую, -уешь (по-ᵖ)**
(+ acc.) to feel (something)

чуде́сный (17) wonderful

шампа́нское (n adj) (12) champagne,
sparkling wine

ша́пка (14) gen.pl. **ша́пок** hat (no
brim); cap

ша́ркн/утьᵖ (30) **-у, -ешь (ша́рка/ть**˙ **-ю,
-ешь)** to shuffle

шестна́дцать (22.3) sixteen

шесть (22.3) six

шестьдеся́т (22.3) sixty

шестьсо́т (22.3) six hundred

ши́ре (18) wider

широ́кий (18) wide

широча́йший (30) widest

шко́ла (7) school

шокола́д (3) chocolate

шофёр (13) driver

шту́ка (30) thing, piece

шу́мно (14) noisy, it's noisy

шу́мный (26) noisy

шути́ть˙ (23) **шучу́, шу́тишь (по-ᵖ)** to
joke

шу́тка (11) gen.pl. **шу́ток** joke

щёголь (m) (30) dandy

щи (pl) (1) gen. **щей**, dat. **щам**, inst.
ща́ми, prep. **щах** cabbage soup

экза́мен (23) **(на)** examination

экономи́ческий (28) economic

экску́рсия (17) excursion

электробри́тва (21) electric razor

эмигри́р/овать/ᵖ (23) **-ую, -уешь** to
emigrate

эне́ргия (28) energy

эпо́ха (23) era, epoch

Эрмита́ж (11) the Hermitage

эта́ж (7) **(на)** gen.sg. **этажа́** floor,
storey

э́то (3) this/that/it

э́тот (7) (T4) this

юг (14) **(на)** south

ю́жный (18) southern

я (4) I (T4)

я́беднича/ть**˙ (30) **-ю, -ешь** to tell tales,
sneak

я́блоко (30) pl. **я́блоки**, gen.pl. **я́блок**
apple

явля́/ться˙ (16) **-юсь, -ешься** (+ inst.)
to be

яйцо́ (8) **[yee-tsó]** pl. **я́йца**, gen.pl. **яи́ц**,
dat.pl. **я́йцам** egg

яи́чница (16) **[ye͑esh-nee-tsa]** fried
eggs

янва́рь (m) (17) gen.sg. **января́**
January

язы́к (4) gen.sg. **языка́** language

427

ENGLISH–RUSSIAN VOCABULARY

This quick-reference list will enable you to trace any Russian word you may have forgotten since you met it in one of the lessons. For more grammatical information about the Russian words, refer to the Russian–English list.

Abbreviations:

acc.	accusative	m	masculine
adj	adjective	n	neuter
adv	adverb	nom.	nominative
coll	colloquial usage	past	past tense
comp	comparative	p	perfective
dat.	dative	pl.	plural
dim	diminutive	pol.pl.	polite plural
f	feminine	PPP	past passive participle
fam	familiar	prep.	prepositional
fut.	future tense	pres.	present tense
gen.	genitive	sg.	singular
i	imperfective	s.o.	someone
imper	imperative	sth	something
indecl	indeclinable	T	Grammatical Table
inf	infinitive		(see pages 378–86)
inst.	instrumental		

ability **спосо́бность** (f) 28

about **о** (5) + prep.

above **над** (16) + inst.

abroad **за грани́цей** (28) (place);
 за грани́цу (28) (motion)

absent-minded **рассе́янный** (19)

accent **акце́нт** (23)

accept **принима́ть**ᴵ (27) **(приня́ть**ᴾ**)**

according to **по** (12) + dat.

achieve **добива́ться**ᴵ (28) **(доби́ться**ᴾ**)**

acquaintance **знако́мая** (f adj.) (26),
 знако́мый (m adj.) (26)

acquire **приобрета́ть**ᴵ (27)
 (приобрести́ᴾ**)**

across **че́рез** (6) + acc.

actor **актёр** (27)

actress **актри́са** (27)

add **добавля́ть**ᴵ (28) **(доба́вить**ᴾ**)**,
 прибавля́тьᴵ (28) **(приба́вить**ᴾ**)**

address **а́дрес** (26)

Admiralty **Адмиралте́йство** (29)

admirer **покло́нник** (27)

advanced **передово́й** (28)

adviser **сове́тник** (30)

aeroplane **самолёт** (20)

Africa **А́фрика** (27)

after (a period of time) **че́рез** (6) + acc.

after **по́сле** (10) + gen.

again **ещё раз** (15), **опя́ть, сно́ва**
 (17)

aged **престаре́лый** (23)

agent **аге́нт** (27)

ago **наза́д** (13)

agree (reach agreement)
 догова́риватьсяᴵ (19)
 (договори́тьсяᴾ**)**

agreement **согла́сие** (28)

aim **цель** (f) (28)

airmail envelope **авиаконве́рт** (10)

all **весь** (11) (T4)

allow **разреша́ть**ᴵ (15) **(разреши́ть**ᴾ**)**

allowed: it's allowed **мо́жно** (14)

almost **почти́** (13)

alone **оди́н** (m)/**одна́** (f)/**одно́** (n) (22)

along **по** (12) + dat.

already **уже́** (6)

also (in addition) **кро́ме того́** (12),
 та́кже (7)

although **хотя́** (16)

always **всегда́** (8)

America **Аме́рика** (13)

American (adj.) **америка́нский** (7)

American (man) **америка́н(е)ц** (8)

American (woman) **америка́нка** (18)

among **среди́** (17) + gen.

ancient **дре́вний** (18)

and **и** (4)

and/but (slight contrast) **а** (3)

angry **гне́вный** (21)

animal (wild) **зверь** (m) (18)

annihilation **уничтоже́ние** (28)

anniversary **годовщи́на** (14)

announce **объявля́ть**ᴵ (27)
 (объяви́тьᴾ**), заявля́ть**ᴵ (21)
 (заяви́тьᴾ**)**

announcement **объявле́ние** (2)

answer **отвеча́ть**ᴵ (13) **(отве́тить**ᴾ**)**

any (any kind of) **како́й-нибудь** (26),
 (any one you like) **любо́й** (15),
 (none at all) **никако́й** (24)

anyone **кто́-нибудь** (26)

anything **что́-нибудь** (9), (anything
 whatever) **что́-либо** (26)

anywhere (motion) **куда́-нибудь** (26)

anywhere (place) **где́-нибудь** (26)

apart from **кро́ме** (10)

apartment **кварти́ра** (7)

apologize **извиня́ться**ⁱ (19)
(извини́тьсяᵖ**)**

applaud **аплоди́ровать**ⁱ (27)

apple **я́блоко** (8)

application **заявле́ние** (22)

approximately **о́коло** (10) + gen.,
приме́рно (22)

April **апре́ль** (m) (17)

architectural **архитекту́рный** (29)

argue **спо́рить**ⁱ (27) **(по-**ᵖ**)**

arm **рука́** (22)

arrival (by transport) **прие́зд** (23)

arrive (by air) **прилета́ть**ⁱ (20)
(прилете́тьᵖ**)**

arrive (by transport) **приезжа́ть**ⁱ (13)
(прие́хатьᵖ**)**

arrive (on foot) **приходи́ть**ⁱ (12)
(прийти́ᵖ**)**

article **статья́** (26)

as far as **до** (9)

as for **что́ каса́ется** + gen.

Asia **А́зия** (18)

ask (a question) **спра́шивать**ⁱ (13)
(спроси́тьᵖ**)**

ask (s.o. to do sth) **проси́ть**ⁱ (15)
(по-ᵖ**)**

assignment **командиро́вка** (19)

astound **ошеломля́ть**ⁱ (30)
(ошеломи́тьᵖ**)**

at **в/на** (4), (at the house of) **у** (10)

at the time of (under) **при** (5) (28)
+ prep.

atmosphere **атмосфе́ра** (26)

attached to **при** (5) (28) + prep.

attention **внима́ние** (24)

attitude **отноше́ние** (21)

attractive **краси́во** (14), **краси́вый**
(7)

August **а́вгуст** (17)

author **а́втор** (21)

authorities **вла́сти** (f pl.) (24)

autocracy **самодержа́вие** (28)

autumn **о́сень** (f) (16)

avenue **проспе́кт** (4)

average **сре́дний** (10)

away from **от** (9) + gen.

awkward **неудо́бно** (10)

back (adv.) **наза́д** (13)

back (noun) **спина́** (30)

backwardness **отста́лость** (f) (28)

bad **плохо́й** (8)

bag (handbag) **су́мка** (24), (sack)
меш(о́)к (25)

Baltic Sea **Балти́йское мо́ре** (11)

banana **бана́н** (10)

bank **бе́рег** (18)

bar **бар** (18)

barber's **парикма́херская** (f.adj.)
(23)

bathroom **ва́нная** (f.adj.) (7)

bay **бу́хта** (29)

be **быть**ⁱ (11), (repeatedly/often)
быва́тьⁱ (23), **явля́ться**ⁱ (16)

be able **мо́чь**ⁱ (13) (15) **(с-**ᵖ**)**

be afraid **боя́ться**ⁱ (15)

be angry **серди́ться**ⁱ (11) **(рас-**ᵖ**)**

be born **роди́ться**ᵖ (13)

be called (of thing) **называ́ться**ⁱ (11)

be interested **интересова́ться**ⁱ (16)
(за-ᵖ**)**

be keen on **увлека́ться**ⁱ (16)

be patient **терпе́ть**ⁱ (21) **(по-**ᵖ**)**

be situated **находи́ться**ⁱ (15)

be surprised **удивля́ться**ⁱ (26)

(удиви́тьсяᵖ**)**
be upset **пережива́ть**ⁱ (24)
beard **борода́** (28)
beautiful **краси́во** (14), **краси́вый** (7), **прекра́сный** (24)
beauty **красота́** (11)
because **потому́ что** (12)
because of **из-за** (11)
become free **освобожда́ться**ⁱ (15) **(освободи́ться**ᵖ**)**
become **станови́ться**ⁱ (16) **(стать**ᵖ**)**
bed **крова́ть** (f) (21)
bedroom **спа́льня** (7)
beer **пи́во** (20)
beetroot soup **борщ** (3)
before (prep.) **пе́ред** (16) + inst.
before (adv.) **ра́ньше** (16), **пре́жде** (26)
begin **начина́ть(ся)**ⁱ (11) **(нача́ть(ся)**ᵖ**), стать**ᵖ (ᵖ only) (16)
beginning **нача́ло** (18)
behind **за** + acc. (6) (motion), + inst. (place)
believe **ве́рить**ⁱ (21) **(по-**ᵖ**)**
beloved **люби́мый** (16)
bench **скамья́, скаме́йка** (26)
beside **ря́дом** (7) (16) **с** + inst.
best **лу́чший** (18)
better **лу́чше** (18)
between **ме́жду** (16)
big **большо́й** (7)
bigger **бо́льший** (18)
billion (US) **миллиа́рд** (22) (thousand million)
bird **пти́ца** (18)
birth **рожде́ние** (17)
birthday **день рожде́ния** (17)
black **чёрный** (8)
boiling water **кипят(о́)к** (21)

book **кни́га** (7)
border **грани́ца** (18)
bore (verb) **надоеда́ть**ⁱ **(надое́сть**ᵖ**)**
boring: it's boring **ску́чно** (14) [sko´o-*sh*na]
both **о́ба** (m/n)/**о́бе** (f) (22.4), **и . . . и** (22.4)
bottle **буты́лка** (9)
bow **кла́няться**ⁱ (30) **(поклони́ться**ᵖ**)**
bowl **ми́ска** (28)
boy **ма́льчик** (13)
boyar (powerful landowner) **боя́рин** (28)
brandy **конья́к** (25)
bread **хлеб** (8)
break **переры́в** (17)
break up **распада́ться**ⁱ (22) **(распа́сться**ᵖ**)**
breakfast (verb) **за́втракать**ⁱ (16) **(по-**ᵖ**)**
breakfast (noun) **за́втрак** (16)
bridge **мост** (7)
briefcase **портфе́ль** (29) (m)
bring (by carrying) **приноси́ть**ⁱ (20) **(принести́**ᵖ**)**
bring (by leading) **приводи́ть**ⁱ (20) **(привести́**ᵖ**)**
bring (by transport) **привози́ть**ⁱ (20) **(привезти́**ᵖ**)**
bring up (s.o.) **воспи́тывать**ⁱ (19)
Britain **Великобрита́ния** (27)
British **брита́нский** (7)
brother **брат** (3)
build **стро́ить**ⁱ (11) **(по-**ᵖ**)**
building **зда́ние** (15)
bundle **у́з(е)л** (30)
bureaucrat **чино́вник** (27)
bus **авто́бус** (4)

business trip **командиро́вка** (19)
businessman **бизнесме́н** (29)
busy **за́нят** (25)
but **но** (4)
butter **ма́сло** (8)
buy **покупа́ть**ᐟ (8) (12) **(купи́ть**ᵖ**)**
by **у** (10) + gen.
by chance **случа́йно** (24)

cabbage **капу́ста** (12)
cabbage soup **щи** (pl.) (1)
call **звать**ᐟ (4) **(по-**ᵖ**)**
call in **заходи́ть**ᐟ (20) **(зайти́**ᵖ**)**
campaign **кампа́ния** (27)
cap **ша́пка** (14)
car **маши́на** (10)
carpenter **пло́тник** (28)
carriage **ваго́н** (20)
carry **носи́ть**ᐟ (20), **нести́**ᐟ (20) **(по-**ᵖ**)**
carry across **переноси́ть**ᐟ (21)
    (перенести́ᵖ**)**
carry away **уноси́ть**ᐟ (27) **(унести́**ᵖ**)**
case (incident, instance) **слу́чай** (22)
case (suitcase) **чемода́н** (29)
cash desk **ка́сса** (1)
catch sight of **уви́деть**ᵖ (12)
cathedral **собо́р** (15)
cause (of) **причи́на** (21) (+ gen.)
caviare (fish roe) **икра́** (25)
celebrate **отмеча́ть**ᐟ (14) **(отме́тить**ᵖ**)**
central **центра́льный** (20)
centre **центр** (5)
century **век** (17)
certain (some) **не́которые** (17),
    ко́е-каки́е (26)
chair **стул** (29)
chairman **председа́тель** (m) (16)
champagne **шампа́нское** (n.adj.) (12)
change **меня́ть(ся)**ᐟ (23)

change (money returned) **сда́ча** (9)
change (transport) **переса́живаться**ᐟ
    (15) **(пересе́сть**ᵖ**)**
chapter **глава́** (28)
chase **гоня́ть**ᐟ (20), **гнать**ᐟ (20) **(по-**ᵖ**)**
cheap **дешёвый** (18)
check **проверя́ть**ᐟ (21) **(прове́рить**ᵖ**)**
cheerful **весёлый** (18)
cheese **сыр** (8)
cherry **ви́шня** (30)
Chicken Kiev **котле́ты по-ки́евски**
    (12)
chief **глава́** (28)
child **ребён(о)к** (10) pl. **де́ти**
childhood **де́тство** (17)
children **де́ти** (10)
chin **подборо́д(о)к** (30)
China **Кита́й** (18)
Chinese (noun) **кита́(е)ц** (30)
chocolate **шокола́д** (3)
choose **выбира́ть**ᐟ (27) **(вы́брать**ᵖ**)**
church **це́рковь** (f) (24)
cinema **кино́** (n indecl) (11),
    кинотеа́тр (20)
circuit **сеть** (f) (21)
circumstance **обстоя́тельство** (24)
city **го́род** (7)
civilization **цивилиза́ция** (28)
clamber **ла́зить**ᐟ (20), **лезть**ᐟ (20)
    (по-ᵖ**)**
class **класс** (30)
clean (adj.) **чи́стый** (18)
clean (verb) **очища́ть**ᐟ (28),
    (очи́ститьᵖ**)**
clever **у́мный** (18)
client **клие́нт** (15)
climb up **поднима́ться**ᐟ (19)
    (подня́тьсяᵖ**)**
climb **ла́зить**ᐟ (20), **лезть**ᐟ (20) **(по-**ᵖ**)**

clock **часы́** (17) (pl. of **час**)

close **закрыва́ть(ся)**ⁱ (17) **(закры́ть(ся)**ᵖ**)**

coat **пальто́** (n indecl) (7)

coffee **ко́фе** (m indecl) (5)

cognac **конья́к** (25)

cold **холо́дный** (7), (it's cold) **хо́лодно** (14), (noun) **хо́лод** (11)

coldly **хо́лодно** (14)

collect **собира́ть**ⁱ (26) **(собра́ть**ᵖ**)**

colour **цвет** (21)

come (by transport) **приезжа́ть**ⁱ (13) **(прие́хать**ᵖ**)**

come (on foot) **приходи́ть**ⁱ (12) **(прийти́**ᵖ**)**

come back **возвраща́ться**ⁱ (14) **(верну́ться**ᵖ**)**

common **распространённый** (23)

Communism **коммуни́зм** (29)

company **фи́рма** (23), **компа́ния** (14) (27)

compare **сра́внивать**ⁱ (22) **(сравни́ть**ᵖ**)**

compel **обя́зывать**ⁱ (28) **(обяза́ть**ᵖ**)**

complain **жа́ловаться**ⁱ (21) **(по-**ᵖ**)**

completely **совсе́м** (10), **по́лностью** (28)

comprehensible **поня́тно** (14)

comrade **това́рищ** (25)

concern **каса́ться**ⁱ (21)

concerning **о** (5) + prep.

concert **конце́рт** (11)

concession **усту́пка** (30)

condition **усло́вие** (28)

conduct **проводи́ть**ⁱ (17) **(провести́**ᵖ**)**

conflict **конфли́кт** (22)

congratulate **поздравля́ть**ⁱ (23) **(поздра́вить**ᵖ**)**

congratulation **поздравле́ние** (26)

congratulations! **поздравля́ю!** (6)

consequently **поэ́тому** (9)

consider **счита́ть**ⁱ (13)

contact **конта́кт** (23)

contemporary **совреме́нный** (13)

content(s) **содержа́ние** (27)

continue **продолжа́ть(ся)**ⁱ (11)

contract **контра́кт** (23)

conversation **разгово́р** (10)

converse **разгова́ривать**ⁱ (16)

cook **гото́вить**ⁱ (16) **(при-**ᵖ**)**

corner **у́г(о)л** (19)

cost **сто́ить**ⁱ (9)

cottage (peasant's) **изба́** (25)

count **счита́ть**ⁱ (13) **(со-**ᵖ**)**

country (opposite of town) **дере́вня** (19)

country (state) **страна́** (12)

couple **па́ра** (22)

course (of a meal) **блю́до** (12)

course (of study) **ку́рсы** (pl. of **курс**) (13)

courtyard **двор** (26)

cover **покрыва́ть**ⁱ (28) **(покры́ть**ᵖ**)**

crawl **по́лзать** (20), **ползти́** (20) **(по-**ᵖ**)**

create **создава́ть**ⁱ (17) **(созда́ть**ᵖ**)**

creation **созда́ние** (28)

Crimea **Крым** (5)

Crimean **кры́мский** (12)

cross **переходи́ть**ⁱ (19) **(перейти́**ᵖ**)**

crossing (street) **перехо́д** (15)

crowded: it's crowded **те́сно** (25)

cry **пла́кать**ⁱ (15) **(за-**ᵖ**)**

cucumber **огур(е́)ц** (28)

cultural **культу́рный** (28)

culture **культу́ра** (21)

cup **ча́шка** (21)

currency **валю́та** (24), **валю́тный** (9) (adj.)

433

custom **обы́чай** (28)

customer **посети́тель** (m) (12)

cut **нареза́ть**' (28) **(наре́зать**ᵖ**)**

dad **па́па** (m) (3)

date **число́** (17)

daughter **до́чь** (f) (5.6)

day (not night) **д(е)нь** (m) (3)

day (twenty-four hours) **су́тки** (f pl.) (23)

day before yesterday **позавчера́** (18)

day off **выходно́й день** (17)

dear (expensive) **дорого́й** (8)

dear (nice) **дорого́й** (8), **ми́лый** (30)

death **смерть** (f) (7)

December **дека́брь** (m) (17)

decide **реша́ть**' (13) **(реши́ть**ᵖ**)**

decision **реше́ние** (27)

deep **глубо́кий** (18)

defend **защища́ть**' (22) **(защити́ть**ᵖ**)**

define **определя́ть**' (29) **(определи́ть**ᵖ**)**

definitely **обяза́тельно** (15)

degree **сте́пень** (f) (17)

deliberately **наро́чно** (21)

demand **тре́бовать**' (21) **(по-**ᵖ**)**

depart (of train) **отходи́ть**' (20) **(отойти́**ᵖ**)**

department (of shop) **отде́л** (8)

departure **отъе́зд** (26)

depend **зави́сеть**' (19)

deputy **замести́тель** (m) (23)

development **разви́тие** (21)

dictionary **слова́рь** (10) (m)

die **умира́ть**' (23) **(умере́ть**ᵖ**)**

difficult **тру́дный** (13), (it's difficult) **тру́дно** (14)

difficulty **тру́дность** (f) (24)

dimension **разме́р** (10)

dine **обе́дать**' (12) **(по-**ᵖ**)**

dinner **обе́д** (12)

direct (adj.) **прямо́й** (12)

direct (verb) **направля́ть**' (28) **(напра́вить**ᵖ**)**

director **дире́ктор** (23)

dirty **гря́зный** (20)

discuss **обсужда́ть**' (27) **(обсуди́ть**ᵖ**)**

disease **боле́знь** (f) (11)

disgusting **проти́вно** (30)

divide up **разделя́ть**' (21) **(раздели́ть**ᵖ**)**

divorce **разво́д** (14)

divorced **разведённый** (27)

do **де́лать**' (8) (12) **(с-**ᵖ**)**

doctor **врач** (16)

dog **соба́ка** (10)

dollar **до́ллар** (9)

don't mention it **пожа́луйста** (3)

door **дверь** (f) (3)

down **вниз** (15)

drag **таска́ть**' (20), **тащи́ть**' (20) **(по-**ᵖ**)**

dream **с(о́)н** (17)

dress (oneself) **одева́ть(ся)**' (11) **(оде́ть(ся)**ᵖ**)**

dress (n.) **пла́тье** (25)

dried **сушёный** (28)

drink **пить**' (12) **(вы́-**ᵖ**)**

drive **гоня́ть** (20), **гнать**' (20) **(по-**ᵖ**)**

drive across **переезжа́ть**' (13) **(перее́хать**ᵖ**)**

driver **шофёр** (13)

drop **роня́ть** (30) **(урони́ть**ᵖ**)**

drunk **пья́ный** (14)

during **во вре́мя** (17)

each **ка́ждый** (9)

each other **друг дру́га** (30)

ear **у́хо** (25)

earlier **ра́ньше** (16)

early **ра́но** (16)

earth **земля́** (2)

east **восто́к** (18)

eastern **восто́чный** (18)

easy **лёгкий** (18)

eat **есть**ⁱ (12) **(съесть**ᵖ**)**

economic **экономи́ческий** (28)

egg **яйцо́** (8)

eight **во́семь** (9)

eight hundred **восемьсо́т** (9)

eighteen **восемна́дцать** (9)

eighty **во́семьдесят** (9)

elder **ста́рший** (18)

electricity socket **розе́тка** (21)

electric razor **электробри́тва** (21)

electrician **монтёр** (21)

eleven **оди́ннадцать** (9)

embassy **посо́льство** (7)

emigrate **эмигри́ровать**ⁱ/ᵖ (23)

end **кон(е́)ц** (18), **оконча́ние** (28)

endure **терпе́ть**ⁱ (21) **(по-**ᵖ**)**

energy **эне́ргия** (28)

engineer **инжене́р** (16)

England **А́нглия** (5)

English **англи́йский** (10)

English: in English **по-англи́йски** (4)

Englishman **англича́нин** (5)

Englishwoman **англича́нка** (3)

enormous **огро́мный** (18)

enough **доста́точно** (19)

enter **входи́ть**ⁱ (13) **(войти́**ᵖ**)**

enter (university) **поступа́ть**ⁱ (13)

  (поступи́тьᵖ**)**

entrance **вход** (19)

entrance (of block) **подъе́зд** (19)

envelope **конве́рт** (10)

envy **зави́довать**ⁱ (23) **(по-**ᵖ**)**

epoch **эпо́ха** (23)

era **эпо́ха** (23)

essential **необходи́мо** (14)

European (adj) **европе́йский** (21)

European (noun) **европе́(е)ц** (28)

even **да́же** (14), **хоть** (23)

evening (adj.) **вече́рний** (7)

evening (noun) **ве́чер** (16)

ever **когда́-нибудь** (26)

every (each) **ка́ждый** (9)

every (all) **весь** (11) (Т4)

everybody **все** (11) (Т4)

everything **всё** (10) (Т4)

exactly **то́чно** (9), **как раз** (20)

examination **экза́мен** (23)

excellent **отли́чный** (26)

except **кро́ме** (10)

exclaim **восклица́ть**ⁱ (30)

  (воскли́кнутьᵖ**)**

exclude **исключа́ть**ⁱ (27)

  (исключи́тьᵖ**)**

excursion **экску́рсия** (17)

excuse (me) **прости́(те)** (3),

  извини́(те) (11)

execute **казни́ть**ⁱ/ᵖ (28)

exercise **упражне́ние** (3)

exist **существова́ть**ⁱ (28) **(про-**ᵖ**)**

exit **вы́ход** (15)

expect **ожида́ть**ⁱ (11)

expensive **дорого́й** (8)

expression **выраже́ние** (21)

extent **сте́пень** (f) (17)

extraordinarily **необыча́йно** (29)

eye **глаз** (25)

façade **фаса́д** (29)

face **лицо́** (21)

factory **заво́д** (16)

fairly **дово́льно** (15)

faithful **ве́рный** (29)

fall **па́дать¹ (упа́сть**ᵖ**)**

family (adj) **семе́йный** (22)

family (noun) **семья́** (12)

famous **знамени́тый** (7)

far **далеко́** (12), (adj) **далёкий** (18)

farewell (noun) **проща́ние** (30)

fast **бы́стро** (13)

fasten **застёгивать¹**

   (застегну́тьᵖ**)**

fat (adj) **то́лстый** (30)

fat (noun) **жир** (28)

father **от(е́)ц** (6), **па́па** (m) (3)

favourite **люби́мый** (16)

February **февра́ль** (m) (17)

feel **чу́вствовать¹** (21) **(по-**ᵖ**)**

female **же́нский** (15)

festival **пра́здник** (17) [práz-neek]

few (several) **не́сколько** (9)

few (not many) **ма́ло** (9)

fifteen **пятна́дцать** (9)

fifty **пятьдеся́т** (9)

film **фильм** (11)

find **находи́ть¹** (13) **(найти́**ᵖ**)**

find oneself **ока́зываться¹** (20) (26)

   (оказа́тьсяᵖ**)**

find out **узнава́ть¹** (28) **(узна́ть**ᵖ**)**

fine **прекра́сный** (24)

finger **па́л(е)ц** (16)

finish **конча́ть¹** (13) **(ко́нчить**ᵖ**)**

firm (company) **фи́рма** (23)

firmly **кре́пко** (26)

first (adj) **пе́рвый** (7)

first (at first) **снача́ла** (16)

fish **ры́ба** (10), **ры́бный** (10) (adj)

five hundred **пятьсо́т** (9)

five **пять** (9)

flat **кварти́ра** (7)

floor **эта́ж** (7)

fly **лета́ть¹** (20) **лете́ть¹** (20) **(по-**ᵖ**)**

fly in **влета́ть¹** (20) **(влете́ть**ᵖ**)**

fly out **вылета́ть¹** (20) **(вы́лететь**ᵖ**)**

fly past/through **пролета́ть¹** (20)

   (пролете́тьᵖ**)**

fog **тума́н** (11)

following **сле́дующий** (8)

food **проду́кты** (m pl.) (8)

food shop **гастроно́м** (17)

foot **нога́** (25)

for (benefit, purpose) **для** (10) + gen.

for (in return for) **за** (6) + acc.

for (to fetch) **за** (16) + inst.

for (time) **на** (23) + acc.

for example **наприме́р** (18)

for some reason **почему́-то** (26)

for the sake of **ра́ди** (10) + gen.

force **вынужда́ть¹** (27) **(вы́нудить**ᵖ**)**

forced **вы́нужден** (PPP) (27)

foreign **иностра́нный** (10),

   зарубе́жный (17)

foreigner **иностра́н(е)ц** (16)

forename **и́мя** (noun) (6) (T4)

forest **лес** (5)

forget **забыва́ть¹** (13) **(забы́ть**ᵖ**)**

form **вид** (18), **о́браз** (29)

former **бы́вший** (16)

fortunately **к сча́стью** (12)

forty **со́рок** (9)

forward **вперёд** (20)

found **осно́вывать¹** (29) **(основа́ть**ᵖ**)**

four **четы́ре** (9), **че́тверо** (22.10)

four hundred **четы́реста** (9)

fourteen **четы́рнадцать** (9)

fourth **четвёртый** (15)

free **свобо́дный** (10)

French **францу́зский** (18)

French: in French **по-францу́зски** (4)

frequent **ча́стый** (21)

fresh **све́жий** (8)

Friday **пя́тница** (17)

fried eggs **яи́чница** (16)

[ye'esh-nee-tsa]

friend (female) **подру́га** (4)

friend **друг** (8), **прия́тель** (m) (30),

това́рищ (25)

friendship **дру́жба** (1)

from (out of) **из** (10) + gen.

from (off) **с** (10) + gen.

from (a person) **от** (9) + gen.

from behind **из-за** (30) + gen.

from here **отсю́да**

from there **отту́да** (23)

from where **отку́да** (30)

fruit (piece of fruit) **фрукт** (8)

frying-pan **сковорода́** (28)

full **по́лный** (30)

funny **смешно́** (23)

further **да́льше** (16)

future (adj) **бу́дущий** (17)

garden **сад** (5)

gates **воро́та** (n pl.) (29)

gather **собира́ть**¹ (26) **(собра́ть**ᴾ**)**

generation **поколе́ние** (26)

genuine **настоя́щий** (16)

German (adj) **неме́цкий** (18)

German: in German **по-неме́цки** (13)

Germany **Герма́ния** (20)

get **получа́ть**¹ (9) **(получи́ть**ᴾ**)**

get angry **серди́ться**¹ (11) **(рас-**ᴾ**)**

get divorced **разводи́ться**¹ (19)

(развести́сьᴾ**)**

get drunk **напива́ться**¹ (14)

(напи́тьсяᴾ**)**

get off **сходи́ть**¹ (20) **(сойти́**ᴾ**)**

get tired **устава́ть**¹ (15) **(уста́ть**ᴾ**)**

get up **встава́ть**¹ (16) **(встать**ᴾ**)**

get worse **ухудша́ться**¹ (28)

(уху́дшитьсяᴾ**)**

giggle **хихи́кать** (30) **(за-**ᴾ**)**

girl **де́вушка** (9)

give **дава́ть**¹ (12) **(дать**ᴾ**)**

give (present) **дари́ть**¹ (24) **(по-**ᴾ**)**

give away **отдава́ть**¹ (25) **(отда́ть**ᴾ**)**

glad **рад** (short adj) (29)

glass (tumbler) **стака́н** (25)

go (by transport) **е́здить**¹ (20), **е́хать**¹

(20) **(по-**ᴾ**)**

go (on foot) **ходи́ть**¹ (20), **идти́**¹ (20)

(пойти́ᴾ**)**

go ahead (please do) **пожа́луйста**

(3)

go away (on foot) **уходи́ть**¹ (12)

(уйти́ᴾ**)**

go down **сходи́ть**¹ (20) **(сойти́**ᴾ**)**,

спуска́ться¹ (15) **(спусти́ться**ᴾ**)**

go on foot (there and back) **ходи́ть**¹

(9) (20) **(с-**ᴾ**)**

go out **выходи́ть**¹ (15) **(вы́йти**ᴾ**)**

go past/through **проходи́ть**¹ (19)

(пройти́ᴾ**)**

go to bed **ложи́ться**¹ (25) **(лечь**ᴾ**)**

goal **цель** (f) (28)

gold **зо́лото** (18)

good **хоро́ший** (8)

good day **до́брый день** (3)

goodbye **до свида́ния** (3)

graduate from **ока́нчивать**¹ (13)

(око́нчитьᴾ**)**

gram(me) **грамм** (9)

grand **торже́ственный** (29)

grandfather **де́душка** (m) (6)

grandmother **ба́бушка** (19)

grease **жир** (28)

great **вели́кий** (11)

Great Britain **Великобрита́ния** (27)

greetings (coll) **привéт** (26)

groceries **продýкты** (m pl.) (8)

grocery (adj) **продовóльственный** (17)

group **грýппа** (24)

grow **растú**' (24) **(вы́-ᵖ)**

guest **гóсть** (m) (12)

guide (person) **гид** (16)

guidebook **путеводúтель** (m) (10)

guitar **гитáра** (16)

habit **привы́чка** (16)

hairdresser's **парикмáхерская** (f adj) (23)

half **половúна** (17)

half a kilo **пóлкилó** (n indecl) (9)

half an hour **полчасá** (20)

ham **ветчинá** (30)

hand **рукá** (22)

happen **случáться**' (16) **(случúться ᵖ)**

happiness **счáстье** (26) **[shshá-]**

hardly **вряд ли** (21)

harmful **врéдно** (14)

harmonious **гармонúчный** (29)

hat **шáпка** (14)

have (own) see 10.2

have (+ abstract noun) **имéть**' (10)

have supper **ýжинать**' (16) **(по-ᵖ)**

have time (to do sth) **успевáть**' (15) **(успéть ᵖ)**

he **óн** (3) (T4)

head **головá** (28)

health **здорóвье** (26)

hear **слы́шать**' (11) **(у-ᵖ)**

heart **сéрдце** (15)

heavy **тяжёлый** (28)

hello **здрáвствуй(те)** (3)

help (noun) **пóмощь** (f) (19)

help (verb) **помогáть**' (12) **(помóчь ᵖ)**

her **её** (indecl) (6)

here (motion) **сюдá** (20)

here (place) **здесь** (4), **тут** (25)

here (when pointing) **вóт** (3)

here and there **кóе-где** (26)

here you are (giving) **пожáлуйста** (3)

Hermitage **Эрмитáж** (11)

hero **герóй** (21)

hide **прятать**' (21) **(с-ᵖ)**

hill **горá** (18)

hinder **мешáть**' (25) **(по-ᵖ)**

his **егó** (indecl) (6) **[ye-vó]**

history **истóрия** (16)

holiday **прáздник** (17) **[práz-neek]**

Holland **Голлáндия** (28)

holy **святóй** (m adj) (23)

home (motion) **домóй** (4)

home (place) **дóма** (7)

homeland **рóдина** (21)

hope **надéяться**' (11)

host **хозяин** (25)

hot (of weather) **жáркий,** it's hot **жáрко** (14)

hot (to touch) **горячий** (8)

hotel **гостúница** (4)

hotel room **нóмер** (5) (21)

hour **час** (6)

house **дóм** (3)

how **как** (4)

how many **скóлько** (9) + gen.

how much **скóлько** (9) + gen.

hundred **стó** (9)

hurry **спешúть**' (24) **(по-ᵖ)**

husband **муж** (6)

I (T4) **я** (4)

I'm sorry **простú(те)** (3), **извинú(те)** (11)

identical **одина́ковый** (21)

if **е́сли** (8)

image **о́браз** (29)

imagine **представля́ть**/
предста́витьᵖ **себе́** (29)

immediately **сра́зу (же)** (21)

important **ва́жный** (13)

impossible **невозмо́жно** (14),
нельзя́ (14)

in **в** (4) + prep.

in addition **та́кже** (7)

in front of **пе́ред** (16) + inst.

in my opinion **по-мо́ему** (13)

in no way **ника́к** (24)

in spite of **несмотря́ на** (26) + acc.

in that case **тогда́** (12)

include **включа́ть**ᵢ (27) **(включи́ть**ᵖ**)**

independently **самостоя́тельно** (24)

indifferently (with indifference)
равноду́шно (13)

industrial **промы́шленный** (28)

industry **промы́шленность** (f) (28)

information (piece of) **спра́вка** (24)

inhabitant **жи́тель** (m) (9)

initiative **инициати́ва** (22)

insist **наста́ивать**ᵢ (21)

instead of **вме́сто** (16) + gen.

institute **институ́т** (5)

institution **учрежде́ние** (23)

insufficiently **недоста́точно** (27)

intend to **собира́ться**ᵢ (26)

interest **интере́с** (16)

interesting **интере́сно** (14),
интере́сный (7)

international **междунаро́дный** (27)

interrupt **прерыва́ть**ᵢ (23)
(прерва́тьᵖ**)**

interval **переры́в** (17)

introduce (s.o.) **знако́мить**ᵢ (16) **(по-**ᵖ**)**

invent **приду́мывать**ᵢ (24)
(приду́матьᵖ**)**

investigation **иссле́дование** (22)

invite **приглаша́ть**ᵢ (18)
(пригласи́тьᵖ**)**

island **о́стров** (18)

it **э́то** (3), **оно́** (3) (Т4)

it doesn't matter **ничего́** (11)
[nee-chye-vó]

it's time (to do sth) **пора́** (14) (+ inf)

its **его́** (indecl) (6) **[ye-vó]**

jam **варе́нье** (16)

January **янва́рь** (m) (17)

joke (noun) **шу́тка** (11), **анекдо́т** (18)

joke (verb) **шути́ть**ᵢ (23) **(по-**ᵖ**)**

journalist **журнали́ст** (13),
журнали́стка (27)

journey **пое́здка** (21)

joy **ра́дость** (f) (13)

juice **сок** (10)

July **июль** (m) (17)

jump in/up **вска́кивать**ᵢ (25)
(вскочи́тьᵖ**)**

jump out **выска́кивать**ᵢ (25)
(вы́скочитьᵖ**)**

June **ию́нь** (m) (17)

junior **мла́дший** (18)

just (very recently) **то́лько что** (15)

just (exactly) **как раз** (20)

keep silent **молча́ть**ᵢ (16) **(за-**ᵖ**)**

kettle **ча́йник** (21)

kilo(gram) **кило́** (n indecl) (8),
килогра́мм (8)

kind **до́брый** (7)

king **коро́ль** (m) (27)

kiosk **кио́ск** (1)

kiss **целова́ть**ᵢ (26) **(по-**ᵖ**)**

kitchen **ку́хня** (7)

knee **коле́но** (28)

knock **стуча́ть**¹ (25) **(по-**ᵖ**)**

know **знать**¹ (4)

know how to **уме́ть**¹ (13)

known: it's known **изве́стно** (22)

kopeck (1/100th of a rouble) **копе́йка** (9)

Kremlin (fortress) **Кремль** (m) (7)

lag behind **отстава́ть**¹ (28) **(отста́ть**ᵖ**)**

lake **о́зеро** (18)

land **земля́** (2)

landscape **ландша́фт** (29)

language **язы́к** (4)

large **большо́й** (7)

last (final) **после́дний** (7)

last (previous) **про́шлый** (11)

late **по́здно** (16) [pó-zna]

lateness **опозда́ние** (11)

laugh **смея́ться**¹ (11) **(за-**ᵖ**)**

lead **води́ть**¹ (20), **вести́**¹ (20) **(по-**ᵖ**)**

learn (to do sth) **учи́ться**¹ (28) **(на-**ᵖ**)**

learn (sth) **учи́ть**¹ (13) **(вы́-**ᵖ**)**

leave (by transport) **уезжа́ть**¹ (14) **(уе́хать**ᵖ**)**

leave (on foot) **уходи́ть**¹ (12) **(уйти́**ᵖ**)**

leave (sth) **оставля́ть**¹ (15) **(оста́вить**¹**)**

lecture **ле́кция** (18)

lecturer **преподава́тель** (m) (13)

left: on the left **сле́ва** (15)

left: to the left **нале́во** (5)

leg **нога́** (25)

lemon **лимо́н** (16)

less **ме́нее** (18), **ме́ньше** (9) (18)

lesson **уро́к** (16)

let (command) **пусть** (15)

let (in/out) **пуска́ть**¹ (25) **(пусти́ть**ᵖ**)**

letter **письмо́** (5)

level **у́ров(е)нь** (m) (26)

library **библиоте́ка** (23)

lie (be in a lying position) **лежа́ть**¹ (21) **(по-**ᵖ**)**

lie down **ложи́ться**¹ (25) **(лечь**ᵖ**)**

life **жизнь** (f) (19)

lift **поднима́ть**¹ (25) **(подня́ть**ᵖ**)**

like (prep.) **вро́де** (30) + gen.

line **ли́ния** (12)

lip **губа́** (30)

listen **слу́шать**¹ (12) **(по-**ᵖ**)**

literature **литерату́ра** (13)

little (adj) **ма́ленький** (7)

little (a little) **немно́го** (13) + gen.

little (not much) **ма́ло** (9) + gen.

little girl **де́вочка** (25)

live **жить**¹ (4) **(прожи́ть**ᵖ**)**

long (adj) **дли́нный** (18)

long (for a long time) **до́лго** (11)

long ago **давно́** (13)

look **смотре́ть**¹ (11) (13) **(по-**ᵖ**)**, **гляде́ть**¹ (25) **(по-**ᵖ**)**

look for **иска́ть**¹ (11) **(по-**ᵖ**)**

look out **выгля́дывать**¹ (30) **(вы́глянуть**ᵖ**)**

loud **гро́мкий** (14)

love **люби́ть**¹ (6) **(по-**ᵖ**)**

love affair **рома́н** (13)

low **ни́зкий** (18)

luck **сча́стье** (26) **[shshá-]**

lucky: I was lucky **мне повезло́** (13)

machine **маши́на** (10)

magazine **журна́л** (1)

magnificent **великоле́пный** (29)

maid (servant) **го́рничная** (f adj) (21)

main **гла́вный** (7)

maintenance **ремо́нт** (21)

majestic **торже́ственный** (29)

majority **большинство́** (17)

make **де́лать**' (8) **(с-ᵖ)**

male (adj) **мужско́й** (14)

man **мужчи́на** (m) (18)

manage to **мочь**' (13) **(с-ᵖ)**

manager **администра́тор** (21), **дире́ктор** (23)

manner **о́браз** (29)

many **мно́го** (9) + gen.

many (people) **мно́гие** (pl.adj) (13)

map **ка́рта** (10), (of town) **план** (7)

March **март** (17)

mark (celebrate) **отмеча́ть**' (14) **(отме́тить**ᵖ**)**

market **ры́н(о)к** (8)

marriage **брак** (22)

married (of a man) **жена́т** (30) (short adj)

marry (of a man) **жени́ться**'/ᵖ (28)

marry (of a woman) **выходи́ть/ вы́йти**ᵖ **за́муж** (29)

master (noun) **хозя́ин** (25)

master (verb) **вы́учить**ᵖ (13), **изучи́ть**ᵖ (13)

material **материа́л** (26)

matter **де́ло** (19)

May **май** (17)

meal **обе́д** (12)

meaning **значе́ние** (24)

meat **мя́со** (8)

medicine **медици́на** (28)

meet (have a meeting with) **встреча́ться**' (19) **(встре́титься**ᵖ**)**

meet (become acquainted with) **знако́миться**' **(по-**ᵖ**)**

meeting **встре́ча** (23), **заседа́ние** (28), **свида́ние** (9)

memory **па́мять** (f) (17)

mental **у́мственный** (28)

menu **меню́** (n indecl) (3)

merchant **куп(е́)ц** (28)

metro **метро́** (n indecl) (5)

midday **по́лдень** (17)

middle (adj) **сре́дний** (10)

middle (noun) **середи́на** (26)

midnight **по́лночь** (17)

military **вое́нный** (28)

milk **молоко́** (8), **моло́чный** (8) (adj)

million **миллио́н** (22)

mineral (adj) **минера́льный** (12)

ministry **министе́рство** (23)

minute **мину́та** (6)

mist **тума́н** (11)

model **моде́ль** (f) (29)

modern **совреме́нный** (13)

Monday **понеде́льник** (17)

money **де́ньги** (pl.) (8)

Mongolia **Монго́лия** (18)

month **ме́сяц** (9)

mood **настрое́ние** (14)

more **бо́лее, бо́льше** (9) (18) (22), **ещё** (9)

morning **у́тро** (3)

Moscow **Москва́** (3), **моско́вский** (17) (adj)

most (majority) **большинство́** (17)

most (forms superlative) **са́мый** (18), **наи-** (18), **наибо́лее** (29)

mother **мать** (f) (3) (5.6), **ма́ма** (11)

mother-in-law (wife's mother) **тёща** (19)

mountain **гора́** (18)

move (house) **переезжа́ть**' (13) **(перее́хать**ᵖ**)**

move (resettle) **переселя́ть**' (21) **(пересели́ть**ᵖ**)**

move away **отходи́ть**' (20) **(отойти́**ᵖ**)**

much **мно́го** (9) + gen.

much (with comparatives) **гора́здо**
(18), **намно́го** (18)
Muscovite **москви́ч** (17)
museum **музе́й** (5), **музе́йный** (29)
(adj)
mushroom **гриб** (12), (adj) **грибно́й**
(28)
music **му́зыка** (6)
musician **музыка́нт** (16)
must **на́до** (14), **до́лжен** (19)
my **мой** (6) (T6)

name (first name) **и́мя** (n) (6) (T4)
name (of thing) **назва́ние** (16)
name (surname) **фами́лия** (6)
name (verb) **называ́ть**ⁱ (11)
(**назва́ть**ᵖ)
nation **наро́д** (13)
national **национа́льный** (26)
native **родно́й** (28)
nature **приро́да** (17)
near **бли́зкий** (18)
near **о́коло** (10) + gen., **у** (10) + gen.
nearby **ря́дом** (7) (16) **с** + inst.
nearest **ближа́йший** (18) (23)
necessary (adj) **ну́жен** (short adj)
(29), **ну́жный** (29)
necessary: it's necessary **ну́жно** (11),
на́до (14)
necessity **необходи́мость** (f) (28)
negotiations **перегово́ры** (m pl.) (23)
neighbour **сосе́д** (11)
neighbouring **сосе́дний** (20)
neither . . . nor **ни . . . ни** (24)
network **сеть** (f) (21)
never **никогда́** (16) (24)
nevertheless **всё-таки** (19)
new **но́вый** (7)
New Year (adj) **нового́дний** (26)

newspaper **газе́та** (3)
next (nearest) **ближа́йший** (18) (23)
next (then) **пото́м** (12), **зате́м** (17)
next (following) **сле́дующий** (8)
next (next door) **сосе́дний** (20)
night **ночь** (f) (9)
nine **де́вять** (9)
nine hundred **девятьсо́т** (9)
nineteen **девятна́дцать** (9)
ninety **девяно́сто** (9)
no **нет** (3)
no (none at all) **никако́й** (24)
no longer **уже́ не** (24)
nobleman **дворяни́н** (28)
nobody **никто́** (24), (there is nobody)
не́кого (24)
noisy **шу́мный** (26), (it's noisy)
шу́мно (14)
north **се́вер** (18)
northern **се́верный** (18)
not **не** (4)
not allowed **нельзя́** (14)
not bad **непло́хо** (6)
not far **недалеко́** (14)
not much **ма́ло** (9) + gen.
not yet **пока́ нет** (15)
note **запи́ска** (15)
note down **запи́сывать**ⁱ (19)
(**записа́ть**ᵖ)
nothing **ничто́** (24), (there is nothing)
не́чего (24)
novel **рома́н** (13)
November **ноя́брь** (m) (17)
now **тепе́рь** (4), (at this moment)
сейча́с (6)
nowhere (motion) **никуда́** (24), (there
is nowhere) **не́куда** (24)
nowhere (place) **нигде́** (24), (there is
nowhere) **не́где** (24)

number **но́мер** (5) (21), **число́** (22)

object **возража́ть** (14) **(возрази́ть^p)**
obliged **до́лжен** (19)
obtain **достава́ть** (18) **(доста́ть^p)**
occupied **за́нят** (25)
occupy **занима́ть** (18) **(заня́ть^p)**
occur **происходи́ть** (22)
  (произойти́^p)
ocean **океа́н** (29)
o'clock **час** (17)
October **октя́брь** (m) (17)
off **с** (10) + gen.
offend **обижа́ть** (25) **(оби́деть^p)**
office **бюро́** (n indecl) (17)
often **ча́сто** (12)
oil (cooking, lubrication) **ма́сло** (8)
OK **хорошо́** (4)
old **ста́рый** (7)
old man **стари́к** (26)
old woman **стару́шка** (26)
olive **масли́на** (28)
on **на** (4) + prep.
on foot **пешко́м** (20)
once **одна́жды** (23)
one **оди́н** (m)/**одна́** (f)/**одно́** (n) (9)
one and a half **полтора́** (22)
one day **одна́жды** (23)
oneself (emphatic) **сам** (13) (T4)
onions **лук** (28)
only **то́лько** (8), **всего́** (10)
onwards **да́льше** (16)
open **открыва́ть(ся)** (11)
  (откры́ть(ся)^p)
opinion **взгляд** (21)
opponent **проти́вник** (28)
opportunity **возмо́жность** (f) (13)
opposite (adj) **противополо́жный** (20)

opposite (adv) **напро́тив** (10)
opposite (prep.) **про́тив** (10) + gen.
or **и́ли** (9)
orange **апельси́н** (8)
orchard **сад** (5)
order (command) **прика́з** (28)
order (for goods, services) **зака́з** (27)
order (s.o. to do sth) **прика́зывать**
  (13) **(приказа́ть^p)**
order (goods or services)
  зака́зывать (23) **(заказа́ть^p)**
organization **организа́ция** (16)
organize **устра́ивать** (21)
  (устро́ить^p) организова́ть^{i/p} (27)
organizer **организа́тор** (28)
original (noun) **оригина́л** (13)
our **наш** (6) (T6)
out of **из** (10) + gen.
outstanding **выдаю́щийся** (28)
overcoat **пальто́** (n indecl) (7)
overcome **преодолева́ть** (28)
  (преодоле́ть^p)
own (of family relationships) **родно́й**
  (28)
own **свой** (21), **со́бственный** (21)
owner **хозя́ин** (25)

palace **двор(е́)ц** (29)
pancake **блин** (8)
paper **бума́га** (21)
parents **роди́тели** (m pl.) (9)
park **парк** (20)
part **часть** (f) (18)
participate **уча́ствовать** (27)
parting **проща́ние** (30)
party **ве́чер** (16), **засто́лье** (26)
pass (sth to s.o.) **передава́ть** (15)
  (переда́ть^p)
past (prep.) **ми́мо** (10) + gen.

patronymic **о́тчество** (6)

pay **плати́ть**' (24) **(за-ᵖ)**

pay attention to **обраща́ть**' **(обрати́ть**ᵖ**)** **внима́ние** (24) **на** + acc., **уделя́ть**' (28) **(удели́ть**ᵖ**) внима́ние** + dat.

peace **мир** (12)

peasant **крестья́нин** (11)

pencil **каранда́ш** (16)

peninsula **полуо́стров** (29)

people **лю́ди** (16), (nation) **наро́д** (13)

pepper **пе́р(е)ц** (28)

per cent **проце́нт** (22)

performance **спекта́кль** (m) (22)

perhaps **мо́жет быть** (9)

period of time **срок** (23)

perish **погиба́ть**' (28) **(поги́бнуть**ᵖ**)**

permit **пуска́ть**' (25) **(пусти́ть**ᵖ**)**

person **челове́к** (18), **лицо́** (21)

personal **со́бственный** (21)

physical **физи́ческий** (28)

pick up **поднима́ть**' (25) **(подня́ть**ᵖ**)**

pie (large) **пиро́г** (10), (small) **пирож(о́)к** (8)

pineapple **анана́с** (24)

pity: it's a pity **жа́лко** (14), **жаль** (14)

place **ме́сто** (8)

plan **план** (7), **прое́кт** (29)

plane **самолёт** (20)

plate **таре́лка** (20)

play **игра́ть**' (16) **(сыгра́ть**ᵖ**)**

pleasant **прия́тно** (4), **прия́тный** (10)

please **пожа́луйста** (3)

please (verb) **нра́виться**' (12) **(по-ᵖ)**

pleasure **удово́льствие** (16)

plod along **брести́**' (20) **(по-ᵖ)**

plot **за́говор** (28)

plug in **включа́ть**' (21) **(включи́ть**ᵖ**)**

poet **поэ́т** (23)

poetry **поэ́зия** (23), **стихи́** (23) (pl. of **стих**)

police **мили́ция** (21)

popular **популя́рный** (13)

porridge **ка́ша** (16)

port **по́рт** (11)

possess **облада́ть**' (27)

possibility **возмо́жность** (f) (13)

possible **возмо́жный** (27)

possible: it's possible **мо́жно** (14)

post office **по́чта** (5)

postage (adj) **почто́вый** (10)

potatoes **карто́фель** (m)

pound (weight and currency) **фунт** (9)

power **власть** (f) (24)

precisely **ро́вно** (17), **то́чно** (9)

prepare **гото́вить**' (16) **(при-ᵖ)**

present (gift) **пода́р(о)к** (19)

present (verb) **представля́ть**' (27) (29) **(предста́вить**ᵖ**)**

president **президе́нт** (27)

previous **про́шлый** (11)

price **цена́** (10)

primarily **пре́жде всего́** (26)

prime minister **премье́р-мини́стр** (27)

principle **при́нцип** (23)

probably **должно́ быть** (19), **наве́рное** (21)

problem **пробле́ма** (21)

professional (noun) **профессиона́л** (16)

professor **профе́ссор** (19)

programme **програ́мма** (27)

progressive **передово́й** (28)

project **выступа́ть**' (29) **(вы́ступить**ᵖ**)**

proportion **пропо́рция** (29)

prospect (wide street) **проспе́кт** (4)

publish **издава́ть**' (28) **(изда́ть**ᵖ**)**

publishing house **изда́тельство** (23)

punish **нака́зывать**¹ (15) **(наказа́ть**ᵖ**)**
pupil **учени́к** (30)
pure **чи́стый** (18)

quality **ка́чество** (28)
quantity **коли́чество** (22)
quarter **че́тверть** (f) (22)
question **вопро́с** (27)
quick **бы́стрый** (18)
quickly **бы́стро** (13)
quiet **ти́хий** (18), (it's quiet) **ти́хо** (14),
  (noun) **тишина́** (17)
quite **дово́льно** (15)

radio **ра́дио [o]** (n indecl) (5)
railway **желе́зная доро́га** (30)
rain **до́ждь** (m) (11)
rare **ре́дкий** (18)
reach (by flying) **долета́ть**¹ (20)
  (долете́тьᵖ**)**
reach (by transport) **доезжа́ть**¹ (20)
  (дое́хатьᵖ**)**
reach (on foot) **доходи́ть**¹ (15)
  (дойти́ᵖ**)**
reach an agreement **догова́риваться**¹
  (19) **(договори́ться**ᵖ**)**
read **чита́ть**¹ (12) **(про-**ᵖ**)**
ready **гото́в** (short adj) (29)
real **настоя́щий** (16)
realize **поня́ть**ᵖ (13)
reason (for) **причи́на** (21) (+ gen.)
recall **вспомина́ть**¹ (13) **(вспо́мнить**ᵖ**)**
receive **получа́ть**¹ (9) **(получи́ть**ᵖ**)**
recently **неда́вно** (11)
recognize **узнава́ть**¹ (28) **(узна́ть**ᵖ**)**
red **кра́сный** (7)
reduction **усту́пка** (30)
reform **преобразова́ние** (28),
  рефо́рма (28)

refuse **отка́зываться**¹ (25)
  (отказа́тьсяᵖ**)**
regard (treat) **относи́ться**¹ (13)
regret **сожале́ние** (10)
remain **остава́ться**¹ (14) **(оста́ться**ᵖ**)**
remarkable **замеча́тельный** (17)
remember **по́мнить**¹ (18)
remind **напомина́ть**¹ (15)
  (напо́мнитьᵖ**)**
repair(s) **ремо́нт** (21)
repeat **повторя́ть**¹ (26) **(повтори́ть**ᵖ**)**
replace **заменя́ть**¹ (28) **(замени́ть**ᵖ**)**
request **про́сьба** (21)
research **иссле́дование** (22)
reside **прожива́ть**¹ (22)
resident **прожива́ющий** (m adj) (21)
resolutely **реши́тельно** (28)
respect (noun) **уваже́ние** (26)
respect (verb) **уважа́ть**¹ (21)
respected **уважа́емый** (26)
rest **отдыха́ть**¹ (12) **(отдохну́ть**ᵖ**)**
restaurant **рестора́н** (5)
result **результа́т** (27)
return (noun) **возвраще́ние** (26)
return (verb) **возвраща́ться**¹ (14)
  (верну́тьсяᵖ**)**
revolution **револю́ция** (16)
revolutionary **революционе́р** (16)
rich **бога́тый** (18)
right **пра́во** (24)
right: to the right **напра́во** (5)
ripe **спе́лый** (30)
rise **поднима́ться**¹ (19) **(подня́ться**ᵖ**)**
river **река́** (7)
road **доро́га** (25)
role **ро́ль** (f) (24)
roll **ката́ть**¹ (20), **кати́ть**¹ (20) **(по-**ᵖ**)**
room **ко́мната** (14)
rouble **рубль** (m) (3)

round **по** (12) + dat.
run **бе́гать**' (20), **бежа́ть**' (20) **(по-ᵖ)**
run (there and back) **бе́гать**' (20) **(с-ᵖ)**
run about **бе́гать**' (20) **(по-ᵖ)**
run away **убега́ть**ᵖ (20) **(убежа́ть**ᵖ**)**
run out **выбега́ть**' (20) **(вы́бежать**ᵖ**)**
Russia **Росси́я** (4)
Russian: in Russian **по-ру́сски** (4)
Russian (adj and noun) **ру́сский** (adj) (7)
Russian woman **ру́сская** (f adj)

sack **меш(о́)к** (25)
sacred **свято́й** (m adj) (23)
sadness **печа́ль** (f) (26)
sail **пла́вать**' (20), **плыть**' (20) **(по-ᵖ)**
sailor **матро́с** (29)
saint **свято́й** (m adj) (23)
salad **сала́т** (12)
salami **колбаса́** (8)
sale **прода́жа** (24)
sales assistant **продав(е́)ц** (8)
salt **со́ль** (f) (28)
salted **солёный** (28)
same **то́т же** (28)
samovar **самова́р** (21)
satisfaction **удово́льствие** (16)
Saturday **суббо́та** (14)
saucepan **кастрю́ля** (28)
say **говори́ть**' (4) (12) **(сказа́ть**ᵖ**)**
scale **масшта́б** (29)
scenery **приро́да** (17)
school **шко́ла** (7)
scissors **но́жницы** (pl.) (28)
sea **мо́ре** (5), **морско́й** (29) (adj)
seat **ме́сто** (8)
second **второ́й** (7)
secretary (male or female) **секрета́рь**
  (m) (15)

section (of shop) **отде́л** (8)
see **ви́деть** (11) **(у-ᵖ)**
seek **иска́ть**' (11) **(по-ᵖ)**
seem **каза́ться**' (11) **(по-ᵖ)**
seize **хвата́ть/схва́тывать**' (25)
  (схвати́тьᵖ**)**
self **себя́** (21)
sell **продава́ть**' (8) **(прода́ть**ᵖ**)**
send **посыла́ть**' (23) **(посла́ть**ᵖ**)**
senior **ста́рший** (18)
sentence to **пригова́ривать**' (28)
  (приговори́ть'**) к** + dat.
separate **отде́льный** (18)
September **сентя́брь** (m) (17)
serf **крепостно́й** (m adj) (28)
serfdom **крепостни́чество** (28)
seriously **серьёзно** (19)
serve **служи́ть**' (30) **(по-ᵖ)**
serve (food) **подава́ть**' (22) **(пода́ть**ᵖ**)**
settle **поселя́ться**' (26)
  (посели́тьсяᵖ**)**
seven **семь** (9)
seven hundred **семьсо́т** (9)
seventeen **семна́дцать** (9)
seventy **се́мьдесят** (9)
several **не́сколько** (9)
shameful **сты́дно** (14)
share **разделя́ть**' (21) **(раздели́ть**ᵖ**)**
sharply **ре́зко** (28)
shave (oneself) **бри́ть(ся)** (11) (28)
  (по-ᵖ)
she **она́** (3) (T4)
ship **кора́бль** (m) (28)
shoes **ту́фли** (f pl.) (21)
shop **магази́н** (6)
shopping bag **су́мка** (24)
shore **бе́рег** (18)
short **коро́ткий** (18) (23)
shout **крича́ть**' (20) **(за-ᵖ)**

show (performance) **спекта́кль** (m) (22)

show (verb) **пока́зывать**' (7) (12)
(**показа́ть**ᵖ)

Siberia **Сиби́рь** (f) (3)

side **сторона́** (15)

sign **подпи́сывать**' (23) (**подписа́ть**ᵖ)

significance **значе́ние** (24)

silence **тишина́** (17)

silly **глу́пый** (29)

simple **просто́й** (18)

simply **про́сто** (10)

simultaneously **одновреме́нно** (28)

since (a time) **с** (17) + gen.

since (because) **так как** (10)

sing **петь**' (16) (**с-**ᵖ)

sister **сестра́** (14)

sit (be sitting) **сиде́ть**' (14) (**по-**ᵖ)

sit down **сади́ться**' (15) (**сесть**ᵖ)

situated **располо́жен** (29)

six **шесть** (9)

six hundred **шестьсо́т** (9)

sixteen **шестна́дцать** (9)

sixty **шестьдеся́т** (9)

size **разме́р** (10)

skilled workman **ма́стер** (21)

skis **лы́жи** (f.pl.) (29)

sleep (noun) **с(о)н** (17)

sleep (verb) **спать**' (16) (**по-**ᵖ)

slice (noun) **ло́мтик** (28)

slice (verb) **нареза́ть**' (28)
(**наре́зать**ᵖ)

slippers **та́почки** (f.pl.) (11)

slope **скло́н** (29)

slow **ме́дленный** (18)

small **ма́ленький** (7)

smell (of) **па́хнуть**' (30) (+ inst.)

smile (noun) **улы́бка** (26)

smile (verb) **улыба́ться**' (11)
(**улыбну́ться**ᵖ)

smoke **кури́ть**' (4) (**по-**ᵖ**, за-**ᵖ)

snackbar **буфе́т** (10)

snow **снег** (20)

so **так** (6), (consequently) **так что**
(26)/**поэ́тому** (9), (that means)
зна́чит (10)

so many **сто́лько** (10) + gen.

so much **сто́лько** (10) + gen.

solve **реша́ть**' (13) (**реши́ть**ᵖ)

some (certain) **не́который** (17)

some (some kind of) **како́й-то** (26)

some (various) **ко́е-каки́е** (26)

somehow **ка́к-то** (26)

someone **кто́-то** (26), **ко́е-кто́** (26)

something **что́-то** (26), **ко́е-что́** (26)

sometime **когда́-то** (26), (in the future)
когда́-нибудь

sometimes **иногда́** (9)

somewhere (motion) **куда́-то** (26)

son **сын** (6)

son of a tsar **царе́вич** (28)

song **пе́сня** (25)

soon **ско́ро** (20), **вско́ре** (28)

sound (verb) **звуча́ть**' (23)

sour cream **смета́на** (3)

south **юг** (14)

southern **ю́жный** (18)

Soviet Union **Сове́тский Сою́з** (22)

spark **и́скра** (30)

speak **говори́ть**' (4) (**по-**ᵖ)

special **осо́бый** (26)

specialist **специали́ст** (18)

specially **осо́бенно, специа́льно**
(10)

spend (time) **проводи́ть**' (17)
(**провести́**ᵖ)

spend the night **ночева́ть**' (25) (**пере-**ᵖ)

spoon **ло́жка** (16)

spring **весна́** (16)

square **пло́щадь** (f) (5)

stadium **стадио́н** (20)

staircase **ле́стница** (20)

stamp **ма́рка** (10)

stand **стоя́ть**' (11) **(по-**ᴾ**)**

star **звезда́** (30)

start **стать**ᴾ (ᴾ only) (16)

state (adj) **госуда́рственный** (28)

station **вокза́л** (5), (metro/in country)
ста́нция (7)

stay **остава́ться**' (14) **(оста́ться**ᴾ**)**

still **ещё** (9)

stock **запа́с** (18)

stop (halt) **остана́вливать(ся)**' (13)
(28) **останови́ть(ся)**ᴾ

stop (cease) **перестава́ть**' (15)
(переста́тьᴾ**)**

stop (noun) **остано́вка** (20)

storey **эта́ж** (7)

stove **печь** (f) (25)

straight **прямо́й** (12)

straight on **пря́мо** (5)

strange **стра́нно** (20)

street **у́лица** (4)

street map **план** (7)

strong **кре́пкий** (18)

student **студе́нт** (22)

study (something) **изуча́ть**' (4) (13)
(изучи́тьᴾ**)**, **занима́ться**' (16)

study (somewhere) **учи́ться**' (13)

study trip **командиро́вка** (19)

stupid **глу́пый** (29)

style **стиль** (m) (21)

such **тако́й** (10)

suddenly **вдруг** (13)

sugar **са́хар** (8)

suitcase **чемода́н** (29)

summer **ле́то** (22) (noun), **ле́тний** (7)
(adj)

summon **вызыва́ть**' (21) **(вы́звать**ᴾ**)**

Sunday **воскресе́нье** (17)

supper **у́жин** (16)

surname **фами́лия** (6)

surprise (noun) **сюрпри́з** (10)

surprise (verb) **удивля́ть**' (27)
(удиви́тьᴾ**)**

survey **опро́с** (27)

sweet **ми́лый** (30)

swim **пла́вать**' (20), **плыть**' (20) **(по-**ᴾ**)**

swings **каче́ли** (pl.) (26)

switch on **включа́ть**' (21)
(включи́тьᴾ**)**

table **стол** (16)

take **брать**' (10) (12) **(взять**ᴾ**)**

take (transport) **сади́ться**' (15)
(сестьᴾ**) на** + acc.

take a walk **гуля́ть**' (17) **(по-**ᴾ**)**

take across **переводи́ть**' (13)
(перевести́ᴾ**)**

take fright **пуга́ться**' (25) **(ис-**ᴾ**)**

take off **снима́ть**' (30) **(снять**ᴾ**)**

take somewhere (by carrying)
относи́ть' (20) **(отнести́**ᴾ**)**

take somewhere (by transport)
отвози́ть' (20) **(отвезти́**ᴾ**)**

take (lead) **води́ть**' (20), **вести́**' (20)
(по-ᴾ**)**

talk (converse) **разгова́ривать**' (16)

talk (speak) **говори́ть**' (15) **(по-**ᴾ**)**,
разгова́ривать' (16)

talk (tell) **расска́зывать**' (12)
(рассказа́тьᴾ**)**

talks **перегово́ры** (m pl.) (23)

tall **высо́кий** (18)

tape recorder **магнитофо́н** (13)

tasty **вку́сный** (8)

tax **нало́г** (28)

taxi **такси** (n indecl) (3)

tea **чай** (3)

teach **преподавать** (13)

teacher (school) **учитель**' (m) (16)

teacher (institute, university)
   преподаватель (m) (13)

teapot **чайник** (21)

tear **слеза** (30)

tease **дразнить**' (30)

telephone (noun) **телефон** (15)

telephone (verb) **звонить**' (12) **(по-**ᵖ**)**

television set **телевизор** (13)

tell **рассказывать**' (12) **(рассказать**ᵖ**)**

ten **десять** (9)

territory **территория** (18)

than **чем** (18)

thank you **спасибо** (3)

that **это** (3), **тот** (7) (T4)

that (conjunction) **что** (5.8) [shto]

that is (i.e.) **то есть** (22)

theatre **театр** (7)

their **их** (indecl) (6)

theme **тема** (16)

then (at that time) **тогда** (12)

then (in that case) **то** (12)

then (next) **потом** (12), **затем** (17)

there (motion 'thither') **туда** (9)

there (place) **там** (5)

there (when pointing) **вот** (3)

there is/are **есть** (7) (8)

there isn't/aren't **нет** (10) + gen.

there is no time **некогда** (24)

there is nothing **нечего** (24)
   [nyé-chye-va]

there is nowhere (motion) **некуда** (24)

there is nowhere (place) **негде** (24)

they **они** (4) (T4)

thin **тонкий** (30), **худой** (18),
   худенький (30)

thing **вещь** (f) (10), **штука** (30)

think **думать**' (19) **(по-**ᵖ**)**

third (adj) **третий** (7) (T6)

third (fraction) **треть** (f) (22)

thirteen **тринадцать** (9)

thirty **тридцать** (9)

this **это** (3), **этот** (7) (T4)

thought **мысль** (f) (26)

thousand **тысяча** (9) (22)

three **три** (9), **трое** (22.10)

three hundred **триста** (9)

through **через** (6) + acc.

throw/throw away **бросать**' (25)
   (броситьᵖ**)**

Thursday **четверг** (17)

ticket **билет** (10)

ticket office **касса** (1)

tight **тесно** (25)

time **время** (9), (a time) **раз** (9)

time limit **срок** (23)

to (a person) **к** (12) + dat.

to (a place) **в/на** (6) + acc.

to (in order to) **чтобы** (21) **[shtó-bi]**

today **сегодня** (7) **[sye-vód-nya]**

toe **пал(е)ц** (16)

together **вместе** (16)

toilet **туалет** (5)

toilet paper **туалетная бумага** (21)

tomato **помидор** (12)

tomorrow **завтра** (6)

too (also) **тоже** (4)

too (excessively) **слишком** (10)

topic **тема** (16)

touch **касаться**' (21) **(коснуться**ᵖ**),**
   трогать' (16) **(тронуть**ᵖ**)**

tourist **турист** (15)

towards **к** (12) + dat.

tower **башня** (16)

town **город** (7)

trade **торго́вля** (28)

trader **торго́в(е)ц** (24)

traffic light **светофо́р** (19)

train **по́езд** (17)

tram **трамва́й** (15)

transfer **переноси́ть**' (21)
  (перенести́ᵖ)

transfer **переводи́ть**' (13)
  (перевести́ᵖ)

translate **переводи́ть**' (13)
  (перевести́ᵖ)

translator **перево́дчик** (21)

transmit **передава́ть**' (15)
  (переда́тьᵖ)

transport **вози́ть**' (20), **везти́**' (20)
  (по-ᵖ)

travel **е́здить**' (20), **е́хать**' (20)
  (по-ᵖ), **путеше́ствовать**' (21)

travel (there and back) **е́здить**' (20)
  (съ-ᵖ)

travel past **проезжа́ть**' (15) (20)
  (прое́хатьᵖ)

travel through **проезжа́ть**' (15) (20)
  (прое́хатьᵖ)

travelling companion **спу́тник** (16)

tree **де́рево** (26)

triple **тройно́й** (29)

trolleybus **тролле́йбус** (4)

trousers **брю́ки** (pl.) (22)

true **ве́рный** (29)

truth **пра́вда** (11)

tsar (emperor) **царь** (m) (5)

Tuesday **вто́рник** (17)

turn (a corner) **завора́чивать**' (19)
  (заверну́тьᵖ)

turn (change direction) **повора́чивать**'
  (15) **(поверну́ть**ᵖ)

turn away (from) **отвора́чиваться**'
  (30) **(отверну́ться**ᵖ)

turn off **свора́чивать**' (20)
  (сверну́тьᵖ)

turn out **ока́зываться**' (20) (26)
  (оказа́тьсяᵖ)

turn pale **бледне́ть**' (30) **(по-**ᵖ)

twelve **двена́дцать** (9)

twenty **два́дцать** (9)

two **два** (m/n), **две** (f) (9), **дво́е**
  (22.10)

two hundred **две́сти** (9)

Ukraine **Украи́на** (5)

uncle **дя́дя** (m) (3)

under **под** (16) + inst. (place)/(25)
  + acc. (motion)

under (a ruler) **при** (28) + prep.

underground (adj) **подзе́мный** (15)

underground (railway) **метро́**
  (n indecl) (5)

understand **понима́ть**' (4) **(поня́ть**ᵖ)

unexpected **неожи́данный** (26)

unfortunately **к сожале́нию** (10)

uniform **мунди́р** (30)

United States of America
  Соединённые Шта́ты Аме́рики
  (12)

university **университе́т** (5)

until (conjunction) **пока́ . . . не** (14)

until (prep.) **до** (9) + gen.

up to (and including) **по** (17.12) (23)
  + acc.

uprising **восста́ние** (28)

Urals **Ура́л** (17)

urgent **сро́чный** (19)

urgently **сро́чно** (21)

use **по́льзоваться**' (21) **(вос-**ᵖ)

usually **обы́чно** (13)

variety **разнообра́зие** (29)

various **ра́зный** (9)

vegetables **о́вощи** (m pl.) (9)

vegetarian **вегетариа́н(е)ц** (12), **вегетариа́нка** (9), **вегетариа́нский** (12) (adj)

very **о́чень** (4)

view **взгляд** (21), **вид** (18)

village **дере́вня** (19)

vinegar **у́ксус** (28)

visa **ви́за** (23)

visit (a place) **посеща́ть** (28) (**посети́ть**ᵖ), **побыва́ть**ᵖ (24)

visit (a person) **быть в гостя́х у/идти́ в го́сти к** (12)

vodka **во́дка** (3)

voice **го́лос** (14)

wait **ждать** (15) (**подо-**ᵖ)

waiter **официа́нт** (12)

waitress **официа́нтка** (12)

walk (noun) **прогу́лка** (17)

walk (go on foot) **ходи́ть** (20), **идти́** (20) (**пойти́**ᵖ)

walk (take a walk) **гуля́ть** (17) (**по-**ᵖ)

walk about **ходи́ть** (20) (**по-**ᵖ)

wall **стена́** (16)

wallpaper **обо́и** (m pl.) (21)

wander **броди́ть** (20) (**по-**ᵖ)

want **хоте́ть** (12.5) (**за-**ᵖ)

war **война́** (14)

warm **тёплый** (7), (it's warm) **тепло́** (14)

warn **предупрежда́ть** (12) (**предупреди́ть**ᵖ)

wash thoroughly **промыва́ть** (28) (**промы́ть**ᵖ)

watch (timepiece) **часы́** (pl. of **час**) (17)

watch (verb) **смотре́ть** (11) (**по-**ᵖ)

water **вода́** (8)

way **путь** (m) (20)

we **мы** (4) (T4)

wealth **бога́тство** (29)

wear **носи́ть** (28)

weather **пого́да** (7)

wedding **сва́дьба** (22)

Wednesday **среда́** (17)

week **неде́ля** (6)

weekday **бу́дний д(е)нь** (23)

weekdays **бу́дни** (pl.) (23)

well (adv) **хорошо́** (4)

well (particle) **ну** (25)

well-known **изве́стный** (27)

west **за́пад** (18)

western **за́падный** (7)

what **что** (3) [shto]

what (what kind of) **како́й** (7)

when **когда́** (5)

where (motion 'whither') **куда́** (4)

where (place) **где** (3)

whether **ли** (13)

which **кото́рый** (18)

white **бе́лый** (8)

who (interrogative pronoun) **кто** (5) (T4)

who (relative pronoun) **кото́рый** (18)

why **почему́** (4)

wide **широ́кий** (18)

widespread **распространённый** (23)

wife **жена́** (6)

willingly **охо́тно** (25)

wind **ве́т(е)р** (27)

window **окно́** (3)

wine **вино́** (3)

wineglass **бока́л** (21)

wing **крыло́** (29)

winter **зима́** (16), **зи́мний** (7) (adj)

wish **жела́ть** (21) (**по-**ᵖ)

with **с** (16) + inst.

without **без** (10) + gen.

without fail **обязáтельно** (15)

woman **жéнщина** (14)

wonderful **чудéсный** (17)

wood (forest) **лес** (5)

wood (material) **дéрево** (26)

word **слóво** (8)

work (noun) **рабóта** (6), **труд** (26)

work (verb) **рабóтать**ⁱ (4) **(по-ᵖ)**

work for (an aim) **добивáться**ⁱ (28)
  (добитьсяᵖ**)** + gen.

worker **рабóчий** (m adj) (28)

world **мир** (18)

worry **беспокóиться**ⁱ (14),
  переживáтьⁱ (24)

worse **хýже** (18)

write **писáть**ⁱ (13) **(на-ᵖ)**

writer **писáтель** (m) (17)

yard **двóр** (26)

year **гóд** (6)

yes **да** (3)

yesterday **вчерá** (10)

yet **ещё** (9)

you **ты** (4) (T4), **вы** (4) (T4)

young **молодóй** (13)

young man **молодóй человéк** (18)

younger **молóже** (18), **млáдший** (18)

your **твóй** (6) (T6), **ваш** (6) (T6)

KEY TO EXERCISES AND
TRANSLATIONS OF TEXTS

1/1

1 **[ba-re´es]** Boris. 2 **[da]** yes. 3 **[nyet]** no. 4 **[balʲ-shóy]** big. 5 **[spa-se´e-ba]** thank you. 6 **[ro´o-ska-ya áz-boo-ka]** Russian alphabet. 7 **[borshsh]** beetroot soup. 8 **[chay]** tea. 9 **[sá-har]** sugar. 10 **[zhoor-nál]** magazine.

1/2

1 **[a-e-ra-pórt]**. 2 **[boo-fyét]**. 3 **[ga-ste´e-nee-tsa]**. 4 **[dee-ryék-tar]**. 5 **[za-krí-ta]**. 6 **[za-prye-shshye-nó]**. 7 **[een-too-re´est]**. 8 **[ká-ssa]**. 9 **[ksye-byé]**. 10 **[nye koo-re´etʲ]**. 11 **[at sye-byá]**. 12 **[pa-reek-má-hyer-ska-ya]**. 13 **[póch-ta]**. 14 **[rye-mónt]**. 15 **[rye-sta-rán]**. 16 **[too-a-lyét]**.

1/3

1 BAR. 2 PRAVDA (the newspaper). 3 TAXI **[tak-se´e]**. 4 STOP. 5 MOSCOW **[mask-vá]**. 6 LOS ANGELES. 7 PIZZA HUT **[-hat]**. 8 Vladimir Lenin **[vla-de´e-meer lyé-neen]**. 9 IZVESTIYA (newspaper) **[eez-vyé-stee-ya]**. 10 NEW YORK **[nʲyoo-yórk]**. 11 glasnost ('openness') **[glás-nastʲ]**. 12 ROLLS-ROYCE. 13 The Beatles. 14 Shakespeare. 15 HELSINKI **[hyélʲ-seen-kee]**.

2/1

Ленинград   Москва   Киев

Достоевский Пастернак

водка пиццерия Брежнев

Горбачёв Прокофьев Набоков

Бернард Шоу Лидз

2/2

[ve´e-skee] whisky
[een-flyá-tsi-ya] inflation
[már-kye-teenk] marketing
[myo´o-zeekl] a musical
[nó-oo-há-oo] know-how
[pyer-sa-nál'-ni kam-p'yo´o-ter] personal computer
[pree-va-tee-zá-tsi-ya] privatization
[rok-mo´o-zi-ka] rock music
[streep-te´es] striptease
[ek-sklyoo-ze´ev-na-ye een-ter-v'yo´o] exclusive interview

2/3

1 **[shsheet]**
2 **[shit]**
3 **[brat]**
4 **[za-la-ta-va-ló-sa-ye]**
5 **[za-shshee-shshá-yoo-shshee]**
6 **[na-ka-oo-te´e-ra-vat']**
7 **[ek-spye-ree-myen-te´e-ra-vat']**
8 **[da-sta-pree-mye-chá-tyel'-na-stee]**
9 **[chye-la-vye-ka-nye-na-ve´est-nee-chye-stva]**

3/1

Да   Нет   Это   Спасибо

Доброе утро   Добрый день

До свидания   Простите

Пожалуйста   Здравствуйте

Что Где   один два три

четыре   пять

3/2

1 Вóт онá.
2 Вóт óн.
3 Вóт онó.
4 Вóт óн.
5 Вóт онá.
6 Вóт онó.

3/3

1 Э́то чай.
2 Э́то рубль.
3 Нет, э́то винó.
4 Вóт онó.

3/4

1 Здрáвствуйте.
2 Простúте, чтó э́то?
3 Э́то винó.
4 Спасúбо.

5 Пожа́луйста.

6 Нет, э́то бо́рщ.

7 Где смета́на?

8 Прости́те, пожа́луйста, где Ва́ня?

9 Во́т о́н.

10 Спаси́бо. До свида́ния.

3/5

1 **[vla-dee-va-stók]** (m) о́н. 2 **[ska-va-ra-dee-nó]** (n) оно́. 3 **[ab-loʹo-chye]** (n) оно́. 4 **[chee-tá]** (f) она́. 5 **[slyoo-dyán-ka]** (f) она́. 6 **[bay-kálʹsk]** (m) о́н. 7 **[mask-vá]** (f) она́.

3/6

1 **[hree-stee-án]** = Christian (m). 2 **[yoo-lee-án]** = Julian (m). 3 **[ar-ká-dee]** = Arkadii (m). 4 **[má-ya]** = Maya (f). 5 **[eʹe-garʹ]** = Igor (m). 6 **[yoo-deʹefʹ]** = Judith (f). 7 **[lyoo-bófʹ]** = Liubov ('Love') (f). 8 **[nee-nyélʹ]** = Ninel' (a female name created by spelling Lenin backwards).

4.13

(1) Here are Vladimir Smirnov and Mary Robinson. They are in Moscow, in the Hotel Russia. They are speaking Russian.

VS: Hello, my name is Volodia. And what's your name? MR: Mary. I'm English. VS: You speak Russian well. MR: I'm studying Russian here in Moscow. (And) do you speak English? VS: I understand English but I don't speak (it). Where do you live, Mary? MR: In Volgin Street. And you? VS: On Peace Prospekt.

(2) V: Hello, Natasha. Are you going home by bus? N: Hello, Vania. No, I'm going by trolleybus.

(3) A: Why is Mary going by trolleybus and not by metro? B: I don't know.

(4) V: What's your name? E: My name is Eva. And what's yours? V: Vadim.

(5) E: This is Natasha. V: Pleased to meet you. I'm Vadim. N: Pleased to meet you.

4/1

1 **зна́ю** 'I don't know.' 2 **говори́т** 'He doesn't speak Russian'. 3 **говори́те** 'You speak English well.' 4 **живёте** 'Where do you live?' 5 **живу́ в Ло́ндоне** 'I live in London.' 6 **изуча́ем** 'We are studying Russian.' 7 **живёт в Москве́** 'Mary lives in Moscow.' 8 **е́дет на авто́бусе е́дет на тролле́йбусе** 'Ivan is going by bus and

Mary is going by trolleybus.' 9 **éдут** 'They are going home.'

4/2

1 **Прости́те.** 2 **Я не зна́ю.** 3 **Я не понима́ю.** 4 **Вы говори́те по-англи́йски?** 5 **Где вы живёте?** 6 **Как вас зову́т?**

4/3

1 Misha, Vania, Marie. 2 Misha: Vavilov Street (**у́лица Вави́лова**). Vania: Volgin Street (**у́лица Во́лгина**). Marie: in Moscow. 3 She knows English, she's studying Russian and already speaks it pretty well; she doesn't know French.

Translation:

A: Hello, Vania. Where are you going? B: Home, to Volgin Street. Are you going to the university? A: No, I'm going home too. I live in Vavilov Street now. B: Let me introduce you. This is my friend Marie, she's English. She's studying Russian here in Moscow. Marie, this is Misha. V: Hello, Misha. A: Excuse me/I'm sorry, are you called Mary? V: No, Marie. It's a French name. But I don't speak French.

5.12 **Dialogues**

(1) A: Where's Moscow? B: In Russia. (2) A: Where's London? B: In England. (3) A: Where's Kiev? B: In the Ukraine. (4) A: Where's Yalta? B: In the Crimea. (5) A: Where does Uncle Vania work? B: In (St) Petersburg. (6) A: What are you talking about? B: About Russia. (7) A: Are you talking about Mary? B: No, we're talking not about her but about you (fam). (8) A: Where do you live/Where are you staying? B: In the Hotel 'Russia'. A: And where are John and Margaret staying? B: In the 'Russia' too. (9) A: Where is Irkutsk? B: In Siberia. (10) A: Where does Mary Robinson live? B: In Moscow, in Volgin Street. But in England she lives in Bristol. (11) A: Tell me please, where is Volgin Street ('Street of Volgin')? B: Straight on and turn right. (12) A: Tell (me) please, where is the toilet here? B: On the left. A: Thank you. B: You're welcome. (13) A: (And) where do you live, Ivan Petrovich? B: I live in Voronezh, in the centre. (14) A: Is Mary studying Russian at the university? B: No, she's studying Russian at the/an institute. (15) A: Excuse me, please, do you (don't you) know where the post office is here? B: House (building) number 2. A: And where's that? B: Over there on the right. A: Thank you. B: You're welcome.

5/1

1 В Ло́ндоне. 2 В Росси́и. 3 В гости́нице. 4 В Нью-Йо́рке. 5 В Австра́лии 'in Australia'. 6 В Аме́рике 'in America'. 7 В го́роде 'in the town/city'. 8 В Сиби́ри. 9 В Крыму́. 10 В до́ме. 11 На у́лице. 12 На пло́щади.

5/2

1 О Ва́не. 2 О Мари́и. 3 Об Ива́не. 4 Об Анн Бра́ун. 5 О ней. 6 О нём.

5/3

1 Где туале́т? 2 Э́то борщ? 3 Вы живёте (pol)/Ты живёшь (fam) в це́нтре? 4 Я живу́ в А́нглии, в О́ксфорде. 5 Мы говори́м о вас (pol)/о тебе́ (fam).

5/4

1 Dublin Ду́блин. 2 Hamburg Га́мбург, Germany Герма́ния. 3 Anton Pavlovich Chekhov Анто́н Па́влович Че́хов. 4 Rostov-on-Don Росто́в-на-Дону́.

5/5

1 [mask-vá]. 2 [zdrá-stvooy-tye]. 3 [shto é-ta?]. 4 [pa-zhál-sta]. 5 [é-ta kó-fye?] (rise-fall on [kó-]). 6 Спаси́бо. 7 Пожа́луйста. 8 До свида́ния. 9 Прости́те. 10 Что́ э́то? 11 Э́то чай? 12 Прости́те, как вас зову́т? 13 Вы зна́ете, где метро́? 14 Вы говори́те по-англи́йски? 15 Я живу́ в А́нглии/Ма́нчестере/Ду́блине. 16 Я не зна́ю. 17 Я говорю́ по-ру́сски. 18 Я е́ду на авто́бусе. 19 Они́ е́дут домо́й. 20 Он живёт в Москве́. 21 Они́ живу́т в Сиби́ри. 22 На пло́щади. 23 Она́ изуча́ет ру́сский язы́к в Росси́и.

6/1

1 Мой сын. 2 На́ша дочь. 3 Его́ мать. 4 Ва́ша/Твоя́ гости́ница. 5 Её муж.

6/2

1 Я люблю́ му́зыку. 2 Она́ лю́бит му́жа? 3 Позови́те, пожа́луйста, Любо́вь Влади́мировну. 4 Подожди́те мину́ту. 5 Спаси́бо за чай. 6 Спаси́бо за во́дку.

6.17 Dialogues

V: Are you fond of music? E: Very. I like Glinka and Borodin. V: And (do you like) Prokofiev? E: Not very much.

KM: Hello, Mikhail Petrovich, how are you?

MP: Not bad, Konstantin Mikhailovich. And how are you?

KM: I'm all right too.

MP: Where are you going?

KM: To work. And you?

MP: I'm going to the shop. And how is your wife, Natalia Borisovna?

KM: She's well. Tomorrow she's going to Moscow. Our daughter Nina has been living there for a year. Do you know her husband Andrei?

MP: Yes, I know him.

KM: And their son is called Misha.

MP: Their son? So you're already a grandfather, Konstantin Mikhailovich. Congratulations!

6/3

1 Позови́те, пожа́луйста, Ива́на. 2 Позови́те И́горя Петро́вича. 3 Позови́те, пожа́луйста, Ната́шу. 4 Позови́те, пожа́луйста, Ната́лью Алекса́ндровну.

6/4

1 Здра́вствуйте/До́брое у́тро, Ива́н Петро́вич. 2 Где на́ша гости́ница? 3 Спаси́бо за вино́. 4 Пожа́луйста, подожди́те мину́ту. 5 Э́то ва́ша жена́?

6/5

Михаи́л Серге́евич, Людми́ла Андре́евна. Ма́рк Тве́н (Mark Twain) Сэ́линджер (Salinger), А́гата Кри́сти (Agatha Christie).

7/1

1 За́падная. 2 Ру́сский. 3 Но́вая. 4 Кра́сная. 5 Больша́я. 6 Ма́ленькое. 7 Пу́шкинская. 8 Брита́нское.

7/2

1 После́дняя. 2 Зи́мнее. 3 Тре́тий. 4 Тре́тья.

7.18 Dialogues

A: Moscow is a large city. Moscow has an attractive river and a famous university. You already know Red Square, the Bolshoi Theatre and Tverskaia Street. B: I do.

Tverskaia Street is the main street. A: (Points (to them) on the map) Here is Tverskaia, here is New Arbat, and here is the old Arbat, a very old street. This is the Hotel 'Russia', a very large hotel. Here is the Kremlin, nearby is the Great Stone Bridge, and this is the British Embassy, on the embankment. Here is the American Embassy, and here's the Canadian (one).

A: Good morning. B: Good day. A: Why are you in (= wearing) a winter coat? The weather is warm today. B: This isn't a winter coat, it's a summer one.

We live in Moscow. We – that's me Pavel Pavlovich Petrov, my wife Svetlana Aleksandrovna and our daughter Elena. At school they call her Lena but at home we call her Lenusha. My mother, Zinaida Egorovna, lives in Moscow too. She lives in an old house in the centre, while we live in a new flat in a new block in the south-west. Our block is on Prospekt Vernadskovo **[pras-pyékt vyer-nát-ska-va]**. Do you know the 'Yugo-Zapadnaia' (underground) station? We live on the third floor (second floor in Britain). In our flat there is a hall, a large-room (= a living room) and a bedroom. There is also a small kitchen, a bathroom and a toilet.

7/3

1 **В За́падной Сиби́ри** He lives in Western Siberia. 2 **Вы зна́ете но́вую гости́ницу?** Do you know the new hotel? 3 **Они́ иду́т на Кра́сную пло́щадь** They are going to Red Square. 4 **Она́ в зи́мнем пальто́** She's wearing a winter coat. 5 **Вы зна́ете мою́ втору́ю жену́?** Do you know my second wife? 6 **В э́том магази́не рабо́тает моя́ до́чь** My daughter works in this shop. 7 **Она́ пока́зывает но́вое зи́мнее пальто́** She is showing (her) new winter coat. 8 – **Кака́я сего́дня пого́да? – Тёплая** 'What's the weather like today?' 'Warm.'

7/4

1 **Где Кра́сная пло́щадь?** 2 **Она́ на Кра́сной пло́щади.** 3 **Мы идём** (on foot)/**е́дем** (by transport) **на Кра́сную пло́щадь.** 4 **Эта кни́га ва́ша/твоя́?** or **Это ва́ша/твоя́ кни́га?**

7/5

1 Along Nikol'skaia Street **(Нико́льская у́лица)** and north-east across Lubianskaia Square **(Лубя́нская пло́щадь).** 2 Manezhnaia Square **(Мане́жная пло́щадь).** 3 Go straight on (north) up **Мане́жная у́лица** to **Мане́жная пло́щадь,** turn left into **Тверска́я у́лица** and go straight on to **Пу́шкинская пло́щадь.**

8/1

1 **у́лицы** 'streets'. 2 **тролле́йбусы** 'trolleybuses'. 3 **университе́ты** 'universities'.
4 **шко́лы** 'schools'. 5 **музе́и** 'museums'. 6 **продавцы́** 'sales assistants'.
7 **пи́сьма** 'letters'. 8 **пло́щади** 'squares'. 9 **мину́ты** 'minutes'. 10 **неде́ли**
'weeks'. 11 **фами́лии** 'surnames'. 12 **кни́ги** 'books'. 13 **языки́** 'languages'.
14 **пирожки́** 'pies'. 15 **до́чери** 'daughters'. 16 **дома́** 'houses'. 17 **англича́не**
'Englishmen'. 18 **леса́** 'forests'. 19 **такси́** 'taxis'. 20 **сыновья́** 'sons'. 21 **имена́**
'names'. 22 **я́блоки** 'apples'. 23 **друзья́** 'friends'.

8/2

1 **ру́сские кни́ги** 'Russian books'. 2 **э́ти языки́** 'these languages'.
3 **ле́тние дни** 'summer days'. 4 **на́ши сыновья́** 'our sons'. 5 **ста́рые города́**
'old towns'. 6 **мои́ друзья́** 'my friends'. 7 **больши́е магази́ны** 'big shops'. 8 **те
го́ды** 'those years'. 9 **ва́ши места́** 'your places (seats)'. 10 **э́ти упражне́ния**
'these exercises'.

8.12

(1) *Groceries/Food*. M: What kinds of food do Russians buy in a/the shop? V: In
a/the shop we buy salami, cheese, milk, eggs, butter, potatoes, sugar. And bread,
of course, black and white. Russian bread is very good ('tasty'), always fresh. We
are fond of making ('very like to make') open sandwiches. M: What about fruit
('fruits')? V: Fruit we buy at the market. It's ('They are') expensive but fresh. We buy
apples and oranges, if there are (any). M: Where do you buy meat? V: In the shop
the meat is bad. There is good, fresh meat only at the market.

(2) *Fruit*. A: Where do they sell oranges? B: Only at the market. A: What about
apples? B: There are apples in the shop, but they're bad.

(3) *At the Market*. A: Are these pies yours? B (a trader): Yes ('Mine'). A: Are they
fresh? B: (They're) fresh, very good. A: Give me a kilo, please.

(4) *In the Shop*. M: Tell (me), please, in which section do they sell kefir (yogurt-
type drink)? Sales Assistant: In the dairy (section). M: What about eggs? SA: In the
dairy section too. M: Thank you.

8/3

1 **Есть ко́фе?/Ко́фе есть?** 2 **Есть све́жие бутербро́ды?/Све́жие
бутербро́ды есть?** 3 **Где ва́ши/твой друзья́?** 4 **Я люблю́ ру́сские блины́.**
5 **Чёрный хлеб, пожа́луйста.** 6 **Да́йте э́ти апельси́ны, пожа́луйста.**

8/4

1 **белору́с** Belorussian (White Russian). 2 **валли́(е)ц** Welshman (mobile **е** after a vowel replaced by **й**). 3 **венгр** Hungarian. 4 **ирла́нд(е)ц** Irishman. 5 **испа́н(е)ц** Spaniard. 6 **латы́ш** Latvian. 7 **лито́в(е)ц** Lithuanian. 8 **не́м(е)ц** German. 9 **поля́к** Pole. 10 **францу́з** Frenchman. 11 **ру́сский** Russian (the only nationality whose Russian name is an adjective). 12 **укра́ин(е)ц** Ukrainian. 13 **швед** Swede. 14 **шотла́нд(е)ц** Scot. 15 **эсто́н(е)ц** Estonian.

9/1

1 рубля́. 2 письма́. 3 сы́на. 4 же́нщины. 5 Москвы́. 6 кни́ги. 7 до́чери. 8 молока́. 9 свида́ния. 10 ко́фе (indeclinable).

9/2

1 **Две копе́йки.** 2 **Нет са́хара/Са́хара нет.** 3 **Три сло́ва.** 4 **Два сы́на.** 5 **Две неде́ли.** 6 **у́лица Во́лгина.** 7 **Муж Ма́ши** (**и** after ш). 8 **Буты́лка вина́.** 9 **Но́мер до́ма.** 10 **Ча́я нет/Нет ча́я.**

9/3

1 **рубле́й** '5 roubles'. 2 **домо́в** '10 houses'. 3 **ноче́й** '6 nights'. 4 **жи́телей** '300 inhabitants'. 5 **этаже́й** '7 floors'. 6 **книг** '126 books'. 7 **упражне́ний** '12 exercises'. 8 **враче́й** '19 doctors'. 9 **бутербро́дов** '5 sandwiches' 10 **мест** '20 places (seats)'. 11 **газе́т** '40 newspapers'. 12 **апельси́нов** '9 oranges'. 13 **америка́нцев** '200 Americans'. 14 **ты́сяч** '5000'. 15 **я́блок** 'a kilogram of apples'. 16 **друзе́й** '6 friends'. 17 **де́нег** 'There's no money'. 18 **копе́ек** '40 kopecks'. 19 **пи́сем** '11 letters'. 20 **англича́н** '70 Englishmen'. 21 **неде́ль** '11 weeks'. 22 **лет** '450 years'. 23 **море́й** '7 seas'. 24 **имён** '8 names'. 25 **англича́нок** '90 Englishwomen'.

9/4

1 **Де́сять рубле́й три́дцать копе́ек.** 2 **Пять часо́в.** 3 **Пятна́дцать мину́т.** 4 **Пять неде́ль.** 5 **Во́семьдесят апельси́нов.** 6 **Пятьдеся́т до́лларов.** 7 **Два́дцать дней.** 8 **Пять ме́сяцев.** 9 **Сто́ слов.** 10 **Две́сти шестьдеся́т кварти́р.**

9/5

1 **мину́ты** (gen.sg. after 3) '3 minutes'. 2 **мину́т** '5 minutes'. 3 **мину́та** '21 minutes'. 4 **го́да** '2 years'. 5 **лет** '10 years'. 6 **дня** '123 days'. 7 **до́ллар** '1261 dollars'. 8 **до́чери** '4 daughters'. 9 **одна́ копе́йка** '41 kopecks'. 10 **одного́ студе́нта** 'I know 21 students' (**anim acc.**).

9/14

(1) A: Please give me three coffees, three teas, five open sandwiches and five pies. B: That will be ('From you') 4 roubles 28 kopecks. A: Here you are. B: Here's (your) change – 5 roubles 72 kopecks. A: Thank you. B: You're welcome.

(2) A: Please give me 200 grams of cheese and half a kilo of salami. B: 7 roubles 26 kopecks.

(3) A: What (How much) does this cost? B: 12 roubles a kilo. A: 400 grams, please. B: Here you are. 4 roubles 80 kopecks.

(4) A: Please give me a kilo of apples. B: Anything else? A: How much are the oranges? B: 14 roubles. A: Half a kilo, please. B: That will be ('From you') 16 roubles.

A: How many inhabitants are there in Moscow. 2 or 3 million? B: No, more. 8 million. But in St Petersburg there are fewer inhabitants – 4 million. A: And how many in Russia? B: I don't know exactly. Perhaps 150,000,000.

9/6

1 **два́дцать оди́н**. 2 **ты́сяча две́сти**. 3 **ты́сяча восемьсо́т се́мьдесят три**. 4 **де́вять ты́сяч** (gen.pl. of **ты́сяча**). 5 **семьсо́т пятьдеся́т пять**. 6 **пятьдеся́т два**. 7 **пятьдеся́т**. 8 **три́дцать пять**. 9 **три́дцать шесть рубле́й шестьдеся́т копе́ек**.

9/7

Q.1 Eleven weeks, four days. Q.2 Two or three times a week. Q.3 'Sadko' is expensive and she gets only £120 a month from her parents.

V: How many months have you been ('are you already') in Moscow, Mary? M: Three months, or, to be precise ('if precisely'), eleven weeks and four days. V: How are you getting on? ('How are you living?') You're a vegetarian, aren't you ('you know'), and Russians are very fond of meat. M: I buy a lot of food at the market. I go there two or three times a week. Sometimes I go to the 'Sadko' foreign currency shop. There they have ('there are') various dairy products, a lot of vegetables and fruit, but everything is ('costs') expensive. A kilogram of cheese costs five pounds, ten eggs cost two pounds. I get ('receive') only £120 a month from my parents, so I buy very little there.

10/1

1 Does Vadim have a wife? 2 He has a Russian female friend. 3 Does Eva have a brother? 4 She doesn't have a brother (stress on doesn't – so **нет** at end). 5 **У вас есть бе́лое вино́?** 6 **У них есть до́чь и два сы́на.** 7 **У неё есть де́ньги?**

10/2

1 **ру́сского дру́га** Mary receives letters from her Russian friend.
2 **Большо́го теа́тра** There is a metro station near the Bolshoi Theatre. 3 **Воло́ди** Volodia is not at home ('Of Volodia there is not at home'). 4 **друзе́й, хоро́шего вина́** For our friends we are buying a bottle of good wine. 5 **рабо́ты, Са́ши** Today after work everybody except Sasha is going to the theatre. **6 килогра́мма све́жей колбасы́** Please give me two kilos of fresh salami.

10/3

1 Do your Russian friends have any children? 2 Why haven't you any fresh fruit? 3 Near our house there is an institute of foreign languages. 4 They are not at home. 5 **Во́т письмо́ от мое́й ру́сской подру́ги.** 6 **(Одно́) кило́ э́тих больши́х я́блок, пожа́луйста.** 7 **У нас есть не́сколько кни́г для ва́ших/твои́х друзе́й.** 8 **Две буты́лки кра́сного вина́ и одна́ буты́лка ру́сской во́дки.** 9 **У него́ (есть) мно́го интере́сных книг.** 10 **У нас нет ру́сских де́нег.**

10/4

1 **мои́х америка́нских друзе́й** 'She knows my American friends.'
2 **америка́нских до́лларов** 'Thirty-five American dollars.' 3 **больши́х буты́лок/одну́ ма́ленькую буты́лку** 'She is buying five large bottles of juice and one small bottle of wine.' 4 **иностра́нных** (gen.pl.) **языка́** (gen.sg.) 'Mary knows three foreign languages.'

10.17

(1) A: Do you have tea? B: No, but there's juice. A: And is there coffee? B: Yes (There is). (2) A: Do you have any bananas? B: No. There aren't any. A: What

have you got then? B: There are apples. There is no other fruit. (3) A: (And) what have you got to drink? B: Wine. White (and) red. There's no vodka. A: Please give (me) a bottle of white wine. B: Here you are.

A: Tell me please, do you have ('don't you have') any airmail envelopes? B: Yes. A: And what does such an envelope cost? B: An airmail envelope costs fifty-four kopecks. A: Two envelopes, please. B: 1 rouble 8 kopecks. A: OK.

A: Tell me please, do you have a map of the town? B: Unfortunately, we haven't any at the moment, but there's a guidebook. A: What about maps of Russia? ('And are there maps of Russia?') B: Yes, we have maps. Have a look at this one. A: No, this map is too small. Don't you have a big one? B: There aren't any big ones., But there's this medium-sized one ('here such [a map], of average dimensions'). A: OK. I'll take ('I take') this one. How much is it? B: Fourteen kopecks. A: Only fourteen kopecks! So little! What a pleasant surprise!

Customer: Tell me please, you don't have any meat, do you? Assistant: No, this is a fish shop. Fish is what we don't have. Where they don't have meat is at the shop opposite.

10/5

V: Do you have any (postage) stamps? I have three letters for my English (British) friends but I have no stamps at all. E: I have only two six-kopeck stamps. Ask ('at') my parents. V: That's awkward. I borrow ('take') so many different ('various') things from ('at') them – yesterday *several English newspapers*, this morning *two English dictionaries* . . . [answer to Q.1]. E: Since *they don't have a son* [Q.2 Eva has no brothers], you are like a son to them. You have the right (10.4) to take (borrow) anything you like ('anything that you want'). V: And who am I to ('for') you – your brother, am I? E: Of course not. You are simply one of my friends. V: Thank you. So I am simply one of your friends. But *your parents are fond of me* ('love') me. E: Yes, *today mother is making an apple pie* ('pie of fresh apples'), *specially for you* [Q.3 Evidence that she does].

10.6

1 **Я не понима́ю.** 2 **Вы говори́те по-англи́йски?** – normal form. Also possible: **Говори́те ли вы по-англи́йски?** 3 **Вы живёте в Москве́? (Живёте ли вы в Москве́?)** 4 **Вы (не) зна́ете, где по́чта?/Скажи́те, пожа́луйста, где по́чта?** 5 **Он не говори́т по-ру́сски.** 6 **Спаси́бо за письмо́.** 7 **Как** ('how') **её и́мя и о́тчество?** 8 **Я иду́ (е́ду) на Кра́сную пло́щадь.** 9 **Я не о́чень люблю́ Бородина́** (if emphasis on Borodin)/**Я Бородина́ не о́чень люблю́** (if emphasis on 'not very fond'). 10 **Ка́жется, Макдо́налдс на Пу́шкинской пло́щади.** 11 **Мои́ друзья́ живу́т на э́той у́лице.** 12 **Два́дцать пять**

до́лларов. 13 Вот дом моего́ дру́га Ива́на (gen.). 14 Сего́дня нет молока́.
15 У вас есть англи́йские кни́ги? 16 Прости́те/Скажи́те, пожа́луйста, у
вас есть ко́фе? 17 У меня́ (есть) мно́го ру́сских друзе́й. 18 У Ната́ши есть
два ма́леньких сы́на. 19 Да́йте буты́лку хоро́шего бе́лого вина́,
пожа́луйста. 20 Вы зна́ете/Ты зна́ешь э́тих де́вушек?

11/1

1 **был** Ivan was in Moscow. 2 **была́** Masha was in Moscow too. 3 **был**
(man)/**была́** (woman) I was in Kiev (for) two days. 4 **рабо́тали** They worked all
day. 5 **рабо́тал** (man)/**рабо́тала** (woman) I worked/was working yesterday.
6 **зна́ли, была́** Did you know that she was/had been in Berlin? 7 **ви́дели** Have
you seen/Did you see my husband? 8 **могла́** She couldn't work. 9 **шли** We were
walking slowly. 10 **ви́дел/ви́дела, шёл** When I saw him, he was going to the
shop. 11 **бы́ли** Did you have friends in Moscow? 12 **был** She had a Russian
friend. 13 **не́ было** There was no milk in the snackbar. 14 **не́ было** We had no
Russian money.

11/2

1 улыба́ется. 2 одева́лись. 3 открыва́ется. 4 открыва́лись. 5 начина́ется.

11.9

(1) VP: Have you been in Petersburg? E: Yes. Last year. I was there for four days.
VP: What did you see there? E: I saw Nevskii Prospekt, the (River) Neva, the Peter
and Paul Fortress, I was in the Hermitage, of course. I didn't know that Petersburg
was such a beautiful city. I had heard a lot about the ('that') city but all the same I
didn't expect such beauty.

(2) E: When does the concert begin ('itself')? V: At seven o'clock, I think. Why are
you smiling? E: I know that there are no tickets left ('already no tickets'). But there's
a good American film on at the cinema. Mother saw ('watched') (it) yesterday. She
says that everybody was laughing.

(3) KM: Welcome! Come on in! Take your coat off ('Undress yourself'). Here are
some slippers. AB: Klara Mikhailovna, I'm sorry I'm late ('Excuse for lateness'). I
hope you're not angry. I spent so long looking for a taxi. KM: Never mind. Please,
go through (to the main room). AB: There were no free cars at all. I didn't know
what to do. KM: Let me introduce you. This is our neighbour, Vladimir Petrovich.
He was in London recently. AB: Pleased to meet you. My name is Anna Borisovna.
And what did you see there? VP: Unfortunately, because of the fog I didn't see

anything. AB: Really? Why are you laughing? VP: It's a joke, of course. There weren't any fogs. But it rained all the time.

11/3

The Russian Tsar Peter the Great considered it necessary ('that it is necessary') to build a new port on the Baltic Sea. This was (is) the city of Saint Petersburg, or Petersburg, as it is usually called. This new 'window on to ('into') Europe' was built ('[they] built') on the River Neva, *where the Peter and Paul Fortress already stood on an island* [Q.1 so the site was not empty]. Petersburg was built ('built itself') quickly. For the construction of the city thousands of peasants were sent every year from all corners of Russia. *They worked in the (winter) cold, it rained constantly, it was windy, they stood up to their knees in water and mud. Every year thousands of people perished from diseases, hunger and overwork* [Q.2].

12/1

1 Я помогу́. 2 Вы помо́жете/Ты помо́жешь? 3 Мы уви́дим её за́втра. 4 Мы пойдём/пое́дем на Кра́сную пло́щадь. 5 Они́ не пое́дут. 6 Я куплю́ э́ту кни́гу. 7 Мы отдохнём. 8 О́н не придёт. 9 Я беру́ э́ту кни́гу. 10 Я скажу́ два сло́ва.

12/2

1 Что́ вы хоти́те/Что́ ты хо́чешь? 2 Я хочу́ пое́хать° в Сиби́рь. 3 Мы не хоти́м. 4 Они́ хотя́т купи́ть° во́дку. 5 Ты (не) хо́чешь вы́пить°?

12/3

1 **вам** I'll give you 5 dollars. 2 **мне** Will you help me? 3 **Жене́** I'll show the letter to (my) wife. 4 **Е́ве и Вади́му** I'll phone Eva and Vadim. 5 **сча́стью** Fortunately, the Russians want peace.

12/4

1 **мое́й жене́** to my wife. 2 **ва́шему ру́сскому дру́гу Воло́де** to your Russian friend Volodia. 3 **э́тому интере́сному англича́нину** to that interesting Englishman.

12/5

1 **на́шим роди́телям** to our parents. 2 **э́тим у́лицам** along these streets. 3 **тем америка́нцам** He's helping those Americans. 4 **мои́м друзья́м** I'll phone my

467

friends. 5 **Соединённым Шта́т<u>ам</u>** She's an expert on the United States.

12/6

1 **ру́сск<u>им</u> друзь<u>я́м</u> о на́ш<u>их</u> де́т<u>ях</u>** I told our Russian friends about our children. 2 **вс<u>ех</u> ру́сск<u>их</u> дом<u>а́х</u>, о Соединённ<u>ых</u> Шта́т<u>ах</u>** In all Russian homes (houses) people often talk about the USA. 3 **э́т<u>их</u> магази́н<u>ах</u>, нам** We don't like the food in these shops.

12.19

Waitress: Hello. Customer: Hello. W: What do you want. C: We want to have a meal. W: Certainly. C: What have you got? W: We have mushrooms in sour cream, fish salad, meat rissoles, Beef Stroganov, Chicken Kiev. What would you like? C: My wife will have ('take') the mushrooms and the Chicken Kiev and I'll have ('take') the mushrooms and Beef Stroganov. Is there any mineral water? W: Yes. C: And what (alcoholic) drinks have you got? W: There's champagne and wine. C: Please bring my wife a bottle of mineral water and red wine for me ('to me'). W: All right. I'll bring you our Crimean red.

C: Waiter, excuse me ('Be so good'). W: What can I do for you? ('I'm listening to you.') W: I'm a vegetarian. Do you have vegetarian dishes? W: Yes. Would you like fish? C: No, I only eat vegetables. W: All right, I'll bring you potatoes, cabbage and tomatoes. C: Thank you.

E: Where shall we go? V: Let's go to (see) your friends. E: Which ones? ('To whom shall we go?') V: (To) Vera and Oleg.

V: Would you like a drink? E: No thank you. I want a sandwich – and Pepsi, if there is any. V: I'll have a drink. E: I warn you: if you (will) drink a lot, (then) I'll leave without you.

12/7

E: Let's go and see ('to') my friends. V: Vera and Oleg? E: No, Natal'ia Petrovna and her family. V: I don't want to go there ('to them'). *They live in Sokol'niki, don't they? That's a very long way* [Q.1 First objection]. E: There's a direct metro line (i.e. no changes). V: On top of that, *Natal'ia Petrovna constantly talks about small children. I find that boring* [Q.1 Second objection]. E: Her husband will talk to you (tell you) about the countries of Western Europe. Boris Karlovich is an expert on the European Union, he often travels around these countries. V: *I don't want to listen to an economics lecture* [Q.1 Third objection]. Let's go and see Vera. E: *I think ('To me it seems') you don't want to go and see Natal'ia and Boris only*

because they don't drink. (While) Vera will let you have a drink. V: How can you?!
*(You should be ashamed.) You know very well (**же** is for emphasis) that I like the*
sober lifestyle of Natal'ia Petrovna and her husband. E: In that case, let's go to visit
my abstainers. [Q.2 Eva manoeuvres Vadim into protesting that he's not looking for
vodka and admires her sober friends]. I'll just ring them/I'll ring them right now,
and then we'll ring mother to say that we won't be in for dinner ('we to dinner won't
come').

13/1

Eva and Vadim *were walking* (action in process, unfinished) along Tverskaia
Street and *talking* (action in process, unfinished) about her friends. Suddenly Eva
remembered (single completed event) that she *had forgotten* (single event) *to*
phone (**забы́ть** is followed by p infinitive, meaning one hasn't done what one
should have done) Vera. Usually she *rang* (repeated action) her every morning, but
today she *hadn't rung* (failed to do what she should have done). 'I *want* (present
tense) *to make a phone call* (single event),' she *said* (single completed event) to
Vadim. 'We need *to find* (single event with a result) a phone box.' They *searched*
(action in process, unfinished) ('for it') for ten minutes and finally *found*
(completed; result achieved) one near the 'Intourist' Hotel.

13/2

1 We asked if she knew ('knows') Boris Petrovich. 2 Eva didn't know whether she
would see ('will see') Vadim. 3 **Я не зна́ю, говори́т ли о́н по-ру́сски.** 4 **Я не**
зна́ю, позвони́тᵖ **ли она́ за́втра.** 5 **Мы не зна́ли, говори́т ли она́** ('if she
speaks') **по-англи́йски.** 6 **Она́ спроси́ла**ᵖ**, америка́нец** (m)/**америка́нка** (f) **ли**
я ('whether I am') 7 **Я спрошу́**ᵖ **её, хо́чет ли она́ пойти́**ᵖ **в теа́тр.**

13.9

NN: When did you begin to study Russian? M: Four years ago. NN: Do you like
Russian? M: Very much. But it's very difficult. NN: What languages do you know,
apart from Russian? N: I speak a little French. In our schools almost all children
learn French. And I can read German but I don't speak it. NN: Is Russian popular
in your country ('at you', 'chez vous'). M: Many people want to study it, because
everybody knows that it is a very important language nowadays ('in the modern
world'). But there aren't many opportunities in our schools. I myself went to
evening classes. I was lucky: in my town there is an institute where they have been
teaching Russian for a long time. In general the English (British) are not very
interested in foreign languages ('regard foreign languages indifferently'). They

usually think that the whole world speaks English. NN: And why did you decide to study Russian? M: The thing is that several years ago I began to read the novels of Dostoevskii – in English, of course. Then I got the urge to read Russian literature in the original. That's why I decided to take a course ('enrol on a course'). I don't know whether I'll manage to master the language, but I've already read three Dostoevskii novels in Russian. NN: I think you've already mastered it.

A journalist was conducting a survey on the streets of Moscow. 'Excuse me, where were you born?' 'In St Petersburg'. 'And where did you go to (finish) school?' 'In Petrograd.' 'And where do you live now?' 'In Leningrad.' 'And where would you like to live?' 'In St Petersburg.'

13/3

Vera was born in Moscow. She lived there for three years, then the family moved to Irkutsk. There she finished school and entered an institute. When she was studying at the institute, she fell in love with a young lecturer. Since he taught English and was translating (**action in process**) an English novel, she decided that she too wanted ('wants') to study English. So she started to go to evening classes.

13/4

1 Я изуча́ю (ог учу́) ру́сский язы́к (уже́) три ме́сяца. 2 Мы хоти́м вы́учить ру́сский язы́к. 3 Мэ́ри перее́хала в Москву́ и бы́стро вы́учила ру́сский язы́к. 4 Я не зна́ю, говори́т ли Вади́м по-англи́йски. 5 Е́сли о́н говори́т по-англи́йски, я ему́ дам э́тот рома́н.

13/5

Brezhnev was travelling in his car along a Moscow avenue. *He decided to take a look at the living standards of ('how lives') the Soviet people* [Q.1]. He ordered his chauffeur to stop the car at a tall block of flats. He went into the block and rang the bell of ('into') the first flat. The door was opened by a small boy. *Brezhnev asked the boy if his home had a television* [Q.2]. 'Yes,' answered the boy. 'Is there a refrigerator?' 'Yes.' 'A tape recorder?' 'Yes.' 'Well then, it was I who gave you all these things!' The boy laughed with joy. 'Mummy, Daddy, Uncle Misha has come from America!' [Q.3 **The family could only afford luxury goods thanks to the generosity of a relative in the West.**]

14/1

1 Я бу́ду в Москве́. 2 Она́ бу́дет до́ма за́втра? 3 Мы бу́дем изуча́ть (учи́ть)

ру́сский язы́к. 4 **За́втра я бу́ду рабо́тать.** 5 **В Москве́ я бу́ду говори́ть то́лько по-ру́сски.** 6 **Они́ бу́дут звони́ть ка́ждый день.**

14/2

1 When we are ('shall be') in Moscow, we'll stay (be staying) at the 'Russia' Hotel. 2 If you write ('will write') her a letter, she'll answer. 3 If Vadim drinks ('will drink') a lot, Eva will leave without him. 4 We'll tell you when you come ('will come'). 5 When we've had dinner ('shall finish having dinner'), we'll watch television (for a while)/ After dinner we'll watch some television. 6 **Когда́ я бу́ду** ('shall be') **в Москве́, я бу́ду говори́ть то́лько по-ру́сски.** 7 **Когда́ Е́ва придёт/прие́дет** ('will come'), **Вади́м позвони́т нам/нам позвони́т.** 8 **Е́сли вы дади́те ему́ де́сять до́лларов, он даст вам биле́ты.** 9 **Я не зна́ю, бу́дет ли она́ до́ма.**

14/3

1 'Aren't you cold?' 'No, I'm actually ('even') warm.' 2 In Moscow in August we were hot. 3 'May I open the window?' 'Please do/Go ahead, but it will be noisy.' 4 Tomorrow it will be necessary to (we'll have to) buy a hat. 5 **Здесь мо́жно купи́ть во́дку?** (Put the place word **здесь** at the beginning unless it's stressed.) 6 **В э́той ко́мнате о́чень хо́лодно.** 7 **Вам/Тебе́ не бу́дет ску́чно.** 8 **Вади́му нельзя́ пить.**

14.8

V: Will you object if I go ('will go') to Alësha's place ('to Alësha') on Saturday? We're going to celebrate the anniversary of his divorce. Men only ('in male company'), of course, no women. E: I see. So you're going to drink vodka all evening. You know drinking's bad for you ('While to you to drink is harmful'). V: I'll drink a little, just to relax a bit. I know that I mustn't drink too much ('one must drink in moderation'). E: If you get drunk, you'll feel ashamed afterwards. V: Don't worry.

14/4

VP: Where are you going to spend your summer holiday? AM: In the south, in the Crimea, not far from Yalta. It's very beautiful there. VP: *I don't like the Crimea in summer. It's very hot. And it's hard to find somewhere to stay ('to find a room')* [Q.1 Two of the reasons]. AM: And may I ask you what you're going to do (be doing) in August? VP: You'll think this is funny, but we've decided to stay in Moscow. We're going to stay ('sit') at home and watch television. AM: *But that'll be boring, won't it?* [Q.2] VP: On the other hand, *it'll be peaceful. All the neighbours*

471

KEY TO EXERCISES AND TRANSLATIONS OF TEXTS

will go away, we won't hear any drunken voices, any swearing or any loud rock music [Q.1 The third reason]. AM: In our block the soundproofing is good. VP: Ours is very noisy ('In our place is very noisy'). Then in autumn, when everybody returns ('will return') to Moscow, *we'll take a holiday in Sochi, at my sister's place* [Q.3].

15/1

1 **Да́йте**. 2 **Послу́шай(те)**. 3 **Одева́йся/Одева́йтесь**.

15/2

1 **Принеси́те**. 2 **Уходи́/Уходи́те**. 3 **Купи́/Купи́те**. 4 **Посмотри́(те)**.

15/3

1 **Оста́нься/Оста́ньтесь**. 2 **Отве́ть/Отве́тьте**. 3 **Забу́дь** (familiar form going with the intimate form **Ва́ня**).

15/4

1 Come and see us on Saturday (' invitation). 2 Would you open the window? (ᵖ request). 3 'May I smoke?' 'Go ahead' (' a general invitation, not a command). 4 Answer two questions (ᵖ single command). 5 Give me your telephone (number) (ᵖ single command/request). 6 Do have a pie (' invitation). 6 Don't go away (' negative command/prohibition).

15/5

1 **Позвони́(те) мне за́втра**. 2 **Скажи́те, пожа́луйста, где вокза́л?** 3 **Не забу́дь(те) принести́ со́к**. 4 **Пиши́(те) нам ча́сто**. 5 **Сади́сь/Сади́тесь**. 6 **Да́йте два биле́та, пожа́луйста**. 7 **Не открыва́й(те) окно́. В э́той ко́мнате хо́лодно**.

15/6

1 Let's have a drink. 2 Let's go and see Eva and Vadim. 3 Don't be angry. Let them go if they want to. 4 If Volodia phones, tell him I've left. Tell him to (Let him) phone tomorrow. 5 **Дава́й(те) говори́ть** (**поговори́м**ᵖ) **по-ру́сски**. 6 **Дава́й(те) позвони́м**ᵖ **Е́ве**. 7 **Дава́й(те) не бу́дем ду́мать о рабо́те**. 8 **Пусть изуча́ет** (**у́чит**ᵖ) **францу́зский (язы́к), е́сли (о́н) хо́чет**.

15/7

Yu: Have you read [15.11 (8)] the novel *Anna Karenina*? Sh: Not yet. I bought [15.11 (9)] it last year. I wanted/intended [15.11 (3)] to read [15.11 (9)] it, but I was working a lot [15.11 (2) (3) (6)], I got very tired [15.11 (6)] and hadn't time to do anything [15.11 (4) (6)]. But this August ('Here in August') I'll be on holiday [15.11 (3)], then I'll definitely read it [15.11 (9)/15.12 (b)]. Yu: When you've read it [15.11 (11)], we'll talk/have a talk [15.11 (9)] about whether Tolstoi understood [15.11 (3)] the female heart/how women feel.

15.14

Tourist: Could you tell me how to get to the station? V: Take trolleybus number 4, get out at the square and change there to any tram.

Tourist: Could you tell me how to get to ('reach') the 'Russia' Hotel? E: Let's look at the city map. Here's the hotel, not far from the Kremlin. We're here, near McDonald's on Pushkin Square. Turn right and go straight on along Tverskaia Street. At the 'National' Hotel you'll see a pedestrian subway. Go down the steps ('Go down'), then straight on, then find the exit to Red Square. Go towards St Basil's ('the cathedral of Vasilii the Blessed'). To the left of the cathedral you'll see a large modern building. That's the 'Russia'.

E: Excuse me, could I speak to Vadim, please? NN: He's just gone out. Is that Eva? E: Yes. NN: He rang you [¹ no result 15.11 (2), 15.12 (c)] ten minutes ago, but you weren't at home. E: Tell him that I'll be at home in the evening. Ask him to ring again. NN: I'll do that.

LP: Tania! What are you doing? Stop it! T: But I want to. LP: I don't allow it! You mustn't! T: Why mustn't I? LP: Tania, that's enough! T: I'm not afraid of you. LP: I'll punish you. T: If you punish me, I'll cry.

15/8

B: Could I speak to R, please? *('Please call R')* Secretary: I'm afraid he's busy. Ring in an hour. B: *Don't hang up, please. Could you tell him that B rang?* S: OK, I'll tell him. B: *Ask him to ring me on 125-36-47* [Q.1]. S: Don't worry, I'll tell him.

B: Excuse me for troubling you. This is Evgenii Matveevich Borisov. Could I speak to R, please? S: He's already left. B: How can he have left? Why didn't he ring? S: I don't know. *I told him you rang.* B: Please remind him again tomorrow. S: Will do. [Q.2 She couldn't call R because he was busy. She didn't hang up. She says she told R that B rang but she doesn't mention having asked R to ring B. So she carried out at least two of the instructions.]

B: Hello. It's Borisov. Is R in? He's in but he's expecting a client. B: *When he's free, remind him that I asked him to ring me* [Q.3]. S: *OK, I'll leave him a note* [Q.4].

15/9

1 **Я хочу купи́ть**ᴾ **ша́пку**. 2 **Мы жи́ли**ᴵ **в гости́нице «Интури́ст»**. 3 – **Вы чита́ли**ᴵ**/Ты чита́л(а)**ᴵ **рома́н «А́нна Каре́нина»?** – **Нет, не чита́л(а)**ᴵ. 4 **Мы ча́сто звони́ли**ᴵ **Вади́му и Е́ве**. 5 – **Вы придёте**ᴾ**/Ты придёшь**ᴾ **за́втра?** – **Я приду́**ᴾ, **е́сли смогу́**ᴾ. 6 **Е́сли за́втра у нас бу́дет вре́мя (за́втра), мы позвони́м**ᴾ **(на́шим) друзья́м**. 7 **Мы бу́дем ждать**ᴵ **вас/тебя́**. 8 **Я отдохну́**ᴾ, **пото́м я пойду́**ᴾ **на Кра́сную пло́щадь**. 9 **Невозмо́жно/Нельзя́ откры́ть**ᴾ **э́ту дверь**. 10 **Пожа́луйста, принеси́те**ᴾ **мне буты́лку минера́льной воды́**. 11 **Пожа́луйста, не открыва́й(те)**ᴵ **окно́. Нам хо́лодно**. 12 **Пиши́**ᴵ **мне ча́сто. Я бу́ду писа́ть**ᴵ **тебе́ ка́ждую неде́лю** (acc.). 13 **Не забу́дь(те)**ᴾ, **что за́втра мы идём/е́дем** (pres.) **к Ната́лье Петро́вне**. 14 **Сади́тесь. Я приду́ че́рез не́сколько мину́т. Мне на́до позвони́ть де́тям**. 15 **Дава́й(те) не бу́дем говори́ть**ᴵ **о де́тях**.

16/1

1 **варе́ньем**. 2 **ло́жкой**. 3 **у́тром**. 4 **жено́й и до́черью**. 5 **Са́шей**. 6 **царём Никола́ем**.

16/2

1 **сёстрами**. 2 **буты́лками**. 3 **детьми́**. 4 **америка́нцами**.

16/3

1 **ру́сской му́зыкой** I have been studying/involved with Russian music for a long time. 2 **бра́том** My brother and I were on holiday in the Crimea. 3 **молоко́м, апельси́новым со́ком** Vadim is drinking coffee with milk and Mary is drinking vodka with orange juice. 4 **мои́ми ру́сскими друзья́ми** I want to introduce you to ('acquaint you with') my Russian friends. 5 **ней, на́ми** What's the matter with her? Why doesn't she want to talk to ('with') us?

16.11

In the morning my brothers Sergei and Aleksandr and I get up early, get dressed and go to the kitchen. We usually breakfast with father. He sits at ('behind') the table, drinking coffee with milk and reading the paper with interest. He hardly ever speaks to ('with') us at ('behind' as in **за столо́м** 'at table') breakfast. He used to be a schoolteacher and while breakfasting always prepared lessons. That's why he's in the habit ('has such a habit') of reading in silence at the table. But when we sit down at (**3a + acc. = motion behind**) the table, he says: 'Good morning, boys. Good morning, my little girl ('daughterlet'). How did you sleep?' 'Well, dad,' we answer. Then we start to eat. My brothers usually have kasha. Serëzha eats with a spoon and Sasha with his fingers, since he knows that father isn't looking at him. I have bread and cheese. We drink tea with lemon or jam. Sometimes Mum fries me some eggs with salami, but usually she gets up late. Our mother doesn't like breakfast. She gets up after us and goes to the factory where she is chief engineer ('works as chief engineer'). In the evening she comes back home, Dad makes supper, and we all have supper together. After supper we sit in front of the television, but usually we don't watch it. Mum sits between me and my brothers and we talk. I enjoy that. Unfortunately, sometimes instead of our talk Serëzha plays the guitar and Sasha sings. Although I'm interested in music, I can't listen to them when they give such a concert. They say they want to become professionals but in my view they'll never be real musicians. When they start, I say that I have to study and I leave the room. But Dad is very keen on these concerts and enjoys listening to his sons.

16/4

V: Where do you want to go today? M: I want to get to know the sights of Moscow. Will you be my guide? V: With pleasure. Let's go to the centre. I'll just get a city map. Right. Let's go first to *Okhotnyi Riad. That used to be Marx Prospekt* [**Q.1 One**]. Going along it we'll reach *Theatre Square – it used to be called Sverdlov Square* [**Q.1 Two**]. And, see, here is the famous Bolshoi Theatre. Beside it is the Malyi Theatre. Then we'll continue to *Lubianka Square. After the Revolution Lubianka was for a long time called Dzerzhinskii Square* [**Q.1 Three**]. M: Who was Dzerzhinskii? If I'm not mistaken, he became famous for something rather unpleasant. V: Feliks Edmundovich Dzerzhinskii was one of the first Chekists (secret policemen). To be more precise, *he was the chairman of the All-Russia Special Commission Against Counter-Revolution and Sabotage (the Cheka)* [**Q.2**]. M: *Feliks Edmundovich?* Was he a foreigner? [**Q.3 Mary thinks, correctly, that his name doesn't sound very Russian.**] V: By birth he was Polish. M: And what happened to his Special Commission? V: That organization changed its name several times: now it's the KGB, the Committee of State Security. If you like, I'll tell you Dzerzhinskii's life-story. M: Thank you, I don't suffer from insomnia. V: I'm sorry, I don't follow. M: It was a joke. Why are you so interested in that subject? V: My favourite subject at school was history. I was very interested in the Old

Bolsheviks – Lenin, *Krupskaia* [Q.4 f ending], Trotskii, Bukharin, Kamenev, Zinov'ev, *Kollontai* [Q.4 since the person is female, the m **-ай** ending doesn't decline], Dzerzhinskii and others. For a long time now I've been working particularly on Dzerzhinsky and his assistants. *Although many now consider that the Chekists were criminals, even murderers, I think that they were genuine revolutionaries, passionate believers in Lenin's ideas ('devoted to the ideas of Lenin')* [Q.5]. M: Perhaps we'll come back to the subject in the evening. But what about our route round Moscow? V: OK. Then we'll go along Nikol'skaia Street. In front of you you'll see ('will open itself') a view of Red Square, the Lenin Mausoleum and, behind the Mausoleum, the Kremlin wall with its towers.

17/1

1 On Sunday. 2 It is now six o'clock. 3 It is now twenty-five past two. 4 **В сре́ду.** 5 **Де́сять мину́т пя́того.** 6 **Без двадцати́ двена́дцать.**

17/2

1 She'll come at five to eight. 2 Let's go there on Saturday at half past two. 3 The film begins at ten past seven. 4 We'll arrive at ten p.m. 5 **Я приду́ (прие́ду) в сре́ду в шесть (часо́в** – can be omitted in conversation). 6 **Фильм начина́ется без десяти́ семь.** 7 **О́н позвони́т в полови́не пя́того.** 8 **В Ло́ндоне оди́ннадцать часо́в ве́чера (два́дцать три часа́).**

17/3

1 The main holidays in the USSR were 1 January, 1 May, 9 May, 7 November. 2 Lenin was born on 22 April 1870. 3 They arrived at 6 p.m. on Monday, 31 December 1990. 4 **Шесто́го апре́ля ты́сяча девятьсо́т девяно́сто пе́рвого го́да.** 5 **В де́вять часо́в утра́ в пя́тницу оди́ннадцатого января́.** 6 **Без пятна́дцати (че́тверти) шесть деся́того октября́ ты́сяча девятьсо́т се́мьдесят седьмо́го го́да.**

17/4

(1) A: How old are you? B: I'm thirty-four. A: When's your birthday? B: On 23 March. A: How old are your children? B: My son is ten and my daughter is eight. A: Have you been in Moscow long? B: Since last Friday.

(2) A: Vania, in which year did you become a teacher? B: In (19)63. A: How old were you then? B: Twenty-three.

(3) A: Could you say when this shop is open ('works')? B: From 9 a.m. to 10 p.m.

(4) A: It's now a quarter past four. B: What ('How')?! On my watch it's not yet four ('yet isn't of four' (**gen. after нет**).

(5) Tourist: Could you tell me when the Russian Museum is open? Eva: Every day except Tuesday, from nine to six. T: Thank you. E: You're welcome.

(6) A: Could you tell me when this shop opens? B: At eleven. A: And when's the lunch break? B: From two to three.

(7) A: When is GUM's lunch break? B: GUM doesn't have one.

(8) A: Which day are the food shops closed? B: Food shops don't have days off.

17.15

M: When do Muscovites have lunch ('have a meal in the afternoon')? V: Some (lunch) at twelve, some at one, some at two, some even at three. Some shops close from three to four, sometimes even from four to five. Many shops don't close for lunch. M: And when do they open in the morning? V: Food shops at ('from') eight, other shops (non-food shops) at ('from') ten. M: When do they close? V: Late. Most stay open until eight, some until ten. But offices close earlier, about five. M: What about weekends ('Saturday and Sunday')? V: Food shops are open every day. Offices are closed on these days.

Guest: When does the train leave for Voronezh? Girl: At eleven p.m. Gu: And when will I be able to pick up my ticket? Gi: Tomorrow morning. Gu: OK. I'll come at eight. Gu: That's (too) early. The office opens at nine. Gi: But tomorrow I won't be able to come at nine. Our city tour ('excursion round the city') will start at eight-thirty. Gu: In that case we'll expect you ('be waiting for you') after the excursion. We're open ('work') until eight p.m.

17/5

1 Ско́лько ей лет? 2 Мне три́дцать шесть (лет). 3 В ты́сяча девятьсо́т во́семьдесят восьмо́м году́ ему́ бы́ло со́рок (лет). 4 Я приду́/прие́ду во вто́рник без пятна́дцати (че́тверти) три дня. 5 Пожа́луйста, позвони́(те) мне деся́того по́сле шести́ (часо́в). 6 Мы бу́дем в Сиби́ри с девя́того ма́я по шестна́дцатое (до шестна́дцатого) ию́ня. 7 Я живу́ в Ло́ндоне с (ты́сяча девятьсо́т) се́мьдесят тре́тьего го́да.

17/6

1 Pëtr Il'ich Chaikovskii (Tchaikovsky) was born in the Urals in 1840 (Q.1 **в**

тысяча восемьсот сороковом году). He started to compose music when he was still a child. He received his musical education at the St Petersburg Conservatoire. From 1885 (Q.1 **с тысяча восемьсот восемьдесят пятого года**) Chaikovskii lived near (in the vicinity of) the town of Klin, not far from Moscow. He moved into the house which is now the Chaikovskii Museum in May 1892 (Q.1 **в мае тысяча восемьсот девяносто второго года**). Here was everything which Chaikovskii had sought for so long: wonderful countryside, peace and quiet, and the chance to compose. [Q.2:] *He got up between seven and eight* [1], *until nine he studied English and read* [2]. *At nine-thirty he started work* [3]. *He worked until one p.m.* [4]. *He spent an hour on lunch* [5], *and then went for a walk which lasted exactly two hours* [6]. He always ('without fail') walked alone, since during these walks he almost always composed. *From five to seven again he worked* [7]. *After work he went for a walk or played the piano* [8]. *At eight supper was served.* [9] *After supper Chaikovskii entertained ('spent time with') his guests, or, if he had no guests, read* [10]. *At eleven he went to his room, where he wrote letters* [11] *and before bed did some more reading* [12]. In this house Chaikovskii composed ('created') his last works, among which was the brilliant Sixth Symphony. Nowadays Klin is Chaikovskii's town. His house in Klin has become a museum. Twice a year, on *7 May* [Q.3], *Chaikovskii's birthday* [Q.4], and on *6 November* [Q.3], *the day of his death* [Q.4], *musicians from Russia and abroad come here* [to the museum]. *And here once again Chaikovskii's wonderful music is heard* [Q.4]. Then many listeners recall the words of the great Russian writer Anton Pavlovich Chekhov: 'I am willing to mount a day-and-night guard of honour at the door of the house which is the residence of Pëtr Il'ich.'

18/1

1 Which wine is better? 2 These oranges are dearer. 3 Do come and see us a little more often. 4 Hurry up a bit, please, it's already half past seven. 5 Eva is younger than Vera. 6 In Moscow the weather was better than in Petersburg. 7 Russian is much more difficult than French. 8 *War and Peace* is a longer novel than *Anna Karenina*. 9 Vera was wearing a more expensive dress than Eva. 10 Mary is a lot more interesting than Eva. 11 Mary is less interested in Dzerzhinskii than Volodia *is* (*not* 'than in Volodia') 12 Please give me something easier to do ('work which is a bit easier').

18/2

1 **лучше** In London life is better. 2 **медленнее вас/тебя (, чем вы/ты).**

3 **намно́го (гора́здо) доро́же, чем в магази́не** Vodka costs much more (is much more expensive) in a restaurant than in a shop. 4 **бо́льше Е́вы (, чем Е́ва).** 5 **бо́лее интере́сные писа́тели, чем Толсто́й.** 6 **ча́ще (бо́лее ча́сто), чем во́дку** (acc.) I buy wine more often than than (I buy) vodka.

18/3

1 We'll buy the most expensive tickets. 2 We live (are staying) in the best hotel. 3 Lake Baikal is the biggest in the world. 4 **Он купи́л са́мую дешёвую во́дку.** 5 **Э́то са́мое лёгкое упражне́ние.**

18/4

1 **кото́рая** (nom.f sg.). 2 **кото́рой** (inst. f sg.). 3 **кото́рые** (acc. pl.). 4 **кото́рую** (acc. f sg.). 5 **кото́ром** (prep. m sg.). 6 **кото́рого** (acc. m anim sg.).

18.12

V: Do you remember Viktor? M: Is he that young man you were talking to ('with whom you were talking') in the bar yesterday? V: No. He's the one who got us tickets to the Taganka Theatre. M: He isn't that thin man who(m) we talked to at Vera's? V: Come now! That's a different Viktor. I'm talking about the ('that') Viktor you wanted to get to know better ('with whom you wanted to become a bit more closely acquainted'). The tall one, taller than me, with a nice voice. M: Oh yes, I remember. Who tells jokes better than anyone else. V: That's the one. Well then, he remembers you and wants to invite you to a lecture which he's giving ('reading') on Wednesday. M: On what subject? I hope his lecture will be more interesting than the one on the Chekists you took me to the day before yesterday. V: Don't worry. Viktor is our finest expert on the Russian theatre.

18/5

Siberia occupies the greater (**бо́льший** 'larger') part of Northern Asia *from the Ural Mountains in the west to the Pacific in the east and from the shores of the Arctic Ocean in the north to the southern steppes and the border with Mongolia and China* [Q.1]. The Siberian rivers Ob', Enisei and Lena are among the ten biggest in the world. Apart from rivers, Siberia has very beautiful large and small lakes with extremely pure water. One of them, *Lake Baikal, is the oldest, deepest and largest freshwater lake in the world* [Q.2]. Siberia has more than half of all Russia's natural resources: coal, oil, gas, gold, diamonds and rare metals. *And it is the world's number one source of hydroelectric power* [Q.3]. Siberia has a most varied range of wild animals ('most various wild animals . . .') and birds, it has very valuable fish – for example, sturgeon and salmon. Geographers normally divide Siberia into Western Siberia, Eastern Siberia and *the Far East, which they consider a separate region [from Siberia]. The Far East is an enormous territory which includes Kamchatka, Iakutia and the island of Sakhalin* [Q.4]. Its most important cities are Khabarovsk and Vladivostok.

19/1

1 If she had spoken more slowly, I would have understood (If she spoke more slowly, I would understand). 2 If we had known that you would be ('you will be') in Moscow, we would have phoned. 3 Vadim would write Eva a letter if he had time (Vadim would have written Eva a letter if he had had time). 4 Vera would like ('would want') to talk to you ('have a talk with you').

19/2

1 Если бы он был в Москве, он бы нам позвонил (он позвонил бы нам). 2 Они бы пришли (бы), если бы вы их пригласили. 3 Если бы Ева знала, что Вадим пьёт с нами вино (с нами), она бы рассердилась (бы). 4 Я бы хотел(а) (бы) вас пригласить.

19/3

1 должна. 2 должен был. 3 должны будем.

19/4

1 *to give back* or *give away* money. 2 *to hand over* or *transmit* a letter. 3 *to cease to love* a husband *('dislove').* 4 friends and *foes. 5 to look around* a town/city. 6 *a suburb* of Moscow. 7 *departure* from work. 8 *to rebuild* (extensively alter) a house. 9 *to reach* ('travel as far as') the station. 10 *a stray* ('homeless') dog. 11 *penultimate* day. 12 *to foresee* the result.

19.9

M: Excuse me, do you know where Professor Mirchanov is? He was supposed to meet me here at two o'clock. What ('How') do you think, should I wait? Secretary: Yes, yes, I remember that you and Il'ia Egorovich agreed to meet today. He must have forgotten. I think he's already gone home. I would have reminded him, but unfortunately I was with the dean all morning. M: If I had known he was so absent-minded, I would have telephoned in the morning. But how I am to find him? It's urgent. Tomorrow I'm going on a study trip to Zabaikal'e (the area beyond (**за**) Lake Baikal). S: You must go out of the institute, go straight on, then turn the corner at the shop called 'Podarki' ('Gifts'). Cross the street there, go as far as the traffic lights, walk past the metro entrance, find house number 6, go in at the third entrance, climb up to the fourth [third in UK] floor and ring the bell of flat 42. M: Thank you, I've noted all that down.

19/5

A year ago Elena and Pavel Sidorov had a daughter, Tania. Lena thinks that life would be easier if grandmother was close by. *'I wouldn't object if my mother lived with us,'* says Lena. *'She would help me to cook and to bring up Tanechka.'* [Q.1 **Elena wants her mother to move in to help her cook and bring up her one-year-old daugher.**] 'I think I help you enough,' Pavel objects. *He thinks that his mother-in-law should stay in the country* [Q.2]. *'If you didn't help me, I'd divorce you!'* Lena answers seriously. *'But all the same it would be better if I didn't depend only on your help.'* [Q.3 **She doesn't, though she implies that he's not the world's best househusband.**]

20/1

1 Last year we went (m) to New York (**and came back**). 2 Every day my wife takes (m) the children to school by car (**she makes round trips**). 3 Yesterday she took (m) her small son to the park (**and they came back**). 4 Where are you lugging ('dragging') (u) those huge dictionaries to (**one direction**)? 5 Usually I get up at eight, have breakfast and at nine go (u) to work) (**stressing the trip *to* work; obviously I come back from work, but not at nine in the morning**). 6 Time flies (u) (**in one direction only, at least in the world we and the Russians inhabit**)! 7 Run (u) (**one direction**)! The film starts in five minutes. 8 Every year my husband and I go (m) to the seaside (**there and back**). 9 Have you ever flown (m) in a Russian plane (**number of directions irrelevant**)? 10 I can't (don't know how to) swim (m) (**direction irrelevant, since I don't succeed in moving in any direction**). 11 Don't go (m) to that film (**no motion**). You'll be bored. 12 Don't go (u) so quickly, we still have time (**you're already moving in a particular direction and I want you to keep moving, only not so fast**). 13 We don't like running (jogging) (m) before breakfast (**direction irrelevant**).

20/2

1 **ходи́ли** (there and back). 2 **лета́ем** (round trips). 3 **идёт**. 4 **ползёт** (see ex 20/1 (6)). 5 **броди́ли** (many directions). 7 **несёт** ((a) the champagne is on a one-

way trip; (b) even though the waiter is going to go back again, remember that
i multidirectional verbs can be used for a *single* round trip *only in the past tense* –
20.2 (1).

20/3

1 We walked around the shops then went to (set off for) the cinema. 2 We made a
three-day trip to Paris. 3 The children ran around in the park for a while, got tired
and went home. 4 This morning we took Tania to the doctor (and brought her
back). 5 We're going to swim in the pool every morning (in many directions or
direction irrelevant). 6 Would you run to the shop for some bread (and come back
with it)?

20/4

1 He will soon arrive in London. 2 She entered the room. 3 He left (went out of) the
shop. 4 When you reach the corner, turn right. 5 Please move away from the
window. 6 Let's cross the road at the traffic lights. 7 He went up to her. 8 Go away.

20/5

1 **идём** (u). 2 **летим** (u). 3 **бегут** (u) (somewhere). 4 **ходите** (m) (round trips).
5 **ездили** (m). 6 **поедем**ᵖ (u) (**съездим**ᵖ (m)) **в город**. 7 **везёт** (u). 8 **ходи(те)**
(m) Don't go to that bar. The beer's bad there. 9 **приходит**. 10 **приедет**ᵖ.
11 **убежала**ᵖ. 12 **принесёт**ᵖ. 13 **привезите**ᵖ. 14 **вышли**ᵖ. 15 **приезжали**.

20.10

'Tania, please take this dirty plate (away) to the kitchen and bring a clean one.'
Tania ran off. Ten minutes later I went to look for her: I went into the kitchen [and
came out again], she wasn't there, then I went into the bedroom to see
grandmother. 'Did Tania pop in here [run in and out]?' 'No. I think I heard her voice
in the flat next door.' 'Strange,' I said. 'The Abramovs went to Germany a month
ago.' I ran next door ('to the neighbours'). It turned out that the Abramovs had just
flown in from Frankfurt. Tania had heard them arriving ('how they arrived') and had
run out on to the stairs. 'Yes, Tania is with us,' said the neighbours, laughing. 'She
came (running) about fifteen minutes ago. We'll bring her back home soon.'
'Daddy, look what lovely things they've brought (by transport)!' shouted Tania. 'I
want to go and live in Germany!'

A: How do I get to the Central Stadium? B: It would be best to take the metro to
('as far as') 'Sportivnaia'. A: How long does it take ('how much [time] there to

travel')? B: I think it takes half an hour.

A: Excuse me, how do I get to the 'Russia' Hotel? B: You'll have to get on a bus and travel three stops. A: Thank you. B: You're welcome.

A: Excuse me, how do I get to ('reach') the 'Russia' Hotel? B: Take the metro to 'Kitai-gorod' ('China-Town'). A: Can I get there by bus? B: Yes. Take the 24. It goes along Kitaiskii Prospekt ('Chinese Avenue'). But the metro is better.

20/6

IP: Write down how to get to our place. *You should take the metro and go as far as 'Profsoiuznaia' ('Trade Union Street'). Walk towards the last carriage (i.e. make for the exit at the rear end of the train) and out to the street. Turn left . . .* E: Hang on. I'm writing it down: out on to the street and turn which way? IP: Turn left, *go to the corner and cross over. Turn left again and go along the avenue until you reach our street* [Q.1]. E: Ivan Petrovich, isn't there a simpler way? IP: If you're going to be at Vadim's, it's better to take the bus. *The 57 goes along his (Vadim's) street. You need to travel four stops and get off at the fifth, by the cinema.* You won't go past it, it's a big cinema, right opposite the stop. *Go along the avenue a little way until you come to our block* [Q.2]. *You can also take the number 10 but it turns left into Narodnoe Opolchenie ('People's Militia'/'Home Guard') Street and doesn't go as far as the cinema* [Q.3].

20/7

1 **Куда́ ты идёшь?** 2 **Я иду́ на Кра́сную пло́щадь.** 3 **Они́ пошли́ в Кремль.** 4 **Я ча́сто хожу́ в кино́ (ча́сто).** 5 **В сре́ду я е́здил(а) в Но́вгород (в сре́ду).** 6 **Мы е́здим в Росси́ю почти́ ка́ждый го́д.** 7 **Я люблю́ бе́гать** (m) **пе́ред за́втраком.** 8 **Че́рез три дня́ я полечу́ (улечу́) в Та́ллинн (че́рез три дня́).** 9 **Мы хоти́м пойти́ на ры́нок.** 10 **Официа́нт несёт (прино́сит) бо́рщ.** 11 **Куда́ вы нас ведёте (нас)?** 12 **Ча́сто идёт до́жды/До́ждь идёт ча́сто?**

20/8

1 I don't know **(зна́ю).** I don't speak **(говорю́)** French. I live **(живу́)** in England. 2 I'll give **(дам)** five dollars. 3 We're sorry we're **(пришли́)** late. We couldn't **(могли́)** find a taxi. 4 Show **(Покажи́те)** (me) that, please. Give **(Да́йте)** me two, please. 5 If I knew **(зна́л(а)),** I would phone/If I had known, I would have phoned **(позвони́л(а)).** 6 Please may I speak to ('Please call') Mariia Fёdorovna **(Мари́ю Фёдоровну)** or Ivan Petrovich **(Ива́на Петро́вича)?** 7 I can't open this door **(э́ту дверь).** 8 Please bring five bottles **(буты́лок)** of mineral water **(минера́льной**

воды), three teas (**чáя**) and five pies (**пирожкóв**). 9 I (**меня́**) have no Russian money (**ру́сских де́нег**). 10 Viktor is a specialist on Russian theatre (**ру́сскому теа́тру**). 11 Help them (**им**), please. Help these tourists (**э́тим тури́стам**). 12 Let me introduce you to my new friend (**мои́м но́вым дру́гом**). 13 I want to meet your friends (**ва́шими друзья́ми**). 14 Do you have any books in English (**англи́йском языке́**)? 15 We talked/were talking about him (**нём**). 16 **Входи́те (Заходи́те), пожа́луйста. Сади́тесь.** 17 **Я хоте́л(а) бы пойти́ в Большо́й теа́тр.** 18 **Скажи́те, пожа́луйста, как прое́хать в институ́т (дое́хать до институ́та) на метро́?** 19 **Пожа́луйста, да́йте (мне) два биле́та. Фильм начина́ется в полови́не восьмо́го?** 20 **Извини́те (Прости́те) за опозда́ние. Бы́ло о́чень тру́дно найти́ ваш дом.** 21 **Вчера́ я говори́л(а) с Влади́миром Смирно́вым (вчера́). Он сказа́л, что я до́лжен/должна́ (мне на́до/ну́жно) (вам) позвони́ть вам.** 22 **В мое́й ко́мнате хо́лодно. Кро́ме того́, о́чень шу́мно/И о́чень шу́мно. Окно́ не закрыва́ется/Нельзя́ закры́ть окно́.** 23 **Нет туале́тной бума́ги. Пожа́луйста, не говори́те, что я до́лжен/должна́ купи́ть «Пра́вду».** 24 **Я перечита́л(а) письмо́/прочита́л(а) письмо́ ещё раз. Я не могу́ его́ поня́ть/Я его́ не понима́ю.** 25 **Перейди́те (че́рез) доро́гу, пройди́те ми́мо магази́на и поверни́те (сверни́те) напра́во.**

21/1

Why doesn't Ivan know where his (**его́**) ticket is? Why can't he find his (**свой**) ticket? He doesn't know where his ticket is because his (**его́**) wife gave his (**его́**) ticket to her (**свое́й**) friend.

21/2

1 **свою́**. 2 Omit (**своё** also possible). 3 **Его́ жена́ – мой секрета́рь.** 4 **своё, своё.**

21/3

1 **Возьми́(те) её с собо́й.** 2 **Расскажи́(те) нам о себе́.** 3 **Она́ счита́ет себя́ о́чень интере́сной.**

21/4

1 **Мы е́дем в Росси́ю, что́бы изуча́ть ру́сский язы́к.** 2 **Я хочу́, что́бы они́ пришли́/прие́хали за́втра.** 3 **Он хо́чет, что́бы вы позвони́ли ве́чером.** 4 **Да́й(те) (мне) две копе́йки, что́бы позвони́ть.** 5 **Мы сказа́ли, что́бы она́ взяла́ (своё) пальто́.**

21.10

Tour-Group Translator: Hello. I have a request to make. Mr Thornthwaite wants to be given another room. He says that his room has no power socket and he wants to make himself a cup of coffee. Manager: There *is* a power socket, behind the bed. But as a general rule we don't like residents to plug in heating appliances. Tell him that the maid will give him boiling water from her samovar. T: All right, I'll tell him. *Ten minutes later.* T: Mr Thornthwaite is not satisfied ('Mr T that does not suit'). He says he doesn't want to use the maid's samovar. He says that the maid's samovar is probably dirty, that he has his own kettle and that his own kettle is what he's going to use. M: And did he find the power point? T: He did, but he claims that it doesn't work. He also complains that he can't plug in his electric razor, that there's no toilet paper and that he doesn't like the colour of the wallpaper. M: All right, I'll call the electrician to check the socket and I'll tell the maid to bring toilet paper. As for the wallpaper, there's nothing I can do. All the rooms are the same. T: Speaking for myself, I can't stand Mr Thornthwaite. He thinks only of himself, he's always angry and loses his temper over everything. When we were in our hotel in Moscow and he couldn't find his shoes, he demanded that I call the police immediately. The police came and it turned out that the shoes were under his bed. Instead of apologizing, he announced that the maid had deliberately hidden his shoes in order to sell them later on the black market. *An Englishman approaches with an angry expression on his face.* T: Mr Thornthwaite demands to be moved to another room immediately. M: All right. We have rooms free on the ninth [eighth in UK] floor, although there's redecoration going on there and he's unlikely to be any better off. I can request that he be moved up there. T: Thank you very much. M: Tell Mr Tiran . . . what's his name . . . tell the English guest to go back to his room. I'll get the maid to help him move his things.

21/5

The well-known Russian writer Ivan Sergeevich Turgenev, author of the novel *Fathers and Sons* ('Fathers and Children'), was born *on 28 October (9 November new style* [i.e. by the Western calendar introduced in Russia after the 1917 Revolution]) *1818* [Q.1], *in the town of Orël* (or Orel) [**Ор(ё)л** 'Eagle' Q.2], south of Moscow. *Although Turgenev felt a deep love for his homeland and his people, and for his people's culture and language, he spent a lot of time abroad ('beyond the border')* [Q.3]. He studied in Berlin, spent a long time in Paris, travelled in the countries of Western Europe and visited England, where in 1860 he spent three weeks on the Isle of Wight and in 1879 received an honorary degree from the University of Oxford. *It is generally considered that the main reason for his* *frequent journeys abroad was his attachment to the French singer Pauline Viardot, whom he met in 1843. But many people think that he felt more comfortable ('better') in Western Europe than in Russia* [Q.4]. Although he wrote about the problems of his own country, he was a European writer. He published his best novel, *Fathers and Sons*, in 1861. Many people in the West know this novel and its hero, the 'nihilist' revolutionary Bazarov. Turgenev respected his strong hero, but he did not share his views. In order to understand his ambiguous attitude to Bazarov, one must bear in mind that *Turgenev was well aware of all the problems of his backward country, but he considered himself a liberal, not a revolutionary. He didn't believe that Russia needed a revolution. He was a westernizer, that is, he considered the western European, capitalist path of development appropriate for Russia* [Q.5 Neither, but he believed that backward Russia had lots of problems which could be tackled by learning from the more liberal West].

22/1

1 He'll come between 3 and 5 o'clock. 2 She earns more than $4,300 a month. 3 Our shop sells books in eighty-two languages.

22/2

1 **одиннадцати** (gen.) 2 **двумя** (inst.). 3 **восьми** (prep.). 4 **тридцати одного** (gen.).

22/3

1 **тридцати двух** We were/have been in thirty-two countries. 2 **полтора** (nom./acc. form) We travelled for an hour and a half. 3 **девяти, пяти** The shop is open ('works') from 9 a.m. to 5 p.m. 4 **обеими** (f inst.) I met (got to know) both girls. 5 **многих** We visited (were in) many Russian cities/towns. 6 **несколькими** We talked to ('with') several Russian engineers.

22/4

1 **двухсот пятидесяти** We walked about 250 km. 2 **двести пятьдесят** We walked approximately 250 km. 3 **пятьюстами сорока** He arrived with $540. 4 **пятьсот сорок** When he arrived, he had $540. 5 **десятью и одиннадцатью** I'll come between ten and eleven o'clock. 6 **одиннадцатом** I'll come between ten and eleven ('in the eleventh hour'). 7 **шести миллионов пятисот тысяч** More than 6.5 million people live in Moscow. 8 **шесть миллионов пятьсот тысяч** The population of Moscow exceeds 6.5 million.

22/5

1 **У нас дво́е дете́й.** 2 **Нас тро́е.** 3 **На́до е́хать тро́е су́ток.** 4 **Нас жда́ли дво́е мужчи́н.** 5 **У меня́ бы́л<u>о</u> бо́льше** (or **бо́лее** in formal style) **ста до́лларов.**

22.14

In 1982 the population of the USSR was more than 268 million people, of whom about five million were students studying in 900 universities and institutes. In 1982 there were about one million doctors. In the same year Moscow had more than 8,350,000 inhabitants, who watched performances in twenty-six theatres. Moscow children attended 1,000 schools.

22/6

If one compares ('If to compare') the number of divorces in a year with the number of married couples existing at the beginning of the year, one finds that ('then') in the course of the year only *about 1.5 per cent* [Q.1] of married people ('spouses') get divorced, that is, in a year only about 15 out of every 1,000 families break up. *In 1950 for every 1,000 marriages there were 32 divorces. In 1977 for every 1,000 marriages there were already 323 divorces* [Q.2]. Research has shown that *one-third of all divorces take place during the first year of married life and another one-third affect families which have existed for between one and five years. Of every 100 marriages* ('new married couples'), 11 break up in the first year, and *22 break up within five years* [Q.3: 22 per cent]. We know that in the case of married couples without children (*a quarter of divorcing couples* [Q.4]), husbands take the initiative in half the divorces. But in families with children, women are more likely to initiate proceedings – two-thirds of all divorce applications involving families with one or two children were filed by women (70 per cent of all divorces involve one or two children ['of such are 70 per cent of all breaking up families']; only 5 per cent involve a larger number of children). In this way women seek to protect children from family conflicts. They consider that the children will be better off without a father than with a bad one.

23/1

1 **в суббо́ту в семь (часо́в).** 2 **В э́том году́.** 3 **на про́шлой неде́ле.** 4 **Во вре́мя войны́ (В войну́).** 5 Mary sees ('meets') Volodia **четы́ре ра́за в неде́лю.**

23/2

1 два́дцать мину́т. 2 неде́лю/одну́ неде́лю. 3 на три ме́сяца. 4 на пять мину́т. 5 за две неде́ли (also possible в ('within') две неде́ли – stressing the speed). 6 за час.

23/3

1 Когда́ (or по́сле того́ как) я вы́учу ру́сский язы́к. 2 пока́ Ёва не позвони́т. 3 You must hide the bottle до того́ как Ёва вернётся (до возвраще́ния Ёвы).

23/4

1 В про́шлом году́ мы е́здили в Росси́ю (в про́шлом году́). 2 Жизнь бу́дет лу́чше в два́дцать пе́рвом ве́ке. 3 На сле́дующей (бу́дущей) неде́ле мы пое́дем (if you mean to do it on foot say пойдём пешко́м) в Сиби́рь. 4 Ле́том Ёва и Вади́м (с Вади́мом) пое́дут в Я́лту на ме́сяц. 5 В тот (э́тот) день мы вста́ли в шесть (часо́в) утра́. 6 Ива́н Петро́вич жил/прожил^p в Аме́рике два го́да. 7 Он бу́дет рабо́тать всю неде́лю (acc.) 8 Я был(а́) там два ра́за. 9 Мэ́ри прочита́ла «Войну́ и мир» за (в) шестьдеся́т два часа́. 10 Во вре́мя войны́ они́ рабо́тали во́семьдесят часо́в в неде́лю.

23.7

V: Congratulate me! In a month's time they're sending me on a business trip to London. E: Congratulations, but I'm jealous too. How long will you be in England (Britain)? V: From 29 May to 1 June. Unfortunately, I'm only going for four days. E: What will you manage to see in such a short time? V: Probably only the City, St Paul's Cathedral and perhaps Big Ben. After all, I'll be in meetings ('conducting negotiations') in various offices ('institutions') all day. E: Are you going by train or by plane? V: By plane, of course. By train it takes ('one has to travel') almost forty-eight hours ('two days and nights'), while by plane I'll get there in three and a half. I've got to order the ticket today ('already today'), before five o'clock. What are your plans for the day? E: I'm going to the library. Then I'll call on Viktor Pavlovich at ('into') the institute for half an hour. From there I'm going to the hairdresser. I'll phone you about six, after I get back. V: I won't be back from the town before (I'll return from town not before') half past five. I won't get my ticket in less than three hours. Then I'll call on Volodia. But I won't leave until you ring. E: You're going to see Volodia? V: Don't worry. You know very well (**же** – emphasis) that we never drink on weekdays.

23/5

KI: Good morning. My name is Kuznetsov, Konstantin Ivanovich. I'm the deputy director in charge of contacts with foreign publishers. RP: Good morning, Konstantin Ivanovich. My name is Pope. Richard Pope. KI: You speak Russian with almost no accent. Do you visit Russia often? RP: No. In the last twenty years I've been here only three times. But *I've been speaking Russian since I was a child. My father emigrated from Russia at the beginning of the twenties, during the Civil War. His surname was Popov* [Q.1] then, but two years after arriving in England he decided to change it to ('become') Pope. KI: Why? 'Pope' means the head of the Catholic Church, doesn't it? RP: *Although Popov* ['son of the priest' **(nóп)**] *is one of the commonest surnames in Russia, in England it sounds funny* [Q.2 Popov sounds like 'pop off']. For example, when in the eighties elderly Soviet leaders – Brezhnev, Andropov, Chernenko – were dying one after the other, the English joked that the next one would be called Popov, and the one after him would be Abouttopopov. As for the name Pope, my father was well acquainted with the work of the eighteenth-century English poet Alexander Pope. Of course, most English people are rather indifferent to poetry, but my father, as a real Russian, had great respect for poets, including foreign ones ('both his own and foreign'). KI: Very interesting. But I must interrupt you. It's time to meet the director. *He is usually here only in the afternoons, but this morning he has come from the ministry specially to see you. He is very keen that we should sign ('He very hopes that we will be able to sign') a contract with your firm in (the course of) the next two or three days.* RP: How times change! *When I was last in Russia, at the end of the seventies, I phoned the then director of this (publishing) firm three times a day, but he had no desire to see me* [Q.3].

24/1

1 **внима́ния** Pay no attention to them. 2 **ни одного́ пода́рка** I didn't buy/haven't bought a single present. 3 **э́того** We don't want that. 4 **взгля́дов** Turgenev didn't share Bazarov's views.

24/2

1 **Я вам не дам (вам) ни одно́й копе́йки.** 2 **Почему́ ты не купи́ла вина́** (gen.)? 3 **Не покупа́й(те) э́ту кни́гу** (acc). 4 **Не Вади́м купи́л вино́/Э́то не Вади́м купи́л вино́/Вино́ купи́л не Вади́м.** 5 **Я приду́/прие́ду не в пя́тницу, а в суббо́ту.**

24/3

In each case either choice is possible, but the preferable ones are: 1 **вина́** – gen. (any wine). 2 **биле́та** – gen. (any ticket); **биле́т** – acc. (possible if stress on **не доста́ла**). 3 **А́ню** – acc. (definite person, and stress on 'didn't see'). 4 **вре́мени** – gen. (any time).

24/4

1 **никогда́ не помога́ет.** 2 **ничего́ не понима́ем.** 3 **ниче́м.** 4 **ни от кого́.** 5 **не́ было ничего́.** 6 **нет нигде́.**

24/5

1 In this town there's nothing to do in the evening. There's nowhere to go. There's nowhere to drink coffee or beer. We're bored. 2 Vadim doesn't know, Vera doesn't know, Marina and Viktor don't know either. There's no one else to ask. 3 I'm sorry, I can't help you. I don't have time, I'm very late ('I very hurry'). 4 There was no one in the café. There was no one to talk to. 5 Mary read (all) Turgenev at home in England, because she knew that in Moscow she wouldn't have time to read.

24.10

E: Was it you who brought the pineapple? VP: No, I didn't bring any pineapple. Where did you see a pineapple? E: Tania says there's a pineapple in a bag in the kitchen. VP: Pay no attention to what Tania says. She's never seen a pineapple in her life. She doesn't even know what a pineapple is.

V: Eva, why did you tell Marina there was a pineapple in the kitchen? E: It wasn't me. It was Tania. She was the one who invented (it). V: No, she didn't invent that pineapple. I happened to find it ('I bought it by chance') at the market. I wanted to give it to Marina and Viktor as a present. Now it's no longer a surprise. E: Don't be upset. It doesn't matter. It's still a splendid present.

M: I can't buy any bananas. There aren't any anywhere. V: And there's no point in looking for them. I have never seen bananas anywhere in Russia, neither at the market, nor in the hands of ('at', 'in the possession of') speculators. Bananas don't grow here. M: And do you think there will never be any under any circumstances? V: No, I don't say that. We used not to have any foreign (convertible) currency, there was nothing to buy them with ('on'). But soon everyone will have hard currency, then you won't be able to move for banana sellers.

24/6

T: Excuse me, can you suggest how to get to Sergievskii Posad? I've heard that there are many attractive churches there. *I want to go alone, without a guide.* I: Unfortunately, I can't help you. *We only sell tickets for excursions. We don't give information. If you want to go independently, then, unfortunately, I can't help you in any way.* T: I want to go to Sergievskii Posad, and nobody can help me, and they can't even suggest how I can get there. I: They'll tell you everything at the station. But *we are a commercial organization, we sell services and tickets for excursions* [Q.1]. T: I see. But all the same I want to visit Sergievskii Posad. I: By all means ('Please do'), you can go with a group on Friday. T: Thank you. But *I don't want to go with a group. I want to go by myself ('self'), independently* [Q.2]. I: In that case you can order a car and a guide *twenty-four hours before the trip* [Q.3]. T: Can I go there with a guide on any day I like? I: Any day except weekends. T: Tell me, why not at weekends? T: In principle you can, but *the church authorities asked us not to send tourists at weekends. They would prefer not to be disturbed during services* [Q.4]. T: I see. Thank you. I: You're welcome.

25/1

1 **копе́йка** 'kopeck'. You wouldn't have a one-kopeck coin, would you [pol.]?
2 **биле́т** 'ticket'. Could I have your ticket, dear [friendly, as if talking to a child]?
3 **буты́лка** 'bottle'. Could I trouble you for a bottle of mineral water [pol.]?
4 **Татья́на** 'Tat'iana'; **ша́пка** 'hat'. Tanechka, be a good girl and put your hat on [talking to a child]. 5 **Еле́на** 'Elena'; **пла́тье** 'dress'. Just look at Lenochka. What a lovely little dress [tenderness]! 6 **вода́** 'water'. Give the pussy cat some water [talking to a child]. 7 **чай** 'tea'. How about a nice cup of tea [polite, friendly]?
8 **икра́** 'caviare'. Could I interest you in some nice caviare [ingratiating]? 9 **рука́** 'hand'. What dirty little hands you have [talking to a child]! 10 **дверь** 'door'. Close the (car) door [not specially polite, since a car door is a small door and is commonly called **две́рца**]. 11 **мину́та** 'minute'. Just a moment, please [**мину́точка** from **мину́тка** is a double diminutive – 'little tiny minute' – meant to suggest the shortest possible of delays]. 12 **окно́** 'window'. Take a look out of the window, dear. Perhaps it's stopped raining.

25/2

1 I'm sorry, I didn't mean to offend you. 2 I'm sorry, I seem to have taken ('occupied') your seat ('place'). 3 Excuse me, I hope I haven't disturbed you. 4 Excuse me, if it isn't too much trouble, could you bring a clean glass? 5 Excuse me, could you tell me where the (nearest) post office is ('where here is post office')?

25/3

(a) A: Ow! B: I'm sorry, it was accidental. A: That's all right.

(b) A: Let's go to my place. I've got some good cognac (at home). B: I don't object! V: I've no objections either! A: Serëzha, will you come with us? My wife will make us supper. S: Count me in. Delighted. A: What about you, Volodia? V: Gladly. I'm game. A: Well then, let's go.

(c) A: Vadim, is that you? We're all ('We've all gathered') at my place, we're celebrating this ('one' meaning 'a certain') friend's birthday. Come on round ('Call in'). V: Quite impossible. I'm very busy. A: Well just come for a quick drink. V: Out of the question. No way! You *know* Eva doesn't allow it. A: Well, how about a glass of tea? V: I don't feel like it. Let's leave it until tomorrow ('Let's better tomorrow'). A: Listen, forget about Eva. Think of us. Don't forget your friends! Get a taxi and come round! V: No, and I mean it. I don't want to hurt Eva. A: You absolutely refuse? A pity.

25/4

Once upon a time, [We've added this phrase to compensate for the untranslated folk-tale diminutives] a fox was walking along a road and found a rolling-pin. She picked it up and walked on. She came to a village and knocked at the door of the first cottage. 'Knock-knock.' 'Who's there?' 'It's me, little sister fox, can you put me up for the night?' *'We're short of space as it is'* [Q.1] ('In our house even without you is tight'). *'But I won't get in your way: I myself will lie down on the bench, my little tail will go under the bench and my rolling-pin will go under the stove* [Q.2]' They let her in. She (herself) lay down on the bench, with her tail under the bench and her rolling-pin under the stove. *Early in the morning the fox got up, burnt the rolling pin, and then asked 'Where's my rolling-pin then? I want a hen for it'* ('Give [using the imperfective, which as a request is impolite compared with **Дáйте**] me in return for it a hen'). *The peasant had no choice* ('there was nothing to be done' – 24.8*) but to give her a hen for the rolling-pin* [Q.2]. The fox took the hen and goes along singing [the change from past to present tense is quite common in Russian narratives]: 'A fox was walking along a road, she found a rolling-pin. For the rolling-pin she got ('took') a hen!' She arrived at another village: 'Knock-knock.' 'Who's there?' 'It's me, little sister fox, can you put me up for the night?' 'We're short of space as it is.' 'But I won't get in your way: I ('myself') will lie down on the bench, my little tail will go under the bench and *my hen will go under the stove.*' They let her in. The fox lay down on the bench with her tail under the bench and the hen under the stove. *Early in the morning she got up* nice and quietly, *seized the hen, ate it* [Q.4] and then said ('says'): 'Where's my hen? I want a goose for it.'

There was no help for it, the host had to give her a goose for the hen. The fox took the goose and goes along singing: 'A fox was walking along a road, she found a rolling-pin, for the rolling-pin she got ('took') a hen, for the hen she got a goose!' She arrived in the evening at a third village. 'Knock-knock!' 'Who's there?' 'It's me, little sister fox! Can you put me up for the night?' 'We're short of space as it is.' 'But I won't get in your way: I myself will lie down on the bench, my little tail will go under the bench and my little goose will go under the stove.' They let her in. She lay down on the bench with her tail under the bench and the goose under the stove. Early in the morning the fox jumped up, seized the goose, ate it and then said ('says'): *'But where's my goose? Give me a girl for it!'* [Q.5]. But the peasant didn't want to part with a girl. *He put a large dog in a sack and gave it to the fox* [Q.5]. 'Here's ('Take!' – invitation 15.3 (4)) a girl for you, fox!' So the fox took the sack, went out on to the road and says: 'Little girl, sing to me ('sing songs')!' But the dog in the sack started to growl.

The fox took fright, threw down the sack and started to run. At this ('Here') the dog jumped out of the sack and gave chase ('after her'). The fox ran away from the dog as fast as she could and ran into a burrow under a tree-stump. She sits there and says 'Ears, ears! What did you do?' 'We kept listening.' 'And you, legs, what did you do?' 'We kept running.' 'And you, eyes?' 'We kept watch.' *'And you tail?'* *'I kept getting in your way ('I all the time hindered your running').'* 'Ah, you kept getting in the way! Well, just you wait, I'll show you!' *And she thrust her tail out of the burrow: 'Eat it, dog!' At this the dog seized the fox by the tail, pulled her out of the burrow and gave her a thrashing!* [Q.6]

25/5

1 **шести́ города́х** (prep. pl.) In six days we visited six cities/towns. 2 **тремя́ ру́сскими студе́нтами** (inst.) We talked to three Russian students. 3 **четырёх до́лларов** (g.pl.) I won't give you more than four dollars. 4 **одну́ неде́лю** (acc.) We'll be in Petersburg for one week. 5 **Она́ лю́бит то́лько себя́.** 6 **Они́ в своём но́мере/Они́ у себя́ (в но́мере).** 7 Мы прие́хали в Росси́ю, что́бы говори́ть по-ру́сски. 8 Я хочу́, что́бы он извини́лся. 9 Она́ здесь одна́. 10 У них тро́е дете́й. 11 **Нас че́тверо.** 12 Я никого́ не зна́ю в Ирку́тске. 13 Она́ не понима́ет ни одного́ сло́ва. 14 **Не́кого спроси́ть.** 15 **Ей не́ с кем бы́ло говори́ть/разгова́ривать.**

A: Mr Smith, my wife and I want to invite you to our house ('to ourselves at home'). Б: **С удово́льствием.** A: Will you be able to come the day after tomorrow, on Friday? Б: **К сожале́нию, я не могу́. Я бу́ду в Ки́еве три дня.** A: Then come on the twenty-seventh. Б: **В тот день я за́нят.** A: On the thirtieth? Б: **Ка́жется, у меня́ совсе́м нет встреч (никаки́х встреч нет) по́сле два́дцать девя́того.**

A: Fine. We expect you on the thirtieth, after seven o'clock.

26/1

1 что́-то. 2 что́-нибудь. 3 ничего́. 4 что́-нибудь. 5 кто́-нибудь. 6 куда́-то, каки́м-то. 7 Почему́-то. 8 когда́-нибудь.

26/2

1 Тебе́ звони́ла кака́я-то же́нщина. 2 Она́ что́-то купи́ла. 3 В Москве́ нет бана́нов. 4 На столе́ лежа́ла ру́сская кни́га. 5 Кни́гу принесла́ Мэ́ри (Э́то Мэ́ри принесла́ кни́гу). 6 Я тебе́ позвоню́ за́втра. 7 За́втра я позвоню́ Вади́му.

26.13 Letter, Note, Greetings

Dear Professor Nikifirov, I'm sorry that I haven't written for so long. I was intending to write to you immediately after my return from Moscow, but I had too many things to do. Last week I read your splendid book about the Bolshoi Theatre. I liked it very much. A couple of weeks after my return to Bristol I telephoned our National Theatre and spoke to your acquaintance (the woman you know there). She said that she had already collected a number of materials for you, so, when you are in London in August, you will be able to start work immediately on your article about the Bolshoi's tours in England. If nothing prevents it, (then) Richard and I will be in Moscow again somewhere around the middle of July. If I can help you in any way (pass on something from your acquaintance or anything else whatever), telephone me. Thank you again for the excellent book. Best wishes. Yours sincerely, Barbara Pope.

My dear Annushka, Greetings to you from Paris. There are so many interesting things here that I've no time to write letters. I'll be back on Thursday, after six. Come and visit me, I'll tell you all about it. Love and kisses ('I kiss firmly'), Iura.

Dear Pëtr Ivanovich, May all sorrows remain in the old year. May happiness come to live in your house! I wish you a cheerful New Year party, smiles, joy and health. I wish you success in your life and work. I wish you the things you wish yourself. Yours sincerely, Eva Antonova.

26/3

Volodia and Mary entered the courtyard of a five-floor block of flats. Although the busy ('noisy') avenue was not far away, the yard was quiet, there were big old trees, and in the very centre there was a children's playground with swings. Old men and women sat on benches while children played in front of them. 'Good morning,' 'Hello,' Volodia kept repeating. 'Do you know everybody here?' asked Mary in surprise. 'Of course. I grew up in this yard, you know. There's a special atmosphere in these old Moscow houses. Sometimes two or three generations live in them. These old women over there knew my grandfather and grandmother, they watched my father growing up, they watched me growing up, and my sister Masha too. They've spent their life here. And they love both this building and all the people who live in it.'

26/4

Dear Mrs Pope, Please do not be surprised by my unexpected letter, in spite of the fact that it's already eight months since we met. The thing is that only you can help me and my friends. But first of all I'll remind you of a few things about myself. My name is Vera. I'm from *Minusinsk*. That tiny little *Siberian provincial town* which you and your husband visited on business in May last year. I'm very sorry that I didn't write this letter immediately after your departure, but as we say here 'Better late than never.' After I met you *in our museum* [Q.1] I had an idea which has never left me since. *My idea is that I want somehow to get to know more about your country, its customs and its people* [Q.2]. This has now become more realistic than it used to be. Probably *that is primarily connected with the thaw in political and cultural relations between our countries, but apart from that, having become a student, I've taken up ('started to study') English, which is taught quite well ('at a not bad level') at our institute* [Q.3]. So *I would like you to help me to make contact with someone at the university in Bristol who is interested in the history of Siberia* [Q.4]. If I can help you in any way, I'll be pleased to. I wait eagerly for your reply. My address: 660022 Krasnoiarsk (**the г is for го́род** 'city'), Abakanskaia Street, 33/2/315 (see 26.10), Vera Petrishcheva. Excuse me for troubling you. Yours sincerely, Vera.

27/1

1 Everything will be done. 2 The shop called GUM was built in the nineteenth century. 3 This novel was written by Tolstoi. 4 No one and nothing is forgotten. 5 The festival was organized by students. 6 We were invited to a party in the House of Friendship. 7 Not all the questions were dealt with ('solved', 'decided'.) 8 The work is finished. 9 The oranges were imported ('brought by transport') from Africa. 10 The programme will tell about ('In the programme will be told about') life in Siberia. 11 Two-thirds of the films shown at the festival were bought by Americans. 12 Many of the students accepted by ('into') the institute are foreigners.

27/2

1 пока́зан. 2 за́няты. 3 решён. 4 за́дан ру́сским журнали́стом. 5 закры́т.
6 объя́влено. 7 при́нят.

27/3

1 **Все биле́ты про́даны.** 2 За́втра музе́и бу́дут закры́ты (за́втра). 3 Э́то
ме́сто за́нято? 4 Биле́ты бу́дут зака́заны за́втра. 5 В на́ших магази́нах
тру́дно найти́ кни́ги, напи́са<u>нные</u> (от кото́рые (бы́ли) напи́са<u>ны</u>)
совреме́нными ру́сскими писа́телями.

27/4

(a) On Wednesday it was announced that all the tickets had already been sold.
We were very surprised, because in the director's letter it was written that tickets
for us would be bought on Thursday.

(b) On Wednesday they announced that they had already sold all the tickets. We
were very surprised, because in his letter the director wrote that they would buy
tickets for us on Thursday.

27/5

Gone with the Wind [Q.1] ('Carried away by the wind')

In 1937, after the decision to make a film of the novel *Gone with the Wind* was
taken, Russell Birdwell, the agent of the producer David Selznick, launched a
campaign in America: the novel's admirers were asked who should play Scarlett
and Rhett. People stopped discussing a real-life melodrama – the love affair of
King Edward VIII and the divorced American Wallis Simpson (as a consequence of
which the British king was forced to abdicate). At mealtimes every family argued
about the relative claims of Gary Cooper, Errol Flynn and Clark Gable. Ninety-five
per cent of those who took part in the survey named Clark Gable as the only
possible Rhett Butler. As for Scarlett O'Hara, 45 per cent were in favour of Bette
Davis, who already had two Oscars. But she refused. Selznick chose the English
theatre actress Vivien Leigh. The film made Vivien Leigh a superstar. In 1943, four
years after the première, during her concerts in North Africa she was applauded
by General Eisenhower and General Montgomery. The film of *Gone with the Wind*
was first shown in Russia in October 1990. Earlier it had been included in the
programme of one of the Moscow international film festivals but for some reason it
was excluded at the last minute. *Probably certain bureaucrats took a dislike to the
contents of the film* [Q.2]. The rights to show *Gone with the Wind* were acquired

from ('at') the American company United International Pictures. At the première in the October Cinema, the film was presented by the president of UIP, Ted Turner. There were many guests, including Jane Fonda, the well-known English actor Ben Kingsley and his wife, and the journalist Carol Thatcher, daughter of the then British prime minister.

[Q.3] Names are transcribed into Russian as far as possible according to how they *sound* in English, not by the letters. So 'Leigh' is not **Леигх** but **Ли**, 'Gable' is not **Габле** but **Гейбл**, 'United' is not **Унитед** but **Юнайтед**. When transliterating the other way, from Russian into English, we use the opposite principle and work by *letters*. So **Достоéвский** is written in English as 'Dostoevskii' even though Russians pronounce his name Dastayéfskee.

[Q.4] **прúнято** (from **принять**) 'taken', 'accepted'
зáдан (from **задáть**) 'asked', 'posed'
вúнужден (from **вúнудить**) 'forced'
покáзан (from **показáть**) 'shown'
включён (from **включúть**) 'included'
исключён (from **исключúть**) 'excluded'
приобретенú (from **приобрестú**) 'acquired'
предстáвлен (from **предстáвить**) 'presented'

28/1

1 Knowing that Eva would return late, Vadim drank a glass of vodka. 2 Driving past the theatre, we learnt that Chekhov's *Three Sisters* was on. 3 Holidaying in the Crimea, Mary met an interesting professor. 4 We walked without hurrying, there was plenty of time. 5 (By) studying three hours every day, Volodia learnt English in two years.

28/2

1 After travelling three stops, Mary got out at the University station. 2 Having bought nothing in the shop, Vera decided to go to the market. 3 Having become interested in the Chekists, Volodia began to spend all his free time in libraries. 4 Before we reached ('Not having reached') the avenue, we turned left. 5 Vadim left without closing ('not having closed') the window.

28/3

1 **Не знáя** or **Так как** (since) **онá не знáла**ⁱ Russian, Carol couldn't find her hotel. 2 Eva left **не сказáв** or **а (нó) не сказáла**ᵖ, where she was going.

3 **Вы́пив** or **По́сле того́ как** (23.6) **он вы́пил**[p] two glasses of vodka, Vadim decided to call on Vera. 4 **Оде́вшись,** my brothers and I go for breakfast or **Мы с бра́тьями одева́емся, пото́м идём за́втракать** (We get dressed, then . . .).

28.9

Peter was born on 30 May 1672. In 1689 he married Evdokiia Lopukhina, the daughter of a Moscow boyar. He became Tsar in 1696. Possessing outstanding mental abilities and enormous energy, he studied constantly. Knowing that Russia lagged behind the advanced countries of the West, he fully understood the need for economic, military and cultural reforms. In 1697 he went abroad. In Holland he learnt to build ships, working as a simple carpenter. He visited factories and schools and took an interest in medicine. In England he studied naval matters, visited the observatory and attended a sitting of Parliament. In August 1698, having learnt of the streltsy uprising in Moscow, Peter had to rush home. Abroad Peter got to know the everyday life and customs of Europeans. On his return ('Having returned') to Moscow, he took determined measures to introduce Russian noblemen and merchants to European civilization. When the boyars and noblemen came to welcome Peter home ('congratulate Peter on ['with'] his arrival'), he cut off their beards with scissors. Soon an order was issued requiring noblemen to dress in European style and shave their beards. Peter allowed merchants to wear beards, but for this they paid a tax. Peter gave a lot of attention to the development ('questions of the development') of industry and trade. As well as giving ('While giving') merchants money to start ('for the creation of') industrial enterprises, he drove state peasants into the towns as serf workers. In the achieving of ('While working for') his goals he stopped at ('before') nothing. When building the city of St Petersburg he paid no attention to the harsh conditions. Labouring in the cold and rain, standing up to their knees in water and mud, thousands of peasants perished from disease, hunger and overwork. Peter dealt with his opponents mercilessly, sometimes resorting to their physical annihilation. In 1698, having established that the streltsy uprising had been led by the Miloslavskii boyar family, he executed the organizers and more than a thousand streltsy. Some time later Peter did not spare his own son Aleksei, having found out that the Tsarevich was a member of ('participating in') a plot. In 1718, with his father's permission, Aleksei was condemned to death. Peter's reforms ('The reforms conducted by Peter' 27.7) facilitated the Europeanization of Russia. However, he could not completely overcome the country's backwardness since his reforms were at the same time intended to strengthen ('directed at strengthening') autocratic rule and serfdom. Under Peter, the life of the (common) people got considerably worse.

28/4

Per ('to') 500 gm of fresh mushrooms, 1 kg of fresh cabbage, 1 pickled cucumber, 1 onion, 2 tablespoons of tomato purée, 1 or 2 teaspoons of sugar, 2 tablespoons of butter/oil [Q.1 No].

Chop up the cabbage and put it in a saucepan, add the butter/oil and a little water. Simmer ('Stew') for about an hour [Q.2 first part]. Fifteen to twenty minutes before the end (of the simmering) add the tomato purée, the sugar, salt, pepper, a bay leaf and vinegar. After cleaning and washing the mushrooms (boletus, brown, saffron milk-cap or whatever [Russians are enthusiastic mushroom gatherers, and all these terms belong to everyday vocabulary]), put them in boiling water for ten to fifteen minutes. Then slice them and fry them in butter/oil. After putting the mushrooms in a bowl, use the same frying-pan to brown the onion and then mix it with the mushrooms, adding ('having added') the sliced (PPP 27.7) cucumber, salt and pepper. *Put half of the stewed cabbage in a greased* (PPP 27.7) *frying-pan, spread out the prepared* (PPP 27.7) *mushrooms over the cabbage and cover with* [inst. case] *the remaining cabbage. Sprinkle rusks and butter/oil over the cabbage and put it in the oven to bake.* [Q.2 second part]. *Before serving one may add ('put on') a slice of lemon or olives* [Q.3 (1)]. *Mushroom solianka can also be made with sour cabbage (sauerkraut)* [Q.3 (2)], but in this case leave out the vinegar. *The fresh mushrooms can be replaced by pickled or dried ones* [Q.3 (3)].

[Q.4] **очи́стив** (from **очи́стить**ᴾ) having cleaned
промы́в (from **промы́ть**ᴾ) having washed thoroughly
наре́зав (from **наре́зать**ᴾ) having cut, having sliced
положи́в (from **положи́ть**ᴾ) having put
доба́вив (from **доба́вить**ᴾ) having added
посы́пав (from **посы́пать**ᴾ) having sprinkled
не добавля́я (from **добавля́ть**ⁱ) not adding, without adding

29/1

1 **вести́** 'to lead'. We walked along a/the road *leading* into a/the forest. 2 **писа́ть** 'to write'. Everybody respects writers who write ('*writing*') the truth about Communism. 3 **стро́ить** 'to build'. Mr Pope meets/is meeting a businessman (who is) *building*/who builds new factories in Siberia. 4 **уме́ть** 'to know how to'. For our shop we seek/are looking for women who know how to ('*knowing how to*') dress well ('beautifully'). 5 **существова́ть** 'to exist'. In this Siberian town, which has existed ('*existing*') for only ten years, there are already more than 5,000 inhabitants. 6 **отка́зываться** 'to refuse'. The director is meeting workers who

refuse ('*refusing*') to work on Sunday.

29/2

1 The students *who were late* for the examination were very worried. 2 There are now very few people *who saw* Lenin. 3 The woman *who found* (from **найти** 'to find') the (hand)bag is asked ('one asks') to see ('go up to') the theatre manager.

29/3

1 **жела́ющих** (gen.) or **кото́рые жела́ют**. 2 **занима́ющимися** (inst.) or **кото́рые занима́ются**. 3 **писа́вших** (prep.) or **кото́рые писа́ли**. 4 **прие́хавших** (anim acc.) or **кото́рые прие́хали**.

29/4

IE: Hello, Vera Petrovna. I'm glad to see you. VP: I'm glad too, Il'ia Egorovich. IE: Are you ready? VP: I'm (already) ready. IE: Please would you pass my briefcase, I need it. VP: Your briefcase is like a suitcase. IE: That's true. But your handbag would be like a suitcase too if you were as busy [PPP – notice same endings as short adjectives] as I am.

29/5

1 **Я был(á) рáд(а).** 2 **Онá похóжа на (своегó) отцá.** 3 **Э́то хорошó.** 4 **Э́то дóрого.** 5 **Им нужны́ дóллары** (stress on 'dollars')/**Дóллары им нужны́** (stress on 'need'). 6 **Тáня, ты готóва?** 7 **Мы бýдем готóвы чéрез пять минýт.** 8 **Шáпка ей великá.**

29.9

Vladivostok is situated on a peninsula projecting (pres. act. part.) into the Pacific Ocean. It is a huge port. The most interesting part of the city is the quay/promenade ('embankment'). Here is the tall column ('Here rises the column') with the model of the ship which landed the sailors ('from which disembarked the sailors') who founded (past act. part.) Vladivostok in 1880. The city, which slopes down ('descending [pres. act. part.] on slopes') to the sea, is very attractive (short form – bookish). The unique landscape and the subtropical vegetation ('nature') are striking adornments.

29/6

Even if you have paid only one visit to the Hermitage, you remember it, seeing in your imagination the grandly beautiful Winter Palace. *The Palace is the most remarkable and most impressive of the five buildings which make up the Hermitage Museum* [Q.1]. Built in 1754–62 to the plans of Francesco Bartolomeo Rastrelli (1700–1771), it determined the form of the magnificent architectural ensemble *on the bank of the Neva [Q.2 first detail]*. By the scale, richness and variety of its architectural decoration and the relative proportions of its parts the Winter Palace, constructed in the style known as Russian baroque, creates an image of harmony and splendour. *Two wings on the west side face the Admiralty* [Q.2 second detail]; *the main façade*, which *overlooks Palace Square* [Q.2 third detail] is the grandest. In the central, projecting, part is the triple arcade of the entrance gates with their magnificent decorated ironwork.

[Q.3] Active participles:

побыва́вший (**побыва́ть** 'to visit') who has visited
впечатля́ющее (**впечатля́ть** 'to impress') impressive ('impressing')
выходя́щий (**выходи́ть** 'to go out') looking out
выступа́ющей (**выступа́ть** 'to project', 'step out') projecting
Verbal adverb: **представля́я себе́** (**представля́ть** 'to present') imagining ('presenting to onself')

Passive participles:

постро́енный (**постро́ить** 'to build') built (long form)
испо́лненный (**испо́лнить** 'to carry out') carried out, executed
обращены́ (**обрати́ть** 'to turn') turned
укра́шенных (**укра́сить** 'to adorn', 'decorate') adorned (long form)

30.6

At the Nikolaevskii Station two friends met. One was fat, the other thin. The fat one had just dined at the station, and his grease-coated lips gleamed like ripe cherries. He smelt of sherry and orange blossom. The thin one, on the other hand, had just got off a train and was weighed down with suitcases, bundles and cardboard boxes. He smelt of ham and coffee grounds. Behind him could be seen a thinnish woman with a long chin – his wife, and a tall schoolboy with one eye partly closed – his son. 'Porfirii!' the fat one exclaimed, seeing the thin one. 'Can it be you? My dear, I haven't seen you for years.' 'Good gracious!' cried the thin one. 'Misha! My childhood friend! Where have you sprung from?' The friends exchanged the traditional three kisses and then gazed at each other with tears in their eyes. Both were pleasantly shocked. 'My dear!' the thin one began after the greetings.

'I didn't expect this. What a surprise! Well let's have a good look now! The same handsome fellow you always were. The same smart well-dressed charmer! Good heavens! Well, how are you doing then? Are you rich? Married? I'm married now, as you see . . . This is my wife here, Luiza, née Wanzenbach . . . a Lutheran . . . And this is my son Nafanail, he's in the third form. This, Nafania, is a friend from my childhood! We were at grammar-school together!' Nafanail thought for a moment and took off his cap. 'We were at grammar-school together!' the thin one went on. 'Do you remember what they called you? They called you Herostratos because you burnt a hole in one of the school's books with a cigarette, and they called me Ephialtes because I liked sneaking on people. Ho-ho . . . We were children! Don't be afraid, Nafania, come a bit closer .. . . And this is my wife, née Wanzenbach . . . a Lutheran.' Nafanail thought for a moment and hid behind his father's back. 'Well, how are you getting on, my friend?' asked the fat one, gazing with delight at his friend. 'Are you working for the government? Have you got on?' 'Yes, old pal! I made collegiate assessor two years ago and I've got my St Stanislas. The salary's bad . . . but then that's life! My wife gives music lessons, I make wooden cigar-cases in my free time. They're splendid cigar-cases! I sell them for a rouble a time. If you buy ten or more, then I give a reduction. We get by. I was working in a government department, you know, and now I've been transferred here as a section head, still in the same department . . . So I'll be working here. Well how about you? You're probably a grade five already, eh?' 'No, my dear, go a bit higher,' said the fat one. 'I've got to grade three . . . I've got two stars.' The thin one suddenly turned pale and his body went rigid, but soon his face wriggled itself into the broadest of grins; his face and eyes seemed to be showering sparks.

His body became shrivelled, hunched and even thinner. His suitcases, bundles and boxes became shrivelled and creased . . . His wife's long chin became even longer; Nafanail stood to attention and fastened all the buttons of his uniform . . . 'I, Your Excellency . . . Delighted, Sir! A childhood friend, so to speak, and suddenly such an important personage, Sir! He-he-he.' 'Come, enough of that!' said the fat one, frowning. 'Why this change of tone? We're childhood friends – what's the point of this servility!' 'Pardon me . . . How could you, Sir . . .' giggled the thin one, becoming even more shrunken. 'The gracious attention of Your Excellency . . . is like the finest wine . . . Here you have, Your Excellency, my son Nafanail . . . my wife Luiza, a Lutheran, in a manner of speaking . . .' The fat one was going to protest, but the thin one's face wore such an expression of awe, delight and abject deference that the privy councillor felt disgusted. He turned his face away from the thin man and extended his hand in farewell. The thin one pressed three fingers, bowed with his whole body and giggled like a Chinese: 'He-he-he.' His wife smiled. Nafanail clicked his heels and dropped his peaked cap. All three were pleasantly shocked.

GLOSSARY OF
GRAMMATICAL TERMS

accusative: case form primarily used for the person or thing affected by an action – 'Ivan kissed *her*', **Ивáн прочитáет газéту** ('Ivan will read the newspaper').

active: verb form in which the person carrying out the action is also the subject[t] of the verb: 'opened' in 'Ivan opened the door'. Cf. passive.

adjective: a word which can fill the gap in 'It's a ____ thing' (e.g. fine, blue, beautiful).

adverb: a word which can fill the gap in 'Ivan did it ____' (e.g. slowly, yesterday, well). Russian adverbs (always indeclinable) typically end **-o** (**хорошó** 'well').

agree: (of verbs or adjectives) match the gender/number/case/person to the gender/person/case/person of the relevant noun. In **Мáленькая Тáня убежáла** 'Little Tania ran away', the endings (feminine singular) of **мáленькая** and **убежáла** agree with the feminine singular noun **Тáня**.

animate: a Russian noun denoting a person or an animal, e.g. **Ивáн** 'Ivan', **собáка** 'dog', **лицó** 'person'.

aspect: how the action takes place in time. 'The door was opening' (unfinished *imperfective*[t] action), 'Ivan opened the door, then closed it' (completed *perfective*[t] actions).

bookish: used in formal style, not in everyday conversation. 'Construct' is a bookish equivalent of 'build'.

case: an ending (sometimes meaningful, sometimes not very) on a noun, pronoun or adjective which links the noun, pronoun or adjective to other words in the sentence. **Дóм Ивáна** (genitive case) 'Ivan's house', **Мáшу** (accusative case) **лю́бит Ивáн**

503

(nominative case) 'Ivan loves Masha'.

clause:	sentence component consisting of a finite[1] verb with its subject[1] (if it has one) and any dependent words. 'Ivan, who is always helpful, opened the door and showed them in' contains three clauses: 'Ivan *opened* the door', 'who *is* always', 'and *showed* them in'.
colloquial:	used in informal style, not in formal situations or official letters. 'Hi' is a colloquial equivalent of 'Good morning'.
conjugation:	list of the personal forms of any verb (in the present, past or future). The present conjugation of **знать** 'to know' is: **знáю, знáешь, знáет, знáем, знáете, знáют**.
conjunction:	a word which joins phrases or clauses, e.g. 'and', 'but', 'although', 'that' in 'I know *that* she's married.
dative:	case form whose primary meaning is 'to'. **Ивáну** 'to Ivan'.
declension:	list of all the case forms (singular and plural) of a noun, pronoun or adjective. **Стóл** 'table': **стóл, стóл, столá, столу́, столóм, столé, столы́** . . . etc.
diminutive:	noun with a suffix[1] suggesting smallness, tenderness, intimacy – **стóлик** 'small table', **Вéрочка** 'dear Vera'.
finite verb:	any verb form with a nominative subject: 'He *opens* the door', 'She *was opening* the door'.
first person:	the 'I' form (first person singular) or the 'we' form (first person plural) of any tense of any verb.
genitive:	case form whose primary meaning is 'belonging to'. **Дóм Ивáна** 'Ivan's house'.
hard:	any consonant pronounced without a [y] sound. Cf. soft[1].
imperative:	the form of the verb used to tell someone to do something – '*Open* the door', **Открóйте дверь**.
imperfective:	the Russian verb aspect[1] which names the action or state without saying anything about completion – **открывáть**[1] 'to open', **онá читáла**[1] 'she read/was reading'.
impersonal:	a Russian construction in which the person affected is either in the dative or omitted. **Ему́ нáдо идти́** 'He has to go', **Мóжно открыть окнó?** 'Is it possible to (May I) open the window?'
inanimate:	any Russian noun not denoting a person or animal, e.g. **стóл** 'table', **красотá** 'beauty'.
indeclinable:	a word which has only one grammatical form, so that its ending never changes, e.g. **егó** 'his', **хорошó** 'well', **Мэ́ри** 'Mary'.
infinitive:	dictionary form of a verb, e.g. 'to open'; in Russian, usually ends

504

ть in, e.g. **откры́ть** 'to open'.

instrumental:	case form whose primary meaning is 'by means of': **Ива́н ест ло́жкой** 'Ivan is eating *with* a spoon'.
intransitive:	a verb which cannot be followed by 'him' in English or the accusative in Russian: 'The door *opens*', 'Ivan *smiled*'.
neutral:	a word which can be used in any style or situation (unlike book-ish' or colloquial' words). Most words – 'house', 'build', 'red' – are neutral.
nominative:	the case form in which nouns, pronouns and adjectives are given in word lists; the case form used for the subject': **Ива́н, она́, но́вый**.
noun:	a word which can fill the gap in 'He's talking about (a/the) ____' (e.g. book, Natasha, beauty).
participle:	verb form with the features of an adjective or adverb – **Рабо́та была́ сде́лана** (f sg.) 'The word was *done*', **пи́шущий** 'writing', **зна́я** '(while) knowing'.
particle:	a (usually short) word which occurs with other words, never on its own, to indicate emphasis, speaker's attitude, emotion or grammatical structure, e.g. **же** (emphasis), **ведь** (expecting agreement), **ли** ('whether'), **не** ('not').
partitive:	a use of the genitive which means 'some'. **Бери́те хле́ба** (gen.) 'Take some bread'.
passive:	verb form in which the subject' of the sentence is the person or thing affected by the action: 'was opened' in 'The door *was opened* by Ivan'.
perfective:	the Russian verb aspect which describes an action as a completed whole, e.g. **откры́ть**ᴾ 'to open' (completed act), **Она́ прочита́ла**ᴾ **кни́гу** 'She read (and finished) the book.
possessives:	words, similar to adjectives, which indicate ownership, i.e. my, your, our, his, her, its, their.
predicate:	the part of a sentence or clause which contains the verb and its dependent words; everything which isn't the subject'. In 'Little Tania went to visit the neighbours', 'Little Tania' is the subject and 'went to visit the neighbours' is the predicate.
prefix:	piece added to the beginning of a word, e.g. un- (meaning 'not') in '*un*friendly', or **по-** (meaning 'a little') in **побо́льше** 'a little more'.
preposition:	any word which can fill the gap in 'Ivan talks ____ the table' (e.g. under, near, by, about).

prepositional:	Russian case form used after the prepositions **в** 'in', **на** 'on', **о** 'about', **при** 'attached to'.
pronoun:	a word which can replace a noun and whose meaning depends on the context, e.g. he, it, this, that, self.
reflexive:	a verb ending **-ся**, sometimes corresponding to 'oneself' in English, e.g. **одеваться** 'to wash oneself'.
root:	the basic part of a word, the core to which prefixes, suffixes and endings are added, e.g. '*friend*' in 'un*friend*ly'.
second person:	the 'you' form of any tense of any verb. In Russian, **ты** is the second person singular, and **вы** is the second person plural.
soft:	any consonant pronounced with a [**y**] sound. In Russian, consonants are soft when followed by **е, ё, и, ю, я** or **ь**.
stem:	the part of a word (often the same as the root*) to which the grammatical endings are added. **Зна-** is the stem of the verb **знать** 'to know', **жив-** is the present tense stem of the verb **жить** 'to live', **нов-** is the stem of the adjective **новый** 'new'.
stressed:	a syllable* (marked ´ on its vowel) which is pronounced more prominently than the others, e.g. tó in 'pho*tóg*raphy', **вóд** in **вóдка**.
subject:	the noun or pronoun which determines the ending of the verb, 'Ivan' in 'Ivan opens the door'. In Russian the subject is in the nominative case **Ивáн открывáет дверь**.
subordinate clause:	clause* which could not stand on its own as an independent sentence but depends on a main clause which *could* stand on its own. In 'Ivan knows that Tania is at Masha's', 'Ivan knows' is the main clause and 'that Tania is at Masha's' is a subordinate clause.
suffix:	meaningful piece added to the end of a root*, eg. -ly in 'friend*ly*'.
syllable:	a vowel with its preceding consonants (and the following consonant(s) if it/they are not part of another syllable). 'Manchester' is three syllables: man-che-ster. Syllables are determined by pronunciation, not spelling, so 'house' is one syllable.
tense:	the time of the action in relation to the moment of speech. 'The door opened' (past), 'The door opens' (present), 'The door will open' (future).
third person:	the he/she/it form (third person singular) or the they form (third person plural) of any tense of any verb.
transcription:	representation of the pronunciation of any word. A transcription of **сегóдня** 'today' is **[sye-vód-nya]**. Cf. transliteration*.
transitive:	a verb which can be followed by 'him' in English or the accusative case in Russian: 'Ivan *knows/likes/killed* him'.

transliteration: representation of Russian letters by English ones. A transliteration of **сегóдня** 'today' is *segodnia*. Cf. transcription'.

unstressed: the less prominently pronounced syllables (with no stress mark ´), e.g. pho, gra and phy in '*photógraphy*', or **Моск** in **Москвá** 'Moscow'.

unvoiced: pronounced with little or no vibration of the vocal cords, e.g. p, f, k, s.

verb: word, expressing an action or a state, which will fit in the gap in 'Ivan wants to ____' (e.g. 'kill', 'go', 'sit').

voiced: pronounced with vibration of the vocal cords, e.g. b, v, g, z.

INDEX

This index includes the abbreviations used in the lessons. The figures on the right are lesson section numbers, unless preceded by 'page' or 'table'. The sign ᵗ marks technical terms which are defined in the 'Glossary of Grammatical Terms' above.